WHAT THE BELLS SANG

ESSAYS & REVIEWS

By the Same Author

Newman and his Critics
The Saint Mary's Book of Christian Verse (ed.)
Anglican Difficulties (ed.)
Newman and History
Adventures in the Book Pages: Essays and Reviews
Culture and Abortion
Newman and his Family
Newman and his Contemporaries

What the Bells Sang

ESSAYS & REVIEWS

Edward Short

GRACEWING

First published in England in 2023
by
Gracewing
2 Southern Avenue
Leominster
Herefordshire HR6 0QF
United Kingdom
www.gracewing.co.uk

ISBN 978 085244 996 7

Cover illustration:
Giotto, Nativity, 1303–5, Scrovegni Chapel, Padua

Cover design by Bernardita Peña Hurtado
Typeset by Word and Page, Chester, UK

CONTENTS

ACKNOWLEDGEMENTS

The essays and reviews included in *What the Bells Sang* were written over a number of years for different publications including *The Catholic Herald*, *The Bulletin of the New York C. S. Lewis Society*, *The Weekly Standard*, *The Human Life Review*, *City Journal*, and *Catholic World Report*. Accordingly, I should like to thank the editors of these papers, Luke Coppen, Robert Trexler, Philip Terzian, Anne Conlon, Paul Beston, and Carl Olson.

No acknowledgements would be complete without my expressing my abundant thanks to my publisher, Tom Longford, who made many crucial recommendations for the book's improvement. Gracewing is a godsend of a publisher and I am keenly grateful to Tom and his staff for all of their brilliant support and help, not to mention their patience with an author who often revises interminably.

Once again, I am grateful to the incomparable Clive Tolley, who showed the typesetting of the collection his usual meticulous, artful care.

Another debt that I should like to acknowledge here is to the crack literary scholar and editor of Elizabeth Jennings, Prof. Emma Mason, who has given me generous and welcome encouragement.

I am also grateful to my dear friend Father Carleton Jones, O.P., for graciously reading over the typescript. The son of an English master and terse, witty stylist in his own right, Father Jones has a genius for good copy-editing, though in looking over my musings he only had time to single out my more blatant errors. All remaining slips, all remaining solecisms are mine and mine alone.

Lastly, I am grateful to my darling wife, Karina, and to my children, Sophia and Sebastian, to whom I have dedicated the book.

For my children,

Sophia Thérèse Mariana
and
Edward John Joseph Sebastian

Deo Gratias!

Introduction

Confessions of a Catholic Essayist

Whenever asked what the point of a Catholic essayist is, I am tempted to answer that one is not a Catholic essayist but only an essayist who happens to be Catholic. Of course, this is what Graham Greene, Evelyn Waugh and Muriel Spark would say whenever they were asked whether they considered themselves Catholic novelists. Yet there is a sense in which my Catholic faith does give me a special charge whenever I write essays or review books. After all, I am on my mettle not only to write sensibly but charitably. Knowing one's own flaws and inadequacies, one is not likely to be altogether unsparing about those of others. I am also on my mettle to look at my subjects, as far as I can, *sub specie aeternitatis*. And I try to be bright and amusing. Catholics, after all, have a fairly obsessional sense of sin, fueled by their notoriously bad behavior, and certainly there is no greater literary sin than boring one's reader.

In calling myself an essayist, I have deliberately avoided the invidious obligation of deciding whether to call myself a reviewer or a critic. T. S. Eliot had some interesting things to say on the topic in "Author and Critic," a lecture he gave in 1955 to the Authors Club in London. "There is a vague difference, generally recognised, between reviewing and criticism," he observes in his talk,

> though there is no generally accepted definition of the difference. ... If a review leads the writer far enough, if it contains enough learning or wisdom over and above what is called for by the book reviewed, or if it is a statement of enduring value about a book of enduring value, then it qualifies as criticism. On the other hand, the critical article which is disguised as a review—when the new book has been, in the usual phrase, a "peg to hang the article on"—can be most maddening to the author of the book. I know, because I have written many such articles, which have been collected and reprinted in books (and in view of the fact I have gained the rank of critic). Somebody, let us say, has devoted many years of his life, and much scholarship, to the biography of a great author, or to a definitive edition of his works. Along comes the critic, disguised as reviewer, who, with the connivance of his editor, puts down in print what he thinks about the author in question, at the length of several thousand words. In the first paragraph is a reference to

the new book or the new edition; and an asterisk refers you to the bottom of the page, where the title, author's name, publisher and price are given. As a critic I defend this practice, for it gives the critical intelligence a unique opportunity, sometimes to the benefit of the public, and it gives the critic an article to reprint. But as author I should not care to be the victim of it; and as a publisher I should be exasperated by it.

The conclusion to which Eliot comes after all of this hairsplitting is rather comically inconclusive: "I have wandered from my point. It was incidental to my saying that while there are various criteria for distinguishing between a reviewer and a critic, there is no frontier at which reviewing ends and criticism begins." If even someone of Eliot's acuity could not draw the line between these two literary functionaries, I can hardly be faulted for refusing to draw it myself. Hence, I will persevere in calling myself an essayist and let the reader decide when I am commencing critic, when reviewer and when mere abject scribbler.

In all events, when trying to write well of any subject, one has to bring critical, historical and aesthetic skills to bear, and these skills need to have a certain incisiveness, a certain pith, regardless of one's faith; even if it is also true that these are skills that are always colored and indeed strengthened by one's faith. At the same time, quite faithless writers can shine in the writing of critical essays and reviews, where they might fail in more creative undertakings, like history or fiction or poetry. And, on this score, I have always thought Virginia Woolf's best work not her fiction or polemics but the literary essays and reviews she wrote for various papers. Like her father, Leslie Stephen, she was a voracious reader; she could turn a phrase; she had a rich, mocking, elegant wit; and her subjects ranged from Gibbon, Jane Austen, Thackeray, and George Eliot to the Brontës, Henry James, George Moore, and Arnold Bennet. Nonetheless, she had nothing but haughty contempt for reviewers, having been on the receiving end of some rather well-deserved wiggings from those who found her fiction anaemic and affected. Indeed, she looked forward to the day that reviewers could be shown off the stage altogether by an enlightened, cultivated, mandarin public, one which would treat the author, not as reviewers had treated him, as a "figure of fun," a "hybrid between the peacock and the ape," but "as an obscure workman doing his job in the darkness of the workshop," and, as such, "not unworthy of respect."

How odd that it is often the thing that we do best that we should least respect! And, conversely, that we should most wish to do the very thing that we cannot do well. What are those lines from Eliot's *The Confidential Clerk*?

> the thing I cannot do,
> The art that I could never excel in,

Seems the one thing worth doing, the one thing
That I want to do.

When it comes to the utility of the reviewer, however, there is another point to make, and, strangely enough, it puts me at odds with Saint John Henry Cardinal Newman. Newman reviewed books for a good portion of his long life and some of his best work was done for the periodical press, or even the daily press. *The Tamworth Reading Room*, for example, which exploded the peculiarly modern notion that education is possible without the teaching of theology, was done for *The Times*. Nevertheless, the Cardinal shared Woolf's low opinion of book reviewing. To his brother Frank, for instance, an indefatigable contributor to the periodical press, he once wrote: "I wonder you can for a moment lay stress on the *dicta* of reviewers. You must have had surely enough experience how utterly worthless, for the most part, the formal criticisms of the day are."

No one knows the truth of this worthlessness better than authors, whose books are often misunderstood or simply abused by lazy, malicious or stupid reviewers. Yet the Cardinal's impatience with reviewing fails to take into account its modest but real virtues. Reviewing may be a lowly enterprise, but it is precisely its lowliness that ensures its usefulness, for good reviewing—and, I would argue, proper Catholic reviewing espe-cially—demands careful, imaginative, judicious reading. Then, too, good reviewing requires humility and self-effacement, and no reviewer will appreciate these virtues more keenly than the Catholic reviewer, whose familiarity with the confessional cannot leave him unaware of the envy, pettiness, conceit, malevolence and spite, to which reviewers and indeed all writers are peculiarly prone.

Another question that the Catholic essayist needs to be prepared to answer is whether describing oneself as a Catholic essayist leaves one open to the charge of bias. And my answer to that is that all writing is biased, and certainly a Catholic bias is better than a Marxist or, indeed, a secular bias, both of which tend to underestimate or ignore good and overestimate bad books. Catholic bias, after all, gives one depth and balance, as well as sympathy and zest. And it puts one beyond the pale of fashion, which is a good place to be, when so many within that pale spend most of their days following the silliest or, as the case may be, the most sinister hula hoops. The good Catholic essayist is a sign of contradiction; a just, sympathetic, generous guide to the good work of others; but always a defender of the good, the beautiful and the true, even when being so exposes him to opprobrium or marginalization.

Apropos this, I was delighted when my publisher Bloomsbury brought out a new and updated edition of Roger Scruton's *Fools, Frauds and Fire-brands: Thinkers of the New Left*, which includes these timely words of

3

wisdom: "The pursuit of equality at all costs, and of a purely noumenal emancipation, is vain and even contradictory. Yet, however devastating the proof that equality can be pursued only at the cost of liberty, and unmediated liberty only at the cost of consensual politics, the leftist position bounces back." Why? Scruton makes a brilliant point when he says that, at heart, the leftist yearns for something that he otherwise affects to despise: religion—he longs for something "that no amount of rational thought ... can ever eradicate. And that longing is more easily recruited by the abstract god of equality than by any concrete form of social compromise." Or, one might add, by Our Lord and Saviour, than whom there is nothing more concrete or more gratifyingly real. Since Scruton's death, the religious longings of the left have grown more implacable and more irrational still in the religion of wokery. The essays and reviews in *What the Bells Sang* are an implicit repudiation of that false, degrading, dehumanizing religion.

Yet, if I am convinced that wokery is the pseudo-religion of a bankrupt, rapacious State, I also know that my powers of persuasion when it comes to convincing my neighbor of this reality may not be all that they might be. Why? Well, I have read Eliot, and if Eliot was not convinced of his powers of persuasion in this line, neither can I be of mine. What is it that the redoubtable rhetorician in Eliot says in one of his later essays:

> We are all, in fact, trying to persuade other people; that is, we appeal to their emotions, and often indeed to their prejudices, as well as to their reason ... We can at least try to understand our own motives, passions, and prejudices, so as to be conscious of what we are doing when we appeal to those of others. This is very difficult, because our own prejudice and emotional bias always seem to us so rational. We are perpetually engaged in pointing out the extent to which other people's reasoning is deflected by their sentiments. I am quite aware that I have been trying to persuade, though I may not be quite sure of what. But although I should be discouraged if nobody agreed with anything I have said, I should be thoroughly alarmed if everybody agreed; because a statement upon which everyone can agree, in the discussion of topics such as these, is pretty certain not to mean much. I hope, however, that my main motive has been to unsettle your minds, rather than to impose a theory; and while I have gone on defining, I have not been thinking of convincing, though you may have been thinking of your next cocktail party

If I succeed in sending my readers away *unsettled*, however unpersuaded, I shall consider my labors to have been a success. The world in its present state needs unsettling.

Often, I am asked whether I believe reviewing and essay writing can be creative. And to that I always give an emphatic affirmative: reviewing and essay writing can and should be richly creative. Many of the figures I took up in my last book of essays, *Adventures in the Book Pages: Essays and Reviews* — G. K. Chesterton, W. H. Auden, T. S. Eliot, Graham Greene, Evelyn Waugh, Penelope Fitzgerald — wrote reviews and essays expressly to sustain and refine their own creative work, whether in poetry, fiction, history, apologetics or criticism. Graham Greene, for example, was an excellent critic, and all of his criticism grew out of his reviewing and essays. Evelyn Waugh was another superb reviewer, especially of the work of unknown or unsung fellow novelists. His pieces on William Trevor, Flannery O'Connor, Muriel Spark and Sybille Bedford, all younger contemporaries, who gained enormously from his critical attention, are uniformly insightful, indeed prescient. The edition of his collected work being undertaken by Oxford University Press shows how he sustained his own creative work by keeping abreast of what others were doing, especially the innovative young.

Waugh, however, was an exception. He was not only sympathetic when reviewing, he was conscientious. Thomas Hardy's experience of reviews was perhaps more representative, as his biographer Michael Millgate points out in his biography of the poet. After Macmillan brought out his *Moments of Vision* (1919), Hardy was sent a batch of fifty or so reviews and while most were "friendly enough," he was appalled to find that all but five or six were "deplorably inept, purblind, & of far less *value* than the opinion of one's grocer or draper." The poet could not understand why there should be such a propensity to dullness in reviewers. Although never a reviewer himself, he was confident that if he did review, he would make a proper job of it. "I always fancy I could point out the best, & the worst, in a volume of poems," he wrote. He was also annoyed by how stereotypical reviewers' notions of poets tended to be. For most reviewers, "true poets" must be cut out of a certain conventional cloth: "they must all be impractical in the conduct of their affairs, nay, they must almost, like Shelley or Marlowe, be drowned or done to death, or like Keats die of consumption." Of course, in our time, such uncritical groupthink is still with us, though, instead of being drowned or dying of consumption, poets must be left-wing, atheist, dismissive of traditional form, and, perhaps most indispensably, reliant for their livelihoods on ruthlessly ideological, conformist academies.

One reason why I am always grateful to editors for allowing me to review this or that book or to write a long essay of my own choosing is that they are giving me an opportunity to learn about a subject or an author or an author's work that could very well serve as good creative grist to my own work. T. S. Eliot did this with Dante and Lancelot Andrewes; Graham Greene with Henry James; Chesterton with Dickens; and Auden with an enormous range of different authors, from Betjeman, Beerbohm, Houseman, Boswell, and Byron to Sidney Smith, Goethe, Yeats, Shakespeare and someone who may be rather undeservedly forgotten, Charles Cochrane, the Canadian who wrote that fascinating book, *Christianity and*

Culture: A Study of Thought and Action from Augustus to Augustine (1944), which is still very much worth reading.

There are a few authors whom I cover in my last book—Jane Ridley, for instance, the biographer of Edwin Lutyens, Edward VII and, most recently, George V—from whom I have learned a great deal, and this has given my reviewing and essay writing very distinct, practical benefits. Reading Ridley is an education not only in biography and history but narrative and interpretation, not to mention that often elusive, subtle thing, style. Speaking of Princess Alexandra at Bertie's coronation, Ridley observes: "She was fifty-six, heavily made up, allegedly bald, and almost stone deaf, but she seemed like a queen from a fairy tale." That is wonderfully stylish writing.

Another writer from whom I have learned more recently is R. W. Southern, whose forays into the mediaeval world of Saint Anselm and the Schoolmen have convinced me that the scholastic project is not only fascinating but unfinished. It may be true that our age's rejection of the God that made scholasticism and all of its civilizing achievements possible has consigned the world to a new primitivism, one intoxicated with the blood sacrifice of abortion and the taboos of a seemingly endless parade of political witch doctors, but it is also true that the Schoolmen can help us find our way out of the labyrinth of this primitivism by reacquainting us with the creative joy that only God's Love can bestow. If this collection does little more than inspire a few bright young things to dip into Southern's *Scholastic Humanism and the Unification of Europe*, I shall consider my endeavors to have succeeded. If we are to take arms against our sea of troubles, we must have proper arms, and I do not know that there are any better on offer than those supplied by the perennial philosophy of St. Thomas.

Since the subjects I cover are fairly eclectic, culled as they are not only from Cardinal Newman and his nineteenth-century milieu, but from literature, history, biography, art, music and theatre, I am often asked who my favorite subjects are, and here I must admit that my favorites are too numerous for singling out. I tend to review books by or about figures from the English nineteenth century, only because I am keen on learning as much as I can about Newman's immediate historical context. Accordingly, there are pieces in my last book of essays, to which this current collection is a companion, on Henry Mayhew, the author of *London Labour and the London Poor*, the Victorians and the Bible, John Ruskin, nineteenth-century Venice, the Neo-Gothic, A. W. N. Pugin, Gladstone, Thackeray, Edward Burne-Jones, Henry Irving, and Gerard Manley Hopkins. But I certainly did not limit myself to the Victorian ethos: I also wrote pieces about Renaissance portraiture, Europe *entre deux guerres*, and the twentieth-century American popular music that Wilfrid Sheed loved. Then, again, I wrote a long essay on fox hunting, primarily so I could quote a passage about the brave, unsentimental fox from Evelyn Waugh's country neighbor, Frances

Donaldson, the daughter of the playwright Freddy Lonsdale. Donaldson wrote a charming memoir, *Child of the Twenties* (1959), with which some of my readers will doubtless be familiar. It is one of the best things ever written about London after the Great War.

In *What the Bells Sang* there are essays on poets from Lord Tennyson and Thomas Hardy to Rudyard Kipling and Robert Lowell; on the novelists Anthony Trollope, Henry James, J. K. Huysmans, James Joyce, Italo Svevo, Evelyn Waugh and Graham Greene; on such admirable historians as Christopher Dawson, R. W. Southern, and Andrew Roberts; on Edmund Burke; on Samuel Johnson; on T. S. Eliot; on C. S. Lewis; on the utopian socialism that once again besots the young; on the beleaguered family, which is so essential to the civilization that we all see fast disappearing from our increasingly disordered societies; on two great statesmen, one relatively neglected and the other incessantly assailed by the censorious young, Calvin Coolidge and Winston Churchill; on the indomitable Abigail Adams; on Walter Bagehot; on the Great War; and on the painter George Romney, whose portraiture captures so movingly and so brilliantly the creativity of the Georgians, those exuberant men and women who are such a standing indictment of the littleness and barbarity of our own derisory age. Lastly, there are a number of pieces on Saint John Henry Newman, which I wrote leading up to and after his canonization.

Since the present collection includes several essays on poets, I should make readers aware that I have written the essays expressly with the collection of Christian poetry in mind that I recently chose and introduced for Gracewing entitled *The Saint Mary's Book of Christian Verse*. When published, I shall be hawking both books together, since they are complementary.

Some of the pieces included in this collection are longish reviews but most are fairly involved, meditative essays, undertaken for editors of publications generous enough to let me have my say at a certain leisurely length. Some are footnoted; others are not. I am grateful to my publisher Tom Longford for agreeing to bring the essays and reviews together in *What the Bells Sang* not only because they give readers a chance to see the wide and interrelated interests that inform my work on Newman but because they make so bold as to be contributions to what used to be regarded, not too very long ago, as the art of the essay.

Four hundred and forty-one years ago, the quizzical Gascon Michel de Montaigne (1533–92) could hardly have known how much livelier he would make the world by publishing his *Essais* (1581), and yet, in addition to giving Shakespeare fodder for *Hamlet, King Lear* and the *Tempest*, he inspired generations of other writers to sit down and write essays of their own, the best of whom made the essay one of the most supple, versatile and enchanting of literary forms. To name a few of the essayists at work in the course of those centuries is to name some of the most brilliant writers in the English language. Sir Francis Bacon, Jonathan Swift, Joseph Addison, Richard Steele, Samuel Johnson, Oliver Goldsmith, David Hume, Charles Lamb, William Hazlitt, Lord Macaulay, William Makepeace Thackeray, St John Henry Newman, James Anthony Froude, Walter Bagehot, Henry James, Max Beerbohm, R. L. Stevenson, G. K. Chesterton, Hilaire Belloc, T. S. Eliot, Virginia Woolf, G. M. Young, V. S. Pritchett, Graham Greene, George Orwell, and James Grant all owe the Frenchman who spent most of his days in a chateau in Perigord a fundamental debt. Of course, not all of these essayists might have Montaigne's acute appreciation for the multiplicity of life, but they do share his ebullient intelligence, his readiness to test convictions, his delight in God's good variousness. Their essays certainly corroborate the truth of Montaigne's conviction that "La plus grande chose du monde, c'est de savoir être à soi." Whether my own essays show that I have managed this grand thing is now up to my gentle readers to decide.

Edward Short
20 January 2023
Feast of Saint Sebastian
Astoria, New York

Bells pealing. The pleasure of hearing them. It leads the mind to a longing after some thing I know not what. It does not bring past years to remembrance. ... What does it do? We have a kind of longing after something dear to us and well known to us, very soothing. Such is my feeling at this minute, as I hear them.

John Henry Newman, March 1819

Silence that dreadful bell!
It frights the isle from her propriety.

Shakespeare, *Othello*

Towards the river
A pealing swells:
They cost me a quiver—
Those prayerful bells!

Thomas Hardy,
"Evelyn G. of Christminster"

9

Poets

What the Bells Sang:
Belief, Unbelief and Thomas Hardy

I

Readers who come to the poetry of Thomas Hardy keen on hearing what
he has to say of the Christian faith must always be wary of the notion, still
widely, if vaguely held, that he was an agnostic whose ingrained pessi-
mism prevented him from entering into the reality of religious faith.[1] Poem
after poem of Hardy's nine-hundred odd poems record his yearning for
the Christian faith to which he could not bring himself to subscribe. Yes,
he disavows belief, but he is never content with the brittle assumptions of
unbelief. As for his pessimism, it is more often than not an expression of
dismay—spiritual, not temperamental dismay.

There was no exhibitionistic ennui in Hardy: he had too much zest.
His gloomiest poems tend to be his most exuberant. In "Thoughts from
Sophocles," for instance, he gives voice to the Greek tragedian's gloom
with an almost rollicking buoyancy. "What are song, laughter, what the
footed maze / Beside the good of knowing no birth at all," he writes, before
describing old age as a place "Where sunshine bird and bloom frequent no
more / And cowls of cloud wrap the stars' radiancy."[2] Here, it is the "stars'
radiancy," the very radiancy that led the magi to the Christ Child, not the
"cowls of cloud" that arrests the reader, though the choice of the word *cowl*
complicates the poem's pagan pessimism, a cowl being a monk's hooded
cloak, *vestis caputiata*, worn especially during the night office, when the
monk keeps vigil with the promises of Christ.

1 There are some good exceptions to this uncritical view, most admirably Raymond
Chapman, "'Arguing about the Eastern Position': Thomas Hardy and Puseyism," *Nine-
teenth-Century Literature*, vol. 42, no. 3 (December 1987), 275–94.

2 All of the poems by Hardy quoted in the essay are from *The Complete Poems of
Thomas Hardy*, ed. James Gibson (London: Macmillan, 1978). "Thoughts from Sophocles,"
one of the poet's uncollected verses, written in the 1890s, first appeared in Evelyn Hardy:
"Some Unpublished Poems by Thomas Hardy," *The London Magazine*, 3/1 (January 1956).

The tragic sense that animates so many of Hardy's poems comes of his tragic estrangement from his Maker. His poems, in this light, can almost be seen as prayers *manqué*: their seeming longing for death a longing for the life after death. Take the lovely, bleak, implacable "Bereft" (1901):

> In the black winter morning
> No light will be struck near my eyes
> While the clock in the stairway is warning
> For five, when he used to rise.
> Leave the door unbarred,
> The clock unwound,
> Make my lone bed hard—
> Would 'twere underground!
>
> When the summer dawns clearly,
> And the appletree-tops seem alight,
> Who will undraw the curtain and cheerly
> Call out that the morning is bright?

Here the wife's lament for her absent husband could easily be the agnostic's lament for his absent God. If Hardy had been truly convinced of the cogency of the rationalist dismissal of God, it is questionable whether he would have composed such laments. Far from redounding to that suppositious cogency: they undermine it. No, Hardy is an uneasy unbeliever, and many of his poems are expressions of that spiritual unease. Like Cleopatra, he had immortal longings, which unbelief could only leave unrequited. Take another baleful bagatelle, "Let Me Believe":

> Let me believe it, dearest,
> Let it be
> As just a dream—the merest—
> Haunting me,
> That a frank full-souled sweetness
> Warmed your smile
> And voice, to indiscreetness
> Once, awhile!

Is this a rejection of matrimonial love or a cry for its endurance? Hardy's poems about Christian faith strike a similar note. Here is "The Oxen," one of his poems about Christmas, the feast which inveterately exposed the ambiguity of his agnosticism.

> Christmas Eve, and twelve of the clock.
> "Now they are all on their knees,"
> An elder said as we sat in a flock
> By the embers in hearthside ease.
>
> We pictured the meek mild creatures where

They dwelt in their strawy pen,
Nor did it occur to one of us there
To doubt they were kneeling then.

So fair a fancy few would weave
In these years! Yet, I feel,
If someone said on Christmas Eve,
"Come; see the oxen kneel,

"In the lonely barton by yonder coomb
Our childhood used to know,"
I should go with him in the gloom,
Hoping it might be so.

The reference to the oxen being "all on their knees" is an allusion to Isaiah
1:3: "the ox knoweth its owner and the ass his master's crib: but Israel
does not know, my people doth not consider." If there was an agnostic in
Hardy, there was also a chronicler, a remembrancer, [3] who was at pains to
record that in the wake of what Newman called the "great *apostasia*,"[4] the
wisdom of the elders and the delighted faith of children were not what
they had been. Indeed, priests were not what they had been. In his won-
derful little gem of a novel, *Nina Balatka* (1867), Trollope has one servant
say to another, "the priests are not the men they used to be, Souchey. And
it is not exactly their fault neither. There are so many folks about in these
days who care nothing who goes to glory and who does not, and they are

3 *Remembrancer* is nicely deployed by the fine English critic and translator Michael
Alexander, who says, apropos Walter Scott: he "recreated for poetry one of its oldest
roles, that of remembrancer. ... Thomas Hardy especially honored him for reclaiming
this role for poetry." Michael Alexander, *Medievalism: The Middle Ages in Modern Eng-
land* (New Haven: Yale University Press, 2007), 59. Cf., Hardy's lovely poem, "One
We Knew" (1902), the penultimate stanza of which brilliantly exemplifies Alexander's
point. "With cap-framed face and long gaze into the embers / We seated around her
knees / She would dwell on such dead themes, not as one who remembers / But rather
as one who sees."

4 Upon being made a cardinal in 1879 by Pope Leo XIII, Newman gave his "Bigli-
etto Speech" in which he told his English and Italian audience in Rome: "Hitherto the
civil Power has been Christian. Even in countries separated from the Church, as in
my own, the *dictum* was in force, when I was young, that: 'Christianity was the law of
the land'. Now, everywhere that goodly framework of society, which is the creation
of Christianity, is throwing off Christianity. ... As to Religion, it is a private luxury,
which a man may have if he will; but which ... he must not obtrude upon others, or
indulge in to their annoyance. The general character of this great *apostasia* is one and
the same everywhere." *Addresses to Cardinal Newman with his Replies 1879–81*, ed. W. P.
Neville (London: Longmans, Green & Co, 1905), 65–6. See Edward Short, *Newman and
his Contemporaries* (London: T&T Clark, 2011), 8, 213.

too many for the priests."[5] Such unvarnished truth telling recalls G. K. Chesterton's criticism of Hardy:

> I have been blamed for an alleged attack on Hardy, in a sketch of Victorian literature; it was apparently supposed that talking about the village atheist brooding on the village idiot was some sort of attack. But this is not an attack on Hardy; this is the defence of Hardy. The whole case for him is that he had the sincerity and simplicity of the village atheist; that is, that he valued atheism as a truth and not a triumph.[6]

In spiritual matters, since the loss of their traditional faith as a result of their English Reformation, the English have had little "hearthside ease."[7] Yet their very displeasure with their national faith proved the importunity of that traditional faith, not its superannuation. Moreover, that Hardy should capture belief in the Christian faith with the tenderness he does in "The Oxen" bespeaks the residual affection he felt for the faith of his childhood and young manhood, which neither his later dismissal nor even his derision of it could ever dispel. The lines: "Come; see the oxen kneel / In the lonely barton by yonder coomb / Our childhood used to know" are of an exquisite tenderness, though he was equally tenderly attentive to the "frail moan from the martyred saints" of a cathedral façade:

> At the ancient faith's rejection
> Under the sure, unhasting, steady stress
> Of Reason's movement, making meaningless
> The coded creeds of old-time godliness.[8]

In "Christmas in the Elgin Room," Hardy writes a variation on Milton's "On the Morning of Christ's Nativity" where, again, a certain tenderness presides. The ancient deities react to the Christian feast with a longing to know what it means as acute as his own.

---

5 Anthony Trollope, *Nina Balatka*, introduced by Angela Thirlwell (London: Folio Society, 1996), 142.

6 G. K. Chesterton, *The Autobiography of G. K. Chesterton*, ed. Randall Paine (San Francisco: Ignatius Press, 1988), 262–3. See also Ian Ker, *G. K. Chesterton: A Biography* (Oxford: Oxford University Press, 2008), 238–9. In *The Victorian Age in Literature* (1913), Chesterton had written: "Hardy became a sort of village atheist brooding and blaspheming over the village idiot" — a jibe which, as we shall see, stuck in Hardy's craw. G. K. Chesterton, *The Victorian Age in Literature* (Oxford: Oxford University Press, 1946), 88.

7 See Christopher Haigh, *English Reformations* (Oxford: Oxford University Press, 1993) and John Joseph Scarisbrick, *The Reformation and the English People* (Oxford: Oxford University Press, 1984).

8 These lines are from "A Cathedral Façade at Midnight" from *Human Shows, Far Phantasies, Songs and Trifles* (1925).

> Demeter too, Poseidon hoar,
> Persephone, and many more
> Of Zeus' high breed,—
> All loth to heed
> What the bells sang
>   that night which shook them to the core.

Walter de la Mare is wonderfully good on this quality in Hardy's verse. "No God, it is true, could loom more phantasmal and remote from our trivial and agonizing affairs," he writes,

> than the "all-Immanent Will" that drives us into the world in "rabble rout," mutters in slumber or mocks, or sighs out of his tenebrous abiding-place in consciousness, at "the momentous moil of strained hard-run Humanity." But anthropomorphic deities are usually flattering reflections of their creators. This deity is infinitely less compassionate, tender, magnanimous, and faithful than the poet whose workmanship he is, and who in every word he writes is present with us. Wherefore relenting and tenderness often steal into the limning of his Divine conception, and pity smiles from the eye-holes of the cold mask of the ironic:

> Thou shouldst have learnt that Not to Mend
> For Me could mean but Not to Know[9]

De la Mare's quoting of the pivotal lines in "God-Forgotten" may evince some grudging tenderness on the part of Hardy's "all-Immanent Will," but the poet himself, feeling as deeply as he did, in his grave, meditative way, was made for tenderness. One can see this tenderness in the many rueful, longing-laced poems he wrote for his first wife Emma after her death

> And when you come to me
> To show you true,
> Doubt not that I shall infallibly
> Be waiting you.

Philip Larkin, so much of whose poetry hearkens back to that of Hardy, in its assiduous unbelief, speculated that the intensity of the earlier poet's love of his first wife showed "the basic insincerity in human affection … a flaw built deeply into the working of the emotions," a rather striking contention, especially since it might have led to the composition of "An Arundel Tomb."[10] Hardy, after all, is the poet who taught Larkin the lesson

---

9 Walter de la Mare, "Thomas Hardy's Lyrics," *Private View* (London: Faber & Faber, 1953), 98.

10 Philip Larkin, "Mrs. Hardy's Memories," *Required Writing: Miscellaneous Pieces 1955–1982* (New York: Farrar, Straus & Giroux, 1983), 147.

that what will survive of us is our love. For Larkin to have accused Hardy of insincerity shows the extent to which his own difficulties with love stemmed from his obsessional unbelief.[11] Rejecting the love of God, *pace* those who would have us settle for the cold comforts of secular humanism, is never inconsequential. Moreover, to read "At Castle Boterel," one of Hardy's most unforgettable poems, is to encounter a sincerity that only the most hard-hearted would deny.

> Primaeval rocks form the road's steep border,
>   And much have they faced there, first and last,
> Of the transitory in Earth's long order;
>   But what they record in colour and cast
>   Is—that we two passed.
>
> And to me, though Time's unflinching rigour,
>   In mindless rote, has ruled from sight
> The substance now, one phantom figure
>   Remains on the slope, as when that night
>   Saw us alight.
>
> I look and see it there, shrinking, shrinking,
>   I look back at it amid the rain
> For the very last time; for my sand is sinking,
>   And I shall traverse old love's domain
>   Never again.

That Hardy should have composed this "full-souled" love poem to his first wife when he had already taken his second shows a certain ruthlessness when it came to the prosecution of his art, though it also shows the depth of his capacity for love.[12] The suddenness of Emma's death left Hardy full of unavailing remorse: he had no time to reconcile with the disenchanted wife whom he knew he had wronged, though the precise nature of the wrong remains undefined.[13] If there was an unhappiness in the marriage, there was also great love. As François Mauriac once said, "Husbands and wives of long standing never hate each other as much as they think they do."[14] In any case, there is no poem expressing his disbelief in the promises

---

11 For Larkin's difficulties with love, see John Sutherland, *Monica Jones, Philip Larkin and Me: Her Life and Long Loves* (London: Weidenfeld & Nicolson, 2021).

12 Hardy's breezy tactlessness on this score can be seen in a letter he wrote to Florence shortly after their marriage in which he confessed: "I wonder if it will surprise you when I say that according to my own experience the second marriage does not, or need not, obliterate an old affection, though it generally assumed that the first wife is entirely forgotten in such cases." Michael Millgate, *Thomas Hardy: A Biography Revisited* (Oxford: Oxford University Press, 2004), 456.

13 See Millgate, *Thomas Hardy*.

14 François Mauriac, *The Knot of Vipers* (1932), in *A Mauriac Reader*, trans. Gerard

of Christianity that has anything like the power of his late love lyrics, and yet it is these lyrics that call into question not only the nature of love, but the nature of time, the relationship between the living and the dead, and the promises of hope.

II

Thomas Hardy (1840–1928) was born in the Dorset hamlet of Higher Bockhampton, the first of four children of a stonemason. Born six months after his parents' marriage, he was presumed stillborn and only saved by the attentions of a vigilant midwife. Due to his sickly youth, he received no schooling until the age of eight, spending most of his childhood at home, from which he acquired that delight in the countryside evident in all of his books. From an early age, he loved hymns and the rituals of the Anglican church service. Taught the violin by his father, he often played with him and his paternal uncle at local gatherings, an unforgettable music-making, "elusive as a jack-o'-lanthorn's gleam," which he immortalizes in "To My Father's Violin" (1916). Music, as his delightful novel *Under the Greenwood Tree* (1874) shows, was another of his great loves. [15] Indeed, music proves how indissolubly bound the artist in Hardy was to the countryman.[16] "To dwellers in a wood," he writes at the opening of that charming book, "almost every species of tree has its voice as well as its feature. At the passing of the breeze the fir-trees sob and moan no less distinctly than they rock; the holly whistles as it battles with itself; the ash hisses amid its quiverings; the beech rustles while its flat boughs rise and fall. And winter, which modifies the note of such trees as shed their leaves, does not destroy its individuality." After attending an Anglican, nonconformist and commercial school, Hardy taught himself Greek and Latin and resolved to go on to Cambridge to prepare himself for the church. Of all the authors he read, he was especially steeped in Homer, the Greek Tragedians and Virgil. In 1862, he left Dorchester for London, where he abandoned his plans to apply to Cambridge and became instead a draughtsman in the offices of a prominent Gothic architect. Once in London, he became an avid theatre

Hopkins (New York: Farrar, Straus & Giroux, 1968), 373.

15 "Under the Greenwood Tree is a novel for all time," the good critic Angela Thirlwell writes of the book, "an unsentimental novel of rural affairs for both town and country readers; it has a perennial bloom that lodges in the soul." See "Introduction," *Under the Greenwood Tree or the Mellstock Quire*, introduced by Angela Thirlwell (London: Folio Society, 1989), xvii.

16 With Hardy in mind, Ralph Vaughan Williams wrote his bold, brooding Ninth Symphony (1958), which re-envisions the pastoral, in very Hardyesque terms, as a place of immemorial mystery.

and gallery goer and resumed the wide-ranging self-education that he had begun in Dorset. In 1870, he married Emma Lavinia Gifford (1840–1912), the daughter of a Plymouth solicitor. Upon the publication of Darwin's *On the Origin of Species* (1859), his once fervent Christian faith began to fade. At the same time, he resolved on becoming a writer. His first successful novel, *A Pair of Blue Eyes* (1872) drew heavily on his Cornish courtship of Emma. This was followed by a series of novels that consistently garnered critical as well as commercial success, *Far from the Madding Crowd* (1874), *The Return of the Native* (1878), *The Mayor of Casterbridge* (1886), and *Tess of the D'Urbervilles* (1891). It was only after the public outcry against *Jude the Obscure* (1895), his final novel, regarded in many quarters as objectionable for its criticism of the country's marriage and education laws, that he decided to devote himself fully to the writing of poetry. As Tim Armstrong, the editor of a good edition of Hardy's selected poems, recognized: "the novels had become testaments to a failure of hope" and consequently "he could not easily have written on."[17] Poetry for Hardy, amongst other things, offered a way out of this impasse. In 1875 he returned to Dorchester, where he would remain until his death, living at Max Gate, the red-brick villa he designed himself. A member of both the Athenaeum and the Savile Club, he would never cut ties with London. His first collection of poems, *Wessex Poems*, appeared in 1898 when he was fifty-eight. Seven volumes followed, all of an undiminishing richness. In 1912, Emma died. In 1914, Hardy married Florence Dugdale, a friend of his sister and an admirer of his work. Rather than his wives, it was a lady unmoved by his amorous attentions who left the most vivid account of Hardy's person, observing that he was "slightly below the middle height, but strongly built, with rugged, aquiline features, pallid complexion, a crisp, closely trimmed brown beard, and mustache short enough to disclose an infrequent smile of remarkable sweetness." In 1928, at the time of his death, the stonemason's son was worth £95,428 or what would be somewhat over £7 million today.[18]

In his poetry, no less than in his prose fiction, Hardy was preeminently a storyteller, and many of the poems can best be seen as expressing the views of his hardboiled rustics as much as himself. As he pointed out to his readers, there was a difference in any man's poetry "between the expression of fancy and the expression of belief."[19] The poem "The Ruined Maid" is a good example of Hardy's fancy:

17 *Thomas Hardy: Selected Poems*, ed. Tim Armstrong (London and New York: Routledge, 2014), 1.

18 For a good biographical overview of Hardy, including the description of his person from Hardy's lady friend, see Millgate's entry in the *ODNB*.

19 Hardy to Alfred Noyes (19 December 1920), Florence Emily Hardy, *The Later Years of Thomas Hardy* (London: Macmillan, 1930), 217.

"O 'Melia, my dear, this does everything crown!
Who could have supposed I should meet you in Town?
And whence such fair garments, such prosperity?" —
"O didn't you know I'd been ruined?" said she.

In *Thomas Hardy: Half a Londoner* (2006), Mark Ford gets the tragic irony of "The Ruined Maid" terribly wrong when he speculates that Hardy "found something liberating in the kinds of self-invention that the city made possible," as though desperate country girls turning to prostitution were somehow something to admire.[20] No, self-destruction, not self-invention was the upshot of those sad stories, as the shrewd countryman in Hardy well knew. To appreciate the truly tragic force of "The Ruined Maid" — without sentimental anachronism — one must turn to Mayhew. "At the corner of Drury Lane, I saw three women standing talking together," the author of *London Labour and the London Poor* (1851–62) wrote.

> They were innocent of crinoline, and the antiquity of their bonnets and shawls was really wonderful, while the durability of the fabric of which they were composed was equally remarkable. Their countenances were stolid, and their skin hostile to the application of soap and water. The hair of one was fringed with silver. They were inured to the rattle of their harness; the clank of the chains pleased them. They had grown grey in prostitution.[21]

Lytton Strachey, who reviewed *Satires of Circumstance* (1924) when it first came out was right to remark that "The originality of [Hardy's] poetry lies in the fact that it bears everywhere upon it the impress of a master of prose fiction. Just as the great seventeenth-century writers of prose, such as Sir Thomas Browne and Jeremy Taylor, managed to fill their sentences with the splendour and passion of poetry, while still preserving the texture of an essentially prose style, so Mr. Hardy, by a contrary process, has brought the realism and sobriety of prose into the service of his poetry."[22] And to illustrate his point, he quotes the delightfully apt "At the Draper's," which describes a dying man admitting to his wife how he had seen her in a shop looking at widow's weeds.

---

20 Mark Ford, *Thomas Hardy: Half a Londoner* (New Haven: Yale University Press, 2006), 89.

21 Henry Mayhew, *London Labour and the London Poor*, ed. Christopher Hibbert (London: Folio Society, 1998), 424. It is true that Catherine Walters (1839–1920), the celebrated courtesan, otherwise known as "Skittles," did well enough out of prostitution to have a house in Mayfair in the same Bolt Street in which Henry James lived but she was an exception. As Mayhew copiously documents, the majority of tarts came to very dismal ends. Romanticizing such ends shows a certain blithe hardheartedness.

22 Lytton Strachey, "Mr. Hardy's New Poems" (1914), *Literary Essays* (London: Chatto & Windus, 1948), 221–2.

"You were viewing some lovely things. 'Soon required
For a widow, of latest fashion';
And I knew 'twould upset you to meet the man
Who had to be cold and ashen

"And screwed in a box before they could dress you
'In the last new note in mourning,'
As they defined it. So, not to distress you,
I left you to your adorning."

No narrative verse of which I am aware encapsulates the life of its tale with anything like this bravura concision. Hardy's penchant for the dramatic also shows why the critical editor of the poems, Samuel Hynes is so wrong when he characterizes the poet as making "a fine and private art."[23] No, like Dickens, Hardy was theatrical to his fingertips, in both his poetry and his fiction. Playing to the gallery was of his very essence; and his art, especially the art of his poetry, is a very public witnessing to cares and desiderations, loves and miseries that the entertainer in him knew his audience shared. And here he was not only the consummate storyteller but the consummate countryman, who "must know all about those invisible ones of the days gone by," as the novelist wrote in *The Woodlanders* (1887), "whose feet have traversed the fields which look so grey from his windows … whose creaking plough has turned those sods … whose hands planted the trees that form a crest to the opposite hill; whose horses and hounds have torn through that underwood … what bygone domestic dramas of love, jealousy, revenge or disappointment have been enacted in the cottages, the mansions, the street or on the green." This was hardly the stuff of a "private art," though after Emma died it was his own "bygone domestic dramas of love" that consumed his theatrical muse.

Apropos the poet's fondness for deploying voices in his verse, Michael Millgate, Hardy's biographer, quotes an interesting exchange between Florence and Lady Hoare, a friend of the couple, who would often invite Hardy to her husband's Palladian country house, Stourhead in Wiltshire. Hardy had married Florence in 1914, a young lady 38 years his junior, not only because she shielded him from the bores of fame but shared his love of literature. She was a woman who had come into his life, Hardy was convinced, "To soothe a time-torn man."[24] Reading *Satires of Circumstance*, Florence was aggrieved by the impassioned love it expressed for her predecessor, not to mention its relentless negativity. "It seems to me," she wrote

23 Thomas Hardy, *Selected Poems*, ed. Samuel Hynes (Oxford: Oxford University Press, 1994), xxiv.

24 The phrase comes from Hardy's poem "A Broken Appointment," in *Poems of the Past and the Present* (1901).

Lady Hoare, "that I am an utter failure if my husband can publish such a *sad, sad* book. … I cannot get rid of the feeling that the man who wrote those poems is utterly weary of life—& cares for nothing in the world. If I had been a different sort of woman, & better fitted to be his wife—would he, I wonder, have published that volume?"[25] Lady Hoare tried to console her friend by pointing out that many of the poems were dramatic monologues and, as such, not necessarily reflective of the sentiments of the poet himself, though Florence would not be assuaged. The fact that her famous husband did nothing to help her advance what she hoped, deludedly, by all accounts, might have been her own literary career only exacerbated her sense of grievance. She also resented the honorable pecuniary care that he showed his many necessitous relatives, whom she, or, perhaps, the ghostwriting Hardy, nicely dubbed his "little crowd of annuitants."[26]

Lady Hoare, however, had a point. Hardy is at his most inventive when he gives voice to other voices. A charming example can be found in a poem entitled "Queen Caroline to Her Guests," which appeared in *Human Shows* (1925), where he has his spurned, convivial queen plead:

> Dear friends, stay!
> Lamplit wafts of wit keep sorrow
> In the purlieus of tomorrow:
> Dear friends, stay!
>
> Haste not away!
> Even now may Time be weaving
> Tricks of ravage, wreck, bereaving:
> Haste not away!

In another example, "Christmas Ghost Story" (1896), he has a most arresting ghost pass along a Christmas greeting, which may not be to everyone's taste but certainly tallies with the toughminded Catholic recognition of what Newman nicely called our "aboriginal calamity," without which there should have been no need for the birth of Our Lord and Saviour.

> South of the Line, inland from far Durban,
> A mouldering soldier lies—-your countryman.

25 Millgate, *Thomas Hardy*, 459–60. Despite Florence's complaining of Hardy's gloom, she was not without gloom of her own, being, as Millgate points out, "the possessor of a temperament scarcely less depressive than his own." Indeed, "over the years she would prove capable of descents deep into melancholy, impulsive confidences to people believed to be sympathetic, and suspicions, jealousies, and resentments, sometimes justified, sometimes not, of those who seemed to threaten her position … Her husband's continuing tenderness towards Emma's memory … was just one such irritant she could have lived without." Millgate, *Thomas Hardy*, 457.

26 Millgate, *Thomas Hardy*, 499.

Awry and doubled up are his gray bones,
And on the breeze his puzzled phantom moans
Nightly to clear Canopus: "I would know
By whom and when the All-Earth-gladdening Law
Of peace, brought in by that Man Crucified,
Was ruled to be inept, and set aside?
And what of logic or of truth appears
In tacking "Anno Domini" to the years?
Near twenty-hundred liveried thus have hied,
But tarries yet the Cause for which He died."

Christmas Eve, 1899.

In "He Never Expected Much," Hardy has still another voice explain, with the ghostly echoing reverberation typical of his supernatural poems, why he cannot be counted among the disillusioned. Not surprisingly, Larkin included it in his selection of the poet's work for his *Oxford Book of Twentieth-Century Verse* (1973). In the case of both poets, what Hardy called the "bell of quittance" always called them to lively attention.[27] Indeed, this grim sally could almost have served as a kind of *vade mecum* for the resolutely unillusioned poet of Hull:

Well, World, you have kept faith with me,
Kept faith with me;
Upon the whole you have proved to be
Much as you said you were.
Since as a child I used to lie
Upon the leaze and watch the sky,
Never, I own, expected I
That life would all be fair.

In poems like this, it is almost as though Hardy were trying to convince the rationalists in his midst that he, too, was the foursquare rationalist that he was reputed to be. Moreover, since his association with Leslie Stephen had opened doors to social and literary London that he might not otherwise have entered, this was an image he was careful to cultivate. In his introduction to Stephen's correspondence, Frederick Maitland's quotes Hardy's account of how he answered Stephen's call for a life-defining testimonial, which is worth quoting, since Stephen, as editor of the *Cornhill*, where *Far from the Madding Crowd* was serialized, was one of Hardy's key readers and publishers.

One day [23 March 1875], I received from Stephen a mysterious note asking me to call in the evening, as late as I liked. I went, and found him alone, wandering up and down his library in slippers; his tall

27 The phrase is from Hardy's poem "Afterwards" from *Moments of Vision* (1917).

thin figure wrapt in a heath-coloured dressing gown. After a few remarks on our magazine arrangements, he said he wanted me to witness his signature to what, for a moment, I thought was his will; but it turned out to be a deed renunciatory of holy orders, under the Act of 1870. He said grimly that he was really a reverend gentleman still, little as he might look it, and though he thought it as well to cut himself adrift of a calling for which, to say the least, he had always been utterly unfit. The deed was executed with due formality. Our conversation then turned upon theologies decayed and defunct, the origin of things, the constitution of matter, the unreality of time and kindred subjects. He told me that he had "wasted" much time on systems of religion and metaphysics, and that the new theory of vortex rings had a "staggering fascination" for him."[28]

The boy who had believed the oxen in the barton kneeling before the Christ Child out of reverent love turned into a man who sought the approval of the professionally apostate, the approval of a more socially superior, more highly educated world which Darwin's granddaughter Gwen Raverat describes so vividly in *Period Piece* (1952) as one "where to speak openly of religious matters would have been terribly embarrassing."[29] Hardy, in other words, was something of a climber. Indeed, in a dramatic monologue entitled "An Evening in Galilee," he even ascribes climbing to Our Lady, whom he describes deploring the company her Son keeps.

"Would he'd not mix with the lowest folk—like those fishermen—
The while so capable, culling new knowledge, beyond our ken! ..."

Yet how attached Hardy was to the unbelieving world, for all his aspiring to endear himself to it, is a lively question. "Wessex Heights" (1896)—with its marvelous line—"mind-chains do not clank where one's next neighbor is the sky"—suggests that the attachment was only tenuous. If we contrast "He Never Expected Much" with "The Voice," we can see how much richer the love poem is and how much more expressive of Hardy's true nature. The dying fall of its dactyls are at once plaintive and insistent; the ghostly setting of its rendezvous between the living and the dead stark and harrowing; the longing of its love reminiscent of that love that Eliot so nicely described as being "most nearly itself / When here and now cease to matter."[30] Hardy may have personally given out that he fully subscribed to the rationalist agenda of agnostics like Leslie Stephen;[31] in a letter to

---

28 Hardy quoted in *The Life and Letters of Leslie Stephen*, ed. Frederick Maitland (London: Duckworth & Co, 1906), 287–8.
29 Gwen Raverat, *Period Piece* (London: Faber & Faber, 1952), 222.
30 T. S. Eliot, "East Coker," in *Four Quartets* (London: Faber & Faber, 1943).
31 See *The Life and Letters of Leslie Stephen*, ed. Frederick Maitland (London: Duckworth & Co, 1906).

the Catholic convert, Alfred Noyes, which Hynes quotes in an appendix to his edition for Oxford Authors, he insists that his view of "the Cause of Things" is that it is "neither moral nor immoral, but unmoral: loveless and hateless"; yet the unbiddable lyric poet who writes so much of the great love lyrics confounds the autodidact's trumpery speculations.[32]

> Woman much missed, how you call to me, call to me,
> Saying that now you are not as you were
> When you had changed from the one who was all to me,
> But as at first, when our day was fair.
>
> Can it be you that I hear? Let me view you, then,
> Standing as when I drew near to the town
> Where you would wait for me: yes, as I knew you then,
> Even to the original air-blue gown!
>
> Or is it only the breeze, in its listlessness
> Travelling across the wet mead to me here,
> You being ever dissolved to wan wistlessness,
> Heard no more again far or near?
>
> Thus I; faltering forward,
> Leaves around me falling,
> Wind oozing thin through the thorn from norward,
> And the woman calling.

Tom Paulin clearly stretches matters when he claims that Hardy "could see the Virgin Mary in Emma's blue eyes. And he could see heaven, all eternity there, as well as the many Italian pictures he saw in the National Gallery which use the Marian colour."[33] But the Belfast poet is right to stress that in the most intense of the love poems we see Hardy's religious sensibility at its most appealing. One cannot have immortal longings and no faith. By the same token, one has to be careful about making too much of Hardy's preoccupation with the supernatural. After all, Yeats made a great deal of the supernatural but no one could sensibly consider him Christian.

In struggling with belief and unbelief in his love poetry, Hardy puts one in mind of Browning's witty anatomy of the unfair dilemma posed by unbelief in his "Bishop Blougram's Apology." (1855)—at least from the standpoint of the doctrinaire agnostic. "How can we guard our unbelief / Make it bear fruit to us," he asks in the poem. If unbelief can be no more

32 Hardy to Alfred Noyes (19 December 1920), *Thomas Hardy: The Oxford Authors*, ed. Samuel Hynes (Oxford: Oxford University Press, 1984), 502.

33 *Thomas Hardy: Poems Selected by Tom Paulin*, ed. Tom Paulin (London: Faber & Faber, 2001), xxi.

certain than belief, why not plumb for the latter? Even resolute unbelief—resolute unbelief very much like Hardy's—can never be sure that belief will not reassert itself. Why?

> Just when we are safest, there's a sunset-touch,
> A fancy from a flower-bell, some one's death,
> A chorus-ending from Euripides,—
> And that's enough for fifty hopes and fears
> As old and new at once as nature's self,
> To rap and knock and enter in our soul,
> Take hands and dance there, a fantastic ring,
> Round the ancient idol, on his base again,—
> The grand Perhaps!

Hardy worked strenuously to deny this "grand Perhaps," though the very fact that he could never entirely dismiss it gives his poetry its tension and its zest. In refusing to concede even the possibility of Browning's proposition that:

> soon or late you hit
> Some sense, in which it might be, after all.
> Why not, "The Way, the Truth, the Life?"

Hardy betrays the fragility of his agnosticism. The unbeliever in him protests too much.

III

John Henry Newman, to whose work Hardy paid close attention, was insistent that there could be no real commingling of doubt and faith: to believe was necessarily to reject doubt, but Hardy shows that one could have a great deal of doubt and still not be able to rule out faith entirely.[34] In this regard, he is something of an epitome of the unsettled men and women of his time, so many of whom had their faith in Christianity undermined by what Ruskin called the "dreadful hammers" of the geologists, forever chipping away at orthodox Christianity, without entirely losing their receptivity to the Revelation.[35] The historian G. M. Young, author of the classic

---

34 For a fascinating glimpse into Newman's eminently realistic understanding of belief and unbelief from the standpoint of the unconverted or the would-be converted, see John Henry Newman to Louisa Simeon (25 June 1869), *Letters and Diaries of John Henry Newman*, xxiv, 274–6.

35 Ruskin to Henry Acland quoted in Tim Hilton, *John Ruskin: The Early Years* (New Haven: Yale University Press, 1985), 167. "You speak of the flimsiness of our own faith," Ruskin wrote. "Mine, which was never strong, is being beaten into gold leaf, and flutters in weak rags from the letter of its old forms ... If only the geologists

Victorian England: Portrait of an Age (1936), has some memorable things to say about this aspect of my subject that are worth quoting at length.

> We misread the Victorian age if we do not apprehend how deep, how intimate, and how sincere were the feelings that gathered round, and sustained, its customary life, its religion, and its domestic order. ... And of all of this Hardy is the poet ... This is what the late Victorian age meant, this is what it stands for in the history of the English mind. Here we see with what presuppositions men of a good intelligence thought, what themes engaged their minds and stirred their sympathies, by what causes they judged of things: the pressure of custom, the breaking up of custom, the anxious view into a world where custom had dissolved: the craving for serenity of soul, not sovereign over circumstance, but at least in harmony with itself. And there we may leave the poet, as the darkness gathers about him and his world, wistfully speculating on an alliance, by means of the "interfusing effect of poetry," between "religion, which must be retained unless the world is to perish," and "complete rationality," without which the world will also perish, and, for the last time, circling home to the place from which he had come, to the prayers, the music, and the very stones of the village church.[36]

That Hardy, the son of a stonemason, began his career as an architect, charged with the restoration of churches, was a droll irony. He even composed a prayer of sorts to express his thanks for being freed of what he regarded as his distasteful duties, though it is important to note that he was an accomplished, hard-working, learned architect.

> From restorations of Thy fane,
> From smoothings of Thy sward,
> From zealous Churchmen's pick and plane
> Deliver us O Lord! Amen!

In the critical detachment with which Hardy viewed the vogue for the Gothic in his contemporaries, he demonstrated that he was highly appreciative of the aspirations and limitations of the Tractarians. As he wrote in *Jude the Obscure*: "the most real [Oxonian ghosts] to Jude Fawley were the founders of the religious school called Tractarian; the well-known three, the enthusiast, the poet, and the formularist, the echoes of whose teachings had influenced him even in his obscure home." Raymond Chapman is worth reading on this aspect of the poet, though he confuses the Tractarians

---

would let me alone, I could do very well, but those dreadful hammers! I hear the clink of them at the end of every cadence in the Bible verse."

36 G. M. Young, "Thomas Hardy," in *Victorian Essays* (Oxford: Oxford University Press, 1962), 201–2.

with the High Church, a vulgar error which accountable church historians should be expected to eschew.[37] For Chapman, Hardy's "attitude to what he generally calls 'High Church' principles and practices tends to be cool. It is in essence the attitude of a conservative churchman of the time ... preferring the middle of the road ... to any extremes." His wariness of the Oxford Movement, to which he would give such dramatic expression in *Jude the Obscure*, "is not a simple antipathy to change" but to "a false antiquarianism." For Chapman, Tractarianism could never appeal to "the polarities that were important in [Hardy's] own philosophy," which were "on the one hand, a deep sense of the continuity of life and of the strata of history that were the foundations of the present" and, on the other, an alertness to unpredictable change. As Chapman points out, Hardy

> did not share the hankering of many of his contemporaries for an imagined golden age in any period, but ... drew a sense of stability and even of comfort from the evidence of human patterns constantly repeated. On the other hand, he was uneasily accepting the new age, the "ache of modernism" which might bring forth terrible but essential changes.[38]

Church restoration also gave Hardy a useful excuse for gratifying his taste for the macabre, and to exhibit his occasional inability to tell the story of man's destiny as anything other than an ugly enigma. In "The Church Builder," he has one of his voices describe all of the exacting work he did to restore churches. Yet at the end of his labors, the builder admits to feeling a certain despair.

> My gift to God seems futile, quite;
> The world moves as erstwhile;
> And powerful wrong on feeble right
> Tramples in olden style.
> My faith burns down,
> I see no crown;
> But Cares, and Griefs, and Guile.

Here was a frank admission of the futility of the Anglican investment in the Gothic: it never succeeded in papering over the moral and theological vacuities of the National Church. In Hardy's poem, the remedy for this failure has nothing if not a certain brave simplicity, as the hero of the poem relates:

37 No one conflated the High Church and Tractarianism more licentiously than the confused and blessedly forgotten librarian, Peter Nockles in his ahistorical monograph, *The Oxford Movement in Context Anglican High Churchmanship, 1760–1857* (Cambridge: Cambridge University Press, 1997).
38 Chapman, "'Arguing about the Eastern Position'," 279–80.

Well: Here at morn they'll light on one
Dangling in mockery
Of what he spent his substance on
Blindly and uselessly! ...
"He might," they'll say,
"Have built, some way.
A cheaper gallows-tree!"

Browning was a useful model for Hardy's storytelling in verse. "Browning," J. I. M. Stewart says in a good essay on Hardy in his *Eight Modern Writers* (1963), "was the most important literary influence upon his verse, but it was an influence exercised over one already firmly wedded to the lucidity of hymns and ballads."[39]

Hardy's hymnal clarity has had an enduringly salutary influence on the best of our more recent poets, from W. H. Auden, John Betjeman and Philip Larkin to Charles Causley, James McAuley and Dana Gioia, all of whom have Hardy's gift for negotiating complex subject matter in perspicuous English. One can see the fruits of this pellucidity in Gioia's poem on loss and conation, "The Lost Garden":

The trick is making memory a blessing.
To learn by loss subtraction of desire,
Of wanting nothing more than what has been,
To know the past forever lost, yet seeing
Behind the wall a garden still in bloom.[40]

Hardy took from Browning not only his storytelling but something of his idiomatic energy and his dramatic sense, while nothing of his tedious obscurity, the ruinous effects of which have blighted so many fine poetic talents—none more so than that of incomprehensible Geoffrey Hill, who nonetheless admired Hardy, seeing his poetry, not altogether reliably, as "great lyrical dramas of sexual—particularly marital—solipsism and suicidal introversion."[41] The problem with too much of Hardy's fiction is that it takes its cue not from Browning but from the marriage-hating Ibsen, which makes it at once so impassioned and so wooden.

39 J. I. M. Stewart, *Eight Modern Writers* (Oxford: Oxford University Press 1963) 50. When Larkin received his honorary doctorate from Oxford, Stewart regaled him with an eyewitness account of Hardy's funeral, which he said, "looked like an animated Beerbohm cartoon." Larkin to Robert Conquest (13 July 1984), *Selected Letters of Philip Larkin*, ed. Anthony Thwaite (London: Faber & Faber, 1992), 712.

40 Dana Gioia, "The Lost Garden," *Interrogations at Noon* (Minneapolis: Greywolf Press, 2001), 68.

41 Geoffrey Hill, *Collected Critical Writings*, ed. Kenneth Haynes (Oxford: Oxford University Press, 2008), 417.

One can see two modes—the one scolding, rationalist, and gloomy and the other enraptured, fond and celebratory—contending for mastery throughout Hardy's verse. They are particularly striking in "To an Unborn Pauper Child."

> Breathe not, hid Heart: cease silently,
> And though thy birth-hour beckons thee,
>   Sleep the long sleep:
>   The Doomsters heap
> Travails and teens around us here,
> And Time-wraiths turn our songsingings to fear.
>
> Hark, how the peoples surge and sigh,
> And laughters fail, and greetings die:
>   Hopes dwindle; yea,
>   Faiths waste away,
> Affections and enthusiasms numb:
> Thou canst not mend these things if thou dost come.
>
> Had I the ear of wombèd souls
> Ere their terrestrial chart unrolls,
>   And thou wert free
>   To cease, or be,
> Then would I tell thee all I know,
> And put it to thee: Wilt thou take Life so?
>
> Vain vow! No hint of mine may hence
> To theeward fly: to thy locked sense
>   Explain none can
>   Life's pending plan:
> Thou wilt thy ignorant entry make
> Though skies spout fire and blood and nations quake.
>
> Fain would I, dear, find some shut plot
> Of earth's wide wold for thee, where not
>   One tear, one qualm,
>   Should break the calm.
> But I am weak as thou and bare;
> No man can change the common lot to rare.
>
> Must come and bide. And such are we—
> Unreasoning, sanguine, visionary—
>   That I can hope
>   Health, love, friends, scope
> In full for thee; can dream thou wilt find
> Joys seldom yet attained by humankind!

If the first five stanzas are given over almost entirely to the pinchbeck pity of the abortionist, the last redeems matters with a genuine show of fellow feeling, and a concomitant renunciation of the impulse to regard the unborn child as though he would be somehow better off either dead or in a world of the poet's own devising, where "some shut plot" could guarantee his being spared tears or qualms. When it came to the poet's meretricious pity, Auden was suitably severe: "The worst that can be said against Hardy is that, in unguarded moments, he falls into that most dangerous of all modern heresies, the heresy of pity, that secular parody of Christian sympathy and compassion."[42] This was one of those moments.

The stanzas also remind one of the Book of Job, of the question God poses to all of those who imagine they can arrange things better than the God who created them: "Where were *you* when I laid the foundation of the earth?" (Job 38:4). The literary critic Cynthia Ozick is brilliant on Job's interrogations of God, interrogations which get at the essence of Hardy's own quarrels with his Creator.

> God's answer to Job lies precisely in His not answering; and Job with lightning insight comprehends, ... God denies us a god of our own devising, a god that we would create out of our own malaise or complaint, or desire, or hope, or imagining ... We are part of God's design: can the web manufacture the spider? The Voice out of the whirlwind warns against god-manufacture — against the degradation of a golden calf surely, but also against god-manufacture even in the form of the loftiest visions. Whose visions are they? Beware: they are not God's; they are ours.[43]

Now, of course, Hardy himself might never have agreed with any of this himself, but the last stanza of the poem does. As the poet critic Donald Davie insightfully recognized, "we encounter in his poems things that are not dreamed of in his philosophy," and one of them is the humility to realize that "god-manufacture," especially in the case of the "unreasoning," "sanguine," and "visionary," is not a wise enterprise.[44]

Chesterton had occasion to admire this aspect of Hardy when he met him in a publisher's office and saw that there was no side or swank to the famous novelist: he behaved as though he were "a new writer awaiting his first publisher," a modesty that led the Catholic apologist to conclude that "the rather tremendous truth about Hardy" was that "he had humility."[45] The poet Frances Cornford, Rupert Brooke's friend, corroborated Chesterton's impression after meeting the writer in 1910: "I never saw anyone

42 W. H. Auden, "Thomas Hardy: An Aspect of his Poetry," in *The Complete Works of Auden: Prose: Volume III, 1949–1955* (London: Faber & Faber, 2008), 681.

43 Cynthia Ozick, "The Impious Impatience of Job," in *Quarrel & Quandary* (New York: Knopf, 2000), 71–2.

44 Donald Davie, *Thomas Hardy and British Poetry* (London: Routledge and Kegan Paul, 1973); 45.

45 Chesterton, *Autobiography*, 261–3.

so modest, or so needing appreciation. … The poems are such splendid real things."[46]

It was Hardy's complicated relationship with his first wife Emma that gives so many of his poems about women their *éclat*. Emma was an unusual lady. When Robert Louis Stevenson's wife Fanny met her, she was convinced that Hardy's betrothed was one of the most hideous women she had ever beheld. Later, she wrote to the art critic Sidney Colvin, "What very strange marriages literary men seem to make."[47] But if Emma was not a looker, she was decided in her opinions. Returning from a holiday in Calais, she recommended that one skip the cathedral: it was "not important," containing as it did "the usual paraphernalia of a Continental Roman Catholic country."[48] She also made censorious mention of the insalubrity of the city's drains, a common Protestant complaint, the backwardness of Catholic town planning being regarded as emblematic of the backwardness of the Catholic religion. The tune to which Emma shared the opposition of the Protestant Alliance to "all encroachments of Popery" was extraordinary: she belonged to every No Popery organization in London.[49] Larkin speculated that the poet's "rather unnerving taste for the macabre, his temperamental sunlessness, and his lifelong intense awareness of women exacerbated Emma's peculiarities."[50] Then, again, she was childless. Virginia Woolf noticed in Emma's successor Florence "the large sad lack lustre eyes of a childless woman."[51] The daughter of Leslie Stephen might have seen the same sadness in Emma. Sadness and a certain fierceness, for Emma was a strong, beguiling, irrepressible personality, and she had a great influence over her husband, though it might have been at once oblique and belated. The woman who inspired "Beeny Cliff" (1913), surely one of the loveliest love poems in the language, was no inconsiderable woman.

> O the opal and the sapphire of that wandering western sea,
> And the woman riding high above with bright hair flapping free—
> The woman whom I loved so, and who loyally loved me.[52]

---

46 Cornford quoted in Christopher Hassell, *Rupert Brooke: A Biography* (London: Faber & Faber, 1964), 215. Cornford wrote an amusing poem about Brooke before he was killed in the war: "A young Apollo, golden-haired / Stands dreaming on the verge of strife / Magnificently unprepared / For the long littleness of life."
47 Millgate, *Thomas Hardy*, 250.
48 Millgate, *Thomas Hardy*, 421
49 Millgate, *Thomas Hardy*, 440.
50 Larkin, *Selected Letters*, 143.
51 Virginia Woolf quoted in Millgate, *Thomas Hardy*, 523.
52 "An unforgettable experience to me, scampering up and down the hills on my beloved mare alone, wanting no protection, the rain going down my back often and my hair floating in the wind." Cf. *Some Recollections of Emma Hardy*, ed. Evelyn Hardy and Robert Gittings (Oxford: Oxford University Press, 1961), 50–1.

For all of the great love they bore one another, Emma eventually put Hardy off marriage—what he has one of his voices in "The Christening" (1905) refer to as "sweet Love's sepulchring!" If Ibsen influenced him in this regard, Emma obsessed him. Her misery, no doubt exacerbated by the loneliness she felt sharing a home with a man who did little else but write, became the marriage's misery, and confirmed her husband's long-standing habit of seeing the commandment not to covet one's neighbor's wife as unjustly oppressive. Nevertheless, towards the end of her life, Emma found solace in her faith and wrote in her diary, "outward circumstances are of less importance if Christ is our highest ideal. A strange brilliance shines around our path, penetrating and dispersing difficulties with its warmth and glow."[53] Hardy burned most of Emma's journals. By all accounts, a good deal of what she had to say of him was not flattering. But he did not burn the foregoing. Even before she died—of impacted gallstones, of all things—Hardy put himself to school to her sorrow and made from it some of his most beautiful poetry.

> Where touched the check-floored chancel
> My knees and his?
> The step looks shyly at the sun,
> And says, "'Twas here the thing was done,
> For bale or else for bliss!"
> Of all those there I least was ware
> Would it be that or this
> When touched the check-floored chancel
> My knees and his!
>
> Here in this fateful chancel
> Where all's the same,
> I thought the culminant crest of life
> Was reached when I went forth the wife
> I was not when I came.
> Each commonplace one of my race,
> Some say, has such an aim—
> To go from a fateful chancel
> As not the same.
>
> Here, through this hoary chancel
> Where all's the same,
> A thrill, a gaiety even, ranged
> That morning when it seemed I changed
> My nature with my name.
> Though now not fair, though gray my hair,
> He loved me, past proclaim,

---

53 Emma Hardy, quoted in Millgate, *Thomas Hardy*, 439.

Here in this hoary chancel,
Where all's the same.

IV

Many of Hardy's poems put one in mind of his character, Gabriel Oaks, the shepherd in *Far from the Madding Crowd* (1874), whose yearning for love mirrors his own.

> His Christian name was Gabriel, and on working days he was a young man of sound judgment, easy motions, proper dress, and general good character. On Sundays he was a man of misty views, rather given to postponing, and hampered by his best clothes and umbrella: upon the whole, one who felt himself to occupy morally that vast middle space of Laodicean neutrality which lay between the Communion people of the parish and the drunken section, — that is, he went to church, but yawned privately by the time the congregation reached the Nicene creed, and thought of what there would be for dinner when he meant to be listening to the sermon.

Gabriel epitomizes the "broad church" Anglican whom no amount of Tractarianism of the sort that attracted the hero of *Jude the Obscure*, Jude Frawley could budge, though it is important to keep in mind that it is in the midst of his contemporaries' "Laodicean neutrality" that Hardy presents his aloof, indifferent, yet inescapable God. The Gloucester poet Ivor Gurney offered one interpretation of Hardy's understanding of this "neutrality" when he wrote a correspondent from the trenches: "The truth is, as Hardy says, that the English fall back on stoical fatalism; and whatever it is they believe it is not Christianity. They go to Church, and desire something spiritual, but it is nothing the Churches give them. They … are self-reliant not relying on God."[54] One can agree with this only up to a point. The self-reliance of the English did not breed unbelief: it bred mistrust of unbelief.

Still, this Laodicean neutrality," as Hardy called it, can be seen throughout his work. For example, there is the scene in *Far from the Madding Crowd* where Bathsheba and Gabriel overhear the children's choir singing Newman's "Lead, Kindly Light" in the village church.

> Whilst she stood and read and meditated the tones of the organ began again in the church, and she went with the same light step round to the porch and listened. The door was closed, and the choir was learning a new hymn. Bathsheba was stirred by emotions which

---

54 Gurney to Marion Scott (8 October 1916), *Ivor Gurney War Letters*, ed. R. K. R. Thornton (London: The Hogarth Press, 1984), 106.

35

latterly she had assumed to be altogether dead within her. The little attenuated voices of the children brought to her ear in distinct utterance the words they sang without thought or comprehension—

> Lead, kindly Light, amid the encircling gloom,
> Lead Thou me on.

No sooner does Bathsheba begin listening to the children singing Newman's hymn than she is stirred to her core.

> Something big came into her throat and an uprising to her eyes— and she thought that she would allow the imminent tears to flow if they wished. They did flow and plenteously ... She would have given anything in the world to be, as those children were, unconcerned at the meaning of their words, because too innocent to feel the necessity for any such expression.

What is striking here is that Hardy has Bathsheba envy the children not for their faith, but for their ignorance of the meaning of the words they sing, while Gabriel is utterly indifferent to the hymn or its words. As Newman wrote in his King William Street lectures, "It is no work of a day to convince the intellect of an Englishman that Catholicism is true."[55] Hardy certainly took pains to have Jude confirm Newman's view of his countrymen's ineducability on this score. "At dusk that evening he went into the garden and dug a shallow hole, to which he brought out all the theological and ethical works that he possessed, and had stored here. He knew that, in this country of true believers, most of them were not saleable at a much higher price than waste-paper value, and preferred to get rid of them in his own way, even if he should sacrifice a little money to the sentiment of thus destroying them." The crack about "true believers" here shows the satirical Hardy at his best, confirming as it does the man's mocking recognition that he is not the only one in Anglican England who did not believe in the National Church. Then comes the book burning: "Lighting some loose pamphlets to begin with, he cut the volumes into pieces as well as he could, and with a three-pronged fork shook them over the flames. They kindled, and lighted up the back of the house, the pigsty, and his own face, till they were more or less consumed." Who were the authors of the books thus burned? Jeremy Taylor, Butler, Doddridge, Paley, Pusey, and Newman. And the moral of the book burning? Just this: Jude "might go on believing as before, but he professed nothing, and no longer owned and exhibited engines of faith which, as their proprietor, he might naturally be supposed to exercise on himself first of all. In his passion ...

---

55 John Henry Newman, *Difficulties of Anglicans*, ed. Edward Short (Leominster: Gracewing, 2021), I, 435. The page number in Newman's last revised edition is 399.

he could not stand as an ordinary sinner, and not as a whited sepulchre." Newman, very likely, would have been amused to see his Tractarian work included in this bonfire of the Anglicans. After he converted to the Church of Rome, as we can see from his excoriation of the Oxford Movement and all of its pedigree in *Anglican Difficulties*, he held no brief for what he called its "mimic Catholicism."[56] However, he might have seen the work of Hardy himself as something of an illustration of that memorable passage of his in *The Idea of a University* (1875) where he exhorts his readers, "Quarry the granite rock with razors, or moor the vessel with a thread of silk; then may you hope with such keen and delicate instruments as human knowledge and human reason to contend against those giants, the passion and the pride of man."[57]

V

In assessing Hardy's relationship to Christianity, one has to keep in mind that he wrote a fair amount of nonsense on the subject. Indeed, he was not above giving out that poetry and religion were really one and the same. In his "Apology" for *Late Lyrics and Earlier* (1922), he declares that "poetry, pure literature in general, religion—I include religion, in its essential and undogmatic sense, because poetry and religion touch each other, or rather modulate into each other; are, indeed, often but different names for the same thing." This was nonsense when Arnold asserted it in the nineteenth century: and it was no less so when Hardy reasserted it in the twentieth. Here is Arnold:

> I believe that Christianity will survive because of its natural truth. Those who fancied that they had done with it, those who had thrown it aside because what was presented to them under its name was so unreceivable, will have to return to it again, and to learn it better. ... Neither will the old forms of Christian worship be extinguished by the growth of a truer conception of their essential contents. Those forms ... will not disappear. They will survive as poetry.[58]

56 Newman, *Difficulties of Anglicans*, I, xiii, lxxxvi, 14.
57 John Henry Newman, *The Idea of a University: Defined and Illustrated* (London: Longmans, Green & Co., 1907), 121
58 Matthew Arnold, *Last Essays on Church and Religion* (London: John Murray, 1903), xxiii. It was none other than Newman who gave Arnold and, indeed, Pater, the idea that poetry could somehow act as a substitute for religion, an idea he floated in response to John Keble's immensely popular collection of Anglican devotional poems, *The Christian Year* (1827), which went into 95 editions in Keble's lifetime alone. For Newman, Keble had succeeded in giving Anglicans a version of their religion in verse that the National Church itself had failed to give them. See Edward Short, *Newman and his Contemporaries*, 337–9.

In response, Eliot was contemptuous of what he nicely referred to as the poet's "conjuring trick." "For Arnold," Eliot wrote in *The Use of Poetry and the Use of Criticism* (1933), "the best poetry supersedes religion and philosophy ... The most generalized form of my own view is simply this: that nothing in this world or the next is a substitute for anything else; and if you find that you must do without something, such as religious faith or philosophic belief, then you must just do without it."[59]

In attempting to understand Hardy, Eliot can be a useful figure. If the Dorset poet grew up and came to manhood in Victorian England, his poetry was the early twentieth-century bridge between Arnold and Eliot. After all, Hardy was still writing when Eliot published *The Waste Land* (1922); indeed, he was giving center stage to the question of faith that the great Modernist poem was written, in part, to address. It is true that Eliot was not altogether appreciative of Hardy's genius. "The later work of Thomas Hardy is an interesting example of a powerful personality uncurbed by any institutional attachment or by submission to any objective beliefs," Eliot wrote, somewhat mystifyingly, if one considers his own freedom, when he first made his mark, from "any institutional attachment or ... objective beliefs." It is also strange that he should rate Hardy for being "unhampered by any ideas":[60] the very thing for which he famously praised Henry James, whose "critical genius," he contended, "comes out most tellingly in its mastery over, his baffling escape from Ideas; a mastery and an escape, which are perhaps the last test of a superior intelligence."[61] Then, again, it was simply false of Eliot to claim that Hardy was unhampered "by what sometimes acts as a partial restraint upon inferior writers, the desire to please a large public." Hardy never left off deliberately and quite brilliantly entertaining a large and miscellaneous audience. Eliot's other strictures against Hardy were no less unpersuasive: "He seems to have written as nearly for the sake of 'self-expression' as a man well can; and the self which he had to express does not strike me as a particularly wholesome or edifying matter of communication. He was indifferent even to the prescripts of good writing; he wrote sometimes overpoweringly well, but always very carelessly."[62] The note of uncritical prejudice in such observations is patent. Indeed, Eliot himself regretted them, telling Stephen Spender in the wake of the publication of *After Strange Gods* (1934) that his com-

59 T. S. Eliot, *The Use of Poetry and the Use of Criticism* (London: Faber & Faber, 1933), 113.

60 T. S. Eliot, *After Strange Gods: The Page-Barbour Lectures at the University of Virginia, 1933* (London: Faber & Faber, 1934), 54.

61 T. S. Eliot, "Henry James" (1918) from *Selected Prose of T. S. Eliot*, ed. Frank Kermode (London: Faber & Faber, 1975), 151.

62 Eliot, *After Strange Gods*, 54–6.

ments had been made "for the purpose of proving one's point"; and when writing polemical criticism, "it is necessary to know one's authors from cover to cover—and I didn't. … I ought to have read the whole of Hardy … without any design whatever, and have known it ever so well, before generalising about it. … I mean that you don't really criticise an author to whom you have never surrendered yourself."[63] If Eliot had followed his own eminently sage advice, he would have found that Hardy's poetry is not only a corroboration of the untenability of unbelief inaugurated by Arnold but a foreshadowing of his own acting on that untenability both in his conversion and his composition of such Christian works as "Ash Wednesday," "The Journey of the Magi" and *Four Quartets*.

Yet there is another affinity between Hardy and Eliot: the poets in them were both transformed by the tormented love they bore their first wives. Take Emma and Vivienne out of the equation and neither poet would be recognizable. Certainly, Eliot's rueful meditations on his marriage after the death of Vivienne were no less lacerating than those Hardy suffered after Emma's going. For both, retrospection became penitential. In 1960, five years before his death, Eliot acknowledged that while the marriage "had brought no happiness" to Vivienne, it had brought to him "the state of mind out of which came *The Waste Land*." His marital ordeals, in other words, had paid unexpected dividends to his poetry. Indeed, Eliot gratefully acknowledged his debt to the wife whose mental troubles had consumed so much of his youth. "Vivienne nearly was the death of me," he confessed, "but she kept the poet alive. In retrospect, the nightmare agony of my seventeen years with Vivienne seems to me preferable to the dull misery of the mediocre teacher of philosophy which would have been the alternative."[64] Nowadays, of course, Eliot is pilloried by a society that does not believe in sacramental penance—only pillorying—but he knew how to express contrition with a conscientious exactitude that would have impressed the compunctious Hardy. In "Little Gidding," Eliot considers the "gifts reserved for age" and sees only

> the rending pain of re-enactment
> Of all that you have done, and been; the shame
> Of motives late revealed, and the awareness
> Of things ill done and done to others' harm
> Which once you took for exercise of virtue.
> Then fools' approval stings, and honour stains.

63 Eliot to Stephen Spender (9 May 1935), *The Letters of T. S. Eliot, Volume 7: 1934–1935*, ed. Valerie Eliot and John Haffenden (London: Faber & Faber, 2017), 617.

64 Eliot quoted in Ann Pasternak Slater, *The Fall of a Sparrow: Vivien Eliot's Life and Writings* (London: Faber & Faber, 2020), 492–3.

Having found himself in the dark wood at about the same age as Dante, Eliot converted. Yes, he wrote his poetry to negotiate his sense of sin, but he had a religion that helped him to atone for the sin. Hardy did not have any religion to help him sort out his sense of sin. And this is one reason why he might have inclined to imagine that poetry offered a serviceable substitute for religion. What makes his grasping at this peculiar driftwood ironic, however, is that it was derived in his case from a misreading of Newman's *Apologia Pro Vita Sua* (1864), about which he wrote in his diary:

> Newman's *Apologia*, which we have all been talking about lately. A great desire to be convinced by him ... Style charming, and his logic really human, being based not on syllogisms but on converging probabilities. Only — and here comes the fatal catastrophe — there is no first link to his excellent chain of reasoning, and down you come headlong. Poor Newman! His gentle childish faith in revelation and tradition must have made him a very charming character.[65]

Later, Hardy would reveal that although Newman's "Lead, Kindly Light" was one of his favorite hymns, he could never regard his prose as persuasive. Why? For Hardy, "Newman was no logician ... the *Apologia* was simply a poet's work, with a kind of lattice-work of logic in places to screen the poetry."[66] Elsewhere, contrasting Newman with Carlyle, he wrote:

> The former's was a feminine nature, which first decides, and then finds reasons for having decided. He was an enthusiast with the absurd reputation of a logician and reasoner. Carlyle was a poet with the reputation of a philosopher. Neither was truly a *thinker*.[67]

The notes that Hardy made in response to his reading of the *Apologia* clearly show, as the astute critic Jan Paweł Jędrzejewski shows, that the poet focused on those passages of the book dealing with the difficulties confronting Christian belief *per se*, rather than Newman's own grounds for conversion to Catholicism.[68] In this case, it was Hardy, not Newman, who first decided and then found reasons for having decided.

Still, if Hardy followed Arnold in touting the fallacy that poetry could be a kind of religion, he also suffered the anguish Arnold suffered for abandoning what he knew, *ex corde*, he could not abandon.[69] And it is this that

---

65 Hardy, quoted in Robert Gittings, *Young Thomas Hardy* (New York: Little Brown, 1975), 70.

66 Hardy, quoted in Jan Paweł Jędrzejewski, "Thomas Hardy and Roman Catholicism," *The Thomas Hardy Journal*, vol., 9, no. 1 (February 1993), 31. This is an unusually good essay, well worth reading.

67 Hardy, quoted in Jędrzejewski, "Thomas Hardy and Roman Catholicism," 30.

68 Jędrzejewski, "Thomas Hardy and Roman Catholicism," 29–30.

69 See Edward Short, "Culture and Hollowness: Newman and Matthew Arnold,"

makes him worth reading on religious matters. He could never be stayed from his heart's desire even in the place that Eliot recognized as "a place of disaffection."[70] The last concluding stanza of "The Darkling Thrush," the best of his poems about the Christian faith, amply proves that.

> So little cause for carolings
> Of such ecstatic sound
> Was written on terrestrial things
> Afar or nigh around,
> That I could think there trembled through
> His happy good-night air
> Some blessed Hope, whereof he knew
> And I was unaware.

Does this make Hardy a Christian poet *malgré lui?* In his introduction to the Penguin edition of the poet's selected poems, Robert Mezey says that Hardy "is a Christian who is simply no longer able to believe in Christian doctrine."[71] In 1885, the poet himself gave some sanction to this otherwise dubious characterization by writing to the liberal politician and rationalist John Morley: "I have sometimes had a dream that the church, instead of being disendowed, could be made to modulate by degrees (say as the present incumbents die out) into an undogmatic, non-theological establishment for the promotion of that virtuous living on which all honest men are agreed — leaving to voluntary bodies the organisation of whatever societies they may think best for teaching their various forms of doctrinal religion."[72] Of course, Newman would only have seen well-meaning Socinianism in such a dream. "From the age of fifteen, dogma has been the fundamental principle of my religion," he told his readers in the *Apologia*, "I cannot enter into the idea of any other sort of religion; religion as a mere sentiment, is to me a dream and a mockery."[73] The American poet John Crowe Ransom, in calling Hardy "a disaffected religionist," might have been nearer the truth of what in any case was an odd religiosity.[74] Of all Hardy's commentators, however, Ivor Gurney is perhaps the most perceptive when it comes to the poet's relationship to the Christian religion, holding as he did that

---

in *Newman and his Contemporaries* (London: T&T Clark, 2011), 335–60.

70 T. S. Eliot, "East Coker," in *Four Quartets*.

71 *Thomas Hardy Selected Poems*, ed. Robert Mezey (London: Penguin Books 1998), xxv.

72 Hardy, quoted in Millgate, *Thomas Hardy*, 247.

73 John Henry Newman, *Apologia pro Vita Sua*, ed. Martin Svaglic (Oxford: Oxford University Press, 1967), 54. In the last edition Newman saw through the press the page number is 49.

74 *Selected Poems of Thomas Hardy*, ed. John Crowe Ransom (New York: Macmillan, 1961), xxxiii.

"Hardy's sins are chiefly the result of a narrow spiritual outlook, and a dryness of soul."[75]

Flannery O'Connor once said that "Smugness is the Great Catholic Sin. I find it in myself."[76] For the cradle or convert Catholic, the salutary thing about reading Hardy is that it disabuses one of smugness. He shows what a mysterious and, indeed, inestimable gift faith is, especially in light of the difficulties those without faith experience in struggling to apprehend, let alone possess it. "God's Funeral" drives home Hardy's appreciation of the indispensability of faith—and, what is perhaps even more important, the diffidence he felt in following rationalists like Leslie Stephen in assuming it somehow dead and gone.[77] Yes, in his cocky, provocative way, he had once joked, "I have been looking for God for 50 years and I think that if he had existed, I should have discovered him,"[78] but this was certainly not the poet speaking, the poet "whose consciousness of sorrow"[79] is indissolubly linked to his need for the God whom his flippant theorizing has sent away.

> Still, how to bear such loss I deemed
> The insistent question for each animate mind

The whole intellectual, moral and religious history of nineteenth-century England is summed up in these two lines, not to mention Hardy's own history.

Another interesting quality about Hardy's verse is that so much of it captures the sensibility of a man who may not have assented to faith but has nevertheless the impulses of a man of faith, especially when it comes to conscience-laden contrition. After all, the poems he wrote with his first wife Emma in mind are all poems of contrition. Then, again, in 1922, he

---

75 Gurney to Mrs. Voynich (late September 1915) in *Ivor Gurney War Letters*, 40. Ethel Lillian Voynich (1864–1960) was a composer whom Gurney had met at the Royal College of Music, one of whose compositions was a cantata in honor of the Irish nationalist Roger Casement, whom the English executed for treason during the Great War.

76 O'Connor to "A" (17 January 1956), *The Habit of Being: Letters of Flannery O'Connor,* ed. Sally Fitzgerald (New York: Farrar, Straus, Giroux, 1979), 131.

77 In a letter to Edmund Gosse (18 July 1913), Hardy had written that "'God's Funeral' would have been enough in itself to damn me for the Laureateship, even if I had tried for or thought of it, which of course I did not. Fancy Nonconformity on the one hand, and Oxford on the other, pouring out their vials on poor Mr. Asquith for such an enormity!'" As it was, the English Establishment accepted Hardy as one of their own: he was buried in Westminster Abbey.

78 See *ODNB*.

79 The phrase appears in the second stanza of "God's Funeral"—and is a nice confirmation of Davie's incisive point that "Time and again [Hardy] writes in ways that it seems his declared intentions and his professed ideolog would have ruled out." Donald Davie, *Thomas Hardy and British Poetry* (London: Routledge and Kegan Paul, 1973), 41.

wrote a poem of excoriating self-examination that towers above anything any Catholic poets were writing at the time. If not explicitly Christian, it is certainly not atheist. It also confirms a good point that Auden makes about Hardy: that his putative pessimism was really a rejection of the "doctrine of automatic progress, the elimination of evil by the mere flow of history."[80] In other words, Hardy saw evil as evil: and what is more, he saw evil in himself.

Surview
"Cogitavi vias meas"[81]

A cry from the green-grained sticks of the fire
Made me gaze where it seemed to be:
'Twas my own voice talking therefrom to me
On how I had walked when my sun was higher—
My heart in its arrogancy.

"You held not to whatsoever was true,"
Said my own voice talking to me:
"Whatsoever was just you were slack to see;
Kept not things lovely and pure in view,"
Said my own voice talking to me.

"You slighted her that endureth all,"
Said my own voice talking to me;
"Vaunteth not, trusteth hopefully;
That suffereth long and is kind withal,"
Said my own voice talking to me.

"You taught not that which you set about,"
Said my own voice talking to me;
"That the greatest of things is Charity ..."
—And the sticks burnt low, and the fire went out,
And my voice ceased talking to me.

Donald Davie excluded Hardy from his *New Oxford Book of Christian Verse* (1981) on the grounds that, although some of his poems "wish to believe, though they cannot" (he cited "The Oxen"), none of them were properly Christian.[82] For Davie, the son of a Yorkshire Baptist, who only converted to his own rather fanciful "broad church" understanding of the Anglican Church in his fifties while teaching in California, Christian poetry must

---

80 W. H. Auden, "Thomas Hardy: An Aspect of his Poetry," in *The Complete Works of W. H. Auden, Prose, Volume III, 1949–1955* (London: Faber & Faber, 2008), 681.

81 This is a quotation from Psalm 119:59: "Cogitavi vias meas et converti pedes meos in testimonia tua," "I thought on my ways and turned my feet unto thy testimonies."

82 *The New Oxford Book of Christian Verse*, ed. Donald Davie (Oxford: Oxford University Press: 1981), xx.

be defined with a certain astringency as appealing to a "body of dogma," to "some one or more of the distinctive doctrines of the Christian church: to the Incarnation ... Redemption, Judgement, the Holy Trinity, the Fall";[83] otherwise we should have to cast definition aside and open the flood-gates to what he called "*religious* verse," to "yeasty yearnings towards 'the transcendent.'"[84] Was this just? I should say that while Davie had a point about the need to define Christian poetry, I do not know that trying to define it in strictly dogmatical terms is possible. Lyrical poetry, by its very nature, cannot be expected to be dogmatical. Instead, Davie might have simply asked himself what good artful poets in his various periods had to say of Christianity, or of themes pertaining to Christianity, and made his choice in accordance with those criteria. For him to regard Hardy's preoccupations with transcendence as somehow *outré* was far too astringent. After all, not all interest in the transcendental is Emersonian bosh. Yes, Hardy himself might not have been a Christian, but he did manage to write poems replete with Christian impulses, one of which, "On a Discovered Curl of Hair," shows how the poet never stopped yearning for love—love beyond the grave, resurrected love.

> When your soft welcomings were said,
> This curl was waving on your head,
> And when we walked where breakers dinned
> It sported in the sun and wind,
> And when I had won your words of grace
> It brushed and clung about my face.
> Then, to abate the misery
> Of absentness, you gave it me.
>
> Where are its fellows now? Ah, they
> For brightest brown have donned a gray,
> And gone into a caverned ark,
> Ever unopened, always dark!
>
> Yet this one curl, untouched of time,
> Beams with live brown as in its prime,
> So that it seems I even could now
> Restore it to the living brow
> By bearing down the western road
> Till I had reached your old abode.

In one of his last poems, Hardy took a swipe at Chesterton, claiming that the paradoxical author was a "literary contortionist" given to imputing

---

83 Davie, *Christian Verse*, xx–xxi.
84 Davie, *Christian Verse*, xx.

blasphemy to those whose views he did not share.[85] This was in response to Chesterton calling the poet a "village atheist" fifteen years earlier—even though GKC later explained that he had resorted to the epithet not in censure of the older writer's honesty, but in praise.[86] Why this *contretemps* should have preoccupied Hardy on his deathbed is a nice question. Could it have been because the dying man could not die before he had refuted the imputation of blasphemy? True blasphemers revel in blasphemy: Thomas Hardy did not. Of course, he was inclined to argue that belief was insupportable and unbelief man's only rational option; but the poet in him—the extraordinarily good poet—only succeeded in showing that man is made for belief, not unbelief, a condition of his nature which no amount of agnosticism or rationalism or even blasphemy can alter.

85 "Epitaph for G. K. Chesterton." In another context, Hardy had called GKC: "a phrasemongering literary contortionist," *The Personal Notebooks of Thomas Hardy*, ed. Richard H. Taylor (London: 1978), 259.
86 Chesterton, *Autobiography*, 266–7.

Kipling:
The Unheralded Christian Poet

I

In the barbarous cultural circumstances in which we find ourselves, no writer is more unfairly traduced than Rudyard Kipling. Charles McGrath nicely captured this recently in a *New Yorker* essay:

> Rudyard Kipling used to be a household name. Born in 1865 in Bombay, where his father taught at an arts school, and then exiled as a boy to England, he returned to India as a teen-ager, and quickly established himself as the great chronicler of the Anglo-Indian experience. He was Britain's first Nobel laureate in literature, and probably the most widely read writer since Tennyson. People knew his poems by heart, read his stories to their children. The Queen wanted to knight him. But in recent years Kipling's reputation has taken such a beating that it's a wonder any sensible critic would want to go near him now. Kipling has been variously labelled a colonialist, a jingoist, a racist, an anti-Semite, a misogynist, a right-wing imperialist warmonger; and—though some scholars have argued that his views were more complicated than he is given credit for—to some degree he really was all those things. That he was also a prodigiously gifted writer who created works of inarguable greatness hardly matters anymore, at least not in many classrooms, where Kipling remains politically toxic.

The beauty of McGrath's testimony to this lamentable state of affairs is that it comes with a certain ungainsayable authority. After all, McGrath is a hireling of the cancel culture to which he refers. No one could possibly write for the *New Yorker* who was not. Thus, for him to suggest that this implacable culture might be going just a little too far in banishing Kipling from the classroom says a lot, though one could cite many other literary functionaries to the same effect. "All anthologists cower at the thought of their omissions and hard choices," Daniel Karlin, Professor of English at the University of Bristol wrote in his introduction to his excellent critical

47

edition of Kipling's poems and verse for the Oxford Authors series; "but the selector of Kipling fears hate mail."

Since I recently finished compiling *The Saint Mary's Book of Christian Verse* for the English Catholic publisher Gracewing, I can empathize with Karlin. With regard to my own anthology, I agonize over the hard choices I made with respect to Kipling's verse every day—obsessively, unavailingly; though I can honestly say that I do not lose sleep over running afoul of the woke brigade. Neither an academic nor a journalist, I am immune to the menaces of those bullying louts. They can neither cancel nor intimidate me. The person I am loth to rub the wrong way is the general reader. Being a general reader myself, I naturally expect anthologists to make their choices sensibly. Indeed, one reason why I am writing the present essay is to make some atonement for what I know is the inadequate selection I was constrained to make of the riches of Kipling's verse. When Prof. Karlin admits in his preface that "A complete and magnificent volume could be compiled from what I have left out," I could not be in more sympathetic agreement with him. Here, I shall discuss some of what I regard as the real glories of Kipling's verse, which I had no space to showcase in my collection, particularly his Christian verse. But before I do that I should start by addressing why Kipling remains so *outré* for certain readers.

The best place to start for this enterprise of clarification is Kipling's famous, or perhaps I should say, infamous poem, "Recessional,"

God of our fathers, known of old,
Lord of our far-flung battle-line,
Beneath whose awful Hand we hold
Dominion over palm and pine
Lord God of Hosts be with us yet,
Lest we forget—lest we forget!

The tumult and the shouting dies;
The Captains and the Kings depart:
Still stands Thine ancient sacrifice,
An humble and a contrite heart.
Lord God of Hosts, be with us yet,
Lest we forget—lest we forget!

Far-called, our navies melt away;
On dune and headland sinks the fire:
Lo, all our pomp of yesterday
Is one with Nineveh and Tyre!
Judge of the Nations, spare us yet,
Lest we forget—lest we forget!

If, drunk with sight of power, we loose
Wild tongues that have not Thee in awe,

Such boastings as the Gentiles use,
Or lesser breeds without the Law
Lord God of Hosts, be with us yet,
Lest we forget—lest we forget!

For heathen heart that puts her trust
In reeking tube and iron shard,
All valiant dust that builds on dust,
And guarding, calls not Thee to guard,
For frantic boast and foolish word
Thy mercy on Thy People, Lord!

Many readers over the years have oddly misread the poem. Despite its recognition of the perils of power and its calls for humility, they have contrived to see it as an endorsement of empire. Written at the end of Queen Victoria's Jubilee in 1897, the poem is not an endorsement, but a chastisement of empire.

The poem is also suffused with Biblical references. *God of our fathers* is a phrase found in Deuteronomy 26:7 and many other places; *Lord God of Hope* also shows in many places, including 2 Samuel 5:10; *Lest we forget* recalls Deuteronomy 4:9: "Only take heed to thyself, and keep thy soul diligently, lest thou forget the things which thine eyes have seen, and lest they depart, from thy heart all the days of thy life, but teach them thy sons, and thy sons' sons." Then, again, *The tumult and the shouting dies* both alludes to and transforms Amos 2:2: "Moab shall die with tumult, with shouting, and with the sound of the trumpet." *The Captains and the Kings depart* recalls Zechariah 10:11: "the pride of Assyria shall be brought down, and the sceptre of Egypt depart away." *A humble and a contrite heart* is another phrase taken directly from the Bible: Psalm 51:17: "The sacrifices of God are a broken and a contrite heart, O God, thou will not despise." *Judge of the Nations* echoes Isaiah 2:4: "And he shall judge among the nations."[1] If Kipling were somehow an uncritical advocate of empire, he chose to advocate it in peculiarly admonitory terms. The admonitions, moreover, to which he helped himself were those not of politicians but sacred Scripture. And this is one reason why his verses have their power. He never writes to curry favor. Even in "Danny Deever," one of his most justifiably popular verses, he will not sentimentalize his hero to endear himself to the soldiers whose dignity he so much respects: Danny is a "sneakin', shootin' hound." Why? He shot someone asleep whom he should have shot face-to-face. This is not the sort of wit to amuse civilians—it is too bloody-minded—but it is the sort that those who follow the profession of arms, with all its horrors and

---

1 For all of these references and more, see *Rudyard Kipling: Stories and Poems*, ed. Daniel Karlin (Oxford: Oxford University Press, 2015), 666–8.

bleak, crazy comedy—naturally relish. Admirers of Owen and Sassoon and the other First World War poets might not be inclined to agree but "Danny Deever" is one of the best war poems ever written precisely because it is one of the best soldier poems ever written.

II

George Orwell was one of Kipling's most incisive critics, deploring what he saw as his meretriciousness and yet always honest about his merits. In an essay on Kipling written in 1936, Orwell put the controversial author's preoccupations with empire in perspective:

> What is much more distasteful in Kipling than sentimental plots or vulgar tricks of style, is the imperialism to which he chose to lend his genius. The most one can say is that when he made it the choice was more forgivable than it would be now. The imperialism of the 'eighties and 'nineties was sentimental, ignorant and dangerous, but it was not entirely despicable. The picture then called up by the word "empire" was a picture of overworked officials and frontier skirmishes, not of Lord Beaverbrook and Australian butter. It was still possible to be an imperialist and a gentleman.

The reference here to the imperialist Beaverbrook is apt, though it should be remembered that he was the inspiration of one of Kipling's bitterest *bons mots*, which he gave to Stanley Baldwin for one of his speeches: "What the proprietorship of these papers is aiming at is power and power without responsibility—the prerogative of the whore throughout the ages."

Throughout the ages ... Kipling's sense of time, his sense of wrong and the foolishness of man is always shown in terms of the long, never the short term. He would be amused, not angered to see his reputation so vexed by the purveyors of political correctness. After all, those purveyors have confirmed his sagest prognostications.

> When desperate Folly daily laboureth
> To work confusion upon all we have,
> When diligent Sloth demandeth Freedom's death,
> And banded Fear commandeth Honour's grave—
> Even in that certain hour before the fall,
> Unless men please they are not heard at all.

An added twist here is that no author ever endeavored more to please than Kipling—his mastery of the various forms in which he worked shows this—and yet, despite the elaborate pleasure he offers his readers, especially those of his readers in positions of power, he is not heard. His warnings fall on deaf ears.

In a later essay of 1941, Orwell was quick to point out to readers that, although Kipling was an imperialist, the attitude to imperialism that he expressed in "Recessional" was far from jingoistic. He was never a believer in "might makes right" nor any burly nationalism defiant of law. "And yet the 'Fascist' charge has to be answered," Orwell recognized, "because the first clue to any understanding of Kipling, morally or politically, is the fact that he was *not* a Fascist. He was further from being one than the most humane or the most 'progressive' person is able to be nowadays." The woke brigade might not be capable of recognizing this but the rest of us should be.

> An interesting instance of the way in which quotations are par-roted to and fro without any attempt to look up their context or discover their meaning is the line from "Recessional"—"Lesser breeds without the Law". This line is always good for a snigger in pansy-left circles. It is assumed as a matter of course that the "lesser breeds" are "natives", and a mental picture is called up of some pukka sahib in a pith helmet kicking a coolie. In its context the sense of the line is almost the exact opposite of this. The phrase "lesser breeds" refers almost certainly to the Germans, and especially the pan-German writers, who are "without the Law" in the sense of being lawless, not in the sense of being powerless. The whole poem, conventionally thought of as an orgy of boasting, is a denunciation of power politics, British as well as German.

This is not only balanced, it is brilliant criticism, and it is interesting to see how Kipling's own prophetic work bears out Orwell's interpretation of it. Nothing Kipling ever wrote is as prophetic as "Justice" (1918), though now it is not so much the Germans we think of when we read it as our own proud, faithless, antinomian selves.

> A People and their King
>   Through ancient sin grown strong,
> Because they feared no reckoning
>   Would set no bound to wrong;
> But now their hour is past,
>   And we who bore it find
> Evil Incarnate held at last
>   To answer to mankind.
>
> For agony and spoil
>   Of nations beat to dust,
> For poisoned air and tortured soil
>   And cold, commanded lust,
> And every secret woe
>   The shuddering waters saw—
> Willed and fulfilled by high and low—
>   Let them relearn the Law

As it happened, the people who "feared no reckoning" and "set no bound to wrong" might have proved themselves "Evil Incarnate" in the First World War, but they would also get up to even more staggering barbarity in the Second. Manifestly, they did not "relearn the Law." Nor have we. The Allies, who might have claimed some moral victory when they defeated the Nazis, are now little better than their erstwhile foe. They certainly share with them a delight in the engines of tyranny: state control, state propaganda, state thuggery and, of course, state eugenics. It is no piece of muddled equivalence to say that we are all fallen—obscenely fallen.

And it is to this reality that Kipling, who, by all accounts had a very bad brush with Calvinism as a child, speaks most eloquently in his poetry. Whenever he goes into his prophetic mode—a mode he handles rather well—he always returns to the pride and vanity of man. He is fascinated by Original Sin. He is fascinated by the failure of man. He is fascinated by how this failure risks involving man in a kind of final failure. One can see all of this clearly in "The Deep Sea Cables":

The wrecks dissolve above us; their dust drops down from afar—
Down to the dark, to the utter dark, where the blind white sea-snakes are.
There is no sound, no echo of sound, in the deserts of the deep,
Or the great grey level plains of ooze where the shell-burred cables creep.

Here in the womb of the world—here on the tie-ribs of earth
Words, and the words of men, flicker and flutter and beat—
Warning, sorrow and gain, salutation and mirth—
For a Power troubles the Still that has neither voice nor feet.

They have wakened the timeless Things; they have killed their father Time
Joining hands in the gloom, a league from the last of the sun.
Hush! Men talk to-day o'er the waste of the ultimate slime,
And a new Word runs between: whispering, "Let us be one!"

Kipling's critics are always ready to see his summons to virtue and hope—the convictions expressed in his ever-popular poem "If"—as simple-minded and crude, the implication being that the complexity of our moral nature was somehow lost on him. *Pace* these detractors, "The Deep-Sea Cables" shows that Kipling realized all too well that it is our shared susceptibility to the wrecks of sin that beckons us to true communion and redemption, not our ideological affiliations.

However, he also realized that there were perils in worldly communions. A fair outsider most of his life in whichever swim he found himself, he was always intrigued by how men form clubs of various sorts—enclaves of would-be exclusivity—to fend off the fear of "not belonging."

The Stranger within my gate,
He may be true or kind,

But he does not talk my talk—
I cannot feel his mind.
I see the face and the eyes and the mouth,
But not the soul behind.

The men of my own stock
They may do ill or well,
But they tell the lies I am wonted to,
They are used to the lies I tell.
And we do not need interpreters
When we go to buy and sell.

The Stranger within my gates,
He may be evil or good,
But I cannot tell what powers control—
What reasons sway his mood;
Nor when the Gods of his far-off land
Shall repossess his blood.

The men of my own stock,
Bitter bad they may be,
But, at least, they hear the things I hear,
And see the things I see;
And whatever I think of them and their likes
They think of the likes of me.

This was my father's belief
And this is also mine:
Let the corn be all one sheaf—
And the grapes be all one vine,
Ere our children's teeth are set on edge
By bitter bread and wine.

Here, again, Kipling resorts to Scripture—Ezekiel 18:1–4, 25–32 and Jeremiah 31:29—to remind his club-loving readers, imperialists and anti-imperialists alike, that we are all strangers where exile and sorrow are the lot of sinful man,

Samuel Johnson, speaking of Isaac Watts, one of England's better Christian poets, said that "His ear was well-tuned, and his diction was elegant and copious." But he regarded his devotional poetry, "like that of others" as uniformly "unsatisfactory." Why? "The paucity of its topics enforces perpetual repetition, and the sanctity of the matter rejects the ornaments of figurative diction." The poet critic Donald Davie might have given Watts a generous showing in his *Oxford Book of Christian Verse*; Johnson could only bring himself to say that "It is sufficient for Watts to have done better than others what no one man has done well."[2] When one reads Kipling's

2 Johnson, quoted in *Boswell's Life of Johnson*, ed. George Birkbeck Hill and L. F.

Christian verse, one can see that he agreed with Johnson, for he takes a certain paucity of theme for granted. For Kipling, what we need to know about Christianity in the straits in which we find ourselves is not extensive or unduly nuanced. We are at odds with the majesty of our Creator and the sooner we recognize the fact the better.

> *Non nobis Domine!* —
> Not unto us, O Lord!
> The Praise or Glory be
> Of any deed or word;
> For in Thy Judgment lies
> To crown or bring to nought
> All knowledge or device
> That Man has reached or wrought.
>
> And we confess our blame —
> How all too high we hold
> That noise which men call Fame,
> That dross which men call Gold.
> For these we undergo
> Our hot and godless days,
> But in our hearts we know
> Not unto us the Praise.
>
> O Power by Whom we live —
> Creator, Judge, and Friend,
> Upholdingly forgive
> Nor fail us at the end:
> But grant us well to see
> In all our piteous ways —
> *Non nobis Domine!* —
> Not unto us the Praise!

If there is a simplicity, an austerity about this, it is one that Johnson would have approved. "Sacred history," he says in his essay on Cowley in the *Lives of the Poets*, "has always been read with submissive reverence, and an imagination overawed and controlled. We have been accustomed to acquiesce in the nakedness and simplicity of the authentic narrative, and to repose on its veracity with such humble confidence, as suppresses curiosity. We go with the historian as he goes, and stop with him when he stops. All amplification is frivolous and vain; all addition to that which is already sufficient for the purposes of religion, seems not only useless, but in some degree profane." [3] A good deal of Kipling's Christian verse

Powell (Oxford: Clarendon Press, 1934), 6 vols., iii, 358.

3 Samuel Johnson, *The Lives of the Most Eminent English Poets*, 3 vols. (London: Methuen, 1896), i, 40.

comports with this wise, astringent aesthetic.

As a parting shot to those who would take Kipling and his marvelous work out of the classroom, and, indeed, out of the study, if they could, I shall quote a final poem by this masterly poet to remind them that while in Time's eye the work of the political class scarcely lasts a day, poetry is forever.

> Cities and Thrones and Powers
>   Stand in Time's eye,
> Almost as long as flowers,
>   Which daily die:
> But, as new buds put forth
>   To glad new men,
> Out of the spent and unconsidered Earth
>   The Cities rise again.
>
> This season's Daffodil,
>   She never hears
> What change, what chance, what chill,
>   Cut down last year's;
> But with bold countenance,
>   And knowledge small,
> Esteems her seven days' continuance,
>   To be perpetual.
>
> So Time that is o'er-kind
>   To all that be,
> Ordains us e'en as blind,
>   As bold as she:
> That in our very death,
>   And burial sure,
> Shadow to shadow, well persuaded, saith,
>   "See how our works endure!"

Robert Lowell and the Sanity of Art

Robert Lowell: Setting the River on Fire: A Study of Genius, Mania and Character,
Kay Redfield Jamison (Knopf). 527 pages.

In his "Memory of W. B. Yeats," W. H. Auden wrote how, once dead, the poet "became his admirers." I thought of this a few months ago when I came upon a piece by Seamus Heaney on Robert Lowell, of whose work the Irish poet was exceedingly fond. And this is what he found to admire about the dead Lowell: "Lowell deliberately took upon himself—sometimes by public apostrophe and rebuke, sometimes by introspective or confessional example—the role of the poet as conscience of his society." This may very well have been true; for years Lowell tried to play in America the same public role that Yeats had played in Ireland. Certainly, the support he gave the anti-war movement on American campuses around the country in 1968 was public enough, though he never managed to parry Diana Trilling's objections to what she regarded as the malign effects of his "radical piety." In a letter to *Commentary*, she had asked: "What does Mr. Lowell think of the moral spectacle of the Columbia uprising, how does he feel about students kidnapping an officer of the University, rifling the personal files of the President and broadcasting their contents, urinating on floors, spitting at their teachers, destroying the research of one of their professors, shouting obscenities?" Lowell's response was rather feeble: "They are only us younger and the violence that has betrayed our desires will also betray theirs if they trust to it." How much naivety and how much moral vanity played in this particular public stance is hard to say. In trying to argue that Lowell was indeed the "conscience of his society," Heaney had recourse to the sort of moral gibberish that was not altogether unusual with Harvard's poet-in-residence: "Conscience, if we press upon its etymology, can mean our capacity to know the same thing together, yet such knowledge also makes us vulnerable to poetry as a reminder of what, together, we may have chosen to forget and this admonitory function is one which Robert Lowell exercised, more or less deliberately, all his life." One virtue of Kay Redfield Jamison's new biography of the poet, *Robert Lowell: Setting the River on Fire: A Study of Genius, Mania and Character*, which insists on seeing its subject through the lens of his struggles with manic depression, is that it

57

forces us to question anew the poet's public stances. Yet whether the lens of mental health itself gives us a reliable picture of the poet and his work is even more questionable. Admirers, in all events, are not invariably the best stewards of a poet's reputation.

Certainly, there is merit in knowing how frequently Lowell was not in his right mind; how his periodical madness manifested itself; how he strove to recover from a disorder that often left him hospitalized, physically shattered, estranged from loved ones and profoundly guilt-ridden. Answering these questions, however, does not provide any omniscient key to the man or his work. If, anything, by giving these questions the sort of prominence that they are given here, the author has proven just how elusive her subject is, for, despite her trying to argue otherwise, madness does not explain her subject's complex personality; it does not explain his friendships, his marriages or his family life; and it most decidedly does not explain his poetry.

Descended on his mother's side from the Winslows, who came to America on the Mayflower and on his father's side from the poets James Russell Lowell and Amy Lowell, Robert Lowell (1917–77) was born in Boston and educated first at St. Mark's School, where he studied under the poet Richard Eberhart, and then at Harvard, where he stayed only a year before moving on to Kenyon College to study under the poet John Crowe Ransom. There he met two of his lifelong friends, the short story writer Peter Taylor and the poet Randall Jarrell, as well as the novelist Jean Stafford, whom he would later marry, though the couple separated in 1946. In "The Old Flame," Lowell recalled their marriage in Damariscotta Mills, Maine with wry affection: "how quivering and fierce we were / there snowbound together / simmering like wasps / in our tent of books!" After graduating from Kenyon in 1940, Lowell went on to study with the New Critics, Cleanth Brooks and Robert Penn Warren at Louisiana University. One of the best things Lowell took away from his studies with Ransom, Warren and Brooks was a mellifluous Southern drawl, which gives his readings of his work a marvelous *frisson*. As with G. M. Hopkins, the obscurities in Lowell often vanish if he is read aloud.

In 1943, after being turned down twice for naval service in World War II, the mercurial poet wrote to President Roosevelt declaring his conscientious objection to serving in the war on the fanciful grounds that while it might have been undertaken in 1941 "to preserve our lives, our fortunes and our sacred honor against the lawless aggressions of a totalitarian league," by 1943 it had led to America "collaborating with the most unscrupulous and powerful of totalitarian dictators to destroy law, freedom, democracy, and above all, our continued national sovereignty." For Heaney, this was a good example of Lowell acting as "conscience for his society" because the American war effort was guilty, as Lowell put it, of "Machiavellian

contempt for the laws of justice and charity between nations." The Mach-
iavellian Department of Justice, however, saw matters differently and duly
incarcerated the poet.

In the wake of his five-month stint in prison, Lowell emerged with his
first collection of poems, *The Land of Unlikeness* (1944), about which Allen
Tate wrote in an astute introduction: "Christopher Dawson has shown in
a long historical perspective that material progress may mask social and
spiritual decay. But the spiritual decay is not universal, and to a young
man like Lowell, whether we like his Catholicism or not, there is at least a
memory of the spiritual dignity of man, now sacrificed to mere seculariza-
tion and a craving for mechanical order." Lowell told his mother that the
poems in the collection were "cries for us to recover our ancient freedom
and dignity, to be Christians and build a Christian society." Although a
diligent and learned poet, Lowell had no long apprenticeship. In a poem
from this first outing called "The Boston Nativity" we can hear something
of the playful acerbity of the mature poet:

> Child, the Mayflower rots
> In your bred-out stock. Brave mould, here all
> The Mathers, Eliots and Endicots
>   Brew their own gall
> Here Concord's shot that rang
> Becomes a boomerang

Lowell's second collection, *Lord Weary's Castle* (1946) revealed the tech-
nical and thematic boldness that were the natural issue of the seriousness
with which he regarded his art. As one friend put it, Lowell had set his
heart on becoming America's Milton. The God-haunted sea music of "The
Quaker Graveyard in Nantucket" shows that the young poet was not
entirely unentitled to his lofty ambitions.

If Lowell had converted to Catholicism in 1941 under the influence of
the Neo-Thomist Etienne Gilson, by the late 1940s he had lapsed, though
towards the end of his life he would embrace High Church Episcopalianism.
In all events, he had a strong affinity for Catholic writers, especially Flan-
nery O'Connor, whom he met at Yaddo, the writer's colony. O'Connor did
not know at first what to make of the distraught poet, who, as she recounted,
"had the delusion that he had been called on some kind of mission of puri-
fication and was canonizing everybody." After learning of O'Connor's death
at 38 of lupus, Lowell wrote that she reminded him of "a commanding,
grim, witty child, who knew she was destined to live painfully and in ear-
nest … rather like … a Catholic saint with a tough innocence, well able to
take on her brief, hardworking, hard, steady, splendid and inconspicuous
life." Before her death, O'Connor would say of Lowell: "I feel almost too
much about him to get to the heart of it. He is one of the people I love."

Gentle, gregarious and witty, the poet inspired a similar response from others. As Peter Levi, the Oxford don noted, "He was a man one actually loved." Of course, he could also be boorish, egomaniacal and violent, but even those closest to him—his wives, for example—chose to see the gentle as the true Cal. (He was nicknamed "Cal" after Caligula and Caliban by his St. Mark classmates for what they saw as his puerile savagery.)

In 1959, Lowell stripped down his elaborate style to produce *Life Studies*, an incandescent collection, which nevertheless ushered in the confessional vogue in American poetry and reams and reams of bad poetry. Sylvia Plath and Anne Sexton were perhaps its two most flamboyant devotees. It is ironic that Lowell should have instigated the vogue because his own autobiographical poems are rarely confessional. Where others might confess, the artist in Lowell usually opts for rhetorical flourishes. ("Can I be forgiven the life-waste of my lifework / Was the thing worth doing worth doing badly?) The evils of his influence notwithstanding, no poet ever coaxed more life from autobiography, or made the history of that life more captivating.

Lowell's next volume, *For the Union Dead* (1964) took this new style and gave it a supple immediacy. In one piece, Lowell follows the lugubrious musings of a crapulous sot whose wife has bolted.

> Her absence hisses like steam,
> the pipes sing ...
> even corroded metal somehow functions.
> He snores in his iron lung,
> and hears the voice of Eve
> beseeching freedom from the Garden's
> perfect and ponderous bubble. No voice
> outsings the serpent's flawed, euphoric hiss.

In 1949, Lowell married the writer Elizabeth Hardwick and took up residence in New York, Maine and Harvard, where he taught poetry. Like Auden, he was always keen to mine his far-ranging reading for subject matter for his poems. One can see this especially in such uneven collections as *History* (1973), though autobiography, often rather licentious autobiography would continue to animate his work. In *The Dolphin* (1973), for example, he actually "versified," as he put it, bits of Hardwick's correspondence. Betraying confidential letters, however, was the least of Lowell's sins when it came to Hardwick. As Jamison remarks: "Lowell's affairs brought him distraction, pleasure, discomfort, and poems. To others, especially Elizabeth Hardwick, they brought pain." Later, he would express rather facile remorse for these serial transgressions.

> I have sat and listened to too many
> words of the collaborating muse,
> and plotted perhaps too freely with my life,

not avoiding injury to others
not avoiding injury to myself—

In 1972, Lowell moved to England to take a teaching post at the University of Essex, where he was surprised to find his English students (compared to those at Harvard) "rather retarded." In London, he fell in love with and subsequently married the Anglo-Irish writer and heiress Lady Caroline Blackwood, whose acid sense of humor may have appealed to him but whose mental instability and fondness for strong drink did no favors for his own psychic travails. When Hardwick learned of the *folie à deux* that would lead to her husband's betrayal of her and their daughter, she was excoriating: "My utter contempt for both of you for the misery you have brought to two people who had never hurt you knows no bounds."

Lowell's last volume, *Day by Day* (1977) ends with "Epilogue," one of his finest poems, which makes a fairly unrepentant plea for the candor of his work.

> Those blessèd structures, plot and rhyme—
> why are they no help to me now
> I want to make
> something imagined, not recalled?
> I hear the noise of my own voice:
> *The painter's vision is not a lens,*
> *it trembles to caress the light.*
> But sometimes everything I write
> with the threadbare art of my eye
> seems a snapshot,
> lurid, rapid, garish, grouped,
> heightened from life,
> yet paralyzed by fact.
> All's misalliance.
> Yet why not say what happened?

On the afternoon of 12 September 1977 Lowell died in a taxi cab on his way from the airport to the apartment at West 67th Street that he had shared with his wife and daughter, to both of whom he meant to return after his life with Blackwood had come to smash, though he was found in the cab clutching a portrait of Caroline by Lucian Freud (her former husband), which the strapped heiress had asked him to have appraised in New York. No one would have savored the droll circumstances of his death more than Lowell himself. Later, Hardwick would look back on her long, turbulent life with Lowell and remark: "I didn't know what I was getting into, but even if I had, I still would have married him. He was not crazy all the time—most of the time he was wonderful. The breakdowns were not the whole story. I feel lucky to have had the time—everything I know I learned from him."

After Lowell's death, the long delay in the release of his *Collected Poems* (2003) left his reputation in limbo for decades. By the time that hefty volume appeared, the sort of ambitious poetry in which Lowell specialized, at every stage of his development, had gone out of fashion. Lowell may have transformed the way poetry was written after the long shadows of Eliot, Pound and William Carlos Williams had receded, but his influence could not ward off the ineptitude, imposture and banality that are now staples of American poetry, despite the best efforts of good poets like Richard Wilbur and Anthony Hecht to come to its rescue. What continues to set Lowell's work apart, at its best, is its consummate art. "As his taste for metaphysical verse flagged," the shrewd biographer of James Joyce, Richard Ellmann remarked, "[Lowell] strove to present feelings that would be 'raw" rather than 'cooked,' to use the once famous distinction. At the same time he worked very hard at his poems, as if aware that even steak tartare requires the utmost finesse in preparation."

The rave reviews that Jamison's book has received testify to the tenacity with which the Romantic notion of the artist as someone whose creativity is reliant on derangement persists, a notion shared by a progressive establishment averse to art exerting any genuinely critical rigor. To remain pliable for the establishment's ideological purposes, it must be kept as uncritical as possible.

When we attempt to make a proper assessment of Jamison's book we have our task complicated at every turn by Lowell himself. Why? A part of the mythologizing poet would have agreed with Jamison that his life and work can be seen through the lens of madness, even though this very mythologizing was itself the product of mania. Jamison quotes the well-known lines that Lowell wrote about his fellow poets:

> Ah the swift vanishing of my older
> Generation — the deaths, suicides, madness
> Of Roethke, Berryman, Jarrell and Lowell.

By including himself in this ill-fated roll call, the mythologist in Lowell might be seen to be sanctioning Jamison's biographical approach. If Lowell defined himself as mad, why should his biographer not follow suit? The wary reader, however, has to ask himself whether the mythologizing Lowell is the true Lowell, or whether that rather more inscrutable creature lies elsewhere. After all, it was the critic in Lowell who said, only half facetiously: "Everything is real until it's published."

Yet, even though Lowell might not dissuade others from seeing himself as the mad Romantic poet, he could be admirably truthful in his work — truthful and sane. And this came out of a kind of irrepressible love. Indeed, throughout his poetry, he treats his subjects, whether his wives, his parents, his fellow poets, his contemporaries, his ancestors or the famous dead, as

though they were all part of one great tribe—a tribe of which Lowell him-
self is always the stage-managing paterfamilias. If his parents had never
managed to put together a loving family in real life—always mired as they
were in quarrels over Lowell's hapless father, both as a naval officer and
stockbroker—Lowell would create a family of his own in his poetry. The
problem was that he often confused the two, imagining that the damage
he had done to his family in real life could be somehow mended in his
poetry. Nevertheless, in making the pain of family the marrow of his art,
he put himself to school to a demanding empathy. Speaking of his cousin
Harriet Winslow, for example, in "Soft Wood," he writes:

> This is the season
> when our friends may and will die daily.
> Surely the lives of the old
> are briefer than the young.
>
> Harriet Winslow, who owned this house
> was more to me than my mother.
> I think of you far off in Washington
> breathing in the heat wave
> and air-conditioning, knowing
> each drug that numbs alerts another nerve to pain.

This tendency of seeing the world in terms of family doubtless arose from
his Bostonian background. One can hear the same note in Henry Adams,
the quintessential Bostonian, whom Lowell considered "the subtlest and
least hollow of American minds." In a letter to Henry James, Adams wrote
in 1903: "The painful truth is that all of my New England generation,
counting the half-century, 1820–1870, were in actual fact only one mind
and nature, the individual was a facet of Boston." Here, the city is the
family, but Adams anticipates Lowell's understanding of the inescapable
clairvoyance of family.

> We knew each other to the last nervous centre, and feared each
> other's knowledge. We looked through each other like microscopes.
> There was absolutely nothing in us that we did not understand
> merely by looking in the eye. There was hardly a difference even
> in depth, for Harvard College and Unitarianism had made us all
> shallow. We knew nothing—no! but really nothing! of the world. One
> cannot exaggerate the profundity of ignorance of Story in becoming
> a sculptor, or Sumner in becoming a statesman, or Emerson in
> becoming a philosopher. Story and Sumner, Emerson and Alcott,
> Lowell and Longfellow, Hillard, Winthrop, Motley, Prescott, and all
> the rest, were the same mind—and so, poor worm!—was I!

History, Lowell's book of sonnets, commemorating as it does everyone
from King David to Bobby Kennedy, is full of the same sort of appropriation

in which Adams engages. All men are men of Lowell's kith and kin, even though, like a good imperialist, he is careful to leave their own identity intact. The critic Helen Vendler, who studied with Lowell at Harvard, recalled that he would treat poets with the same intimate familiarity in his poetry classes. "This, in the end, seems to me the best thing Lowell did for his students," she wrote; "he gave them the sense, so absent from textbook notes, of a life, a spirit, a mind and a set of occasions from which writing issues—a real life, a real mind, fixed in historical circumstances, and quotidian abrasions." This preoccupation on Lowell's part with both art and life was nicely summed up by the poet himself in one of his sonnets in *For Lizzie and Harriet*: "Nothing seems admirable until it fails / but it's only people we should miss."

Appropriately enough, some of Lowell's best autobiographical portraits are of figures who would have known nothing of poetry. One can readily imagine Lowell relishing bringing this St. Mark's contemporary into the fold.

> The labour to breathe that younger, rawer air:
> St. Mark's last football game with Groton lost on the ice-crust,
> the sunlight gliding the golden polo coats
> of boys with country seats on the Upper Hudson.
> Why does the stale light stay? First form hazing,
> first day being sent on errands by an oldboy,
> Bobby Delano, cousin of Franklin Delano Roosevelt—
> deported soused off the Presidential yacht
> baritoning *You're the cream in my coffee* ...
> His football, hockey, baseball letter at 15;
> At 15, expelled. He dug my ass with a compass,
> forced me to say "My mother is a whore."
> My freshman year, he shot himself in Rio,
> odious, unknowable, as inspired as Ajax.

Of course, in Lowell's tribe, the poet often figures himself, and towards the end of his life these self-portraits show how fine a lyric gift he had. Jamison devotes a stupefying number of pages throughout her lengthy book to describing the epidemiology of manic depression. In many parts of the book, one has the disorienting impression that one has somehow picked up the wrong book and is reading not a biography of Lowell but a textbook on mania, and a rather repetitive one at that. Yet there is nothing in Jamison's pages that can begin to explicate this cry of mortal man:

> Dull, disagreeable and dying,
> the old men—
> they were setups for my ridicule,
> till time, the healer, made me theirs.

In the old New York, we said,
"If life could write,
it would have written like us."
Now the lifefluid goes
from the throwaway lighter,
its crimson, cylindrical, translucent
glow grows pale—
O queen of cities, star of morning.

The age burns in me.

The path is cleared and cleared each year,
each year the brush closes;
nature cooperates with us,
then we cooperate no more.

There is no madness in any of that, no mania, no depression. Here is only the sanity of art. And this sanity, this fellow feeling, this lament for fellowship's end, was what finally enabled Robert Lowell to produce his finest work, among which one must always include "For the Union Dead" (1964), with its masterly, vivid, heartbreaking lines about Colonel Robert Gould Shaw, who was killed while leading the first black regiment in the North in an assault against Fort Wagner in South Caroline in July of 1863.

Two months after marching through Boston,
half the regiment was dead;
at the dedication,
William James could almost hear the bronze Negroes breathe.

Their monument sticks like a fishbone
in the city's throat.
Its Colonel is as lean
as a compass-needle.

He has an angry wrenlike vigilance,
a greyhound's gentle tautness;
he seems to wince at pleasure,
and suffocate for privacy.

He is out of bounds now. He rejoices in man's lovely,
peculiar power to choose life and die—
when he leads his black soldiers to death,
he cannot bend his back.

That Lowell should compare this honorable man and his honorable charge with a late-twentieth-century Boston intent only on building more parking garages for its "giant finned cars" makes Tate's point that Lowell, even in an age of headlong decadence, never lost sight of the "spiritual dignity of man."

If readers wish to understand the poet in Lowell, as well as the man, they should get Ian Hamilton's 1982 "warts and all" biography, which still crackles with the recollections of those who knew Lowell. Paul Mariani's *Lost Puritan: The Life of Robert Lowell* (1994), in addition to being well researched and well written, has the sense to see that poetry and madness are not one and the same. It is also excellent on Lowell's religious sensibility, which has not always been given the attention it deserves. No one can read Mariani's book without seeing that his subject was always "jolting between salvation and demolition," as Lowell himself said of Israel. Catholics might wonder if the poet's conversion to the Church of Rome was anything more than a show of kinship with Hopkins and his dear friend Flannery O'Connor, but it still exhibited his recognition of the vitality of faith in a world where rationalism rules the decaying roost. Then, again, Sarah Payne Stuart's wonderfully funny piece in *The New York Times*, "'Bobby Was a Difficult Child': My Cousin Robert Lowell" captures the patrician comedy in Lowell's makeup, which the poet's more solemn critics often miss. One person close to Lowell who appreciated this was his daughter Harriet, who said of her father: "Above all he was a poet ... He had a terrible disease, but he was charming, mischievous and full of fun." If Jamison's study had adhered more to this balanced view, her book would have been less objectionable. What the reader needs to know about Lowell is not how he succumbed to mania but how he overcame mania to write the admirable poetry he wrote. In Lowell, the sane, not the mad laureate is the true laureate, for as he said himself, with the sanity that only comes of humility,

> imperfection is the language of art.
> Even the best writer in his best lines
> is incurably imperfect, crying for truth, knowledge
> honesty, inspiration he cannot have—

Hats Off to Valerie!
The Complete Prose of T. S. Eliot

The Complete Prose of T. S. Eliot: The Critical Edition, edited by Ronald Schuchard *et al*. 8 vols. (Johns Hopkins University Press).

Writing in 1920 of the poet Algernon Swinburne, the appeal of whose enraptured lyricism was not self-evident to the generation that had survived the Great War, T. S. Eliot pronounced, in that marvelously authoritative tone of his, that "It is a question of some nicety to decide how much must be read of any particular poet," before delivering the sort of definitive verdict that his readers came to relish.

> There are some poets whose every line has unique value. There are others who can be taken by a few poems universally agreed upon. There are others who need be read only in selections, but what selections are read will not very much matter. Of Swinburne, we should like to have the Atalanta entire, and a volume of selections which should certainly contain "The Leper," "Laus Veneris," and "The Triumph of Time."

That Eliot should have given serious reconsideration to a poet whom many of his contemporaries thought *passé* was characteristic. Throughout his career, he would come to the defense of other unfashionable poets, particularly Dryden, Tennyson and Kipling, each of whom, as some of the uncollected early pieces of this magnificent edition show, had a strong influence on his fledgling talent. Yet to come to the defense of Swinburne in 1920 showed great critical confidence. Here, in a reassessment of what most critics might have regarded as the poet's greatest liability, we can see the emergence of an altogether new critical intelligence.

> Language in a healthy state presents the object, is so close to the object that the two are identified. They are identified in the verse of Swinburne solely because the object has ceased to exist, because the meaning is merely the hallucination of meaning, because language, uprooted, has adapted itself to an independent life ... In Swinburne ... we see the word "weary" flourishing in this way independent of

the particular and actual weariness of flesh or spirit. The bad poet dwells partly in a world of objects and partly in a world of words, and he never can get them to fit. Only a man of genius could dwell so exclusively and consistently among words as Swinburne.

Then, again, Eliot also saw in Swinburne precisely the sort of poet critic—Dryden, Johnson, Coleridge, and Arnold were others—whom he was working to emulate. For Eliot, "Swinburne's essays have the value of notes of an important poet upon important poets." And the proof of that was that, like Eliot himself, "He read everything, and he read with the single interest in finding literature." No one who revisits both the pieces gathered here on Swinburne will fail to concede Eliot's contention, which is as true of himself as it is of Swinburne, that "The author of Swinburne's critical essays is also the author of Swinburne's verse: if you hold the opinion that Swinburne was a very great poet, you can hardly deny him the title of a great critic."

Since Eliot's death in 1965, admirers of the poet's work have often criticized his literary executor, Valerie Eliot, for not bringing out her late husband's complete prose sooner. After all, if it had been made available sooner, many of the attacks on Eliot's reputation might have been more easily parried. Yet, now that this laudable edition is finally appearing, it is clear that she proved an admirably meticulous, thorough, and, above all, responsible executor of her husband's literary estate. This edition will stand as a monument to her good judgement and her good taste, especially since she chose Ronald Schuchard, who has done such splendid work on Oxford's *Collected Letters of W. B. Yeats*, as editor-in-chief. Here, he has overseen a body of annotation that promises to be a veritable intellectual biography of Eliot. The searchable online edition (which is also available as hardcover books) includes all of Eliot's collected essays, reviews, lectures, commentaries from *The Criterion*, and letters to editors, including more than 800 uncollected and 150 unpublished pieces from 1905 to 1965.

As Schuchard shows, Eliot was ambivalent about the quality of his uncollected prose, telling his crippled friend, John Hayward, whom he initially thought to make his literary executor, that he could never revisit his scattered pieces "without acute embarrassment." Indeed, Eliot dissuaded Hayward from preparing any of his uncollected pieces for publication because, as he said, "I have had to write at one time or another a lot of junk in periodicals the greater portion of which ought never to be reprinted." Later, after making Valerie his executor, he relaxed this astringency. Yet Schuchard is certainly right to quote something Eliot wrote of Baudelaire in 1927 to justify his exhaustive edition.

> It is now becoming understood that Baudelaire is one of the few poets who wrote nothing, either prose or verse that is negligible.

To understand Baudelaire you must read the whole of Baudelaire. And nothing that he wrote is without importance. He was a great poet; he was a great critic. And he was also a man with a profound attitude toward life, for the study of which we need every scrap of his writing.

One can revel in many of the uncollected pieces included here without denying that the fastidious judge in Eliot saved the *crème de la crème* for the collections published in his own lifetime, including *The Sacred Wood* (1920), *For Lancelot Andrewes* (1928), *Selected Essays* (1932, 1934, 1951), and *On Poetry and Poets* (1957). Nevertheless, while both the collected and uncollected pieces enhance Eliot's stature as a critic of genius, they also show him to have been an impassioned champion of what Cardinal Newman once called "the sovereignty of Truth." Moreover, many of the pieces show that, for all of his brashness, Eliot had a certain humility, which makes his brilliance doubly winning. In a letter of 1959 recalling the tutorial course he taught at University College, London in 1916, he wrote:

> I was working in a bank during the day-time, and reviewing for two or three periodicals at night-time. The transport between Southall and Marylebone, where I lived, was sometimes interrupted too by the primitive air raids which took place during that war ... But I was happy in my classes and I must admit that I learnt more about English literature than my class did, in as much as I had to read a good many books which I ought to have read but had not read, in order to take my pupils over the ground properly.

Most of the pieces in the first two volumes are either philosophical papers written when Eliot was contemplating a career in philosophy at Harvard or literary pieces. What is striking about the philosophy papers is that they have the same witty self-assurance as the literary essays. On the idealist philosopher T. H. Green, for example, Eliot observes: "Green's philosophy, like most others, is built upon facts which everyone can acknowledge, but he proceeds in the familiar way by throwing a rope in the air and clambering up it; and it is not until he has disappeared from view that we break the spell and realise that the magician was on the ground the whole time." Certainly, Eliot could lay down the law in the philosophical realm with admirable dispatch. "Second Thoughts on Humanism" (1929) is included in the third volume but its force is characteristic of all of Eliot's philosophical pieces:

> Man is man because he can recognize spiritual realities, not because he can invent them. Either everything in man can be traced as a development from below, or something must come from above. There is no avoiding that dilemma: you must be either a naturalist or a supernaturalist. If you remove from the word "human" all

that the belief in the supernatural has given to man, you can view him finally as no more than an extremely clever, adaptable, and mischievous little animal.

The literary pieces are nicely exemplified by an essay on the French playwright and novelist Marivaux, written in 1919, where Eliot's grasp of cultural history makes an early appearance, as does his delight in provocative generality.

> When Marivaux began to write plays, the age of Molière was well over; several years of weak imitation had prepared Paris for receiving favourably something entirely new; something making use of different machinery, investigating different emotions, disregarding all traditions and laying hold on a new world as the material of its art. Then came perhaps not the greatest, but certainly the most civilised period of French art and letters. Magniloquence and rhetoric were discarded; sentimentalism had not yet appeared. Moralists are replaced by observers. Instead of Rochefoucauld, we have Vauvenargues; instead of Madame de Sévigné, Madame du Deffand; instead of Molière, Marivaux; and instead of Racine also, Marivaux. Between Claude and Poussin on the one hand, and Greuze on the other, is Watteau; and the similarity between Watteau and Marivaux, both the men and the work, is more than superficial. Perhaps the temper which I am endeavouring to localise existed only in a very few men; but very few ever can be civilised. The age, at least, was propitious, and the painting of Watteau, the *Dialogues des Morts* of Fontenelle, and the plays and novels of Marivaux are the result. In England, there was Chesterfield, perhaps Horace Walpole. Since Rousseau, the flood of barbarism has left very few peaks. It is difficult to be civilised alone.

Another hallmark of the writing assembled here is its *brio*. Eliot was the brilliant critic he was because he loved good writing and he gave unforgettable expression to that love. Some of us who become writers, whether good, bad or indifferent writers, do so because in our youth we were passionate readers. It is the passionate reader in Eliot who gives the critic in him his exhilarating perspicacity. One can see this in a passage of his on the incomparable tribute that Samuel Johnson paid to Shakespeare, a tribute which I remember first reading in the little Clarendon edition of Johnson's prose & poetry that my father gave me when I was scarcely out of grammar school. Even then I found its music delightful, and Eliot nicely reminds me of my old delight. "To pass from Dryden to Johnson is to make the journey from one oasis to another," Eliot writes.

> After the critical essays of Dryden, the Preface to Shakespeare by Samuel Johnson is the next of the great pieces of criticism to read. One would willingly resign the honour of an Abbey burial for

the greater honour of words like the following, from a man of the greatness of their author:

> The poet, of whose works I have undertaken the revision, may now begin to assume the dignity of an ancient, and claim the privilege of established fame and prescriptive veneration. He has long outlived his century, the term commonly fixed as the test of literary merit. Whatever advantages he might once derive from personal allusions, local customs, or temporary opinions, have for many years been lost; and every topick of merriment, or motive of sorrow, which the modes of artificial life afforded him, now only obscure the scenes which they once illuminated. The effects of favour and competition are at an end; the tradition of his friendships and his enmities has perished; his works support no opinion with arguments, nor supply any faction with invectives; they can neither indulge vanity, nor gratify malignity; but are read without any other reason than the desire of pleasure, and are therefore praised only as pleasure is obtained; yet, thus unassisted by interest or passion, they have passed through variations of taste and changes of manners, and, as they devolved from one gener-ation to another, have received new honours at every trans-mission.

What a valedictory and obituary for any man to receive! My point is that if you assume that the classical criticism of England was grudging in its praise of Shakespeare, I say that no poet can ask more of posterity than to be greatly honoured by the great; and Johnson's words about Shakespeare are great honour.

Apropos the seventeenth-century devotional poet, George Herbert, the reader in Eliot again comes to the fore in an essay on the poet that he wrote in 1962 to record the pleasure this most accomplished of poets gave him over the years. If Eliot continues to win the loyalty and affection of readers, despite the obloquy that has been heaped on him by the custo-dians of wokery, it is because they see in him a reflection of their own joy in reading. His observations on Herbert epitomize this joy.

> Two of [Herbert's] poems are such as would be considered, if written by a poet to-day, merely elegant trifles: "The Altar" and "Easter Wings." In each, there is a disposition of longer and shorter lines so printed that the poem has the shape, the one of an altar and the other of a pair of wings. Such a diversion, if employed frequently, would be tedious, distracting and trying to the eyesight and we must be glad that Herbert did not make further use of these devices: yet it is evidence of Herbert's care for workmanship, his restless explora-tion of variety, and of a kind of gaiety of spirit, a joy in composition which engages our delighted sympathy. The exquisite variations

of form in the other poems of *The Temple* show a resourcefulness of invention which seems inexhaustible, and for which I know no parallel in English poetry.

Apropos Gerard Manley Hopkins, the reader in Eliot shows that while he can appreciate style, he never loses sight of the content that style forms and reveals. If Newman is often praised for his style by those heedless of the profoundly Christian import of his work, Hopkins is similarly praised for his style by those who cannot be bothered with the Christian sensibility that inspired the style. Indeed, Norman White, in his wrongheaded critical biography of the poet, even goes so far as to argue that Hopkins's Christian devotion stymied his art. Eliot does not suffer from this error, an error which has become too pervasive to be easily dispelled; he understands the Catholic poet in Hopkins well enough to know that his Catholic faith, his Catholic reason, his Catholic feeling transformed everything he wrote. "One peculiarity to which I should call attention," Eliot writes in volume six, "is his passionate love of nature, and the minute and loving care with which, in his private diary as well as in his poems, he describes its appearances. In this love of nature he is extremely English, in the tradition from Wordsworth. But in Hopkins the nature-worship of the Romantics is taken up into something higher, and reaches its consummation by being re-integrated into an orthodox Christian view of life. To have accomplished this is a great achievement." Now, it is incumbent on those of us who delight in Hopkins's poetry to disabuse the young from imagining that Hopkins's solicitude for Nature has anything to do with the cynical pantheism that animates the environmental policies of the left.

As a whole, the pieces here exhibit the apprenticeship of an intelligence that might have distinguished itself in history, philosophy or theology, but plumbed instead for literary criticism because this was the discipline that could not only prompt his poetry but accommodate his interests in history, philosophy and theology. In his Clark Lectures on the Metaphysical Poets (1926), Eliot gave his readers a good idea of the sort of eclectic criticism that he meant to produce. "The literary critic must remain a critic of literature," he writes, "but he must have sufficient knowledge to understand the points of view of the sciences into which his literary criticism merges. You cannot know your frontiers unless you have some notion of what is beyond them." Yet knowledge for the sake of knowledge always incurred Eliot's mistrust. As he insists in "Tradition and the Individual Talent" (1919), "a poet ought to know as much as will not encroach upon his necessary receptivity and necessary laziness." And for corroboration of this, he adduced the fact that "Shakespeare acquired more essential history from Plutarch than most men could from the whole British Museum."

This creative understanding of knowledge accentuates the highly practical character of Eliot's criticism. After all, although splendidly well read and full of self-deprecatory charm, he was never a litterateur. Nor was he a critic in any *l'art pour l'art* sense. He wrote his essays, whether on the Elizabethan drama, Dante, Shakespeare, Marvell, Arnold, Pater, Seneca, or the darling of the music halls, Marie Lloyd, not merely to make sense of European culture, but to revitalize it. Indeed, he founded *The Criterion*, which ran from 1922 to 1939, precisely to advance that often quixotic object.

A good example of the far-sightedness of Eliot's practical criticism can be seen in his animadversions on religion and education. In the seventh volume of the set, for example, in a long essay entitled, "The Aims of Education" (1950), Eliot speaks of the consequences of the assault on the publicity of religion that appeals more pressingly to our society than it did to his. "The assertion that a man's religion is his private affair, that from the point of view of society it is irrelevant, may turn out in the end to lead to a situation very favorable to the establishment of a religion, or a substitute for religion, by the State," he says, in his wonderfully dry, caustic way.

> The religious sense, and the sense of community, cannot be finally divorced from each other. They are first formed, certainly, in the family; and when they are defective in the family, the defect cannot be supplied by the school and the university. But on the other hand, the contrast between a community life in which religion has no place, and a family life for which it is reserved, cannot be long endured; and the weakening of the social side of religion in the outside world will tend to weaken it in the family also; and the weakening of the religious bond between members of the same household, beginning at that early age at which we first think that we are thinking for ourselves, will leave the family reduced to the insecure bond of affection and sentiment. Thus, when religion comes to be more and more an individual matter, and is no longer a family tie; when it becomes a matter of voluntary association on one day a week when the weather is neither too good nor too bad, and of a traditional and more and more meaningless verbiage in the pulpit and at times on the political platform; when it ceases to inform the whole of life; then a vacuum is discovered, and the belief in religion will be gradually supplied by a belief in the State. That part of the social life which is independent of the State will be diminished to the more trivial. The necessity will appear for a common belief in something to fill the place of religion in the community; and the liberals will find themselves surrendering more and more of the individual freedom which was the basis of their doctrine.

In the Age of Wokery, our own liberals are surrendering their individual freedoms with an almost entranced abandon. Clearly, when Eliot made his dire forecast, he knew what he was about.

For another good example of the practicality of Eliot's criticism, we can turn to what he has to say in volume six on prosody. Here are insights useful not only to the aspiring poet but to the reader keen on understanding how good poets, grounded in the work of past poets, lay claim to the tradition of verse by at once restoring and renewing it.

> In the Latin language, the natural rhythms of the language were overlaid by a metric adopted from the Greek: and again, this classical GraecoLatin metric has been imposed by classical scholarship upon English. To read a line of Shakespeare's simply as five iambic feet, is to ignore the music of it. For English syllables are not always and everywhere of the same length and value; the length or strength of a syllable depends upon its context, and upon the meaning of the phrase, which imposes particular stresses and intonations. The English verse line is better conceived on the analogy of a musical phrase, composed of bars of equal value though not of an equal number of notes. There are not many actors capable of reciting Shakespeare so as to bring out all the musical value; the tendency of most is either to deliver the line as a monotonous series of thumps, or, if they feel that this is too remote from speech, to deliver it as if it was prose. It is putting this point in an exaggerated way to say that since the middle of the seventeenth century a great deal of the musical possibilities of English verse has been ignored in obedience to supposed rules of versification. The speech quality—the foundation of the dramatic quality—of our blank verse was very gravely damaged by Milton, who, being a very great poet as well as a remarkable linguist and classical scholar, made it the vehicle for a different kind of music than that native to English speech. I believe that the blank verse line is a kind of norm for English verse, that it is the right length for the English voice; but in order to recover it, we have to depart from it, if we are to restore in the speech of our own time anything of the flexibility and range that it had in the time of Shakespeare. Hence, while modern English poetry has been influenced to some extent by Walt Whitman, and by experiments on the borders of prose and verse in other languages, I regard it rather as tending to recover the music and speech values of three hundred and more years ago, than as tending to a new kind of prosody

Of course, in Eliot's own case, the way Donne had negotiated these options exerted a profound influence on the way he wrote not only his own verse but looked at the verse of others. Donne's witty discriminations were the school from which a good deal of his judgment and taste were formed. In a fascinating untitled lecture he gave in 1940 on religious verse, Eliot has occasion to say of this metaphysical poet whose influence ran so deep not only on Eliot but, through Eliot, on so many of his contemporaries:

Donne certainly had, from his beginning, that always present sense of Death and Mortality which none of his contemporaries, however irreligious, was without; a sense of Death no doubt sharpened by the reminder of frequent recurrences of plague; and in his religious phase he adds an awareness of damnation and of penitence, supported by his great theological learning. Some of the finest of his religious poems are sonnets:

> Batter my heart, three person'd God; for you
> As yet but knock, breathe, shine and seek to mend;
> That I may rise, and stand, o'erthrow me, and bend
> Your force, to break, blow, burn and make me new.
> I, like an usurpt town, to another due,
> Labour to admit you, but Oh, to no end,
> Reason your viceroy in me, me should defend,
> But is captiv'd, and proves weak or untrue.
> Yet dearly I love you, and would be loved faine,
> But am betroth'd unto your enemy:
> Divorce me, untie, or break that knot again;
> Take me to you, imprison me, for I,
> Except you enthrall me, never shall be free,
> Nor ever chaste, except you ravish me.

You would not, however, grasp the full influence of Donne upon his younger contemporaries, only from reading his religious verse. The love poems which he wrote in youth were widely known, and established his style. In these early poems all the innovations of his idiom are displayed: a style at once natural and highly sophisticated, catching the tone and rhythm of ordinary speech and expressing also the most refined intellectual subtleties

What set Eliot apart from his contemporaries was his recognition that such aesthetic judgments necessarily required understanding the nature of tradition. In other words, for Eliot, tackling questions of tradition required tackling questions of belief and unbelief. Readers of his own time might not have realized the degree of this necessity; twenty-first century readers, confronted all around them with what ensues when poets are not so much negligent as utterly ignorant of tradition, can see this degree all too clearly. In "Shakespeare and the Stoicism of Seneca" (1927), Eliot writes of Donne: "In making some very commonplace investigations of the 'thought' of Donne, I found it quite impossible to come to the conclusion that Donne believed anything. It seemed as if, at that time, the world was filled with broken fragments of systems, and that a man like Donne merely picked up, like a magpie, various shining fragments of ideas as they struck his eye, and stuck them about here and there in his verse." This could be a description of the Eliot misunderstood by many Modernists, before he succumbed to what the poet and critic William Empson sneeringly called "malign neo-Christianity."

Yet Eliot was never indifferent to faith. Even before converting to Christianity, his reading had given him a respect for the culture of Christianity. As he remarks in the piece on Seneca, "The problem of belief is very complicated and probably quite insoluble," though he also recognized that it was not a problem that one could shirk.[1] "The germ of skepticism," he writes as early as 1913 in an uncollected piece on Kant and agnosticism, "is quickened always by the soil of system (rich in contradictions). As the system decomposes, the doubts push through, and the decay is so general and fructifying that we are no longer sure enough of anything to draw the line between knowledge and ignorance."

The use of the word "fructifying" here might seem odd, unless we appreciate that, for Eliot, as he wrote in his introduction to "The *Pensées* of Pascal" (1931), "the demon of doubt ... is inseparable from the spirit of belief." At the same time, he was unimpressed with the Absolute posited by the British idealist, Francis Herbert Bradley, on whom he wrote his doctoral thesis. "This Absolute is mystical, because desperate," Eliot writes. "Ultimate truth remains inaccessible; and it only remains for [sceptics} to shatter what little Bradley has left standing, by urging upon us that we have no right to affirm ... that there is truth at all." Which led the 25-year-old Eliot to pose the overwhelming question that Prufrock could never bring himself to ask: if there is an Absolute that can reaffirm objective truth, 'what is it?'"

Thus, even in these early years, the appeal of Christianity had already become importunate for a poet who would not be fobbed off with philosophical abstractions. By the time the Battle of Britain had brought the fight between good and evil to a fiery crescendo, Eliot became attuned more deeply still to the creative appeal of the faith with which his nineteenth-century predecessors were so implacably consumed. Indeed, the lonely fire brigade warden in Eliot drew comfort from recalling these past poets, especially Christina Rossetti, about whose place in the development of religious poetry in England he is insightful. "Not only two-hundred years of religious history, but two-hundred years of literary history, make

---

1 Apropos the influence that Seneca (indirectly) had on the good Catholic poet St Robert Southwell, SJ, Eliot makes an interesting point when he says in an untitled lecture given in April of 1940: "The verse [of Southwell's 'The Burning Babe'] is really the old 'fourteener,' the fourteen-syllable line used by the translators of Seneca. But Southwell, in spite of a certain uncouthness, is a good poet who influenced his successors more than is generally recognised." *The Complete Prose of T. S. Eliot: The Critical Edition: The War Years, 1940–1946*, ed. David Chintz and Robert Schuchard (Baltimore: John Hopkins, 2019), vi, 48.

the religious poetry of the nineteenth century very different from that of the seventeenth," he writes. "The earlier poetry, in comparison, is impressively impersonal: it is the work of men who were Christians in a Christian society. It is not only free from autobiography, but from the consciousness on the part of the author of being a Christian. The writer vanishes from his own mind, in the presence of what he contemplates. After the Romantic Movement, a poet, and especially a religious poet, is more conscious of himself." And, as Eliot shows, Christina Rossetti epitomized this change in self-consciousness. "For the Christian poet, there is not only the consciousness of a certain isolation in the world; there is also the consciousness of the struggle by which his faith is won," he writes,

> the consciousness, in short, of the convert: though perhaps a convert as an adult back to the faith into which he was born. Add to this the fact that Christina Rossetti was a woman, and it is not surprising that her poetry should be a kind of reticent confession, an *aveu*. The biography of the poet takes on a certain importance for understanding the poetry. In the work of Christina Rossetti, we recognise a wistfulness for the normal satisfactions of life which her lonely situation denied her; and the fact that she rejected one lover because he belonged to another communion, and a second, and more important lover, because his Christianity was at best frail, is useful to know. What emerges triumphantly from the reserved autobiography of her poems is a surrender to the will of God, an inspired passivity, which is perfectly expressed in her best-known, and one of her finest poems:

> > Passing away, saith the World, passing away:
> > Chances, beauty and youth sapped day by day:
> > Thy life never continueth in one stay.
> > Is the eye waxen dim, is the dark hair changing to grey
> > That hath won neither laurel nor bay?
> > I shall clothe myself in Spring and bud in May:
> > Thou, root-stricken, shalt not rebuild thy decay
> > On my bosom for aye.
> > Then I answered: Yea.

> > Passing away, saith my Soul, passing away:
> > With its burden of fear and hope, of labour and play;
> > Hearken what the past doth witness and say:
> > Rust in thy gold, a moth is in thine array,
> > A canker is in thy bud, thy leaf must decay.
> > At midnight, at cockcrow, at morning, one certain day
> > Lo, the Bridegroom shall come and shall not delay:
> > Watch thou and pray.
> > Then I answered: Yea.

Passing away, saith my God, passing away:
Winter passeth after the long delay:
New grapes on the vine, new figs on the tender spray,
Turtle calleth turtle in Heaven's May.
Though I tarry, wait for Me, trust Me, watch and pray.
Arise, come away, night is past and lo it is day,
My love, My sister, My spouse, thou shalt hear Me say.
Then I answered: Yea.

In his wonderful essay on the seventeenth-century Anglican divine, Lancelot Andrewes, published in 1926, Eliot speaks again of the appeal of Christianity by sharing with his contemporaries the inimitable prose of someone of whom most of them had probably never heard. Bradley might have understood metaphysics as "the finding of bad reasons for what we believe on instinct," but Andrewes saw the supernatural in altogether different terms.

I know not how, but when we hear of saving or mention of a Saviour, presently our mind is carried to the saving of our skin, of our temporal state, of our bodily life, and farther saving we think not of. But there is another life not to be forgotten, and greater the dangers, and the destruction more to be feared than of this here, and it would be well sometimes we were remembered of it. Besides our skin and flesh a soul we have, and it is our better part by far, that also hath need of a Saviour.

In yet another uncollected piece, the Christian critic in Eliot considers what we ought to mean when we refer to "Christian thinking." What is striking about the volumes of the complete prose is how frequently he addresses the common reader, how disinclined he was to play the mandarin. And here is a good example of that.

Now, I have mentioned "Christian thinking," and I want to explain what I mean. Consider the five points recently put forward by His Holiness the Pope ... [Here he was referring to the Christmas message of Pope Pius XII, *The Pope's Five Peace-Points: Address (in questo giorno) of Pope Pius XII to the Sacred College of Cardinals on Christmas Eve delivered in 1939*, which was published by the Catholic Truth Society.] As nearly everyone can accept them, we are apt to overlook the possibility of our giving them different interpretations, and accepting them only on our own terms. It will make a vast difference how much phrases like "the laws of God," "Divine vocation," and "God's gifts to the whole world" happen to mean to you. The full meaning is tremendous. But if they come to you like familiar quotations, as something which you need make no fresh effort to understand, they will probably be lost on you. This is one instance of what I mean by the necessity for Christian thinking. I mean thinking as Christians. We need to know what it is that we profess to believe, and without believing which we are not Christian. We must know the dogmas of our faith—and if you do not know what a dogma is, or why it is vitally important, then the first thing that you can do to help towards a Christian Britain is to find out. For otherwise your social thinking is not likely to be particularly Christian. Christian feeling is not enough. By itself, it may lead us to suppose that we do our social duty if we support any scheme of reform which appears to have humane and generous aims. Or it may lead us to assume that any programme elaborated by Christians is necessarily a Christian programme. Our so-called Christian programme may be merely a secular programme warmed by the glow of Christian sentiment—or perhaps only illuminated by the chilly light of Christian phrases.

In a world such as ours in which the Roman Church finds herself misled by a ramshackle Jesuit Peronist whose "Christian programme"—to use Eliot's phrase—is no different from the secular program of the international left, such discriminations could not be more welcome.

Together, these fascinating volumes of Eliot's complete prose chart not only an arduous conversion but the extent to which conversion was essential to the development of an altogether dazzling critical intelligence. Readers who treat themselves to the volumes are in for an incomparable critical feast.

The Maker's Workshop: Auden's Complete Prose

The Complete Works of W. H. Auden: Prose, Volume 1: 1926–1938, Volume 2: 1939–1948, Volume 3: 1949–1955, Volume 4: 1956–1962, Volume 5: 1963–1968, Volume 6: 1969–1973, edited by Edward Mendelson (Princeton University Press).

"At the beginning of the 21st century," Edward Mandelson writes in his entry on W. H. Auden in the *Oxford Dictionary of National Biography*, "many readers thought it not implausible to judge his work the greatest body of poetry in English of the previous hundred years or more." Even allowing for a literary executor's special pleading, this is an extravagant claim. Auden's poetry is full of good things but it is also full of bad things. And the latter are usually the result of bad rhetoric. That Auden regarded "September 1, 1939," for example, his famous poem about the outbreak of World War II, as "infected with an incurable dishonesty" says something for his critical probity. If he was capable of writing nonsense, he was also capable of owning up to writing nonsense.

Some of the bad rhetoric that marred Auden's work can be blamed on his left-wing politics. Valentine Cunningham's study, *British Writers of the Thirties* (1990) brilliantly supplies the cultural and historical context for those politics. Yet Auden also acquired his rhetorical excesses from Yeats, whose public persona he initially tried to emulate. Robert Lowell also played the Yeatsian public poet with regrettable results. The only poet who has managed to play a responsible public role in our time is Dana Gioia, who has nothing of Yeats's or Lowell's fondness for the showy, empty effect. His work for the National Endowment for the Humanities was as selfless as it was substantive. One had to be more than a brilliant rhetorician to get the Boeotian bureaucrats who run America's public schools to allow Shakespeare back in the classroom, though now it is lamentable to see all of his good work being undone by the barbarians of wokery.

One of the virtues of Princeton's magnificent edition of Auden's complete prose, which covers his essays and reviews from 1926 until his death in 1973, is that it shows how the poet gradually renounced the public stage for a more self-effacing, meditative, private life, especially after settling in America in 1939 at the age of 32. "When the ship catches fire," he wrote in a piece on Rilke, "it seems only natural to rush importantly to the pumps, but perhaps one is only adding to the general confusion and panic: to sit still and pray seems selfish and unheroic, but it may be the wisest and most helpful course." Later, in 1972, speaking with *The Paris Review*, he insisted, "A poet, *qua* poet, has only one political duty, namely, in his own writing to set an example of the correct use of his mother tongue which is always being corrupted." This echoes what Eliot had to say in his essay "What Dante Means to Me" (1950), where he tells his readers that "To pass on to posterity one's own language, more highly developed, more refined, and more precise than it was before one wrote it ... is the highest possible achievement of a poet as poet."

How Auden regarded this duty can be seen in the moving eulogy that he wrote for his friend Louis MacNeice, "The Cave of Making" (1964), in which he celebrated the demands of the art to which he devoted his life.

> After all, it's rather a privilege
> amid the affluent traffic
> to serve this unpopular art which cannot be turned into
> background noise for study
> or hung as a status trophy by rising executives,
> cannot be "done" like Venice
> or abridged like Tolstoy, but stubbornly still insists upon
> being read or ignored

One can agree or disagree with the charge brought by Randell Jarrell and Philip Larkin that Auden's intellectual interests stultified his poetry, but one cannot maintain that the essays in which he pursued those interests are stultifying. They exude zest. For Auden, reviewing not only paid the bills but helped shape his protean poetry. The relationship between the state and the individual, history and human suffering, cultural vitality and cultural decay, talent and the snares that entrammel talent: these are the constant preoccupations of his poetry, and they are abundantly explored in these six volumes. Since Auden only published two collections of essays in his lifetime, *The Dyer's Hand* (1962) and *Forewords and Afterwords* (1973), there is much uncollected and unpublished work gathered here, and most of it, as Mendelson shows, is highly revelatory of his personal development. Indeed, in 1964, in a review of autobiographies by Leonard Woolf and Evelyn Waugh, he wrote an autobiography of his own of sorts, in which he gives expression not so much to self-revelation or nostalgia as to the exile's inexorable loneliness.

The range of Auden's subjects is staggering: Goethe, Gogol, Hardy, James, Stravinsky, Mozart, Sainte-Beuve, Dickens, Shakespeare, Dante, Wagner,

Cervantes, Johnson, Beerbohm, Waugh, Wilde, Scott — these and many more make lively appearances in the pages of this well-edited edition. A particularly amusing piece on Kierkegaard describes what it would be like for the Danish gadfly and Sydney Smith to have been condemned to Purgatory together. As Auden relates, the witty Anglican vicar in Smith would recoil at the "prospect of being confined to the company of a fanatical dissenter with no sense for the conventions of polite conversation." And Kierkegaard would see in Smith a replica of the frivolous Christians he deplored in Copenhagen. But after a few centuries, "Kierkegaard would discover that his worldly, society-loving colleague had been banished, at the age of thirty-eight to a rural parish in Yorkshire, where, instead of taking to drink, he served his rustic flock devotedly for the next twenty years." And Smith "would discover that Kierkegaard was not a fanatic but a serious thinker, and under his influence would come to see that he had been wrong when he said, 'There is no enthusiasm in the Gospels.'"

If love of neighbor is at the core of Auden's Christianity, it is also at the core of his criticism. All of these volumes testify to his *caritas*, as well as his abounding sense of fun. In a review of a book on Tennyson, Auden relates how the great poet was dining one night with Benjamin Jowett, the Master of Balliol, and after reciting one of his new poems, Jowett was impelled to say: "I shouldn't publish that poem if I were you, Tennyson," to which the poet replied without skipping a beat: "Well, if it comes to that, Master, the sherry you served us before dinner was filthy."

Journalists will be amused by a long piece that Auden submitted to *Life* magazine in 1966 on the fall of Rome, in which he observed certain parallels between the third and twentieth centuries:

> Instead of Gnostics, we have Existentialists and God-is-dead theologians, instead of Neo-Platonists, devotees of Zen, instead of desert hermits, heroin addicts and Beats (who also, oddly enough, seem averse to washing), instead of mortification of the flesh, sado-masochistic pornography; as for our public entertainments, the fare offered by television is still a shade less brutal than that provided by the Amphitheatre, but only a shade and may not be so for long.

Mendelson relates that *Life* was willing to pay the poet $10,000 for the piece, if only he toned it down. Auden refused, and was paid nothing. Not many of the journalists I know, God bless them, would have been capable of such costly incorruptibility.

In the same piece, Auden is worth quoting on the Desert Fathers, about whom he says:

> We owe the Desert Fathers more than we generally realise. The classical world knew many pleasures, but of one which means a great deal to us, it was totally ignorant until the hermits discovered

it, the pleasure of being by oneself. Nothing could better illustrate the relentlessly public character of classical civilization than an anecdote of Augustine's, in which he tells of his utter astonishment when he saw a hermit reading to himself without pronouncing the words aloud; this was a new world.

The pieces here on poetry shed light on Auden's poetic ambitions. "The difference between major and minor poetry has nothing to do with the difference between better and worse poetry," he observes. "Indeed, it is frequently the case that a minor poet produces more single poems which seem flawless than a major one, because it is one of the distinguishing marks of a major poet that he continues to develop, that the moment he has learnt how to write one kind of poem, he goes on to attempt something else, new subjects, new ways of treatment or both, an attempt in which he may quite possibly fail." The very versatility of Auden's poetic output—with its impressive array of different forms—shows how keen he was to achieve "major" status, though his stylistically conservative poems tend to be his best. "For the Time Being" (1944) and "The Mirror and the Sea" (1944) are full of technical virtuosity but shorter, less bravura poems like "The Memory of W. B. Yeats" (1939) and "The Shield of Achilles" (1955) are more memorable.

Nonetheless, Auden has amusing things to say on form. "Rhymes, meters, stanza forms, etc. are like servants. If the master is fair enough to win their affection and firm enough to command their respect, the result is an orderly happy household. If he is too tyrannical, they give notice; if he lacks authority, they become slovenly, impertinent, drunk and dishonest." A good history of American poetry could be culled from that instructive analogy.

The judgements he lays down on various matters show not only his critical smarts but his charm. Of Max Beerbohm, he writes: "One can very well understand why he was pampered, for few people can have been by nature so adapted to a life of cozy domesticity. He was charming, affectionate, intensely loyal, good-tempered; and none of the common threats to a happy home life, like promiscuity, the bottle, or the race track seem ever to have tempted him." Although Max moved among the rich and well-born easily enough, he did not envy them their opulence, and Auden quotes him to good effect on the most curious of all the memorials left behind by the grandees of the eighteenth century. "The great English country houses are built for gods," Max observed; "an exaggerated conception of the human being led to their scale. It is nightmarish to think of living in those terribly big rooms." Quoting Max on the capaciousness of these homes, I suppose, was one way for Auden to reconcile himself to living in the shoebox he rented in St. Mark's Place in New York's East Village.

Max is a good essayist with whom to compare the essayist in Auden, for, in a way, they exhibit the same appeal in different ways. Like Richard

Steele, Lamb and William Hazlitt, Max is the personal essayist; we delight in what he has to say on anything on which he chooses to write because we delight in Max the person: he is so charming, so witty, so companionable. The essayist in Auden is also someone whom we read because we enjoy Auden the person, though since he is a poet critic, it is a good deal more than simply his charm that attracts us. We like his easy learning, his range of learning, his aesthetic good sense, his understanding of history, his honesty about the role of the author in a world mad to enlist authors in its ideological fisticuffs. Asked to respond to a questionnaire about the American involvement in Vietnam, for example, the poet writes with refreshing common sense:

> Why writers should be canvassed for their opinion on controversial political issues, I cannot imagine. Their views have no more authority than those of any reasonably well-educated citizen … If, as a social human being, I am asked my opinion about some political issue in England, Europe, or the United States, my answer, however stupid or prejudiced, is at least in part based upon personal knowledge. I have traveled in the countries concerned, I know something about their inhabitants, their history, their language, their ways of thinking. But what do I, or any other writer in the West, know about Vietnam, except what we can glean from newspapers and a few hurriedly written books? … It goes without saying that war is an atrocious corrupting business, but it is dishonest of those who demand the immediate withdrawal of all American troops to pretend that their motives are purely humanitarian. They believe, rightly or wrongly, that it would be better if the Communists won.

On his fellow poets, Auden is at once generous and insightful. Of Alexander Pope, he observes, "if Wordsworth had Pope in mind as the enemy when he advised poets to write 'in the language really used by men,' he was singularly in error." Pope writes as men normally speak: it is Wordsworth and the Romantics who go in for "poetic" language. In the case of Lord Byron, Auden points out that while the author of *Don Juan* might have been a master of form, and, particularly, comic form, he never managed "deep emotions" or "profound thoughts." Why? Auden quotes Lady Byron, who once said of the poet: "He is the absolute monarch of words, and uses them as Bonaparte did lives, for conquest, without regard to their intrinsic value." Considering the strictures that would be increasingly levelled against Auden's own technical facility, this is a striking observation. Then, again, with regard to the poet who had such a formative influence on him, Auden says that "Yeats is probably the only poet in [the twentieth century] who has written great poetry on political subjects," which can be read as an admission of his own rather poor showing in that usually inadvisable vein. Of Marianne Moore, he writes, "Those who believe, as I do, that what any poem says should be true and that, in our own noisy, overcrowded age, a quiet and intimate poetic speech is the only genuine way of saying it, will find in *O to Be a Dragon* exactly what they are looking for." Again, the lesson of the evils of bad rhetoric had left its mark.

Regarding Eliot, Auden says that while he was "one of the most idiosyncratic of poets, both in his subject matter and in his technique," and therefore impossible to imitate, he still exerted a sobering influence on a poet who was never averse to the exuberance of art. "None of us, I think, imitated him exactly by taking to a bowler hat and a tight-rolled umbrella," Auden recalled, "but he certainly taught us to think that it was unbecoming to dress or behave in public like the romantic conception of a poet." When living a fairly bohemian existence in Manhattan's St Mark's Place, Auden may have appeared inveterately rumpled—his fingers stained an insalubrious saffron from smoking too many unfiltered cigarettes, his hair askew, his opera slippers dusty and abraded—but his suits were always Brooks Brothers suits of the most conventional cut, however much in need of dry cleaning.

Now that Princeton has completed this superb edition, a wonderfully discerning, erudite, life-enhancing critic has been restored to us. Auden may not have been the greatest poet of the twentieth century but he was certainly one of our most enjoyable critics.

Elizabeth Jennings and the Poetry of Faith

Elizabeth Jennings: The Inward War, Dana Greene (Oxford University Press). 258 pages.

Before his early death at forty-four, Robert Louis Stevenson confided to one of his best friends from his Samoan hideaway: "Were it not for my health which made it impossible, I could not find it in my heart to forgive myself that I did not stick to an honest commonplace trade when I was young … *David Balfour* is a nice little book, and very artistic and just the thing to occupy the leisure of a busy man; but for the top flower of a man's life it seems to be inadequate … I ought to have been able to build lighthouses and write *David Balfour* too."

Dana Greene's excellent biography of the English poet Elizabeth Jennings (1926–2001) puts one in mind of this quote because Jennings, like Stevenson, would never have any career other than writing, though, unlike Stevenson, despite all of the difficulties she braved to pursue her vocation, she never regretted it. Greene notes how Jennings, at the end of her career, would always field the question, "Are you still writing?" by responding, "Are you still breathing?" For Jennings, as Greene shows in her terse, lucid, incisive pages, poetry "was her 'moon and sun' … it could not be turned off and on." If scores of previous critics have complained that Jennings wrote too much and too unevenly, Greene shows that it was her very profuseness that proved how vital poetry was to her.

Towards the end of her life, this investment in her chosen art only intensified. As Greene writes, Jennings "claimed it was a sacrament, a gift and a way to pray. It could heal the lonely and lost, haunt readers, and speak over continents. It was a gift of kindness and helped readers to grapple with fears. It brought contrition, fostered justice, and served as a harbinger of peace." Although the occasional censures of reviewers could unduly upset her, she was always careful to persist in her accustomed copiousness. For Jennings, there was an "arc of good" in her work—all 27 volumes of it—and she never allowed her critics to keep her from seeing it flourish. Greene's book does full justice to Jennings's dedication to her art by showing how much it was nurtured and sustained by her Catholic faith.

More than Philip Larkin or even John Betjeman (both good popular poets), Jennings was the darling of the general reader, or what Samuel Johnson called the "common reader," by whose "common sense ... uncorrupted by literary prejudice ... must finally be decided all poetical honours." Certainly, Michael Schmidt was right to claim that his bestselling Carcanet author was "the most unconditionally loved writer" of her generation. Writing of the things that preoccupy most readers—family, faith, love, loss, illness, hope, atonement, redemption—she not only won her readers' trust but their affection. In light of the many false reputations that disfigure our literary landscape, Jennings's unfashionably popular work is tonic, especially since so much of its appeal derives from its Catholic character.

II

Catholicism, in one way or another, meant a good deal to Jennings. Born in Boston, Lincolnshire, the daughter of a medical examiner, Jennings was educated at Rye St. Anthony, a Catholic private school and at Oxford High School before going on to St. Anne's College, Oxford, where she studied English, acted in plays and made friends with Larkin and Kingsley Amis. It was hearing Chesterton's poem "Lepanto" read aloud that first inspired her to be a poet. Several extended trips to Rome when she was in her thirties not only steeled her desire to be a poet but deepened her faith. Greene is particularly perceptive about how Jennings's sense of religious and artistic vocation intertwined, a reality which few of her contemporary critics understood or respected.

Greene is also good when it comes to showing how Jennings stood out from her contemporaries. When the poet and historian of Stalinist Russia Robert Conquest included Jennings's work in an anthology of young British poets, which included Larkin, Amis, Donald Davie, and Thom Gunn, the group was dubbed "The Movement," though its members would never have much in common beyond their insistence on clarity and their use of traditional forms. What set Jennings apart from the other poets of her time can be summed up in a few lines from her last collection: "You said we only share what intellect / Provides us with. I can't agree with you / Surely we share our love." In other words, it was her Catholic recognition of the primacy of love (true love, not the counterfeit article of the pop culture) that set her apart. In one of her last poems, she writes of how

> Matter never satisfies for long
> Power dwindles fast and leaves us wondering
> Why we pursued it. In the soul a strong
> Yearning for a personal truth brings
> Us to our knees and keeps us there.

For those similarly prostrated, Jennings's honesty about her spiritual struggles is always endearing. As she entreats her Maker in a poem called "Prayer for Holy Week":

Teach me how you love and have to die
And I will try
Somehow to forget myself and give
Life and joy so dead things start to live
Let me show now an untrammeled joy
Gold without alloy."

Jennings's ability "to forget herself" in her work and write of others is another of her virtues as a writer, about which Greene is perceptive.

Jennings' ability to enter into the sufferings of others was born of her own vulnerability and strengthened by her religious commitment. She wrote of women who were single or infertile or who had miscarriages or abortions, adopted children, the elderly, the poor, the sick, prisoners, even murderers. Her capacity to empathize them was one of the unique qualities of her poetry and in part explains its popularity. In order to write in the first person about the shattered lives of outcasts Jennings needed artistry, craftsmanship, and a talent for "imagined experience."

After working briefly at Chatto and Windus as a publisher's reader, wading through reams of the usual unreadable rubbish, Jennings took a post as librarian at the Oxford City Library. After returning to Oxford from Rome in 1960, however, she resolved to make her living from her pen, a decision which may have reduced her to occasional beggary but kept her lyric gift in good serviceable trim. While readers may need to sift through dross here and there in Jennings abounding output, her gold is never far away. Here is a little effusion called "Rain."

Beautiful rain
Falling so softly
Such a delicate thing

The harvests need you
And some of the flowers
But we too

Because you remind
Of coolness and quiet
Of tenderest words

Come down rain, fall
Not too harshly, but give
Your strange sense of peace to us.

89

Although she would never marry, Jennings was fond of children. A beautiful child herself—the photographs that Greene includes in the book of the poet as a girl show her to have had "a beauty beyond beauty"—she never lost the ability to practice both her faith and her art with a child's wholeheartedness. Indeed, as a poet, she approached her subjects, as Thomas Traherne approached his, with a child's wonder. "Your *Centuries* are noble, rich, serene," she writes in homage to Traherne, "Leaping with love and dancing with delight / And it is clear exactly what you mean." A good deal of her own poems can be seen as variations on Traherne. In one of her late poems, for example, after describing what we in America call "Indian summer," she writes:

> I am a Summer child whose birthday
> Is in July but here was Summer all over
> Again, all over the late grass of our meadows ...
> I wanted to praise, I needed a new *Book of Hours*
> Painted by unseen holy ones, enchanted
> By God as man and creator of the world.
> O it is sweet to be
> Suddenly warm in October in suddenly green
> Fields ...

In another poem, she confides to her readers:

> There is no dead
> Place for me. I have a pulsating land
> Peopled with saints and children. These I need
> To help me see in joy and pain, God's hand.

In light of lines like these, with their stark pellucidity, it is no wonder that Jennings won little attention from the charlatans who pass for critics in the academy.

Traherne was such an abiding touchstone for Jennings because in his evocation of Eden her own sense of Eden's allure and loss would always find an insistent echo. That one of Jennings's favorite poets, Edward Thomas was also fond of Traherne must also have endeared the seventeenth-century devotional poet to her. No one can read anything by Jennings without seeing how much her poetry recalls Traherne's catalogue of childhood's graces. Here is a characteristic passage from the *Centuries of Meditations*, which Thomas quotes in his travelogue, *The South Country* (1906):

All appeared New, and Strange at the first, inexpressibly rare, and Delightfull, and Beautifull. I was a little Stranger which at my Enterance into the World was Saluted and Surrounded with innumerable Joys. My Knowledg was Divine. I knew by Intuition those things which since my Apostasie, I Collected again, by the Highest REASON My very Ignorance was Advantageous. I seemed

as one Brought into the Estate of Innocence. All Things were Spotles
and Pure and Glorious: yea, and infinitly mine, and Joyfull and
Precious. I Knew not that there were any Sins, or Complaints, or
Laws. I Dreamed not of Poverties Contentions or Vices. All Tears and
Quarrels, were hidden from mine Eys. Evry Thing was at Rest, Free,
and Immortal. I Knew Nothing of Sickness or Death, or Exaction,
in the Absence of these I was Entertained like an Angel with the
Works of GOD in their Splendor and Glory; I saw all in the Peace
of Eden; Heaven and Earth did sing my Creators Praises and could
not make more Melody to Adam, then to me. All Time was Eternity,
and a Perpetual Sabbath. Is it not Strange, that an Infant should be
Heir of the World, and see those Mysteries which the Books of the
Learned never unfold?

In a poem entitled "From Light to Dark" from her collection, *A Dream
of Spring* (1980), Jennings gives her own sense of these mysteries when
she writes of how

> a strange homesickness
> Haunts us, not for some place where we have been
> Happy. It is for one place we've not seen
> But where we feel we fit. An Eden is
> Our long desire.

And to make sure her readers do not imagine that she is gratifying any
vague nostalgia in speaking of this "strange homesickness," she ends the
poem by describing our collective lost Eden.

> Among its many trees
> One stands and mocks us, one whose fruit is gone
> This is our lost home. Cannot we put back
> The forbidden fruit? We can't, since we lack
> The proper love, the selfless one. We're sick
> With an old pain.

In another poem entitled "Eden," she is more explicit still about why this
loss is so acute: "Something is / Wrong at the heart of us."

The theme of Eden also informs Jennings's understanding of art. In her
poem, "Order," she insists that our yearning for order in art is akin to our
yearning for the order of the prelapsarian Eden.

> After we
> Were driven from that garden, we've shown how
> There must be patterns. We lost liberty
> Of one kind but we've fashioned others. Now
>
> In our wild world of misrule we insist
> On shapeliness and balance. Most of us
> Do this to our gardens. Tough weeds persist

Until we've plucked them. We make curious
Designs for garden-beds. O we exist
To make new order since our Eden loss.

III

In the mid-1960s Jennings began to suffer bouts of mental illness, which the
ministrations of a smug Freudian psychiatrist from the Radcliffe Infirmary
only exacerbated. A wonderfully witty riposte to this sadist (too long to
quote here) can be found in her poem entitled "The Interrogator." Luckily,
she had many good, loyal, and resourceful friends — including Vivian
Greene, Graham Greene's estranged wife and Veronica Wedgewood, the
popular historian — all of whom came to her rescue at different periods in
her often troubled life. Even the actor John Gielgud sent her gifts of money
now and again, though he never met the beneficiary of his eleemosynary
largesse.

If Jennings's mental distress brought out the kindness of friends and
well-wishers, it also brings out the virtues of her biographer. Although
unfailingly sympathetic, Greene never gives way to psychobabble. On
page after page of this admirable book, it is clear that she has had her
prayer answered for what Robert Lowell called "the grace of accuracy."
No unseemly tittle tattle mars her pages. She pays attention to the poems
as poems, and leaves speculations as to how the messy life might have
influenced the writing of the poems to others.

Greene shows that some of Jennings's best poems are those treating of
hospitals; and, here, we can contrast her with Eliot. In "East Coker," Eliot
sees hospitals as a useful metaphor for the irredeemable world.

> The whole earth is our hospital
> Endowed by the ruined millionaire,
> Wherein, if we do well, we shall
> Die of the absolute paternal care
> That will not leave us, but prevents us everywhere.

In "Sequence in Hospital," Jennings kicks away such rhetorical stilts and
descends instead into the actual world of infirmity and fear that hospitals
never entirely allay.

> Though death is never talked of here,
> It is more palpable and felt —
> Touching the cheek or in a tear —
> By being present by default.
> The muffled cries, the curtains drawn,
> The flowers pale before they fall —
> The world itself is here brought down

To what is suffering and small.
The huge philosophies depart,
Large words slink off, like faith, like love,
The thumping of the human heart
Is reassurance here enough.

Unlike Sylvia Plath and the American confessional poets, Jennings never exploited her illness to gratify the prurience so marked in those who had rather read about the poet's troubles than the poet's work. As the literary critic and biographer Julian Symons nicely put it: "No one has ever written less hysterically of hysteria." This is doubtless why Jennings wrote so fondly of clowns and scapegoats. Illness elicited from her a wry detachment. In a poem about visiting the sick in hospital, she writes:

You are the one to whom I bring distress
The troubles, dreams, and all the broken things.
The roles reverse and I'm the one who brings
Solicitude and help and tenderness
And yet it is a mask I wear, an act
Where terror hides behind the look of tact.

In sharing such experiences so candidly, Jennings brought them into the very making of her poetry, which is another reason why she managed to command such unusual popularity. She saw the same relation between Traherne and his readers, as she pointed out in an essay on the poet in her collection of essays, *Every Changing Shape* (1961):

Traherne wears no masks, casts no concealing shadow. He is, in the deepest sense, a man possessed. What possesses him is a sense of God, and this he wishes to share ... But his sharing is not done from any lofty height; he demands neither reverence nor awe, not because his work is not penetrated with these things but because we, his readers, are admitted to the heart of his experiences where reverence and awe have other names. Traherne's work becomes, in fact, our property, part of our life.

This is good criticism, confirming as it does what Thomas admired in Traherne, which was his respect for his neighbor's dignity. Thomas, for example, was struck by Traherne making no bones about the fact that "One soul in the immensity of its intelligence is greater and more excellent than the whole world." Similarly, Jennings won so many readers precisely because her poems showed how she prized their dignity, which is something altogether different from pandering to what publishers imagine the popular taste.

IV

In sub-titling her biography, "The Inward War," Greene stresses Jennings's debt to another Catholic poet, Gerard Manley Hopkins, whose spiritual struggles resembled Jennings's own. In his poem on Saint Alphonsus Rodriguez, Hopkins described how:

> Honour is flashed off exploit, so we say;
> And those strokes once that gashed flesh or galled shield
> Should tongue that time now, trumpet now that field,
> And on the fighter, forge his glorious day.

This was one type of heroism. Yet Hopkins knew that his own heroism would be quite different. Strokes that gash flesh or gall shield make visible war.

> But be the war within, the brand we wield
> Unseen, the heroic breast not outward-steeled,
> Earth hears no hurtle then from fiercest fray.

This is the interior war that Hopkins chronicled with such unflinching fidelity. Jennings's spiritual struggles were similarly fierce, though, unlike Hopkins, she lived to survive their harrowing, thanks, in large measure, to her indomitably faithful art. In "Against the Dark" from her collection *Tributes* (1989), she speaks of this survival with no-nonsense gratitude.

> I have lived in a time of opulent grief
>   In a place also of powers
> Where self-indulgence can break your purchase on life
>   But now I inhabit hours
>
> Of careful joy and rousing gratitude
>   My spirit has learnt to play
> And I have willed away the darker mood
>   And now I want to say
>
> That verse is hostile to shadows and casts you out
>   When you have mourned too long.
> Images always rise from the root of light
>   And I must make my song
>
> Truthful, yes, obstinate, too and yet
>   Open to love that takes
> Language by the hand and ignores regret
>   And also our heartbreaks.

This lovely poem is central to understanding Jennings's work as a whole and should be read in *toto*, exhibiting as it does her hard-earned artistry, Fortunately, readers can read this and all of the poems quoted here in Prof.

Emma Mason's wonderfully rich edition of Jennings's *Collected Poems* (2012), published by Carcanet.

V

In 1987, Jennings received an honorary Doctor of Divinity from Durham University and in 1993 she was made Commander of the Most Excellent Order of the British Empire (CBE), though the English tabloids mocked her for turning up for the honor in characteristically inelegant dress. Nonetheless, there are moving photographs in the book of Jennings shaking hands with Queen Elizabeth and standing with her sister after she had received her CBE. It is a tribute to Greene's book that by the time the reader encounters these photographs in her pages, he feels a personal affection and esteem for their subject.

Poets are not inveterately well served by biographers. Take, for example, the plodding biography that Robert Crawford recently wrote of T. S. Eliot (whom he has the effrontery to address as "Tom") or the equally impertinent biography of Robert Lowell by Kay Redfield Jamison, who effectively claims that the poet's periodical mental illness, not his art, produced his poetry. What distinguishes Greene from these duffers is not only her good judgement but her tact, indeed, her self-effacement. In "Seers and Makers" from *In the Meantime* (1996), Jennings memorably extols this *sine qua non* of good art.

> There is one quality in common which
>   Artists and men of prayer
> Display when we think back on them. They were
>   Eager to disappear
> Within the words, paint, sound, and praying: each
> Wished to be hidden. Thus we can
> Always mark off the honest from the sham.

In *Elizabeth Jennings: The Inward War*, Dana Greene has written an exemplary life of a praiseworthy poet by revealing not only the hidden artist in Jennings but the faithful pilgrim as well.

Desire and Loss
in the Poetry of Dana Gioia

Each thing is good and beautiful by its proper form.

St. Thomas Aquinas

I

"Verse is dressed up that has nowhere to go," the poet critic John Wain once said in one of his own verses, "Apology for Understatement." I thought of the line the other day when thinking of Dana Gioia's poetry because, although his poems may not be "dressed up" in the sense of being over-dressed, they are definitely smartly dressed and they always know where they are going, even when their destination is the most unravellable mystery. A good example of this can be seen in the final lines of his sonnet, "The Road":

> He noticed then that no one chose the way
> All seemed to drift by come collective will.
> The path grew easier with each passing day,
> Since it was worn and mostly sloped downhill.
> The road ahead seemed hazy in the gloom.
> Where was it that he had meant to go, and with whom?

If at some point in our checquered lives, we have not paid any mind to the road we go, or asked ourselves why, where and with whom we go, what an unexamined life we live! And yet Gioia realizes why we may be tempted to forgo such inquiries. In the dramatic monologue of "Interrogations at Noon," the speaker finds himself asking himself questions that are not easily answered.

> "Who is the person you pretend to be?"
> He asks, "The failed saint, the simpering bore,
> The pale connoisseur of spent desire,
> The half-hearted hermit eyeing the door?"

97

As those who have followed Gioia's career know, form, the appropriate dress of verse, whether free or unfree, has always preoccupied him—"how," as he says in one of his essays, "a poet best shapes words, images, and ideas into meaning." And yet it is never form for form's sake that interests him but form for the sake of clarity, memorability, order, concinnity.[1] In "All Souls'," he marshals the order of form to portray what the experience of death might be like where there is no life after death:

> Suppose there is no heaven and no hell,
> And that the dead can never leave the earth,
> That, as the body rots, the soul breaks free,
> Weak and disabled in its second birth.
>
> And then invisible, rising to the light,
> Each finds a world it cannot touch or hear,
> Where colors fade and, if the soul cries out,
> The silence stays unbroken in the air.

The very matter-of-fact orderliness of the verse accentuates the horror of an afterlife where there is no touch, no sound, no color; where cries, like the cries of nightmares, go unheard and unheeded. Here is a vision of desolated loss entirely in keeping with Robert Graves's evocation of the "sinister, long, brass-bound coffin-box" of death. Gioia's unrisen dead remain forever excluded from life. These are the dead not of ghost stories or senior common rooms but of the most consequential apostasy.

> they are silent as a rising mist,
> A smudge of smoke dissolving in the air.
> They watch the shadows lengthen on the grass.
> The pallor of the rose is their despair

Here, we can also see that symbols are another element of poetry that engage Gioia's attention. The poem's pallid rose is an anti-rose: a symbol not of love but of lovelessness. And yet its inadequacy when it comes to capturing the full force of the lovelessness that issues from denial of what our Lord and Saviour calls "the resurrection and the life' is patent. The reader is obliged to imagine himself what the poem can only encourage him to imagine in all its terrifying nihilism—a nihilism, incidentally, which

---

1 Gioia took his understanding of form as a young man from the class in versification that he took with the poet and translator Robert Fitzgerald, who "cautioned" his students "that metre was only one of several features operating in a poem. 'Verse is not just metre,' [Fitzgerald] observed, 'but also diction, rhetoric and syntax.' Separate the elements, even for pedagogical purposes, and one risked teaching abstract simplifications. The beauty of poetry arose from the intricate dance of its parts." Dana Gioia, *Studying with Miss Bishop: Memoirs from a Young Writer's Life* (Philadelphia: Paul Dry Books, 2021), 78.

Larkin captured, too, in his very last published poem, "Aubade." Indeed, Gioia's poem might almost be a response to Larkin's, especially these memorable lines, which express so pitiably Larkin's *timor mortis*.

This is a special way of being afraid
No trick dispels. Religion used to try,
That vast moth-eaten musical brocade
Created to pretend we never die,
And specious stuff that says *No rational being*
Can fear a thing it will not feel, not seeing
That this is what we fear—no sight, no sound,
No touch or taste or smell, nothing to think with,
Nothing to love or link with,
The anaesthetic from which none come round.

In "Autumn Inaugural," Gioia again admits that symbols can only be approximations of the things they signify. The road as a symbol of the pilgrimage of desire has, of course, an ancient warrant. Yet Gioia recognizes that one reason why symbols cannot be entirely the things we wish them to be is that they are of our own devisal.

Symbols betray us.
They are always more or less than what
Is really meant. But shall there be no
Processions by torchlight because we are weak?
What native speech do we share but imperfection?

Gioia may concede that symbols savor of the imperfection central not only to our speech but to our very being, but he also chides those who imagine that "the still star of painted plaster / Praised creation less than the evening star." Symbols, in other words, for all their limitations, are one of our pro-creative means of sharing in God's creativeness. As the poem will go on to show, they are how we receive and pass on the life of marriage, the life of baptism. They accompany the sacraments on their way to grace. And this is not to mention how they enable a poet with as much music in him as Gioia to sing.[2]

Praise to the rituals that celebrate change,
Old robes worn for new beginnings,
Solemn protocol where the mutable soul,
Surrounded by ancient experience, grows
Young in the imagination's white dress.

---

2 Another good example of the music of Gioia's verse is a line from his "Psalm to Our Lady, Queen of the Angels," which appears in his forthcoming collection of poetry, *Meet Me at the Lighthouse*: "She will not abandon her divided pueblo," a beautiful, noble line.

Praise, celebration, mutability, growth, rejuvenation: for all of these things to be jostling one another in a stanza of five lines is proof not only of the poet's economy but of the power of form, symbols, rituals, rites.

> Because it is not the rituals we honor
> But our trust in what they signify, these rites
> That honor us as witnesses—whether to watch
> Lovers swear loyalty in a careless world
> Or a newborn washed with water and oil.

In his essay, "Can Poetry Matter?" (1991), Gioia rankled many vested interests when he called attention to the ill-formed poetry produced in reams by America's academic establishment. "Seeing so much mediocre verse not only published but praised," he wrote, "slogging through so many dull anthologies and small magazines, most readers now assume that no significant new poetry is being written. This public skepticism represents the final isolation of verse as an art form in contemporary society." Yet in "Autumn Inaugural," he relents and treats his refractory critics to a lesson in song. He practices what he preaches. If such critics will not concede the points he makes in his essay, they might at least listen to his music, a music replete with form's enrapturing alchemy.

> So praise to innocence—impulsive and evergreen—
> And let the old be touched by youth's
> Wayward astonishment at learning something new,
> And dream of a future so fitting and so just
> That our desire will bring it into being.

II

Born in 1950 in Los Angeles of Mexican and Sicilian parentage, Gioia has led a life driven by desire. If desire is a theme that commands constant attention in his poetry, it shaped his life. He was such a good scholar as a boy that he went on to Harvard and Stanford. It was while studying for a year in Vienna that he first decided to consider poetry as a profession. At Harvard, he studied with Flannery O'Connor's good friend, Robert Fitzgerald, the crack translator of Homer, who taught him the niceties of poetic form. He also studied with and befriended the poet Elizabeth Bishop before leaving what he feared would be the stultifying hot house of academe. From 1977 to 1991, he pursued a successful business career in New York, though even as a businessman he never stopped writing poetry. Like T. S. Eliot and Wallace Stevens, he decided to make his living in business, rather than poetry, and the bet paid off. The competence made possible by the earnings of business freed him to master the art of poetry— his heart's desire. Indeed, in 1986, while still an executive with General

Foods, he published his first book of poems, *Daily Horoscope*. Four highly acclaimed and commercially successful volumes of poetry would follow. A new collection is in the offing.

Gioia left business to dedicate himself fully to poetry a year after the publication of *The Gods of Winter* (1991), one of the few American volumes ever chosen as the main selection of England's Poetry Book Society. Although he has cited Hardy, Frost, Stevens, Eliot, Auden, Bishop and Larkin as influences on the technical aspects of his work, he has also championed less popular or well-known poets such as Robinson Jeffers and Weldon Kees.

From 2003 to 2009, Gioia headed up the National Endowment for the Arts with creative aplomb. Many poets aspire to play public roles, usually out of moral vanity: Gioia played his with a selfless efficiency that benefited the American young profoundly by giving them an access to Shakespeare that many of them might not otherwise have had. In his recognition of the pedagogical point of Shakespeare, a point the appalling bureaucrats who run our schools can never be expected to understand, Gioia was one with Lady Antonia Fraser, who recalled of her own schooldays at the Dragon School: "To know three Shakespeare plays virtually by heart, to love them, before the age of twelve, to realize there was a whole Shakespearean world and it was part of History — these were inestimable gifts."

In addition to his poetic work, Gioia is an accomplished librettist, having written the texts for four operas and collaborated with the composers Dave Brubeck, Morten Lauridsen and James MacMillan. Anyone attuned to music will see in a trice Gioia's natural affinity for its ineffable swing. The opening lines of "New Year" are good examples of his assured musicality:

> Let other mornings honor the miraculous
> Eternity has festivals enough
> This is the feast of our mortality
> The most mundane and human holiday.

Married with two sons, Gioia lives in the hills of Sonoma Valley, which he describes in one of his poems as:

> A hiding place, a shrine for dragonflies
> and nesting jays, a sign that there is still
> one piece of property that won't be owned.

As this brief overview of his life shows, Gioia has always been fascinated by the fortunes of desire, whether in forming or in failing its object. In "Convergence of the Twain" (1912) Hardy responded to the loss of the Titanic by showing what become of human vanity and the pride of life when their desires come to smash.

> Jewels in joy designed
> To ravish the sensuous mind

101

Lie lightless, all their sparkles bleared and black and blind.

Gioia's take on the miscarriage of desire is rather more subtle. In his poem, "The Apple Orchard," he sets desire in its natural, indeed, its supernatural habitat where "perfume of blossoms" is "mingled with the dust."

> You won't remember it—the apple orchard
> We wandered through one April afternoon,
> Climbing the hill behind the empty farm.
>
> A city boy, I'd never seen a grove
> Burst in full flower or breathed the bittersweet
> Perfume of blossoms mingled with the dust.
>
> A quarter mile of trees in fragrant rows
> Arching above us. We walked the aisle,
> Alone in spring's ephemeral cathedral.
>
> We had the luck, if you can call it that,
> Of having been in love but never lovers—
> The bright flame burning, fed by pure desire.
>
> Nothing consumed, such secrets brought to light!
> There was a moment when I stood behind you,
> Reached out to spin you toward me ... but I stopped.
>
> What more could I have wanted from that day?
> Everything, of course. Perhaps that was the point—
> To learn that what we will not grasp is lost.

Reading the poem, one is given a jolt by the last line. It seems, at first, so discordant. One expects the line to cast a wry look back at lost romance, something along the lines of Hardy's little poem, "A Thunderstorm in Town."

> She wore a "terra-cotta" dress,
> And we stayed, because of the pelting storm,
> Within the hansom's dry recess,
> Though the horse had stopped; yea, motionless
> We sat on, snug and warm.
>
>> Then the downpour ceased, to my sharp sad pain,
>> And the glass that had screened our forms before
>> Flew up, and out she sprang to her door:
>> I should have kissed her if the rain
>> Had lasted a minute more.

Instead, Gioia invites the reader to reconsider desire, time, action, will, love, loss. A casual would-be dalliance has impressed upon the poet—and his readers—the meaning of choices in a mortal world where the stakes are immortal. The *carpe diem* poem is often little more than a summons to hedonism. Laugh and lie down because who knows what tomorrow will bring. Marvell, unless I misread him, does not have rendering an account in mind when he bids his coy mistress to keep in view that:

> The Grave's a fine and private place,
> But none I think do there embrace.

Gioia sets up the usual expectations inherent in the *carpe diem* poem to frustrate them—or perhaps, one should say, to redirect them. Desire partakes not merely of passing fancy but of our moral quintessence. Men are perpetually moralists but only gallants by chance. When we finish the poem, instead of Marvell, we think of the summons to exploration that closes out the last of T. S. Eliot's *Four Quartets*, "Little Gidding"—an exploration "Costing not less than everything."

III

In Gioia's poetry, loss and desire are intertwined. The poem "The Lost Garden" could almost be a companion piece, a gloss on "The Apple Orchard."

> If ever we see those gardens again,
> The summer will be gone—at least our summer.
> Some other mockingbird will concertize
> Among the mulberries, and other vines
> Will climb the high brick wall to disappear.

Again, the setting is both natural and supernatural, particular and universal. The mulberries recall the tale of Pyramus and Thisbe, the comic star-crossed lovers in Shakespeare's *A Midsummer Night's Dream*, who find their death beneath a mulberry tree, about which Quince nicely remarks:

> Gentles, perchance you wonder at this show
> But wonder on till truth make all things plain.

That the mulberry is also an emblem of patience gives this plea a certain aptness. Gioia, too, pleas for patience. Indeed, to beguile the pain of loss, he even resorts to rifling the cards of contingency.

> Still, thinking of you, I sometimes play a game.
> What if we had walked a different path one day,
> Would some small incident have nudged us elsewhere
> The way a pebble tossed into a brook
> Might change the course a hundred miles downstream?
>
> The trick is making memory a blessing,
> To learn by loss subtraction of desire,

Of wanting nothing more than what has been,
To know the past forever lost, yet seeing
Behind the wall a garden still in blossom.

Whether the trick actually works is another matter. Such counterfactual suppositions might keep historians from falling into the fallacy of imaging events inevitable, but they offer scant consolation to losers in love. In "The Lunatic, the Lover and the Poet," Gioia wonders "if the only purpose of desire / Were to express its infinite unfolding." And as for the past being "forever lost," Gioia has some rather arresting things to say of that in a poem strikingly entitled, "Nothing is Lost."

Nothing is lost. Nothing is so small
that it does not return.
 Imagine
that as a child on a day like this
you held a newly minted coin and had
the choice of spending it in any way
you wished.
 Today the coin comes back to you,
the date rubbed out, the ancient mottoes vague,
the portrait covered with the dull shellac
of anything used up, passed on, disposed of
with something else in view, and always worth
a little less each time.
 Now it returns,
and you will think it unimportant, lose
it in your pocket change as one more thing
that's not worth counting, not worth singling out.
That is the mistake you must avoid today.
You sent it on a journey to yourself.
Now hold it in your hand. Accept it as
the little you have earned today.
 And realize
that you must choose again but over less.

Here, rendering an account, which had only been implicit in "The Apple Orchard," becomes explicit. Desire and memory, choice and loss are all a part of the same accountancy. In Gioia's poetry, time's wingèd chariot hurrying near is more than simply a *memento mori*: it is a reminder that the books need balancing. That Gioia should have chosen to have an estate accountant narrate his bravura narrative poem, "Counting the Children" was no unconsidered choice. After he beholds the dead woman's doll collection—with all of her dolls, plucked for years from city trash cans, arranged row upon row, from floor to ceiling—the accountant muses:

Was this where all lost childhoods go? These dim
Abandoned rooms, these crude arrangements staged
For settled dust and shadow, left to prove

That all affection is outgrown or show
The uniformity of our desire?
How dismal someone else's joy can be.

IV

This preoccupation with what amounts to a metaphysical accountancy
might have been what impelled Gioia to write "Money," his witty gloss on
Wallace Stevens's immortal jibe, "Money is a kind of poetry."

> Money, the long green,
> cash, stash, rhino, jack
> or just plain dough.
>
> Chock it up, fork it over,
> shell it out. Watch it
> burn holes through pockets.
>
> To be made of it! To have it
> to burn! Greenbacks, double eagles,
> megabucks and Ginnie Maes.

To get a comparative sense of the geniality of Gioia's attitude towards
what Balzac in *Eugénie Grandet* (1833) regarded as "the one god who yet
finds worshippers in modern times," we can look at what Robert Graves
had to say of money. In "The Virus," he is rather less forbearing.

> We can do little for these living dead
> Unless to help them bury one another ...
> They are, we recognize, past praying for—
> Only among the moribund or dying
> Is treatment practical.
>
> Faithfully we experiment, assuming
> That death is a still an undetected virus
> And most contagious where
> Men eat, smoke, drink and sleep money:
> Its monstrous and unconscionable source.

Gioia, by contrast, is too humane a satirist to give way to bitterness. In
his send-up of the degree to which we are attached to money there is a
comic gaiety entirely missing in Graves's withering screed. The master of
language in Gioia also relishes the opportunity the subject gives him of
celebrating the idiomatic genius of English, for if we are unduly attached to

money, we express our attachment with a certain eloquence. Roget would surely delight in how Gioia sets out the varieties of our attachment.

It greases the palm,
feathers a nest, holds heads
above water, makes both ends meet.

Money breeds money.
Gathering interest, compounding daily.
Always in circulation.

Money. You don't know where it's been,
but you put it where your mouth is.
And it talks.

The exclamation points in the third stanza here—"To be made of it! to have it / to burn!"—show what a superb comedian Gioia is. Whenever he means to be funny, he never misses the mark. This is difficult enough to do in prose. After all, why else would James Joyce have thought so highly of Flann O'Brien or Evelyn Waugh of P. G. Wodehouse if not that both writers were so brilliantly funny in their prose. To be truly funny in verse—rather than simply amusing—is much more difficult. Any anthology of comic verse will prove, *pace* Gavin Ewart, *pace* John Gross, how poetry, as a rule, even when it means to be, is seldom funny. As Samuel Johnson was fond of saying, "Nothing is more hopeless than a scheme for merriment." Yet Gioia's "Progress Report" is sublimely funny.

It's time to admit I'm irresponsible.
I lack ambition. I get nothing done.

I spend the morning walking up the fire road.
I know every tree along the ridge.

Reaching the end, I turn around. There's no point
to my pilgrimage except the coming and the going.

Then I sit and listen to the woodpecker tapping away.
He works too hard.

Tonight I will go out to watch the moon rise.
If only I could move that slowly.

Precisely because of its wit, the poem makes a serious point. The writing of poetry, which also includes preparing to write poetry, requires more meditative idleness, more leisure, more *otium* than our middle-class obsession with business can often tolerate, much less understand. Then, again, unlike too many contemporary poets, convinced of what they imagine the dividends of slapdash spontaneity, Gioia plays the long game; he is content to let a poem's gestation take its own sweet time; he is never in a hurry.

V

Words obsess Gioia, as they should all good poets. His sense of form, after all, is never focused on the old debate about whether poetry should be "cooked" or "uncooked" but whether it should be well made or poorly made, whether its words should be true, though he is never unaware, as he says in "Words, Words, Words," that:

> The truest words subvert what we intend.
> They bring no ease.
> The cost is always more than we can spend.

In the precision and wit with which he chooses his words, Gioia never shies away from the obligation all good poets have of "purifying the dialect of the tribe," to use the Dantescan phrase of which Eliot was so fond. Accordingly, those who insist on regarding Gioia as merely a publicist for the "new formalism" get him terribly wrong. For no poet are labels more misleading than the versatile Gioia. Form is not a matter for him simply of rhyme and metre or of no rhyme and metre: he is as much at home in free as he is in traditional verse. No, for this most accomplished of poets, form is the condition of style. In this sense, he is one with Swift, the most economical of the great Georgian stylists, who neatly defined style as putting "proper words in proper places." Indeed, Gioia's entire *oeuvre* as a poet could be summarized as a compiling of "a rosary of words," as he says in "The Litany," with the understated exactitude with which he always speaks of prayer, a rosary

> to count out time's
> illusions, all the minutes, hours, days
> the calendar compounds as if the past
> existed somewhere—like an inheritance
> still waiting to be claimed.

Gioia is thus aware that, to an extent that few of us may recognize, we live by words. This is why we must contrive to make sure that the words by which we live are true. This is why dogma in the understanding of the profession and practice of faith is so profoundly important. This is why we cannot live by words which are demonstrably false. It might be true, as the poet says in "Words," that "The world does not need words"; but that does not mean that we do not need them.

> To see a red stone is less than seeing it as jasper—
> metamorphic quartz, cousin to the flint the Kiowa
> carved
> as arrowheads

Gioia's choice of the word "jasper" here is well chosen. It reminds one of Ronald Knox's niece, the novelist Penelope Fitzgerald (1916–2000). Precisely because she had something of a soft spot for her fun, faithful, fastidious uncle, she had a soft spot for the Church of Rome, even though she never abandoned the broad-church Anglicanism of her childhood. Indeed, during a visit to the Holy Land in 1992, she took outdoor communion at St. Peter's Church and then "took a perfectly flat, smooth, pale red pebble home to remind herself of it. "I think it may have some jasper in it," she wrote, "and it shines a little in a good light." The poet, too, as we shall see, has a personal attachment to the precious stone.

For Gioia, this is why getting words right is so consequential: it helps us to understand the meaning of our lives. He does not subscribe to what Craig Raine nicely referred to as "the modishly perverse platitude that language is always an obstacle to expression." If our lives are buried lives, to use Arnold's phrase, one of poetry's charges is to excavate the buried. And obviously this is not only vital for poets, but for the common reader for whom the poet writes—the reader, as Johnson says in his life of Gray, "uncorrupted by literary prejudices." No one can read Gioia's work without seeing the solicitude he shows these common readers, the allowances he makes for their collaborative contribution to his work. Frost, not the confessional Lowell is his model, the same Frost, about whom he once wrote: "he is never autobiographical but always personal."

Gioia's investment in the personal has always this attentiveness to communion: it is the reverse of narcissistic. "No possession is joyous," St. Thomas Aquinas recognized, "without a companion." In choosing to treat the common reader as his audience, not the secluded, footling academy, Gioia has chosen his companions well. After all, they bind him to the real world, with which all of us, poets, readers and saints—saints especially—must inveterately contend. Falstaff may have daffed the world aside and bid it pass but poets do so at the risk of losing touch with the very thing that gives their art life. And this inescapable connection between words and the world, words and life, words and the inner life, words and prayer, is one that Gioia returns to again and again. It gives his work its great unity. In "Speaking of Love," he could almost be giving his readers a primer in why the poetry bound to this respect for reality matters.

> Speaking of love was difficult at first.
> We groped for those lost, untarnished words
> That parents never traded casually at home,
> The radio had not devalued.
> How little there seemed left to us.
>
> So, speaking of love, we chose
> The harsh and level language of denial

Knowing only what we did not wish to say,
Choosing silence in our terror of a lie.
For surely love existed before words.

But silence can become its own cliché,
And bodies lie as skillfully as words,
So one by one we spoke the easy lines
The other had resisted but desired,
Trusting that love renewed their innocence.

In the debates of whether poetry in our own time has become debased—whether as a result of the general debasement of the language or by the conformism of the academy that demands and applauds only the sort of poetry that feeds its ideological pathologies—Gioia is always salutary by reminding readers that the damage "easy lines" wreak is never inconsequential. After all, the narrator of his dramatic monologue succumbs to an easy line himself when he imagines that he and his lover have left no words unsaid. Of course, they have left no borrowed words unsaid, and this makes all the difference.

Our borrowed speech demanded love so pure
And so beyond our power that we saw
How words were only forms of our regret.
And so at last we speak again of love,
Now that there is nothing left unsaid,
Surrendering our voices to the past,
Which has betrayed us. Each of us alone,
With no words left to summon back our love.

As he often does, Gioia follows up avowals from various voices in his poems with disavowals of his own. In "Unsaid," he tells his reader what the narrator of "Speaking of Love" has chosen to forget—or, perhaps, conceal.

So much of what we live goes on inside—
The diaries of grief, the tongue-tied aches
Of unacknowledged love are no less real
For having passed unsaid. What we conceal
Is always more than we dare confide.
Think of the letters we write our dead.

VI

In all of his poetry of desire, Gioia is ultimately concerned with loss, and this complicates and enriches his engagement with what the eighteenth-century poet Matthew Prior once called "the idiom of words." Like the great short story writer and novelist, William Trevor (1928–2016), Gioia is often at pains to tell the stories of those whose lives baffle storytelling—the well-spoken murderer in "The Homecoming," the accountant charged with making sense of the dead collector of damaged dolls in "Counting the Children," the monk who once could have learned the secrets of the dead in "Haunted." And yet nowhere is Gioia's genius better displayed than in his portrayal of the story-defying lives of children in hospital destined to die.

In "Special Treatments Ward," the reader is given a poem that exhibits at once the failure and the triumph of words. Ted Hughes once invited his readers to gaze into the eyes of a famous poet to see what he characterized as "the haggard stony exhaustion of a near-/finished variety artist." Well, in this first-person poem Gioia may invite his readers to accompany him into a place where desire and loss collide, a place where his skills as a poet are tested to their limit; but he does so not as a "near-finished variety artist" but as a Christian poet alive to the exactions of the Cross. He does so as someone who has survived a harrowing at the very core of human and of divine love. I will not quote all of the poem—I do not wish to spoil it for those who may not have read it as yet—but what I have quoted here will show my readers what I mean. This is poetry of a very high order.

So this is where the children come to die,
hidden on the hospital's highest floor.
They wear their bandages like uniforms
and pull their iv rigs along the hall
with slow and careful steps. Or bald and pale,
they lie in bright pajamas on their beds,
watching another world on a screen.

The mothers spend their nights inside the ward,
sleeping on chairs that fold out into beds,
too small to lie in comfort. Soon they slip
beside their children, as if they might mesh
those small bruised bodies back into their flesh.
Instinctively they feel that love so strong
protects a child. Each morning proves them wrong.

No one chooses to be here. We play the parts
that we are given—horrible as they are.
We try to play them well, whatever that means.
We need to talk, though talking breaks our hearts.
The doctors come and go like oracles,
their manner cool, omniscient, and oblique.
There is a word that no one ever speaks.

II

I put this poem aside twelve years ago
because I could not bear remembering

the faces it evoked, and every line
seemed—still seems—so inadequate and grim.

What right had I, whose son had walked away,
to speak for those who died? And I'll admit
I wanted to forget. I'd lost one child
and couldn't bear to watch another die.

Not just the silent boy who shared our room,
but even the bird-thin figures dimly glimpsed
shuffling deliberately, disjointedly
like ancient soldiers after a parade.

Whatever strength the task required I lacked.
No well-stitched words could suture shut these wounds.
And so I stopped ...
But there are poems we do not choose to write.

Here, Gioia notes in passing that he has lost a son. He did indeed lose a
son, his first, Michael Jasper Gioia, from sudden death syndrome. He thus
comes to his meditations of these melancholy matters with *bona fides*. He
comes to them as a man of battered, not simply tested faith. Then, again, in
"Prayer," desire and loss find expression in a poem of unforgettable beauty.
Gioia may be the heir of Frost in charging the most seemingly ordinary
language with the most extraordinary point—the line "in the brief violet
darkening the sunset" does this with masterly ease—but he is no one's heir
when it comes to giving his verse the music of aggrieved longing.

Seducer, healer, deity or thief,
I will see you soon enough—
in the shadow of the rainfall,

in the brief violet darkening a sunset—
but until then I pray watch over him
as a mountain guards its covert ore

and the harsh falcon its flightless young.

VII

When we speak of desire and loss, we must perforce speak of love. And
this is a story Gioia tells with exquisite fidelity. In his poem, "An Old Story,"
he tells it in a variation of the villanelle

Our story is an old story, the tale of two,
Who met in our feverish, infallible youth
And woke transfigured in a world made new.

We walked through gardens of such stark perfume

That merely breathing left us drunk for days.
We rolled in brambles with our skin unbruised.

We shined in sunlight and in moonlight glowed,
As radiant as angels drawn by Blake.
How could such fiery brightness not explode?

In "The Present," Gioia's metaphysical wit toys with the gift-giving of love. Ben Jonson and John Donne would have enjoyed his elegant, mischievous sense of fun. In the anthology of metaphysical poets that Helen Gardner compiled she rightly singled out "concentration" and "a sinewy strength of style" as the first attribute of metaphysical poets, the second being a fondness for improbable conceits. Well, Gioia's poems possess both. Here, while he does not venture an actual conceit, he does impel the reader to think twice about what he might otherwise be inclined to imagine an unremarkable convention.

The present that you gave me months ago
is still unopened by our bed,
sealed in its rich blue paper and bright bow.
I've even left the card unread
and kept the ribbon knotted tight.
Why needlessly unfold and bring to light
the elegant contrivances that hide
the costly secret waiting still inside?

In his essay, "The Metaphysical Poets" (1921), T. S. Eliot posited the bold theory that between Donne or Lord Herbert of Cherbury and Tennyson and Browning—that is to say, between, roughly, 1635 and 1832—the reflective and the intellectual parted ways in English poetry; a "dissociation of sensibility" set in. Whereas Donne could both think and feel in his verse, the theory goes, Gray could only feel, and since the feeling is undisciplined by any proper thought, the feeling is crude. Yet whether Donne was capable of expressing thought *and* feeling (something C. S. Lewis and A. D. Nuttall rather doubted), or whether Gray was capable only of factitious feeling and no thought, it is true that few poets, of any period, manage to capture both feeling and thought. Dana Gioia is one of the few. And this has everything to do with the quality of his response to love—both human and divine.[3]

3 In the obituary for the poet Charles Tomlinson (1927–2015) that appeared in *The Guardian* (27 August 2015), Michael Schmidt quotes the poet as saying that "the English have rather sloppy ideas about the relation between mind and feelings and one can only sigh and go on believing there is such a thing as passionate intellect." To which Schmidt adds: "He looked to the Italians and the French for poetry of 'sensuous cerebration': feeling thinks and thinking feels." He might also have looked to Dana Gioia.

Take, for instance, his poem, "Prophecy," which is shot through with what one might call the thought of feeling, a sort of feeling we rarely encounter in the arid rationalism of our base, dehumanizing techno culture. It is also apt that it should be written in Dante's *terza rima*—the same Dante who is the master of thoughtful feeling.

> For what is prophecy but the first inkling
> of what we ourselves must call into being?
> The call need not be large. No voice in thunder.
>
> It's not so much what's spoken as what's heard—
> and recognized, of course. The gift is listening
> and hearing what is only meant for you.
>
> Life has its mysteries, annunciations,
> and some must wear a crown of thorns. I found
> my Via Dolorosa in your love.
>
> And sometimes we proceed by prophecy,
> or not at all—even if only to know
> what destiny requires us to renounce.

Again, we encounter the theme of desire and loss. But we also encounter the primacy of prayer where renunciation alone equips us to read "the signature of things to come." And in Gioia's prayer, feeling and thought are indissolubly one.

> O Lord of indirection and ellipses,
> Ignore our prayers.
> Deliver us from distraction.
> Slow our heartbeat to a cricket's call.
>
> In the green torpor of the afternoon,
> bless us with ennui and quietude.
> And grant us only what we fear, so that
>
> Underneath the murmur of the wasp
> we hear the dry grass bending in the wind
> and the spider's silken whisper from its web.

Here, we can see how fine an ear Gioia has. We can also see what an instructive awareness of aesthetics his poetry displays. Like Shakespeare, he often writes not only to articulate but to exhibit the understanding of art that his poems embody. Indeed, the last triplet here puts one in mind of what Berowne has to say to his fellow courtiers in the court of Navarre in *Loves Labours Lost*, which could almost be an *apologia* for precisely the sort of thoughtful feeling that suffuses Gioia's work.

> love, first learned in a lady's eyes,
> Lives not alone immured in the brain;

But, with the motion of all elements,
Courses as swift as thought in every power,
And gives to every power a double power,
Above their functions and their offices.
It adds a precious seeing to the eye;
A lover's eyes will gaze an eagle blind;
A lover's ear will hear the lowest sound,
When the suspicious head of theft is stopp'd:
Love's feeling is more soft and sensible
Than are the tender horns of cockl'd snails.

In another of Eliot's essays, his most famous, "Tradition and the Individual Talent" (1919), he gave out, in his best pontifical manner, that "The more perfect the artist, the more completely separate in him will be the man who suffers and the mind which creates." Well, now that we have the letters that Eliot wrote when he was composing some of his greatest poetry in London after the First World War, we can see that this was not entirely the case with Eliot himself. The man who suffers and the poet who creates were inseparable in Vivienne Haigh-Wood's beleaguered husband. His endeavoring to appear otherwise was an attempt on the part of a rather private man, for all of his confessional compulsions, to leave his wounds unbared. Gioia, too, can be seen as an artist whose suffering has been inseparable from the development and dispatch of his considerable talents. As he once told an interviewer, "I admire poetry that conveys hard wisdom won from and still inseparable from experience." The suffering may not have caused the creativity, but it has given the creativity not only its mettle but its wisdom.

To conclude, I shall quote one of Gioia's best poems, "Marriage of Many Years," which can be read as a kind of coda to the central preoccupations that animate his work, though its theme is the love that not only transcends but transfigures desire and loss. It is also, incidentally, a moving rebuttal to the Wain poem with which I began, especially its ill-considered contention that "We only utter what we lightly know." No, sometimes, with the grace of gratitude, we actually mange to utter what we profoundly know, as Dana Gioia proves so splendidly here:

Most of what happens happens beyond words.
The lexicon of lip and fingertip
defies translation into common speech.
I recognize the musk of your dark hair.
It always thrills me, though I can't describe it.
My finger on your thigh does not touch skin —
it touches *your* skin warming to my touch.
You are a language I have learned by heart.

This intimate patois will vanish with us,
its only native speakers. Does it matter?
Our tribal chants, our dances round the fire
performed the sorcery we most required.
They bound us in a spell time could not break.
Let the young vaunt their ecstasy. We keep
our tribe of two in sovereign secrecy.
What must be lost was never lost on us.

MORALISTS

Abigail Adams Unvarnished

I

In 1778, John Adams wrote his wife Abigail from France, where he was sorting out peace terms after the American Revolutionary War, of how pleased he was that "so many respectable strangers" were visiting with her in his absence because, as he said, it gave his wife a chance of "speculating upon these illustrious characters," and it gave them "an opportunity of observing that their new Ally can boast of Female Characters equal to any in Europe." John himself had received renewed proof of just what an admirable wife he had married in Abigail when she wrote him earlier in the year of how her "greatest comfort and consolation" in the otherwise lacerating absence of her husband and their 10 year-old son John Quincy was "the Belief of a Superintending providence, to whom I can with confidence commit you since not a Sparrow falls to the ground without his Notice." John could also see what an admirable mother his wife was in her stern remonstrance to her precocious son. "Dear as you are to me," she told John Quincy, " I had much rather you should have found your Grave in the ocean you have crossed, or any untimely death crop you in your Infant years ... than see you an immoral profligate or a Graceless Child." One of the "respectable strangers" to whom John had referred in his letter was the admiral of the French fleet, the Comte Charles-Henri Théodat d'Estaing, whose fleet of twelve ships had been narrowly thwarted by Lord Howe's smaller fleet from attacking the British garrison, first, in New York and, then, in Newport. After sailing from Newport, the comte had put up in Boston Harbor and invited Abigail and as many family members as she wished to come and dine with him on his flagship, the 64-gun *Languedoc*. Abigail reported back to John that the dinner for thirteen had been "an entertainment fit for a princess." Clearly, the comte saw that his guest of honor was a "Female Character equal to any in Europe." Thanks to Abigail's letters, which for insight, verve, charm and perspicacity, rival those of Madame de Sévigné, we, too, can enter into the peculiar brilliance of her character. In this essay I shall revisit Abigail's life and letters in order to show that while neither her husband nor her French friend was mistaken about the distinction of that character, some of our contemporaries are, especially those who see her, not, as she must be seen, in her own historical context, as a wife, mother and grandmother, but as what one of her biographers, Woody Holton, calls a "prototypical" feminist, a label she would have scorned.

II

Abigail Adams (1744–1818) was born in Weymouth Massachusetts, the daughter of a country parson, William Smith and his wife, Elizabeth Quincy Smith. Besides her character, what was perhaps most striking about Abigail was her beauty. David McCullough, in his classic biography of John Adams, relates how the portrait painter Gilbert Stuart regretted that he had not painted Abigail in youth, so convinced was he that she would have made "a perfect Venus." For the historian Bernard Bailyn: "Abigail's face is extraordinary, not so much for its beauty, which ... is clearly ... there, as for the maturity and the power of personality it expresses." One can see this clearly in the redoubtably poised young lady of twenty-two that Benjamin Blythe painted in 1766. While Abigail received no formal schooling, she read widely in her Congregationalist father's library in literature, history and French. Among her favorite authors were Joseph Addison and Richard Steele, who had made the *Spectator* so popular among Georgian readers; Samuel Richardson, whose realistic depiction of female virtue betrayed in his novel *Clarissa* (1748) fascinated an early America cognizant of how vital protecting this virtue was for the establishment and flourishing of civil society; the great moralist, lexicographer and poet critic, Samuel Johnson, and the political philosopher, Edmund Burke, whose *Reflections of the French Revolution* was widely read in post-Revolutionary America, together with Thomas Paine's *Rights of Man*. A good sense of Abigail's critical smarts can be seen in her reading of Lord Chesterfield's *Letters to his Son* (1774), about which she wrote her friend and frequent correspondent Mercy Otis Warren:

> A collection of his Lordships Letters came into my Hands this winter which I read, and though they contain only a part of what he has written, I found enough to satisfy me, that his Lordship with all his Elegance and graces, was a Hypocritical, polished Libertine, a mere Lovelace [the character in Richardson's novel who leads Clarissa astray], but with this difference, that Lovelace was the most generous Man of the two, since he had justice sufficient to acknowledge the merit he was destroying, and died penitently warning others, whilst his Lordship not content himself with practicing, but is in an advanced age, inculcating the most immoral, pernicious and Libertine principals into the mind of a youth whose natural Guardian he was, and at the same time calling upon him to wear the outward

Garb of virtue knowing that if that was cast aside, he would not be so well able to succeed in his pursuits.

Since "inculcating the most immoral, pernicious and Libertine principles" into the mind of youth is of the essence of most feminist education, we should keep this passage in mind when we consider whether Abigail's views on education justify her being branded a feminist.

Abigail married John Adams in 1764 when she was nineteen and he was twenty-eight. Curiously enough, John's literary debut was a temperance tract against taverns, which, being a drinker himself, he later regretted as hypocritical, though his wife would have seen its point, having a brother and two sons who suffered from alcoholism. The Adams had six children, of whom only four survived, Abigail ("Nabby"), John Quincy, Charles, Thomas Bolyston and Elizabeth. Susannah was born in December of 1768 and died in February of 1770. Elizabeth was stillborn on 11 July 1770. In 1813, when her son John Quincy's English wife lost her fourth child Louisa in infancy in Russia, Abigail wrote her one of her most heartfelt letters, one which pro-lifers will particularly appreciate.

> How shall I address a Letter to you, how share and participate in your Grief without opening afresh the wound which time may in some measure have healed? Distance excluded me from knowing Your distress, or sharing your Sorrows, at the time when you most needed consolation but neither time, or distance has banished from my Bosom, that Sympathy which although, Billows rise; and oceans Roll between us; like mercy is not confined to time or space, but crosses the Atlantic and mingles tears with you over the grave of your Dear departed Babe, whom with an Eye of faith, I behold with other Innocents, surrounding the Throne of their Maker, and singing Hallelujahs to the most high; or who knows but they may be called "to act as Seconds to Some Sphere unknown"

While John was away for long stretches in Philadelphia with the Continental Congress during the American Revolution and afterwards in Europe, where he helped to put American diplomacy on the map, Abigail managed the family farm and began what would become her abounding correspondence. For fifteen years of their fifty-four-year marriage John and Abigail were separated. While they crossed swords now and again, they never stopped loving one another. John's letters might be occasionally reserved—there was always the possibility that enemies might intercept them—but they nonetheless reveal how much he delighted in the wife he aptly nicknamed Portia. "Is there no way for two friendly souls to converse together although the bodies are four hundred miles off," he asked in one missive. "Yes, by letter. But I want a better communication. I want to hear you think or to see your thoughts." For the passionate thinker in John, this was no idle compliment. After Abigail relayed how the American colonists had repulsed the British at Bunker Hill, without suffering anything like the casualties they feared, he was exultant. "The account you give me of the numbers slain on the side of our enemies is … a glorious proof of the bravery of our worthy countrymen. Considering all the disadvantages under which they fought, they really exhibited prodigies of valor. Your description of the distresses of the worthy inhabitants of Boston and the other seaport towns is enough to melt a stone." If John Adams had had nothing to do with the founding of the United States of America, he would still merit the esteem of his compatriots for being the first to recognize the genius of Abigail's letter writing.

As for Abigail herself, being separated from her husband, especially at times of crisis not only for the family but for the country, could give her letters a rhapsodic eloquence. "I dare not express to you, at three hundred miles' distance, how ardently I long for your return," she wrote in 1774 when the colonies' secession from the Mother Country was not altogether decided. "The whole collected stock of ten weeks' absence knows not how to brook any longer restraint, but will break forth and flow through my pen. May the like sensations enter thy breast, and (spite of all the weighty cares of state) mingle themselves with those I wish to communicate … You cannot be, I know, nor do I wish to see you, an inactive spectator; but if the sword be drawn, I bid adieu to all domestic felicity, and look forward to that country where there is neither wars nor rumors of war, in a firm belief, that through the mercy of its King we shall both rejoice there together." That country would always appeal to an age not entirely dissevered from its Christian moorings, though once the sword was drawn, Abigail showed her patriotism for a different, less ethereal land. "A fine, quiet night," she wrote John in March of 1776. "No alarms—no cannon. The more I think of our enemies quitting Boston, the more amazed I am that they should leave such a harbor, such fortifications, such intrenchments, and that we should be in peaceable possession of a town which we expected would cost us a river of blood, without one drop shed. Surely it is the Lord's doings, and it is marvelous in our eyes. Every foot of ground which they obtain now they must fight for, and may they purchase it at a Bunker Hill price."

From 1784 to 1788, Abigail lived abroad with her husband and eldest son in France and England. Of the latter country's society, she remarked in a retrospective letter to her husband that she thought it "distant, haughty and unpolite," though she also qualified this by saying that "We must allow something for their feelings, humbled as they really are, in the eyes of Europe, at the triumphs and victories obtained over them by land, and by sea. It is only Americans who forgive their enemies, and hug them too!" When her husband assumed the vice presidency in 1789, Abigail joined him, first, in New York and, then, in Philadelphia. In 1797, after

John became the nation's second president, Abigail joined him in the executive mansion in Philadelphia. In 1800, John and Abigail became the first residents of the White House in Washington. Years of managing her own smaller households in America and in Europe gave her the confidence she needed to tackle the much more demanding appointments of the White House, which First Ladies from Martha Washington to Melania Trump would appreciate. "The house is upon a grand and superb scale, requiring about thirty servants to attend and keep the apartments in proper order, and perform the ordinary business of the house and stables," she wrote her daughter "Nabby."

an establishment very well proportioned to the President's salary. The lighting of the apartments, from the kitchen to parlours and chambers, is a tax indeed; and the fires we are obliged to keep to secure us from daily agues is another very cheering comfort. To assist us in this great castle, and render less attendance necessary, bells are wholly wanting, not one single one being hung through the whole house, and promises are all you can obtain.

In the same year, their son Charles, a failed lawyer and philandering rake, died at the age of thirty of cirrhosis of the liver. "His parents' grief," James Grant remarks in his splendid biography of John Adams, "was doubly reproachful—towards themselves and him," proof that they were not perfect parents. In 1801, after her husband's defeat in the presidential election to Thomas Jefferson, Abigail left Washington and returned to their country estate, the Old House in Quincy. On 28 October 1818, Abigail died of typhoid. Before handing in his own dinner pail, John assured his son that he could endure his last separation from Abigail because he knew it would be relatively brief. With a fine patriotic flourish, he then contrived to die on Independence Day, 1826.

In a diary entry on the day of her death, John Quincy Adams summed up the woman who meant so much not only to him and his family but to later generations of the extraordinary Adams family as well, including his son, Charles Francis Adams and *his* son, Henry Adams, the mandarin historian and author of *Monte Saint-Michel and Chartres* (1904), a paean to the Blessed Virgin that could only have been written by the great grandson of Abigail. "My mother was an angel upon earth," John Quincy wrote.

She was a minister of blessing to all human beings within her sphere of action. Her heart was the abode of heavenly purity. She had no feelings but of kindness and beneficence; yet her mind was as firm as her temper was mild and gentle. She had known sorrow, but her sorrow was silent. She was acquainted with grief, but it was deposited in her own bosom. She was the real personification of female virtue, of piety, of charity, of ever active and never intermit-

123

ting benevolence. Oh God! could she have been spared yet a little longer! My lot in life has been almost always cast at a distance from her. I have enjoyed but for short seasons, and at long, distant intervals, the happiness of her society, yet she has been to me more than a mother. She has been a spirit from above watching over me for good, and contributing by my mere consciousness of her existence to the comfort of my life. That consciousness is gone, and without her the world feels to me like a solitude. Oh! what must it be to my father, and how will he support life without her who has been, to him its charm? Not my will, heavenly Father, but thine, be done.

III

The contention that Abigail was a feminist before her time is typically based on three things: a letter she wrote her husband when he was attending the Continental Congress in Philadelphia; her negotiation of the law of coverture in her conduct of the family properties; and her views on the education of women. Here is the celebrated passage from the letter she wrote John in March of 1776 enjoining him to "Remember the Ladies":

> I long to hear that you have declared an independency. And, by the way, in the new code of laws which I suppose it will be necessary for you to make, I desire you would remember the ladies and be more generous and favorable to them than your ancestors. Do not put such unlimited power into the hands of the husbands. Remember, all men would be tyrants if they could. If particular care and attention is not paid to the ladies, we are determined to foment a rebellion, and will not hold ourselves bound by any laws in which we have no voice or representation. That your sex are naturally tyrannical is a truth so thoroughly established as to admit of no dispute; but such of you as wish to be happy willingly give up the harsh title of master for the more tender and endearing one of friend. Why, then, not put it out of the power of the vicious and the lawless to use us with Supreme Being make use of that power only for our happiness.

John's response showed his readiness to spar with his brilliant wife, but also his appreciation of how husbands and wives in eighteenth-century America lived in practice, not theory.

> As to your extraordinary code of laws, I cannot but laugh. We have been told that our struggle has loosened the bands of government everywhere; that children and apprentices were disobedient; that schools and colleges were grown turbulent; that Indians slighted their guardians, and negroes grew insolent to their masters. But your letter was the first intimation that another tribe, more numerous and powerful than all the rest, were grown discontented. This is

rather too coarse a compliment, but you are so saucy, I won't blot it out. Depend upon it, we know better than to repeal our masculine systems. Although they are in full force, you know they are little more than theory. We dare not exert our power in its full latitude. We are obliged to go fair and softly, and, in practice, you know we are the subjects. We have only the name of masters, and rather than give up this, which would completely subject us to the despotism of the petticoat, I hope General Washington and all our brave heroes would fight; I am sure every good politician would plot, as long as he would against despotism, empire, monarchy, aristocracy, oligarchy, or ochlocracy.

Abigail's bantering response to this suggests that she might not have entirely disagreed with its analysis of the "give and take" that necessarily obtained between spouses in the "masculine systems" of eighteenth-century America. In this instance, as in many others, she was never averse to the "give and take" of debate, in contrast to the doctrinaire refusal to debate that we see in many feminists, especially those enamoured of abortion. "I cannot say that I think you are very generous to the ladies," Abigail wrote: "for, whilst you are proclaiming peace and good-will to men, emancipating all nations, you insist upon retaining an absolute power over wives. But you must remember that arbitrary power is like most other things which are very hard, very liable to be broken; and, notwithstanding all your wise laws and maxims, we have it in our power, not only to free ourselves, but to subdue our masters."

John would not have disagreed. Certainly, he never wielded absolute power in his own marriage. Indeed, more often than not, he was happy to defer to Abigail, especially since her judgement proved so reliable, whether with respect to the demands of the family farm, the purchase and disposal of the family properties, the management of their respective households, or the education of their children. Since he would often find himself tortured, as men of affairs are, by what he nicely referred to as the "Folly, Littleness, and Knavery in this World," he always accounted himself blessed to be able to rail at such things with a wife as bright and discriminating as Abigail. "Amidst all your afflictions," he wrote her after the death of her mother, "I am greatly rejoiced to find that you all along preserve so proper and so happy a temper—that you are sensible 'the Consolations of Religion are the only sure Comforters.'"

Despite all of their separations, or, perhaps, because of them, it was their shared Christian faith that gave their marital bond its hoops of steel. "You and I, my dear, have reason, if ever mortals had ... to look ... beyond the transitory scene," John wrote Abigail in reaffirmation of this unwavering faith. And it was precisely Abigail's trust in the world beyond the "transitory scene" that gave her the strength that John found so admirable. "It gives me more pleasure than I can express," he wrote her in the summer of 1775, when Boston was under siege, "to learn that you sustain with so much fortitude the shocks and terrors of the times. You are really brave, my dear. You are a heroine." Both John and Abigail would have been amused to hear of what the prodigious English letter writer, Horace Walpole made of the Bostonians' stand against their British masters in the gathering insurrection. "If you have any inspiration about you," Walpole wrote his cousin, Henry Conway, the soldier, statesman, and critic of Lord North's American policy, when that policy was becoming less and less tenable, "I assure you it will be of great service—we are at our wit's end—which was no great journey."

What we see in most feminist interpretations of the "Remember the Ladies" exchange between Abigail and John is a thoroughly ahistorical misreading of Abigail in her own historical setting. As the scholar Carl Degler points out in his balanced study, *At Odds: Women and the Family in America from the Revolution to the Present* (1980): "Rather than denying in any way wifehood or motherhood as the role of women, Abigail Adams merely asked for an improvement in the traditional relationships with husbands." To contend, as some feminist historians do, that Abigail was somehow at fundamental odds with her husband—a husband, who, according to Elizabeth Evans in her feminist study, *Weathering the Storm: Women of the American Revolution* (1975) "was quite bullheaded about women's rights and refused to take them seriously"—is to miss the affectionate raillery that animates so much of their correspondence. It also fails to take into account how much Abigail rejoiced in her role as wife. "Good night," she signed off one letter to John in 1777, "friend of my heart, companion of my youth, husband and lover. Angels watch thy repose!" This is hardly the language of a wife who found her husband "bullheaded."

Edith Gelles, the least unreliable of Abigail's biographers, appreciates that such licentious revisionism "perpetuates the very misinterpretations" that good historians should endeavor to dispel. As she writes in her thematic biography, *Portia: The World of Abigail Adams* (1992), "The prevailing female role of the eighteenth century—the domestic role that Abigail herself valued as the greatest in her life—is overshadowed [in such feminist revisionism] by a mythical political activism that reflects late twentieth-century ideology." In other words, the historical Abigail Adams has been pushed aside to make way for an anachronistic Abigail Adams designed expressly to endorse and promote the feminist cause.

Another aspect of Abigail's character often cited in support of her suppositious feminism is the fondness she showed for amassing property at a time when the law of coverture stipulated that, in the case of married couples, only the husband could own property. Yet the ingenuity with which Abigail eluded the technical limitations of married women owning property proves the law's porousness. While it is true that coverture held that husband and wife were one under law and that it was the husband who technically owned the married couple's property, it is also true that as a result of John's frequent absences from the family, it was Abigail who amassed and managed the family properties. If the law of coverture had been as oppressive as feminist historians contend, Abigail should never have been able to purchase and manage the property she did. Moreover, that she handled the family properties with inveterate aplomb was always acknowledged by her grateful husband. "Your Reputation, as a Farmer, or any Thing else you undertake I dare answer for," he wrote Abigail in a letter of April 1776. "Your Partners Character as a Statesman is much more problematical."

Abigail's call for the formal education of women is yet another facet of her character cited to suggest that she was a pioneering feminist. Yet, even here, the claim is unpersuasive. After lamenting the poor state of education in the country, Abigail wrote her husband in August of 1776 that: "If we mean to have heroes, statesmen, and philosophers, we should have learned women." Indeed, she was convinced that America should have "some more liberal plan laid out and "executed for the benefit of the rising generation," ensuring that "our new constitution may be distinguished for Learning and virtue." That the Bradford Academy in Massachusetts alone among America's colleges opened its doors to women and then not until 1803 could only have reinforced Abigail in her criticism of the country's educational character. (The Ursuline Academy, founded in New Orleans in 1727 and run by the Order of the Sisters of St. Ursula, had been educating girls on the primary and secondary level since 1727.) At the same time, Abigail was convinced, as she wrote in 1814, that "There are so few women who may be really called learned, that I do not wonder they are considered as black swans. It requires such talents and such devotion of time and study, as to exclude the performance of most of the domestic cares and duties which exclusively fall to the lot of most females in this country. I believe nature has assigned to each sex their particular duties and sphere of action, and to act well their part, 'there all the honor lies'"

If Abigail's concern for the education of women was shared by many in the eighteenth century—Lady Mary Wortley Montague and Jonathan Swift, most notably—few of these could be styled feminists *manqué*. Then, again, in the nineteenth century, Abigail's great grandson, Henry Adams (1838–1918) was also critical of the education on offer in New England at the time. "The clergy and the bar took charge of politics," he wrote in his *History of the United States during the Administration of Thomas Jefferson* (1891);

> the tavern was the club and the forum of political discussion; but for those who sought other haunts, and especially for women, no intellectual amusement other than what was called "belles-lettres"

existed to give a sense of occupation to an active mind. This keen and innovating people, hungry for the feast that was almost served, the Walter Scotts and Byrons so near at hand, tried meanwhile to nourish themselves with husks.

For the fastidious Henry, no one in Jeffersonian America was being properly educated. However, simply because he recognized that women were particularly deprived of any adequate tutelage would be no grounds for our treating him as though he had been a would-be feminist; the same goes for Abigail. It is true that the poetess and essayist Judith Sargent Murray (1751–1820) advocated for female education in a way that the more sentimental feminists of today might approve but it is hard to imagine Abigail making the case for the education of women by pleading for poor Eve in such fatuous terms as these. "Let us examine her motive," Murray wrote in a piece entitled "The Equality of the Sexes" published in 1791. "It doth not appear that she was governed by any one sensual appetite; but merely by a desire of adorning her mind; a laudable ambition." It is also important to stress that what Abigail understood by education and what many present-day feminists understand by the term are worlds apart. Abigail, after all, prized not only the classical education that most learned men of the eighteenth century would have received in America or Europe but religious instruction. No one can read her letters—or those of her husband—without recognizing how seriously she took the puritanical charge to steep children in the Christian virtues. Taking these convictions into account, we can see that Abigail would have had nothing but contempt for the "gender studies" that our own feminists promulgate in a present-day academy antagonistic alike to learning and virtue. In this regard, she was entirely in agreement with her husband, in one of whose letters we can hear both parents' clear appreciation for the sort of didactical education favored by most eighteenth-century American Protestants. "The education of our children is never out of my mind," John wrote Abigail in 1774.

> Train them to virtue. Habituate them to industry, activity, and spirit. Make them consider every vice as shameful and unmanly. Fire them with ambition to be useful. Make them disdain to be destitute of any useful or ornamental knowledge or accomplishment. Fix their ambition upon great and solid objects, and their contempt upon little, frivolous, and useless ones.

That two of their sons, Charles and Thomas Boylston chose to flout these strictures by drinking themselves to death does not invalidate the strictures, nor discredit the parents, whose expostulations, after all, were warrantable at a time when alcoholism was rampant in America. The prominent historian of the early American Republic, Gordon S. Wood, in his magisterial history of the period, notes that even in "staid New England" there were "more taverns than churches," and one temperance society in Delaware was not exaggerating matters when it warned its compatriots that "we are actually threatened with becoming a nation of drunkards."

If one wishes to see the mother in Abigail at her most characteristic, one can revisit her relationship with her troubled son, Charles, "a mere Adonis, a perfect beauty," as one relative recalled, whose inability to swear off drink inspired his mother's most loving cajolery. "I have conjured the unhappy Man by all that is dear; Honour, reputation, and Fame, his Family and Friends, to desist," she told a relative, "and to strive to regain what he was daily losing in the estimation of the World. I have painted before him the misery he was bringing upon himself, his amiable wife and lovely innocent Children, but all has been lost upon him." When the bleak end came, Abigail wrote one of her most moving letters, which has an almost Johnsonian gravity about it. "Upon your part, you have the consolation of having performed your duty, no remembrance of any unkindness has deterred your fulfilling it," she wrote Charles's devoted, devastated wife.

> Even to the last distressing scene, may you be rewarded by a self-approving conscience; until fatal propensities took entire possession of this poor deluded man. He was kind, and affectionate, beloved by all his acquaintance, an Enemy to no one but a favorite where ever he went, in early Life no child was more tender and amiable; but neither his mind, or constitution could survive the habits he but too fatally pursued, in the midst of his days his course is stopped and his years numbered. May I be enabled in silence to bow myself in submission to my maker whose attributes are Mercy, as well as judgments.

As for the grandchildren left fatherless by Charles's intemperance, they brought out the indominatable grandmamma in Abigail, who would never allow reversals, personal or political, to get in the way of her continuing to do her duty. "The Children will be ever dear to me," she told their mother, "may they be trained up in the way in which they should go. I will supply to them as far as in my power the parent they have lost." For Abigail, especially in light of fallen man's propensity for error, for profligacy, for self-destructive selfishness, for sin, education must always be focused on inculcating moral virtue.

Since the object of most feminist education is the acquisition and retention of political power, especially insofar as it serves and aggrandizes the interests of the abortion trade, enlisting Abigail Adams as its champion flouts the real woman's real sentiments. No one as philoprogenitive as Abigail, or as Christian, would ever have seen abortion as anything other than flagitious. Similarly, she was familiar enough with the nature of political power never to romanticize, or, worse, idolize it, as so many feminists do. "I am more and more convinced that man is a dangerous creature," she wrote her husband in November of 1775, "and that power, whether vested in many or a few, is ever grasping, and, like the grave, cries, 'Give, give!' The great fish swallow up the small; and he who is most strenuous for the rights of the people, when vested with power, is as eager after the prerogatives of government. You tell me of degrees of perfection to which human nature is capable of arriving, and I believe it, but at the same time lament that our admiration should arise from the scarcity of the instances."

This toughmindedness reflects Abigail's critical reading, a reading which actually made her far more discerning than many of her formally educated countrymen, including Benjamin Franklin and Thomas Jefferson, neither of whom was as shrewd as Abigail when it came to taking the measure of those clamoring for the rights of man. One can see this clearly in her estimate of Burke's *Reflections on the Revolution in France* (1790). "I have read Mr. Burke's letter," she wrote in 1791, "and though I think he paints high, yet strip it of all its ornament and colouring, it will remain an awful picture of liberty abused, authority despised, property plundered, government annihilated, religion banished, murder, rapine and desolation scourging the land." As to Richard Price, the deluded English divine whose embrace of the Revolution inspired Burke's strictures against it, Abigail was generous but unsparing: "I am sorry that my worthy and venerable divine should expose himself, at this late period of his life, to so severe a censure. I love and venerate his character, but think his zeal a mistaken one, and that he is a much more shining character as a divine, than politician." As for her own countrymen, she was adamant: "I trust that they will not follow France and lop off heads." That one of the heads the Jacobins lopped off happened to be that of her irreproachable friend, the comte d'Estaing gave Abigail's revulsion an extra horror.

IV

As this shows, the political power so prized by our own feminists was seen by Abigail as something about which we should be wary. She certainly never saw it as the end of education. Intellectually, Abigail might occasionally part ways with her husband. About Samuel Johnson, for example, John was dismissive, calling him a "pedant," "cynic," and "monk"; whereas Abigail was discerning enough to recognize that "he was a very accurate observer of Human Life & manners." Nevertheless, when it came to the evils of the French Revolution Abigail and John saw eye to eye. "Dragon's teeth have been sown in France and will come up as monsters," John was convinced, and, certainly, in our time, no monsters have shared that Revolution's obsession with radical equality more than our feminists. To include Abigail in their number is ahistorical propaganda for a faith she never espoused. But, on this matter, as on so many others, it is best to let Abigail speak for herself. To John, she wrote gratefully in January of 1795:

I received by our Thursday post, yours of December 18 and 23 together with the Bennet's Strictures. You may be sure Bennet is a favorite writer with me for two reasons. The first is that he is ingenious enough, to acknowledge and point out the more than Egyptian Bondage, to which the Female Sex, have been subjugated, from the earliest ages, and in the second place that he has added his Mite, to the cultivation, and improvement of the Female Mind. Much yet remains to be done. There is however more attention paid to the Education of Females in America, within these last 15 years than for a whole century before, and the rising Generation will be benefitted by it. Conjugal fidelity holds the first place in the Rank of Female Virtues, and whilst that Source is uncorrupted, we may hope to see the united efforts of parents exerted towards the improvement and cultivation of the minds and morals of their offspring regardless of the Sex, affording to each an Education to qualify them to move with honour and dignity in their proper Sphere.

C. S Lewis and Samuel Johnson: A Study in Affinity

The unique, formative affinity that C. S. Lewis had for Samuel Johnson, the great eighteenth-century poet, critic, editor, lexicographer, biographer and essayist, can be demonstrated in many ways. Let me begin, if I may, by quoting from a piece by Lewis called "Dogma and the Universe," which he wrote for the then Anglican paper, the *Guardian* in 1943.

> When any man comes into the presence of God he will find, whether he wishes it or not, that all those things which seemed to make him so different from the men of other times, or even from his earlier self, have fallen off him. He is back where he always was, where every man is. *Eadem sunt omnia semper.* (Not a memo that our friends on the Gender Crusade ever received!) Do not let us deceive ourselves. No possible complexity which we can give to our picture of the universe can hide us from God: there is no copse, no forest, no jungle thick enough to provide cover. We read in Revelation of Him that sat on the throne "from whose face the earth and heaven fled away." It may happen to any of us at any moment. In the twinkling of an eye, in a time too small to be measured, and in any place, all that seems to divide us from God can flee away, vanish, leaving us naked before Him, like the first man, like the only man, as if nothing but He and I existed. And since that contact cannot be avoided for long, and since it means either bliss or horror, the business of life is to learn to like it. That is the first and great commandment.

Now, to appreciate the profound Johnsonian quality of this passage, the cadences of which fall upon the ear with the tolling of the most solemn unambiguous bell, I shall quote from one of the great moral essays that Johnson wrote for a periodical of his called *The Rambler*, which he composed from 1750 to 1752. The theme of number 185 is forgiveness and it is one of the noblest things that Johnson ever wrote, ruthlessly exposing as it does the tragic self-love that thwarts forgiveness. Here, as in the passage from Lewis, Johnson addresses his reader on a matter of immense moral gravity and he does so with unsparing directness. "He who has often brooded over his wrongs, pleased himself with schemes of malignity, and glutted his pride

133

with the fancied supplications of humbled enmity will not easily open his bosom to amity and reconciliation," Johnson writes, "or indulge the gentle sentiments of benevolence and peace." Here, we can detect something of the resentment that Johnson felt when he was a Grub Street writer seething under the condescension of lesser, more powerful men. Before receiving a pension of £300 per annum from George III, Johnson toiled in that part of London given over to ill-paid literary hack work. Alexander Pope wrote of its unremitting drudgery in his great satirical poem, *The Dunciad* (1728). Yet Johnson, in his *Rambler* essay, disavows all embittered pride. "Of him that hopes to be forgiven it is indispensably required, that he forgive. It is therefore superfluous to urge any other motive. On this great duty eternity is suspended, and to him that refuses to practice it, the throne of mercy is inaccessible, and the Saviour of the world has been born in vain."

In both passages, Lewis and Johnson address their readers as unabashed moralists. A basal moral truth has become a part of the very marrow of each man's being and he is keen on sharing it with his readers. As I will show, Lewis should never have addressed his readers with this forthright moral purpose without the example of Johnson before him, an example he admired from boyhood until the day he died. In this respect, it is interesting to note that one of Lewis's earliest references to Johnson should have been to James Boswell's *Life of Johnson* (1791)—which his father had sent him in the two-volume Everyman edition when he was a soldier in the trenches in France. R. W. Chapman (1881–1960)—one of the greatest of all Johnsonians—also read Johnson in the Great War. Indeed, in the summer of 1918, he edited Johnson's and Boswell's accounts of their journey to the Hebrides, averring in the preface:

> This edition was planned, and in great part executed, in Macedonia, in the summer of 1918. I had a camp ... on the left bank of the Vardar, and a six-inch gun (Mark XI, a naval piece, on an improvised carriage; "very rare in this state") with which I made a demonstration in aid of the French and Greek armies, when they stormed the heights beyond the river ... This was in the early hours of the morning, and a very pretty display of fireworks. Twelve hours later, I remember Mark XI was still too hot to touch.

I

That Lewis was a keen admirer of Johnson's moral essays in *The Rambler* is clear from his correspondence. "I have read a good deal of the *Rambler*," he writes in 1928 to his brother. "You know that the *Rambler* ... infuriates the French critics, who say that they haven't come to their time of life to be told that life is short and that wasted time can never be recovered." Yet Lewis was always appreciative of the power of Johnson's insights into the abiding moral truths of life, those inescapable, consequential truths to which so many of us pay lip service, without ever taking to heart or heeding. In his reliably sympathetic brother Warnie, Lewis knew that he could share his delight in Johnson's four square approach to the moral life without fear of being thought trite. "Better still, this on marriage," Lewis wrote Warnie, quoting Johnson himself:

> "Marriage is not otherwise unhappy than as life is unhappy." I can't say that would be a whole novel with the moderns because the whole novel would not get as far as that. The author would make a great fuss about how Pamela got on Allen's nerves and how in the end they decided that life was a failure, and would be praised for his fearless criticism of the institution of marriage without ever getting one glimpse of the fact that he was merely describing the general irritatingness of daily life as it happens in the case of married people. Johnson knocks a whole silly literature aside. He has been through all that (Ibsen and Wells and such) before it was written.

Lewis was right to single out the *Rambler* essays on marriage because they nicely exemplify the psychological astuteness with which Johnson surveyed the miseries that often bedevil that honorable estate. In Number 45, for example, Johnson observes how "it is indeed common to hear both sexes repine at their change, relate the happiness of their earlier years, blame the folly and rashness of their own choice, and warn those whom they see coming into the world against the same precipitance and infatuation."

> But it is to be remembered that the days which they so much wish to call back, are the days not only of celibacy but of youth, the days of novelty and improvement, of ardour and of hope, of health and vigour of body, of gaiety and lightness of heart. It is not easy to surround life with any circumstances in which youth will not be delightful; and I am afraid that whether married or unmarried, we shall find the vesture of terrestrial existence more heavy and cumbrous the longer it is worn.

Lewis admits that Johnson's moral essays are largely based on "moral platitudes." Yet Lewis was never above belaboring platitudes himself. What was it that he says in *Surprised by Joy* (1955)? "Term, holidays, term, holidays, till we leave school; and then work, work, work, till we die." Then, again, in *The Screwtape Letters*, he has Wormwood observe how "The Enemy loves platitudes." Why?

> Of a proposed course of action He wants men, so far as I can see, to ask very simple questions: Is it righteous? Is it prudent? Is it possible? Now if we can keep men asking: Is it in accordance with the general

movement of our time? Is it progressive or reactionary? Is this the way that History is going? they will neglect the relevant questions.

A good deal of why so much history in our time is so modish and so shallow can be attributed precisely to this refusal to engage with fundamental questions. Elsewhere, in *Screwtape*, Lewis has Wormwood explicitly explain how he and his colleagues have devilishly distorted the study of history. "Only the learned read old books and we have now so dealt with the leaned that they are of all men the least likely to acquire wisdom by doing so," he writes.

> We have done this by inculcating the Historical Point of View. The Historical Point of View, put briefly, means that when a learned man is presented with any statement in an ancient author, the one question he never asks is whether it is true. He asks who influenced the ancient writer, and how far the statement is consistent with what he said in other books, and what phase in the writer's development, or in the general history of thought, it illustrates, and how it affected later writers, and how often it has been misunderstood ... To regard the ancient writer as a possible source of knowledge — to anticipate that what he said could possibly modify your thoughts or your behavior — this would be rejected as unutterably simple-minded. And since we cannot deceive the whole human race all the time, it is most important thus to cut every generation off from all others, for where learning makes a free commerce between the ages there is always the danger that the characteristic errors of one may be corrected by the characteristic truths of another. But thanks be to Our Father and the Historical Point of View, great scholars are now as little nourished by the past as the most ignorant mechanic who holds that "history is bunk."

What gives the affinity between Lewis and Johnson its reassuring appeal is that it is like the communion of saints, where the differences separating men of different ages dissolve in their shared love of God and the goodness of His creation. There is no freer commerce between the ages than that.

What gives Johnson's *Rambler* essays their abiding appeal is the philosophical acuity with which they delve into what too many of us are apt to regard as the emptiness of platitudes. Why, Johnson asks himself, are so many of the married so captious when it comes to their chosen mates? That marriage is suffused with fault-finding might be a platitude but in answering why this tends to be the case Johnson is anything but platitudinous.

> Wives and husbands are, indeed, incessantly complaining of each other; and there would be reason for imagining that almost every house was infested with perverseness or oppression beyond human

sufferance, did we not know upon how small occasions some minds burst out into lamentations and reproaches, and how naturally every animal revenges his pain upon those who happen to be near, without any nice examination of its cause. We are always willing to fancy ourselves within a little of happiness, and when, with repeated efforts, we cannot reach it, persuade ourselves that it is intercepted by an ill-paired mate, since, if we could find any other obstacle, it would be our own fault that it was not removed.

Another aspect about Johnson's moral essays that Lewis enjoyed was their sheer satirical fun. If Johnson deplored the folly of fallen man, he was never above finding that folly funny.

When I see the avaricious and crafty, taking companions to their tables, and their beds. without any inquiry, but after farms and money; or the giddy and thoughtless uniting themselves for life to those whom they have only seen by the light of tapers at a ball; when parents make articles for their children, without inquiring after their consent; when some marry for heirs to disappoint their brothers, and others throw themselves into the arms of those whom they do not love, because they found themselves rejected where they were more solicitous to please; when some marry because their servants cheat them, some because they squander their own money, some because their houses are pestered with company, some because they will live like other people, and some only because they are sick of themselves, I am not so much inclined to wonder that marriage is sometimes unhappy, as that it appears so little loaded with calamity ...

By the ancient custom of the Muscovites, the men and women never saw each other till they were joined beyond the power of parting. It may be suspected that by this method many unsuitable matches were produced, and many tempers associated that were not qualified to give pleasure to each other. Yet, perhaps, among a people so little delicate, where the paucity of gratifications and the uniformity of life, gave no opportunity for imagination to interpose its objections, there was not much danger of capricious dislike, and while they felt neither cold nor hunger, they might live quietly together, without any thought of the defects of one another.

Amongst us, whom knowledge has made nice, and affluence wanton, there are, indeed, more cautious requisites to secure tranquility; and yet, if we observe the manner in which those converse, who have singled out each other for marriage, we shall, perhaps, not think that the Russians lost much by their restraint. For the whole endeavour of both parties, during the time of courtship is to hinder themselves from being known, and to disguise their natural temper, and real desires, in hypocritical imitation, studied compliance, and continued affection. From the time that their love is avowed, neither sees the other but in a mask, and the cheat is managed often with so much art, and discovered afterwards with so much abruptness, that each has reason to suspect that some transformation has happened on the wedding night, and that by a strange imposture, one has been courted and another married.

II

In his admiration for Johnson's witty exposure of the ways in which men and women routinely deceive and, indeed, betray themselves, Lewis might very well have begun to form in his mind what he would do with *The Screwtape Letters* (1942), which are deliciously Johnsonian in their exposure of the pretense and self-deception that often estrange men from God, although, of course, he presents these proclivities from the standpoint of the devils who incite them. "The deepest likings and impulses of any man are the raw material, the starting-point, with which the Enemy has furnished him," says Wormwood to his nephew.

> To get him away from those is therefore always a point gained, even in things indifferent it is always desirable to substitute the standards of the World, or convention, or fashion, for a human's own real likings and dislikings. I myself would carry this very far. I would make it a rule to eradicate from my patient any strong personal taste, which is not actually a sin, even if it is something quite trivial such as a fondness for county cricket or collecting stamps or drinking cocoa. Such things, I grant you, have nothing of virtue in them; but there is a sort of innocence and humility and self-forgetfulness about them which I distrust. The man who truly and disinterestedly enjoys any one thing in the world, or its own sake, and without caring two-pence what other people say about it, is by that very fact forearmed against some of our subtlest modes of attack. You should always try to make the patient abandon the people or food or books he really likes in favour of the "best" people, the "right" food, the "important" book.

The fascinating thing about this Johnsonian foray into the psychology of the moral life is how much it describes Johnson himself, a man whose own moral and literary strengths can be seen to have been based, in large measure, on his refusal to hide or abandon his "real likings or dislikings" in order to curry favor with the World. We can see this, most strikingly, in his literary criticism. Johnson was never hesitant to say what he truly thought of books and authors, regardless of whether his opinions met with favor or not. His dislike of John Milton's use of pastoral in "Lycidas" (1638) is a famous example. For Johnson, Milton's mixing of "heathen deities" with the "most awful and sacred truths" was "indecent," indeed it smacked of "impiety," even though he was sure that it was not something of which the poet was conscious. Yet what really annoyed Johnson about the poem is that although it was written as a eulogy, it was altogether too artificial to express proper mourning. "It is not to be considered as the effusion of real passion," he complained, "for passion runs not after remote allusions and obscure opinions. Passion plucks no berries from the myrtle and ivy, nor calls upon Arethuse and Mincius, nor tells of rough 'satyrs' and 'fauns' with cloven heel. Where there is leisure for fiction there is little grief." At the same time, Johnson could not have been more candid about Milton's greatest poem.

> *Paradise Lost* is one of the books which the reader admires and lays down, and forgets to take up again. None ever wished it longer than it is. Its perusal is a duty rather than a pleasure. We read Milton for instruction, retire harassed and overburdened, and look elsewhere for recreation; we desert our master, and seek for companions.

Lewis was equally unafraid to go against the critical consensus of his age by deploring what he regarded as the joylessness in John Donne's love poetry, despite or, perhaps one should say, because of its manic badinage, and this at a time when Donne's reputation, thanks to H. J. C. Grierson, T. S. Eliot and Helen Gardner, was at its zenith. "The effect of all these poems is somehow serious," Lewis observed in the deeply learned, witty volume that he contributed to the *Oxford History of English Literature* on the literature of the sixteenth century. "Seldom profound in thought, not always passionate in feeling, they are none the less the very opposite of gay. It is as though Donne performed in deepest depression those gymnastics which are usually a sign of intellectual high spirits." Moreover, when the literary critic F. R. Leavis was still trying to lay down the literary law for the academic teaching of literature, Lewis refused to join the Leavisite band-wagon. "Leavis demands moral earnestness," Lewis once dryly remarked; "I prefer morality … I mean I'd sooner live among people who don't cheat at cards than among people who are earnest about not cheating at cards."

III

Another noteworthy aspect about these two superb critics is how they always wrote for the general reader, not the specialist. One of Lewis's abiding objections to the work of Eliot was that it was written by a man who seemed to disdain the common man and often presented Christianity, at least in his published prose writings, as though it were a religion that only refined, well-read people could properly apprehend — an understandable but false accusation, as I note elsewhere, especially in light of the way the American academy lionized the poor man. And it was precisely because of Lewis's interest in speaking to the common man that he left the donnish swim of Oxford to give the talks that would eventually make up *Mere Christianity* (1943), talks which, stylistically, he deliberately pitched to appeal to a general, not a mandarin audience. Much is made of the accessibility, grace and succinctness of Lewis's prose style, but I doubt a better definition of it can be found than the one that Johnson recommended in his life of Addison in the *Lives of the Poets*. "His prose," Johnson wrote, referring to the prose of the essays Addison wrote for *The Spectator*, which revolutionized the way English was written in the eighteenth century, "is the model of the middle style, on grave subjects not formal, on light occasions not groveling, pure without scrupulosity, and exact without apparent elaboration; always equable, and always easy."

At the same time, there was an admirable reticence about both Johnson and Lewis. Johnson, in his life of the poet Edmund Waller, objects to what he considers the impertinence of a good deal of sacred poetry. "Thanksgiving," he writes, "the most joyful of all holy effusions ... is confined to a few modes, and is to be felt rather than expressed. Repentance, trembling in the presence of the judge, is not at leisure for cadences and epithets. Supplication of man to man may diffuse itself through many topicks of persuasion, but supplication to God can only cry for mercy." Lewis, in *A Grief Observed* (1961) finding himself desolate before the majesty of Our Lord, is equally humble. "I mustn't, because I have come to misunderstand a little less completely what a pure intelligence might be, lean over too far. There is also, whatever it means, the resurrection of the body. We cannot understand. The best is perhaps what we understand the least."

Although Johnson's own style could be wonderfully elaborate—Hilaire Belloc said that the great Doctor's prose was "like the rhythmical swell of deep water"—Lewis and Johnson in their different ways wrote for as large and as miscellaneous an audience as they could muster. Johnson memorably expressed what might have been their motto when it comes to this matter when he wrote in his Life of Gray in his *Lives of the Poets*: "I rejoice to concur with the common reader; for by the common sense of readers, uncorrupted by literary prejudices, after all the refinements of subtilty and the dogmatism of learning, must be finally decided all claim to poetical honours."

Unlike so many men of his time, and indeed of ours, Johnson actually went out of his way to sing the praises of the common man, realizing, precisely because of his own great learning, that learned men could have blind spots every bit as blind as anyone else. Indeed, in this regard, he would have agreed with Nathaniel Hawthorne, when he pointed out that: "the influential classes, and those who take upon themselves to be leaders of the people, are fully liable to all the passionate error that has ever characterized the maddest mob. Clergymen, judges, statesmen,—the wisest, calmest, holiest persons of their day." are often "the loudest to applaud the work of vilification, the latest to confess themselves miserably deceived." The response of many of our own "clergymen, judges, and statesmen to the slaughter of the innocents that arises from our legalization of abortion certainly bears this out. Johnson, on the other hand, came to the defense of those for whom his contemporaries had the least sympathy. His magnificent essay, "On the Bravery of the English Common Soldiers" (1767) is a case in point.[1]

> Whence then is the courage of the English vulgar? It proceeds, in my opinion, from that dissolution of dependance which obliges every man to regard his own character. While every man is fed by his own hands, he has no need of any servile arts: he may always have wages for his labour; and is no less necessary to his employer, than his employer is to him. While he looks for no protection from others, he is naturally roused to be his own protector; and having nothing to abate his esteem of himself, he consequently aspires to the esteem of others. Thus every man that crowds our streets is a man of honour, disdainful of obligation, impatient of reproach, and desirous of extending his reputation among those of his own rank; and as courage is in most frequent use, the fame of courage is most eagerly persued. From this neglect of subordination I do not deny that some inconveniences may from time to time proceed: the power of the law does not always sufficiently supply the want of reverence, or maintain the proper distinction between different ranks: but good and evil will grow up in this world together; and they who complain, in peace, of the insolence of the populace, must remember, that their insolence in peace is bravery in war.

Now, since my learned audience this evening knows better than I what a prodigious memory C. S. Lewis had for books that met with his approval, I am certain that this was one of those passages from Johnson that he could have quoted from memory. Surely, he echoed Johnson's appreciation for the power of courage when he wrote himself in *The Screwtape Letters*: "Courage is not simply one of the virtues but the form of every virtue at the testing point, which is the point of highest reality."

---

1 On Georgian England's contempt for its soldiery, Sir John Fortescue is eloquent: "There was no idea in those days of making a hero of the soldier, not even for a day. When he had served his purpose he was cast aside and went back to his old status of a plague of the nation … Not until Miss Nightingale went out to the hospitals in the Crimea did the nation awake to the fact that this outcast was after all a man, very patient, very gentle, very courteous, and so devoted to her, who cared for them, that they would kiss her shadow on the wall. It was a wholesome lesson for us, even though it had cost us two centuries to learn." *Johnson's England*, ed. Turberville, 2 vols. (The Clarendon Press: Oxford, 1933), i, 81–7.

IV

In order to further parallels between Lewis and Johnson, I shall have to say something of Johnson's life, about which Lewis never tired of reading and re-reading in James Boswell's incomparable *Life*. There are some good twentieth-century biographies of Johnson—John Wain, Lewis's student at Magdalen wrote one, as did the critical biographer, Walter Jackson Bate—but the best of the lot remains the one that Boswell put together, where, as Lord Macaulay wrote in his famous essay, "The old philosopher is still among us in the brown coat with the metal buttons and the shirt which ought to be at wash, blinking, puffing, rolling his head, drumming with his fingers, treating his meat like a tiger, and swallowing his tea in oceans." The love of tea, incidentally, was another fondness Lewis shared with Johnson. As the great comic Irish writer Flann O'Brien might have put it, they were both "tea sots."

Johnson's life can be seen best as a study in indomitability. He was born in the cathedral town of Lichfield in 1709, half-blind and scarred with scrofula. His father was a bookseller and his mother a peevish, implacable, devout woman who married beneath herself and lived to regret it. Johnson's struggles began in the cradle: "I was born almost dead," he recalled, "and could not cry for some time." At Lichfield Grammar School, he related having Latin beat into him by a schoolmaster, who would cry out as he thrashed his charges: "this I do to save you from the gallows." Johnson escaped the gallows but not debtor's prison. Poverty dogged him all his days until George III awarded him a pension in his fifties. Johnson could only afford to spend a year at Oxford and when he returned dejectedly to Lichfield he suffered the first of his two crack-ups, which nearly relieved him of his sanity. After failing to make a living as a schoolmaster, he moved to London and put himself to school to the arts of Grub Street, where he gradually established himself as "that great Cham of literature," as the satirical novelist Tobias Smollet called him.

The works on which Johnson's literary reputation is based include the pioneering *Life of Savage* (1744); the long poem, *The Vanity of Human Wishes* (1749), which T. S. Eliot thought superior to Gray's *Elegy* and "the perfect theme for his abilities"; his great *Dictionary* (1755), on which Noah Webster and James Murray based their dictionaries; *Rasselas: The Prince of Abyssinia* (1759), an Oriental tale featuring some of Johnson's wittiest prose, which he polished off in two weeks to bury his mother; *A Journey to the Western Isles of Scotland* (1775) a caustic account of his trip to the Hebrides with Boswell; a fascinating edition of the works of Shakespeare (1765); and his magnificent *Lives of the English Poets* (1779–81), which Oxford recently released in a superb five-volume set edited by Roger Lonsdale. Johnson also wrote some of the greatest essays in the language, including, as we have seen, a series of moral essays for a periodical called *The Rambler* (1750–2) and a series of more light-hearted essays for two other periodicals, *The Adventurer* (1754) and *The Idler* (1758–60).

In 1735, Johnson married Elizabeth Porter, a widow 20 years his senior, who fell in love with the genius of her unlikely suitor, if not his grotesque person, telling her daughter: "This is the most sensible man that I ever saw in my life." Her death inspired Johnson's greatest sermon, which he wrote to bear the seemingly unbearable trial of bereavement. "The only end of writing," he once wrote, "is to enable the reader better to enjoy life, or better to endure it." In his sermon for Tetty, Johnson wrote a piece that has helped generations to endure the loss of loved ones; it might also have been one of the inspirations for Lewis's *A Grief Observed* (1961), his meditation on the loss of his own wife, where he expresses the profound Johnsonian truth: "You never know how much you really believe until its truth or falsehood becomes a matter of life and death to you."

Since one of Johnson's deepest convictions was that "a decent provision for the poor is the true test of civilization," he made his successive London homes a haven for necessitous strays and misfits and often walked the streets at night to put pennies in the palms of sleeping homeless children. Still, when it came to poverty, and the problems that perpetuate poverty, Johnson was no "liberal"; he believed in alms, not government hand-outs. And he also believed in something our own liberals abominate: personal responsibility. "Resolve not to be poor," Johnson urged the extravagant Boswell, "spend less. Poverty is a great enemy to human happiness; it certainly destroys liberty, and it makes some virtues impracticable."

Johnson's house in Gough Street—which was miraculously spared in the bombing of London by Goering's Luftwaffe—was a scene of continual discord. Since it included lodgers that Johnson had taken in out of charity—particularly, the bibulous doctor Robert Levet, the blind poetess Anna Williams and the black servant from Jamaica, Francis Barber, whom Johnson would later make his legatee—peace was never the rule of the day. Levet, Johnson admitted, was "a brutal fellow," even though he enjoyed his company, "for his brutality," as he said, was "in his manners, not his mind." And Williams, although a learned woman, was equally unrefined, always losing her temper and eating her meals with her fingers. The fights between Frank and Williams were fierce, Frank complaining of Williams's bossiness and Williams complaining of Frank's laziness. Indeed, Williams's rages became so unbearable that Johnson often had to flee to Fleet Street taverns to get out of ear shot of the constant caterwauling of his ill-assorted house-mates. No wonder he told John Hawkins, one of his early biographers, that "a tavern-chair was the throne of human felicity."

On this score, Lewis would have commiserated with Johnson, for, as he wrote a correspondent later in life, referring to his own domestic menagerie, which included his alcoholic brother Warnie and the difficult Mrs. Moore:

> I have lived most of it (my private life) in a house which was hardly ever in peace for 24 hours, amid senseless wranglings, lyings, back-bitings, follies and *scares*. I never went home without a feeling of terror as to what appalling situation might have developed in my absence. Only now that it is over do I begin to realize quite how bad it was.

Yet it is worth noting that, despite all of their familial woes, neither Johnson nor Lewis ever had anything but good things to say about the primacy of the family. Lewis is particularly worth attending to on this point. "If Christian teachers wish to recall Christian people to domesticity — and I, for one, believe that people must be returned to it — the first necessity is to stop telling lies about home life, and to substitute realistic teaching." Accordingly, to arrive at this "more realistic teaching," Lewis lays out five principles in his essay, "The Sermon and the Lunch" (1945), all of which speak to us as much as the war-weary Britain for which it was initially composed. The first principle is that "The family, like the nation, can be offered to God, can be converted and redeemed, and will then become the channel of particular blessings and graces. But, like everything else that is human, it needs redemption." The second states that "By the conversion or sanctification of family life we must be careful to mean something more than the preservation of love in the sense of natural affection." The third principle offers an even more fundamental home truth: "What distinguishes domestic behavior is often its selfishness, slovenliness, incivility — even brutality. And it will often happen that those who praise home life most are the worst offenders in this respect: they praise it ... because the freedoms in which they indulge themselves at home have ended by making them unfit for civilized society." (This, incidentally, is one of Henry James's great themes.) The fourth principle follows from the third: if we are not to behave as self-centered brutes in our own homes, how are we to behave? Lewis insists that we must see home life as demanding "its own rule of courtesy — a code more intimate, more subtle, more sensitive and therefore, in some ways, more difficult, than that of the outer world." And the fifth and final principle reconfirms that proper homes need proper rules. Why? Because "The alternative to rule is not freedom but the ... tyranny of the most selfish member." If only we could manage to inculcate these principles into our own society, the number of those resorting to our divorce courts would precipitately drop. In all events, Lewis would have agreed with Johnson wholeheartedly when he counseled Boswell in a letter of 21 December 1776: "When once a discordant family has felt the pleasure of peace, they will not willingly lose it."

V

On Monday, 16 May 1762, Boswell met Johnson in Tom Davies's bookshop and it is from that momentous day that he began to draft his own largely eye-witness account of Johnson's life in London, which he lived in company with some of the greatest figures of the age, including Edmund Burke, Joshua Reynolds, Oliver Goldsmith, David Garrick, and Edward Gibbon, all of whom were also members of Johnson's famous Club, where Boswell heard and recorded many of the brilliant conversations that give his biography so much of its exuberant life. The similarities between the Club and the Inklings are striking, especially when one considers how inclined both Johnson and Lewis were to surround themselves with talented, learned, witty friends. And yet for all of their gregariousness, both were also men who knew how to put solitude to good use, as all devout men must.

Catholic readers might be surprised to discover how sympathetic Johnson was to Roman Catholicism at a time when the Faith in England was still synonymous with what William Cobbett called "monkish ignorance and superstition." If Lewis has perplexed many—including the convert, Joseph Pearce, whose book, *C. S. Lewis and the Catholic Church* (2003) is worth reading—for coming close to converting to the ancient faith without taking the final step, he shared this appreciation of the claims of Rome with Johnson. In Boswell's *Life*, Johnson is quoted as saying that, "a good man, of a timorous disposition, in great doubt of his acceptance with God, and pretty credulous, might be glad to be of a church where there are so many helps to get to Heaven. I would be a Papist if I could. I have fear enough; but an obstinate rationality prevents me." In one sense, no man was less timorous than Johnson—he knocked down the impudent bookseller Osborne with a folio, and Osborne was a big man—but, in another, deeper sense, he recognized how holy fear, which for Johnson was always the beginning of wisdom, might dispose a man to put rational misgivings aside and embrace "a church where there are so many helps to get to Heaven."

On Purgatory, the defining issue of the continental Reformation, about which English Protestants have always been understandably ambivalent, Johnson showed how little he credited the distortions of Protestant reformers. "Why, Sir, it is a very harmless doctrine," he told Boswell. "They [Roman Catholics] are of an opinion that the generality of mankind are neither so obstinately wicked as to deserve ever-lasting punishment, nor so good as to merit being admitted into the society of blessed spirits; and therefore that God is graciously pleased to allow of a middle state, where they may be purified by certain degrees of suffering." Johnson's own belief in the doctrine is evident from his prayers for his wife, Tetty: "O Lord, so far as it may be lawful in me, I commend to thy fatherly goodness the soul

145

of my departed wife; beseeching thee to grant her whatever is best in her present state, and finally to receive her to eternal happiness." Indeed, in his sermon for Tetty's funeral, he enjoins his auditors to "remember that the day of life is short, and that the day of grace may be much shorter; that this may be the last warning which God will grant us, and that, perhaps, he who looks on this grave unalarmed, may sink unreformed into his own." Like all good homilists, Johnson is adamant about doing the good deed now, not tomorrow.

On the Catholic sacrament of Penance, Johnson told Boswell: "Why, I don't know but that is a good thing. The scripture says, 'Confess your faults one to another,' and the priests confess as well as the laity." He was equally sympathetic about what might be thought the sins of the Roman Church. In the Harwich stage coach one afternoon in 1763, Johnson and Boswell encountered a woman who was railing against the Inquisition. Johnson, to what Boswell describes as the "utter astonishment of all the other passengers," defended it, maintaining that "false doctrine should be checked on its first appearance; that the civil power should unite with the church in punishing those who dared to attack the established religion, and that such only were punished by the Inquisition." Indeed, Johnson routinely spoke so well of the Roman Church that Bennet Langton's father believed he was actually Catholic.

Some will always attribute this partiality to sophistry, to what Boswell refers to as Johnson's "spirit of contradiction." By recommending the unpopular doctrines of Catholicism, so this thinking goes, Johnson only wished to exhibit what an ingenious advocate he could be. But this is to deny him his accustomed independence of mind. He was, after all, very High Church and loyal to the Stuarts.[2] It would have been strange if he had not been partial to Catholicism. In all events, in his love of good debate, his respect for rhetoric, his respect for good writing, his care for the poor, and his humble appreciation for the binding force of religion, Johnson never ceased to be an exemplary figure for Lewis.

2 Cf. Johnson quoted in *Boswell's Life of Johnson*, ed. Birkbeck Hill and Powell, 6 vols. (Oxford: Clarendon Press, 1934), i, 354. "It has now been fashionable, for near half a century, to defame and vilify the house of Stuart, and to exalt and magnify the reign of Elizabeth. The Stuarts have found few apologists, for the dead cannot pay for praise; and who will, without reward, oppose the tide of popularity? Yet there remains still among us, not wholly extinguished, a zeal for truth, a desire of establishing right in opposition to fashion."

VI

At the top of this talk, I quoted from Lewis describing the choice facing all of us as being one of choosing "between bliss and horror." For both Lewis and Johnson, the devout life was an imperative, not an optional thing. And, for both, there was something horrifying about failing to recognize and act on that truth. In the case of Johnson, this was alone grounds for one's having holy fear. The notion now prevalent, even in Catholic circles, that God is really an easy-going Latitudinarian who wishes somehow to spare us the unpleasantness of holy fear would have struck Johnson as presumptuous folly. Still, he never neglected charity. Boswell's *Life* abounds with examples of his kindness to those in distress, from the mad poet Christopher Smart, who insisted on people praying with him in the street, to one of his old schoolfellows down on his luck, whose face, Boswell recalled, "had the ruddiness of one who is in no haste to leave his can." In one of his sermons, Johnson takes the respectable to task for withholding alms from a misguided aversion to vice. "It is always to be carefully observed that we are not to refuse any man relief, because he is wicked, but to afford it in such a manner, as may not contribute to confirm his vices; the crime and the criminal are always to be carefully distinguished, and the detestation that we may properly indulge against the one, ought never to harden our hearts against the other."

About the consequences for those who omit charity, Johnson was insistently lurid. "At that day, when all the generations of the earth shall stand forth in the immediate presence of God … they, who have looked with indifference upon the calamities of others, who have scoffed at the mourner and insulted the captive; who have diverted the uneasiness of sympathy by vicious enjoyments, and suffered others to languish in pain or poverty … shall be condemned to an everlasting society, with those beings, whose depravity incites them to rejoice at the destruction of mankind." Again, here is the grave, unsparing tone of the Dutch uncle, which we often hear Lewis making his own in *The Screwtape Letters*, though in creating Wormwood he would give the Dutch uncle an altogether new satirical twist. In that incomparably witty book, which my dear Father passed along to me when I was all but fifteen, the great calamity is not eternal perdition but eternal salvation. And therefore Wormwood, in his Johnsonian way, never minces his words when it comes to the stakes of the moral life. If Johnson is concerned — rightly — with the need for all proper Christians to give alms, Lewis is equally concerned with how wary the same Christians need to be about confusing social justice with the truth of the Christian faith. "Certainly we do not want men to allow their Christianity to flower over into their political life, for the establishment of anything like a really just society would be a major disaster," says Wormwood.

On the other hand we do want, want very much, to make men treat Christianity as a means to their own advancement, but failing that, as a means to anything—even to social justice. The thing to do is to get a man at first to value social justice as a thing which the Enemy demands, and then work him on to the stage at which he values Christianity because it may produce social justice. For the Enemy will not be used as a convenience. Men or nations who think they can revive the Faith in order to make a good society might just as well think they can use the stairs of Heaven as a short cut to the nearest chemist's shop. Fortunately, it is quite easy to coax humans round this little corner. Only today I have found a passage in a Christian writer where he recommends his own version of Christianity on the ground that "only such a faith can outlast the death of old cultures and the birth of new civilizations.' You see the little rift? Believe this, not because it is true, but for some other reason. That's the game.

Here, Lewis shows us yet another way in which he both learned from and came to resemble Johnson. In his preface to the *Life of Johnson*, Boswell said of his hero that

In him were united a most logical head with a most fertile imagination, which gave him an extraordinary advantage in arguing; for he could reason close or wide, as he saw best for the moment. Exulting in his intellectual strength and dexterity, he could, when he pleased, be the greatest sophist that ever contended in the lists of declamation ... but he was too conscientious to make errour permanent and pernicious by deliberately writing it; and in all his numerous works he earnestly inculcated what appeared to him to be the truth; his piety being constant, and the ruling principle of all his conduct.

That the same could be said of Lewis measures just how formative his affinity for Johnson became.

To prove the affinity between Lewis and Johnson still more, I could, I assure you, enumerate parallels between the two long into the night, so long as even to make the poor church mouse here droop, but since I can see from your pitiably impatient faces that I have totted up quite enough already, I shall take this opportunity to desist.

Ladies and Gentleman, thank you for joining me this evening!

Edmund Burke's Family Legacy

The present state of things in France is not a transient evil, productive, as some have too favourably represented it, of a lasting good ... the present evil is only the means of producing future, and (if that were possible) worse evils.

Edmund Burke, *An Appeal from the New to the Old Whigs* (1791)

I

In his great riposte to the revolution that toppled the most tragic of the Bourbon kings, *Reflections on the Revolution in France* (1791), Edmund Burke reminded his English readers that the source of their constitutional liberties was the principle of inheritance, a principle which was of the very essence of the family. By remaining loyal to this principle, the English might not meet with the approval of France's *philosophes*, who saw only oppressiveness and irrationality in the family, but they certainly confirmed their reliance on the natural law, and in defending and, indeed, celebrating that law Burke showed how fundamental the family is to the acquisition and exercise of liberty.

> Through ... conformity to nature ... and by calling in the aid of her unerring and powerful instincts, to fortify the fallible and feeble contrivances of our reason, we have derived several ... benefits, from considering our liberties in the light of an inheritance. Always acting as if in the presence of canonized forefathers, the spirit of freedom, leading in itself to misrule and excess, is tempered with an awful gravity. This idea of a liberal descent inspires us with a sense of habitual native dignity, which prevents that upstart insolence almost inevitably adhering to and disgracing those who are the first acquirers of any distinction. By this means our liberty becomes a noble freedom. It carries an imposing and majestic aspect. It has a pedigree and illustrating ancestors. It has its bearings and its ensigns armorial. It has its gallery of portraits; its monumental inscriptions; its records, evidences, and titles. We procure reverence to our civil institutions on the principle upon which nature teaches us to revere individual men; on account of their age; and on account

of those from whom they are descended. All your sophisters cannot produce any thing better adapted to preserve a rational and manly freedom than the course that we have pursued, who have chosen our nature rather than our speculations, our breasts rather than our inventions, for the great conservatories and magazines of our rights and privileges.

In pointedly praising the natural law for fortifying what he nicely referred to as "the fallible and feeble contrivances of our reason," Burke showed how thoroughly he differed from the *philosophes*, whether Diderot or d'Alembert, Voltaire or Rousseau, all of whom regarded these contrivances as instrumental to forging a new, improved, more rational society. Again and again, throughout his writings, but especially in his *Reflections*, Burke held up the idea of inheritance—with all of its manifold affections, duties and obligations—to refute the *philosophes*, and since this is an idea that lies at the very heart of both family and tradition, it is one that we might profitably revisit. Accordingly, in this essay, I shall endeavor to show not only how Burke opposed the revolutionary ideas of the *philosophes* but how he made the family the touchstone of his vision of good governance.

Writing after Burke's death, the radical essayist William Hazlitt realized that the orator could not be dismissed as a mere reactionary. If Burke was at heart a conservative two generations before the term was coined—indeed, he is rightly hailed as the father of conservatism—he also appreciated that "A state without the means of some change, is without the means of its conservation." When it came to the essence of Burke's conservative vision, Hazlitt applauded its fundamental humanity.

> He thought that the wants and happiness of men were not to be provided for, as we provide for those of a herd of cattle, merely by attending to physical necessities. He thought more nobly of his fellows. He knew that man had affections and passions and powers of imagination, as well as hunger and thirst, and the sense of heat and cold. He took his idea of political society from the pattern of private life, wishing, as he himself expresses it, to incorporate the domestic charities with the order of the state, and to blend them together.

That the radical Hazlitt should have agreed with the conservative Burke on the advisability of statesmen basing their conduct of affairs on "domestic charities" says a good deal for the essayist's fairmindedness. Yet it also argues that there is something about Burke's insistence on family as a model for our polity that transcends party. If the political philosopher Thomas Hobbes (1588–1679) considered men to be necessarily at war with one another, animated as he considered them to be by "a perpetual and restless desire of power after power, that ceaseth only in death," Burke saw his fellows in a far more generous light. "You will observe, that from

Magna Charta to the Declaration of Right," he wrote in the *Reflections*, "it has been the uniform policy of our constitution to claim and assert our liberties, as an *entailed inheritance* derived to us from our forefathers, and to be transmitted to our posterity; as an estate specially belonging to the people of this kingdom without any reference whatever to any other more general or prior right." For Burke, that England's constitution should be founded on the laws of inheritance was "the result of profound reflection; or rather the happy effect of following nature, which is wisdom without reflection, and above it." Conversely, while no antiquarian, he would always look askance at change for change's sake. "A spirit of innovation is generally the result of a selfish temper and confined views. People will not look forward to posterity, who never look backward to their ancestors. Besides, the people of England well know, that the idea of inheritance furnishes a sure principle of conservation, and a sure principle of transmission; without at all excluding a principle of improvement. It leaves acquisition free; but it secures what it acquires. Whatever advantages are obtained by a state proceeding on these maxims, are locked fast as in a sort of family settlement; grasped as in a kind of mortmain for ever."

Revolutionary critics might charge Burke with simply defending the interests of the propertied, but he saw property in a metaphysical, as well as a material sense. For Burke, "the institutions of policy, the goods of fortune, the gifts of Providence, are handed down, to us and from us." Seen thus, England's conforming her constitution to the natural law bespoke a certain humility.

> Our political system is placed in a just correspondence and symmetry with the order of the world, and with the mode of existence decreed to a permanent body composed of transitory parts; wherein, by the disposition of a stupendous wisdom, moulding together the great mysterious incorporation of the human race, the whole, at one time, is never old, or middle-aged, or young, but in a condition of unchangeable constancy, moves on through the varied tenour of perpetual decay, fall, renovation, and progression. Thus, by preserving the method of nature in the conduct of the state, in what we improve, we are never wholly new; in what we retain we are never wholly obsolete.

Burke returned to this theme of how the "pattern of private life" should furnish the model for the state again and again. "We begin our public affections in our families," he was convinced. "No cold relation is a zealous citizen." Indeed, for the family man in Burke, a tender, liberal, gregarious man, whom friends and family alike found delightful company, it became almost axiomatic that: "To be attached to the subdivision, to love the little platoon we belong to in society, is the first principle (the germ as it were) of public affections. It is the first link in the series by which we proceed towards a love to our country and to mankind." Readers interested in Burke's fascinating life will enjoy F. P. Lock's magisterial two-volume biography, even though it concludes by declaring that "Burke's supreme gift ... was not his wisdom but his eloquence," as though the two were somehow different.

II

The son of a Protestant Dublin solicitor and a Catholic mother from a well-to-do family in Cork, Edmund Burke (1730–97) was educated at an excellent Quaker school in Kildare and at Trinity College, before entering the Middle Temple in London. In 1756, after working for Robert Dodsley, the bookseller who helped launch Samuel Johnson's literary career, he married a Catholic Irishwoman, Jane Mary Nugent, with whom he had two boys, only one of whom survived. Happily married for over forty years, Burke and his wife were well matched. Indeed, a good deal of Burke's ability to turn his extraordinary talents to account must be attributed to his marriage. Often mocked in public by such unsparing caricaturists as Gillray and Rowlandson as an unscrupulous Irishman, a crypto-Catholic or even a madman, he drew fortitude and serenity from a wife whose strong Catholic faith encouraged him to disregard the opprobrium to which public life exposed him. In 1765, Burke became secretary to the Whig magnate Lord Rockingham, with whom his political fortunes would be long associated, and in the same year he entered Parliament. There he gave the famous speeches on America, Ireland, France and India that made his reputation. In 1768, he purchased the costly estate at Beaconsfield that would be the family home until his death. In later life, he generously helped to promote the literary careers of the poet George Crabbe (a favorite of Cardinal Newman) and the novelist Fanny Burney (Johnson's friend), who so exulted in Burke's company when she first met him at one of Joshua Reynold's dinners, that she went away convinced that she was in love with him: "quite desperately and outrageously in love." Later, she wrote of the *Reflections*, "it is the noblest, deepest, most animated, and exalted work that I think I have ever read." Burke, in turn, found Burney's novels unputdownable. "In an age distinguished by producing extraordinary women," he wrote to her after reading *Cecilia* (1782), "I hardly dare to tell you where my opinion would place you amongst them—I respect your modesty, that will not endure the commendations which your merit forces from every body." Such happy meetings, however, were not unalloyed. When Burke's only surviving son Richard died in 1794, aged 36, a month after he was to take his father's seat in Parliament, Burke was devastated. "The storm has gone over me," he wrote; "and I lie like one of those oaks which the late hurricane has scattered about me ... I am torn up by my roots … I have none to meet my enemies in the gate. Indeed, my lord, I greatly deceive myself if I would give a peck of refuse wheat for all that is called fame and honour in the world." Reading this, no one could ever accuse Burke of having been a "cold relation."

The intellectual historian, Jonathan Clark, in his superb critical edition of the *Reflections* (2001), may be right to downplay Burke's Irishry and his connection to the Church of Rome, which have been exaggerated. As his writings abundantly show, Burke saw himself as a Protestant Englishman, not as an Irishman *per se* or crypto-Catholic. Nevertheless, Burke's experience of the divisions of Ireland cannot be discounted; going back and forth from Dublin to Cork as a boy left him with an indelible sense of the injustice at the heart of Irish society, which would always animate his political thinking. In 1750, before leaving Ireland for London, he gave moving expression to this sense.

> Whoever travels through this Kingdom will see such poverty as few nations in Europe can equal … It is no uncommon sight to see half-a-dozen children run quite naked out of a cabin, scarcely distinguishable from a dunghill, to the great disgrace of our country with foreigners, who would doubtless report them savages, imputing that to choice which only proceeds from their irremediable poverty. Let anyone take a survey of their cabins, and then say whether such a residence be worthy … of a human creature.

For Burke, the moral of such degradation was inescapable: "I fancy many of our fine gentlemen's pageantry would be greatly tarnished, were their gilt coaches to be preceded and followed by the same miserable wretches, whose labour supports them." The same solicitude for those on the receiving end of oppression would guide all of his great writings on America, France and India. Then, again, as Conor Cruise O'Brien observed in his biography of Burke: "In all of Burke's great campaigns there was, as Yeats discerned, one constant target … the abuse of power." Of course, the shape this abuse took would vary, but in each case, Burke would always insist on two principles: that power be accountable and that it serve liberty. Moreover, if he understood that: "The greater the power, the more dangerous the abuse," he was equally aware that: "Nothing turns out to be so oppressive and unjust as a feeble government," a truth to which the ramshackle rule of the Jacobins spectacularly attested. (Burke, always ready to call a spade a spade, neatly defined Jacobinism as "the revolt of the enterprising talent of a country against its property.") He also saw that the anarchy caused by the Jacobins would pave the way for the authoritarian rule of Napoleon, which Burke prophesied nearly twelve years before the ambitious Corsican assumed power.

It was apt that O'Brien should have based his biography on Yeats's poem, "The Seven Sages" (1929), in which the poet hailed the statesman for being a hater of Whiggery, which he memorably defined as "A leveling, rancorous, rational sort of mind / That never looked out of the eye of a saint / Or out of a drunkard's eye" because the poet admired Burke's deep respect for tradition. Reading Burke's works as a whole, one can see this understanding of the appeal of tradition at every turn. "To innovate is not to reform," Burke declares in *A Letter to a Noble Lord* (1796). In his *Reflections*, he is no less categorical: "Those who attempt to level never equalize." Speaking of the Jacobins and their newfangled schemes for improving the social order, he is even more admonitory: "In the groves of *their* academy, at the end of every vista, you see nothing but the gallows." During the Reign of Terror, which would occur two years after Burke made his prescient observation, 40,000 French men and women had their heads removed by the guillotines of Robespierre's Committee of Public Safety. That our own culture of death is also advanced by appeals to public safety is surely no coincidence.

III

Burke wrote his *Reflections* to refute the radical Richard Price (1723–91) who had commended the French Revolution for spreading "the ardour for liberty," seeing in it "the dominion of kings changed for the dominion of laws; and the dominion of priests giving way to the dominion of reason and conscience." Burke took up his pen to show his contemporaries that Robespierre and his friends were spreading not liberty but tyranny. And he did this, in large measure, by showing that what Price considered the enlightened good sense of the lawyers who made up the majority of France's Third Estate was really little more than small-minded greed.

> Judge, Sir, of my surprise, when I found that a very great proportion of the Assembly ... was composed of practitioners in the law. It was composed not of distinguished magistrates, who had given pledges to their country of their science, prudence, and integrity; not of leading advocates, the glory of the bar; not of renowned professors in universities; — but for the greater part, as it must in such a number, of the inferior, unlearned, mechanical, merely instrumental members of the profession. There were distinguished exceptions; but the general composition was of provincial advocates, of stewards of petty local jurisdictions, country attornies, notaries, and the whole train of the ministers of municipal litigation, the fomentors and conductors of the petty war of village vexation.

In taking the measure of these revolutionary parvenus, Burke confirmed one of his governing principles. "Never wholly separate in your mind," he told the young Frenchman to whom he dedicated his *Reflections*, "the merits of any political question from the men who are concerned in it." And from this insistence on judging of the real merits of real men, as opposed to those theoretical abstractions that tend to be the stock and trade of revolutionaries, Burke drew conclusions that have a perennial appeal.

> Who could conceive, that men who are habitually meddling, daring, subtle, active, of litigious dispositions and unquiet minds, would easily fall back into their old condition of obscure contention, and laborious, low, unprofitable chicane? Who could doubt but that, at any expense to the state, of which they understood nothing, they must pursue their private interests, which they understood but too well? It was not an event depending on chance or contingency. It was inevitable: it was necessary; it was planted in the nature of things. They must ... [gravitate to] any project which could ... lay open to them those innumerable lucrative jobs which follow in the train of all great convulsions and revolutions in the state, and particularly in all great and violent permutations of property. Was it to be expected that they would attend to the stability of property, whose existence had always depended upon whatever rendered property question-able, ambiguous, and insecure? Their objects would be enlarged with their elevation, but their disposition and habits, and mode of accomplishing their designs, must remain the same.

By first vilifying France's Catholic clergy and then confiscating their property, these revolutionary *arrivistes* consolidated their power. Yet it was remarkable that Burke should have foreseen so clearly how these men would lead the Revolution to its confiscatory apotheosis. Again, one cannot underestimate the tune of Burke's prescience. According to the historian Alfred Cobban: "If accurate prophecy is the test of a political thinker, Burke stands supreme. He prophesied that France would first fall under the con-trol of an oligarchy of *nouveaux riches*, made wealthy by the acquisition of confiscated estates, and then by the way of terror and disorder would pass into the hands of a military despotism, more powerful, more destructive of the peace of the world, and more disastrous in its historical sequel than any that Western civilization had known." Nearly six million civilian and military lives were lost as the result of Napoleon's misadventures. Nev-ertheless, here it is useful to recall what Francois-René de Chateaubriand (1768–1848) had to say of the almost festive complicity of the French in the anarchy that gave rise to such a costly authoritarian reaction: "The breaches of the laws, the emancipation from duties, customs and proprieties ... all add to the interest of ... disorder. The human race perambulates the streets in holiday mood, having got rid of its schoolmasters and returned for a moment to a state of nature, and does not begin to feel the need for social restraint until it bears the yoke of the new tyrants engendered by license."

Taking into account the confiscation of lucrative church lands that inau-
gurated and sustained the Revolution, it is difficult to deny Burke's own
contention, which he makes in *An Appeal from the New to the Old Whigs* (1791)
that "what the assembly calling itself national had held out as a large and
liberal toleration, [was] in reality a cruel and insidious religious persecu-
tion, infinitely more bitter than any which had been heard of within this
century." And to prove his point, Burke contended that this unparalleled
"new persecution [was] not against a variety in conscience, but against all
conscience." In fine, the revolutionaries set out to undermine all liberty,
which would necessarily include not only the prerogatives but the very
lifeblood of the family.

When the *Reflections* was first published, the antiquarian and Whig
politician Horace Walpole called it "sublime, profound and gay. The wit
and satire are brilliant and the whole is wise ... If it could be translated ...
I should think it would be a classic book in all countries, except in *present*
France. To their tribunes it speaks daggers." In *The Rights of Man* (1791–2),
Thomas Paine came to Price's defense, castigating Burke for his "unpro-
voked attack" on France's National Assembly. "Every age and generation,"
he declared, "must be free to act for itself ... The vanity and presumption
of governing beyond the grave is the most ridiculous and insolent of all
tyrannies."

Burke was adamant that none of us is free to act as he pleases irrespective
of his obligations and duties to previous, present and future generations.
"We have obligations to mankind at large," he pointed out, "which are
not in consequence of any voluntary pact. They arise from the relation of
man to man, and the relation of man to God, which ... are not matters of
choice." Children, for example, do not choose their parents, nor can parents
abrogate their duties to children, whether born or unborn.

Although Burke's book sold 30,000 copies in two years, Paine's far out-
stripped it, selling over 200,000. In the debate that ensued as to what ought
to be the basis for good governance, two positions took abiding shape.
William Doyle, in his *Oxford History of the French Revolution* (1989), encap-
sulates how those favorable to the Revolution perceived the positions: "The
French were now in the process of giving themselves a rational, equitable,
established constitution, whereas that of Great Britain, so vaunted by Burke,
was nothing but a random and arbitrary collection of unjust customs going
back to no better title than conquest by a Norman adventurer. Now was
the time for all peoples to follow the French example by abolishing nobility
and titles, and proclaiming the regeneration of man."

Burke's response to this caricature was to reject the putative wisdom
of any nation disowning her ancestors. "If the last generations of your
country appeared without much lustre in your eyes," Burke counseled the
revolutionaries, "you might have passed them by, and derived your claims

from a more early race of ancestors. Under a pious predilection for those ancestors, your imaginations would have realized in them a standard of virtue and wisdom, beyond the vulgar practice of the hour: and you would have risen with the example to whose imitation you aspired. Respecting your forefathers, you would have been taught to respect yourselves. You would not have chosen to consider the French as a people of yesterday, as a nation of low-born servile wretches until the emancipating year of 1789." Burke also pointed out to his French friends that they had been culpably precipitate in toppling a monarchical constitution that still had much about it that was worthy of conservation. Indeed, he spoke of the *ancien regime*, with all of its pockmarks, as though it had been a marriage between the French and their monarchy—imperfect, yes, but certainly not warranting dissolution.

> Your constitution, it is true … suffered waste and dilapidation; but you possessed in some parts the walls, and in all the foundations, of a noble and venerable castle. You might have repaired those walls; you might have built on those old foundations. Your constitution was suspended before it was perfected; but you had the elements of a constitution very nearly as good as could be wished … You had all these advantages in your ancient states; but you chose to act as if you had never been moulded into civil society, and had everything to begin anew.

When it came to anatomizing rationalist arrogance—which has always been at war with the perceived failings not only of established constitutions but the prototype of all constitutions, the primordial family—Burke was in his element, recognizing the impatience and vainglory of those who consider their own private judgment superior to the authority of tradition. He also looked forward to perhaps the best French critic of the Revolution, Gustav Flaubert (1821–80), whose unfinished comic novel, *Bouvard and Pecuchet* (1881) burlesques the *hubris* of the *philosophes* by having his two village copy clerks set out to make themselves masters of all knowledge, only to have their mania for omniscience devolve into farcical futility. Burke, referring to the *philosophes* as "literary men" and "politicians" and "the whole clan of the enlightened among us," described the principles by which they were motivated in their revolutionary endeavors with damning precision. "They have no respect for the wisdom of others; but they pay it off by a very full measure of confidence in their own," he wrote.

> With them it is a sufficient motive to destroy an old scheme of things, because it is an old one. As to the new, they are in no sort of fear with regard to the duration of a building run up in haste; because duration is no object to those who think little or nothing has been done before their time, and who place all their hopes in discovery. They conceive, very systematically, that all things which

give perpetuity are mischievous, and therefore they are at inexpiable war with all establishments. They think that government may vary like modes of dress, and with as little ill effect. That there needs no principle of attachment, except a sense of present convenience, to any constitution of the state. They always speak as if they were of opinion that there is a singular species of compact between them and their magistrates, which binds the magistrate, but which has nothing reciprocal in it, but that the majesty of the people has a right to dissolve it without any reason, but its will. Their attachment to their country itself, is only so far as it agrees with some of their fleeting projects; it begins and ends with that scheme of polity which falls in with their momentary opinion.

Another arresting characteristic that Burke recognized about France's rationalist revolutionaries was their genius for self-promotion. Burke had many talents: he was an incisive historian of an event that struck most of his contemporaries as unfathomably chaotic; he was alive to the duplicity of those who give out that they are coming to the aid of the poor, when they are only pillaging the rich; he knew how revolutionary adventurers acquire and retain power by manipulating language; yet he was also a redoubtable psychologist, especially when it came to unpacking the stratagems by which his rationalist oligarchs shaped public opinion.

They were possessed with a spirit of proselytism in the most fanatical degree; and from thence by an easy progress, with the spirit of persecution according to their means. What was not to be done towards their great end by any direct or immediate act, might be wrought by a longer process through the medium of opinion. To command that opinion, the first step is to establish a dominion over those who direct it. They contrived to possess themselves, with great method and perseverance, of all the avenues to literary fame. Many of them indeed stood high in the ranks of literature and science. The world had done them justice; and in favour of general talents forgave the evil tendency of their peculiar principles. This was true liberality; which they returned by endeavouring to confine the reputation of sense, learning, and taste to themselves or their followers. I will venture to say that this narrow, exclusive spirit has not been less prejudicial to literature and to taste, than to morals and true philosophy.

Plus ça change, plus c'est la même chose is a phrase that occurs to the reader frequently as he turns Burke's surprisingly topical pages, but nowhere more than here:

These Atheistical fathers have a bigotry of their own; and they have learnt to talk against monks with the spirit of a monk. But in some things they are men of the world. The resources of intrigue are called in to supply the defects of argument and wit. To this system of literary monopoly was joined an unremitting industry to blacken and discredit in every way, and by every means, all those who did not hold to their faction.

As we can all attest, such rationalist principles are with us still. Indeed, they continue to ravage what is left of Western civilization. When Burke first got wind of them, he thought to oppose them by claiming that the English opposed them as well, though the phenomenal sales of Paine's tract must always qualify that claim. Nevertheless, even if only a slender majority in his own country agreed with Burke, the sentiments he puts into the mouths of his Englishmen are still those that all sensible men share when confronted with the manifest evils of rationalism. "Thanks to our sullen resistance to innovation, thanks to the cold sluggishness of our national character, we still bear the stamp of our forefathers," he says in one of the book's most bravura passages, invoking again his respect for the natural law as the warrant of all good sense and all good faith in the public, as in the private sphere.

We are not the converts of Rousseau; we are not the disciples of Voltaire; Helvetius has made no progress amongst us. Atheists are not our preachers; madmen are not our lawgivers. We know that we have made no discoveries, and we think that no discoveries are to be made, in morality; nor many in the great principles of government, nor in the ideas of liberty, which were understood long before we were born, altogether as well as they will be after the grave has heaped its mould upon our presumption, and the silent tomb shall have imposed its law on our pert loquacity. In England we have not yet been completely embowelled of our natural entrails; we still feel within us, and we cherish and cultivate, those inbred sentiments which are the faithful guardians, the active monitors of our duty, the true supporters of all liberal and manly morals. We have not been drawn and trussed, in order that we may be filled, like stuffed birds in a museum, with chaff and rags, and paltry blurred shreds of paper about the rights of man. We reserve the whole of our feelings still native and entire, unsophisticated by pedantry and infidelity. We have real hearts of flesh and blood beating in our bosoms. We fear God; we look up with awe to kings; with affection to parliaments; with duty to magistrates; with reverence to priests; and with respect to nobility. Why? Because when such ideas are brought before our minds, it is natural to be so affected; because all other feelings are false and spurious, and tend to corrupt our minds, to vitiate our primary morals, to render us unfit for rational liberty; and by teaching us a servile, licentious, and abandoned insolence, to be our low sport for a few holidays, to make us perfectly fit for, and justly deserving of slavery, through the whole course of our lives.

In a social order like ours, which has seen innovations in morality lead to the legalizing of abortion, the redefining of marriage, the travestying of gender, and the sanctioning of euthanasia, to name only a few of the dehumanizing novelties that degrade our already coarsened culture, all sedulously advanced by the tyrannical censorship of political correctness, Burke's defense of the prejudices that proceed from respect for the natural law is particularly salutary.

> You see, Sir, that in this enlightened age I am bold enough to confess, that we are generally men of untaught feelings; that instead of casting away all our old prejudices, we cherish them to a very considerable degree, and, to take more shame to ourselves, we cherish them because they are prejudices; and the longer they have lasted, and the more generally they have prevailed, the more we cherish them. We are afraid to put men to live and trade each on his own private stock of reason; because we suspect that this stock in each man is small, and that the individuals would do better to avail themselves of the general bank and capital of nations and of ages. Many of our men of speculation, instead of exploding general prejudices, employ their sagacity to discover the latent wisdom which prevails in them. If they find what they seek (and they seldom fail) they think it more wise to continue the prejudice, with the reason involved, than to cast away the coat of prejudice, and to leave nothing but the naked reason; because prejudice, with its reason, has a motive to give action to that reason, and an affection which will give it permanence. Prejudice is of ready application in the emergency; it previously engages the mind in a steady course of wisdom and virtue, and does not leave the man hesitating in the moment of decision, skeptical, puzzled, and unresolved. Prejudice renders a man's virtue his habit; and not a series of unconnected acts. Through just prejudice, his duty becomes a part of his nature.

That prejudice in favor of the self-evident benefits of the natural law should now be under such plenary assault by a ruling class in Europe that makes the Jacobins look like choir boys should attract more readers to Burke's counter-revolutionary writings.

Certainly these readers will find it of interest that a defining aspect of the "new fanatical Religion," as Burke called it, "of the Rights of Man, which rejects all establishments, all discipline, all ecclesiastical, and in truth all civil order," was its contempt for marriage. Of course, this was inseparable from its contempt for the family, and it inspired some of Burke's most vitriolic criticism. In his first *Letter on a Regicide Peace* (1796), the defender of sacred tradition in Burke spoke passionately of the revolutionaries' attacks on an institution that has since suffered no end of attacks. "All their new institutions (and with them every thing is new) strike at the root of our social nature," he wrote. "Other Legislators, knowing that marriage is the origin of all relations, and consequently the first element of all duties, have endeavoured by every art to make it sacred. The Christian Religion, by confining it to the pairs, and by rendering that relation indissoluble, has, by these two things, done more towards the peace, happiness, settlement, and civilisation of the world, than by any other part in this whole scheme of Divine Wisdom." For Burke, the fact that the National Assembly should pronounce that "marriage was no better than a common civil contract" was bad enough; but what was even worse was their producing a prostitute at the bar "whom they called by the affected name of 'a mother without being a wife'" to mock and undermine the principle of inheritance by putting illegitimate children on the same legal footing as "the issue of lawful unions." To make sure that no one should be in any doubt as to the point of these proceedings, they "gave a licence to divorce at the mere pleasure of either party, and at four day's notice. With them the matrimonial connexion was brought into so degraded a state of concubinage, that, I believe, none of the wretches in London, who keep warehouses of infamy, would give out one of their victims to private custody on so short and insolent a tenure. … Their law of divorce, like all their laws, had not for its object the relief of domestick uneasiness, but the total corruption of all morals, the total disconnection of social life."

In the same letter, Burke reminded his readers that the corruption of manners, which the Assembly was thus hastening to effect, was neither trifling nor accidental. "Manners are of more importance than laws," he wrote. "Upon them, in a great measure the laws depend. The law touches us but here and there, and now and then. Manners are what vex or sooth, corrupt or purify, exalt or debase, barbarize or refine us, by a constant, steady, uniform, insensible operation, like that of the air we breathe … They give their whole form and colour to our lives. According to their quality, they aid morals, they supply them, or they totally destroy them. Of this the new French Legislators were aware; therefore, with the same method, and under the same authority, they settled a system of manners, the most licentious, prostitute, and abandoned that ever has been known, and at the same time the most coarse, rude, savage, and ferocious." Nevertheless, to put Burke's censures in some context, it should be borne in mind that neither the 1791 Penal Code nor Napoleon's Penal Code (1810) legalized abortion. If hostile to marriage, the revolutionary and post-revolutionary French were not prepared to legalize the killing of unborn children.

IV

Against the libertine rationalism of the French *philosophes*, Burke offered a vision of the social order as a compact made up not only of the living and the dead but of those yet to be born, which makes him a natural ally of all pro-lifers. Here, there is no honored place for harlotry or concubinage. "In this choice of inheritance, we have given to our frame of polity the image of a relation in blood," he wrote in a justly celebrated passage, "binding up the constitution of our country with our dearest domestic ties; adopting our fundamental laws into the bosom of our family affections; keeping inseparable and cherishing with the warmth of all their combined and mutually reflected charities our state, our hearths, our sepulchres and our altars."

The reference to "sepulchres," here, is vital to Burke's understanding of the virtuous polity, since "People will not look forward to posterity, who never look backward to their ancestors." That virtue was indeed crucial to this compact was clear if one appreciated, as Burke did, that "Among a people generally corrupt liberty cannot long exist." The historian Lewis Namier regarded Burke's insistence on virtue in government as so much "cant," camouflage behind which ruthless self-interest could go its merry way. Yet Burke saw virtue ensuring for government a kind of aristocracy of talent, which it might not otherwise have. "There is no qualification for government," he wrote, "but virtue and wisdom, actual or presumptive. Wherever they are actually found, they have, in whatever state, condition, profession or trade, the passport of Heaven to human place and honour."

As for Burke's own probity, the historian Paul Langford makes an incisive point when he says: "Irishmen of minor gentry or professional background were conventionally portrayed in England as fortune-hunters and Burke sometimes among them. In his case it was a particularly absurd charge, for at all the crucial points in his career he had turned his back on promotion for its own sake." Langford also gets to the heart of what made Burke tick when he says: "For many of his generation the deity of the early Enlightenment was little more than a stage prop in a rationally ordered existence. For Burke it was an intense and all-pervading spiritual reality." And this was another reason why he recognized how the new religion of the Rights of Man would triumph over Christian civilization if the English were to emulate France's apostasy. This is also why Burke, although not the crypto-Catholic that many of his contemporary critics claimed (he was necessarily Anglican), still recognized the indispensability of the Catholic Church in a world rife with apostasy. Asked late in life whether he thought Catholics should be admitted to the Irish Parliament, Burke was categorical: the Catholic Church should be "cherished" and "given positive encouragement." Why? Because he understood that "the serious and earnest belief and practice of it by its professors forms, as things stand, the most effectual barrier, if not the sole barrier, against Jacobinism."

V

That liberty inheres in inheritance, in the lawful acquisition, protection and transmission of property is a truism of which many of the young are now lamentably unfamiliar, but it is foundational to Burke because it is foundational to the family and the tradition that the family makes possible. It is also a truism that reminds us of how vital it is that we draw the right lessons from a Revolution that still supplies a blueprint for those avid to undermine the family and its traditions. Burke recognized more than any of his contemporaries that the French Revolution would constitute a baleful precedent. "In France is the bank of deposit and the bank of circulation of all the pernicious principles that are forming in every state," he wrote. Had he lived to see the rise of totalitarianism in twentieth-century Russia, Italy, and Germany, not to mention the now pathological rationalism that animates our tweny-first-century progressives, he would have seen the awful accuracy of his prescience. "I am not going to make an idle panegyric on Burke (he has no need of it)," wrote Hazlitt in his essay on the great man, "but I cannot help looking on him as the chief boast and ornament of the English House of Commons. What is said of him is, I think, strictly true, that 'He was the most eloquent man of his time; his wisdom was greater than his eloquence.'" Burke's magnificent writings, especially those extolling the blessings of the family, show why Hazlitt, *pace* Lock, was right. Yet for our purposes, no one summed up this wise champion of the family better than Paul Langford: "Burke saw with a fearful clarity what seemed to him the ultimate obscenity of a creed, the 'rights of man', that degraded humanity while professing to serve it."

Christopher Dawson and the Embattled Family

When I was a boy, back in the last century, my father would often speak at the dinner table of his favorite authors. In his lovely, deep, amused and amusing voice, a voice always alive to the serendipities of wit, he would read aloud from the various writings of Max Beerbohm, including that imperishable bagatelle, *Zuleika Dobson* (1911), as well as from the authors of the Catholic revival of the nineteenth and twentieth centuries, writers such as John Henry Newman, G. K. Chesterton, Hilaire Belloc, Ronald Knox and Evelyn Waugh. Yet of all these authors, the one about whom he spoke with the most admiration was the great Catholic historian Christopher Dawson (1889–1970). After all, in those faraway days, the old Cold War was still on, and no one articulated the stakes of that struggle with Dawson's admonitory precision. For Dawson, the showdown between totalitarian Russia and the liberal West had had instructive dress rehearsals. First, in the ancient world, there had been the successful struggle mounted by the free Greek city-states to resist the tyranny of Persia. Then, there was the rise of the Catholic Church and its struggle with the Roman Empire, which, Dawson recognized, "had lost the ideals of citizenship and political freedom and was rapidly becoming a vast servile state like those of the ancient East." No one can read Dawson's characterization of this struggle without seeing its pertinence for the Cold War. Here was a battle, like the one Stalin waged against dissenters in his gulags, "fought out under the shadow of the executioners' rods and axes in praetoria and amphitheatres and concentration camps from Germany to Africa and from Spain to Armenia, and its heroes were the martyrs." Thus, for Dawson, the Christians opposed the Romans to witness to their love of their Saviour, but, in doing so, they also fought for what those in the liberal West fought for against the Bolsheviks—the "idea that men possess rights even against the state and that society is not a totalitarian political unity but a community made up of a complex variety of social organisms, each possessing an autonomous life and its own free institutions." And, for Dawson, at the heart of this "autonomous life," properly understood, was the family, within whose relations, under God, men and women were uniquely free to embody the life-affirming, religious culture that makes civilization possible. In this essay, I shall revisit Dawson's life and work to show how vital the family was to his understanding of history and how prescient this understanding became when he turned his thoughts to the repudiation of the moral law, especially as it relates to the family, which constituted in his own time and, continues to constitute in ours, the greatest threat to the Christian civilization he so deeply prized.

Yet before I delve into these lively, involved matters, I should say a few words about Dawson's life, because his personal fortunes had an abiding influence on how he saw not only the world but the history of the world.

Christopher Henry Dawson was born in 1889 at Hay Brecknockshire in Wales, the only son of Colonel Henry Philip Dawson (1850–1933), a Yorkshire country gentleman, and his wife Mary Louisa, the eldest daughter of Archdeacon William Lathan Bevan of Hay Castle, which, as I write, is being meticulously restored. Dawson was educated at Winchester and Trinity College, Oxford, where he left with a second class degree in history in 1911. Although, at Winchester, he enjoyed the liberty he was given to read what he pleased, and, at Oxford, he formed his lasting friendship with the Catholic historian, E. I. Watkin, he did not acquire his love of learning from either of these redoubtable institutions. In an autobiographical fragment vividly describing his Victorian childhood, which can be found in the appendix of his daughter, Christina Scott's excellent biography of the historian, Dawson makes plain that he was educated mostly by his father (as I was by mine) and by his appreciation of the history of place. "I got nothing from school, little from Oxford, and less than nothing from the new post-Victorian urban culture," he declared in 1925; "all of my 'culture' and my personal happiness came from that much-derided Victorian rural home life." In other words, it was his family, first and foremost, that educated him. This, and that ineradicable sense of place that always accompanies and reinforces the tutelage of family. "There is something about running water that appeals to a child's mind," Dawson recalled about the days he spent as a child beside the river Wharfe in Yorkshire.

> On summer days the brown waters giggling and chattering among the rocks were a constant companion and friend, but better still were the days of sudden storm, when it was changed into a roaring torrent, rising foot by foot and hour by hour until the whole appearance of the valley was transformed. I think these early impressions of the elemental force of nature have a great importance in one's education … Moreover this love of the river had a certain literary and religious significance. For it was in the Old Testament, and there only, that I found these things written about, and it seemed to me that in those days they felt about these things as I did. "Deep calleth to deep …"

The place where his childhood was spent was significant for another reason for the child who would grow up to write such brilliant Catholic history. "The fragments of the Anglian high crosses and the ruins of the great northern abbeys recalled the times when the Church had been more of a power here than in most parts of England," he noted. "Nowhere was the destruction of the monasteries more bitterly resented than in Craven." In his father's decision to leave Wales to build his own country house, Hartlington, next to the gloriously scenic Yorkshire dales, Dawson saw a curiously Catholic impulse. Although fond of Dante and such Catholic devotional writers as St. Ignatius Loyola and Jean Baptiste Avrillon, Dawson's father had remained loyal to the Church of England, convinced as he was that no man had a right to leave the church of his fathers; yet, for his son, Henry Philip Dawson was hardly consistent "in his social traditionalism," since "his return to Craven was in part a deliberate reaction against the Protestant tradition and an attempt to recover lost spiritual roots in a past which he felt to be Catholic."

In light of these torn affinities, it is noteworthy that when Dawson converted to Catholicism, shortly after leaving Oxford, it was his father who accepted his secession from the National Church, while his mother, the daughter of an Anglican church historian, always regarded it as an unaccountable betrayal. The division in his own family would always impress upon Dawson, as it had impressed upon Newman, how deep-seated the English aversion was to the Church of Rome, which gave so much of his own work its personal and its public purpose. If the English and, indeed, the Welsh needed to be reacquainted with the historical, living richness of their traditional faith, he was the man to do it.

Many factors contributed to Dawson's conversion. In 1909, he had visited Rome during Easter Week and, like Newman before him, he was impressed by the unexpected appeal of the ancient faith. Then, again, his close friend Edward Watkins was a Catholic, and he introduced Dawson to other Catholics, including the learned Catholic priest, Father Francis Burdett, who, according to Dawson's daughter, may have "looked like an Edwardian aesthete" in youth but in old age "resembled an eighteenth-century French abbé, with a flowing mane of white hair." Like Dawson, Burdett was highly original in his thinking, and fastidiously learned. Finally, listening to Newman's biographer, Wilfrid Ward expound on Newman's *Apologia pro Vita Sua* (1864) also pointed Dawson in the direction of Rome.

However, it was his extraordinary wife, Valery Mills, a bright, beautiful, dedicated lady, the daughter of the Oxford architect Walter Edward Mills, whom he had met in Oxford at a party given by friends in their house on Folly Bridge (from which Zuleika's young admirers jump to their deaths), who finally prevailed upon Dawson to convert. He was received at what was then the Jesuit Church of St. Aloysius on 5 January 1916. After the couple had become engaged, Dawson wrote his fiancé: "I loved you before I knew you." which in his case, was the literal truth. Even before meeting Valery, Dawson had seen and fallen in love with her in a photograph in which she was dressed as Joan of Arc. Apropos their eventual courtship, Dawson's daughter nicely observes: "It was a romantic attachment but love and courtship were never so romanticized and idealized since the ages of chivalry than they were in the years before the First World War before the arrival of the Bloomsbury cult, the Jazz Age and the sexual revolution."

A good deal less convincingly, his daughter claims that "Personal reasons, even the influence of his future wife, counted for little in his conversion in comparison with intellectual and historical ones." On the contrary, I would argue that since the future historian's love for his Catholic fiancé and his respect for the historical and theological grounds for conversion were inseparable, it is likelier that Valery did play a decisive role. After all, if he had somehow lost his nerve and *not* converted, he would have lost the girl of his dreams. As one of his friends noted: "When [Dawson] was a boy of thirteen or fourteen, the writings of Catholic saints and mystics, mediated through the Anglo-Catholic tradition, made a profound, indeed an indelible impression on his mind." For young Dawson, Valery dressed as St. Joan was the very embodiment of this irresistible sanctity. Moreover, as a good student of Newman, Dawson was never unduly reliant on what Newman himself characterized as "the aggressive, capricious, untrustworthy intellect."

In making sense of his conversion after the fact, the historian in Dawson pointed to Newman's *Essay on the Development of Christian Doctrine* (1845), which the antinomian Cardinal Walter Kaspar and his friends continue to misrepresent. For Dawson, "There were but two paths: the way of faith and the way of unbelief, and as the latter led through the halfway house of Liberalism to Atheism, the former led through the halfway house of Anglicanism to Catholicism."

Yet one must also keep in mind that before marrying Valery, Dawson sent her a copy of *Aucassin and Nicolette,* a charming thirteenth-century tale of courtly love about the misadventures that the son of a Christian count has to endure before rescuing and marrying his one true love, Nicolette, a captive of the Saracens. In all events, the couple married in 1916, after Dawson's father settled a modest income on his scholarly, frail son, a competence which would allow him to write his books outside the academy without distraction or fear of want.

Once the Great War broke out, Dawson duly presented himself at Cowley Barracks but was turned down for active service for health reasons. Afterwards, he took a teaching post in the Cowley Road, not far from a bicycle shop run by a man named Morris, who would later go on, as Lord Nuffield, to make Cowley the site of his famous automobile factory, which transformed sylvan, sequestered Oxford into the tawdry city that it remains today. In what one of his friends recalled as his hermitical seclusion, Dawson read uninterruptedly for fourteen years before publishing his first book, *The Age of the Gods* (1928), an immersion in his chosen field of ancient and modern history that gave him a well-nigh inexhaustible fund of learning on which to draw for the rest of his life.

Yet, here again, Valery played an indispensable role, which shows how formative family was in the education of the great historian. As Dawson's daughter writes: "His marriage ... was linked with [his] destiny, for only with the love and devotion of a wife such as Valery could he have supported the lonely life of a freelance scholar and writer. In fact, it was a harder life for her than for him. For while she was completely devoted to him and his work, she was not mentally equipped to share the intellectual side of it with him. For most of her married life she was deprived also of the social life to which she was naturally inclined." It was only after Dawson was given the Charles Chauncey Stillman Chair of Roman Catholic Studies at Harvard in 1958, when he was sixty-eight, that Valery began to enjoy something of this formerly elusive social life. Valery was also instrumental in joining her husband in seeing to the happiness of their own family, giving loving support to her two daughters and one son. Nevertheless, throughout the scholarly career of the inveterately impractical Dawson, it was Valery who ensured that the lights were kept on by attending to the practicalities of their various households in England and America—never an unimportant portion of the familial division of labor. At Harvard, Valery told Chauncey Stillman how amused she was by the deference she was shown by the intellectuals of the place. Obviously, they thought she must be a high-brow too. "But I am not," she said. "I just like music and laughter."

Thanks to Catholic University of America Press, and to the editor-in-chief of their edition of *The Works of Christopher Dawson*, Prof. Don J. Briel, who holds the Blessed John Henry Newman Chair of Liberal Arts at the University of Mary in Bismarck, North Dakota, most of Dawson's works are available in deftly annotated, reasonably priced editions. All of his best works are featured in this edition, including *Progress and Religion* (1929), *The Making of Europe* (1932), *Enquiries into Religion and Culture* (1933), *The Judgement of the Nations* (1942), *Religion and Culture* (1948), and *The Gods of Revolution* (1972). Ignatius Press has also published his Harvard lectures in two volumes, one entitled *The Formation of Christendom* and the other, *The Dividing of Christendom*, the latter of which comes with an excellent overview of Dawson's work by the great monastic historian, David Knowles (1896–1974). Apropos the still underrated historian, Knowles observed: "His mind had the clarity of wisdom, not the simplicity of the superficial, and his style was lucid and free." After cutting short his Harvard appointment for poor health reasons, Dawson died in Devon in 1970 at the age of eighty-one. It was a mark of how unappreciated his life's achievement was in his own country that it was only acknowledged by the editors of the *National Dictionary of Biography* in their *Missing Persons* volume in 1993, over twenty years after his death.

In nearly all of his works, Dawson shows how religion is the key to history because it is the key to culture, without which there can be no civilization, and in this the primacy of family is always patent. He is especially insightful on how both religion and culture animated the rise of Christianity before and after the fall of the Roman Empire, a necessary riposte to the great Enlightenment historian, Edward Gibbon, whose *Decline and Fall of the Roman Empire* (1776–88) still hornswoggles readers into imagining that the rise of Christianity can be properly treated in merely external, rationalist terms. No one can read Dawson without appreciating the spiritual and transcendent character of that unprecedented historical reality. Or something his perspicuous daughter says in her biography of her father: "He viewed the disintegration of Western culture as a far worse disaster than the fall of Rome."

Dawson is also a good guide to the threats that Christian civilization received not only from Luther's Reformation but from precisely the forces of revolutionary rationalism unleashed by the Enlightenment, whether in the guise of the French or the Russian Revolution.

Like his friend, T. S. Eliot, Dawson was convinced that the West could only withstand the challenge of atheist totalitarianism by reacquainting itself with its own Christian culture. In this respect, we can hear Dawson's appreciation of the consequences of the West losing its Christian inheritance in Eliot's musings on this melancholy subject. "I know very little about Russia," Eliot wrote in a piece entitled "Christianity and Communism" (1932).

> I do not know whether the experiment being made there will turn out to be, in the worldly sense, a failure or a success. If the system can be made to work, and if the Russians can be adapted to it, or bred into the sort of being who can flourish under it, that is their affair. But I should not like it any the better for that: for Russian communism is a religion, and a religion which is not mine. Of course, other and better qualified critics — among them Mr. Maynard Keynes — remarked this fact before; and it is indeed patent enough; but the full implications do not seem to me to me to have yet come home to all. If you like the Russian religion, I cannot expect to make any impression upon you. But if you do not like it, then you must keep in mind that you can never fight a religion except with another religion.

Of course, in our own age, we face a similar threat from the culture of death. The question is whether we will fight that peculiarly satanic religion by returning to our Christian roots and reasserting the Church's commitment to the moral law, or whether we will repudiate those roots and, in effect, acquiesce in the very dehumanizing antinomianism that gives the culture of death so much of its unique menace. No one recognized the centrality of this battle more keenly than Pope John Paul II. "The family is placed at the centre of the great struggle between good and evil, between life and death, between love and all that is opposed to love," the great saint wrote in his *Letter to Families* (1994). "To the family is entrusted the task of striving, first and foremost, to unleash the forces of good, the source of which is found in Christ the Redeemer of man."

Dawson saw the primacy of the family mostly in the ways in which it embodied what Pope John Paul II called "the civilization of love and life." And he saw it as clearly as he did as a result of his lifelong study of the rise of Christianity. "The reconstitution of Western civilization was due to the coming of Christianity and the re-establishment of the family on a new basis," he wrote in "The Patriarchal Family in History" (1933), which can be found *The Dynamics of World History* (1956), a collection of his essays spanning nearly his entire career.

> Though the Christian ideal of the family owes much to the patri-archal tradition which finds such a complete expression in the Old Testament, it was in several respects a new creation that differed essentially from anything that had previously existed. While the patriarchal family in its original form was an aristocratic institution which was the privilege of a ruling race or a patrician class, the Christian family was common to every class, even to the slaves. Still more important was the fact that the Church insisted for the first time on the mutual and bilateral character of sexual obligations. The husband belonged to the wife as exclusively as the wife to the husband. This rendered marriage a more personal and individual relation than it had been under the patriarchal system. The family was no longer a subsidiary member of a larger unit, the kindred or "gens." It was an autonomous self-contained unit which owed nothing to any power outside itself.

Dawson rightly recognizes that it is the family's very autonomy that makes it obnoxious to the state and those who wish to organize society entirely under the insatiate authority of the state. In this regard, it is no wonder that the globalist statists in both America and Europe continue to kowtow to the impeccably statist red Chinese. For Dawson, "It is precisely this character of exclusiveness and strict mutual obligation which is the chief ground of objection among the modern critics of Christian morality. But whatever may be thought of it, there can be no doubt that the resultant type of monogamous and indissoluble marriage has been the foundation of European society and has conditioned the whole development of our civilization." Tragically, even in the twenty-first century, this is something that some in the Catholic episcopate have still to learn.

What is striking about Dawson's analysis of the threats that face marriage and family life is how prescient it is. After all, he wrote this in 1933, decades before it became evident what the sexual revolution had up its pernicious sleeve. And yet how eerily accurate they are!

> The problem that faces us today is … not so much the result of an intellectual revolt against the traditional Christian morality; it is due to the inherent contradictions of an abnormal state of culture. The natural tendency, which is even more clearly visible in America than in England, is for the Puritan tradition to be abandoned and for society to give itself up passively to the machinery of modern cosmopolitan life. But this is no solution. It leads merely to the breaking down of the old structure of society and the loss of the traditional moral standards without creating anything which can take their place. As in the decline of the ancient world, the family is steadily losing its form and its social significance, and the state absorbs more and more of the life of its members. The home is no longer a centre of social activity; it has become merely a sleeping place for a number of independent wage-earners. The functions which were formerly fulfilled by the head of the family are now being taken over by the state, which educates the children and takes the responsibility for their maintenance and health. Consequently, the father no longer holds a vital position in the family: as Mr. Bertrand Russell says, he is often a comparative stranger to his children, who know him only as "that man who comes for week-ends." Moreover, the reaction against the restrictions of family life which in the ancient world was confined to the males of the citizen class, is today common to every class and to both sexes. To the modern girl marriage and motherhood appear not as the conditions of a wider life, as they did to her grandmother, but as involving the sacrifice of her independence and the abandonment of her career.

Of course, there are passages in Dawson's analysis that clearly reflect his time. For instance, he observes how, "The only remaining safeguards of family life in modern urban civilization are its social prestige and the sanctions of moral and religious tradition. Marriage is still the only form of sexual union which is openly tolerated by society, and the ordinary man and woman are usually ready to sacrifice their personal convenience rather than risk social ostracism." Still, such references underscore how degraded our own society has become in comparison. In this regard, they recall something Knowles noticed about the twentieth-century historian: "To some Christopher Dawson may seem to 'date' but when truly assessed he is dateless." Indeed, such references give Dawson's warnings their authority. If he was living in a society that could still see "social prestige" in marriage, he was truly prophetic to see how the fledgling sexual revolution would not only remove that prestige but imperil marriage itself.

Tolstoy was fond of saying that historians are in the habit of asking questions to which no one is interested in learning the answer. Yet this could never be said of Dawson, certainly not by those in our own age who see the desolation and the anarchy to which the methodical destruction of the family has given rise. Dawson was convinced that "if we accept the principles of the new morality," marriage will be effectively "destroyed" and "the forces of dissolution" will be "allowed to operate unchecked." He also saw that other consequences would follow the abandonment of marriage.

> It is true that Mr. Russell, at least, is willing to leave us the institution of marriage, on condition that it is strictly demoralized and no longer makes any demands on continence. But it is obvious that these conditions reduce marriage to a very subordinate position. It is no longer the exclusive or even the normal form of sexual relations: it is entirely limited to the rearing of children. For, as Mr. Russell is never tired of pointing out, the use of contraceptives has made sexual intercourse independent of parenthood, and the marriage of the future will be confined to those who seek parenthood for its own sake rather than as the natural fulfilment of sexual love. But under these circumstances who will trouble to marry? Marriage will lose all attractions for the young and the pleasure-loving and the poor and the ambitious. The energy of youth will be devoted to contraceptive love and only when men and women have become prosperous and middle-aged will they think seriously of settling down to rear a strictly limited family.

For most of Western society today, this scenario is only as it should be. According to its unabashedly selfish lights, there can be nothing wrong with marriage and parenthood being a minority interest. Dawson, however, thought otherwise.

> It is impossible to imagine a system more contrary to the first principles of social well-being. So far from helping modern society to surmount its present difficulties, it only precipitates the crisis. It must lead inevitably to a social decadence far more rapid and more universal than that which brought about the disintegration of ancient civilization. The advocates of birth-control can hardly fail to realize the consequences of a progressive decline of the population in a society in which it is already almost stationary, but for all that their propaganda is entirely directed towards a further diminution in the birth rate.

Today, in many influential quarters, there are individuals who wish to sanction the "situation ethics" that the culture of death deploys to justify birth control. John Paul II was not unaware of these "situation ethics." In *Evangelium Vitae* (1995), he concedes that "while the climate of widespread moral uncertainty can in some way be explained by the multiplicity and gravity of today's social problems, and these can sometimes mitigate the subjective responsibility of individuals," he is also adamant that "it is no less true that we are confronted by an even larger reality, which can be described as a veritable structure of sin." Sin may not be a popular concept in our strenuously Pelagian culture—the word *adultery*, for example, is not used once in *Amoris Laetitia*—but it certainly is one that Pope John Paul II found useful, especially when trying to describe the same peril in which Dawson found the family.

> This reality is characterized by the emergence of a culture which denies solidarity and in many cases takes the form of a veritable "culture of death". This culture is actively fostered by powerful cultural, economic and political currents which encourage an idea of society excessively concerned with efficiency. Looking at the situation from this point of view, it is possible to speak in a certain sense of a war of the powerful against the weak: a life which would require greater acceptance, love and care is considered useless, or held to be an intolerable burden, and is therefore rejected in one way or another. A person who, because of illness, handicap or, more simply, just by existing, compromises the well-being or life-style of those who are more favoured tends to be looked upon as an enemy to be resisted or eliminated. In this way a kind of "conspiracy against life" is unleashed. This conspiracy involves not only individuals in their personal, family or group relationships, but goes far beyond, to the point of damaging and distorting, at the international level, relations between peoples and States. In order to facilitate the spread of abortion, enormous sums of money have been invested and continue to be invested in the production of pharmaceutical products which make it possible to kill the fetus in the mother's womb without recourse to medical assistance. On this point, scientific research itself seems to be almost exclusively preoccupied with developing products which are ever more simple and effective in suppressing life and which at the same time are capable of removing abortion from any kind of control or social responsibility.

The recent vote of the Royal College of Obstetricians and Gynaecologists to abolish nearly all of the restrictions governing abortion in England certainly bears out Pope John Paul II. The college's president, Lesley Regan stated that abortions should be treated like procedures as "mundane as bunion removal."

Here, we can see the stark barbarism of the culture of death and a threat to the family that the family will have all it can do to withstand. Dawson, for his part, anticipated *Evangelium Vitae* in seeing the antidote to such barbarism in terms that Saint John Paul II would richly approve.

The power of the Spirit is the only power that is strong enough to overcome it. In its strength Christians in the past faced and overcame the pagan civilization of the Roman Empire and the pagan savagery of their barbarian conquerors. The new paganism that we have to face today is more terrible than either of these in its cold inhumanity and its scientific exploitation of evil. But if we have faith in the power of the Spirit we must believe that even these evils can be conquered. For the powers of the world, formidable as they appear, are blind powers, which are working in the dark and which derive their strength from negative and destructive forces. They are powerless against the Spirit who is the Lord and Giver of Life. And in the same way all their new and elaborate devices for the enslavement of the human mind are powerless against those higher powers to spiritual understanding and love which are the essential gifts of the Holy Spirit.

Cause for Celebration:
A Last Encore from
The Yale Samuel Johnson

Samuel Johnson: Selected Works, edited by Robert De Maria, Jr., Stephen Fix,
Howard D. Weinbrot (Yale University Press). 818 pages.

In his incomparable biography of Samuel Johnson, Boswell recounts that
while the poet, critic, essayist, and lexicographer was researching his *Lives
of the Poets* (1781), the last of his great literary projects, "the tranquility of
the metropolis of Great Britain was unexpectedly disturbed by the most
horrid series of outrage that ever disgraced a civilized country." The Gordon
Riots broke out, and for six days and nights, the London mob pillaged and
terrorized the city, ostensibly in response to Parliament's relaxation of the
laws against Catholics.

Prisons were emptied, distilleries plundered, Catholic chapels destroyed,
the houses of magistrates ransacked and set afire, and over 200 of the agita-
tors shot dead by the militia sent out to quell them. Lord George Gordon,
who had been accused of instigating the riot, was tried for treason but
acquitted, the court finding that the Scottish peer in charge of the Protes-
tant Association might not be playing with the full shilling but intended
no violence and, in fact, sought to discourage it. "For God's sake go home
and be quiet, make no riot and noise," Gordon urged the mob.

Over one hundred and thirty rioters were arrested on capital offences and
twenty-six were hanged. Conspiracy theories abounded. "What a nation is
Scotland," the diarist Horace Walpole (1717–97) wrote after the riots, "in
every reign engendering traitors to the State, and false and pernicious to
the kings that favour it the most." Edmund Burke (1729–97), perhaps the
most notorious advocate of England's Catholics, defied the mob by refusing
to lie low, adamant that he would be "neither ... forced nor intimidated
from the strait line of what was right."

Johnson sent his dear friend Hester Thrale an eyewitness account of
the riots. "On Friday, the good Protestants met in St. George's Field," he
wrote, "and marching to Westminster insulted the Lords and Commons,

who all bore it with great tameness." While admitting that he could give "no exact Journal of a weeks defiance of Government," he did relay what he saw of the general mayhem.

> On Tuesday night they pulled down Fieldings house [and] ... leaving Fieldings ruins they went to Newgate to demand their companions who had been seized demolishing the Chapel. The Keeper could not release them but by the Mayor's permission which he went to ask, at his return he found all the prisoners released, and Newgate in a blaze. They then went to Bloomsbury and fastened upon Lord Mansfield's house, which they pulled down and, and as for his goods they wholly burnt them. They have since gone to Cane Wood, but a guard was there before them. They plundered some papists I think and burnt a Mass house in Moorfields. ... At night they set fire to the fleet and to the kingsbench, and I know not how many other places; you might see the glare of conflagration fill the sky ... Such a time of terrour you have been happy in not seeing.

The magistrate Sir John Fielding (1721–80) was sympathetic to the Toleration Acts of 1778, which granted concessions to the country's Catholics, as was the judge William Murray, 1st Earl of Mansfield (1705–93). When Benjamin Franklin learned of Mansfield's travails, he was exultant. "Lord Mansfield's house is burnt, with all his furniture, pictures, books and papers," the American diplomat wrote from Paris. "Thus, he, who approved the burning of American houses, has had fire brought home to him." Comically enough, it was the libertine John Wilkes (1725–97) who thwarted the mob from breaking into the Bank of England, a defense of property for which his radical friends never forgave him.

After the rioting was put down, Johnson wrote Mrs. Thrale: "Every body walks, and eats and sleeps in security." He was happy to relate that "Government now acts again with its proper force and we are all again under the protection of the King and the Laws," though he was also certain that "the history of the last week would fill You with amazement, it is without any modern example." Christopher Hibbert, a good Johnsonian in his own right as well as a crack popular historian, wrote his first book on the riots, *King Mob* (1958), which remains the liveliest account.

Order and disorder were abiding preoccupations of Johnson, whether in the realm of ethics, language, literature, or religion, as this splendid *Selected Works* amply demonstrates. The crowning volume in Yale's twenty-three-volume edition of Johnson's collected writings, the anthology includes generous selections from every genre in which "the great cham of literature" shone—essays, fiction, poetry, criticism, sermons, political commentary, biography, travel writing, and, of course, lexicography.

Thanks to Robert DeMaria Jr.'s inspired editing, here are selections from Johnson's *Rambler* and *Idler* essays; his great rendering of Juvenal's satire,

"The Vanity of Human Wishes"; his moving sermon on the death of his wife Tetty; his life of Savage, his philosophical Oriental tale, *Rasselas*; his *Preface* to the Dictionary; his Shakespeare criticism; choice extracts from *A Journey to the Western Islands of Scotland*, a number of complete lives from his critical masterpiece, *Lives of the Poets*, including those of Milton, Cowley, Pope and Gray; and much else. Sumptuously produced and nicely annotated, *Samuel Johnson: Selected Works* will delight old and form many new Johnsonians.

In *On Poetry and Poets* (1957), T. S. Eliot said that the poet in Johnson lay great store by edification, a quality which Eliot approved, even though he acknowledged that in his own time the word had become "an object of derision." If the word "to edify" came into the language meaning "to build," it evolved into one meaning "to build in holiness." Johnson defined the word in his Dictionary as "The act of building up man in the faith; improvement in holiness." Eliot ended his essay by observing that "amongst the varieties of chaos in which we find ourselves ... one is a chaos of language, in which there are ... no standards of writing, and an increasing indifference to etymology and the history of the use of words." Our chaos might be a good deal more fundamental than the one Eliot endured, but that is precisely one reason why we, too, must endeavor to grow in holiness. A confused world can always use more saints. We can also agree with Eliot that "we need to be repeatedly reminded" of "the responsibility of our poets and critics" for "the preservation of the language," and certainly this marvelous anthology of Johnson's edifying work accomplishes that perennial object as well.

What Dr. Johnson
Can Teach Pope Francis

Reading a Catholic paper yesterday, I must say I was rather startled to see the pope of the Roman Church charging the Catholic priests who taught in the elementary schools of Canada with genocide. It is true that the Holy Father does not have the fondest regard for the Catholic priesthood nor the dogmatic proselytism indispensable to evangelization. It is also true that he shares the Marxist view that the history of the Church is, by and large, a history of colonialism, chicane and oppression. But he has never gone so far as to say that the Church is guilty of genocide—until now. Here is the exchange that took place on the airplane after the pope left Canada:

BRITTANY HOBSON, THE CANADIAN PRESS: Good evening Pope Francis. My name is Brittany Hobson. I am a reporter with the Canadian press. You have often spoken on the need to speak clearly, honestly, forthrightly, and with parrhesia. You know that Canada's Truth and Reconciliation Commission described the residential school system as "cultural genocide." This has since been amended to just "genocide." Those who were listening to your apologies the past week did express disappointment that the word genocide was not used. Would you use those words and accept that members of the Church participated in genocide?

POPE FRANCIS: It's true, I didn't use the word because it didn't occur to me, but I described the genocide and asked for pardon, forgiveness for this work that is genocidal. For example, I condemned this too: Taking away children and changing culture, changing mentalities, changing traditions, changing a race, let's say, a whole culture. Yes, it's a technical word, genocide, but I didn't use it because it didn't come to mind, but I described it. It is true; yes, it's genocide. Yes, you all, be calm. You can say that I said that, yes, that it was genocide. [In English] Yes. Yes. Thank you.

After I read this genuinely shocking calumny, I was reminded of a letter that Samuel Johnson (1709–84), the great lexicographer, poet, critic, biographer and moralist wrote in 1766 to Mr. William Drummond, which my fellow co-religionists and, indeed, all men of good faith should read. James Boswell, Johnson's biographer, sets up the context for the letter nicely in his incomparable biography.

[Johnson] wrote this year a letter, not intended for publication, which has, perhaps, as strong marks of his sentiment and style, as any of his compositions. The original is in my possession. It is addressed to the late Mr. William Drummond, bookseller, in Edinburgh, a gentleman of good family, but small estate, who took arms for the house of Stuart in 1745; and during his concealment in London till the act of general pardon came out, obtained the acquaintance of Dr. Johnson, who justly esteemed him as a very worthy man. It seems some of the members of the Society in Scotland for propagating Christian knowledge had opposed the scheme of translating the Holy Scripture into the Erse or Gaelic language, from political considerations of the disadvantage of keeping up the distinction between the Highlanders and the other inhabitants of North Britain. Dr. Johnson being informed of this, I suppose by Mr. Drummond, wrote with a generous indignation as follows.

One should also add here that Johnson actually brought up a slave boy from Jamaica in his various houses in London, Francis Barber (1742–1801), whom he sent to an English school and later made not only his manservant but his legatee. Thus, he took an active, personal, faithful part in the education—particularly the Christian education—of an individual who was not entirely dissimilar from the indigenous peoples of Canada about whom the pope is so misguidedly solicitous. The idea of anyone, let alone a pope, charging the deeply Christian Johnson with having engaged in genocide for indoctrinating Frank in the Faith is too grotesque, but then Pope Benedict XIV, a witty, gentle, civilized man would never have taken it into his head to imagine Christian evangelization reprehensible, nor would Pope Clement XIII, whose authorization of the office of the Sacred Heart was so beloved of the Jesuits of the eighteenth century—Jesuits with whom the present pope has so little in common.

Since the letter to which I refer is one of the noblest Johnson ever wrote, it bears quoting in its entirety:

TO MR. WILLIAM DRUMMOND.
Johnson's Court, Fleet Street, Aug. 13, 1766,

SIR,

I did not expect to hear that it could be, in an assembly convened for the propagation of Christian knowledge, a question whether any nation uninstructed in religion should receive instruction; or whether that instruction should be imparted to them by a translation of the holy books into their own language. If obedience to the will of God be necessary to happiness, and knowledge of his will be necessary to obedience, I know not how he that withholds this knowledge, or delays it, can be said to love his neighbour as himself. He that voluntarily continues ignorance is guilty of all the crimes which ignorance produces; as to him that should extinguish the tapers of a lighthouse, might justly be imputed the calamities of shipwrecks. Christianity is the highest perfection of humanity; and as no man is good but as he wishes the good of others, no man can be good in the highest degree, who wishes not to others the largest measures of the greatest good. To omit for a year, or for a day, the most efficacious method of advancing Christianity, in compliance with any purposes that terminate on this side of the grave, is a crime of which I know not that the world has yet had an example, except in the practice of the planters of America, — a race of mortals whom, I suppose, no other man wishes to resemble.

The Papists have, indeed, denied to the laity the use of the Bible; but this prohibition, in few places now very rigorously enforced, is defended by arguments, which have for their foundation the care of souls. To obscure, upon motives merely political, the light of revelation, is a practice reserved for the reformed; and, surely, the blackest midnight of popery is meridian sunshine to such a reformation. I am not very willing that any language should be totally extinguished. The similitude and derivation of languages afford the most indubitable proof of the traduction of nations, and the genealogy of mankind. They add often physical certainty to historical evidence; and often supply the only evidence of ancient migrations, and of the revolutions of ages which left no written monuments behind them.

Every man's opinion, at least his desires, are a little influenced by his favourite studies. My zeal for languages may seem, perhaps, rather over-heated, even to those by whom I desire to be well esteemed. To those who have nothing in their thoughts but trade or policy, present power, or present money, I should not think it necessary to defend my opinions; but with men of letters I would not unwillingly compound, by wishing the continuance of every language, however narrow in its extent, or however incommodious for common purposes, till it is reposited in some version of a known book, that it may be always hereafter examined and compared with other languages, and then permitting its disuse. For this purpose, the translation of the Bible is most to be desired. It is not certain that the same method will not preserve the Highland language, for the purposes of learning, and abolish it from daily use. When the Highlanders read the Bible, they will naturally wish to have its obscurities cleared, and to know the history, collateral or appendant. Knowledge always desires increase: it is like fire, which must first be kindled by some external agent, but which will afterwards propagate itself. When they once desire to learn, they will naturally have recourse to the nearest language by which that desire can be gratified; and one will tell another, that if he would attain knowledge, he must learn English.

This speculation may, perhaps, be thought more subtle than the grossness of real life will easily admit. Let it, however, be remembered, that the efficacy of ignorance has long been tried, and has not produced the consequence expected. Let knowledge, therefore, take its turn; and let the patrons of privation stand awhile aside, and admit the operation of positive principles.

You will be pleased, Sir, to assure the worthy man who is employed in a new translation, that he has my wishes for his success; and if here or at Oxford I can be of any use, that I shall think it more than honour to promote his undertaking.

I am sorry that I delayed so long to write. I am, Sir, your most humble servant,

SAM. Johnson.

Boswell's response to the letter should also be quoted: "The opponents of this pious scheme being made ashamed of their conduct, the benevolent undertaking was allowed to go on." Whether the pope will register any shame for his vilification of the good work of the priests in Canada remains to be seen, though he should be made aware that keeping native peoples in ignorance of Christianity, let alone the arts and knowledge of civilization is neither faithful nor charitable. As Johnson so unanswerably reminds us, "The efficacy of ignorance has long been tried, and has not produced the consequence expected."

Sophisticates, Primitives and the Veins of Wealth

Flying back from London to New York recently, I was reduced to reading the Sunday magazine of the *Financial Times*, after I found that I had packed away the books I had bought for the flight in my luggage. I share this with my gentle readers because the experience opened my eyes to how aggressively the magazine promotes the culture of death. As a pro-lifer, I was struck by the admirable conviction and indeed unanimity with which the proponents of death make their case. Unlike some in the pro-life camp, the pro-death have nothing wobbly about them. In an adulatory profile of John Le Carré, for example, the fashionable spy novelist made no bones at all about referring to the Catholic Church as "truly perverse," as though none of his readers could ever think otherwise about so self-evidently contemptible an institution. Pro-lifers might take exception to the vituperative character of such a remark, but they cannot fault Le Carre's readiness to meet and engage the enemy. Then, again, in a piece on Marin Alsop, the conductor of the Baltimore Symphony was asked what she thought of assisted suicide and she replied, "I believe in giving people the capacity to make ultimate decisions for themselves." This seemed an odd question to pose in a celebrity interview, even a high-brow celebrity interview. And yet when I went online to verify the conductor's response, I discovered that the Sunday magazine asks this question of all its celebrities, routinely, week after week. And every one of them replies in the affirmative. Jeffrey Archer, Martin Boyce, Felicity Kendal, Jamie Morrison, Joanne Harris, Amanda Wakeley and scores of others all sing the same *macabre* tune: they not only believe in assisted suicide, they champion it, they celebrate it. Ben Fogle speaks for all of his fellow celebrities when he says, with a kind of sublime fatuity, "The ultimate human freedom is making your own choices."

To put these responses in some metaphysical perspective, the magazine then asks the same interviewees if they believe in an afterlife, and *none* of them responds in the affirmative. A few wish to imagine their own lives "spiritual" in some unspecified, consoling, self-congratulatory way; but none of them is willing to go so far as to say that there is life after death.

Indeed, Marin Alsop gives the most eloquent response to the question of whether she believes in the after life when she replies, "Not really."

Here is the wisdom of the age hammered home week after week in one of the establishment's most highly respected papers.

How can those who wish to defend life respond to such relentless, tragic moral error? First and foremost, we must recognize that, when it comes to questions of elemental ethics, which go to the heart of contraception, abortion, and euthanasia, our elites exemplify how terribly misguided our moral intelligence can become if ignorant or defiant of the laws of God. To oppose the culture of death, to oppose the sophisticated opinion-makers who tout the progressive new world order, which has made the evil of contraception and abortion and euthanasia its very cornerstone, we need a countervailing intelligence, one that is animated by God's humanizing love, or we shall find ourselves in the same prison of "ultimate human freedom" of which Ben Fogle is so fond.

To do this, we must stop putting our belief in God to one side and imagining that we can reaffirm and defend the sacredness of life by simply invoking human rights or natural law. We must stop keeping silent on what we rightly regard as the direct bearing that our belief in God has on our understanding of the inviolability of life. And we must stop worrying whether affirming that belief publicly will offend those who believe that killing children in the womb is somehow a requirement of advanced civilization.

Evelyn Waugh, who never passed up an opportunity to mock the progressive new world order, whether in his fiction, travelogues or journalism, is a good case in point. Waugh, of course, was an exceedingly civilized fellow, but he was also a connoisseur of jungles. And he knew, as Blessed John Henry Newman knew, that the sworn enemies of primitive man are not always the bright bulbs they fancy themselves. On the contrary, when it comes to matters of life and death, they can be extraordinarily dim. In *Black Mischief* (1932), Waugh had the European-educated Emperor of a small Ethiopian country named Debra Dowa commission "a large, highly coloured poster well-calculated to convey to the illiterate the benefits of birth control. It was in many ways the highest triumph of the new Ministry ... Copies were placarded all over Debra Dowa; they were sent down the line of every station latrine, capital and coast; they were sent into the interior to viceregal lodges and headmen's huts, hung up at prisons, barracks, gallows and juju trees, and wherever the poster was hung there assembled a cluster of inquisitive, entranced Azanians." And then Waugh nicely describes the advertisement as it appears on the widely distributed poster.

> It portrayed two contrasted scenes. On one side, a native hut of hideous squalor, overrun with children of every age, suffering from

every physical incapacity — crippled, deformed, blind, spotted, and insane; the father prematurely aged with paternity squatted by an empty cook-pot; through the door could be seen his wife, withered and bowed with child-bearing, desperately hoeing at their inadequate crop. On the other side a bright parlour furnished with chairs and table; the mother, young and beautiful, sat at her ease eating a huge slice of raw meat; her husband smoked a long Arab hubble-bubble (still a caste mark of leisure throughout the land), while a single healthy child sat between them reading a newspaper. Inset between the two pictures was a detailed drawing of some up-to-date contraceptive apparatus and the words in Sakuyu: WHICH HOME DO YOU CHOOSE?

Waugh then describes the intense interest the poster inspired and how "Nowhere was there any doubt about the meaning of the beautiful new pictures."

See: on the right hand: there is a rich man: smoke pipe like big chief: but his wife she no good: sit eating meat: and rich man no good: he only one son.

See: on left hand: poor man: not much to eat: but his wife she very good, work hard in field: man he good too: eleven children: one very mad, very holy. And in the middle: Emperor's juju. Make you like that good man with eleven children.

And as a result, despite the admonitions from squire and vicar, the peasantry began pouring into town ... eagerly awaiting the fine new magic of virility and fecundity.

Here, the citizens of Azania echo the wisdom of Mother Teresa, who had no hesitation in seeing that "It is a poverty to decide that a child must die so that you may live as you wish" Unfortunately, not all of the readers of the Sunday magazine of the *Financial Times* possess any comparable discernment. When these highly suggestible readers are shown advertisements for the benefits of birth control and euthanasia (not to mention slack-jawed sacrilege) many respond as the editors of the paper mean them to respond: with servile conformism. But Waugh shows how primitive men, for all of their lack of technical advancement, can often see what parvenus miss, and that is that human life itself is the greatest wealth.

Certainly, as a Catholic convert, Waugh would have seen this in his Church's stalwart rejection of contraception throughout the 1920's and 30s when Marie Stopes was agitating for birth control, with the connivance of nearly all of the English Establishment. But he would also have seen it in the great Victorian art critic John Ruskin, whom he praised for what he referred to as his "exquisite sensibility and stupendous mastery of language."

Ruskin was an only child (a rarity in Victoria's philoprogenitive England) and the son of a rich wine merchant, who, together with his wife, doted on his brilliant boy. After such an upbringing, Ruskin might have turned out a cosseted solipsist. Instead, throughout his work, he exhibited admirable solicitude for the weak and oppressed. In "The Veins of Wealth," for instance, from *Unto This Last* (1862), he recalled encountering servants in a rich man's kitchen who appeared "ill-dressed," "squalid," and "half-starved" and he concluded that the riches of any man who tolerated such a level of want in his own household must be of a "very theoretical" character indeed. But then he went on to make a much more fundamental point about the true nature of wealth, a point which the disciples of the culture of death must always find embarrassing, especially those who put the dictates of feminist ideology before the life of children.

> Since the essence of wealth consists in power over men, will it not follow that the nobler and the more in number the persons are over whom it has power, the greater the wealth? Perhaps it may even appear, after some consideration, that the persons themselves *are* the wealth—that these pieces of gold with which we are in the habit of guiding them, are, in fact, nothing more than a kind of Byzantine harness or trappings, very glittering and beautiful in barbaric sight, wherewith we bridle the creatures; but that if these same living creatures could be guided without the fretting and jingling of the Byzants in their mouths and ears, they might themselves be more valuable than their bridles. In fact, it may be discovered that the true veins of wealth are purple—and not in Rock, but in Flesh—perhaps even that the final outcome and consummation of all wealth is in the producing as many as possible full-breathed, bright-eyed, and happy-hearted human creatures. Our modern wealth, I think, has rather a tendency the other way; most political economists appearing to consider multitudes of human creatures not conducive to wealth.

What those who promote the culture of death think when they read that is anyone's guess, but surely, they cannot claim to have done much themselves to protect the veins of wealth, in all their purple splendor. On the contrary, they are guiltier than anyone of depleting that wealth, so much so that we now face a genuine demographic disaster in the West, though our papers continue to groan under the grossest pro-death advertising.

Confronted with this gathering threat to our civilization, Catholics must refute the proponents of death by showing them how nothing exposes the nihilism of their new world order better than God's abounding love, a love which extends even to those who would betray that love. Giotto recognized this with consummate insight in that marvelous fresco of his in which Christ confronts Judas. Obviously, this is not a reality that will immediately sway the editors of the *Financial Times*; it may take a while before those obdurate souls come round to appreciating how preferable the culture of life is to the culture of death. But that is no good reason for Catholics to put off affirming the truth of God's love, without which the culture of life would be impossible.

Abraham Lincoln, Slavery, and Abortion

With malice toward none, with charity for all, with firmness in the right as God gives us to see the right, let us strive on to finish the work we are in, to bind up the nation's wounds.

Abraham Lincoln

Order my life, O my God. Grant me to know what you would have me do, and to carry it out as I should and as is profitable to my soul.

St. Thomas Aquinas

I

Now that the survival of Roe v. Wade, the 1973 court ruling that made abortion legal in the United States, is under threat by state legislatures opposed to abortion after being held in place for years by the legal principle of *stare decisis* ("to stand by things decided"), it is time to revisit the precedent-honoring principle in light of the options that Americans face with respect to abortion today compared to the options that they faced in the nineteenth century with respect to slavery, especially after the Dred Scott decision of 1857.

To appreciate the force that precedent plays in the Supreme Court's rulings, one has to keep in mind that in the last two centuries it has only reversed 235 decisions. In Planned Parenthood v. Casey (1992), Justices Anthony Kennedy, Sandra Day O'Connor and David Souter had no qualms about putting the perceived legitimacy of the court before the objective merits of Roe v. Wade. It is also useful to remember that it was in this ruling—a colossal punt if ever there were one—that the Justices claimed that "At the heart of liberty is the right to define one's own concept of existence, of meaning, of the universe, and of the mystery of human life. Beliefs about these matters could not define the attributes of personhood were they formed under compulsion of the State"—a truly staggering relativizing of objective truth, which, if applied to slavery, would have given the slave-drivers precisely the grounds they needed to justify their own peculiar notions of "personhood." The rest of the ruling followed suit:

> Men and women of good conscience can disagree, and we suppose some always shall disagree, about the profound moral and spiritual implications of terminating a pregnancy, even in its earliest stage. Some of us as individuals find abortion offensive to our most basic principles of morality, but that cannot control our decision. Our obligation is to define the liberty of all, not to mandate our own moral code ...
>
> It is conventional constitutional doctrine that where reasonable people disagree the Government can adopt one position or the other. That theorem, however, assumes a state of affairs in which the choice does not intrude upon a protected liberty. Thus, while some people might disagree about whether or not the flag should be saluted, or disagree about the proposition that it may not be defiled, we have ruled that a state may not compel or enforce one view or the other ...
>
> The Court's duty in the present case is clear. In 1973, it confronted the already-divisive issue of governmental power to limit personal choice to undergo abortion, for which it provided a new resolution based on the due process guaranteed by the Fourteenth Amendment. Whether or not a new social consensus is developing on that issue, its divisiveness is no less today than in 1973, and pressure to overrule the decision, like pressure to retain it, has grown only more intense. A decision to overrule Roe's essential holding under the existing circumstances would address error, if error there was, at the cost of both profound and unnecessary damage to the Court's legitimacy, and to the nation's commitment to the rule of law. It is therefore imperative to adhere to the essence of Roe's original decision, and we do so today.

Here is a fair specimen of *stare decisis*. And yet it is important to note that none of the distinguished authors of this decision ever mentioned the fact that when Roe v. Wade was first imposed on the American people it nullified the laws prohibiting abortion in every state with the exception of New York. Why it was acceptable to run roughshod over that body of precedent and yet acquiesce in the far less settled precedent of Roe v. Wade the Justices never explained. *Stare decisis* can obviously be a rather selective principle when taken up by those disinclined to incur the wrath of our redoubtable abortion lobby. Moreover, the implicit reasoning behind Casey is no different from the reasoning behind John C. Calhoun's famous speech, "On the Antislavery Petitions of 1837," in which the Southern statesman warned his compatriots that "Abolition and the Union cannot co-exist." For Calhoun, outlawing slavery was out of the question precisely because it would fly in the face of precedent. "Be it good or bad, it has grown up with our society and institutions, and is so interwoven with them, that to destroy it would be to destroy us as a people." If there is a difference between the logic of Casey and that in Calhoun's speech, I am afraid I do not see it.

Susan Collins, the Republican Senator from Maine pointed to the primacy of precedent in her decision to confirm Judge Brett Kavanaugh to the Supreme Court, which shows why even conservative courts have tended to shy away from repudiating Roe v. Wade. "There are, of course, rare and extraordinary times where the Supreme Court would rightly overturn a precedent," the Senator conceded.

> The most famous example was when the Supreme Court in Brown v. The Board of Education overruled Plessy v. Ferguson, correcting a grievously wrong decision, to use the judge's term, allowing racial inequality. But someone who believes that the importance of precedent has been rooted in the Constitution would follow long established precedent, except in those rare circumstances where a decision is grievously wrong or deeply inconsistent with the law. Those are Judge Kavanaugh's phrases. As the judge asserted to me, a long-established precedent is not something to be trimmed, narrowed, discarded or overlooked. Its roots in the Constitution give the concept of *stare decisis* greater weight such that the precedent can't be trimmed or narrowed simply because a judge might want to on a whim. In short, his views on honoring precedent would preclude attempts to do by stealth that which one has committed not to do overtly. Noting that *Roe v. Wade* was decided 45 years ago and reaffirmed 19 years later in Planned Parenthood v. Casey, I asked Judge Kavanaugh whether the passage of time is relevant to following precedent. He said decisions become part of our legal framework with the passage of time and that honoring precedent is essential to maintaining public confidence.

The classic example of the wisdom of the Supreme Court's deciding to flout *stare decisis* is, indeed, Brown v. Board of Education (1954), in which the court ruled against the "separate but equal" precedent set by Plessy v. Ferguson (1896), though the dilatoriness of this otherwise enlightened ruling consigned the country to fifty years of increasingly toxic racial segregation. Now that forty-five years have passed since Roe v. Wade was enacted, we can see what an even ghastlier toll has been exacted from upholding a precedent that issues in abandoning millions of children to the abattoirs of abortion.

II

The Dred Scott decision is instructive for our purposes because it shows how the legitimacy of the Supreme Court, far from being irreproachable, can be very dubious indeed. In light of this occasional fallibility, acknowledging that bad law has damaged the Court's legitimacy, *pace* Justice Kennedy and his colleagues, can be not only salutary but a moral imperative. In the Dred Scott case, the Supreme Court ruled 7–2 that the slave Scott who resided in a free state was not entitled to his freedom; that "a negro whose ancestors were … sold in slavery" was not and could never be a citizen of the United States; and that the Missouri Compromise (1820), which had declared all territories west of Missouri and north of latitude 36°30' free, was unconstitutional. In the decision written by Chief Justice Roger B. Taney, one can see just how bad this particular law was, but also how citing precedent to defend the ruling only made it worse.

> [Black Africans imported as slaves] had for more than a century before been regarded as beings of an inferior order, and altogether unfit to associate with the white race, either in social or political relations; and so far inferior, that they had no rights which the white man was bound to respect; and that the negro might justly and lawfully be reduced to slavery for his benefit. He was bought and sold, and treated as an ordinary article of merchandise and traffic, whenever a profit could be made by it. This opinion was at that time fixed and universal in the civilized portion of the white race. It was regarded as an axiom in morals as well as in politics, which no one thought of disputing, or supposed to be open to dispute; and men in every grade and position in society daily and habitually acted upon it in their private pursuits, as well as in matters of public concern, without doubting for a moment the correctness of this opinion.

What is ironic about Taney's decision is that it was written by a man who was not only a devout Roman Catholic but personally opposed to slavery; before being appointed to the Supreme Court, he freed the slaves he had inherited from his father's estate. Yet he made the calamitous ruling he made because he was convinced that slavery could be treated merely as a matter of state sovereignty; indeed, he was convinced that slavery could be adjudicated without any consideration of whether it was morally right or wrong. Similarly, the Justices in Casey convinced themselves that they could sidestep the moral issue of abortion by claiming that to redress its moral wrongs would be, in effect, to force others to accept their moral code. In other words, they ruled that there is no such thing as objective right and wrong, but only personal opinions as to what is right and wrong, an assertion which if followed to its logical conclusion would make any coherent legal ruling virtually impossible. Certainly, the savior of the Constitution in Abraham Lincoln would have marveled at the incoherent purposes to which the Constitution has been put in the defense of legalized abortion.

Before I proceed, however, with drawing any further parallels between abortion and slavery, I should make one vital distinction. In comparing abortion and slavery, I realize that the two are not entirely comparable. Abortion, after all, results in the destruction of human life, whereas slavery results in turning human life into chattel. Many slaves, it is true, died on slave ships bound for North America—nearly 85,000 of 400,000 by some calculations. And an incalculable number of slaves were murdered by their masters. Yet, in America alone, since 1973, nearly 60 million babies have been murdered as the result of abortion. Nevertheless, if the American slave-drivers of the nineteenth-century were content to justify slavery by pointing to what they considered the inferiority of those they enslaved, their counterparts in the twenty-first century justify abortion by pointing to what they regard as a similar inferiority in those they murder. Hence, to some extent, they are comparable, though only to an extent.

If, as the Justices in Casey remarked, the issue of abortion is of an intense divisiveness, the issue of slavery was no less so—indeed, probably more so. As we all know, the southern states sought to bolster the legality of slavery in their own states by extending it to new states and territories. The various groups of abolitionists opposed this by seeking to rouse public opinion to see the necessity for outlawing slavery in all states. Lincoln was opposed to slavery but leery of outlawing it along the broad lines recommended by the abolitionists because he was fearful that such lines would imperil the Union. To retain the legality of slavery in their own states, he rightly anticipated, the South would be tempted to secede from the Union and repudiate the Constitution.

In succumbing to that temptation, they unleashed a frightful bloodbath. On 17 September 1862, in what became known as the Battle of Antietam, the single bloodiest day in all American military history, 23,000 men lost their lives. As one lieutenant of the North Carolina Infantry recalled,

> Here [the Union soldiers] are, right before us, scarce 50 yards off, but as if with one feeling, our whole line pour a deadly volley into their ranks—they drop, reel; stagger, and back their first line go beyond the crest of the hill. Our men reload, and await for them to again approach, while the first column of the enemy meet the second, rally and move forward again. They meet with the same reception, and back again they go, to come back when met by their third line. Here they all come. You can see their mounted riders cheering them on, and with a sickly "huzza!" they all again approach us at a charge, but another volley sends their whole line reeling back.

A Union eyewitness wrote to his daughters of the day, "The roar of the infantry was beyond anything conceivable ... Imagine from 8,000 to 10,000 men on one side, with probably a larger number on the other, all at once discharging their muskets. If all the stone and brick houses of Broadway should tumble at once the roar and rattle could hardly be greater, and amidst this hundreds of pieces of artillery, right and left, were thundering as a sort of bass to the infernal music." Afterwards, as Shelby Foote recounts in his magisterial narrative, "the armies lay face to face all day, like sated lions, and between them, there on the slopes of Sharpsburg ridge and in the valley of Antietam, the dead began to fester in the heat and the cries of the wounded faded to a mewling." At war's end, all told, approximately 660,000 men would lose their lives in the conflict.

Now, as we have seen, Southern advocates of slavery made their case for what they called their "peculiar institution" largely on the grounds of precedent. In defending this institution, they may not have explicitly invoked the letter of *stare decisis*, but they certainly invoked its spirit. When the vice-president of the Confederacy, Alexander Stephens, gave his infamous "Corner-stone Speech" in Savanah, Georgia on 21 March 1861, he gave an interesting twist to the principle of *stare decisis* by arguing that the South had no alternative but to secede from the Union and adopt a new Constitution in order to honor what the South had always understood to be the true relationship between slavery and Southern society, which the old Constitution at once muddled and subverted.

> The new constitution has put at rest, *forever,* all the agitating questions relating to our peculiar institution—African slavery as it exists amongst us—the proper *status* of the negro in our form of civilization. This was the immediate cause of the late rupture and present revolution. Jefferson in his forecast, had anticipated this, as the "rock upon which the old Union would split." He was right. What was conjecture with him, is now a realized fact. But whether he fully comprehended the great truth upon which that rock *stood* and *stands,* may be doubted. The prevailing ideas entertained by him and most of the leading statesmen at the time of the formation of the old constitution, were that the enslavement of the African was in violation of the laws of nature; that it was wrong in *principle,* socially, morally, and politically. It was an evil they knew not well how to deal with, but the general opinion of the men of that day was that, somehow or other in the order of Providence, the institution would be evanescent and pass away. This idea, though not incorporated in the constitution, was the prevailing idea at that time. The constitution, it is true, secured every essential guarantee to the institution while it should last, and hence no argument can be justly urged against the constitutional guarantees thus secured, because of the common sentiment of the day. Those ideas, however,

were fundamentally wrong. They rested upon the assumption of the equality of races. This was an error. It was a sandy foundation, and the government built upon it fell when the "storm came and the wind blew." Our new government is founded upon exactly the opposite idea; its foundations are laid, its corner-stone rests upon the great truth, that the negro is not equal to the white man; that slavery—subordination to the superior race—is his natural and normal condition.

While Stephens invoked Jefferson and the framers to reject their contention that the individual states of the Union would gradually repudiate the legality of slavery, William Seward, the Governor of New York, who would later go on to serve as Secretary of State in Lincoln's first and second administrations, invoked the framers to argue that they had actually anticipated the irreconcilable impasse between the South and North over slavery. "The strife and contentions concerning slavery," he told an audience in Rochester in 1858, "which gently disposed persons so habitually deprecate, are nothing more than the ripening of the conflict which the fathers themselves not only thus regarded with favor, but which they may be said to have instituted." The same might be said of the "strife and contentions" concerning abortion: they are the ripening of the sexual revolution, which has culminated in the notion that "reproductive rights" somehow trump the rights of developing children in the womb. The fact that Seward was the son of a slave-owning New York farmer opened his eyes to the untenability of slavery. "Assuming ... that all men are equal by the law of nature and of nations," he wrote, "the right of property in slaves falls to the ground; for no one who is equal to another can be the owner or property of another," an observation which demolishes the argument for chattel slavery as elegantly as it demolishes the argument for "reproductive rights."

That Northerners as a whole had a role to play in the gathering conflict—and not just abolitionists in the North—was made clear by Angelina Grimké Weld, the independent-minded daughter of a wealthy South Carolina slave-owner and judge. "Many persons go to the South for a season," she told an audience in Pennsylvania Hall as far back as 1838,

> and are hospitably entertained in the parlor and at the table of the slave-holder. They never enter the huts of the slaves; they know nothing of the dark side of the picture, and they return home with praises on their lips of the generous character of those with whom they had tarried. Or if they have witnessed the cruelties of slavery, by remaining silent spectators they have naturally become callous— an insensibility has ensued which prepares them to apologize even for barbarity. Nothing but the corrupting influence of slavery on the hearts of the Northern people can induce them to apologize for it; and much will have been done for the destruction of Southern

slavery when we have so reformed the North that no one here will be willing to risk his reputation by advocating or even excusing the holding of men as property. The South know it, and acknowledge that as fast as our principles prevail, the hold of the master must be relaxed.

When it came to what Grimké saw as the "corrupting influence" of slavery for all Americans, not just those in the South, the Massachusetts abolitionist Charles Sumner was unforgettably eloquent, though he paid for his eloquence after delivering his speech in favor of keeping Kansas a free state when a South Carolinian congressman beat him on the Senate floor with a cane—a chastening reminder to those who imagine that our own party politics have become somehow unprecedentedly partisan. "One of the choicest passages of the master Italian poet, Dante," Sumner wrote,

> is where a scene of transcendent virtue is described, as sculptured in "visible speech" on the long gallery which led to the Heavenly Gate. The poet felt the inspiration of the scene, and placed it on the wayside, where it could charm and encourage. This was natural. Nobody can look upon virtue and justice, if it be only in images and pictures, without feeling a kindred sentiment. Nobody can be surrounded by vice and wrong, by violence and brutality, if it be only in images and pictures, without coming under their degrading influence. Nobody can live with the one without advantage; nobody can live with the other without loss. Who could pass his life in the secret chamber where are gathered the impure relics of Pompeii, without becoming indifferent to loathsome things? But if these loathsome things are not merely sculptured and painted, if they exist in living reality—if they enact their hideous capers in life, as in the criminal pretensions of Slavery—while the lash plays and the blood spurts—while women are whipped and children are sold—while marriage is polluted and annulled—while the parental tie is rudely torn—while honest gains are filched or robbed—while the soul itself is shut down in all the darkness of ignorance, and while God himself is defied in the pretension that man can have property in his fellow-man; if all these things are present, not merely in images and pictures, but in reality, their influence on character must be incalculable.

Some years ago, in a book called *Culture and Abortion*, I set out to show the many ways in which legalized abortion has corrupted our country by inuring us to a now pervasive culture of death, a travesty of culture which ruthlessly assails the sanctity of life, while mutilating at every turn what Pope Paul VI, in his prophetic encyclical *Humanae Vitae* (1968), referred to as "the whole moral law of marriage." Since my book was released in 2013, what is left of our culture has only become more corrupt, and one measure of that corruption can be seen in how our acquiescing in the horror of abortion has made shipwreck not only of our arts, our manners, our schools and our universities but our very humanity.

III

Senator Sumner, a proud, learned, imperious man, may not have been to every one's taste—he did not suffer fools gladly—but his dedication to eradicating slavery won Lincoln's lasting respect, even affection; after the Civil War, the two men, according to Mrs. Lincoln, became "great chums." What divided them before the war was the timing of emancipation. Certainly, Lincoln came to the implementation of emancipation reluctantly. He is amusing about this in a letter to a gentleman from Kentucky in 1864. "I am naturally anti-slavery," he told his correspondent.

> If slavery is not wrong, nothing is wrong. I cannot remember when I did not so think, and feel. And yet I have never understood that the Presidency conferred upon me an unrestricted right to act officially upon this judgment and feeling. It was in the oath I took that I would, to the best of my ability, preserve, protect, and defend the Constitution of the United States … When, early in the war, Gen. Fremont attempted military emancipation, I forbade it, because I did not then think it an indispensable necessity. When a little later, Gen. Cameron, then Secretary of War, suggested the arming of the blacks, I objected, because I did not yet think it an indispensable necessity. When, still later, Gen. Hunter attempted military emancipation, I again forbade it, because I did not yet think the indispensable necessity had come. When, in March, and May, and July 1862 I made earnest, and successive appeals to the border states to favor compensated emancipation, I believed the indispensable necessity for military emancipation, and arming the blacks would come, unless averted by that measure. They declined the proposition; and I was, in my best judgment, driven to the alternative of either surrendering the Union, and with it, the Constitution, or of laying strong hand upon the colored element. I chose the latter. In choosing it, I hoped for greater gain than loss; but of this, I was not entirely confident. More than a year of trial now shows no loss by it in our foreign relations, none in our home popular sentiment, none in our white military force,—no loss by it any how or anywhere. On the contrary, it shows a gain of quite a hundred and thirty thousand soldiers, seamen, and laborers. These are palpable facts, about which, as facts, there can be no cavilling. We have the men; and we could not have had them without the measure.

However appreciative the constitutional lawyer in Lincoln was to the inopportunity of emancipation at a time when it threatened the preservation of the Union, the moralist in him was never unmindful of the issue's moral stakes. One can see this in his final debate with Judge Stephen Douglas, who tried to argue that even Lincoln's incrementalist approach to slavery, which called for letting slavery stand in the Southern states, without permitting its extension to any additional states, would violate states' rights and foment unnecessary conflict between North and South. Lincoln, for his part, refused to be distracted by sideshows. "The real issue in this controversy — the one pressing upon every mind — is the sentiment on the part of one class that looks upon the institution of slavery as a *wrong*," he wrote, clearly speaking for himself

> and of another class that *does not* look upon it as a wrong. The sentiment that contemplates the institution of slavery in this country as a wrong is the sentiment of the Republican party. It is the sentiment around which all their actions, all their arguments, circle, from which all their propositions radiate. They look upon it as being a moral, social, and political wrong; and while they contemplate it as such, they nevertheless have due regard for its actual existence among us, and the difficulties of getting rid of it in any satisfactory way and to all the constitutional obligations thrown about it. Yet, having a due regard for these, they desire a policy in regard to it that looks to its not creating any more danger. They insist that it should, as far as may be, *be treated* as a wrong; and one of the methods of treating it as a wrong is to *make provision that it shall grow no larger.* They also desire a policy that looks to a peaceful end of slavery at some time, as being wrong. These are the views they entertain in regard to it as I understand them; and all their sentiments, all their arguments and propositions, are brought within this range.

It is clear from Lincoln's remarks here that he addressed the matter of slavery almost in a Socratic vein, seeking not so much to tell his countrymen what he thought they should do *vis-á-vis* slavery as encouraging them to see for themselves what they should do. Moreover, in rereading the debates, one can see the conversion in which Lincoln was engaged in trying to grasp slavery's full gravity. Douglas, by contrast, sought to paint his opponent as an opportunist, who only interjected himself in the matter to win votes, a jibe which Lincoln parried in his best oratorical vein. "Is it true that all the difficulty and agitation we have in regard to this institution of slavery springs from office-seeking, from the mere ambition of politicians?" he asked.

> Is that the truth? How many times have we had danger from this question? Go back to the day of the Missouri Compromise. Go back to the Nullification question, at the bottom of which lay this same slavery question. Go back to the time of the Annexation of Texas. Go back to the troubles that led to the Compromise of 1850. You will

find that every time, with the single exception of the Nullification question, they sprung from an endeavor to spread this institution. There never was a party in the history of this country, and there probably never will be, of sufficient strength to disturb the general peace of the country. Parties themselves may be divided and quarrel on minor questions, yet it extends not beyond the parties themselves. But does not this question make a disturbance outside of political circles?

For Lincoln, the question that needed to be asked was this: if the continuing agitation over slavery could not be attributed to grasping office seekers or party platforms, what could account for it? And here, again, one can see the moral teacher in him, urging his countrymen to ask the questions necessary for them to understand the root of the country's profound division.

> Has anything ever threatened the existence of this Union save and except this very institution of slavery? What is it that we hold most dear amongst us? Our own liberty and prosperity. What has ever threatened our liberty and prosperity, save and except this institution of slavery? If this is true, how do you propose to improve the condition of things by enlarging slavery,—by spreading it out and making it bigger? You may have a wen or cancer upon your person, and not be able to cut it out, lest you bleed to death; but surely it is no way to cure it, to engraft it and spread it over your whole body. That is no proper way of treating what you regard a wrong. You see this peaceful way of dealing with it as a wrong,—restricting the spread of it, and not allowing it to go into new countries where it has not already existed. That is the peaceful way, the old-fashioned way, the way in which the fathers themselves set us the example.

Here, it is evident that the constitutionalist and the moralist in Lincoln were not at odds. In seeking to avoid civil war over the slavery issue, the constitutionalist could serve the moralist by giving the country the wherewithal she needed to resolve her differences without bloodshed.

Still, in these passages, Lincoln was primarily speaking to those who regarded slavery as wrong. What of those who regarded it as *not* wrong? "That is the Democratic sentiment of this day," the opponent of the Democratic Douglas pointed out. Here, Lincoln debated to educate, not merely to refute his opponents. Why? He recognized that not all of them regarded slavery as right. He suspected that if some truly believed that slavery was right, many more would do anything rather than commit themselves openly to so indefensible a position. And in this ambivalence, he saw an opening—as must we when speaking with those ambivalent about abortion.

Another striking thing about Lincoln's animadversions about the wrongness of slavery is how almost incantatory they are. Although usually an economical speaker—his "Gettysburg Address," after all, is a model of succinctness—here he was intent on arresting his auditors in order to make them see how unreal their response to slavery was—an unreality which similarly suffuses our response to abortion.

> If there be among you anybody who supposes that he, as a Democrat, can consider himself "as much opposed to slavery as anybody," I would like to reason with him. You never treat it as a wrong. What other thing that you consider as a wrong do you deal with as you deal with that? Perhaps you say it is wrong, *but your leader never does, and you quarrel with anybody who says it is wrong.* Although you pretend to say so yourself you can find no fit place to deal with it as a wrong. You must not say anything about it in the Free States, *because it is not here.* You must not say anything about it in the Slave States, *because it is there.* You must not say anything about it in the pulpit, because that is religion, and has nothing to do with it. You must not say anything about it in politics, *because that will disturb the security of "my place."* There is no place to talk about it as being a wrong, although you say yourself it is a wrong. But, finally, you will screw yourself up to the belief that if the people of the Slave States should adopt a system of gradual emancipation on the slavery question, you would be in favor of it. You would be in favor of it. You say that is getting it in the right place, and you would be glad to see it succeed. But you are deceiving yourself. You all know that [politicians from St. Louis] … undertook to introduce that system in Missouri. They fought as valiantly as they could for the system of gradual emancipation which you pretend you would be glad to see succeed. Now, I will bring you to the test. After a hard fight they were beaten, and when the news came over here, you threw up your hats and *hurrahed for Democracy.*

Here, one might say, Lincoln was intent on exposing the hypocrisy of those who claimed that they wished a gradual end to slavery but shed no tears over gradualism's failure. Yet he had another object as well. "Take all the argument made in favor of the system you have proposed, and it carefully excludes the idea that there is anything wrong in the institution of slavery." Again, Lincoln was at pains to urge his compatriots not to dodge the moral question of slavery. If Douglas and the Democratic Party sought to remain neutral on the question of the morality of slavery—knowing that such neutrality could best serve their contention that popular sovereignty, not morality, was at issue in the extension of slavery– Lincoln was determined to expose the untenability of such neutrality in light of the intrinsic evil of slavery.

> The Democratic policy in regard to that institution will not tolerate the merest breath, the slightest hint, of the least degree of wrong about it … You may turn over everything in the Democratic policy from beginning to end, whether in the shape it takes on the statute

book, in the shape it takes in the Dred Scott decision, in the shape it takes in conversation, or the shape it takes in short maxim-like arguments,—it everywhere carefully excludes the idea that there is any thing wrong in it. That is the real issue. That is the issue that will continue in this country when these poor tongues of Judge Douglas and myself shall be silent. It is the eternal struggle between these two principles—right and wrong—throughout the world. They are the two principles that have stood face to face from the beginning of time, and will ever continue to struggle.

To appreciate the quality of Lincoln's moral leadership, one has to compare it to Judge Douglas's flippant bigotry. At one point, he even anticipated where Lincoln's own views on slavery were tending when he charged that his opponent was no different from those who "really think that under the Declaration of Independence the negro is equal to the white man, and that negro equality is an inalienable right conferred by the Almighty, and hence that all human laws in violation of it are null and void. With such men it is no use for me to argue. I hold that the signers of the Declaration of Independence had no reference to negroes at all when they declared all men to be created equal. They did not mean negro, nor the savage Indians, nor the Feejee Islanders, nor any other barbarous race. They were speaking of white men." In other words, white men, intent on the exercise of their popular sovereignty could do as they pleased with slaves, just as women in our own society, intent on the exercise of what they fancy their "reproductive rights," can do as they please with children in the womb.

In his brilliant, groundbreaking book, *Slavery, Abortion and the Politics of Constitutional Meaning* (2013), Justin Buckley Dyer puts these supple confusions in useful perspective. "Public policy can no more remain neutral with respect to the morality of abortion than it can with respect to the morality of slavery," Dyer writes, in passage in which he also cites Roy P. Basler, the editor of Lincoln's *Collected Works* (1953).

> As Lincoln insisted in response to Douglas, the contention that "whoever wants slaves" has "a right to have them" is "perfectly logical if there is nothing wrong in the institution; but if you admit that it is wrong, he cannot logically say anybody has a right to do wrong." Like slavery, the right to abortion is perfectly logical if the object of the act is not a human being or if human beings at some early stage of development are not moral persons. Yet the feigned neutrality of liberal public reason prevents engagement with such questions and screens from view the essential continuity of the pro-life argument, stretching from the nineteenth century to today.

That Lincoln was the pioneering figure in this "essential continuity" is clear from his correspondence. In a letter to one of his close friends, for instance, Joshua Speed, the son of a wealthy Kentucky slave owning family, who was opposed to slavery but unwilling to support the limitation of slave owning, Lincoln spoke with the sort of truthful bluntness that was as strikingly rare in his society as it is in ours.

> The slave-breeders and slave-traders, are a small, odious and detested class, among you; and yet in politics, they dictate the course of all of you, and are as completely your masters, as you are the master of your own negroes. You inquire where I now stand. That is a disputed point—I think I am a whig; but others say there are no whigs, and that I am an abolitionist. When I was in Washington I voted for the Wilmot Proviso as good as forty times, and I never heard of any one attempting to unwhig me for that. I now do no more than oppose the *extension* of slavery.

If there was formidable moral accountability in Lincoln, there was nothing of moral grandstanding. Nor any dearth of biting satirical wit. "I am not a Know-Nothing," he told his equivocating friend.

> That is certain. How could I be? How can any one who abhors the oppression of negroes, be in favor or degrading classes of white people? Our progress in degeneracy appears to me to be pretty rapid. As a nation, we began by declaring that *"all men are created equal."* We now practically read it "all men are created equal, *except negroes"* When the Know-Nothings get control, it will read "all men are created equal, except negroes, and *foreigners, and Catholics."* When it comes to this I should prefer emigrating to some country where they make no pretence of loving liberty—to Russia, for instance, where despotism can be taken pure, and without the base alloy of hypocrisy.

Yet, if one wishes to understand what really animated Lincoln's fight to end slavery, while preserving the Union, there is another passage in his letter to Speed that merits quoting.

> You know what a poor correspondent I am. Ever since I received your very agreeable letter of the 22nd of May I have been intending to write you in answer to it. You suggest that in political action now, you and I would differ. I suppose we would; not quite as much, however, as you may think. You know I dislike slavery; and you fully admit the abstract wrong of it. So far there is no cause of difference. But you say that sooner than yield your legal right to the slave—especially at the bidding of those who are not themselves interested, you would see the Union dissolved. I am not aware that *any one* is bidding you to yield that right; very certainly *I* am not. I leave that matter entirely to yourself. I also acknowledge *your* rights and *my* obligations, under the constitution, in regard to your slaves. I confess I hate to see the poor creatures hunted down, and caught, and carried back to their stripes, and unrewarded toils; but I bite

my lip and keep quiet. In 1841 you and I had together a tedious low-water trip, on a Steam Boat from Louisville to St. Louis. You may remember, as I well do, that from Louisville to the mouth of the Ohio, there were, on board, ten or a dozen slaves, shackled together with irons. That sight was a continued torment to me; and I see something like it every time I touch the Ohio, or any other slave-border. It is hardly fair for you to assume, that I have no interest in a thing which has, and continually exercises, the power of making me miserable. You ought rather to appreciate how much the great body of the Northern people do crucify their feelings, in order to maintain their loyalty to the Constitution and the Union.

After reading this, one can see that Lincoln entirely earned his right to school his countrymen in the moral enormity of slavery, to insist that they not excuse themselves from acting responsibly and justly in response to a wrong that could not be ignored. Indeed, if there was one defining aspect of Lincoln's leadership with regard to slavery it was his ability to grow in his understanding of why it needed to be outlawed altogether, even though this growth was a relatively slow growth. It was also an unexpected growth. As Lincoln wrote in his Second Inaugural Speech (1865):

> Neither party expected for the war, the magnitude, or the duration, which it has already attained. Neither anticipated that the cause of the conflict might cease before the conflict itself should cease. Each looked for an easier triumph, and a result less fundamental and astounding.

Of course, here, Lincoln was referring to his *Emancipation Proclamation* (1863) in which he freed the slaves two years before hostilities ended. But he might also have been referring to his own "astounding" moral development. As the literary critic Edmund Wilson pointed out in his fascinating study of the literature of the Civil War, *Patriotic Gore* (1931), if there was no evidence that Lincoln "saw the approaching crisis as an apocalyptic judgment or the possible war as a holy crusade," the ordeal of war transformed him, so much so that "he came to see the conflict in a light more and more religious, in more and more Scriptural terms, under a more and more apocalyptic aspect." Frederick Douglass, one of Lincoln's most caustic critics throughout the war, even saw in the president's speech "a sacred effort." Lincoln, in his typically laconic way, had put the toll of slavery in penitential perspective. That the carnage of the civil war was retribution for the sin of slavery might have been a commonplace among Northern preachers but no one gave the theme anything like the rhetorical force that Lincoln gave it.

> "Woe unto the world because of offenses; for it must needs be that offenses come, but woe to that man by whom the offense cometh."

If we shall suppose that American slavery is one of those offenses which, in the providence of God, must needs come, but which, having continued through His appointed time, He now wills to remove, and that He gives to both North and South this terrible war as the woe due to those by whom the offense came, shall we discern therein any departure from those divine attributes which the believers in a living God always ascribe to Him? Fondly do we hope, fervently do we pray, that this mighty scourge of war may speedily pass away. Yet, if God wills that it continue until all the wealth piled by the bondsman's two hundred and fifty years of unrequited toil shall be sunk, and until every drop of blood drawn with the lash shall be paid by another drawn with the sword, as was said three thousand years ago, so still it must be said "the judgments of the Lord are true and righteous altogether."

Apropos this passage, the historian Eric Foner makes an important point in his superb study, *The Fiery Trial: Abraham Lincoln and American Slavery* (2010):

Lincoln was reminding the country that the "terrible" violence of the Civil War had been preceded by two and a half centuries of the terrible violence of slavery. Yet Lincoln called it "American slavery," not southern slavery, his point being that the nation as a whole was guilty of this sin.

Of course, this is a useful distinction to bear in mind with respect to legalized abortion, because, like slavery, it is not a sin that can be ascribed to any limited group of Americans, not even to those most vociferous in its defense: after forty-five years, the whole country must take responsibility for the murderous devastation it has wrought, those in the Republican camp who deplore it as much as those in the Democratic camp who wish to perpetuate it.

IV

Like those in Lincoln's generation, we find ourselves in twenty-first-century America confronted by a moral abomination that cries out for redress. We can no longer treat the iniquity of abortion as though it is something that we can somehow evade or elude. If the half-measure of outlawing the extension of slavery did not resolve the evil of slavery, neither will the half-measure of *stare decisis* resolve the evil of abortion. Casey, as we all know, was an unfortunate exercise in flapdoodle and evasion. If we persist down that road, we shall only have succeeded in failing the test that God has appointed us. Certainly, letting Roe v. Wade stand in deference to the principle of *stare decisis* will not move us any closer to acknowledging the wrong that has resulted in the murder of over 60 million children, or enable us to begin to redress that wrong. Lincoln's generation had the moral clarity and the courage to outlaw the indefensible scourge of slavery. Will we have the same to outlaw the indefensible scourge of abortion?

Postscript

Stare decisis, *the doctrine on which Casey's controlling opinion was based, does not compel unending adherence to Roe's abuse of judicial authority.*

Justice Joseph Alito, Ruling of Supreme Court in Dobbs v. Jackson

On 24 June 2022, nearly three years after I had written the essay above, Justice Joseph Alito wrote in the ruling overturning Roe v. Wade in Dobbs v. Jackson: "The critical question is whether the Constitution, properly understood, confers a right to obtain an abortion. Casey's controlling opinion skipped over that question and reaffirmed Roe solely on the basis of *stare decisis*. A proper application of *stare decisis*, however, requires an assessment of the strength of the grounds on which Roe was based. The Court therefore turns to the question that the Casey plurality did not consider." And in relentlessly logical terms, step by step, Alito demolished what had been the defense of Roe v. Wade on the grounds that it was a precedent worth upholding. "The doctrine of *stare decisis* does not counsel continued acceptance of Roe and Casey," Alito wrote.

> *Stare decisis* plays an important role and protects the interests of those who have taken action in reliance on a past decision. It "reduces incentives for challenging settled precedents, saving parties and courts the expense of endless relitigation." Kimble v. Marvel Entertainment, LLC, 576 U. S. 446, 455. It "contributes to the actual and perceived integrity of the judicial process." Payne v. Tennessee, 501 U. S. 808, 827. And it restrains judicial hubris by respecting the judgment of those who grappled with important questions in the past. But *stare decisis* is not an inexorable command, Pearson v. Callahan, 555 U. S. 223, 233, and "is at its weakest when [the Court] interpret[s] the Constitution," Agostini v. Felton, 521 U. S. 203, 235. Some of the Court's most important constitutional decisions have overruled prior precedents. See, e.g., Brown v. Board of Education, 347 U. S. 483, 491 (overruling the infamous decision in Plessy v. Ferguson, 163 U. S. 537, and its progeny). The Court's cases have identified factors that should be considered in deciding when a precedent should be overruled. Janus v. State, County, and Municipal Employees, 585 U. S. ___, ___–___. Five factors Cite as: 597 U. S. ____ (2022) 5 Syllabus discussed below weigh strongly in favor of overruling Roe and Casey. Pp. 39–66. (1) The nature of the Court's error. Like the infamous decision in Plessy v. Ferguson,

Roe was also egregiously wrong and on a collision course with the Constitution from the day it was decided. Casey perpetuated its errors, calling both sides of the national controversy to resolve their debate, but in doing so, Casey necessarily declared a winning side. Those on the losing side—those who sought to advance the State's interest in fetal life—could no longer seek to persuade their elected representatives to adopt policies consistent with their views. The Court short-circuited the democratic process by closing it to the large number of Americans who disagreed with Roe. Pp. 43–45. (2) The quality of the reasoning. Without any grounding in the constitutional text, history, or precedent, Roe imposed on the entire country a detailed set of rules for pregnancy divided into trimesters much like those that one might expect to find in a statute or regulation. See 410 U. S., at 163–164. Roe's failure even to note the overwhelming consensus of state laws in effect in 1868 is striking, and what it said about the common law was simply wrong. Then, after surveying history, the opinion spent many paragraphs conducting the sort of factfinding that might be undertaken by a legislative committee, and did not explain why the sources on which it relied shed light on the meaning of the Constitution. As to precedent, citing a broad array of cases, the Court found support for a constitutional "right of personal privacy." Id., at 152. But Roe conflated the right to shield information from disclosure and the right to make and implement important personal decisions without governmental interference. See Whalen v. Roe, 429 U. S. 589, 599–600. None of these decisions involved what is distinctive about abortion: its effect on what Roe termed "potential life." When the Court summarized the basis for the scheme it imposed on the country, it asserted that its rules were "consistent with," among other things, "the relative weights of the respective interests involved" and "the demands of the profound problems of the present day." Roe, 410 U. S., at 165. These are precisely the sort of considerations that legislative bodies often take into account when they draw lines that accommodate competing interests. The scheme Roe produced looked like legislation, and the Court provided the sort of explanation that might be expected from a legislative body. An even more glaring deficiency was Roe's failure to justify the critical distinction it drew between pre- and post-viability abortions. See id., at 163. The arbitrary viability line, which Casey termed Roe's central rule, has not found much support among philosophers and ethicists who have attempted to justify a right to abortion. The most obvious problem with any such argument is that viability has changed over time and is heavily dependent on factors—such as medical advances and the availability of quality medical care—that have nothing to do with the characteristics of a fetus. When Casey revisited Roe almost 20 years later, it reaffirmed Roe's central holding, but pointedly refrained from endorsing most of its reasoning. The Court abandoned any reliance on a privacy right and instead grounded the abortion right entirely on the Fourteenth Amendment's Due Process Clause. 505 U. S., at 846. The controlling opinion criticized and rejected Roe's trimester scheme, 505 U. S., at 872, and substituted a new and obscure "undue burden" test. Casey, in short, either refused to reaffirm or rejected important aspects of Roe's analysis, failed to remedy glaring deficiencies in Roe's reasoning, endorsed what it termed Roe's central holding while suggesting that a majority might not have thought it was correct, provided no new support for the abortion right other than Roe's status as precedent, and imposed a new test with no firm grounding in constitutional text, history, or precedent. Pp. 45–56.

Moreover, Alito rejected Casey's contention that overturning Roe v. Wade would be unacceptably disruptive.

Casey identified another concern, namely, the danger that the public will perceive a decision overruling a controversial "watershed" decision, such as Roe, as influenced by political considerations or public opinion. 505 U. S., at 866–867. But the Court cannot allow its decisions to be affected by such extraneous concerns. A precedent of this Court is subject to the usual principles of *stare decisis* under which adherence to precedent is the norm but not an inexorable command. If the rule were otherwise, erroneous decisions like Plessy would still be the law. The Court's job is to interpret the law, apply longstanding principles of *stare decisis*, and decide this case accordingly. Pp. 66–69.

"*Stare decisis* is not an inexorable command," Justice Alito has wisely reminded not only America but the world. Erroneous past rulings can and should be overturned. There is no right to abortion in the US Constitution. If Americans living in individual states wish to legalize the killing of unborn children in the womb, they can seek to elect representatives to their state legislatures who agree with them: they cannot expect the Supreme Court to impose abortion on the states based on a suppositious right in the Constitution that does not exist.

Anne Lastman's Redeeming Grief

And now why tarriest thou? arise, and be baptized, and wash away thy sins, calling on the name of the Lord.

Acts 22:116

Grief Redeemed: Abortion and Its Pain, Anne Lastman (Gracewing). 258 pages.

Many good things distinguish *Grief Redeemed,* Anne's Lastman's gripping testament to the dehumanizing havoc wrought by abortion. It is the work of a woman who has devoted over seventeen years of her life to helping thousands of fathers and mothers heal from the wounds of abortion. It is an unsparing analysis of the way abortion destroys not only unborn children but the very fabric of the family. And it is the fruit of conversion: Dr. Lastman has come to her courageous testament after two abortions of her own, which she was only able to survive, as she says, because of "the mercy of God" and her own "profound rediscovered love for him."

That contrition should be the foundation of so much of Dr. Lastman's testimony puts her in lively company. One thinks of the great English defender of life, Aleck Bourne (1886–1974), who, despite initially agitating for the legalization of abortion, went on to found the Society for the Protection of the Unborn Child. One also thinks of Dr. Bernard Nathanson (1926–2011), an abortion doctor for many years in New York, as well as an architect of the American pro-abortion lobby, who became one of the most ardent and heroic of pro-lifers.

In addition to these splendid pro-life converts, Mrs. Lastman's career evokes that of an even more illustrious figure. "You can depend on this as worthy of full acceptance," St Paul told St Timothy, "Christ came into the world to save sinners. Of these I myself am the worst. But on that very account I was dealt with mercifully, so that in me, as an extreme case, Jesus Christ might display all his patience, and that I might become an example to those who would later have faith in him and gain everlasting life."

In her impassioned appeal to those unaware or heedless of the real enormity of abortion, and in her solicitude for those beguiled into conniving in the killing of their own unborn children, many of whose stories are

211

woven into the text of *Grief Redeemed*, Dr. Lastman exhibits an altogether compelling, Pauline authority. In this respect, she calls to mind another convert, John Newton (1725–1807), the former slave driver turned abolitionist and hymnologist, who, in repudiating the slave trade, came to personify amazing grace.

Another differentiating virtue of Dr. Lastman's approach is that she recognizes that the essence of abortion is a failure to embrace the God-given gift of life. That life is indeed God's gift is crucial to her case. As she writes early in the book, "for every one of the abortive women whom I have counseled there has been a history in which the Word of God has been totally absent." Consequently, these women often kill their babies out of genuine ignorance of the sanctity of life.

Yet they are not the only ones who fail to grasp the source of life's sanctity. Many pro-lifers preen themselves on making the case for life without making reference to the Lord of Life, as though the all-important relation between the Creator and His creatures had nothing to do with the inviolability of life. Many lose sight of the fact that the guilt suffered by those who betray that inviolability is the voice of conscience, the voice of the Holy Spirit calling the sinner back to the Father of Mercies. Many remain convinced that natural law arguments alone can sway a public opinion ignorant of the God who not only animates but created the moral law. By boldly making God and His love the centerpiece of her study, Dr. Lastman reminds her readers that it is only by understanding and receiving the Love of God that we can understand and protect human love.

Her theological approach also takes into account the full scale of abortion's evil, something from which many pro-lifers shy away. Indeed, it is striking how few reviewers have accurately described *Grief Redeemed*. Far from being a "non-judgmental" therapist's diary, as some have suggested, it is a searing indictment of the satanic viciousness at the core of abortion. Above all else, Dr. Lastman is a truth teller and when she defines her terms she does not shuffle.

> Abortion is ultimately not about rights ... It is about hatred, especially spiritual hatred. It is about the hatred Lucifer bears for God and his creation. It is about the cursing of the seed and the crushing of the head. It is about robbing God of children destined for his Kingdom. It is about wickedness wanting tenants for his own accursed kingdom. It is about violence and degradation. It is about dehumanization and death. It is about the mechanization and finally the death of societal conscience possibly leading to the death of society itself.

If *Grief Redeemed* is full of compassion for those who regret allowing themselves to become agents of this "violence and degradation," it is never "non-judgmental" compassion, which, she recognizes, would trivialize the grief of those who deplore what they have done in killing their own children. As such, her approach reveals the debt Dr. Lastman owes to the most perceptive of all pro-lifers, Pope John Paul, II, whose *Evangelium Vitae* remains the single best book ever written on the topic.

Still another virtue of the book is that it does not avoid addressing aspects of the culture of death that pro-lifers often sidestep. For Dr. Lastman, the tragic rejection of Pope Paul VI's condemnation of contraception, so prophetically set out in *Humanae Vitae*, lay the groundwork not only of legalized abortion but of all of the moral and spiritual disorders that have come to characterize the pro-abortion ethos. She writes:

> *Humanae Vitae* was the document which came out against the social engineers. It attempted to sound the warning bells about possible future disasters. Very sadly it was a document not embraced either by the Catholic world or society in general. Hence the rampant spread of unbridled sexuality, unholy sexuality, contraception on an unimaginable scale, abortions in unprecedented numbers, overt demands for homosexual acceptance as a "normal" lifestyle leading to demands for same-sex marriage, and the slow and insidious disintegration of the family.

That contraception, sodomy and abortion are sins is something one rarely hears from even Catholic pro-lifers. As we all know, in a social order where deploring such sins opens one up to charges of bigotry, silence rules, a silence replete with collusion. It is also a silence which consigns young men and women suffering from post-abortion grief to a solitary, despondent grief, which gives rise to the nihilism and self-destructiveness that now characterize so much of our youth. In taking stock of this "disenfranchised grief," as she calls it, which has become ubiquitous in the wake of Roe v. Wade, Dr. Lastman asks a number of very pointed questions.

> Are the drugs, promiscuity, recklessness their cry to be loved, welcomed, valued, nurtured, guided and directed? Are the dangerous paths embarked upon a rebellion against their perceived lack of value? Are the young consciously atoning for the unjust deaths of millions of their siblings?

Throughout the book, Dr. Lastman makes clear that unless we acknowledge the intrinsic sinfulness of abortion and the other interconnected evils to which it gives rise there can be no hope of our coherently combating the culture of death.

> Often it has been said to me during counseling sessions: "Now I understand what sin is and what sin does." Until this time the sense of sin had not been an issue. "Sin" was what religious fanatics spoke about ... As I listen to these and other similar words I am filled with hope, as I see that the spirit's travail for this loss can be

the energizer for future hope. I can really see that sometimes God allows what appears to be an abhorrent evil to happen in order to achieve a greater overall good.

In encouraging those suffering from post-abortion grief to see for themselves the sinfulness of abortion, Dr. Lastman shows true solicitude for the surviving victims of abortion, not the false solicitude of those who give out that by glossing over this sinfulness they are somehow doing the sinner a favor. Penance, after all, enables the sinner to come to terms with his post-abortion grief and reconciles him to God; impenitence aggravates his grief and estranges him from God.

Then, again, Dr. Lastman shows how an impenitent citizenry attempts to defy its guilt by authorizing the State to have the final say in matters of birth, family, and death, a satanic compact which has set off a tourbillion of deviance.

> A nation which legally mandates that its future citizens may be murdered, has also covenanted itself with death because it has attempted to wrest sovereignty over life and death from God, and placed it in the hands of Caesar … Having done this, it cannot then hope to justly govern its people. Those who have forced the legalisation of abortion cannot then rest because what has been enacted must be protected, and so further abominations must be deemed necessary in order to justify the original act. Thus late term abortions, infanticide, patricide, matricide, euthanasia, same-sex addictions, demands for deconstruction of marriage and demands for same-sex marriage must follow. Beginning with the killing of weakest infants slowly the moral order must collapse.

Particularly odious proof of the collapse of the moral order in England came recently when the Director of Public Prosecutions released a statement on the Crown Prosecution Service's failure to prosecute two doctors exposed by the Daily Telegraph for carrying out abortions based on gender. In his statement, the Director, Keir Starmer said that "there may be circumstances, in which termination of pregnancy on grounds of fetal sex would be lawful." Unconscionable bureaucrats like Starmer may never regret condemning babies to the abattoir, but for those capable of contrition Dr. Lastman has a vital message:

> Human beings were not designed to abort children. They were designed to fulfill a desire to give birth; therefore, the damage which abortion does cannot be repaired by psychological or psychiatric measures (although these measures can help) but by God Himself. Only He can repair the damage to the sacred sanctuary where He encounters the creature of His desire. The healing of abortion grief comes when there is an encounter between the sinner and God.

When this reconciliation is facilitated then solidarity with God and neighbor (including the aborted infant) is reestablished and reintegration into the human and heavenly family is achieved.

The alternative to acknowledging and repenting of the sin of abortion, as Dr. Lastman shows, is set out by the author of *Evangelium Vitae* with great cautionary dispatch: "If it becomes licit to take a human life when it is weakest, wholly dependent on its mother, on its parents, on the strength of human consciences, then what dies is not only an innocent human being but also human conscience itself. And who knows how widely and quickly the cancer of this destruction of conscience will spread." At any rate, Lastman is surely right when she says that at the root of the culture of death is "a death of desire to know our creator God," a death for which our absentee Catholic episcopacy must bear grave responsibility.

Having shared with her readers the fundamental threat that abortion poses to the very survival of our civilized humanity, as well as the lives of unborn children, Dr. Lastman insists that it is precisely in our war with the pro-abortion establishment that our most valiant pro-lifers will emerge.

> Perhaps the greatest and strongest warriors against the enemy of life, abortion, and against abortion providers, will be those individuals who have submitted themselves to the procedure and allowed their baby to be destroyed. Men and women who have experienced an abortion and who know the pain, loss, loneliness, regret, guilt, shame, will slowly surface. With a loud voice they will condemn governments, abortionists, societies and individuals who have lied to them, when told their baby was not a baby and there would be no after effects.

This rousingly hopeful passage will give readers some sense of why *Grief Redeemed* is such a special book and why Anne Lastman is a pro-lifer to celebrate and applaud.

No Summer Progress:
T. S. Eliot and Reviving
Christian Culture

I think that the disintegration of the Imagination is manifest by the separation between those people who cultivate the arts (both as producers and as consumers) and those who cultivate the religious sensibility. The tendency is then for the religious sensibility to be stunted, and for the arts to perish slowly—as the religious imagination atrophies, the imagination tout court disappears also. The arts, in their decline, pass through the stage of sensationalism; theology and philosophy which cease to be nourished by the imagination descend into verbalism.

T. S. Eliot, "Revival of Christian Imagination" (1941)

It has been over sixty years since T. S. Eliot died in 1965, and looking back over that period we can see that the decadence he predicted would overtake the West if it chose to abandon its Christian culture has duly arrived. The only thing about our decadence that might have surprised Eliot is the celerity with which it has come—and its thoroughgoingness. If we look at our social, political, cultural and religious order, we can see how a kind of metastasizing decadence characterizes all of them. By "decadence" I mean what the *Oxford English Dictionary* means: "The process of falling away or declining (from a prior state of excellence, vitality, prosperity, etc.); decay; impaired or deteriorated condition." Robert Louis Stevenson once said that "The obscurest epoch is today," but no amount of obscurity can conceal the fact that if the Christian civilization that Eliot knew was in decline, the one that we know is incommensurably worse. In this essay I shall look at the eight volumes of *The Complete Prose* to show how Eliot responded to the threat of this decadence by returning again and again to the question not only of what constitutes Christian culture but how best to understand, revitalize and prosper it. I shall also look at how the poet's reaction to the pivotal Lambeth Conference of 1930—when the Anglican bishops gave their approval to conception—mars his otherwise shrewd

217

and still instructive anatomy of the crisis of Western Civilization in the twentieth century.

At the heart of the volumes of his collected prose is Eliot's respect for what Cardinal Newman once called "the sovereignty of Truth." Eliot, after all, was insistent that the universities of Europe "should not be institutions for the training of an efficient bureaucracy, or for equipping scientists to get the better of foreign scientists; they should stand for the preservation of learning, for the pursuit of truth, and, in so far as men are capable of it, the attainment of wisdom." In editing his robustly cosmopolitan review, *The Criterion*, from 1922 to 1939, Eliot would work assiduously to give expression to these vital objects, convinced as he was that working to defend European civilization was a consequential enterprise. Since these essays were written at a time when the preoccupation with the Neo-Gothic (first inspired by the novels of Sir Walter Scott in the late 1820s) had not entirely run its course and some Christians still looked to an idealized mediaevalism to renew the Church, it was natural that Eliot should wish to differentiate his own idea of civilization from such a fanciful, antiquarian medievalism. Indeed, in one of his letters, he referred approvingly to something Eric Gill wrote in *Money & Morals* (1934): "We are not a survival of mediaevalism. The mediaeval supremacy of the Church has not survived. We are back in the catacombs—whether we like it or not." Eliot himself was not so much concerned with the proper Christians in the catacombs as with the civilized Christians in places of influence who had done little more than swell the general irreligiousness.

> We are in many ways in a position of advantage over our mediaeval ancestors: we are more humane, cleaner and have better table manners; we may be less saintly than some, but we are less beastly than others; we have material comforts, hygiene, machinery and invention, which we do not wish to dispense with but to manipulate wisely. The forms of social organization in Christian states in the Middle Ages provide much from which we may learn, but little that we can exactly reproduce. We are more civilised than our ancestors, though we ought to be a great deal more civilised than we are, and they have perhaps more reason to be proud of what they did with their talent than we have. Because, instead of preserving affirming and refining their spiritual organisation of society we have progressively secularised it until our values are at war with each other and with life itself.

Nowhere else could one see how civilized man was "at war ... with life itself" more clearly than in Resolution 15 of the Lambeth Conference (1830), which stated:

> Where there is clearly felt moral obligation to limit or avoid parenthood, the method must be decided on Christian principles.

The primary and obvious method is complete abstinence from intercourse (as far as may be necessary) in a life of discipline and self-control lived in the power of the Holy Spirit. Nevertheless, in those cases where there is such a clearly felt moral obligation to limit or avoid parenthood, and where there is a morally sound reason for avoiding complete abstinence, the Conference agrees that other methods may be used, provided that this is done in the light of the same Christian principles. The Conference records its strong condemnation of the use of any methods of conception control from motives of selfishness, luxury, or mere convenience.

Voting: For 193; Against 67.

Of course, Eliot would not live to see how contraception paved the way for the scourge of abortion, with all its dire demographic consequences, let alone its inherent iniquity. Yet he should have seen how his agreement with the Lambeth Conference with regard to contraception put him on the wrong side of the immemorial Christian respect for the inviolability of life. The Anglican bishops, after all, were not only refusing to uphold the unitive and procreative integrity of the marital act but siding with the pitiably deluded birth-control advocate Marie Stopes. Chesterton certainly did not fail to see the point of the resolution. "The excitement of conversion is still open to the atheist and the diabolist," he wrote in *The Well and the Shallows* (1935),

> and everybody can be converted except the convert. In my first outline, I mentioned that one of the crises, which would in any case have driven me the way I had gone already, was the shilly-shal-lying and sham liberality of the famous Lambeth Report on what is quaintly called Birth Control. It is in fact, of course, a scheme for preventing birth in order to escape control. But this particular case was only the culmination of a long process of compromise and cowardice about the problem of sex; the final surrender after a continuous retreat.

Eliot was never a man incapable of remorse, but he seems to have gone to his grave oblivious to how ill-advised he was when he gave out in "Thoughts after Lambeth" (1930) that "The recognition of contraception is, I feel sure, something quite different from a concession to 'modern' opinion. It was a courageous facing of the facts of life." For so discriminating a man as Eliot, this was a surprisingly gross misjudgment, especially in light of the fact that it was not arrived at in haste. Indeed, he sent round a draft of his essay to friends and other counsellors, including William Temple, the Archbishop of York, before publishing it. If he had reservations about the conference, they were not about contraception. "I wonder if I am wrong in feeling (as a result of poring over Lambeth)," he wrote to one correspondent, "that the Anglican Church is a little too ready to approve practices which are worthy of approval and find the theological justifications afterwards ... I am thinking of that difficult matter of mixed communions." In siding with the Anglican bishops on contraception, Eliot was not facing "the facts of life," he was undermining what ought to be our respect and defense of life. The admirable Francis, Cardinal Bourne (1861–1935), who was Archbishop of Westminster at the time of the conference, certainly did not fail to see the tragic significance of the resolution. Fr Mark Vickers, in his brilliant life of Bourne, *By the Thames Divided: Cardinal Bourne in Southwark and Westminster* (2013), quotes the man whom he rightly sees as an early apostle of the pro-life movement—a man who was the absolute reverse of cowardly or shilly-shallying.

> I know the intense surprise and real scandal to the Christian mind which has been caused at home and abroad by this abandonment of unbroken traditional Christian teaching ... Lest, therefore, any be led astray by this resolution of the Lambeth Conference, and placed, thereby, in danger of committing grievous sin, I now reaffirm the teaching of the Catholic Church on this subject, binding on the conscience of every man and every woman. Any direct interference with the natural consequences of the marital relation, namely contraception, whether within the marriage state, or outside of it, is an unnatural vice, sinning against the nature, which the Creator has bestowed upon us, and, therefore, grievously displeasing in His sight.

II

Although the eight volumes of Eliot's recently published *Complete Prose* are full of superb uncollected literary pieces, there are many equally good uncollected pieces touching on philosophy. Apropos a lecture on conscience and Christianity, for *example*, given by a moral philosopher and fellow of New College, Oxford, Eliot writes:

> For Canon Rashdall, "the following of Christ is made easier by thinking of Him ... as the Being in whom that union of God and Man after which all ethical Religion aspires is most fully accomplished." Certain saints found the following of Christ very hard, but modern methods have facilitated everything. Yet I am not sure, after reading modern theology that the pale Galilean has conquered.

The nod to the poet Algernon Swinburne here is nicely glossed by the editors:

> An allusion to ... Swinburne's "Hymn to Proserpine," which represents a noble Roman pagan speaking to Christ after the Emperor Constantine in the Edict of Milan (313 AD) forbade the persecution

of Christians. The epigraph is "Vicisti, Galilæe" (Thou hast con-
quered, O Galilean), and the poem contains the couplet: "Thou
hast conquered, O pale Galilean; the world has grown grey from
thy breath; / We have drunken of things Lethean, and fed on the
fullness of death" (lines 35–6).

The editors might also have mentioned that Theodoret claimed that these
were the dying words of Julian the Apostate in his *Ecclesiastical History*
(*c.* AD 450), with which both Swinburne and Eliot were probably familiar.
Speaking of another Julian, Eliot would include Julian of Norwich's
profound reaffirmation of God's redemptive mercy in the last of his *Four
Quartets* (1944): "And all shall be well and / All manner of thing shall be
well." If Eliot had what Henry James called the "imagination of disaster,"
he was also a man of great Christian hope, as his last major poem so mov-
ingly attests.

In 1927, Eliot wrote the chaplain of Worcester College Oxford:

> What I want to see you about is this: I want your … practical assis-
> tance in getting Confirmation with the Anglican Church. I am sure
> you will be glad to help me. But meanwhile I rely upon you not to
> mention this to anyone. I do not want any publicity or notoriety—
> for the moment, it concerns me alone, & not the public—not even
> those nearest me. I hate spectacular "conversions." By the way, I
> was born & bred in the very heart of Boston Unitarianism.

Whenever Eliot takes up America's peculiar Socinianism, the detached,
ironical, Jamesian view that he took of his compatriots is always in evi-
dence, as here:

> When Emerson as a young man stood in his pulpit and made clear
> to his congregation that he could no longer administer the Com-
> munion, he impressed upon them that he had no prejudice and
> passed no judgment upon those who continued in the practice,
> but that he could take no part himself—because (in his own words)
> it did not interest him. That is an instance of the point of view of
> several thousands of well-bred people in a provincial American
> town; and, arrested at the point of ecclesiastical procedure, it is not
> without an austere grandeur.

This and other pieces show the deliberate eclecticism of Eliot's criticism.
In his Clark Lectures on the Metaphysical Poets, delivered at Cambridge
in 1926, he gave his readers a good idea of the sort of far-ranging criticism
that he was keen on producing. Speaking of "the dilemma which every
honest literary critic, now and in the future, will have to face," he described
how "you cannot treat literary criticism as a subject isolated from every
other subject of study; you must take account of general history, of philo-
sophy, theology, economics, psychology, into all of which literary criticism

merges." Yet, at the same time, "you cannot hope to embrace all of the various points of view implied by these various studies: for not only is such encyclopaedic knowledge impossible to any one man, but, even could you attain it, you would have lost the point of view of literary criticism in the process." The only solution, for the literary critic, was to know as much as he could about these other contiguous studies without straying too far from literature. And so he concluded that "You cannot know your frontiers unless you have some notion of what is beyond them. The only writer who has established a literary criticism which both sticks to the matter in hand and yet implies the other sciences, is of course Aristotle."

Nevertheless, Eliot, although knowledgeable enough himself, never had any interest in knowledge for the sake of knowledge. In "Choruses from *The Rock*" (1934), he made that abundantly plain in verses that anticipate our own digital culture of death.

> All our knowledge brings us nearer to death,
> But nearness to death no nearer to God.
> Where is the Life we have lost in living?
> Where is the wisdom we have lost in knowledge?
> Where is the knowledge we have lost in information?
> The cycles of Heaven in twenty centuries
> Brings us farther from God and nearer to the Dust.

III

Eliot was always amusingly dismissive of his reputation for learning. In a piece on English letter writers, he defended plundering the work of others to serve his own creative purposes, without pretending to an erudition he did not possess.

> I am an extremely ill-educated and ignorant man. I have been trying for some years, indeed, ever since I provided one of my poems with notes, to shatter the fiction that I was a man of vast erudition ... I have a great respect for educated men. I have certainly made use of the few scraps of learning that I possess, I see no reason why I should not use any quotation if it is apposite; but by quoting an author I do not delude myself into believing that I am perfectly acquainted with his works. Nor, until I woke up and found myself burdened by reviewers with the weight of learning which I disclaimed, did I suppose that any one else would believe it either. I am merely a smatterer in a few very narrow fields.

No one can read the notes to Eliot's complete prose, meticulously chron-icling as they do the staggering range of Eliot's reading, without sensing that, here, humility got the better of self-knowledge. Then, again, Eliot's essay on the seventeenth-century divine Lancelot Andrewes shows how brilliantly he mined what he read for his own work. In the essay, Eliot quotes Andrewes's description of the wise men journeying from the East: "It was no summer progress. A cold coming they had of it at this time of the year, just the worst time of the year to take a journey, and specially a long journey in. The ways deep, the weather sharp the days short, the son farther off, in *solstitio brumali*, 'the very dead of winter.'" From Andrewes's account, Eliot would fashion the opening of his "Journey of the Magi," which also includes lines suffused with the crisis of conversion.

> were we led all that way for
> Birth or Death? There was a birth, certainly,
> We had evidence and no doubt. I had seen birth and death,
> But had thought they were different; this Birth was
> Hard and bitter agony for us, like Death, our death.

Here, it is amusing to note in passing, that in 1960 Eliot addressed his fellow clubmen at the Athenaeum on the topic of American religion and noted about his own upbringing as a Unitarian:

> As is usual in American society, we had a house—what Americans call a "cottage"—at the seaside, in Massachusetts, to which we moved for the three summer months. In the fishing port a few miles away, of easy access, there was a Unitarian church: but I do not remember my parents ever attending Sunday service there. Even if they did once or twice, the fact remains that the summer holiday was for my family a holiday from church-going as well as from other serious occupations. This difference came to strike me as remarkable as I approached the age of serious reflection.

In "Virgil and the Christian World (1951), Eliot wrote: "A poet may believe that he is expressing only his private experience; his lines may be for him only a means of talking about himself without giving himself away; yet for his readers what he has written may come to be the expression of their own secret feelings and of the exultation or despair of a generation." Here, Eliot invests a great universal theme with deep, personal significance, which, nonetheless, reaffirms its universality. He can do this with regard to profound things like religious conversion—the only reasonable answer to despair—or he can do it, as he does in what follows, with regard to literary judgment. All men of judgment and taste revel in Sir Max Beerbohm but how nicely Eliot epitomizes our esteem in a contribution he made to a tribute presented to the Incomparable Max on his eightieth birthday, 24 August 1952:

> I am not among those who are entitled to refer to him as "Max." To me he is Sir Max Beerbohm, Hon. Fellow of Merton College, whom I once visited (though he will have forgotten it) at Rapallo, and

whom I once met (though he will not remember it) at a dinner-table in London. He is the defense and illustration of the benefits to a writer of the discipline of the classics; the illustrator, rather than the apologist, of urbanity and the qualities of English prose style now falling into neglect—armed as he is with the sword of wit and the buckler of humour. He once referred to himself as "a link with the past." It would be a sanguine hope for English letters, if we could regard him also as a link with the future.

One has the same "sanguine hope" about Eliot and our own future, though the rancor and crudity of the ideological academy makes it a rather sanguine hope.

IV

Essay after essay in Eliot's *Complete Prose* show how the poet critic's paramount concern was the indispensability of Europe's Christian culture. Unlike Matthew Arnold, he never imagined that the melancholy, long, withdrawing roar of Christianity in retreat was something that one should somehow take in stride. Like John Stuart Mill, he would always be convinced that "Bad men need nothing more to compass their ends, than that good men should look on and do nothing." Indeed, the same can be said for the Christian apostolates of Hilaire Belloc, G. K. Chesterton, Christopher Dawson, Jacques Maritain and Reginald Garrigou-Lagrange, none of whom were prepared to acquiesce in the secularism that has cut our own society adrift from its Christian bearings.

Even before converting to Christianity in 1927, Eliot's extensive reading had given him a respect for the culture of Christianity, which was certainly not typical of his age. "To be able to fill leisure intelligently," the positivist Bertrand Russell wrote in 1930, "is the last product of civilization." And it followed for Russell, as it would doubtless follow for many of his liberal successors today, that "Next to enjoying ourselves, the next greatest pleasure consists in preventing others from enjoying themselves, or, more generally, in the acquisition of power." Eliot would always be keenly appreciative of how this blithely nihilistic view of civilization as nothing more than a scramble for power might take hold in a society avid of hedonism and contemptuous of the Christian faith, hope and charity that had made European civilization possible in the first place. And, as a literary critic, with an incisive historical imagination, he knew that it was not simply the professional atheists like Nietzsche who exemplified this problem. If one of the reasons he had left America for Europe when he was a young man was to seek out, as Henry James before him had sought out, the well-springs of Western civilization, he could see that Americans abroad were no better at reclaiming these springs than Americans at home. Charles Eliot Norton

(1827–1902), the Harvard professor of art and social critic had told young Henry James in 1877 that "Christianity as a creed, & the ascetic morality based on the popular conception of the Christine doctrine have nearly run their course: their influence has become a thing of tradition, rather than an actual force exercising control over the conduct & character of man. And it must take a long time to establish a new morality which is to be the organizing power & animating spirit of the new society." In 1908, the year of Norton's death, Edith Wharton would show how deeply this view of matters had taken hold when she wrote a travelogue of a motor tour that she had made through France, in which, beholding the Cathedral of Amiens, she remarked how:

> The interiors of the great French cathedrals are as a rule somewhat gaunt and unfurnished, baring their structural nakedness sublimely but rather monotonously to eyes accustomed to the Italian churches "all glorious within." Here at Amiens, however, the inner decking of the shrine has been piously continued from generation to generation, and a quite extraordinary wealth of adornment bestowed on the choir and its ambulatory. The great sculptured and painted frieze encircling the outer side of the choir is especially surprising in a French church, so seldom were the stone histories lavished on the exterior continued within the building; and it is a farther surprise to find the same tales in bas-relief animating and enriching the west walls of the transepts. They are full of crowded expressive incidents, these stories of local saints and Scriptural personages; with a Burgundian richness and elaborateness of costume, and a quite charming, childish insistence on irrelevant episode and detail — the reiterated "And so," "And then" of the fairy-tale calling off one's attention into innumerable little by-paths, down which the fancy of fifteenth-century worshippers must have strayed, with oh! what blessedness of relief, from the unintelligible rites before the altar.

It is this religious philistinism, with its concomitant cultural philistinism, that Eliot wrote a good deal of his criticism to redress. As he remarks in one essay, "The problem of belief is very complicated and probably quite insoluble." Yet he was also convinced that it was at the heart of all questions of civilization. In a piece entitled "Christianity and Communism" (1932), Eliot gave a good example of what he meant by this conviction. "If you have any doubt that your problems and their solution must bring you to matters of religion, you have only to turn eastward — towards Russia," he wrote in a piece that illuminates striking parallels between the religion of communism and all other gimcrack faiths.

> I know very little about Russia; I do not know whether the experiment being made there will turn out to be, in the worldly sense, a failure or a success. If the system can he made to work, and if the

Russians can be adapted to it, or bred into the sort of being who can flourish under it, that is their affair. But I should not like it any the better for that: for Russian communism is a religion, and a religion which is not mine. Of course, other and better qualified critics—among them Mr. Maynard Keynes—remarked this fact before; and it is indeed patent enough; but the full implications do not seem to me to me to have yet come home to all. If you like the Russian religion, I cannot expect to make any impression upon you. But if you do not like it, then you must keep in mind that you can never fight a religion except with another religion.

If Eliot were alive to see how the elites of Europe and America, weary of the false promises of secular humanism, now put their faith in wokery to divert themselves from having to think of the horrors of jihadist Islam or expansionist Red China, he might have called their attention to truths that he pointed out in his prophetic essay on communism and Christianity, for they are as applicable to our contemporaries as they were to his. "If we are incapable of a faith at least as strong as that which appears to animate the ruling class of Russia," he wrote, "if we are incapable of dying for a cause, then Western Europe and the Americans might as well be reorganised on the Moscow model at once." Nor did he hold out any hope for there being any adequate political solution to the problem, since "you cannot hope to conquer merely with election cockades: merely with British Conservatism or British Liberalism or British Socialism. Nor will you succeed in inventing another brand new religion to compete with communism. There can only be the two, Christianity and communism: and there, if you like, is your dilemma."

At the same time, Eliot could speak with a certain authority to his skeptical contemporaries because, before converting, he had known something of their own skepticism himself. In the piece on communism and Christianity, Eliot nicely charted his escape from the prison house of unbelief.

> Towards any profound conviction one is borne gradually, perhaps insensibly over a long period of time, by what Newman called "powerful concurrent reasons." Some of these reasons may appear to the outside world irrelevant; some are purely personal; and each individual, perhaps, has some reasons which could concern, some influences which could have influenced, no one but himself. At some moment or other, a kind of crystallization occurs, in which appears an element of faith not strictly definable from any reason or combination of reasons. I am not speaking, mind you, of conversion to Christian faith only, but of conversion in general … In my own case, I believe that one of the reasons was that the Christian scheme seemed to me the only one which would work. I hasten to add that this is not a reason for believing; it is a tenable hypothesis to maintain that there is no scheme which will work.

That was simply the removal of any reason for believing in any-
thing else, the erasure of a prejudice, the arrival at the skepticism
which is the preface to conversion. And when I say "work," I am
quite aware that I had my own notion of what the "working" of a
scheme comprehends. Among other things, the Christian scheme
seemed the only possible scheme which found a place for values
which I must maintain or perish (and belief comes first and practice
second), the belief, for instance, in holy living and holy dying, in
sanctity, chastity, humility, austerity.

For Eliot to cite Newman was apt because the Cardinal did capture the
often inscrutable process of conversion without ever stinting its complexity.
As the editors show, Newman spoke of what he called the "illative sense"
in *An Essay in Aid of a Grammar of Assent* (1870) as one combining intellect
and imagination and "creating a certitude of its truth by arguments too
various for direct enumeration, too personal and deep for words, too pow-
erful and concurrent for refutation." One could also quote something that
Newman wrote to the secretary of the London Evangelisation Society in
1885, when he was a spry eighty-four, in which he described conversion as
"the faint initial stirrings of religion in the heart," though "the darkness,
the sense of sin, the fear of God's judgment, the contrition, the faith, hope
and love, need not be a conscious, clearly defined, experience, but may
be, and commonly is, a slow and silent growth, not broken into separate
and successive stages, but as regards these spiritual acts composite, and
almost simultaneous, strengthening with the soul's strength, advancing
with advancing years, till (after whatever relapses and returns, or whatever
unswerving fidelity) death comes at length, and seals and crowns with
perseverance and salvation what from first to last is a work of grace. Grace
is the beginning and the end of it." For Newman, as for St Augustine and,
indeed, for Eliot, conversion was an arduous, lifelong process.

Moreover, conversion, for Eliot, was preeminently a practical process.
Like some other figures touched upon in this book, including Edmund
Burke and Christopher Dawson, Eliot recognized that it was in the family
that we come to recognize how to be Christians, where we are all in our
slippers and no one can have any doubts about each family member's
desperate need of forbearance and forgiveness, grace and redemption.
"The old-fashioned family-prayers type of Christian life is now unpopular,
and was often perfunctory and unattractive," Eliot observed in a broadcast
entitled "Towards a Christian Britain" (1941):

> but it insisted upon the important truth that Christian life begins
> in the family. It was usually defective in two ways: first, in teaching
> morality as an end in itself, or as a set of prohibitions, instead of as
> a necessary condition of the progress towards spiritual perfection
> which is the Christian goal. Second, in failing to lead the way to

Christian thinking: in assuming that faith was something to be preserved, if possible, from childhood, rather than something to be developed throughout maturity. It sounds as if I was asking a great deal of Christian parents: but it seems excessive because we now tend to expect too much of the schoolmaster. And there is one essential for a Christian start in life which the home, and the home only, can provide: the influence of a Christian atmosphere from the earliest years. Children are more influenced by what their parents are, than by what their parents tell them to be. So the first thing is not that parents should teach their children Christianity, but that they should be Christian parents.

The continuing incidence of Catholic homes in which there is not only no family prayer but no family attendance of Mass corroborates the need for Eliot's point being made and remade again.

Eliot is also sensible about the pitfalls of Christians working with non-Christians, which certain Roman Catholic prelates in our own time choose to flout. Eliot may have allowed himself to be beguiled by the "mimic Catholicism" of Anglo Catholicism, but, for all that, he was realistic enough to recognize that in the interests of false unity Christians could be tempted to barter away their core Christian convictions. The Jesuits, founded to evangelize the ruling class only to have that errant class eventually evangelize them, are the classic example of this perennial pitfall. Indeed, now that so many who pass for Christians, whether Catholic or Protestant, are scarcely Christian at all, Eliot's insistence on Christians understanding these pitfalls is worth keeping in mind. "Even apart from human frailty, we cannot expect individuals or nations who are different to behave in exactly the same way," he writes.

> we must respect their differences as well as their likeness to each other as sons of God. ... Co-operation between Christians and non-Christians is not only possible, it is necessary. But here is where our Christian thinking comes in: we must try to be clear what it is that we are co-operating for, and just where our difference matters and where it does not. We must not confuse the absolute with the relative good: we must remember that we hold a different view of human nature from the non-Christian, and that we have a different conception of the destiny of man. We must co-operate but not surrender. We must remind ourselves that there is no short cut to a Christian Britain

When Eliot was given the Campion Award of the Catholic Club in New York in 1963 in recognition of his own ecumenical efforts, which illness forced him to receive *in absentia*, he wrote a letter of thanks in which he again returned to his understanding of the vitality, as well as the unavoidable limitations of any ecumenical enterprise.

It is no desire to exaggerate the importance of my own work or the extent of my influence, when I say that I have had at heart for many years the cause of true oecumenicity. When I say "true," I mean that I have always looked askance at premature attempts at re-union between any two separated parts of Christendom which might, by a form of re-union, merely have the effect of separating the joined bodies still further from the rest. Reciprocal understanding must be our first aim, and common action where common action is possible and needed to combat the forces of Antichrist.

Unfortunately, few who left the Second Vatican Council would see the object of their dedication to "oecumenicity" in anything like these stark, sensible terms. One can contrast Eliot's level-headed approach to that of the liberal Cardinal Marc Ouellet, who wrote in a paper delivered at the canonization of St. John Henry Cardinal Newman:

The depth of this man of God [Newman] and the place he now occupies in Catholicity, make us aware of the void his absence would have left if he had not been and, consequently, of the theological need for a new ecumenical impetus towards reconciliation and the reconstitution of dislocated elements of Catholic unity. This lack of unity affects the communion of individuals and churches but it points also to a lack of integration of the doctrinal and spiritual riches that adorn the sister Churches and ecclesial communities still separated from Rome. Newman's contribution, which offers the typical qualities of English culture and Anglican tradition, brings about an assessment of what was lost to centuries of separation, polemics and narrowing perspectives, in an attempt to defend confessional identities. The time has thus come to encourage and multiply initiatives, despite the difficulties along the way, for dialogue and reconciliation in order to accomplish full unity among Christians. It is not a question of using Newman's figure to depict the return to the fold. Rather, his life and his theology challenge us to carefully examine the internal difficulties of reconciliation and to take a greater interest in other Christians in order to move together towards a more perfect attainment of the *Catholica*. This requires a conversion from all confessions, starting from the Roman Church, which must be open to eventual transformations that can clear the path towards unity, so desired by the Lord.

The question that any faithful Catholic will naturally ask himself, after reading this startling effusion, is what "eventual transformation" the Canadian cardinal has in mind, if he rules out Newman's accustomed call to Anglicans and other Protestants estranged from the Church "to return to the fold." — that is to say, "the one true fold of the Redeemer," as Newman put it before and after his conversion. Those who know Newman will know the letters he wrote from Littlemore, one of which, to the Tractarian poet,

Isaac William, is worth quoting in this context, Newman never requiring others to do what he was not prepared to do himself.

> My very dear Williams,
>
> I do not like not to send you just a line, though I know how it will distress you. Father Dominic, the Passionist, is coming here to-night on his way to Belgium—He does not know of my intentions, but I shall ask of him the charitable work of admitting me to what I believe to be the one true fold of the Redeemer. He is full of love for religious men among us, and believes many to be inwardly knit to the Catholic Church who are outwardly separate from it—This will not go till all is over—You may suppose how much Bisley has been in my thoughts lately.
>
> This is a short letter, but I have a great many to write—
>
> Ever yours affectionately J. H. N.

The reference to Bisley is to Bisley, Gloucestershire, where Williams was curate and presided over a community of like-minded Protestants, including Keble's brother, all of whom had convinced themselves that their Protestantism had something to do with "catholicity," as they called it. Convinced of the rightness of his own Protestantism, the obdurately Anglo-Catholic Williams always looked askance at Newman's conversion and later accused him of succumbing to, of all things, German rationalism.[1] Newman was not the only nineteenth-century Christian who lacked the ecumenical spirit.

V

Together, Eliot's essays point to the one book that sums up all of his work in poetry and prose, *Notes towards the Definition of Culture* (1948), in which he wrote how "The dominant force in creating a common culture between peoples each of which has its distinct culture, is religion," though he was quick to assure his readers that he was "not setting out to convert anybody": he was "simply stating a fact." In one passage from that prescient volume, he refers to culture as the "incarnation" of a people's religion, which, in itself, measures how much culture we have lost in losing our religion. In another passage, the Aristotelian critic in Eliot gives full expression to his understanding of the fragility of a culture that will only be replaced at incalculable cost.

> It is in Christianity that our arts have developed; it is in Christianity that the laws of Europe have—until recently—been rooted. It is against a background of Christianity that all our thought has signi-

---

1 Edward Short, *Newman and his Family* (London: Bloomsbury, 2013), 283.

ficance. An individual European may not believe that the Christian Faith is true, and yet what he says, and makes, and does, will all spring out of his heritage of Christian culture and depend upon that culture for its meaning. Only a Christian culture could have produced a Voltaire or a Nietzsche. I do not believe that the culture of Europe could survive the complete disappearance of the Christian Faith. And I am convinced of that, not merely because I am a Christian myself, but as a student of social biology. If Christianity goes, the whole of our culture goes. Then you must start painfully again, and you cannot put on a new culture ready made. You must wait for the grass to grow to feed the sheep to give the wool out of which your new coat will be made. You must pass through many centuries of barbarism. We should not live to see the new culture, nor would our great-great-great-grandchildren: and if we did, not one of us would be happy in it.

In light of the demographic shambles that contraception set off in the West, it is ironic seeing Eliot refer to "great-great-great grandchildren." Of course, the birth rate in Europe and the United States has become so calamitously low that many of us will not have "great-great-great grand-children," which brings us back to where we began, with what Eliot styled the "facts of life."

Can there be any real solicitude for Christian culture if there is no solic-itude for the sacredness and protection of actual human life? In retrospect, we can see that nothing subverted Western Civilization as it had come down to the men and women of the twentieth century from the dowry of Mary—not world wars, not Jacobinism, not even the manifold betrayal of the Roman Church from within—quite as disastrously as the bane of contra-ception. Cardinal Gerhard Müller and Stephan Kampowski, in response to the Pontifical Academy for Life's assault on the pro-life principles enshrined in *Humanae Vitae*, recently reaffirmed the vitality of these principles in terms that are as clarion as they are welcome. For them, "the question of contraception is not just a minor issue within a delimited field of special moral theology. Rather the entire ecclesial teaching on sexuality, marriage, and family stands or falls with it: from the moral evaluation of same-sex acts, the issue of pre-marital and extra-marital relations, the meaning of marriage, and the possibility of celibacy for the Kingdom of Heaven." Why?

That sexuality is not a brute force but can be integrated into the order of love and reason, that spouses are truly able to make a gift of themselves and to receive each other with the very freedom of this gift: This is good news. That our sexuality includes, in the very words of the Pontifical Academy for Life's document, a *Gabe* and *Aufgabe*, a gift and a mission (n. 168)—this, too, is good news. That there is a proper context in which to receive this gift and live this mission, namely the institution that marital love gives to itself, which goes by the name of marriage: This is good news. The solution to the Church's current problems—from the abuse crisis to the decline in the number of marriages and baptisms, from the near absence of adult conversions to the increasing numbers of people turning their back on Christ's Mystical Body—is not in giving up the good news she has, but in finally starting to proclaim it with confidence, especially and precisely in the realm of human sexuality. As Elizabeth Anscombe once said, "What can be done? If you want to repair the situation, you will have to preach chastity, the whole doctrine of the Church: the whole package. For it all hangs together."

Eliot might have been a stout and admirable defender of Christian civilization; no one sought to return his contemporaries to its appreciation and defense as eloquently as he did. But his advocacy was not all that it might have been. "The World is trying the experiment of attempting to form a civilized but non-Christian mentality," he warned. "The experiment will fail; but we must be very patient in waiting its collapse; meanwhile, redeeming the time; so that the Faith may be preserved alive through the dark ages before us; to renew and rebuild civilization, and save the World from suicide." Everything he says here is true. Yet in failing to recognise the radical evil of contraception, Eliot willy-nilly lent his sanction to what would become mass suicide. When he had occasion in his talk to the Athenaeum in 1960 to note that "the religion we profess and the religion we live by may not be the same," T. S. Eliot was speaking more wisely than he knew.

HISTORIANS

The Distilled Wisdom
of Edmund Burke

Edmund Burke: Reflections on the Revolution in France and Other Writings, edited and introduced by Jesse Norman (Everyman Library). 1086 pages.

"There is no single speech of Mr. Burke which can convey a satisfactory idea of his powers of mind," wrote William Hazlitt, the essayist and critic; "to do him justice, it would be necessary to quote all his works; the only specimen of Burke is, *all his works.*"

While students of the great orator await the completion of Oxford University Press's mammoth critical edition of *The Writings and Speeches of Edmund Burke,* they could do worse than consult this new Everyman volume, which is smartly edited and introduced by one of Burke's recent biographers, the British politician, Jesse Norman, who is right to remind readers that Burke's greatest writing grew out of his respect for history and memory, "and an Orwellian detestation of those who would erase them." The collection gives an incomparably generous sampling of the political philosopher's responses to the defining crises of his time, including the question of party and the integrity of Parliament; the events leading up to the American Revolution; the question of what ought to be the economic and constitutional relationship between Great Britain and Ireland; the East India Company's egregious misrule of India; and what called forth his most profound animadversions, the French Revolution.

Writing shortly after Burke's death, Hazlitt observed how the genius of the man was not universally acknowledged. "It has always been with me a test of the sense and candour of any one belonging to the opposite party," Hazlitt wrote, "whether he allowed Burke to be a great man." And here he was referring not only to radicals like himself but Whigs and Tories who never trusted the independent, senatorial line that Burke took with regard to economic, constitutional and imperial matters.

> Of all the persons of this description that I have ever known, I never met with above one or two who would make this concession; whether it was that party feelings ran too high to admit of any real candour, or whether it was owing to an essential vulgarity in

their habits of thinking, they all seemed to be of opinion that he was a wild enthusiast or a hollow sophist ... If you said that you though you differed with him in sentiment, yet you thought him an admirable reasoner, and a close observer of human nature, you were answered with a loud laugh.

Although infinitely more radical than Burke, Hazlitt realized that the orator could not be dismissed as a mere reactionary. If Burke was at heart a conservative two generations before the term was coined—indeed, he is rightly hailed as the father of conservatism—he also appreciated that "A state without the means of some change, is without the means of its conservation." When it came to the essence of Burke's conservative vision, Hazlitt applauded its fundamental humanity.

> He thought that the wants and happiness of men were not to be provided for, as we provide for those of a herd of cattle, merely by attending to physical necessities. He thought more nobly of his fellows. He knew that man had affections and passions and powers of imagination, as well as hunger and thirst, and the sense of heat and cold. He took his idea of political society from the pattern of private life, wishing, as he himself expresses it, to incorporate the domestic charities with the order of the state, and to blend them together.

Burke returned to this theme of how the "pattern of private life" should furnish the model for the state again and again. "We begin our public affections in our families," he was convinced. "No cold relation is a zealous citizen." Indeed, for the family man in Burke, a tender, liberal, gregarious man, whom friends and family alike found delightful company, it became almost axiomatic that: "To be attached to the subdivision, to love the little platoon we belong to in society, is the first principle (the germ as it were) of public affections. It is the first link in the series by which we proceed towards a love to our country and to mankind." Readers interested in Burke's fascinating life will enjoy F. P. Lock's magisterial two-volume biography, even though it concludes by declaring that "Burke's supreme gift ... was not his wisdom but his eloquence," as though the two were somehow different.

The son of a Protestant Dublin solicitor and a Catholic mother from a well-to-do family in Cork, Edmund Burke (1730–97) was educated at an excellent Quaker school in Kildare and at Trinity College, before entering the Middle Temple in London. In 1756, after working for Robert Dodsley, the bookseller who helped launch Samuel Johnson's literary career, he married a Catholic Irishwoman, Jane Mary Nugent, with whom he had two boys, only one of whom survived. In 1765, he became secretary to the Whig magnate Lord Rockingham, with whom his political fortunes would be long associated, and in the same year he entered Parliament. There he gave the famous speeches on America, Ireland, France and India that made his reputation. In 1768, he purchased the costly estate at Beaconsfield that would be the family home until his death. When his son Richard died in 1794, aged 36, a month after he was to take his father's seat in Parliament, Burke was devastated: "The storm has gone over me," he wrote; "and I lie like one of those oaks which the late hurricane has scattered about me … I am torn up by my roots … I have none to meet my enemies in the gate. Indeed, my lord, I greatly deceive myself if I would give a peck of refuse wheat for all that is called fame and honour in the world." Reading this, no one could ever accuse Burke of having been a "cold relation."

The intellectual historian, Jonathan Clark, in his superb critical edition of the *Reflections on the Revolution in France* (2001), may be right to downplay Burke's Irishry and his connection to the Church of Rome, which have been exaggerated. As his writings abundantly show, Burke saw himself as a Protestant Englishman, not as an Irishman *per se* or crypto-Catholic. Nevertheless, Burke's experience of the divisions of Catholic Ireland cannot be discounted; going back and forth from Dublin to Cork as a boy left him with an indelible sense of the injustice at the heart of Irish society, which would always animate his political thinking. In 1750, before leaving Ireland for London, he gave moving expression to this sense.

> Whoever travels through this Kingdom will see such poverty as few nations in Europe can equal … It is no uncommon sight to see half-a-dozen children run quite naked out of a cabin, scarcely distinguishable from a dunghill, to the great disgrace of our country with foreigners, who would doubtless report them savages, imputing that to choice which only proceeds from their irremediable poverty. Let anyone take a survey of their cabins, and then say whether such a residence be worthy … of a human creature.

For Burke, the moral of such degradation was inescapable: "I fancy many of our fine gentlemen's pageantry would be greatly tarnished, were their gilt coaches to be preceded and followed by the same miserable wretches, whose labour supports them." Later, in 1780, to show how "Bad laws are the worst sort of tyranny," the conscientious Anglican in Burke would make an appeal to the electors of Bristol.

> A statute was fabricated in the year 1699, by which the saying mass (a church-service in the Latin tongue, not exactly the same as our liturgy, but very near it, and containing no offence whatsoever against the laws, or against good morals) was forged into a crime punishable with perpetual imprisonment. The teaching school, an useful and virtuous occupation, even the teaching in a private family, was in every Catholic subjected to the same unproportioned punishment. Your industry, and the bread of your children, was taxed for a pecuniary reward to stimulate avarice to do what nature

refused, to inform and prosecute on this law. Every Roman Catholic was under the same act, to forfeit his estate to his nearest Protestant relation, until, through a profession of what he did not believe, he redeemed by his hypocrisy, what the law had transferred to the kinsman as the recompense of his profligacy. When thus turned out of doors from his paternal estate, he was disabled from acquiring any other by any industry, donation or charity; but was rendered a foreigner in his native land, only because he retained the religion, along with the property, handed down to him from those who had been the old inhabitants of that land before him.

The same solicitude for those on the receiving end of oppression would guide all of his great writings on America, France and India. As Conor Cruise O'Brien observed in *The Great Melody: A Thematic Biography of Edmund Burke* (1992): "In all of Burke's great campaigns there was, as Yeats discerned, one constant target ... the abuse of power." Of course, the shape this abuse took would vary, but in each case, Burke would always insist on two principles: that power be accountable and that it serve liberty. Moreover, if he understood that: "The greater the power, the more dangerous the abuse," he was equally aware that: "Nothing turns out to be so oppressive and unjust as a feeble government," a truth to which President Obama spectacularly attested.

It was apt that O'Brien should have based his book on Yeats's poem, "The Seven Sages" (1929), in which the poet hailed the statesman for being a hater of whiggery, which he nicely defined as "A leveling, rancorous, rational sort of mind / That never looked out of the eye of a saint / Or out of a drunkard's eye" because the poet in Yeats appreciated the essential man of tradition in Burke. Browsing through this admirably rich anthology, one can see this understanding of the force of tradition at every turn. "To innovate is not to reform," Burke declares in *A Letter to a Noble Lord* (1796). In *Reflections on the Revolution in France* (1790), he is no less categorical: "Those who attempt to level never equalize." Speaking of the Jacobins and their newfangled schemes for improving the social order, he is even more admonitory: "In the groves of *their* academy, at the end of every vista, you see nothing but the gallows."

Against the arrogant rationalism of the French *philosophes*, Burke offered a vision of the social order as a compact made up not only of the living but the dead and those yet to be born. "In this choice of inheritance, we have given to our frame of polity the image of a relation in blood," he wrote, "binding up the constitution of our country with our dearest domestic ties; adopting our fundamental laws into the bosom of our family affections; keeping inseparable and cherishing with the warmth of all their combined and mutually reflected charities our state, our hearths, our sepulchres and our altars."

The reference to "sepulchres" is vital to understanding Burke's understanding of the virtuous polity, since "People will not look forward to posterity, who never look backward to their ancestors." That virtue was indeed crucial to this compact was clear if one appreciated, as Burke did, that "Among a people generally corrupt liberty cannot long exist." And this virtue was particularly required of any country's public servants, for "When the leaders choose to make themselves bidders at an auction of popularity, their talents in the construction of the state will be of no service." Why? "They will become flatterers instead of legislators; the instruments, not the guides of the people." And here it is worth noting that Burke practiced what he preached, for when his views in favor of conciliating the American colonists put him at odds with the electors of Bristol, they voted him out of office.

He could also be bravely defiant of the popular will, when he knew it to be set on evil. During the anti-Catholic Gordon Riots (1780), for example, he made a point, unlike many of his political colleagues, of staying in town and confronting the mob, even though his pro-Catholic sentiments made him a prime target. As Lock points out, "Confident of the rightness of his cause, he preferred an aggressive defiance to skulking behind the barricades." Yet he never lost sight of the good sense of the people, as, here, in his characterization of their likely response to the language of France's confiscatory revolutionaries: "The ears of the people of England are distinguishing. They hear these men speak broad. Their tongue betrays them. Their language is in the patois of fraud; in the cant and gibberish of hypocrisy. The people of England must think so, when these praters affect to carry back the clergy to ... primitive evangelic poverty."

The historian Lewis Namier regarded Burke's insistence on virtue in government as so much "cant," camouflage behind which ruthless self-interest could go its merry way. Yet Burke saw virtue ensuring for government a kind of aristocracy of talent, which it might not otherwise have. "There is no qualification for government," he wrote, "but virtue and wisdom, actual or presumptive. Wherever they are actually found, they have, in whatever state, condition, profession or trade, the passport of Heaven to human place and honour." At the same time, he was never unmindful of fallen man's distaste for virtue. "In doing good we are generally cold, and languid, and sluggish," he told his Bristol constituency in 1780. "But the works of malice and injustice are quite in another style. They are finished with a bold, masterly hand; touched as they are with the spirit of all those vehement passions that call forth all our energies, whenever we oppress or persecute." Nevertheless, Burke was nothing as misanthropic on this score as his fellow Anglo-Irishman Jonathan Swift. In *Thoughts on the Cause of the Present Discontents* (1770) he displayed his accustomed judiciousness. While it might be true that "We must soften into a credulity below the milkiness of infancy to think all men virtuous," it was equally true that "We must be tainted with a malignity truly diabolical, to believe all the world to be equally wicked and corrupt."

As for Burke's own probity, the English historian Paul Langford makes an incisive point when he says: "Irishmen of minor gentry or professional background were conventionally portrayed in England as fortune-hunters and Burke sometimes among them. In his case it was a particularly absurd charge, for at all the crucial points in his career he had turned his back on promotion for its own sake." Langford also gets to the heart of what made Burke tick when he says: "For many of his generation the deity of the early Enlightenment was little more than a stage prop in a rationally ordered existence. For Burke it was an intense and all-pervading spiritual reality."

Now that our own country has elected a president in the political bounder Donald Trump who has pledged to respect the will of the people, even if it means continuing to incur the wrath of many in the state, judiciary and press, who claim that they have the well-being of the people most to heart, by dint of their being professional public men, it might be useful to recall what Burke had to say about the character of the people *vis-à-vis* their representatives. "I am not one of those who think that the people are never in the wrong," he wrote. "They have been so frequently and outrageously, both in other countries and in this. But I do say, that in all disputes between them and their rulers, the presumption is at least upon a par in favour of the people." Indeed, he even went so far as to say that: "In all forms of Government, the people is the true legislator." In light of these judgments, those charged with implementing the new president's populist agenda will warm to Burke's estimation of the force of political protest: "It is a general popular error," he was convinced, "to imagine the loudest complainers for the public to be the most anxious for its welfare."

In his essay on the brilliant orator, Hazlitt assured his readers: "I am not going to make an idle panegyric on Burke (he has no need of it), but I cannot help looking on him as the chief boast and ornament of the English House of Commons. What is said of him is, I think, strictly true, that 'He was the most eloquent man of his time; his wisdom was greater than his eloquence.'" This splendid Everyman collection shows why Hazlitt was right.

G. M. Trevelyan, History and the Schools of St. Mary

I

The other day I was reading an engaging autobiographical essay by the once widely read Whig historian George Macaulay Trevelyan (1876–1962), and I was struck by the fair-minded suavity with which he deals with those whose political and religious convictions he opposed. For example, writing about his childhood, he says:

> During the General Election of 1880, when I was four years old, we were staying at Buxton for Easter, and my brothers were taken to a Liberal meeting in the town. I remember my excitement about it, but I was too young to be allowed to go. My brothers came back and reported that a Tory at the back of the hall, acting after his kind, had cried "boo!" I was much impressed, and it became a joke of the elders to ask me "what do Tories say?" To this question I would reply with a prolonged "boo-o-o."

Of course, his Whig elders would have seen an instructive comedy in Master George's reply, since for them, Tories booed everything worth cheering in public life: they booed reform; they booed progress; they even booed *laissez-faire* liberalism.

Yet Trevelyan was also quick to tell his readers that these same elders, being sound, sturdy, tolerant Whigs, allowed that there were some good Tories, even though they constituted "a select class," including as it did his charming uncle, Harry Holland, later Lord Knutsford, Salisbury's Colonial Minister, and his governess, Miss Martin.

Miss Martin, "though English of the English," taught Trevelyan his French — taught it to him so well that he had to conceal his superior French accent when he went to Harrow to escape being thought "peculiar" by his fellow Harrovians. She also made him "learn dates and poetry by heart, as all children ought to be while their memory is still good and retentive, instead of being stuffed with generalizations about history and criticisms of literature which mean nothing to their empty young minds." Thanks to the Tory Miss Martin, Trevelyan retained his love of literature to the end of his days and would always prize the poetry inherent in history.

For the Whig historian, in other words, Toryism might be objectionable but Tories themselves could be admirable. In fact, for Trevelyan, who regarded a good deal of Christian history as "pietistic flapdoodle," even Roman Catholics could be admirable, as he relates in another childhood memory.

> In 1882 my father became Chief Secretary for Ireland, in succession to his friend Lord Frederick Cavendish who had been murdered in the Phoenix Park. My brothers were in Ireland only for their school holidays, but I, being just six years old, was still at home. I spent much of my time wandering round the wooded circle of the Chief Secretary's grounds, playing chestnuts, marbles and hide-and-seek with a mild, gigantic Irish plain-clothes detective, named Mr. Dunne, whom I regarded as my playmate, and who was incidentally responsible for the safety of my small person in those troubled times. It was startling to discover that he took the opposite side about the battle of the Boyne.

That is to say, Mr. Dunne was a Catholic—he did not exult in King William's victory over the deposed James II in July of 1690 in the battle that became the rallying cry of Ulster's Orangemen, though it is important to note that Pope Alexander VIII supported William of Orange in the battle, James II being too subservient for his tastes to the Gallican Louis XIV. History is rarely without amusing little ironies.

Trevelyan was putting it mildly when he said that the times of his childhood were "troubled": they were atrocious. In May 1882, the "Invincibles," a peculiarly bloodthirsty branch of the Fenian Brotherhood, murdered not only Cavendish but his undersecretary, T. H. Burke in broad daylight with surgical knives. It was a memorable milestone in the history of Irish frightfulness. It even caused the unflappable Charles Stewart Parnell to consider resigning as head of the Home Rule party in Westminster.

Yet how winning of Trevelyan to recall someone for whose putative benefit these outrages were being committed as a "playmate." Nothing could show more clearly his conviction that history was primarily about people, not partisanship, even when people got up to the most abominable partisanship imaginable.

Many years later, Trevelyan would write about the upshot of King William's victory at the Battle of the Boyne in his deservedly popular *History of England* (1926), and it is notable how careful he was to own up to the mismanagement of the same Whig magnets whom Whig historians were otherwise sworn to celebrate and commend. "The restored English rule in Ireland reflected very little of the wise and tolerant spirit of William," he concedes. "In this Catholic island he was powerless to do anything to protect the Catholics whose lot he mitigated in England." The "rash ignorance and prejudice of the Whigs and Tories of the Westminster Parliament … the real overlords of the reconquered dependency" alienated both the Catholic and the Protestant Irish. As for the penal laws, they placed "the Catholics in Ireland under every political and social disadvantage that malice could invent, and pursued and persecuted their priests, the only leaders left to them under the Cromwellian land system." England's Irish policy even incurred the odium of Ulster's Presbyterians, the very men who had "manned the walls of Londonderry and forded the Boyne water." Indeed, it ruined what might have been the thriving Irish cloth trade, with the result that, "Many thousands of Ulster Scots who sought refuge beyond the Atlantic in the Appalachian mountains, had more real wrongs to revenge on England in the War of American Independence than had most of those who followed the standard of Washington." The finest literary boast of this Scotch-Irish tribe, the novelist Henry James would later commend his friend Trevelyan for his "great ability and virtue," for his "great general literary accomplishment," though he could not overlook his "rather limited *grace.*" The rumpled scholar never paid much attention to his dress and was not above appearing in public unshaven.

In reading Trevelyan's autobiographical essay, I was also struck by how his Liberal convictions set him apart at late-Victorian Harrow. "At the General Election of 1892, I was told that I was the only boy in the school who openly said he was a Liberal," he recalled. "And I wouldn't be confirmed,—another eccentricity for which I was taken to task by some of the boys."

He might have been surrounded by more like-minded young men once he went up to Trinity College, Cambridge, but as a schoolboy at Harrow he embraced political and religious convictions that were the reverse of popular. Nevertheless, he largely enjoyed his time at the school, which he credited to an unforgettable *gentilesse.* "The head of my house, James Sandilands, a king among boys, whom I greatly and justly admired, treated me sensibly and kindly, and made my position possible," Trevelyan recalled. "I shall never cease to be grateful to him. He knew how *gauche* I was, but I think he approved of me for taking my own line." Boyhood chivalry, in other words, gave Trevelyan the confidence he needed to pursue his "own line," that and Harrow's commendable aversion to groupthink.

At Harrow, in the sixth form, he pursued his "own line" by pursuing history instead of classics when history was scarcely recognized as a specialized discipline. The influence of "two history masters of rare quality," Robert Somervell and George Townsend Warner guided his decision. "I think I had at Harrow a better historical education than any other schoolboy in England," Trevelyan boasted. "Mr. Winston Churchill [another Harrovian] has gratefully recorded that Somervell taught him the mastery of English,—surely a priceless service to our nation as things have turned out.

Somervell took the Sixth in history. We did Charles II's reign one term, and his teaching of it revealed to me the complexity and interest of the many-sided political past of our country, for I had been brought up at home on a somewhat exuberantly Whig tradition."

This was patrician understatement. Trevelyan was the great nephew of the greatest of all the Whig historians, Thomas Babington Macaulay (1800–59). He was the son of Macaulay's biographer, Sir George Otto Trevelyan. He personified what Herbert Butterfield dubbed the "Whig interpretation of history," which A. J. P. Taylor nicely defined as "the story of English liberty, founded by Magna Carta, consolidated by the Glorious Revolution, expanded by the Great Reform Bill, and reaching its highest achievement with the Labour government." Later in life, Trevelyan might have become a Baldwinite conservative, but only because he thought this exiguous change of allegiance—Baldwin never being a robust conservative—was one of which Macaulay would have approved. In all events, Trevelyan was one of the most popular historians that the world has ever known. It is true that he was unduly partial to the Protestant order that had made England a force in the world, but he also served up histories that were artful, readable, and tolerably well researched. If Trevelyan's popularity incurred the jealous contempt of academic historians, especially when he taught modern history at Cambridge from 1927 to 1940, it endeared him to the common reader. He certainly recognized, as he said in one of his talks, that "When history is used as a branch of propaganda it is a very deadly weapon"—a truth that needs reaffirming today as much as it did after the First World War when totalitarian dictators were gaining power in Europe and the Bolsheviks had Mother Russia by the throat.

II

The influence that Trevelyan's two history masters had on him in helping him to prepare for his choice of career set me wondering how history is taught in our schools here in New York. As it happens, I now work at a school myself, the Schools of Saint Mary, an excellent preparatory academy in Manhasset, Long Island grounded in the Catholic intellectual tradition, with a lower, middle and upper school, and after reading Trevelyan I spoke with two of the school's history instructors, Messrs. Jonathan Marron and Michael King, and they shared with me how they are carrying on some of the good historical traditions to which Trevelyan was loyal

For Mr. Marron, who teaches European history to the upper school and has an incomparable record of preparing students for exceling in Advanced Placement courses: "Studying history provides students the opportunity to develop intellectual and moral skills as well as an appreciation of the past. While studying history students acquire such indispensable life skills as the art of evaluation, comparison, and analysis. In addition, history adds to the development of a student's moral virtue by forming and sharpening his moral sense. The examples of those who have weathered adversity are always inspirational."

Interestingly enough, to exemplify certain benefits of the study of history, he cites the instruction he gives his students in the Renaissance, which "instills in them a love for the beautiful." For Mr. Marron, "it is wonderful to see students explore truly remarkable works of art, and to go on to develop an appreciation and knowledge of some of the great works of art produced by the Old Masters."

The graduate of Chaminade High School and Georgetown's School of Foreign Service adds that, "Instructing students to develop well-reasoned arguments is one of the most important skills that we look to develop. Furthermore, history is filled with individual examples of those who were daring in the pursuit of high ideals, and we always seek to enable the students to appreciate the practical good that such high-achieving individuals accomplish."

Mr. King, who teaches American history at Saint Mary's, is another graduate of Georgetown, where he not only studied finance, international business, and theology but played football for the Hoyas. Like Mr. Marron, he reinforces the school's commitment to rational discourse. "I teach students about both sides of various political issues," he says. "I give them a 'pro' article, which we read and discuss, then a 'con' article, where we do the same. They have a discussion, I play 'devil's advocate' and at the end of the class, they can leave believing whatever they like. My job is to teach them how to construct arguments and to understand the issues—how to think—not to tell them what to think." His methodology is straightforwardly effective:

> Debate and argumentation are a big part of my class. I start off each year with a lesson on the importance of free speech as well as a lesson on the importance of being able to have conversations with those we disagree with, emphasizing that we can learn from our opponents. Indeed, if you want to bring about change in the world, salutary change, you must learn from your opponents, so that you can construct arguments that will appeal to them.

Mr. King stresses that "all opinions are welcome in my class as long as they are respectfully delivered and respectfully received. Students are taught to attack an idea, not the person who holds that idea. Also, when we look at an issue, students are required, like good barristers, to learn the best arguments for both sides. Furthermore, I teach them how to build arguments through claim, reasons, and evidence. When we move into writing, this takes the form of making a thesis statement that will include supporting reasons. Beyond the thesis statement, those reasons must be supported with evidence cited from a reputable academic source."

Nevertheless, Mr. King is not entirely unbiased in his presentation of the history he teaches. Why? "I teach my students about the whole of US History, the good, the bad and the ugly, but I also make clear that, warts and all, this is a very special place."

III

Trevelyan had some interesting things to say about bias and the writing of history. "Clearly, we are hampered and misled in our attempt to find out what our ancestors really thought and felt," he writes, "if we try to fit them into some modern category which did not exist in their time. In that way, bias hinders the search for truth." Yet Trevelyan also recognized that bias could be beneficial to the historian, especially if it helped him "to sympathize with the actual passions of people in the past whose actions it is his business to describe." To enter into such passions, "Clio should not always be cold, aloof, impartial." Sometimes, the historian might even be warranted in sharing the passions of his subject, but only "provided they are the real passions of the past and not a false reflection of some modern dogma or prejudice."

Finally, Trevelyan gave it as his opinion that, "The ideal history, never yet written by any man, would so tell the tale of the Civil War that the reader would not only grasp with his mind but would warmly feel in his heart what Cavaliers and Roundheads respectively felt, and would also understand what they none of them understood. The ideal history requires indeed a more varied combination of heart and of head, of science and of art than any other study undertaken by man." Still, the good historian in Trevelyan, despite all of his own biases, knew that this ideal history was worth keeping in mind, not because it confirmed one's biases but because it enriched one's fellow feeling. Sympathy, after all, not bias, is what makes great history possible—sympathy and wonder. Trevelyan had both, as he made clear when he reminded his readers that, "The poetry of history lies in the quasi-miraculous fact that once, on this earth, once, on this familiar spot of ground, walked other men and women, as actual as we are today, thinking their own thoughts, swayed by their own passions, but now all gone, one generation vanishing into another, gone as utterly as we ourselves shall shortly be gone, like ghosts at cockcrow."

To Raise the Tomb-Door:
Hardy's War Poetry

I

No one can understand how late Victorian and Edwardian England man-
aged to find itself in the trenches of the Great War, with all of its attendant
horrors, without paying attention to Hardy.[1] After all, his tragic sense of life
might almost have prophesied the cataclysmic bloodbath. In this essay, I
shall show that more than any other poet who paid attention to the war—
more than Owen, Thomas, Graves, Blunden, Sassoon, Gurney—Hardy got
at its essence by abstaining from anti-war polemics and seeing the conflict,
instead, in terms that were at once deeply historical and deeply personal.

Like so much of his non-war poetry, Hardy's war poetry is of an incom-
parable beauty and tenderness.

> What of the faith and fire within us
> Men who march away
> Ere the barn-cocks say
> Night is growing gray,
> Leaving all that here can win us;
> What of the faith and fire within us
> Men who march away?

Here, in this haunting aubade, Hardy captured the war's battle cry of
desolation with an unforgettable empathy. The American critic Paul Fussell
misreads the poem on the opening page of his otherwise serviceable *The
Great War and Modern Memory* (1975) by regarding it as simply "patriotic
and unironic."[2] The poet Charles Sorley, who met his end at Loos, thought

---

1 Anyone interested in Hardy's war poetry or that of his contemporaries should read
Tim Kendall's brilliant annotated collection, *Poetry of the First World War: An Anthology*,
ed. Tim Kendall (Oxford: Oxford University Press, 2013).
2 Paul Fussell, *The Great War and Modern Memory* (London: Folio Society, 2014), 3.

it jingoistic.[3] These, it seems to me, are the judgments of those who expect war poetry to be explicitly anti-war; any war poetry less than anti-war must somehow be suspect. Yet, if one reads the poem free of this expectation, one can see that it exemplifies a much subtler response to the war than it is assumed to express. Here, Hardy's accustomed tragic sense is humanized by his fellow feeling, his tenderness, his readiness to enter into the sufferings of others—which, in the case of the Great War, were those of an entire social order. Yes, he composed the poem as a piece of propaganda for a war that he considered just, however lamentable; but the artist in him could never take dictation from the propagandist. It is also worth noting that Edward Thomas liked the poem.[4]

Dana Gioia pointed out to me the other day that Rilke regretted the patriotic poems he wrote: Hardy never regretted his—warrantably so. Laurence Binyon, in his celebrated elegy, "For the Fallen" described the "Men who march away" thus:

> They went with songs to the battle, they were young,
> Straight of limb, true of eye, steady and aglow.
> They were staunch to the end against odds uncounted;
> They fell with their faces to the foe.

Compared to Hardy's lacerating music, this is poor stuff. The popularity of Hardy's poem could not have been more well deserved. Instead of propaganda, Hardy gave his countrymen the music of what would become their bewildered woe. After all, he had done something rather similar in "The Convergence of the Twain," where the sunken Titanic comes to life in a phantasmagoric music that no newsreel could ever rival.

> Over the mirrors meant
> To glass the opulent
> The sea-worm crawls—grotesque, slimed, dumb, indifferent.

3 In November 1914, Sorley wrote his parents: "Needless to say, I do not agree with your criticisms of T. H.'s later work. The actual *Satires of Circumstance* which come in the middle of the book I thought bad poetry. But I think you are too hard on the rest. Hardy explains in the preface to one of his former books of poems that they are expressions of moods and are not to be taken as a whole reading of life, but 'the road to a true philosophy of life seems to be in humbly recording divers aspects of its phenomena as they are forced upon us by chance and change.' And I don't think he writes these poems [for the reason] you suggest, but with a view to helping people on that 'road to a true philosophy of life.' Curiously enough, I think that 'Men who march away' is the most arid poem in the book, besides being untrue of the sentiments of the ranksman going to war: 'Victory crowns the just' is the worst line he ever wrote–filched from a leading article in *The Morning Post*, and unworthy of him who had always previously disdained to insult Justice by offering it a material crown like Victory."

4 Jon Silken, *Out of Battle: The Poetry of the Great War* (Oxford: Oxford University Press, 1972), 51.

Jewels in joy designed
To ravish the sensuous mind
Lie lightless, all their sparkles bleared and black and blind.

Dim moon-eyed fishes near
Gaze at the gilded gear
And query: "What does this vaingloriousness down here?"

In his war poetry, Hardy always pays the betrayed good faith of those who fought in the trenches the ancient respects of pity and awe. Yeats may have taken it into his head to regard pity for what he regarded as "passive suffering" as an improper subject for poetry, but no war poetry—not even Wilfrid Owen's—exposes the odd callous wrongheadedness of such a judgement more unanswerably than Hardy's.[5] In his introduction to the Penguin edition of Hardy's poetry, the poet Robert Mezey nicely captures this aspect of the poet when he says that he "was one of those men who never get over the discovery of how much pain there is in the world, not merely their own pain but that of other creatures, which they seem to feel as keenly as their own; he remained all his life at the mercy of what James Wright calls 'defenseless compassion.'"[6]

The best gloss on Hardy's poem, "Men who march away," can be found in a letter that Henry James wrote to his friend Rhoda Broughton from Lamb House, Rye after the carnage had begun. The novelist could hear the "great guns" from his backyard that Hardy had prophesied so uncannily in "Channel Firing" five months before war was declared. "Black and hideous to me is the tragedy that gathers, and I am sick beyond cure to have lived to see it," James wrote.

> You and I, the ornaments of our generation, should have been spared this wreck of our belief that through the long years we had seen civilization grow and the worst become impossible. The tide that bore us along was then all the while moving us to *this* as its grand Niagara ... It seems to me to undo everything, everything that was ours, in the most horrible retroactive way.[7]

If James could scarcely disagree with the tragic view of the war that Hardy expressed in his verse, he was amusingly dismissive of the poet's fiction. Apropos *Far from the Madding Crowd*, he wrote in *The Nation*: "Farmer Boldwood is a shadow, and Sergeant Troy an elaborate stage-figure.

---

5 *The Oxford Book of Modern Verse 1892–1935*, ed. W. B. Yeats (Oxford: Oxford University Press, 1936), xxxiv.
6 Robert Mezey, "Introduction," *Thomas Hardy: Selected Poems* (London: Penguin, 1998), xxv.
7 James to Rhoda Boughton (10 August 1914), *Henry James Letters*, 4 vols. (Cambridge, Massachusetts and London: Harvard University Press, 1984), iv, 713.

Everything human in the book strikes us as factitious and insubstantial; the only things we believe in are the sheep and the dogs." Hardy, for his part, got his own back by noting in his diary the novelist's "ponderously warm manner of saying nothing in infinite sentences."

In the biography that she wrote of the poet, which Hardy heavily edited before his death, Florence Hardy wrote that "the war destroyed all of Hardy's belief in the gradual ennoblement of man, a belief he had held for many years, as is shown by poems like 'The Sick Battle-God.'" *Ennoblement* might be putting matters a bit too grandly but it is true that the poem expressed his view that warfare was becoming a thing of the past.

> Let men rejoice, let men deplore,
> The lurid Deity of heretofore
> Succumbs to one of saner nod;
> The Battle-god is god no more.

If "Channel-Firing" shows him to have been prophetic, this shows that when it came to what would become the war's unimaginably prodigious butchery he was caught as unawares as everyone else.

Another striking thing about Hardy's war poetry is that it shows that if the man himself continued to tout the irresponsible determinism so beloved of rationalists, the poet in him repudiated it. A. E. Housman, who had "great affection," as he said, for Hardy the man but not so much for his poetry, told a correspondent as late as 1933 that "The Great War cannot have made much change in the opinions of any man of imagination."[8] The war poet in Hardy disproves that flippant misjudgment. Despite so much ink having been spilled to argue otherwise, there was nothing inevitable about the First World War. Readers of Tim Kendall's excellent anthology, *Poetry of the First World War* (2013) will scan its pages in vain to land on better lines than these from "And There was a Great Calm" about the tragic contingency of this most willful of catastrophes. "Time and again," the poet critic Donald Davie recognizes, Hardy "writes in ways that … his declared intentions and his professed ideology would have ruled out,"[9] and here is a good instance of that divergence between poet and poem:

> Calm fell. From Heaven distilled a clemency;
> There was peace on earth, and silence in the sky;
> Some could, some could not, shake off misery:
> The Sinister Spirit sneered: "It had to be!"
> And again the Spirit of Pity whispered, "Why?"

8 Housman to Maurice Pollet (3 February 1933), *The Letters of A. E. Housman,* 2 vols. (Oxford: Oxford University Press, 2007), ii, 329.

9 Donald Davie, *Thomas Hardy and British Poetry* (London: Routledge & Kegan Paul, 1973), 41.

In yet another war poem, "In Time of 'The Breaking of Nations'," the long view Hardy tended to take of men and their follies helped him to put the war in some proper perspective.

I
Only a man harrowing clods
In a slow silent walk
With an old horse that stumbles and nods
Half asleep as they stalk.

II
Only thin smoke without flame
From the heaps of couch-grass;
Yet this will go onward the same
Though Dynasties pass.

III
Yonder a maid and her wight
Come whispering by:
War's annals will cloud into night
Ere their story die.

This clearly influenced Yeats's contribution to the war effort, that and the Anglo-Irishman's understandable desire not to do or say anything that might annoy the prime minister initially charged with conducting the war, H. H. Asquith, who had bestowed a tidy pension on the Irish poet from the Civil List.[10]

I think it better that in times like these
A poet's mouth be silent, for in truth
We have no gift to set a statesman right;
He has had enough of meddling who can please
A young girl in the indolence of her youth,
Or an old man upon a winter's night.

---

10 As to whether Yeats should accept the bounty of the British Government, given his Irish nationalism, Lady Gregory wrote to her friend: "I have never been under the impression that it was impossible for a Nationalist, but I have never gone into the matter. I think you should … get the lists & see what revolutionaries, if any have had it in the past. Standish O'Grady is the only one I know who has it now." Lady Gregory quoted in R. F. Foster, *W. B. Yeats: A Life*, 2 vols. (Oxford: Oxford University Press, 1997), ii, 425. Despite being abused by Sinn Fein journalists as "Pensioner Yeats" for accepting the pension, the poet was glad to have his £600 a year. A gifted polemicist himself, who never eschewed controversy, he rather enjoyed the abuse, especially the bit Foster quotes: "in payment for his patriotism Emmet got the rope but Pollexfen Yeats, the author of "Cathleen ni Houlihan", gets three pounds a week from the British Government." Foster, *Yeats*, ii, 428.

Hardy's conviction that the essence of history is always more a personal than a public thing enriches his war poetry at every turn. For someone who did not go to university, he was remarkably attuned to history, indeed steeped in it. Among other things, history gave him his wonderfully grim sense of humor. Writing to Kitchener regarding the recruitment of troops for the New Army, the author of *The Dynasts* (1904–8) gave it as his opinion that "if something of the old style of doing it—minus the liquor—could be generally adopted, it might have a productive effect." And what would that "old style" be?

> I refer to the systematic and persistent "beating up" through the streets of towns, with a band of fifes and side-drums, two lines four deep of old sergeants (past service) with drawn swords, full uniform, and ribbons and flags flying, followed by a company of recruits who have already joined, also with ribbands in their hats, a halt being made on reaching corners and open spaces, and a brief speech delivered by one of the sergeants. One pound notes were spitted on their swords a hundred years ago, but these would not be essential.[11]

Millgate quotes this without comment, but surely it shows how inveterate the strain of mockery was in Hardy. Writing to his friend Sydney Cockerell on the 15 August 1914, after the scale of the war's brutishness had become all too stunningly plain, Hardy confessed that the brutishness "does not inspire one to write hopeful poetry." Instead, it "made one sit still in an apathy & watch the clock spinning backwards, with a mild wonder if, when it gets back to the Dark Ages, & the Sack of Rome, it will ever move forward again to a new Renascence, & a new literature."[12]

If mockery animated a good deal of what Hardy wrote of war, so, too, did his appreciation for the inexpellable vitality of history. One can see his alertness to the presence of the past in "The Roman Road" (1909):

> The Roman Road runs straight and bare
> As the pale parting-line in hair
> Across the heath. And thoughtful men
> Contrast its days of Now and Then,
> And delve, and measure, and compare;
>
> Visioning on the vacant air
> Helmed legionaries, who proudly rear
> The Eagle, as they pace again
> The Roman Road.

---

11 Hardy to Lord Kitchener (8 November 1914), quoted in Michael Millgate, *Thomas Hardy: A Biography Revisited* (Oxford: Oxford University Press, 2004), 462.
12 Millgate, *Thomas Hardy*, 458.

But no tall brass-helmed legionnaire
Haunts it for me. Uprises there
A mother's form upon my ken,
Guiding my infant steps, as when
We walked that ancient thoroughfare,
The Roman Road.

II

Another reason why Hardy's sense of history is important is that it gave his poems about war their fidelity to experience. He knew in writing his war poems that he was contributing to an historical record. For example, in "The Man He Killed" (1902), about the Boer War, Hardy replicates the personal experience of soldiers, whose relation to their enemy did not always tally with the *casus belli* of politicians.

Had he and I but met
By some old ancient inn,
We should have sat us down to wet
Right many a nipperkin!
But ranged as infantry,
And staring face to face,
I shot at him as he at me,
And killed him in his place.

I shot him dead because—
Because he was my foe,
Just so: my foe of course he was;
That's clear enough; although

He thought he'd 'list, perhaps,
Off-hand like—just as I—
Was out of work—had sold his traps—
No other reason why.

In the case of the Great War, some soldiers might have found themselves in the trenches with no understanding of why they were there, but this cannot be said for the majority of the English and the French, who knew clearly enough that they were fighting to protect their homelands from the ravages of the *Kaiserreich*, a foretaste of which they had seen in how the "Foes of mad mood," as Hardy called them, laid waste Belgium. Walter de is Mate captured something of this love of homeland, when, looking back on his life in old age, he wrote in a poem entitled "England":

All that is dearest to me thou didst give—
Loved faces, ways, stars, waters, language, sea;

Through two dark crises in thy Fate I have lived,
But—never fought for thee.

Nevertheless, Hardy would have recognized the tragic ambivalence that his friend Sassoon saw in the relationship between British soldiers and their German opponents. In the second volume of his Sherston trilogy, where the hero recalls one of his fellow combatants in the line, he writes:

> Allgood was quiet, thoughtful, and fond of watching birds. We had been to the same public school, though there were nearly ten years between us. He told me that he hoped to be a historian, and I listened respectfully while he talked about the Romans in Early Britain, which was his favourite subject. It was easy to imagine him as an undergraduate at Cambridge; travelling in Germany during the Long Vacation and taking a good Degree. But his Degree had been postponed indefinitely. He said he'd always wanted to go to Germany, and there seemed nothing incongruous in the remark; for the moment I forgot that every German we killed was a point scored to our side. Allgood never grumbled about the war, for he was a gentle soul, willing to take his share in it, though obviously unsuited to homicide. But there was an expression of veiled melancholy on his face, as if he were inwardly warned that he would never see his home in Wiltshire again. A couple of months afterwards I saw his name in one of the long lists of killed, and it seemed to me that I had expected it.[13]

Hardy's sense of public war as personal history is most brilliantly exhibited in "Embarcation" (1899), which recounts his experience of seeing off troops on their way to South Africa in the Boer War. As Jon Stallworthy notes in a footnote in his superb Oxford anthology of war poetry, Hardy "despite ill heath ... bicycled 50 miles and back to the pier in Southampton to watch the British soldiers embark."

Here, where Vespasian's legions struck the sands,
And Cerdic with his Saxons entered in,
And Henry's army leapt afloat to win
Convincing triumphs over neighbour land,

Vaster battalions press for further strands,
To argue in the selfsame bloody mode
Which this late age of thought, and pact, and code,
Still fails to mend—Now deckward tramp the bands,

Yellow as autumn leaves, alive as spring,
And as each host draws out upon the sea

---

13 Siegfried Sassoon, *Memoirs of an Infantry Officer* (London: Faber & Faber, 1930), 19–20.

Beyond which lies the tragical To-Be,
None dubious of the cause, none murmuring,

Wives, sisters, parents, wave white hands and smile,
As if they knew not that they weep the while.

All the disillusionment with the "bloody mode" of war that would follow the mad euphoria that greeted the declaration of war was implicit in Hardy's poem—if it had only been heeded. Instead, too many greeted the war as little more than a welcome escape from the routines of peacetime—or, worse, a summons to heroism. Herbert Asquith ("Beb"), the prime minister's son, captured the latter with striking prescience in "The Volunteer" (1912) when he was a lawyer in the City:

Here lies a clerk who half his life had spent
Toiling at ledgers in a city grey,
Thinking that so his days would drift away
With no lance broken in life's tournament
Yet ever 'twixt the books and his bright eyes
The gleaming eagles of the legions came,
And horsemen, charging under phantom skies,
Went thundering past beneath the oriflamme.
And now those waiting dreams are satisfied
From twilight to the halls of dawn he went;
His lance is broken; but he lies content
With that high hour, in which he lived and died.
And falling thus, he wants no recompense,
Who found his battle in the last resort
Nor needs he any hearse to bear him hence,
Who goes to join the men of Agincourt.

In his poem "Then and Now," the wit in Hardy has amusing fun with the notion of the modern soldier negotiating this "high hour":

When battles were fought
With a chivalrous sense of Should and Ought,
In spirit men said,
"End we quick or dead,
Honour is some reward!
Let us fight fair—for our own best or worst;
So, Gentlemen of the Guard,
Fire first!"
    In the open they stood,
Man to man in his knightlihood:
They would not deign
To profit by a stain
On the honourable rules,
Knowing that practice perfidy no man durst

Who in the heroic schools
Was nurst.
    But now, behold, what
Is war with those where honor is not!
Rama laments
Its dead innocents;
Herod howls: "Sly slaughter
Rules now! Let us, by modes once called accurst,
Overhead, under water
Stab first."

III

The anti-war poets of the First World War have come in for a fair amount of criticism by those who claim that they personalized their experience of the war so brilliantly that they ended up misrepresenting the war. Sir Max Hastings, for example, has argued that since the war was one of liberation against the very real prospect of Germany conquering France and taking charge of the Cinque Ports, the rhetorically persuasive anti-war sentiments of the war poets can disable readers from seeing the war's true stakes. Saki's vision of what would happen to London if King Billy had had his way in France is not something anyone should regard as simply the stuff of Edwardian light comedy.[14] "The allies imposed a clumsy peace settlement at Versailles," Hastings concedes in *Catastrophe 1914: Europe Goes to War* (2013), "but if the Germans had instead been dictating the terms as victors, European freedom, justice and democracy would have paid a dreadful forfeit ... those who fought and died in the ultimately successful struggle to prevent such an outcome did not perish for nothing."[15] Here, it is important to realize, that it is not only retrospective historians who weighed matters thus. In August 1914, the novelist Arnold Bennett, speaking of the mood of his compatriots, recorded in his journal that "At the back of the mind of every one is a demi-semi fear lest Germany should after all, by some *coup*, contrive an invasion."[16]

This tallies with what the Liberal journalist H. W. Massingham had to say in the *Nation*: the war "was not a war of adventure" but a "war of defense"; it "was not for colonies, Imperial ambitions, or a balance of power. It was to teach militarism a lesson." When Haig issued the famous Order of the Day in the Spring of 1918, it is dubious whether many questioned its accuracy. "With our backs to the wall, and believing in the justice of our

14 Hector Hugh Munro ("Saki"), *When William Came: A Story of London under the Hohenzollerns* (London: John Lane, 1914).

15 Max Hastings, *Catastrophe 1914: Europe Goes to War* (New York: Alfred A. Knopf, 2013), 563.

16 *The Journal of Arnold Bennett, 1911–1920* (New York: The Viking Press, 1932), 119.

cause, each one of us must fight on to the end." Why? "The safety of our homes and the freedom of mankind alike depend on the conduct of each one of us at this critical moment."[17]

In effect, Hastings's assessment of the grounds for war is no different from the one put forth by Winston Churchill, who contended in his history of the conflict that the war's justification could not have been plainer:

> For four years Germany fought and defied the five continents of the world by land and sea and air. The German Armies upheld her tottering confederates, intervened in every theatre with success, stood everywhere on conquered territory, and inflicted on their enemies more than twice the bloodshed they suffered themselves. To break their strength and science and curb their fury, it was necessary to bring all the great nations of mankind into the field against them. Overwhelming populations, unlimited resources, measureless sacrifice, the Sea Blockade, could not prevail for fifty months. Small states were trampled down in the struggle; a mighty Empire was battered into unrecognizable fragments; and nearly twenty million men perished or shed their blood before the sword was wrested from that terrible hand.[18]

Max Egremont's response to Hastings's objection to the anti-war sentiments of the war poets—an objection shared by such redoubtable First World War historians as Michael Howard and Hew Strachan—merits quoting, precisely because it expresses both agreement and disagreement with the historians. "Surely it's necessary to separate politics, even history from the poetry," Egremont remarks.

> The work of the British First World War poets can be seen as one of the most powerful collective statements not just against what happened on the western front but against all war. But it reflects individual experience rather than objective judgment. How could it do otherwise? Every work of art is restricted by what has inspired it, and war is a more powerful restriction than most. War poetry cannot be isolated from its circumstances—a limitation perhaps and also one that acts against broader historical truth.[19]

---

17 Massingham and Haig quoted in Trevor Wilson, *The Myriad Faces of War: Britain and the Great War 1914–1918* (London: Basil Blackwell, 1986), 852–3.

18 Winston Churchill, *The World Crisis. Volume III: 1916–1918* (London: The Folio Society, 2007), 428. Since the Folio edition follows the text of the first edition of the book, which Thornton Butterworth published in 1927, I believe the page numbers of both editions should be the same. Hardy's view of the war was very much that of Churchill and Hastings: he saw it as defensive—tragic but defensive.

19 Max Egremont, *Some Desperate Glory: The First World War the Poets Knew* (London: Picador, 2014), 262–3.

As an aged non-combatant (seventy-four in 1914 when hostilities began), Hardy was set apart from the other war poets. His war poetry is neither as explicitly anti-war nor as autobiographical as that of Sassoon, Blunden, Owen, Jones and Graves. It is deeply personal, but the personality of his response to the war comes of his sense of the historical and the fatal—a sense always suffused for Hardy with tragic irony. If his engagement with the suffering of soldiers is conducted at a certain remove, it is a remove that allows him to ponder that suffering with the empathy of the artist, which, by its very nature, is more living, more dramatic than anything even the good historian produces.

Hardy's "One We Knew" (1902) exhibits the sort of dramatic empathy I mean. Although written well before the outbreak of the Great War, it still shows the personal lens through which he chose to see war and the experience of war. Accordingly, the poem is dedicated to the memory of Hardy's paternal grandmother, Mary Hardy (1772–1857), who lived with the Hardy family in the hamlet of Bockhampton for the first sixteen years of the poet's life—a vital time for any creative artist. In the course of the poem, Hardy has the old lady recall different aspects, in turn, of the French Revolution. She recalls when the Jacobins guillotined Louis XVI and unleased the Reign of Terror; when Napoleon set about conquering Europe; when the English undertook their "warlike preparations" to repel any invasion along her south coast; and when English children beguiled their sleep with fears of Bony greeting them in the morning. Her memory and Hardy's recreation of her memory show that the poet had what amounts to an aesthetic of remembrance, which renders memory not a retrospective but a living thing. "She would dwell on such dead themes," he tells his readers in the poem, "not as one who remembers, but rather as one who sees." Art, then, when properly deployed, is witness, and witness not simply to the past, but to the living presence of the past, though it is only art that conjures back that presence. And the empathy is in the trouble the artist takes in making that conjuring possible.

> She told how they used to form for the country dances—
> "The Triumph," "The New-rigged Ship" —
> To the light of the guttering wax in the panelled manses,
> And in cots to the blink of a dip.
>
> She spoke of the wild "poussetting" and "allemanding"
> On carpet, on oak, and on sod;
> And the two long rows of ladies and gentlemen standing,
> And the figures the couples trod.
>
> She showed us the spot where the maypole was yearly planted,
> And where the bandsmen stood
> While breeched and kerchiefed partners whirled, and panted
> To choose each other for good.

She told of that far-back day when they learnt astounded
Of the death of the King of France:
Of the Terror; and then of Bonaparte's unbounded
Ambition and arrogance.

Of how his threats woke warlike preparations
Along the southern strand,
And how each night brought tremors and trepidations
Lest morning should see him land.

She said she had often heard the gibbet creaking
As it swayed in the lightning flash,
Had caught from the neighbouring town a small child's shrieking
At the cart-tail under the lash …

With cap-framed face and long gaze into the embers—
We seated around her knees—
She would dwell on such dead themes, not as one who remembers,
But rather as one who sees.

She seemed one left behind of a band gone distant
So far that no tongue could hail:
Past things retold were to her as things existent,
Things present but as a tale.

That the poem should begin with the grandmother's recollections of country dances is another masterstroke, since, here, Hardy recalls the same poem about dancing, "Orchestra" (1596) by the Elizabethan poet Sir John Davies to which T. S. Eliot would allude in *Four Quartets*, written at the time of yet another war.[20]

Dauncing (bright Lady) then began to be,
When the first seedes whereof the world did spring
The Fire, Ayre, Earth, and water did agree,
By Loues perswasion, Natures mighty King,
To learne their first disordred combating:
And, in a daunce such measure to obserue,
As all the world their motion should preserue.

For Eliot, the dancing celebrated by Davies betokens the divine order that war shatters, though it is out of this "disordred combating" that God's love restores order, as the dance brings order to motion.

---

20 The lines in Eliot's "East Coker" speaking of "daunsinge, signifying matrimonie" and "necessarye coniunction / Holding eche other […] Which betokeneth concorde" are taken from his ancestor Sir Thomas Elyot's *The Governour* (1531), though they also point back to Sir John Davies's frequently anthologized poem.

Since when they still are carried in a round,
And changing come one in anothers place,
Yet doe they neyther mingle nor confound,
But euery one doth keepe the bounded space
Wherein the daunce doth bid it turne or trace:
This wondrous myracle did Loue deuise
For Dauncing is Loues proper exercise.

Although Eliot responded to this truth on a philosophical, indeed, theological level, he met his muse, Vivienne Haigh-Wood in a London dance hall.[21] As for Hardy, he exulted in country dancing when he was a young man, not to mention "Joy-jaunts, impassioned flings / Love, and its ecstasy." He shows this in "Great Things" (1917):

The dance it is a great thing,
A great thing to me,
With candles lit and partners fit
For night-long revelry;
And going home when day-dawning
Peeps pale upon the lea:
O dancing is a great thing,
A great thing to me!

"One We Knew" thus captures not only the experience of war through the recollected memories of Hardy's grandmother but the grandmother herself and Hardy's childhood. No example could better show how he saw history in personal terms.

IV

This insistence on humanizing war—and his flair for the dramatic—is brilliantly exhibited in "The Souls of the Slain" (1899), which depicts England's Boer War dead returning to England as spirits and, once returned, hearing how the bereft bemoan their loss. Hardy might have had a fair amount of scepticism when it came to Christianity but he had no hesitation in believing, as he said, "in spectres, mysterious voices, intuitions, omens, dreams, haunted places, etc., etc."[22] Here, the "trooped apparitions" ask their General how their loved ones remember them, and he and those with

21 Lady Antonia Fraser recalls meeting the poet at a ball when she was fresh out of Oxford: "Mr. Eliot's manners being perfect, in due course he asked me to dance ... [he] was an excellent firm dancer and showed every sign of enjoying the activity." Antonia Fraser, *My History: A Memoir of Growing Up* (London: Weidenfeld & Nicholson, 2015), 206.

22 Hardy to Dr. Saleeby (2 February 1915), Florence Emily Hardy, *The Later Years of Thomas Hardy* (London, Macmillan, 1928), 271.

whom he speaks express Hardy's settled belief that it is their home life, not
their deeds as soldiers, that the bereaved most remember.

IX

"A father broods: 'Would I had set him
To some humble trade,
And so slacked his high fire,
And his passionate martial desire;
Had told him no stories to woo him and whet him
To this due crusade!"

X

"And, General, how hold out our sweethearts,
Sworn loyal as doves?"
—"Many mourn; many think
It is not unattractive to prink
Them in sables for heroes. Some fickle and fleet hearts
Have found them new loves."

XI

"And our wives?" quoth another resignedly,
"Dwell they on our deeds?"
—"Deeds of home; that live yet
Fresh as new—deeds of fondness or fret;
Ancient words that were kindly expressed or unkindly,
These, these have their heeds."

XII

—"Alas! then it seems that our glory
Weighs less in their thought
Than our old homely acts,
And the long-ago commonplace facts
Of our lives—held by us as scarce part of our story,
And rated as nought!"

XIII

Then bitterly some: "Was it wise now
To raise the tomb-door
For such knowledge? Away!"
But the rest: "Fame we prized till to-day;
Yet that hearts keep us green for old kindness we prize now
A thousand times more!"

Rather than being anti-war, in the polemical sense in which the poets of
the Great War tended to be anti-war, this is rather more meditative than

polemical. The poem humanizes soldiers and those who mourned the death of soldiers by giving both, in a few bold poignant strokes, something of their personal histories. But it is typical of Hardy and of his restless critical intelligence, that he no sooner seeks to humanize his subjects than he shows how in many cases such humanizing is simply not possible. War, after all, by its very nature, is dehumanizing, and Hardy again turns to drama, a kind of metaphysical drama, to drive home this bitter reality, particularly for the unmourned, the homeless, the forgotten.

XIV

Thus speaking, the trooped apparitions
Began to disband
And resolve them in two:
Those whose record was lovely and true
Bore to northward for home: those of bitter traditions
Again left the land,

XV

And, towering to seaward in legions,
They paused at a spot
Overbending the Race—
That engulphing, ghast, sinister place—
Whither headlong they plunged, to the fathomless regions
Of myriads forgot.

XVI

And the spirits of those who were homing
Passed on, rushingly,
Like the Pentecost Wind;
And the whirr of their wayfaring thinned
And surceased on the sky, and but left in the gloaming
Sea-mutterings and me.

Here, for the poet, is the mystery of war. Answering nothing of the questions we might put to it, war, once its savage work is done, if it is ever done, leaves only sea-mutterings. For Hardy, to raise the tomb-door was to find that mystery deepened, a truth Drummer Hodge nicely confirms, though Rupert Brooke, writing under his English heaven, chose to ignore it.

Young Hodge the Drummer never knew—
Fresh from his Wessex home—
The meaning of the broad Karoo,
The Bush, the dusty loam,
And why uprose to nightly view
Strange stars amid the gloam.

Yet portion of that unknown plain
Will Hodge for ever be;
His homely Northern breast and brain
Grow up a Southern tree,
And strange-eyed constellations reign
His stars eternally.

In the biography of himself that Hardy ghostwrote, he said of the First World War that it "gave the *coup de grace* to any conception he may have nourished of a fundamental ultimate Wisdom at the back of things. With his views on necessitation, or at most a very limited free will, events seemed to show him that a fancy he had often held and expressed, that the never-ending push of the Universe was an unpurposive and irresponsible groping in the direction of least resistance, might possibly be the real truth. "Whether or no," he would say, "'Desine fata Deum flecti sperare precando.'"[23]

Such bleak musings notwithstanding, Hardy could detach himself sufficiently from his war poetry to see that the very act of writing such poetry might be construed as a kind of impertinence, the tragedy of war being so terribly unspeakable. In "I Looked up from My Writing" (1917), he sets before his reader as if in a playhouse an encounter between the moon and himself after the moon interrupts his writing with her "meditative misty head," in which he asks her what she is doing, to which she responds with matter-of-fact mockery:

"Oh, I've been scanning pond and hole
And waterway hereabout
For the body of one with a sunken soul
Who has put his life-light out.

"Did you hear his frenzied tattle?
It was sorrow for his son
Who is slain in brutish battle,
Though he has injured none.

"And now I am curious to look
Into the blinkered mind
Of one who wants to write a book
In a world of such a kind."

Her temper overwrought me,
And I edged to shun her view,
For I felt assured she thought me
One who should drown him too.

---

23 "Cease to think that the decrees of the gods can be changed by prayers", Virgil, *Æneid* VI, 376 (29–19 BC). Florence Hardy, *The Later Years of Thomas Hardy*, 165–6.

Still, despite such lunar visitations, Hardy did write his war poetry. Even in the face of the most staggering evil, he reaffirms that art must continue to go about its business. For art to down tools at such a time would be to abdicate one of its most vital charges, which is to counter human iniquity with human indignation—the watchman's cry of embattled love. After observing how the Dorset dialect echoes German, Hardy curses those who had started the war with a matter-of-factness all his own.

> Then seemed a Heart crying: "Whosoever they be
> At root and bottom of this, who flung this flame
> Between kin folk kin tongued even as are we,
>
> "Sinister, ugly, lurid, be their fame;
> May their familiars grow to shun their name,
> And their brood perish everlastingly."

Again, here, Hardy shows how little he shared the anti-war prejudices of the younger war poets. The war might have been cursed; fighting it might have been an infernal curse; but it was not ill-advisedly fought—or ignoble. The Germans had to be stopped. In this regard, he was one with R. G. Collingwood, who wrote in 1919 in an address to the Belgian Students Association at Fladbury: "The absolutist theory of the state, which drives every state that holds it into a career of aggression, and conquest, and tyranny—a career like that of a mad dog, only to be quieted by death—this theory was the root of the war from which we are now emerging, and it is only the eradication of the theory that can give us peace."[24]

In another essay in this collection, I have occasion to consider what Hardy made of bells celebrating the birth of Christ. In one of his very best war poems, "On the Belgian Expatriation" (1914), the poet returns to this question of what the bells sang, Belgium being famous for its carillons, only to reiterate how the war had left him deaf to what they sang—or could sing.

> I dreamt that people from the Land of Chimes
> Arrived one autumn morning with their bells,
> To hoist them on the towers and citadels
> Of my own country, that the musical rhymes
>
> Rung by them into space at meted times
> Amid the market's daily stir and stress,
> And the night's empty star-lit silentness,
> Might solace souls of this and kindred climes.
>
> Then I awoke; and lo, before me stood
> The visioned ones, but pale and full of fear;
> From Bruges they came, and Antwerp, and Ostend,

24 R. G. Collingwood, *Essays in Political Philosophy*, ed. David Boucher (Oxford; Oxford University Press, 1989), 203.

No carillons in their train. Foes of mad mood
Had shattered these to shards amid the gear
Of ravaged roof, and smouldering gable-end.[25]

In what he saw as a civilization with no bells to solace souls, Hardy saw a civilization captive to its fallenness—irredeemably captive. This, for him, was the lesson of war.

We are getting to the end of visioning
The impossible within this universe,
Such as that better whiles may follow worse,
And that our race may mend by reasoning.

We know that even as larks in cages sing
Unthoughtful of deliverance from the curse
That holds them lifelong in a latticed hearse,
We ply spasmodically our pleasuring.

And that when nations set them to lay waste
Their neighbours' heritage by foot and horse,
And hack their pleasant plains in festering seams,
They may again,—not warily, or from taste,
But tickled mad by some demonic force.—
Yes. We are getting to the end of dreams!

25 In 1906 Hardy submitted a paper, entitled "Memories of Church Restoration," which was read to the Twenty-Ninth General Meeting of the Society for the Protection of Ancient Buildings. The paper was subsequently published in the Society's Annual Report. In it Hardy recounts one or two incidents from his early architectural work and then continues: "My knowledge at first hand of church repair at the present moment is very limited. But one or two prevalent abuses have come by accident under my notice. The first concerns the re-hanging of church bells. A barbarous practice is, I believe, very general, that of cutting off the cannon of each bell—namely, the loop on the crown by which it has been strapped to the stock—and restrapping it by means of holes cut through the crown itself. The mutilation is sanctioned on the ground that, by so fixing it, the centre of the bell's gravity is brought nearer to the axis on which it swings, with advantage and ease to the ringing. I do not question the truth of this; but the resources of mechanics are not so exhausted but that the same result may be obtained by leaving the bell unmutilated and increasing the camber of the stock, which for that matter might be so great as nearly to reach a right angle. I was recently passing through a churchyard where I saw standing on the grass a peal of bells just taken down from the adjacent tower and subjected to this treatment. A sight more piteous than that presented by these fine bells, standing disfigured in a row in the sunshine, like cropped criminals in the pillory, as it were ashamed of their degradation, I have never witnessed among inanimate things."

A Day to Remember:
Revisiting the Somme

Elegy: The First Day on the Somme, Andrew Roberts (Head of Zeus). 292 pages.

"It was a sunny morning, that of July 1st, 1916," the poet Edmund Blunden recalled in a broadcast of 1928.

> The right notes for it would have been the singing of blackbirds and the ringing of the blacksmith's anvil. But, as the world soon knew, the music of that sunny morning was the guns. They had never spoken before with so huge a voice. Their sound crossed the sea. In Southdown villages the school children sat wondering at that incessant drumming and the rattling of the windows. That night an even greater anxiety than usual forbade wives and mothers to sleep. The Battle of the Somme had begun.

The purpose of the "Big Push" was straightforward: to draw German forces away from Verdun and to break the stalemate on the Western Front by inflicting a massive blow against the German defenses in Picardy along an 18-mile front from Gommecourt in the north to Montauban in the south. As it happened, the Somme's first day remains the worst the British Army ever suffered. Very little went as planned and what Churchill referred to as its "melancholy and prodigal slaughter" still staggers the imagination. On that one day alone, the British lost nearly 20,000 men, with 40,000 wounded or missing.

Many good historians, including Denis Winter, Trevor Wilson, Robin Prior, John Keegan, Michael Howard, Gary Mead, and Hew Strachan have produced fascinating studies of the Somme. Now, in *Elegy*, the brilliant historian Andrew Roberts has written a masterly and moving account of the Somme's first day to honor its centennial. It is an evenhanded, elegant overview and does admirable justice at once to the complexity of the battle and the bravery of the men who fought it.

Drawing on the battle's rich historiography, Roberts recreates not only the battle's harrowing first day but the strategy, tactics, and preparations that went into its planning and execution. He also makes incisive use of many contemporary accounts, including Siegfried Sassoon's *Memoirs of an Infantry Officer* (1930) for the British experience of the battle, and Ernst Jünger's novel, *Storm of Steel* (1920) for the German experience.

Once the British went over the top, they encountered a battlefield altogether different from the one that they had been led to expect. Assured that the seven-day pre-battle bombardment would knock out the enemy defenses, they were met, instead, by German machine-gun fire at every turn. The deep German dug-outs withstood the bombardment almost entirely intact, and when it ended, the Germans simply put their machine guns in place and fired at will at the pitiably exposed, advancing enemy. The British also had to contend with the German wire, which the bombardment's shrapnel left uncut. Those who were not immediately hit were pinned down or forced to find shelter in shell-holes.

Tragic irony ruled. General Sir Douglas Haig and General Sir Henry Rawlinson, the chief architects of the battle, assumed that the obliterated enemy trenches would need to be rebuilt. This was their justification for saddling each infantryman with over 60 pounds of equipment. That very few made it past their own trenches, let alone the German trenches, made this a particularly galling miscalculation.

Rawlinson also instructed officers to have their men walk, not run, across no-man's-land, the assumption being that there would be no need for haste before German defenders that had been rendered defenseless. It was only after waves and waves of troops had been mown down that this order was countermanded. Moreover, Rawlinson was convinced that what Germans did survive would make easy targets because of the higher ground the German positions commanded. Yet it was precisely this higher ground that enabled the Germans to see and react to the British infantry's every movement. As Roberts observes, "From the German trenches at ... Beaumont Hamel today, it is easy to spot with the naked eye individuals standing where the Newfoundlanders' trenches were sited." The Newfoundlanders, with whose ordeal Roberts opens the book, suffered some of the worst losses of the day: 89 percent were killed or wounded, for a total of 684, including every one of their 26 officers.

Of course, there were exceptions to the general *debâcle*. The Ulstermen of the 9th Royal Inniskilling Fusiliers, fighting on what was then the 226th anniversary of the Battle of the Boyne, took Schwaben Redoubt, along with 400 prisoners and 4 Victoria Crosses. But they encountered cut wire. And they lost 5,104 men, over a third of the division. Moreover, they could not hold the ground they won: the failure of other divisions to match their advance, not to mention the German counter-attack, made sure of that. When Haig heard of the Ulsterman's gains, he advised that they "advance to the enemy's second line," which elicits from Roberts the mordant reply: "The fog of war was rarely foggier."

Seeing the pre-battle bombardment from the air, in which 1,627,824 shells were fired, Cecil Lewis, the famous ace, and, later, author of *Sagittarius Rising* (1936) was convinced that "Nothing could live under that rain of splintering steel." This was why so many were so convinced of the likelihood of the bombardment's success. And why Haig held an Indian corps of cavalry in reserve in anticipation of the breakthrough he was certain would ensue. What went wrong? In addition to the depth of the German dugouts, the hastily assembled ordnance was often defective, detonating prematurely or not at all. Yet even well-made ordnance could never have knocked out the German trenches. Haig's 400 heavy and 1,000 field guns were simply insufficient for so large a front.

The exact death toll for the British was 35,494 wounded, 19,240 killed; 2,152 missing, and 585 prisoners of war. Nearly half of the 120,000 men who went over the top became casualties. And these numbers have to be seen in terms of the numerical superiority the British enjoyed: their 143 battalions were pitted against 32 German battalions, which made the scale of defeat all the more stunning. Speaking of the crucial contribution that Hiram Maxim's invention made to the battle, Roberts parodies Churchill: "Never in the field of human conflict could so many be killed so quickly by so few." (The Germans lost only 12,000 men.) Certainly, it was providential that Lord Kitchener never lived to see the fate of his New Army. As one wag put it: "Two years in the making and ten minutes in the destroying: that was our history." Still, as one German eyewitness wrote, the first day of the Somme was "an amazing spectacle of unexampled gallantry, courage and bull-dog determination on both sides."

Throughout, Robert brings equanimity and shrewdness to his reading of a battle that is still highly controversial. Although appreciative of Haig's deficiencies—his uncritical confidence in his artillery, his reliance on what proved unreliable intelligence, his excessive planning, his trust in "group think," his mistrust of both his officers and his infantry—he still gives grudging praise to a man who learned from his mistakes and did the best he could with an admittedly poor hand. In this regard, Roberts rejects Ludendorff's oft-repeated clam of dubious provenance that "The English Generals are wanting in strategy. We should have no chance if they possessed as much science as their officers and men had of courage and bravery. They are lions led by donkeys." After all, as Roberts says at the outset, "If there was a way of fighting WWI that did not involve trying to smash frontally through formidable enemy defenses, neither side discovered one."

Nevertheless, Roberts certainly shares Ludendorff's high opinion of the courage of the British infantry. What was it that one of Frederic Manning's characters says in that wonderful novel of the Somme (Hemingway's favorite), *The Middle Parts of Fortune* (1930)? "They can say what they bloody well like … but we're a fuckin' fine mob."

When it comes to Haig, no one could improve on Churchill's amusing portrait in *Great Contemporaries* (1937), where he finds the perfect analogy for the man cordially known as "The Butcher," likening him to "a great surgeon before the days of anesthetics, versed in every detail of such science as was known to him: sure of himself, steady of poise, knife in hand, intent upon the operation; entirely removed in his professional capacity from the agony of the patient, the anguish of relations, or the doctrines of rival schools ... He would operate without excitement, or he would depart without being affronted; and if the patient died, he would not reproach himself. It must be understood that I speak only of his professional actions. Once out of the theatre, his heart was as warm as any man's."

Roberts is adamant that Haig's most notorious battle, for all its horrors, was not futile. Despite Britain's taking 450,000 casualties when it was finally over in November of 1916, it forced Falkenhayn to withdraw heavy batteries from Verdun and wrested the initiative away from the Germans. The Somme might not have broken the stalemate on the Western Front but it certainly paved the way for that otherwise elusive breakthrough.

Roberts also appreciates how Churchill and Sir Alan Brooke learned from the losses of the Somme in their strategic conduct of WWII, in which, as Robert says, they "put off the return to the Continent for four years after the retreat to Dunkirk, preferring to fight in North Africa and Italy, rather than risk a direct assault on France and Germany," which would only have entrapped them in precisely the same war of attrition that bedeviled the Allies on the Western Front. (John Keegan was memorable about Joffre's favorite strategy: "Attrition," he wrote in *The Face of Battle* (1976), "is a game at which two can play.")

What finally makes Robert's book so special is that it never loses sight of the human dimension of the war. The voices of the soldiers whom the Somme changed forever are on nearly every page. Blunden, in the conclusion of his broadcast, gave voice to a truth that has not always been acknowledged: "What men did in the battle of the Somme, day after day, and month after month, will never be excelled in honour, unselfishness and love." Roberts, in his solicitude for the men who underwent this terrible trial, as well as his solid, judicious, revelatory scholarship, proves himself a worthy historian of their embattled good faith.

No More Glory
for the Bold Fenian Men

The Seven: The Lives and Legacies of the Founding of the Irish Republic, Ruth Dudley Edwards (Oneworld Publications). 408 pages.

No history cries out for revision more insistently than Irish history. And no event in Irish history illustrates this better than the Easter Rebellion—the centennial of which is now in full throttle—because no event better epitomizes the vexed question of what constitutes Irish identity and Irish nationhood. As everyone knows, when the band of romantic nationalists occupied the General Post Office in Dublin on that sleepy Monday morning one hundred years ago and proclaimed the founding of the Irish Republic, most of their fellow townsmen looked upon them as mad, disruptive nuisances, especially after the civilian death toll reached 250 and the property damage soared to over £1.8 million. It was only when the unimaginative British started shooting the ringleaders that popular opinion swung round in favor of the rebels. Nevertheless, despite all of the centennial celebrations, it is remarkable how little attention has been paid to the nationalism that inspired the uprising. For centuries, historians of all persuasions have rightly seen nationalism as integral to this and most modern Irish history. And yet few histories marking the centennial have had anything incisive to say of this peculiar phenomenon.

Ruth Dudley Edwards's *The Seven: The Lives and Legacies of the Founding of the Irish Republic* is a brilliant exception. Written with great charm and zest, as well as judicious toughmindedness, the book is an overdue re-examination of the nationalism that led not only to the Easter Rebellion but the Troubles beyond. For anyone keen on understanding why the question of Irish identity and Irish nationhood remains so vexed, Edwards's book is a must.

One governing virtue of the book is that, as a revisionist, Edwards has not come simply to scoff where others have prayed. She understands how English misrule stoked the fires of Irish nationalism, as well as the idealism that often imbued that nationalism. And she certainly understands the sacrifices that individual nationalists made to witness to their faith. Some of the liveliest passages in the book recreate those sacrifices in a narrative full of pathos, irony and wit—proof that good storytelling always distinguishes good history.

Edwards's treatment of the Fenian Thomas Clarke (1858–1916), so much of whose sacrificial zeal animated the Easter Rebellion, nicely demonstrates this. After being dispatched by the Irish-American *Clan na Gael* to blow up London Bridge, Clarke was betrayed by an informer and sentenced at the Old Bailey in 1883 to life imprisonment. It was not until 1898, after fifteen years behind bars, in conditions that were often gratuitously barbarous, that he was released. The *Oxford Dictionary of National Biography* describes Clarke as "shadowy." Edwards's account of the "disciplined, focused teetotaler," who sought "neither status nor recognition" for the work he did to advance his beloved cause brings the man and his trials entirely to life.

Indeed, her vivid account is a model of critical sympathy. It might be true that Clarke, impelled "by a desire for vengeance, an all-pervading hatred for the British, an implacable ambition to get them out of Ireland, a steely determination to do whatever it took and exceptional strength of character … was readying himself to start a revolution," but it is also true, as Edward shows, that he chose to live in "an Irish republican bubble" and had no interest in any culture unless it could somehow help to "damage the British." And this included Irish culture—the genuine article, in all of its richness—not the counterfeit culture peddled by the nationalists. Denied any proper reading by his British captors, Clarke was desperately parochial, and the crude, narrow, fanatical view of Irish identity and Irish nationhood that he bequeathed to the new republic cast a long, lamentable shadow.

Edwards's portraits of the other architects of the rebellion, Seán Mac Diarmada, Éamonn Ceannt, Patrick Pearse, Thomas MacDonagh, Joseph Plunkett, and James Connolly are equally vivid and revelatory. While Pearse and Connolly were trying to keep body and soul together in the blazing GPO, MacDonagh and his Volunteers had their hands full in Jacob's Biscuit factory fending off boredom. As Edwards drolly observes, "A gramophone record of 'God Save the Queen' was played when MacDonagh inspected his troops, the library was raided for books, and there were reading circles." Still, as one British officer noted, MacDonagh faced the firing squad "like a Prince," offering his executioners not only cigarettes but his silver cigarette case. How his wife saw this gallows theatre is another matter. Certainly, after MacDonagh was gone, she must have found his verses tough reading: "Oh, you're my husband right enough / But what's the good of that? / You know you never were the stuff / To be the cottage cat."

Yet it is in her portrait of Patrick Pearse (1879–1916), the poet, schoolmaster and barrister, that Edwards shows how the nationalists' misreading of Irish identity and Irish nationhood was often mirrored in their misreading of themselves. "This tormented man," Edwards writes, "who had

exceptional gifts and deep flaws, could provide enough material to keep
a symposium of psychiatrists arguing for a week." Seeing the Wolf Tones
perform their tribute to Pearse one night, she recalls how:

> It was ... dispiriting to find [an Irish band] still so incurious about
> the real man behind the face and voice of the Easter rising. But then,
> as Pearse pointed out himself, he was hard to understand, which
> is why after his death most republicans settled for some version
> of Pearse the martyr and saint, while a tiny number of doubters
> whispered behind their hands about his being bloodthirsty and a
> paedophile

Apropos this last trait, Edwards relates how Pearse was fond of kissing
the boys in his school (they nicknamed him "Kiss me Hardy"), though his
sublimated homosexuality also suffused his various writings, a tell-tale
fabric, as Edwards characterizes it, "interweaving ... aesthetics, martyrdom,
masculinity and nationhood." Born in London of a free-thinking father from
Birmingham and a devout Irish Catholic mother, Pearse would grow up in
Dublin a bundle of contradictions. Edwards quotes from the Gaelic diary
he kept, which she also plundered for her definitive life, *Patrick Pearse: The
Triumph of Failure* (1977):

> You don't make friends with Gaels. You avoid their company. When
> you come among them you bring a dark cloud with you which lies
> heavily on them ... Is it your English blood that is the cause of that, I
> wonder? ... I suppose there are two Pearses, the somber and taciturn
> Pearse and the gay and sunny Pearse ... I don't like that gloomy
> Pearse. He gives me the shivers. And the most curious part of the
> story is that no one knows which is the true Pearse.

Like so many confused young men, Pearse welcomed the readymade
identity of Irish nationalism and resolved from an early age to emulate the
heroic sacrifices of such legendary Fenians as Wolfe Tone (1763–98) and
John Mitchel (1815–75). He was also enamoured of the Gaelic language
that Douglas Hyde had given such romantic allure.

In 1915, in an oration at the graveside of the Fenian Jeremiah O'Donovan
Rossa (1831–1915), this perfervid acolyte would pave the way for the Easter
Rebellion by reaffirming a central tenet of the Fenian faith. The nationalists,
Pearse insisted, would acknowledge "only one definition of freedom: It is
Tone's definition; it is Mitchel's definition; it is Rossa's definition. Let no
one blaspheme the cause that the dead generations of Ireland served by
giving it any other name and definition than their name and definition."
And his conclusion could not have been more stark: "Ireland unfree shall
never be at peace."

In this bravura piece of nationalist propaganda, Edwards sees something
different: "The use of the dead to justify as well as to dictate the policy of the

living ... would be enthusiastically adopted by subsequent generations of violent republicans," though using Rossa in this way was especially cynical since he had already begun to accept the constitutionalism anathema to Pearse and the nationalists.

One Irishman who consistently rejected Irish nationalism and the preferred language of the nationalists was James Joyce (1882–1941). In fact, Joyce attended one of Pearse's classes in Gaelic but left unimpressed after the revolutionary schoolmaster told him that Gaelic had no word for "thunder," an omission that struck Joyce as proof of the language's superficiality. Moreover, Joyce never surrendered his British passport, even after the Irish Free State was founded in 1922, certain that the British Empire had given the Irish more independence than would any nation state concocted by the nationalists. (Éamon De Valera would prove him prophetic on that score.) Moreover, the years that Joyce spent in Trieste under the Habsburg Empire, where he would create that quintessentially imperial hero, Leopold Bloom, convinced him of the hypocrisy of nationalists, who never tired of claiming that empires were coercive and tyrannical, while turning their own nation states into pagan theocracies. Joyce would give a kind of closure to his otherwise unpropitious encounter with Pearse by coining a new word for "thunder" in *Finnegans Wake* (1939):

> Bababadalgharaghtakamminarronnkonnbronntonn-
> erronntuonnthunntrovarrhounawnskawntoohoohoordenenthurnuk.

Then, again, in light of Yeats's aggrieved response to the pertinacity of the nationalists—"Too long a sacrifice / Can make a stone of the heart"—Joyce doubtless found it amusing that Pearse's father was a stone carver.

Edwards is unsparing about the role that Irish-Americans played in at once fomenting and funding the nationalists' campaigns of violence at a time when the admirable MP and barrister John Redmond (1856–1918)—who was never unsympathetic to the aspirations of the separatists—was trying to put together a constitutional solution acceptable not only to the nationalists and the British but to Ulster as well. While appreciative of the hurdles in his way, Redmond was confident (according to his biographer Lord Bew) that independence could still be won without bloodshed. As it was, the Easter Rebellion was tragic proof that the men of violence, backed to the hilt by bloody-minded Irish America, would prevail over the constitutionalists

In her conclusion, Edwards quotes the Jesuit Francis Shaw to show how the nationalists radically impoverished Ireland's sense of identity and nationhood. "In the commonly accepted view of Irish history," Shaw wrote, "the Irishman of today is asked to disown his own past. He is expected to censure as unpatriotic the common Irishmen who were not attracted by the new revolutionary ideas, but who adhered to an ancient tradition." Then, again, he is told "to apologise for their fellow countrymen who accepted loyally the serious guidance of the Church." Worse still, he is told that he "must despise as unmanly those of their own country who preferred to solve problems, if possible, by peaceful rather than violent means." Here, indeed, was the issue of Irish nationalism in all of its small-mindedness and divisiveness. The Easter Rebellion has inspired some fine historians, including F. S. L. Lyons, J. J. Lee and Charles Townsend. Now, to their illustrious company we can add Ruth Dudley Edwards. In *The Seven* she has written a corker of a book.

Utopians:
Lessons from the New World Order

Paradise Now: The Story of American Utopianism, Chris Jennings (Random House). 488 pages.

In 1908, H. L. Mencken was approached by an editor and author named Robert Rives La Monte, who was keen on persuading the twenty-eight-year-old newspaperman to join him in an epistolary debate about the benefits of socialism: La Monte would argue for and Mencken could argue against them. Despite his misgivings, Mencken agreed, and, shortly thereafter, the now largely forgotten *Man vs. Man* (1910) appeared. The first letter from La Monte was suitably provocative. "If you wish to see better manners, more worthy fiction, higher art, and nobler drama, as I know you do, your only course is to become a Socialist comrade, and give us your aid in hastening the advent of the Social Revolution." Mencken's response was bemused: "Your ideal picture of the best possible world seems to me a fair picture of the worst possible world," and so the exchange proceeded. Looking back, Mencken concluded that although the book proved a commercial and critical failure, it forced him to sort out what he might have called his *Weltanschauung*, which was far from utopian.

> My basic point of view ... went back to my early teens, and has never changed in any essential during the half century since. Under the influence of my father ... I emerged into sentience with an almost instinctive distrust of all schemes of revolution and reform. They were, to me, only signs and symptoms of a fundamental hallucination, to wit, the hallucination that human nature could be changed by passing statues and preaching gospels—that natural law could be repealed by taking thought.

In *Paradise Now: The Story of American Utopianism*, Chris Jennings revisits five utopian groups—the Shakers, the Owenites, the Fourierists, the Icarians, and the Perfectionists—to show that if there was one thing that all of these socialist groups had in common it was a passionate belief not only that the natural law could be repealed but that its repeal would benefit mankind.

Utopianism has a curious history. Although the word *utopia* (from the Greek meaning "nowhere") was coined by St. Thomas More (1478–1535) in his 1516 satire of the same name, in which the great humanist took Europe to task for its lack of Christian *caritas*, the father of the utopianism to which most nineteenth-century utopians subscribed was Henri de Saint-Simon (1760–1825), who fought in the war of American Independence, made a pile speculating in confiscated property, went bankrupt during the Directory, and wrote several highly influential books touting his vision of a techno-cratic socialism. For Saint-Simon, the Industrial Revolution required a more scientific, equitable social order, and enlightened industrialists would lead the way. If not all utopians shared his fanciful trust in the good-heartedness of *capitaines d'industrie*, they did share his conviction, as Jennings notes, that the "golden age of mankind is not behind but before us."

They also shared Saint-Simon's conviction that human nature is perfect-ible. In his magisterial history of the Russian Revolution, *A People's Tragedy* (1996), Orlando Figes quotes a passage from Trotsky, which nicely sums up this quintessentially utopian conviction.

> What is man? He is by no means a finished or harmonious being. No, he is still a highly awkward creature. Man, as animal, has not evolved by plan but spontaneously, and has accumulated many contradictions. The question of how to educate and regulate, how to improve and complete the physical and spiritual construction of man, is a colossal problem which can only be conceived on the basis of Socialism. We can construct a railway across the Sahara, we can build the Eiffel Tower and talk directly with New York, but we surely cannot improve man. No, we can! To produce a new, "improved version" of man—that is the future task of Communism.

Here, in a nutshell, is the utopian belief in social engineering that ani-mates all of Jennings's utopians. And with convictions like these, it was not surprising that American utopians, like their European and Russian counterparts, sought to attain their greater communal good by redefining the family, convinced, as Jennings writes, "that the narrow, superseding loyalties engendered by marriage and the biological family were anathema to progress."

Charles Fourier (1772–1837), for example, the celebrated French utopian, one of whose claims to fame was his belief that we should increase the gaiety of nations by draining the sea of salt to make lemonade, regarded marriage as "nothing more than a prison built to enslave women and lock both of its captives into lives of deceit, intellectual malaise, and sexual nullity." Then, again, John Humphrey Noyes (1811–86), one of the mille-narian Perfectionists who settled in Oneida, New York based his contempt for marriage on the Bible, citing the Gospel of St Matthew, "For in the resurrection they neither marry nor are given in marriage." Jennings has fun with this otherwise serious idiocy by observing, "Noyes had begun to wonder whether there might be a reciprocal relationship between the coming of God's kingdom and the abolition of marriage. If free love was going to define life in the millennium, maybe free love would help trigger the millennium."

Another Frenchman, Étienne Cabet (1768–1856), whose novel, *Voyage en Icaria* (1840) won utopian devotees in Texas, Illinois, Iowa, Missouri and California, might have claimed to be in favor of marriage and the family but it is difficult to see how either could flourish in his earthly paradise, where communal conformity was so strictly enforced. Indeed, as the historian Theodore Zeldin points out in his brilliant two-volume history, *France 1848–1945* (1973), Cabet's ideal state was one in which everyone would wear the same clothes. Why? Because "bizarre and tasteless designs" would be outlawed.

This utopian edict would certainly have met with the approval of the honorary American, P. G. Wodehouse, who went out of his way in his collection of essays, *Louder and Funnier* (1932) to console with those traveling on ocean liners with ill-clad fellow passengers. "When you see a fat man in a yachting cap, horn-rimmed spectacles, plus fours, and black and white buckskin shoes," the great man wrote, "I maintain that there is convincing evidence of premeditation and that the matter should be firmly dealt with by the proper authorities." Cabet and the Icarians would have agreed. Certainly, if any of our contemporary utopians could find a way to outlaw the "bizarre and tasteless" dress of passengers on airplanes, they would do the utopian cause immeasurable good.

In taking up his utopian *illuminés* and their movements, Jennings argues that without utopian convictions of some sort, our political life will stagnate. Indeed, he takes particular issue with the historian Tony Judt for arguing that the charge of sensible political philosophers should be "not to imagine better worlds but rather to think how to prevent worse ones." For Jennings, this is tantamount to "finding the least bad version of the status quo — the assumption being that what we have is well enough and well enough ought to be left alone." Instead, Jennings urges his readers to join his nineteenth-century utopians in re-imagining America in order to create a better America.

For those who might demur, Jennings has his answer ready, arguing that the utopians have much to teach us. "Some of the things that the nineteenth-century utopians got right," he insists, "decades in advance of their fellow citizens — the equality of women, the importance of public education in a democratic society, the need for a social safety net, the edifying vitality of a diverse society, the hazards of unchecked markets — show the social dividends of contemplating idealized futures with a relatively soft commitment to the present state of affairs."

Not all readers will find such pleading persuasive. Mencken, in his unreconstructed way, regarded progressive reform as "only a conspiracy of prehensile charlatans to mulct taxpayers." Even Henry David Thoreau was dubious, telling Emerson of Brook Farm, the Fourierist experiment in communal living about which Hawthorne wrote *Blithedale Romance* (1852): "I'd rather keep bachelor's hall in hell than go to board in heaven."

Readers interested in the pathologies of socialism will benefit from Jennings's lively account of the yearnings of his utopian subjects. Needless to say, such yearnings are still with us, though Jennings often writes as though they were absent in our own ardently progressive age. After all, we are inundated by advocates of what the utopians liked to regard as the "science of society," which would "not just be descriptive," as Jenkins accurately points out, "telling us when and why people act as they do," but would also "allow us to change how people act, to fix every social problem."

Whether such a "science of society" is as benign as Jennings would have his readers believe is another matter. Since so much of the utopianism discussed in *Paradise Now* originated in Europe, readers might wish to look at Michael Burleigh's superb study, *Earthly Powers: The Clash of Religion and Politics in Europe from the French Revolution to the Great War* (2005), which puts this complicated, consequential history in some context.

The best critic of American utopianism, however, remains a high-toned old Christian woman from East Hampton, New York named Catherine Beecher (1800–78), the sister of Harriet Beecher Stowe, the author of *Uncle Tom's Cabin* (1852). Jennings might have given his readers a more critical account of his utopians and their schemes if he had quoted something that this shrewd educator said in 1836 about the Welsh utopian Robert Owen (1771–1858) and his New Harmony community in Indiana, which failed two years after it was founded in 1825, though it still garners wistful praise from our own would-be utopians.

> To collect together a company of persons of all varieties of age, taste, habits, and preconceived opinions, and teach them that there is no God, no future state, no retributions after death, no revealed standard of right and wrong, and no free agency; that the laws that secure private property are a nuisance, that religion is a curse, that marriage is a vexatious restraint, that the family state is needless and unwise, and then to expect such a community to dwell together in harmony, and practice upon the rules of benevolence, what can be conceived more childish or improbable, by any person who has seen the world or known anything of human nature! And yet such is the plan and expectation of the leaders of practical Atheism.

Hotel America

Hotel: An American History, A. K. Sandoval-Strauz (Yale University Press).
375 pages.

In March 1776, James Boswell and Samuel Johnson journeyed by post-
chaise to Blenheim Park to take in the incomparable palace that a grateful
nation had built for John Churchill, Duke of Marlborough, to thank him
for routing the French in the Battle of Blenheim (1705). Since the house they
saw was only a little more than fifty years old (Sir John Vanbrugh finished
it in 1724), its ochre-colored stone must have been radiant. Afterwards,
dining in a nearby inn, Johnson considered the relative merits of private
houses as opposed to inns.

> There is no private house, (said he,) in which people can enjoy
> themselves so well, as at a capital tavern. Let there be ever so great
> plenty of good things, ever so much grandeur, ever so much ele-
> gance, ever so much desire that every body should be easy; in the
> nature of things it cannot be: there must always be some degree of
> care and anxiety. The master of the house is anxious to entertain
> his guests; the guests are anxious to be agreeable to him: and no
> man, but a very impudent dog indeed, can as freely command
> what is in another man's house, as if it were his own. Whereas, at
> a tavern, there is a general freedom from anxiety. You are sure you
> are welcome: and the more noise you make, the more trouble you
> give, the more good things you call for, the welcomer you are. No
> servants will attend you with the alacrity which waiters do, who
> are incited by the prospect of an immediate reward in proportion as
> they please. No, Sir; there is nothing which has yet been contrived
> by man, by which so much happiness is produced as by a good
> tavern or inn.

In his well-researched and well-illustrated account of the history of the
American hotel, A. K. Sandoval-Strauz shows how the purpose-built hotel
evolved from the often improvisational inn. It was George Washington's
presidential tours of the thirteen colonies from 1789 to 1791 that first demon-
strated to the young nation what social, political and economic advantages
good inns could offer. At first, leading citizens, local officials, family mem-

bers and old comrades-in-arms tried to persuade the first President to put up in their private homes, but Washington wisely declined and insisted instead on staying in inns: they would avoid any appearance of favoritism and give him a genuine feel for the pulse of the places and people he visited. The tours helped unify the fractious young nation by giving citizens a common forum where they could debate and resolve disputed issues. In the process, inns became famous for having hosted the President—our own Fraunces Tavern in New York City is proof of that. They also increasingly sought to improve the services and accommodations they offered.

Thus was born the American hotel. Like so many other things in the new republic, its development was rapid. At the beginning of Washington's tours even the best inns were ramshackle affairs of three floors and 20 rooms, costing no more than fifteen thousand dollars; by 1809, less than two decades later, the best hotels could boast as many as seven floors and over 200 hundred rooms, and cost more than a half a million dollars.

Prof. Sandoval-Strauz, who teaches history at the University of New Mexico, charts the history of this quintessentially American institution with admirable élan. The first great New York hotel and indeed American hotel was The City Hotel (1794), which was built in the fashionable Federalist style between lower Broadway and Temple Street. The interior of the City Hotel included a ballroom, public parlors, a bar, stores, offices, and the largest circulating library in the country. Offering 197 rooms, mostly for overnight guests, the hotel was taller than all but the city's tallest churches, and with a price tag of $200,000, it was also the costliest building in the city, with the exception of the newly built headquarters of the New York Stock Exchange on Wall Street. The hotel became so popular with the city's business leaders that they removed the Custom House to its premises. The hotel also offered space for political rallies, caucuses, and receptions for visiting dignitaries. In 1797 the City Hotel hosted a reception for John Adams and then again in 1817 for Andrew Jackson. In 1824, a grand ball was held in honor of General Lafayette.

The economic success of the City Hotel, no less than the prestige it conferred, inspired other hoteliers around the country to attempt to emulate it. When leading merchants in Boston got together to finance and build what they hoped would be the biggest hotel in America the result was the Boston Exchange Coffee House and Hotel (1809), which had more than 200 hundred rooms, a basement kitchen, larder and cellar, a dining room, a ballroom, a bar, a coffee room, shops, a public reading room, an observatory, a newspaper reading room, offices, a Masonic lodge, and several apartments that opened onto the five galleries of the central atrium. One guest in 1818 likened the hotel to a small city.

The author points out that most of the businessmen who backed hotel development had interests in far-flung international trade. They were players in a global economy long before the fall of the Soviet Union and the rise of red China. In the early nineteenth century ninety-percent of Americans might have earned their living from farming but the entrepreneurial elite who were transforming the world economy were dedicated to improving the transportation of goods, and for this they needed places to sleep, places to transact business, places to entertain. "The hotel builders," as the author points out, "came from a small minority for whom wealth derived from the workings of commodities markets that depended upon the exchange of goods, supply and demand, time and distance. Merchants in general and the hotel builders in particular had a vested interest in the speed and reliability of transportation … [In the 1790s alone] the number of post offices increased from 75 to 903, and the total mileage of roads used for mail delivery went from 1,875 to 20,817." The link between railroads and hotels was equally vital. The Hotel Florence (1881) was built expressly in Pullman, Illinois by George Pullman not only for business travelers but tourists eager to see the model community that the railway magnate built for the railway workers responsible for building his famous Pullman sleeping carriages. The red brick building still stands.

Hotels were thus necessarily vital to the country's expansion. When the Erie Canal opened so too did Baltimore's City Hotel (1826), which rivaled the hotels of Eastern cities in size and grandeur. It was also illuminated by gaslight—a dazzling innovation in those Cimmerian days. Its designer, William F. Small, was influenced by Benjamin Latrobe, one of the many talented architects commissioned to design hotel exteriors and interiors. An Englishman educated in Prussia, France and Italy, Latrobe emigrated to the United States in 1796. In addition to designing the United States Capitol, he left behind brilliant architectural plans (1797) for a proposed Richmond Hotel, which was to include a ballroom based on the Hall of Mirrors at Versailles. Alas, the plans were never executed: the then eleventh-largest city in the country found them too grand and too expensive. Jeffersonian husbandry won out over Hamiltonian enterprise. When travelers moved still further West, another Englishman, Fred Harvey built the Montezuma Hotel (1882) and the The Castañeda Hotel (1899) in Las Vegas, both of which featured what were known as the "Harvey Girls," young women who were required to perform their tasks in starched black-and-white uniforms without jewelry or make-up. These were clearly *not* the inspiration for what became the famous Vegas showgirl.

Later developments touched on in the book include the creation of chain hotels—pioneered by the Procrustean E. M. Statler—and the rise of resort hotels in places like the Catskills and Saratoga. Then there was the great movement to make hotels as luxurious as possible, exemplified by Denver's Brown Palace (1892), the Waldorf-Astoria (1893), and the Plaza (1907), which was completed in just two years at a cost of $12.5 million.

The Jumeirah Essex House in New York, once taken over by the Dubai Government, sunk many more millions into its Central Park South property to attain a comparable sumptuousness.

What strikes one in reading *Hotel: An American History* is how soon the hotel as we know it was up and running. By the early nineteenth century, hotels had already become what they continue to be in the twenty-first century: meeting places for politicians and businessmen, reception spaces for the newlywed, retail outlets for shoppers, getaways for tourists, hideaways for adulterers. Henry James saw the hotel as

> an expression of the gregarious state breaking down every barrier but two—one of which, the barrier consisting of the high pecuniary tax, is the immediately obvious. The other, the rather more subtle, is the condition, for any member of the flock, that he or she—in other words especially she—be presumably "respectable," be, that is, not discoverably anything else. The rigour with which any appearance of the pursued or desired adventure is kept down—adventure in the florid sense of the word, the sense in which it remains a euphemism—is not the least interesting note of the whole immense promiscuity.

The first barrier remains as high as ever: rooms at the refurbished Plaza start at $1000. The second has all but vanished. In the nineteenth-century, enterprising prostitutes threatened the good reputation of even the best hotels; books of hotel etiquette warned unwary guests against them. "Have little to say to a woman who is traveling alone without a companion," advised one, "and whose face is painted, who wears a profusion of long curls about her neck, who has a meretricious expression of eye, and who is overdressed. It is safest to avoid her."

Once, as a younger man, I found myself alone in Las Vegas for reasons too complicated to go into, and, sitting at the hotel bar after making a reservation for the dining room, I became engaged in conversation with a lovely young blond lady, whose unaffected friendliness struck me as unusual, living as I did and still do in New York City where one tends to observe a strict, considerate aloofness when it comes to potentially ineludible bores. After buying the lady a glass of wine before she had excused herself to go to the powder room, I turned to the barman and asked him if all the young ladies in Las Vegas were as friendly as my new acquaintance, at which he turned to me and said, somewhat incredulously, "Well, of course, the prostitutes are: they have to be: no friendliness no customers." If I had read some of the manuals of hotel etiquette mentioned by the author of *Hotel Americana* before boarding the airplane at JFK, I might have been spared my ludicrous misapprehension.

In these same manuals, respectable women were urged to behave accordingly. "Any bold action or boisterous deportment in a hotel will expose a lady to the most severe censure of the refined around her, and may render her liable to misconstruction, and impertinence." What was astonishing about my lady friend at the hotel bar in Vegas is that she was the epitome of refinement, the sort of lady one could take back not only to one's mother but one's grandmother. In any case, the Barbizon Hotel on East 63rd Street in New York freed women of having to worry about being misconstrued by giving them a hotel of their own. Sadly, its fanciful jumble of Gothic, Islamic and Italian Renaissance styles is currently obscured by a drab gymnasium.

Now that so many good old New York hotels have closed down altogether or are converting partially or entirely into residential properties — one thinks of the Stanhope, the Plaza, the Carlyle, the Pierre — Samuel Johnson's preference for the public inn over the private house no longer seems the popular choice. Yet, for those expansive souls who like to make noise and give trouble, while calling out for more good things, the public inn will always beat the private house hollow.

Cross Purposes

Gothic Arches, Latin Crosses: Anti-Catholicism and American Church Designs in the Nineteenth Century, Ryan K. Smith (The University of North Carolina Press). 224 pages

"There is no country in the whole world," Alexis de Tocqueville observed in 1840,"in which the Christian religion retains a greater influence over the souls of men than in America." Eighteenth-century *philosophes* might have assured their readers that the diffusion of knowledge would spell the irreversible decline of religion but Tocqueville saw facts disprove this jejune theory. "There are certain populations in Europe whose unbelief is only equaled by their ignorance and their debasement, while in America one of the freest and most enlightened nations in the world fulfils all the outward duties of religion with fervor." *Plus ça change, plus c'est la même chose.* And yet Tocqueville was emphatic that this fervor had nothing to do with forms: "I have seen no country in which Christianity is clothed with fewer forms, figures, and observances than in the United States."

When American Protestants first broke with decades of pious iconoclasm in the 1840s and began adopting the crosses, candles, choir vestments, sanctuary flowers, stained glass windows and Gothic architecture of Roman Catholics a sea-change took place in American religion. Why and in what ways Protestants adopted these Roman Catholic forms is the theme of Ryan K. Smith's *Gothic Arches, Latin Crosses: Anti-Catholicism and American Church Designs in the Nineteenth Century*. Well-researched and engagingly argued, the book is a welcome contribution to a subject that has not received the attention it deserves.

Protestant appropriation of Roman Catholic forms occurred in an America rife with anti-Catholic bigotry. The roots of this bigotry are deep-seated. In his Speech on Conciliation with the Colonies (1775), Edmund Burke recognized how vital dissentient religion was to the colonists.

> The people are protestants; and of that kind which is the most adverse to all implicit submission of mind and opinion … Every one knows that the Roman Catholick religion is at least coeval with most of the governments where it prevails; that it has generally gone hand in hand with them … But the dissenting interests have sprung

up in direct opposition to all the ordinary powers of the world; and could justify that opposition only on a strong claim to natural liberty ... All protestantism, even the most cold and passive, is a sort of dissent. But the religion most prevalent in our Northern Colonies is a refinement of the principle of resistance; it is the dissidence of dissent, and the protestantism of the protestant religion.

Here Burke identified a perennial objection to Roman Catholicism in America: its alleged exaction of "implicit submission of mind and opinion." John Adams echoed this when he told Thomas Jefferson in 1821, "A free government and the Roman Catholick religion can never exist together in any nation or country." Tocqueville, it is true, thought otherwise: "The Catholic religion has erroneously been looked upon as the natural enemy of democracy. Among the various sects of Christians, Catholicism seems to me, on the contrary, to be one of those which are most favorable to the equality of conditions." Still, when the Irish began immigrating into the country in the 1840s, the charge that papal Catholicism held despotic sway over its adherents intensified. There was also the related fear that its adherents were treacherous and inassimilable. The Know Nothing Party responded to this fear by trying to bar Catholics from holding office and insisting on a twenty-year waiting period for naturalization. The Order of the Star Spangled Banner, the Guardians of Liberty, the American Minute Men, the Knights of Luther, and, most spectacularly, the Klu Klux Klan all kept alive the bias that Burke first detected even before the country was founded.

It is only against this background of rabid anti-Catholicism that one can appreciate the irony of not only the Episcopal Church but the Methodist, Presbyterian, Congregationalist, and even Baptist Churches adopting the forms and usages of an otherwise abominated popery. What motivated them to borrow so from their detested neighbors?

First, the sheer number of those neighbors gave them a kind of irresistibility. As Smith shows, the rise of Roman Catholicism in nineteenth-century America was phenomenal. In 1820, there were 124 Roman Catholic churches; in 1860, 2,550—a 1,956 percent increase. At the same time, in 1820 there were 600 Episcopal churches and in 1860, 2,145—only a 258 percent rise. With the enormous influx of Irish, beginning in the 1840s, the Roman Catholic hierarchy in America reasserted the church's traditional splendor. By the 1860s, not only Episcopal but non-prelatical churches were increasingly finding ways to compete with this Roman magnificence. Hence, the "unprecedented market," as Smith shows, for pew-fittings, pulpits, fonts, altars, stalls, lecterns, vestments, altar-cloths, surplices, chasubles, albs, and cassocks—though in appropriating these Roman accoutrements, Protestants were careful to make them serve distinctly Protestant purposes.

Secondly, the Gothic Revival took hold. Kenneth Clark's *The Gothic Revival: An Essay in the History of Taste* (1928) is still the best introduction to this fascinating subject. After Pugin and Ruskin and Gilbert Scott, the Revival's most indefatigable architect, who designed the enormous St. Pancras Station (1868–72) and the Albert Memorial (1862–3), gables, pointed arches and vaulted roofs became all the rage. Still, a good deal of the architecture engendered by the Revival was of questionable merit. "The Albert Memorial," as Clark mordantly observed, "is the expression of pure philistinism, and as such is not a document of much value to the student of taste ... The conscious demands of the philistine are unvarying, and the Albert Memorial has always appealed in the same degree to the same class of people—the people who like a monument to be large and expensive-looking and to show much easily understood sculpture, preferably of animals." Ruskin was even more dismissive of the Revival. "I would rather, for my own part," he confessed, referring to his immensely influential *The Stones of Venice* (1851–3), "that no architects had ever condescended to adopt one of the views suggested in this book, than that any should have made the partial use of it which has mottled our manufactory chimneys with black and red brick, dignified our bank and drapers' shops with Venetian tracery, and pinched our parish churches into dark and slippery arrangements for the advertisement of cheap coloured glass and pantiles." Indeed, Ruskin had nothing but contempt for what he called "the accursed Frankenstein monsters of, indirectly, my own making."

When the Gothic Revival landed in America, cathedrals in Kentucky and Missouri, Philadelphia and New York soon followed. And Protestants made no bones about how fascinating they found them. One Methodist minister visited the Cathedral of St. Peter in Cincinnati in 1847 and drew up an admiring catalogue of the place's "sacred furniture" before writing: "Look, now, upon all that brilliant scene—the brazen fence, the velvet-cushioned cathedra, the marble altar ... and all that array of masterly and affecting pictures—and then ruminate on the design of all this splendor." Rumination led to emulation. In the Gothic style Protestants saw an ideal not only of piety but of refinement and they were determined to make it their own. By the 1840s Protestants could boast of Gothic churches that were as good as the best of their Catholic rivals, including Richard Upjohn's superb Trinity Episcopal Church in New York.

The fact that Gothic became synonymous with refinement would have appalled Ruskin, who insisted that one of the indispensable elements of true Gothic was what he called "savageness." In his great essay, "The Nature of Gothic," he described "this wildness of thought, and roughness of work; this look of mountain brotherhood between the Cathedral and the Alp; this magnificence of sturdy power, put forth only the more energetically because the fine finger-touch was chilled away by the frosty wind, and the eye dimmed by the moor-mist, or blinded by the hail; this outspeaking of the strong spirit of men who may not gather redundant fruitage from the earth, nor bask in dreamy benignity of sunshine, but must break the rock for bread, and cleave the forest for fire, and show, even in what they did for their delight, some of the hard habits of the arm and heart that grew on them as they swung the axe or pressed the plough."

Members of Trinity Episcopal Church might not have seen all of that in their lovely new church but they did see a kind of WASP revenge in it. As one contemporary wrote, "It is pleasant to see the emigrants when they swarm up Broadway from the ships, stop in front of the Church, which they take to be a Roman Catholic Cathedral on a small scale, and kneel before it on the pavement, thanking their God for bringing them safely to land."

Ruskin argued that true Gothic did not derive entirely from papal Christianity. For him, this was evident in the almost pagan delight it exhibited in the natural world, in "the wandering of the tendril and the budding of the flower," which, in turn, prefigured the humanism of the Renaissance. Yet some Protestant advocates of the Gothic refused to acknowledge any debt to Rome. One claimed Biblical precedents for the Gothic. In his *Essay on Gothic Architecture* (1836) the Episcopal bishop John Henry Hopkins traced Gothic back to Palestine and before that to the temple of Solomon. "The style in question," he asserted, "is the most ancient in the world." Mediaeval Roman Catholics were not the first but the last to adopt it. It is amusing to imagine how such a claim would have gone down with Pugin, who once told a friend, that "after a most close and impartial investigation, I feel perfectly convinced that the Roman Catholic Church is the only true one, and the only one in which the grand and sublime style of church architecture can ever be restored."

Drawing on ecclesiastical, architectural and social history, Smith has put together a terse, incisive, thought-provoking book. For the Roman Catholics and Protestants who made the Gothic Revival possible forms were of inestimable importance. Kenneth Clark realized this when he wrote, apropos Pugin, that "The mere names of articles of church furniture were to him like choice wine to an epicure; often the point of an argument is lost while he rolls them round his tongue—'the stoups are filled to the brim; the rood is raised on high; the lamps of the sanctuary burn bright; the saintly portraitures in the glass windows shine all gloriously; and the albs hang in the oaken ambries, and the cope chests are filled with orphreyed baudekins; and pix, and pax, and chrismatory are there, and thurible and cross." There is a kind of Paterian voluptuousness about that. But on the same subject we also have the business-like Newman, who once reminded his readers that: "Forms are the very food of faith."

Coolidge and the Catholics

In September 1924, President Calvin Coolidge gave a speech in Washington to over 100,000 Catholics of the Holy Name Society[1] that exhibits his truly prophetic grasp of the role church and state play in upholding and sustaining America's constitutional order. Now, when that order is beleaguered as never before, the speech should be read and reread by all who prize liberty: it has much to teach us.

In its appreciation of the wellsprings of our constitutional blessings the speech is reminiscent of something Samuel Johnson was told by his cousin, Cornelius Ford, the dissipated parson; "Study the principles of everything," Ford told Johnson when the eighteenth-century poet, critic and lexicographer was a young man, "but grasp the trunk hard only, and you will shake all the branches."[2]

---

1 The Confraternity of the Holy Name Society promotes reverence for the Sacred Names of God and Jesus Christ, obedience and loyalty to the teachings of the Catholic Church, and the personal sanctification and holiness of its members. Founded at the Council of Lyon in the year 1274, the Society contributes to the evangelizing mission of the Church and makes perpetual acts of reverence and love for our Lord and Savior. The Dominicans, who were actively spreading the Christian message in the thirteenth century in a crusade against the Albigensians preached the power of the Holy Name of Jesus. They spread the devotion extremely effectively. In every Dominican church, altars, confraternities and societies were erected in honor of the Holy Name. The first Holy Name Society in the modern sense was founded in the early fifteenth century by Didacus of Victoria, one of the greatest preachers of the devotion to the Divine Name. He founded the "Society of the Holy Name of God" and created a rule for its governance whose purpose was "to suppress the horrible profanation of the Divine Name by blasphemers, perjurers, and by men in their ordinary conversation." Long after Didacus' death in 1450, Pope Pius IV approved the Society on 13 April 1564. The apostolate of the Society is to assist in parish ministries by performing the Corporal and the Spiritual Works of Mercy. In seeking God's grace in order to live a holy life, members are called to receive the sacrament of penance, strengthen themselves with the most Holy Eucharist, nourish their souls on Sacred Scripture, increase their desire of divine love through prayer, and lead their families, friends, and coworkers to Christ Jesus by their acts of charity and piety.

2 Samuel Johnson quoted in *Thraliana: The Diary of Mrs. Hester Lynch Thrale (Later Mrs. Piozzi) 1776–1809*, ed. Katherine C. Balderton (Oxford: The Clarendon Press, 1951), i, 171.

291

Coolidge grasped the "trunk" of America's constitutional order so firmly that it enabled him to speak brilliantly about the natural bond that church and state have in reaffirming America's liberties. Although addressed to Catholics from a speakers' platform that included William O'Connell, Archbishop of Boston and Michael Joseph Curley, Archbishop of Baltimore, both powerful prelates who did much to advance the Church in America, the speech appeals to all Americans, Catholics and non-Catholics.

It begins with an acknowledgement of the vitality of conscience, that "heaven-nursèd plant," as the poet Marvell called it. "Something in all human beings makes them want to do the right thing," Coolidge says. "Not that this desire always prevails; oftentimes it is overcome and they turn towards evil. But some power is constantly calling them back. Ever there comes a resistance to wrongdoing." What is striking about this is that it takes up the theme of conscience to recommend not "liberty of conscience" — as the Founders often did — but the affinity conscience naturally has for goodness, which is something rather more fundamental. Again, Coolidge took hold of underlying principles. He certainly recognized this affinity in the mission of the Holy Name Society when he applauded it for seeking "to rededicate the minds of the people to a true conception of the sacredness of the name of the Supreme Being," to save "all reference to the Deity," as he says, "from curses and blasphemy, and restore the lips of men to reverence and praise."

"Reverence" is not a word that we often hear in the mouths of statesmen, let alone politicians. Yet Coolidge defined it in a way to reassure his compatriots that he knew what he was about in referring to so solemn and so practical a thing; and, what is more, he did the Holy Name Society the honor of acknowledging that they, too, apprehended the consequential force of the word. Indeed, he stressed that:

> The importance of the lesson which this Society was formed to teach would be hard to overestimate. Its main purpose is to impress upon the people the necessity for reverence. This is the beginning of a proper conception of ourselves, of our relationship to each other, and our relationship to our Creator. Human nature cannot develop very far without it. The mind does not unfold, the creative faculty does not mature, the spirit does not expand, save under the influence of reverence. It is the chief motive of an obedience. It is only by a correct attitude of mind begun early in youth and carried through maturity that these desired results are likely to be secured. It is along the path of reverence and obedience that the race has reached the goal of freedom, of self-government, of a higher morality, and a more abundant spiritual life,

The first thing that impresses us about this passage and many others in the speech is that it has been written by a man who uses words with unu-

Coolidge and the Catholics

sual care and precision: he uses words to speak the truth. Of course, our own political class and their agents in the media use words so deceitfully, so carelessly that it is a balm to encounter Coolidge's conscientious truth telling. "The mind does not unfold, the creative faculty does not mature, the spirit does not expand, save under the influence of reverence. It is the chief motive of an obedience." There is a Johnsonian gravity to that. In his Dictionary, the same Dictionary on which the Founders battened, Johnson defined the word "reverence" as "veneration; respect; an awful regard." He illustrates it with a quote from Psalm 89: "God is greatly to be feared in the assembly of the saints, and to be had in *reverence* of all about him." He also quotes Sir Francis Bacon: "When quarrels and factions are carried openly, it is a sign the *reverence* of government is lost." Government, in other words, is answerable to the God to whom reverence is due. It is something more than an unaccountable scrimmage for power.

The second thing that strikes us about the passage is that Coolidge links the word "reverence" to "obedience," which Johnson defines as "submission to authority" and illustrates with a quotation from the seventeenth-century Anglican divine John Tillotson: "Religion hath a good influence upon the people, to make them *obedient* to government, and peaceable one towards another." It is when we read Coolidge's passage in the light of these definitions that we can see what a clear and incisive grasp he had of the truly fundamental relationship between church and state in our constitution, which goes altogether beyond the ban on established religion instituted by the Founders.[3]

As if to remind his auditors that the proper use of language was not merely an attribute of his own, but a clear and bounden duty of responsible statesmanship, "Silent Cal," as he was known, lay out in the speech a kind of metaphysic of terseness. "We read that 'out of the abundance of the heart the mouth speaketh,'" he says.

This is a truth which is worthy of much thought. He who gives license to his tongue only discloses the contents of his own mind. By the excess of his words he proclaims his lack of discipline. By his very violence he shows his weakness. The youth or man who by disregarding this principle thinks he is displaying his determination and resolution and emphasizing his statements is in reality only revealing an intellectual poverty, a deficiency in self-control and

---

3 Apropos these references to Johnson's great Dictionary, the objection might be made that it is anachronistic to cite such definitions; after all, Coolidge was writing in the twentieth century and Johnson published his Dictionary in 1755; but it is precisely because Coolidge was so deeply animated by the principles of America's Constitution that citing Johnson's definitions is in order, since they were the definitions that the Founders themselves consulted in conducting their happy deliberations.

self-respect, a want of accurate thinking and of spiritual insight, which cannot come save from a reverence for the truth.

If the volubility of most politicians abounds in "intellectual poverty," Coolidge's brevity was the soul of wit. In our current circumstances, we hear a good deal about how essential it is for us to rededicate ourselves to inculcating the principles of reasoned discourse in the young, surrounded as they are by rabid misologists; but surely Coolidge's brief speech drives that point home more effectively than reams of white papers. "To my mind, the great strength of your Society lies in its recognition of the necessity of discipline," he told his Catholic friends.

> We live in an impatient age. We demand results, and demand them at once. We find a long and laborious process very irksome, and are constantly seeking for a short cut. But there is no easy method of securing discipline. It is axiomatic that there is no royal road to learning. The effort for discipline must be intensive, and to a considerable degree it must be lifelong. But it is absolutely necessary, if there is to be any self-direction or any self-control. The worst evil that could be inflicted upon the youth of the land would be to leave them without restraint and completely at the mercy of their own uncontrolled inclinations. Under such conditions education would be impossible, and all orderly development intellectually or morally would be hopeless. I do not need to picture the result. We know too well what weakness and depravity follow when the ordinary processes of discipline are neglected.

If lack of discipline and false liberty not only impede but vitiate the education of the young, Coolidge was enough of a man of the world to know whence those things come. To show how repulsed the natural man is by anything redolent of discipline or rule, he quotes from Robert Burns's exuberant cantata "The Jolly Beggars" (1799). Like Johnson, he had no hesitation taking his wisdom from unlikely sources.

> A fig for those by law protected!
> Liberty's a glorious feast!
> Courts for cowards were erected,
> Churches built to please the priest.

Coolidge's gloss on the lines is worth quoting:

> That character clearly saw no use for discipline, and just as clearly found his reward in the life of an outcast. The principles which he proclaimed could not lead in any other direction. Vice and misery were their natural and inevitable consequences. He refused to recognize or obey any authority, save his own material inclinations. He never rose above his appetites.

Coolidge also saw how the Holy Name Society "stands as a protest against this attitude of mind." Church and state, in other words, could always join together where common ground made service to the common good not only possible but imperative.

II

Flaubert once said that "Our ignorance of history makes us libel our own times. People have always been like this." Certainly, we might be tempted to imagine that our own times suffer from an unprecedented unruliness. Yet Coolidge reminds us that his times were just as liable to misrule. Indeed, he was fully aware that "there are altogether too many in the world who consciously or unconsciously ... hold [the] views and follow [the] example" set out in Burns's verses, and his response to this lamentable state of affairs had a certain witty lucidity. "I believe such a position arises from a misconception of the meaning of life," he dryly remarked. Those who feel no reverence and will not submit themselves to discipline "seem to think that authority means some kind of an attempt to force action upon them which is not for their own benefit, but for the benefit of others." For Coolidge, there was a commonsensical objectionableness to such intractability: "To me they do not appear to understand the nature of law, and therefore refuse obedience. They misinterpret the meaning of individual liberty, and therefore fail to attain it. They do not recognize the right of property, and therefore do not come into its possession. They rebel at the idea of service, and therefore lack the fellowship and cooperation of others." Again, Coolidge expresses these immemorial truths with refreshing concinnity. "Our conception of authority, of law and liberty, of property and service, ought not to be that they imply rules of action for the mere benefit of someone else, but that they are primarily for the benefit of ourselves. The Government supports them in order that the people may enjoy them."

In a series of lectures that the future cardinal and saint John Henry Newman gave in London in 1850, he made observations about church and state that put one in mind of Coolidge's speech to the Holy Name Society. "The great principles of the State are those of the Church, and, if the State would but keep within its own province, it would find the Church its truest ally and best benefactor," Newman wrote. "She upholds obedience to the magistrate; she recognises his office as from God; she is the preacher of peace, the sanction of law, the first element of order, and the safeguard of morality, and that without possible vacillation or failure; she may be fully trusted; she is a sure friend, for she is indefectible and undying." The problem, however, as Newman saw it, was that the State was often not interested in any truly collaborative work with the Church. Why? "It is not enough for the State that things should be done, unless it has the doing of them itself; it abhors a double jurisdiction, and what it calls a divided allegiance; *aut Cæsar aut nullus* is its motto, nor does it willingly accept of any compromise."[4] The great value of Coolidge's speech is that he saw very clearly the ways in which church and state could collaborate to achieve the common good, especially at a time when the enemies of liberty and reason were increasingly agitating against such good.

There was a kind of poetic justice in the fact that the president who went out of his way to champion the interests of small businessmen should have reaffirmed this truth in terms of property and the liberty that makes property possible.

> When service is performed, the individual performing it is entitled to the compensation for it. His creation becomes a part of himself. It is his property. To attempt to deal with persons or with property in a communistic or socialistic way is to deny what seems to me to be this plain fact. Liberty and equality require that equal compensation shall be paid for equal service to the individual who performs it. Socialism and communism cannot be reconciled with the principles which our institutions represent. They are entirely foreign, entirely un-American. We stand wholly committed to the policy that what the individual produces belongs entirely to him to be used by him for the benefit of himself, to provide for his own family and to enable him to serve his fellow men.

Coolidge could articulate these truths with such commanding clarity precisely because he recognized that "Liberty is not collective, it is personal. All liberty is individual liberty," a truth corroborated not only by those importunate teachers, experience and reason, but by centuries of Catholic moral theology. Coolidge himself was something of a teacher, as one can see from his animadversions on the genuine genius of our constitutional order.

> Coincident with the right of individual liberty under the provisions of our Government is the right of individual property. The position which the individual holds in the conception of American institutions is higher than that ever before attained anywhere else on earth. It is acknowledged and proclaimed that he has sovereign powers. It is declared that he is endowed with inalienable rights which no majority, however great, and no power of the Government, however broad, can ever be justified in violating. The principle of equality is recognized. It follows inevitably from belief in the brotherhood of man through the fatherhood of God. When once the right of the individual to liberty and equality is admitted, there is no escape

---

4 John Henry Newman, *Difficulties of Anglicans*, volume I, ed. Edward Short (Leominster: Gracewing, 2020), 207. The Latin tag can be translated: "Caesar's way or the highway."

from the conclusion that he alone is entitled to the rewards of his own industry. Any other conclusion would necessarily imply either privilege or servitude. Here again the right of individual property is for the protection of society.

III

Pope Pius XI, no fan himself of collectivism, rejoiced in Coolidge's speech. Socialism and communism were anathema to him, as they are to all properly formed Catholics. Much of his papacy, extending as it did from 1922 to 1939, was given over to opposing totalitarian evil. He also promoted indigenous Catholicism beyond Europe; in 1926, for example, he personally consecrated China's first six bishops. It was only natural that he should concur with Coolidge's masterly defense of liberty. According to the *New York Times*: "The pope placed the congress in Washington of the Holy Name societies among the things which pleased him the most, and expressed gratification that it 'culminated in a speech by the President of the Republic himself, who with appropriate words spoke of the respect due to the Name of God, of the ugliness of blasphemy, and of the divine foundation of human authority.'"[5]

Later, in his papacy, in his encyclical *Divini Redemptoris* (1937), Pius would attest to the consistency with which he and his predecessors had opposed the tyrannical scourge of communism.

> This Apostolic See, above all, has not refrained from raising its voice, for it knows that its proper and social mission is to defend truth, justice and all those eternal values which Communism ignores or attacks. Ever since the days when groups of "intellectuals" were formed in an arrogant attempt to free civilization from the bonds of morality and religion, Our Predecessors overtly and explicitly drew the attention of the world to the consequences of the dechristianization of human society. With reference to Communism, Our Venerable Predecessor, Pius IX, of holy memory, as early as 1846 pronounced a solemn condemnation, which he confirmed in the words of the Syllabus directed against "that infamous doctrine of

5 The news item about the pope in *The New York Times* appeared in the Klu Klux Klan paper, *The American Standard*, which assured its readers in the same number that: "Roman Catholicism and Americanism are not compatible. Roman Catholicism is oriental in origin, pagan in conception and destructive in its results. It is a product of orientalism … the offspring of the colored, enslaved races of mankind. Can you conceive of Roman Catholicism as being a child of the white race, of the Anglo-Saxon mind or of the Nordic spirit? For a white man to be a Roman Catholic is for him to be a traitor to all of the traditions, social customs, sacred instincts, and ideals of his race." *The American Standard* (1 January 1925), 3, 8.

so-called Communism which is absolutely contrary to the natural law itself, and if once adopted would utterly destroy the rights, property and possessions of all men, and even society itself." Later on, another of Our predecessors, the immortal Leo XIII, in his Encyclical *Quod Apostolici Muneris*, defined Communism as "the fatal plague which insinuates itself into the very marrow of human society only to bring about its ruin." With clear intuition he pointed out that the atheistic movements existing among the masses of the Machine Age had their origin in that school of philosophy which for centuries had sought to divorce science from the life of the Faith and of the Church.

Pius himself could not have been clearer about his own opposition to communism. Indeed, he echoes many of the points that Coolidge had made in his speech of 1924.

> Communism … strips man of his liberty, robs human personality of all its dignity, and removes all the moral restraints that check the eruptions of blind impulse. There is no recognition of any right of the individual in his relations to the collectivity; no natural right is accorded to human personality, which is a mere cog-wheel in the Communist system. In man's relations with other individuals … Communists hold the principle of absolute equality, rejecting all hierarchy and divinely constituted authority, including the authority of parents. … Nor is the individual granted any property rights over material goods or the means of production … all forms of private property must be eradicated, for they are at the origin of all economic enslavement.

In light of his own fierce fights with the enemies of liberty, Pius naturally welcomed Coolidge's battle cry against the barbarism inherent in Marxism: "What a wide difference between the American position and that imagined by the vagabond who thought of liberty as a glorious feast unprotected and unregulated by law," the president told the Holy Name Society.

> This is not civilization, but a plain reversion to the life of the jungle. Without the protection of the law, and the imposition of its authority, equality cannot be maintained, liberty disappears and property vanishes. This is anarchy. The forces of darkness are traveling in that direction. But the spirit of America turns its face towards the light.

What gave this modest, this unassuming man—the epitome of small-town America—the confidence that his country possessed the light to overcome the "forces of darkness?" Ironically, it was his humility. "The fame of the advantages which accrue to the inhabitants of our country has spread throughout the world," he told his listeners.

If we doubt the high estimation in which these opportunities are held by other peoples, it is only necessary to remember that they sought them in such numbers as to require our own protection by restrictive immigration.[6] I am aware that our country and its institutions are often the subject of censure. I grieve to see them misrepresented for selfish and destructive aims. But I welcome candid criticism, which is moved by a purpose to promote the public welfare. But while we should always strive for improvement by living in more complete harmony with our ideals, we should not permit incidental failure or unwarranted blame to obscure the fact that the people of our country have secured the greatest success that was ever before experienced in human history.

What Coolidge had to say to the Holy Name Society on that bright September afternoon so many years ago speaks to us as cogently as it spoke to his contemporaries because it is rooted in the Truth, what Johnson called

6 The Immigration Act of 1924 limited the number of immigrants allowed entry into the United States by enforcing a national origins quota. The quota provided immigration visas to two percent of the total number of people of each nationality in the United States as of the 1890 national census, though immigrants from Asia were entirely excluded. Laws dating from 1790 and 1870 excluded people of Asian lineage from becoming naturalized citizens. President Coolidge signed the act into law on 24 May 1924. Majorities in Congress ensured the passage of one of the most astringent immigration laws ever enacted in American history. The popularity of the Johnson–Reed act reflected the concern many Americans had over the negative effect that large-scale immigration would have on wages and job competition. The act was also designed to stop communist agitators from coming into the country from eastern Europe, the threat of communism being a real threat for Coolidge's contemporaries, not the "red scare" that future liberal historians would deplore. Although nativism was not unprevalent in the country at the time, there was a toughminded recognition that prudence, not bigotry justified restrictive immigration. In any case, Rushad L. Thomas, editorial associate at the Calvin Coolidge Presidential Foundation, shows how there was nothing nativist about Coolidge's views on immigration. On the foundation's website, Mr. Thomas writes:

Despite putting his pen to this restrictive law, President Coolidge did not harbor the prejudices and racist attitudes that so often color discussions of migration policy. In his 1926 speech at the dedication of the statue of John Ericsson, the Swede who pioneered the technology for the Monitor class of ships that helped America win the Civil War, he said "when once our feet have touched this soil, when once we have made this land our home, wherever our place of birth, whatever our race, we are all blended in one common country. All artificial distinctions of lineage and rank are cast aside. We all rejoice in the title of Americans." At the 1925 American Legion convention in Omaha, Nebraska Coolidge said "Whether one traces his Americanism back three centuries to the *Mayflower*, or three years of the steerage, is not half so important as whether his Americanism of to-day is real and genuine. No matter by what various crafts we came here, we are all now in the same boat."

"the torch of Truth."[7] But when it comes to so eloquent a witness as Coolidge to the great abiding good that church and state can accomplish in the defense of liberty, we should let this just, sensible man tell us what he has to say in his own words. "Every mother can rest in the assurance that her children will find here a land of devotion, prosperity and peace," Coolidge told his compatriots of the land he loved. "The institutions of our country stand justified both in reason and in experience. I am aware that they will continue to be assailed. But I know they will continue to stand. We may perish, but they will endure. They are founded on the Rock of Ages."

7 Samuel Johnson, *The Rambler*, no. 3 (27 March 1750), in *The Yale Edition of the Works of Samuel Johnson* (New Haven: Yale University Press, 1969), iii, 17.

A Classicist's View of the Cataclysm: Victor Davis Hanson on WWII

The Second World Wars: How the First Global Conflict was Fought and Won, Victor Davis Hanson (Basic Books). 652 pages.

In his six-volume history of the Second World War (1948–53), Winston Churchill gave a well-deserved tribute to Frederick Lindemann, the scientist in the Air Ministry who kept the Conservative M.P. for Epping apprised of Germany's accelerating air capabilities in the mid-1930s, when the Stanley Baldwin and Neville Chamberlain governments were content to look the other way:

> There were no doubt greater scientists than Frederick Lindemann, though his credentials and genius command respect. But he had two qualifications of vital consequence to me. First … he was my trusted friend and confidant of twenty years. Together we had watched the advance and onset of world disaster. Together we had done our best to sound the alarm … [Secondly,] Lindemann could decipher the signals from the experts … and explain to me in lucid, homely terms what the issues were.

Since Harrow and Sandhurst had taught Churchill nothing about science, let alone the science of air defense, this was crucial. "There are only twenty-four hours in the day," Churchill reminded his readers, "of which at least seven must be spent in sleep and three in eating and relaxation. Anyone in my position would have been ruined if he had attempted to dive into depths which not even a lifetime of study could plumb." As it was, Churchill and, indeed, all of the Allies, gained immensely from Lindemann's briefings, before and during the war.

The general reader, as well as the more scholarly specialist, will feel similarly grateful to Victor Davis Hanson for sharing his insights into the complexities of a war that still has much to teach us. *The Second World Wars: How the First Global Conflict Was Fought and Won* is popular history at its very best, offering as it does an overview of the war that is at once scholarly and readable. It is also full of fascinating detail. For example,

Hanson shows how the Germans invaded Russia without knowing that the Russians had T-34 tanks—proof of how threadbare their pre-invasion intelligence was. "The heavy tanks cannot be beaten by our weaponry," one German army report complained. "The men have almost no ammunition left and are being run down by Russian tanks." When the Soviets eventually encircled the German Sixth Army at Stalingrad, sealing Germany's fate on the Eastern Front, it was largely due to the superior firepower and mobility of their T-34s.

Animated by mastery of both strategy and the ordnance with which strategy is carried out, not to mention the often unedifying psychology of war, Hanson's book is a summing up that only an historian of great learning and perspicacity could have produced. That the author draws on his enviable knowledge of the military experience of ancient Greece and Rome gives his analysis of the missteps and oversights of his twentieth-century subjects critical perspective. In his dazzling command of the details and sweep of ancient history, Hanson is reminiscent of another crack historian trained in the classics—Peter Green, the biographer of Alexander and chronicler of the Greco-Persian wars.

Hanson writes of how Italy and Japan confirmed Thucydides' "realist notions of honor and fear" when they threw in their lot with Hitler, convinced that his gamble to make Germany Europe's leading power would not only pan out for the Germans but also benefit their own expansionist ambitions, though it resulted in redrawing borders, redistributing populations, and killing millions—some 60 million, as it turned out, approximately 80 percent of whom were civilians. The opportunism that impelled the Axis powers had its root in the opportunism of the German people themselves. No one is better on this aspect of the war's *casus belli* than Charles Arnold-Baker, the inspired editor of the *Companion to British History* (2001), who wrote in his autobiography, *For He is an Englishman: Memoirs of a Prussian Nobleman* (2007):

> [The Germans] had adopted an abomination which promised them benefits in return for the destruction of law, democracy and certain scapegoats. These benefits went far beyond the tearing up of the Treaty of Versailles ... They would re-establish the frontiers (roughly speaking—what's a few million Slavs between friends?) of the ancient Reich—meaning something golden, glorious, and predatory. The German word *Krieg* (war) is connected with *kriegen* meaning to "get or take," and *Reich* (according to the dictionary "empire") means adjectivally "rich." The Nazis appealed to the myth of the tribal horde with its roistering chieftains ready to fill your hat with gold.

Hanson confirms Arnold-Baker's insight by showing how the German generals acquiesced in Hitler's gambles for their own aggrandizement at the expense of the Wehrmacht. He also shows how "Hitler's blinkered view of geostrategy was abetted by the blinkers of the German General Staff," few of whom "were equipped to think of war in terms of grand strategy or geopolitics." Ben Shepherd's authoritative *Hitler's Soldiers: The German Army in the Third Reich* (2016) exhaustively corroborates this charge. For Shepherd, if Allied superiority in the field, air, and sea finally brought the German army to grief, so too did "the political, economic, strategic and operational failings of the army leadership itself."

As Hanson shows, the very fact that Germany's military leadership connived in the disastrous decision to invade Russia confirms this point. Early in the war, Hitler might have appeared a gambler on a winning streak, going from strength to offensive strength, but by 1943, when his invasion of Russia had stalled, his strategic miscalculations came home to roost. From that point on, despite his no-retreat, no-surrender bluster, the Wehrmacht was forced into a defensive position from which it would never escape. For Hanson, only "unquestioning vicious fighters" in the Waffen SS who "fought as savagely without hope of victory as they once had when assured of conquest" kept the German army going. Such "suicidal zealotry" would also contribute to the scale and destructiveness of the war. Knowing that Germany and Japan would not concede defeat unless entirely ruined, the Allies had no alternative but to ensure their ruin.

This does not let the Allies off the hook for the role they played in failing to prevent the war in the first place. Hanson is unsparing about British appeasement, American isolationism, and Russian collaboration, all of which contributed to making an unnecessary war inevitable. It does, however, explain the necessity of Sir Arthur "Bomber" Harris's incendiary bombing of German cities and President Truman's decision to drop the atomic bomb on Hiroshima and Nagasaki. The military justification of these late bombings may remain controversial, but they did shorten the war and save lives. Harris certainly had no doubts about the warrantability of his actions. "I do not personally regard the whole of the remaining cities of Germany as worth the bones of one British Grenadier," the unrepentant Air Marshal confessed. Even the great Whig historian Lord Macaulay understood that "the essence of war is violence, and moderation in war is imbecility."

Hanson is eloquent when it comes to the American counterpart to Harris, General Curtis LeMay, who did not shrink from incendiary bombing of Japan once its necessity became clear for the dispersal of the enemy's industrial war effort. LeMay, he writes, "enjoyed the role of a take-no-prisoners general, but beneath the crusty exterior, like George S. Patton, he was one of the most introspective, analytical, and naturally brilliant commanders of the war. If he was a frightening man in his single-minded drive 'to put bombs on the target,' he was also an authentic American genius at war."

Yet no one can read Hanson's often harrowing pages without thinking of Thomas Hardy's lines about the Armistice that ended the Great War—lines that must haunt all historians who write of the essential tragedy of war.

> Calm fell. From Heaven distilled a clemency;
> There was peace on earth, and silence in the sky;
> Some could, some could not, shake off misery;
> The Sinister Spirit sneered: "It had to be!"
> And again the Spirit of Pity whispered, "Why?"

For the classicist in Hanson, German's infantrymen recall the Spartans. They were "highly trained and terrifyingly professional" and imbued with "militarist doctrine" but "often deployed for imbecile strategic ends." At times, it is true, they may have been led by generals of the caliber of "the Spartan maverick generals Brasidas, Gylippus and Lysander," but "in addition to a rare Manstein or Rommel, there were also more unimaginative versions of dullard Spartan kings (Generals Alfred Jodl, Wilhelm Keitel, and Walter Warlimont) who ... along with Hitler, would waste their deadly assets." Shepherd, in his study of the German army, shows how this dullness went hand-in-hand with atrocity. Indeed, "the army as a whole was complicit in terror, exploitation and criminality from the start."

In reviewing the comparative strengths and weaknesses of the Allies and the Axis as fighting forces, Hanson shows how superior the Allies were, even though, as a result of their combined fecklessness before hostilities began, it took them a fair amount of time to marshal that superiority. "That the Axis produced rockets, jets and superior torpedoes, Hanson points out, "and yet were the most reliant on horse transportation, is emblematic of their lack of comprehensive industrial policy and pragmatic technological planning—an area where America, Britain and the Soviet Union excelled." When it comes to the upshot of this advantage, Hanson is aphoristic: "We often forget that the Third Reich was postmodern in creative genius but premodern in actual implementation and operations." He observes that the army that invaded the Soviet Union did so "with fifteen thousand Poland peasant wagons, seventy-five divisions powered only by horses, hundreds of different types of looted and often obsolete European vehicles, seventy-three different models of tanks, and fifty-two different makes of anti-aircraft guns."

Strategically, Hanson locates the central flaw of the Third Reich's war plans in Hitler's contention that he could lead the Fatherland to victory by limiting himself to fighting one front at a time. Poland, in other words, would be a discrete war, followed by other limited border wars. "As a self-taught student of history," the author writes, "Hitler felt that he had proceeded, in a ... carefully circumscribed fashion, in direct opposition to

Kaiser Wilhelm II's past nightmare of recklessly incurring an immediate two-theatre war." Here, again, the classicist in Hanson comes to the fore: "Like Hannibal who thought he could reverse the verdict of the First Punic War, and like Hannibal's Carthage, which had been defeated but not emasculated in 241 BC, so Hitler and the Third Reich were convinced that the second time around they would not repeat the strategic mistakes of an earlier generation."

Even after Hitler had entered into a three-front war with Britain, Russia, and the United States, he deluded himself into imagining that he was fighting only a one-front war against Russia, which, once won, would consolidate his gains in Europe. Yet Hanson exhibits his understanding of the complexity of Hitler's nature by showing how the Führer's delusions were not unvisited by moments of lucidity. "Hitler," he writes, "seemed aware of his own failings, manifested in self-doubt," which his megalo-mania never entirely concealed. "To Albert Speer, Hitler confessed shortly before his death that he had always known that Hermann Goering was a drug addict … but he had been too timid to confront [him] … given his earlier key services to the Nazi cause, even as the latter's buffoonery cost tens of thousands of Luftwaffe air crewmen their lives."

If Hitler's definitive biographer Ian Kershaw showed how the Third Reich was often kept going by a kind of rivalrous chaos, Hanson shows that the chaos emanated, to a great degree, from the incoherence and incompetence of Hitler himself, who, the author points out, "had no direct knowledge of anything more than a few hundred miles from his birth-place." Never having been to Europe, Russia, or any of the other places he opposed, he knew little of them other than what maps could tell him. The footage we have of him in conquered Paris underscores this. The erstwhile Austrian corporal is not so much pleased as overwhelmed by his army's capture of so glorious a city. Pitted against opponents of the wide expe-rience, knowledge, and sophistication of Churchill and Roosevelt, Hitler was out of his depth.

Hanson rightly regards Churchill as the best of the war's commanders, whether from the Allied or the Axis camp, because he "possessed the greatest moral courage," though he recognizes Churchill's shortcomings, particularly his sometimes imprudent readiness to allow both Field Marshal Bernard Montgomery and Joseph Stalin free rein and "his constant attention to the effect of operations on Britain's postwar empire." This squares with Sir Max Hastings's overall assessment of Churchill as a war leader: "If the governance of nations in peace is best conducted by reasonable men, in war there is a powerful argument for leadership by those sometimes willing to adopt courses beyond the boundaries of reason, as Churchill did."

An amusing example of Churchill's unorthodox approach to war plan-ning was given by Earl Mountbatten, the Supreme Allied Commander of the South East Asia Command who attended war meetings at Chequers after 1942, when the country house was sufficiently camouflaged to protect the prime minister:

> At 8.30 p.m. the company assembled for drinks and then at about 9 we went in to dinner and a very good dinner it used to be. It went on a long while and then at about ten or 10:15 the ladies left the room and Winston held forth over brandy and a good cigar. It was most entertaining and amusing. At about 10.40 or so we'd get up and join the ladies and we all went up and saw a film. He had a cinema projector at Chequers and always had a film over the weekends. When the film was over, which would be perhaps about 12.30 a.m., we had a nightcap with the ladies, and at about 1 o'clock we'd start work going through all things he wanted to discuss until 2, 3 or 3.30 a.m. On one occasion General Marshall, the Chief of the United States Army, was in the party. We went through this process and at 12.30, when the ladies went to bed, he got up to go. We all said: "You can't go now; it hasn't started yet!"

Hanson also stresses that Churchill, who had fought in the trenches in World War I, was consequently sensible enough never to overrule his chiefs of staff, all of whom had also fought in that war or in Britain's colonial wars. This gave his conduct of the war a certain hardheaded wisdom, despite his incidental eccentricity. Unlike Roosevelt, Churchill never lost sight of the high price the Allies would pay for allying themselves with Soviet Russia, especially once it came time to sorting out postwar Western and Eastern Europe, though he was the first of the Allied commanders to see the indispensability of what was otherwise a distasteful alliance. As Churchill told his private secretary Jock Colville, "If Hitler invaded Hell, I would at least make a favourable reference to the Devil."

Churchill also clearly learned from the mistakes of the First World War. He drew on the experience of the Somme to urge against precipitateness in the timing of the D-Day invasion; he drew on his collaborative relationship with Lloyd George (when that wily man was Minister of Munitions) to ensure against inadequate production of war materiel; and he clearly derived the right lesson from Marshal Josef Joffre's insouciant belief in attrition when he saw to it that the British Expeditionary Force was kept out of the irresistible collapse of France in 1940. In his history of the war, Churchill memorably described how the opening day of the evacuation of Dunkirk affected him and his countrymen:

> There was a short service of Intercession and Prayer in Westminster Abbey on May 26. The English are loth to expose their feelings, but in my stall in the Choir I could feel the pent-up, passionate emotion, and also the fear of the congregation, not of death or wounds or material loss, but of defeat and the final ruin of Britain.

A Classicist's View of the Cataclysm: Victor Davis Hanson on WWII

For students of history, both the celerity and the decisiveness with which the Allies defeated the Axis can be misleading precisely because they can suggest that Allied victory was somehow inevitable. Churchill's recollections nicely explode the falsity of this notion. Many contingencies throughout the war might not have gone the Allies way, and certainly Dunkirk was one of them. In summing up Churchill's conduct of the British war effort, Hanson makes some revelatory comparisons with Britain's experience in the Great War:

> Britain was to fight much longer than in World War I (roughly 71 versus 51 months) on two distant fronts against a much more formidable coalition of enemies. Yet it suffered far fewer deaths (approximately 450,000 versus nearly one million fatalities) in achieving a far more lasting victory in 1918. This was an extraordinary achievement, given that Britain had a continental army far smaller than those of either Germany, Russia or the United States. Although Churchill may have despaired frequently—after the fall of France when an inglorious defeat seemed likely, the ignominious surrenders at Singapore and Tobruk, and in negotiations about the postwar world with undemocratic Joseph Stalin creating facts on the ground throughout Eastern Europe—he was the first Allied leader to see a way to beat Hitler and the only one to fight from the beginning to the end.

Most of this is persuasive, but surely it is dubious that Churchill "frequently despaired" when setbacks arose. On the contrary, his hallmark as a war leader was precisely that he did not despair, even amid setbacks that would have demoralized many lesser men. In this, as Colville recognized, it was the man's very guilelessness that inoculated him against despair. "Strength often marches with simplicity," Colville wrote. "In the war Churchill's burden was lightened and his task simplified by his refusal to be diverted from the single aim of victory; victory at any price, since the alternative was slavery or extinction. This suited his temperament, because although a brilliant tactician and more fertile than most men in imagination and ideas, he was fundamentally a straightforward person ... In August 1940, he considered the clamour for a Statement of War Aims ill-conceived. We had, he said, only one aim: to destroy Hitler."

As good as Hanson is on the strategy and tactics of the Second World War, he can be heartbreaking on the millions of civilians who died as a result of the war. Turning to the Holocaust, he cites Hans Frank, the governor-general of Nazi-occupied Poland, who wrote in his diary in December 1939: "We cannot shoot 2,500,000 Jews. Neither can we poison them. We shall have to take steps, however, designed to extirpate them in some way—and this will be done." Hanson points out a grim irony: "The three major Axis powers directly or indirectly caused about 80 percent of the

307

total World War II dead while suffering somewhere around 20 percent … Rarely in any war of the past had the defeated inflicted such carnage, in such lopsided fashion, on the victorious." In the case of the failed invasion of Russia, the more frustrated the German generals became with what proved an undefeatable Red Army, the more they exhorted their soldiers to gratify their exasperated sadism by slaughtering defenseless Slavs and Jews. If they could not fill their hats with gold, they could spread murder and mayhem.

What ultimately distinguishes Hanson as an historian is his appreciation of the moral dynamics of war. "Men are the city-state," one of his epigraphs from Thucydides states, "and not walls nor ships empty of men." At a time when America and her allies need clear-sighted moral decisiveness as never before, Hanson's book could not be timelier. The way that he sets out his study shows his own moral clarity, which, in a history profession riddled with Marxist determinism and Progressive faddishness, is bracing and salutary:

> Why the Western world—which was aware of the classical lessons and geography of war, and was still suffering from the immediate trauma of the First World War—chose to tear itself apart in 1939 is a story not so much of accidents, miscalculations, and overre-actions (although there were plenty of those, to be sure) as of the carefully considered decision to ignore, appease or collaborate with Adolf Hitler's Nazi Germany by nations that had the resources and knowledge, but not yet the willpower to do otherwise.

While excellent general histories on the Second World War abound—those by Martin Gilbert, John Keegan, Sir Max Hastings, and Andrew Roberts come to mind—Victor Davis Hanson's *Second World Wars* will not only swell but enhance their distinguished company.

History and Truth:
In the Night-Nursery
with R. W. Southern

I

In an essay entitled "The Truth about the Past" (1988), which the medi-
aevalist R. W. Southern (1912–2000) delivered to the St. John's College
Historical Society, he pointed out that it was not until 1850 that Oxford
first included history in its curriculum—seven hundred years after the
university's founding. Now, when the study of history is at the very center
of our increasingly fierce and consequential culture wars, it might be useful
to revisit Southern's understanding of the discipline in light of his preoc-
cupations with scholasticism to see whether he has anything useful to say
to historians and their readers now.

But first I should say a few words about Southern himself. Born in 1912
in Newcastle upon Tyne, the second of the four children of Matthew Henry
Southern, a timber merchant, Southern attended the Royal Grammar School
in Newcastle, and in 1929 he went up to Balliol, where he read modern
history, specifically medieval history under Vivian Galbraith, about whom
he would later write that the "colloquialisms and expletives of his lec-
tures—relics of his army days—were abundant on all occasions ... and the
delight of his audiences." Another of Southern's tutors at Balliol was Francis
Fortescue Urquhart, aka "Sligger," Oxford's first Catholic tutor since the
Reformation, who was instrumental in seeing to it that Ronald Knox was
made Oxford's Catholic chaplain. Indolent and unscholarly, Urquhart was
nevertheless one of the most fondly remembered of all of Oxford's dons,
largely because of his charming personal influence, which he exerted for
many years both in his summer reading parties in the French Alps and the
salon he set up for undergraduates in his rooms over Balliol's back gate.
By recommending that Southern read J. H. Round's *Feudal England* and
John Henry Newman's *The Idea of a University*, Urquhart only deepened
Southern's desire to pursue the life of learning. He also introduced Southern

to Newman's understanding of knowledge, a keynote of scholasticism, which would fascinate him all his days.

> Truth is the object of Knowledge of whatever kind [Newman wrote in the *Idea*]; and when we inquire what is meant by Truth, I suppose it is right to answer that Truth means facts and their relations, which stand towards each other pretty much as subjects and predicates in logic. All that exists, as contemplated by the human mind, forms one large system or complex fact, and this of course resolves itself into an indefinite number of particular facts, which, as being portions of a whole, have countless relations of every kind, one towards another. Knowledge is the apprehension of these facts, whether in themselves, or in their mutual positions and bearings. And, as all taken together form one integral subject for contemplation, so there are no natural or real limits between part and part; one is ever running into another; all, as viewed by the mind, are combined together, and possess a correlative character one with another, from the internal mysteries of the Divine Essence down to our own sensations and consciousness, from the most solemn appointments of the Lord of all down to what may be called the accident of the hour, from the most glorious seraph down to the vilest and most noxious of reptiles.

Although Southern succeeded Galbraith in 1937 as fellow and tutor in medieval history, Maurice Powicke was the Oxford colleague who had the most influence on him, principally by suggesting that his protégé study St. Anselm, whose dictum, "I believe in order that I may understand" would animate everything Southern ever wrote. In 1940, he enlisted in the Oxfordshire and Buckinghamshire light infantry. In 1941 he was commissioned in the Durham light infantry where, as second lieutenant, he trained as a tank commander. In 1943 he was transferred to the political intelligence department of the Foreign Office and in 1944 he was promoted to major. In 1944 he married the widow of an RAF hero, with whom he had two sons. After the war, Southern returned to Balliol, where his dash and brilliance would become legendary. In 1950, upon being diagnosed with tuberculosis, he was obliged to leave Oxford and convalesce for two years, though he turned his unexpected leisure to account by writing his first book, *The Making of the Middle Ages* (1953), In 1961 he left Balliol to become the Chichele Professor of Modern History at All Souls. In 1969, he assumed the presidency of St. John's College, Oxford, a post he held for twelve years. Unlike G. M. Trevelyan, whose popularity incurred the contempt of his fellow academic historians at Cambridge, Southern enjoyed both academic and popular acclaim. In 1974, he was knighted. For the medievalist M. H. Keen, who contributed the entry on Southern to the *Oxford Dictionary of National Biography*, "striking energy" was not the historian's only virtue, for "his personality, grace of manner and playful, almost wayward wit were foils" to his "acute mental power" and "relentless integrity." In addition to the classic *The Making of the Middle Ages,* Southern's books include *Saint Anselm and His Biographer: A Study of Monastic Life and Thought 1059–c.1130* (1963); *Western Society and the Church in the Middle Ages* (1970); *Robert Grosseteste: The Growth of an English Mind in Medieval Europe* (1986); *Saint Anselm: A Portrait in a Landscape* (1990); and *Scholastic Humanism and the Unification of Europe,* 2 vols. (1995, 2001).

II

Why Oxford took so long to acknowledge history as a study worthy of learning was a nice question. First, by its very nature, it was thought incapable of supplying a body of systematic, general truth. Oxford, hitherto, like all the early schools set up in Europe, had looked to theology, law, medicine, arithmetic, geometry, music and the arts of the Trivium—grammar, rhetoric, and logic—for this authoritative truth. Secondly, history, as Southern quotes Samuel Johnson as saying, might tell us "that certain kings reigned" or that "certain battles were fought," but "all the colour, all the philosophy of history" was "conjecture." Why, then, was the new Honour School of Law and Modern History established in 1850? Southern's answer was rather comical: history won its place in the curriculum not so much on its merits as by a kind of desperate default.

> The view of knowledge promoted by the old syllabus—the view, namely that reasonable completeness had been reached on most subjects, and that all that was needed was to transmit the body of ascertained truth from one generation to the next, to complete this body of knowledge in detail—had during the previous century been subjected to hammer-blows which left the whole structure in a state of ruin. It was the collapse of the old body of learning which gave history for the first time a claim to be no worse than any of the other subjects, and just possibly much better. There were not many people in England who were convinced that history could produce anything much better, but there were many who thought that it was at least worth trying.

This readiness to look to history to extricate the university from its metaphysical impasse arose from several factors. Although unlikely to produce the sort of truth that the university had traditionally dedicated itself to extolling, history did nevertheless condition the subjects from which such truth was attained. Indeed, "the queen of the sciences, systematic theology," Southern reminded his readers, "was known to be a growth with many historical roots in the Bible, the Fathers, the Councils of the Church," not to mention "the vast works of critical and historical

elucidation" to which interpretation of these sources gave rise. Develop-
ment, in other words, was essential to these subjects, and there could be
no development without history.

Nevertheless, the paradox remained: while history might be "regarded
as an essential background to systematic knowledge," it was not seen as
"a study in its own right." Even the Tudor historian, G. R. Elton, no fan of
scholasticism, acknowledged that "history does not prove the truth of uni-
versals." And as to why this should have been the case, the good historian
in Southern showed how capable he was of entering into the thinking of
the university prior to 1850 when he explained to his readers that, for the
scholastic university, even though under assault by the "hammer blows"
of the Enlightenment: "the essential substance of history came, not as a
result of historical investigation, but from divine revelation." One can
only imagine how such a statement went down with his largely sceptical
audience. Here was an understanding of knowledge completely at odds
with the doctrinaire uncertainties of modern or post-modern scepticism.
Yet Southern could not have been more foursquare on the matter: "what
was important about this whole body of knowledge was that, though it
had emerged through a long process of accumulation and refinement, the
knowledge it contained was not a product of history, but of Revelation
and Reason—and therefore absolutely unshakable." For the Schoolmen
who had put the university on the map in the first place, and their legion
heirs, "history could accumulate and refine, but God and reason alone
could guarantee the truth of the whole system—including, incidentally,
the truth of a whole system of universal chronology." For Southern, the
moral of this thinking was categorical: "We can understand nothing about
the historical revolution of the last one hundred and fifty years unless we
understand this paradox."

III

As to how the scholastic tradition lost its influence not only over the thinking
but the practical affairs of men, Southern supplies the reader with a rather
questionable *tour d'horizon* of Western apostasy. For the historian, while it
was true that the "alliance between divinely revealed and protected history"
and "rational scientific truth served all the main purposes of European life
till the first half of the nineteenth century," it was also true that "from about
1700" doubts and questions began to assail the alliance, though "for most
people, and even for most intellectuals," the alliance "stood up to criticism
without having to face any unanswerable objections."

By any calculation, this chronology is askew. To take just the case of
Oxford, serious challenges were mounted against the scholastic tradition
earlier than 1700. Putting aside John Wyclif and Lollardy, which David

Knowles nicely called "that urgent, untutored, racy, fiercely independent, half-sour religious zeal that was to become such a powerful and characteristic force in English history," by 1521, books by Luther and Melanchthon were already in circulation at the university, as, later in the century, would be John Jewell's *Apology of the Church of England* (1562), which, in essence was an English version of Melanchthon's *Augsburg Confession* (1530). John Jewell (1522–71), reader at Corpus Christi and later Bishop of Salisbury, was one of the principal architects of the Elizabethan Settlement (1558), which made the new order palatable alike to moderate Calvinists and the more acquiescent Romanists. Jewell's greatest contribution to Elizabeth's "hedge priests," as she called them on her deathbed, was to patronize Richard Hooker, whose *Ecclesiastical Polity* (1594–7) put a supple seal on England's repudiation of Rome. Jewell also famously disputed the papacy and transubstantiation with Thomas Harding, Regius Professor of Hebrew, reminding his former colleague, as the Tudor historian Jennifer Loach notes, that he had once referred to Rome as "the sink of Sodom" and had wished that he had had a voice "equal with the great Belle of Oseney" to resound in "the dull eares of the deafe Papists." (Oseney Abbey was a house of Augustinian canons founded in Oxford in 1129, south of the modern Botley Road, which was relinquished into the king's hands in 1537.) Jewell's view of the recusant priests who made the sacraments available to faithful Catholics during the Elizabethan terror was typical of the Reformation gentry: he referred to them as "those oily, shaven, portly hypocrites." It may be true, as Loach says, that Elizabethan Oxford was not a religiously radical place, and Protestant ideas "might have been accorded no more than the academic courtesy of a careful perusal"; but it is still striking that Southern should ignore the English Reformation in his chronology. Even the historian V. H. H. Green, who had nothing of Southern's command of ecclesiastical history, recognized the grievous cost of the Reformation, which he saw not only in the vandalism of statues, altars, pictures, images, vestments and bells but the loss of several monastic colleges following the dissolution of the great abbeys. Colleges faithful to the ancient faith like New College, Exeter, Trinity and Lincoln were holdouts, but even they would eventually be made to conform to the new Protestant order. Arguing that serious challenges to the scholastic tradition did not arise in England until 1700 betrays the Anglo-Catholic in Southern, who, despite rejoicing in that tradition, could never bring himself to acknowledge what Newman recognized so clearly—the patent heterodoxy, indeed unreality of the Church of England. Coincidentally enough, in 1850, in lectures published as *Anglican Difficulties*, Newman mined ecclesiastical history to show how entirely at variance Anglican theology was with the Fathers and the Councils of the scholastic tradition.

In all events, doubts did persist with regard to Oxford's scholasticism, but since "there was no plausible alternative," as Southern says, they were held at bay. Then, "suddenly the doubts became quasi-certainties, and the first glimmerings of a new, vastly longer chronology began to appear," and the rest was history. As Southern reminds his readers:

> It was really the breakdown of biblical chronology which ruined the whole system, and by about 1800 it had broken down for most people; by 1850, the breakdown had become irreparable. As it penetrated deeper and deeper into society the discovery that the fundamental chronology on which the whole system of a divinely ordered and rationally comprehensible universe had rested, was profoundly untrue, not just in detail, but in its essential framework, gained more and more adherents. It is hard to think of a more deadly assault on the foundations of European thought and life than this. The prospect of the survival of any ordered view of the world seemed very bleak by 1850.

Tennyson's great threnody, "In Memoriam," Queen Victoria's favorite poem, published in 1850, confirms this.

> Behold, we know not anything:
> I can but trust that good shall fall
> At last—far off—at last, to all,
> And every winter change to spring.
>
> So runs my dream: but what am I?
> An infant crying in the night:
> An infant crying for the light:
> And with no language but a cry.

After the publication of Charles Lyell's *Principles of Geology* (1830), which torched the old Biblical timeline, Oxford-educated Victorians constituted a kind of despondent night nursery. John Ruskin, like so many others, could have richly commiserated with Tennyson. "You speak of the Flimsiness of your own faith," the art critic wrote one of his correspondents. "Mine, which was never strong, is being beaten into mere gold leaf, and flutters in weak rags from the letter of its old forms ... If only the Geologists would let me alone, I could do very well, but those dreadful Hammers! I hear the clink of them at the end of every cadence of the Bible verses."

It was characteristic of Southern that he should respond to this reversal not with a chronicler's dispassionateness but Christian pity. "I feel immense sympathy for those who were first exposed to the dreadful fall from certainty into a vast pit of doubt," he wrote; though he was also emphatic that the "historical revolution" beginning in 1850 "was a first attempt to climb out of the pit."

In reviewing how history was revisited from 1850 onwards in an attempt to fill the void left by the desuetude in which the scholastic tradition fell, Southern charted the failure of secular humanism. Initially, it was thought that the best means of studying history to establish general truths was through a study of institutions, particularly the development of Parliament and common law, and, by extension, the development of constitutional liberty, a development which could act as a useful guide not only to the conduct of life but to the challenges of empire, when the English still had an empire for which proconsuls had to be supplied.

Here, in embryo, was the Whig conception of history, according to which all history culminated in the triumph of Whig constitutionalism, and Southern vividly describes the welcome with which it was received two years after the revolutions of 1848 rocked European institutions to their foundations. "It came as a huge liberation from a prison of despair to discover that here in our midst there was something like a divine instrument for the enlargement of human life," Southern writes, "developing through the centuries from the earliest days." Indeed, for those who had despaired of the general truths of Revelation, it offered nothing less than "a kind of secular embodiment of that force which had in the past been particularly associated with the now derelict pattern of Revelation."

Consequently, History, not Theology, came to rule the academic roost. The claims made for the redemptive properties of historical study might now seem, as Southern says, "pure moonshine"; but it did not seem so in 1930, when Southern was an undergraduate. "Indeed, history had succeeded beyond all expectation in giving the university that central position in society which it had had in the thirteenth century and had gradually lost in the intervening centuries." By 1900, one third of all undergraduates were studying history. Fifty years later, historical study had begun to lose and would never regain its fleeting centrality.

What had gone wrong? Well, the Whig approach to history, insisting as it did on continuity, degenerated into a kind of parlor game. As Southern shows in his essay, if the game was to show how a statement in a document of 1215, say, when Magna Carta was ratified, could be related to similar statements in documents of 1166, 1259, 1297 and then back again to the Anglo-Saxons, and forward to 1640, 1832 and 1887, winning the game of "hunt the continuity" would always be fairly easy. For Southern, "Students discovered that … all they had to do was to learn the answers."

Generations of students would duly parrot what passed for the axioms of continuity. "The republican experiment in the seventeenth century was an episode which had no sequel: and even the Norman Conquest made no complete or decisive breach with the past," one English writer declared in 1940. "By retaining the ancient organization in the shires, the Norman kings made possible that interaction of central and local authority which ultimately took shape in Parliament. By observing Parliamentary forms, the autocratic Tudors kept in being a body which in due course showed itself capable of taking over the government of the country. By maintaining the monarchy at the Revolution, Parliament preserved, as it were, a centre of attachment and attraction; a unifying element not above, but within the Constitution itself." The writer of this could have been any number of students at either public school or university for over a hundred years: it just happened to have been written by the historian, G. M. Young, whose *Portrait of an Age: Victorian England* (1936) defined the object of historical study as ascertaining "the origin, content, and articulation of that objective mind which controls the thinking and the doing of an age or race" —not a definition that would have found much favor in his own or our day, though it confirmed Southern's suspicion that history fell out of favor after 1950, partly, because it seemed more and more the handmaiden of an asphyxiating Establishment, something imposed on the university from above by "the socially dominant class in contemporary society." If anything, the political correctness of our own elites has only made such oligarchical priorities more dubious still. As Lord Acton once wrote: "The inner reality of history is so unlike the back of the cards, and it takes so long to get at it, which does not prevent us from disbelieving what is current as history, but makes us wish to sift it, and dig through mud to solid foundations." Even James Anthony Froude, the first English historian to follow Ranke's lead and to delve into archives, recognized the patent absurdity of claiming the art of history a science. In a lecture delivered at the Royal Institution on 5 February 1864, he confirmed that there was

> something incongruous in the very connection of such words as Science and History. It is as if we were to talk of the colour of sound, or the longitude of the rule-of-three. Where it is so difficult to make out the truth on the commonest disputed fact in matters passing under our very eyes, how can we talk of a science in things long past, which come to us only through books? It often seems to me as if History was like a child's box of letters, with which we can spell any word we please. We have only to pick out such letters as we want, arrange them as we like, and say nothing about those which do not suit our purpose.

Then, again, the view of history served up for the Establishment made for an inescapable stasis. If it was the delineation of the development of constitutional liberty, for example, that gave Whig history its *raison d'être*, this development culminated for the Whigs in the late nineteenth century. Yet, for Southern, "It was this conception which gave nobility and universal value to the whole study, just as five hundred years earlier, the application of logic, grammar and rhetoric to the mass of material handed down from the ancient world had given dignity and practical usefulness to the scholastic methods of the early universities"; yet the problem for both remained: "there was no more scope for discovery," not to mention the fact that "the world did not seem much better for all that had so far been achieved." The renaissance of the twelfth century, made possible by the practical benefits of the systematization of Theology, confirmed the salutary universalism of the early schools; there was no renaissance for the liberal academy in the nineteenth and twentieth centuries. It only issued in nihilism. What is that line from Yeats? "Civilisation is hooped together, brought / Under a rule, under the semblance of peace / By manifold illusion." Indeed, now, in the twenty-first century, the fragmented, irrational, ideological university has succumbed to almost complete chaos, the idolatry of power and the obsession with grievance ensuring nothing of that respect for objective truth that made the accomplishments of scholasticism possible.

When after the findings of such Whig constitutional historians as Hallam, Macaulay, Stubbs, Freeman and Maitland were shown the door, and the Marxist and Annales schools were given pride of place, the game might have somewhat changed; the dictatorship of the proletariat and an equally fanciful multiculturalism replacing liberty as the teleological brass ring of historical study; but the old problem only reemerged in different guises: historical study could still offer no universal rule of human development. For Southern, "The greatest weakness of the historical thinking of the century after 1850 was its tendency to think of the present as a climax, with man in command of his destiny. Nothing has done more to impoverish humanity than this absurd delusion of self-sufficiency, which ultimately leads to despair as its falsity comes to be recognized." Julian Barnes was withering about this blithe narcissism in his novel, *Flaubert's Parrot* (1985):

> What a curious vanity it is of the present to expect the past to suck up to it. The present looks back at some great figure of an earlier century and wonders, Was he on our side? Was he a goodie? What a lack of self-confidence this implies: the present wants both to patronize the past by adjudicating on its political acceptability, and also to be flattered by it, to be patted on the back and told to keep up the good work.

The academics most in vogue today—obsessed as they are with gender, class, race and what they now style "white supremacy"—are but the latest exemplars of this "curious vanity."

The only antidote that Southern could offer to this worsening solipsism was humility. For him, "the interesting, perhaps the educative, thing about the people of the past lies in the ways in which they differ from us rather than in what we have in common. They differ from us in their sense of eternity, their wealth of images and symbols, their recognition of their own powerlessness. Of course. no amount of understanding of the thoughts and symbols of the past can bring these lost parts of the human psyche to life again. But in understanding what we have lost, we take a first step towards our regeneration." A first, decidedly modest step, Southern realized, for true regeneration is not something historical study alone can offer, however well-intended. On this score Southern had no illusions. In "learning to understand the beliefs and images of the past, we shall not be brought into a believing or creative frame of mind, but we shall at least come to recognize our poverty in contrast to the wealth of the past." For us to see the stark differences between ourselves and those of our predecessors who had the grace to take advantage of the spiritual and practical blessings of scholasticism, when scholasticism gave Europe not only its unity but its vitality, will at least acquaint us with our radical inadequacies, creatures as we still are of the false assurances of secular humanism. For Southern, the "mere thought of what we have lost is a challenge to explain, perhaps to replace, the defects of the present." History, in other words, if it cannot replace Theology as a source of universal truth, can at least offer the chastening dividends of moral honesty. "We may come to look on the past as a treasury of unused wealth which is open to investigation, perhaps appropriation without any losers," Southern wrote in the conclusion of his essay.

In *The Making of the Middle Ages*, he had another occasion to treat of this crucial matter of self-knowledge, the defiance of which has led so many otherwise sensible men to set sail for shipwreck. "St Bernard owed his influence as a guide to the spiritual life largely to the fact that men's minds had been turning already in the direction along which he impelled them," Southern writes of a time when introspection "ran like fire" through eleventh-century Europe.

> Both St Bernard and St Anselm began their reconstituted ladders of humility with self-knowledge; and this theme of self-knowledge was deeply rooted in the new monastic movements of this time. The first abbot of Cîteaux wrote of his followers as "those to whom grace has been given to know themselves." Guigo, the greatest of the early Carthusian writers, in his *Meditations*, composed between 1110 and 1116, which have been justly compared to the *Pensées* of Pascal, expressed more luminously than any contemporary writer the mystery of the self: "See how ignorant you are of your own self; there is no land so distant or so unknown to you, nor one about which you will so easily believe falsehoods."

IV

If lack of self-knowledge unsettles men, so too does lack of confidence in the promises of peace. During the Battle of Britain, the Anglo-Irish novelist Elizabeth Bowen (1899–1973), who wrote one of England's best wartime novels, *The Heat of the Day* (1949), recalled that the attitude of the Shelburne Hotel in Dublin "to any few wartime travellers who filtered through was one of maternal solicitude." Describing this attitude in her history of the hotel, Bowen wrote:

> It was the rooted belief of all chambermaids that those arriving from London were to be treated as casualties from bomb-shock: voices and footsteps were accordingly muted, soft ministrations were many, and in no night-nursery could one have been more fondly, soothingly, firmly tucked up in bed. "Sleep well tonight," they murmured. "Here nothing will trouble you." Never was one more conscious, through this kindness, of the hotel's primitive human core.

Now, in our own age, when casualties of spiritual bomb-shock strew the post-Christian landscape, we need more than solicitous Irish chambermaids to repair our "primitive human core," and no one fits this bill as handily as Southern, who made good on his recommendation to treat history as "a treasury of unused wealth" by dedicating the last twenty odd years of his life to recreating, in his late masterpiece, *Scholastic Humanism and the Unification of Europe* (1995), the scholastic tradition of the twelfth and thirteenth centuries, on which Christendom, however mutilated, still relies.

The first thing Southern does in the book is to distinguish "scholastic humanism" from what we ordinarily understand by the word "humanism." If "humanism," as defined by the *Oxford English Dictionary*, means "any system of thought or action which is concerned with merely human interests, or with the human race in general," and if its main instrument is scientific knowledge, which it seeks to extend, to the exclusion of the supernatural in human affairs, those who adhere to humanism look down their noses at the Schoolmen, regarding their works as superstitious and retrograde. They especially deplore, as Southern says, "their emphasis on the supernatural end of man, their assumption of the primacy of theology among the sciences, [and] their source in a primarily clerical culture and hierarchical organization under a universal papal authority." Elton, again, is worth quoting on this score. "Humanists can up to a point be identified by their principles as students and teachers: humanism above all was an educational movement," he wrote in an essay entitled "Humanism in England" (1990).

> However, there is surely one characteristic he had to display in order to join the club: he must think *humaniter* and believe in human ability to control human fate. Not all of them need to have fully subscribed to the slogan, "homo mensura"; it was possible to doubt that man is the measure of all things and to allow for the work of God's grace in men nevertheless endowed with free will. What no one properly

to be called a humanist could adhere to was an Augustinian belief in the total and helpless depravity of fallen man.

That the Schoolmen should be tarred with so slapdash a brush might be unfair but it is still proof of the total victory their opponents had over them in the court of intellectual opinion. In other words, humanists have always tended to credit what G. K. Chesterton once called "the loose and largely unverified legend of the Renaissance, that the Schoolmen were all crabbed and mechanical medieval bores." By contrast, humanists have always been regarded as the bright and coming men; it is the badge of their worldliness. The new atheist head chaplain at Harvard, Greg Epstein is typical of such worldly, self-assured humanists. "We don't look to a god for answers," Mr. Epstein recently told *The New York Times*. "We are each other's answers." In *Saint Anselm and his Biographer* (1966), Southern quotes something that the resolutely unworldly saint wrote in one of his letters:

> If the world smiles on you with its favours, do not smile in return. It does not smile that you may smile in the end; but it mocks you with its Prince, that you with its Prince may mourn. Therefore, however it smiles on you, turn from its smile that you may rejoice when the Mocker mourns.

T. S. Eliot, once settled in London after the Great War, took great pleasure in mocking the humanists who had taught him at Harvard when he was an undergraduate there. If alive today, he would doubtless find the appointment of Epstein not only a delicious absurdity but a predictable outcome of the teachings of the Harvard humanist, Irving Babbitt (1865–1933). In "Second Thoughts on Humanism" (1929), for example, Eliot was unsparing:

> Man is man because he can recognize spiritual realities, not because he can invent them. Either everything in man can be traced as a development from below, or something must come from above. There is no avoiding that dilemma: you must be either a naturalist or a supernaturalist. If you remove from the word "human" all that the belief in the supernatural has given to man, you can view him finally as no more than an extremely clever, adaptable, and mischievous little animal.

Here, however, Eliot overlooked one of the signature accomplishments of scholasticism. Apropos the differences between the Schoolmen and their secular humanist successors, Southern rightly shows that the Schoolmen never shackled rational enquiry. On the contrary, by including the supernatural in their studies they were acknowledging "the complexity and richness of the scene of human life": they were not limiting it. Indeed, it was precisely their supernatural studies that gave them their unique understanding of the natural world. In their respect for the natural world, the

Schoolmen were the "direct ancestors" of the secular humanists, without ever falling prey to their parochialism. In other words, they were proper naturalists only because they were supernaturalists.

In the opening pages of *Scholastic Humanism*, Southern captures the understanding of human nature that lies at the heart of scholasticism, which sets it entirely apart from secular humanism and merits quoting in full, epitomizing as it does so much of the mediaevalist's masterly work:

> The first fundamental characteristic of the products of the schools is a strong sense of the dignity of human nature. Without this there can be no humanism of any description, and it is a conspicuous force in the schools of the twelfth and thirteen centuries. That Man is a fallen creature, who has lost that immediate knowledge of God which was the central feature of human nature before the Fall; that human instincts are now deeply disturbed and are often in conflict with reason; that human beings are now radically disorganized and disorientated—all this is common ground to all Christian thinkers at all times. We must not expect a denial of this condition in the Middle Ages, or in the Renaissance for that matter, or any time not blinded by excessive optimism about human capabilities. But what we may reasonably claim for the twelfth-century schools is that they were the first institutions in Europe to make it their main purpose to set about systematically restoring to the fullest possible extent the knowledge that had been forfeited at the Fall. The method employed for effecting this restoration was to study the works of the ancient scholars who had begun the slow process of repairing the ravages of sin in destroying man's knowledge of both the natural and supernatural worlds, and to elucidate and complete this process—so far as is possible in this world—by systemizing and elaborating the truth regained by ancient scholars or revealed in Old Testament prophets, and more fully available to later Christian Fathers and students. The expectation was that, when all had been gathered in, a very great part of the knowledge lost at the Fall would once more be available for the guidance and instruction of human beings.

For Southern, this was the first aim of scholasticism: but it had another, equally important one, which shows why scholastic humanism can be relied upon to extend our knowledge of the natural world in ways humanism cannot.

> Just as human nature has an inherent dignity which, though ruined by the Fall, has not been altogether lost, so too the whole natural order is in a similar situation. The continuing human power to recognise the grandeur and splendour of the universe, to understand the principles of the organization of nature, and to order human life in accordance with nature is symptomatic of the survival of

human dignity, in however depleted a form, after the Fall. But it is also symptomatic of the continuing dignity of the natural world itself that it is intelligible. Consequently, when human beings understand the laws of nature, they not only achieve their true dignity as nature's keystone, holding the whole created order together in an intelligible union, but they also recognise the rationality of nature itself. Further, this position gives human minds access to the divine purpose in the Creation, and therefore, in some degree, access through reason, as well as Revelation, to the divine nature itself.

Given the profundity and practicality of scholasticism, the irony was that the very thing that it was designed to redress—the "ravages of sin"—should be its downfall. If the scholasticism of the early schools wielded great salutary influence in the world by disproving St. Augustine's contention that government could never be anything but organized robbery, it also created a certain amount of competitiveness among scholars, especially where there was not an unlimited number of schools, cathedrals or patrons. "Teachers—it is hard to believe it, but it seems to be true—became a road to profit as well as fame," Southern writes in *The Making of the Middle Ages*. The result of this scramble for place was that some used what they had learned in the schools to prostitute their learning. As Southern points out, "As they consolidated their positions, these scholastically trained career-men developed some clearly marked attitudes, which included a willingness to serve the interests of any employer who could reward them." Although sworn to uphold the hierarchical unity of Christendom, the schools could not control the ambitions of their graduates. Once the services of scholastically trained men became available for the defense of every side of every issue, "the unity of western Christendom, which was the great aim and, in some degree, the achieved result of scholastic training and doctrine, gradually dissolved in a spate of disagreements supported by scholastic arguments." By the fourteenth century, scholasticism had begun to lose its way in such futile disputation. By the late seventeenth century, Southern writes, "it was hard to see the other side of the picture—the wide agreement in principle which these acrimonious disputes presupposed; the hard intellectual discipline; the order and system which the study of logic had diffused throughout the whole body of thought and learning; the awakening of the intellect to the study of itself and the arrangement of its impressions of the outside world; the recognition of the autonomy of reason in the discussion of philosophical and theological problems."

Thus, Southern pleads for what he sees as the continuing usefulness of scholasticism, despite the disrepute into which it fell as a result of its being misapplied, and he manages this largely by helping himself to the encouragement to be found in the study of history. For Southern, the scholastic humanism of the mediaeval schools, "as far removed from the elitism of

Renaissance humanism as it is from the Godlessness of modern secular humanism … whether we consider its inherent grandeur or its influence on the future … has a good claim to be considered the most important kind of humanism Europe has ever produced." It saw England through the invasions of the eleventh century when Viking armies overran the country by persuading Aethelred II to meet the crisis with two decrees: build more ships to repel the invaders and see to it that "every Christian man shall go frequently to confession, and freely confess his sins, and readily make amends as prescribed for him." Later, when Ethelred ordered all the Danes in the country massacred, he might have been grateful for the latter decree. In all events, with the rising demand on the part of kings, bishops, monasteries and great landowners for educated officials, not to mention the rising schools, the Schoolmen lay down codes of behaviour that would seek to advance peace and probity throughout Western Christendom. In the formulation of such codes in such continually inauspicious circumstances Southern rightly saw an admirable confidence. "Regarded simply as an attempt to regulate human life and to direct it in all its aspects towards the attainment of stability on earth and everlasting happiness thereafter, the efforts of the twelfth and thirteenth centuries—coming so soon after the most fragmented period of European invasions and resettlements—have an astonishing assurance of permanence."

Now that we find ourselves in our own night-nursery, with the City of Man in an awful shambles outside the green baize door, and the City of God under unrelenting assault, we could do worse than revisit the work of the historian who recommends this permanent philosophy with such exuberant, solicitous learning.

NOVELISTS

The Prophetical Anthony Trollope

Nothing is more mischievous than the self-complacency of historians who treat the past as though it were an object lesson in why the present is more enlightened than the past. And yet precisely because these historians flatter the self-complacency of their readers, their misjudgments of the past often become conventional wisdom. This certainly occurred with regard to the view of the Victorians that still obtains in many quarters, thanks, in large part, to historians taking it into their heads to portray Victoria's subjects as little more than epitomes of humbug and hypocrisy. Indeed, if we consult the *Oxford English Dictionary*, we can see the figurative sense of the word *Victorian* defined there as *prudish, strict, old-fashioned* and *outdated*, the clear implication being that the successors to the historians are, by contrast, broadminded, liberal, *au courant* and forward-looking. As if to drive home this invidious comparison, the dictionary's editors turned to George Bernard Shaw, who wrote in 1950: *He was helping the movement against Victorian prudery in a very practical way as a nudist.* That says it all.

These distinctions occurred to me recently while reading Anthony Trollope's novel, *The Way We Live Now* (1875). While unnecessary to go into all of the twists and turns of the plot, it is necessary for our purposes to relate that the downfall of the book's hero, Augustus Melmotte, a thoroughly unscrupulous financier involves a host of other characters intent on sharing in what they hope will be the dividends of his dishonest speculations. One of the subsidiary characters is a dissolute young baronet named Sir Felix Carbury, whose enterprising but impecunious mother tries to arrange for his marrying Melmotte's daughter, Marie. Spending most of his time drinking and gambling in his club, the baronet only pursues Marie half-heartedly; he prefers the company of an exuberant young country woman named Ruby Ruggles. Ruby has been put out of her home by her grandfather, whom she calls the "Squire," for refusing to marry an upright miller named John Crumb, who genuinely loves her. Consequently, as the story unfolds, Ruby is living with her Aunt Pipkin in Islington. Meanwhile, Felix has arranged to run away with Marie, convinced that her father will forgive her elopement and settle enough money on her to enable him to continue his life of dissipated improvidence. Before embarking for New York, however, he meets with Ruby one last time, even though her Aunt has told her that if she goes out again with Sir Felix the door will be locked when she returns home.

This is all the plot summary one needs in order to enter into the power of Trollope's treatment of the culminating scene between Sir Felix and Ruby, which nicely proves that, when it comes to *virginibus puerisque*, the Victorians were nothing as benighted as they have been made out to be. "I'm pretty nigh ashamed of myself. Yes, I am," Ruby admits at the beginning of the scene, with a moral clarity that does her justice.

> And now Ruby burst out into tears. "Because I wouldn't have John Crumb, I didn't mean to be a bad girl. Nor yet I won't. But what'll I do, if everybody turns again me? Aunt won't go on for ever in this way. She said last night that—"
>
> "Bother what she says!" Felix was not at all anxious to hear what aunt Pipkin might have to say upon such an occasion.
>
> "She's right too. Of course she knows there's somebody. She ain't such a fool as to think that I'm out at these hours to sing psalms with a lot of young women. She says that whoever it is ought to speak out his mind. There;—that's what she says. And she's right. A girl has to mind herself, though she's ever so fond of a young man."
>
> Sir Felix sucked his cigar and then took a long drink of brandy and water. Having emptied the beaker before him, he rapped for the waiter and called for another. He intended to avoid the necessity of making any direct reply to Ruby's importunities. He was going to New York very shortly, and looked on his journey thither as an horizon in his future beyond which it was unnecessary to speculate as to any farther distance. He had not troubled himself to think how it might be with Ruby when he was gone. He had not even considered whether he would or would not tell her that he was going, before he started. It was not his fault that she had come up to London. She was an "awfully jolly girl," and he liked the feeling of the intrigue better perhaps than the girl herself. But he assured himself that he wasn't going to give himself any "d——d trouble." The idea of John Crumb coming up to London in his wrath had never occurred to him,—or he would probably have hurried on his journey to New York instead of delaying it, as he was doing now. "Let's go in and have a dance," he said.
>
> Ruby was very fond of dancing,—perhaps liked it better than anything in the world. It was heaven to her to be spinning round the big room with her lover's arm tight round her waist, with one hand in his and her other hanging over his back. She loved the music, and loved the motion. Her ear was good, and her strength was great, and she never lacked breath. She could spin along and dance a whole room down, and feel at the time that the world could have nothing to give better worth having than that;—and such moments were too precious to be lost. She went and danced,

resolving as she did so that she would have some answer to her question before she left her lover on that night.

Is this *old-fashioned* or *outdated*? Do young women no longer demand respect from the young men they see? Are they no longer apprehensive lest their fondness for an irresponsible young man betray their dignity, their honor? Should young men no longer feel ashamed when they use young women as though they were nothing more than kept concubines? These are matters of a perennial importance to the young, as they are to any society as a whole reliant on the young for the perpetuation of civil society. In giving them such dramatic reality, Trollope can hardly be said to be "Victorian" in the sense in which the *Oxford English Dictionary* defines the word. On the contrary, his treatment of these deeply consequential matters could not be more *ad rem*. No one can read this riveting scene from *The Way We Live Now* without seeing that its moral preoccupations are our preoccupations. In showing such sympathy and admiration for his brave, incorruptible Ruby, Trollope shows sympathy for an understanding of female dignity without which no civilization can flourish. Indeed, there is a kind of chivalry in Trollope's sympathy, but there is also a very toughminded realism, a recognition that there are stakes attached to how we treat or mistreat women. But rather than gloss the scene, I should let my readers simply read it for themselves.

"And now I must go," she said at last. "You'll see me as far as the Angel, won't you?" Of course he was ready to see her as far as the Angel. "What am I to say to the Squire?"

"Say nothing."

"And what am I to say to aunt?"

"Say to her? Just say what you have said all along."

"I've said nothing all along,—just to oblige you, Felix. I must say something. A girl has got herself to mind. What have you got to say to me, Felix?"

He was silent for about a minute, meditating his answer. "If you bother me I shall cut it, you know."

"Cut it!"

"Yes;—cut it. Can't you wait till I am ready to say something?"

"Waiting will be the ruin o' me, if I wait much longer. Where am I to go, if Mrs. Pipkin won't have me no more?"

"I'll find a place for you."

"You find a place! No; that won't do. I've told you all that before. I'd sooner go into service, or—"

"Go back to John Crumb."

"John Crumb has more respect for me nor you. He'd make me his wife to-morrow, and only be too happy."

"I didn't tell you to come away from him," said Sir Felix.

"Yes, you did. You told me as I was to come up to London when I saw you at Sheepstone Beeches;—didn't you? And you told me you loved me;—didn't you? And that if I wanted anything you'd get it done for me;—didn't you?"

"So I will. What do you want? I can give you a couple of sovereigns, if that's what it is."

"No it isn't;—and I won't have your money. I'd sooner work my fingers off. I want you to say whether you mean to marry me. There!"

As to the additional lie which Sir Felix might now have told, that would have been nothing to him. He was going to New York, and would be out of the way of any trouble; and he thought that lies of that kind to young women never went for anything. Young women, he thought, didn't believe them, but liked to be able to believe afterwards that they had been deceived. It wasn't the lie that stuck in his throat, but the fact that he was a baronet. It was in his estimation "confounded impudence" on the part of Ruby Ruggles to ask to be his wife. He did not care for the lie, but he did not like to seem to lower himself by telling such a lie as that at her dictation. "Marry, Ruby! No, I don't ever mean to marry. It's the greatest bore out. I know a trick worth two of that."

She stopped in the street and looked at him. This was a state of things of which she had never dreamed. She could imagine that a man should wish to put it off, but that he should have the face to declare to his young woman that he never meant to marry at all, was a thing that she could not understand. What business had such a man to go after any young woman? "And what do you mean that I'm to do, Sir Felix?" she said.

"Just go easy, and not make yourself a bother."

"Not make myself a bother! Oh, but I will; I will. I'm to be carrying on with you, and nothing to come of it; but for you to tell me that you don't mean to marry, never at all! Never?"

"Don't you see lots of old bachelors about, Ruby?"

"Of course I does. There's the Squire. But he don't come asking girls to keep him company."

"That's more than you know, Ruby."

"If he did he'd marry her out of hand,—because he's a gentleman. That's what he is, every inch of him. He never said a word to a girl,—not to do her any harm, I'm sure," and Ruby began to cry. "You mustn't come no further now, and I'll never see you again— never! I think you're the falsest young man, and the basest, and the lowest-minded that I ever heard tell of. I know there are them as don't keep their words. Things turn up, and they can't. Or they gets to like others better; or there ain't nothing to live on. But for a young man to come after a young woman, and then say, right out, as he never means to marry at all, is the lowest-spirited fellow that ever was. I never read of such a one in none of the books. No, I won't. You go your way, and I'll go mine." In her passion she was as good as her word, and escaped from him, running all the way to her aunt's door. There was in her mind a feeling of anger against the man, which she did not herself understand, in that he would incur no risk on her behalf. He would not even make a lover's easy promise, in order that the present hour might be made pleasant. Ruby let herself into her aunt's house, and cried herself to sleep with a child on each side of her.

Read in the light of the sexual revolution that has undermined our social order by undermining our commitment to all the virtues and blessings of marriage, this could only be thought *old-fashioned* and *outdated* by those who imagine our need for love, our need for self-respect, our need for civil order *old-fashioned* and *outdated*. "For a young man to come after a young woman, and then say, right out, as he never means to marry at all, is the lowest-spirited fellow that ever was"—if we could only instill this now nearly forgotten truth into the hearts and minds of our own young men, we could begin to revitalize our dying civilization.

This might sound a grandiose claim but I believe it is true, and I base this belief, to some lively extent, on some observations that Trollope himself made about his satirical novel in his *Autobiography* (1883). There he revealed that it was "the commercial profligacy of the age" that inspired him to write the book. Of course, many commentators infer from this that what Trollope found most objectionable about this "profligacy" was its plutocratic extravagance. But this is not actually the case. What troubled Trollope was something more fundamental than mere greed, as he points out in the last chapter of his *Autobiography*.

> Whether the world does or does not become more wicked as years go on, is a question which probably has disturbed the minds of thinkers since the world began to think. That men have become less cruel, less violent, less selfish, less brutal, there can be no doubt;—but have they become less honest? If so, can a world, retrograding from day to day in honesty, be considered to be in a state of progress? We know the opinion on this subject of our philosopher Mr. Carlyle. If he be right, we are all going straight away to darkness and the dogs. ... Nevertheless a certain class of dishonesty, dishonesty magnificent in its proportions, and climbing into high places, has become at the same time so rampant and so splendid that there seems to be reason for fearing that men and women will be taught to feel that dishonesty, if it can become splendid, will cease to be abominable.

Certainly, such moral dishonesty vitiates our own culture at every level, though, as Trollope appreciates, the fact that it permeates the very highest levels of society inures us to its turpitude. "If dishonesty can live in a gorgeous palace with pictures on all its walls, and gems in all its cupboards, with marble and ivory in all its corners, and can give Apician dinners, and get into Parliament, and deal in millions, then dishonesty is not disgraceful, and the man dishonest after such a fashion is not a low scoundrel." This, as Trollope relates, "instigated" him to write *The Way We Live Now*, "to take," as he says, "the whip of the satirist" into his hand, and go "beyond the iniquities of the great speculator" to tackle "other vices" as well; one of which, as we have seen, was "the luxury of young men who prefer to remain single" — young men, that is to say, who, out of concupiscence and solipsism reject the honesty that is at the very heart of sacramental marriage.

In this, curiously enough, Trollope thought he might have overstepped the bounds of warrantable satire. The very forbearance and generosity of the man led him to wonder whether he had been, after all, too harsh in his satirical zeal. "Who," he asks, "when the lash of objurgation is in his hands, can so moderate his arm as never to strike harder than justice would require?" But certainly, we, confronted as we are by a culture of far more baleful dishonesty — a dishonesty that has robbed us of our respect not only for women but for our very humanity — can see that Trollope was not only just in his satire: he was prophetic.

Henry James and the Ties of Family

Recently, we have heard a good deal of the family in our national discontents. Those sworn to the progressive ideology blame the family for perpetuating what the Soviets used to call "dissidence"; they even go so far as to insist that children denounce parents if they fail to salaam before the ideology's implacable gods; while those critical of the ideology deplore the part it continues to play in the breakdown of the family and all the turmoil to which such breakdown inveterately gives rise. However we look at it, the family is a defining factor of our social order, and it is for that very reason that it might be amusing to see what the greatest American novelist had to say of it.

In 1887, Henry James heard from his sister Alice of a daughter who was distraught by her father's remarrying because, as she said, it was "forty years of her mother's life wiped out." This was the genesis of his short story, "The Marriages" (1891), which, in its debt to the theatrical melodrama that James had imbibed as a boy in New York and its psychological acuity, exemplifies his finest fiction.

It also shows how much his art drew upon and was sustained by his own sense of family—in this case, a sense reinforced by his sister Alice, with whom he would always be close, the same Alice who said of their father, the insouciant Swedenborgian, Henry James Senior, "Father, the delicious infant, couldn't even submit to the thralldom of his own whim." Both siblings realized that the love of families is only made possible by the forbearance of families—an important *leitmotif* in "The Marriages."

The plot of the tale is simple. Adela Chart tries to prevent her father, Colonel Chart from remarrying by telling his rich fiancée, Mrs. Churchley that he had broken her mother's heart, a fabrication which affronts her brother Godfrey, who is fond of the fiancée for offering to resolve his "idiotic secret marriage." Godfrey, an imprudent youth, has married an unpresentably cockney woman. In the end, the Colonel's remarriage is prevented, though not for the reasons Adela supposes.

James saw the story's drama inhering in the "pangs of filial piety" and pivoting on what he called "the consciousness, the fond imagination, the possibly poisoned and inflamed judgement" of the daughter who takes it upon herself to hallow her mother's memory. The author's "possibly"

333

leaves it to the reader to decide whether Adela's judgment is "poisoned."

Clearly, no one could consider her judgment slack. There is a pronounced lack of sentimentality about her. "Adela had reason to believe she should never marry, and that someday she should have about a thousand a year," the narrator tells us. "This made her see in the far future a little garden of her own, under a hill, full of rare and exquisite things, where she would spend most of her old age on her knees with an apron and stout gloves ... steeped in the comfort of being thought mad." What James would call "the terrible *fluidity* of self-revelation" is here drolly exhibited.

In thus capturing the peculiar drama of consciousness, James transforms what might have been a potboiler into a short masterpiece. What gives the story an added *frisson* is its scenic briskness, proof that James had learned the lesson of the dramatic master in Maupassant.

In describing Adela's distaste for Mrs. Churchley, James takes full advantage of the exaggerations of melodrama: "Everything about her, to Adela Chart, was enormous. She had big eyes, big teeth, big shoulders, big hands, big rings ... big jewels ... She was high and expansive herself, though not exactly fat; her bones were big, her limbs were long, and she had a loud, hurrying voice, like the bell of a steamboat." At the same time, Adela respects Mrs. Churchley for never breaking her confidence: the rival to her father's affections may be vulgar, even a little absurd, but she is not dishonorable.

Leon Edel, James's best biographer, read the story as a precursor to Freud, showing how "a young girl, under the guise of filial piety and filial self-righteousness can turn passionate jealousy into an exercise of power." Yet trusting Freud to explain Adela's opposition to Mrs. Churchley can hardly account for the story's genuine pathos. When Adela discovers that her brother does not share her view of their father's remarriage, she recognizes why she must be all the more opposed to it. "Their worship of their mother's memory, their recognition of her sacred place in their past, her exquisite influence in their father's life, his fortune, his career, in the whole history of the family ... was like a religion ... to fall away from which was a form of treachery."

Of course, Adela also recognizes that: "This wasn't the way people usually felt in London ... Remembrance there was hammered thin—and to be faithful was to be a bore. ... When they had hustled all sensibility out of their lives, they invented the fiction that they felt too much to utter." If this is merely the guise of filial piety, it is an oddly convincing guise. It also recalls Thackeray's great question: "Who is ever missed in Vanity Fair?"

Seeing the story in Freudian terms also overlooks its comedy. When Adela recoils from Mrs. Churchley "as undomestic as a shop-front and as out of tune as a parrot," it is because her father's intended "would either make them live in the streets or bring the streets into their life—it was the same thing. She had evidently never read a book, and she used intonations that Adela had never heard, as if she had been an Australian or an American." This is the comedy of class, which would have baffled the morose Austrian in Freud. James mines the same comedy when Godfrey's inconvenient wife insists that she be allowed to meet with one of the family: "fice to fice."

When the meeting finally occurs, Adela reels. Her interlocutress has "vivid yellow hair, " a "blue cloth suit with brass buttons, a stick-up collar like a gentleman's, a necktie arranged in a sailor's knot, a golden pin in the shape of a little lawn-tennis racket, and pearl-grey gloves with big black stitchings." At first, Adela mistakes her for an actress, but then she is sure that she is unlike anyone she has ever met. When the "apparition" speaks, it is to insist that Adela's father Colonel Chart must intercede on her behalf and force his son Godfrey to let her accompany him abroad, whither he is going to escape Mrs. Godfrey. The sequel to this demand is blurry.

> What really happened Adela never quite understood; what seemed to be happening was that the room went round and round. Through the blur of perception accompanying this effect the sharp stabs of her visitor's revelation came to her like the words heard by a patient "going off" under ether. She afterwards denied passionately even to herself that she had done anything so abject as to faint; but there was a lapse in her consciousness.

Towards the story's end, Adela, seeing her father's "wasted and jilted air," repents of her meddling, confesses her lies to Mrs. Churchley and begs that she take the Colonel back, whereupon the lady reveals that she never believed Adela's lies. She broke off the marriage because she thought her fiancé's daughter "horrid," not her fiancé. Later, when Adela crows: "Mrs. Churchley can never come back—she's going to marry Lord Dovedale," we are reminded that few Edwardian peers, certainly none strapped for cash, would have objected to the vulgarity that Adela finds so insufferable in her monied *bête noire*.

Whether this confirms Mrs. Churchley's low view of Adela is, of course, arguable. Robert Louis Stevenson, for one, adored James's heroine, as the verses he sent his friend attest: "Adela, Adela, Adela Chart / What have you done to my elderly heart / Of the ladies in paper and ink / I count you the paragon, call you the pink," though it is necessary to add that the reason for this adoration was somewhat barbed: "in all the asylums that cumber the ground / So delightful a maniac was n'er to be found."

The Marriages reaffirms the extent to which Alice James inspired her brother's muse. When the 3rd Duke of Sutherland (1828–92) married Mary Caroline Blair (née Michell) in March 1889, after the death of his first wife, his daughter, Lady Alexandra Leveson-Gower was so upset by the re-marriage and what she regarded as the implicit disrespect shown her mother

335

by it that she actually died three years afterwards. Alice's response to this woeful demise, which she shared with Henry, needs quoting: "Will there be no stirrings of remorse in her father's bosom for the brutalities which rent that delicate fibre?"

Here is the *donnée* that set James's muse afire. Of course, true to the alchemy of art, Adela may not be "delicate," but she nonetheless attests to the profound feeling that courses through what Lancelot Andrewes called "the bands of birth." At the end of *The Marriages*, when Colonel Chart walks away from his inamorato, Adela tells her brother: "Papa gave her up, as it were, for *me*. Fancy the angel, and fancy what I must try to be to him for the rest of his life!" There is nothing "poisoned" in this dénouement to James's moving tribute to the potency of familial love.

While our more agitated neighbors seek to deliver up our unravelling social order to the direction of totalitarian scolds, the rest of us can find solace and sanctuary in the family-friendly Henry James.

J. K. Huysmans
and the Reality of Evil

In the aftermath of the trial of Kermit Gosnell, the doctor found guilty of murdering several children in his abortion clinic in Pennsylvania, commentary followed two tracks. The first argued that the trial exposed the savagery of abortion; the second that it exposed the need to make abortion more efficient by making it more accessible. When subsequent scandals arose from Planned Parenthood being shown on film discussing selling body parts of aborted babies, commentary again followed the same two tracks, one decrying the tapes as proof that abortion is murder and the other calling for more efficient regulation to ensure more efficient abortion. Despite this commentary, the response of the general public to both scandals was oddly muted. Why there was not more widespread outrage is a nice question. Perhaps the inherent grisliness of the scandals was too much for many to confront, let alone denounce. What was it T. S. Eliot once said? "Human kind cannot bear very much reality." Another possible explanation might be not so much that the general public is unable to register reality as that they are unable to register the reality of evil. To explore this possibility, I shall revisit the work of the nineteenth-century French novelist Joris-Karl Huysmans, who took up the issue of evil in several of his books, first in Á Rebours (1882) and then in a lesser known but brilliant tetralogy, comprising La-Bas (1891), En Route (1895), La Cathédrale (1898) and L'Oblat (1903). However, before looking at how these books shed light on the evil of abortion, and on what the author considered to be the only effective antidote to that evil, I should say a few brief words about Huysmans himself.

Joris-Karl Huysman (1848–1907) was born, educated, worked and died in Paris. For most of his adult life, in addition to writing art criticism and fiction, he worked as a civil servant in La Sûreté Géneralé, the government department responsible for state security. His early work was written under the influence of Zola and the pseudo-scientific literary school of naturalism. Indeed, in En Ménage (1881), he wrote what amounts to a fictional tribute to the determinist pessimism of Arthur Schopenhauer (1788–1860), the philosopher whose work animates the fiction of all of the naturalists. In one of his last books, Schopenhauer gave a useful summation of his thinking,

337

which I shall quote at length, if only because the despair at the heart of his philosophy is an essential ingredient of the despair that Huysmans wrote so much of his later fiction to anatomize.

> That human life must be some kind of mistake is sufficiently proved by the simple observation that man is a compound of needs that are hard to satisfy; that their satisfaction achieves nothing but a painless condition in which he is given over to boredom; and that boredom is nothing other than the sensation of the emptiness of existence. For if life, in the desire for which our essence and existence consists, possessed in itself a positive value and real content there would be no such thing as boredom: mere existence would fulfill and satisfy us. As things are, we take no pleasure in existence except when we are striving after something—in which case distance and difficulties make our goal look as if it would satisfy us (an illusion which fades when we reach it)—or when engaged in purely intellectual activity, in which case we are really stepping out of life so as to regard it from outside, like spectators at a play. Even sensual pleasure itself consists in a continual striving and ceases as soon as its goal is reached. Whenever we are not involved in one or other of these things but directed back to existence itself we are overtaken by its worthlessness and vanity and this is the sensation called boredom.

There is a certain dark comedy in this. Indeed, it reminds one of the bleak puzzles of Samuel Beckett's *Waiting for Godot* (1953). Dark comedy appealed to Huysmans, who had a good sense of humor of his own, at once sardonic and farcical. Yet Huysmans' deep discontent and yearning for God eventually turned him away from Schopenhauer and the Naturalism that grew out of his despondent philosophy, and it is the books in which he expresses his wrestling with this discontent that we can find his portrayal of the often unacknowledged evil that makes abortion possible.

I

In 1884, while on honeymoon in Dieppe with his wife, Constance, Oscar Wilde discovered the book that would become what the symbolist poet Arthur Symons called "the breviary of the decadence," Huysmans' *Á Rebours* (Against Nature). Wilde was deeply influenced by the book; indeed, it inspired him to write *The Picture of Dorian Gray* (1891); though it is questionable whether he understood its satirical *raison d'être*. Huysmans' novel chronicles how its epicene hero, the Duc Jean des Esseintes attacks all that is natural by secluding himself from the crass, grasping world of Third Republic Paris to construct his own dandified, alternative world, where the artificial and the deviant predominate. Thus, in one passage, the hero hosts "a farewell dinner, "as he calls it on his black-edged invitations, "to nis dead virility," in which all the food and drink are black, and "nude negresses, wearing slippers and stockings of silver cloth with patterns of tears, serve the guests." In another passage, deciding which color to paint his study, des Esseintes is described as "ignoring the bourgeoisie, whose eyes are insensible to the pomp and splendor of strong, vibrant tones; and devoting himself only to people with sensitive pupils, refined by literature and art, ... convinced that the eyes of those among them who dream of the ideal and demand illusions are generally caressed by blue and its derivatives, mauve, lilac and pearl grey." In yet another passage, the hero introduces a young man of sixteen to a Paris brothel to instill in him such a loathing of the opposite sex as to put him permanently off procreation.

From these passages, it is clear that Huysmans meant his depiction of his strenuously perverse hero to be a satirical criticism, not an endorsement of the unnatural and the decadent. "Dreaming of a refined solitude, a comfortable desert, a motionless ark in which to seek refuge from the unending deluge of human stupidity, " des Esseintes is shown spending his days in his Fontenay retreat deploring what he chooses to regard as the banality of Nature, while concocting various ways to defy and subvert it. In another passage, Huysmans has des Esseintes instruct his readers how they can enjoy the benefits of the seaside without leaving the capital: they can visit the Vigier baths on the Seine where "the illusion of the sea is undeniable" and gaze at photographs of whatever casino they wish to patronize. For des Esseintes, "The secret lies in knowing ... how to concentrate deeply enough to produce the hallucination and succeed in substituting the dream reality for the reality itself." And Huysmans nicely points the moral of this quintessentially decadent preoccupation by stating how "Artifice ... seemed to des Esseintes the final distinctive mark of man's genius."

In this embrace of the nihilism of artificiality, it is not surprising that des Esseintes should be encouraged by his reading of Schopenhauer, most of whose philosophy, as we have seen, turned on the belief that man and indeed the world in which he lives were defined and driven by incessant, irrational, insatiable will. While the plot of *À Rebours* is threadbare, consisting of little more than des Esseintes's ingenious attempts to sustain his make-believe dystopia, it is nevertheless true to the Schopenhauerian logic of its hero's willful despair. And to underscore this, Huysmans is careful to have des Esseintes praise the German philosopher along lines that the convert in him would later roundly reject. For des Esseintes, Schopenhauer was admirable because "He did not affirm the revolting conception of original sin, nor did he feel inclined to argue that it is a beneficent God who protects the worthless and wicked, rains misfortunes on children, stultifies the aged and afflicts the innocent. He did not exalt the virtues of a Providence which has invented that useless, incomprehensible, unjust and senseless abomination, physical suffering."

Huysmans himself, while dying a slow, painful death of jaw and mouth cancer, "in the midst of frightening lucidity," as one of his friends attested, would come to see in physical suffering a necessary, indeed a welcome penance. In fact, he refused all painkillers. "Anyone who hadn't the faith and a ha'porth of courage," he wrote to a friend in his last days, "would have blown his brains out long ago. Well I am not unhappy. The day I said *fiat*, God gave me incredible strength of will and wonderful peace of mind ... I do not wish to be cured, but to continue to be purified so that Our Lady may take me above." And elsewhere he wrote, "Mark well that suffering is the token of divine love. There is not a single saint whom he has not afflicted with it ... So you see he is treating us converts, us repentant rogues as true friends!" Since alleviating physical suffering—at least for the pregnant mother—has always been one of the more dubious justifications for killing unborn children in the womb, not to mention the so-called "mercy killing" of the aged and infirm, Huysmans treatment of this theme throughout his later novels is revelatory of his instinctive pro-life sympathies.

Certainly, he could replicate the arguments of abortionists with brilliant fidelity to their sophistical heartlessness. In one memorable scene in the book, he encounters a group of little boys.

> The little chaps were fighting with one another. They struggled for bits of bread which they shoved into their cheeks, meanwhile sucking their fingers. Kicks and blows rained freely, and the weakest, trampled upon, cried out. At this sight, des Esseintes recovered his animation ... Contemplating the blind fury of these urchins, he thought of the cruel and abominable law of the struggle of existence; and, although these children were mean, he could not help being interested in their futures, yet could not but believe that it had been better for them had their mothers never given them birth. In fact, all they could expect of life was rash, colic, fever, and measles in their earliest years; slaps in the face and degrading drudgeries up to thirteen years; deceptions by women, sicknesses and infidelity during manhood and, toward the last, infirmities and agonies in a poorhouse or asylum.

Here, Huysmans gives eloquent expression to the same nihilistic logic that drives our own abortionists—not only Dr. Gosnell and the sellers of baby parts at Planned Parenthood, but everyone who maintains that there is some justification for killing children in the womb. Of course, Dr. Gosnell killed babies inside and outside of the womb. He and his staff routinely severed the spinal cords of moving, breathing, sentient babies born alive in his abortion clinic. But he was as serenely confident as des Esseintes that abortion was justifiable, if only because it spared unwanted children what he regarded as the miseries of life.

Indeed, the conclusion that des Esseintes draws from these suppositious evils could hardly be more categorical: "How vain, silly and mad it is to beget brats!" With his dim view of human proliferation, it is hardly surprising that des Esseintes should have no use for St Vincent de Paul, who dedicated so much of his life to looking after the abandoned "brats" of the poor. For des Esseintes, one could have nothing but contempt for "those ecclesiastics who had taken vows of sterility, yet were so inconsistent as to canonize Saint Vincent de Paul, because he saved innocent babes for useless torments!" In fine, the duke's objections to St Vincent de Paul's solicitude for the unborn and the unwanted are no different from that of our own professed abortionists: "Children abandoned by their mothers were given homes instead of being left to die quietly without knowing what was happening, and yet the life that was kept for them would grow harder and bleaker day by day … Ah, in the name of pity, if ever futile procreation should be abolished, the time is now!"

With his sharp sense of the incidental comedy of decadence, Huysmans would have been amused to see the Society of St Vincent De Paul join Catholic Charities USA and the Catholic Health Association in 2009 to support President Obama's state health-care plan, which ensures not only mandatory contraceptive and abortion services, but euthanasia, eugenics, and sex education extolling deviance, promiscuity and abortion. Had he ever lived to see the ignominies to which Catholic bureaucracies stoop to perpetuate their often nefarious interests, the Swiftian satirist in him would not have known whether to weep or guffaw.

Flaubert, a good friend of Huysmans, once observed that "Our ignorance of history makes us libel our own times. People have always been like this." Huysmans certainly corroborates this when he has des Esseintes mount his argument for the justification of abortion, which is little different from that mounted by the international pro-abortion lobby for the last forty odd years. "In short, society regarded as a crime the act of killing a creature endowed with life; and yet expelling a foetus simply meant destroying an animal that was less developed, less alive, certainly less intelligent and less prepossessing, than a dog or a cat, which could be strangled at birth with impunity."

II

These animadversions notwithstanding, des Esseintes concedes, at his lowest ebb, that artificiality and perversion, and the contempt for life to which they give rise, do not make for either happiness or peace or the religious fulfillment for which so much of his being craved. As Huysmans's narrator attests, des Esseintes "came at last to perceive that the reasoning of pessimism availed little in comforting him, that impossible faith in a future life alone would pacify him." In the process, he rediscovers the Catholic faith of his childhood by rediscovering the music of the Church, "sad and mournful as a suppressed sob, poignant as a despairing invocation of humanity bewailing its mortal destiny and imploring the tender forgiveness of its Savior!"

At the end of *À Rebours*, after des Esseintes's doctors persuade him that the only cure for his physical and mental debility is to abjure his artificial seclusion and return to the world, the chastened duke resolves to repudiate his unnatural ways and reconcile himself to God and Nature. If the book begins with decadence and despair, it ends with a prayer: "O Lord, pity the Christian who doubts, the sceptic who would believe, the convict of life embarking alone in the night, under a sky no longer illumined by the consoling beacons of ancient faith."

Despite its clear satirical intent, *À Rebours* is embraced in many quarters as an unalloyed paean to decadence. In this respect, it is reminiscent of Anthony Burgess's *A Clockwork Orange* (1962), which continues to be read as a celebration of homicidal hooliganism by readers who see nothing satirical in the author's portrait of Alex, the book's irredeemably depraved hero. Alex is simply a typical *droog*, acting out his naturally rebellious aggressions. Like Burgess's novel, Husyman's *À Rebours* continues to sell briskly precisely because its readers embrace the very decadence that the novelist's satire was meant to expose and denounce, a decadence they see, not as evil, but as something liberating, joyous, indeed exemplary. One can see a good example of this in a piece on Huysmans that appeared recently in *The New Yorker* by Adam Leith Gollner, in which the author discusses the book with the aptly named pop musician Richard Hell.

> When reached to discuss *À Rebours* recently, Hell referred to it still as "the primary source." Which isn't to suggest that Huysmans anticipated punk: despite the book's punkish fascination with boredom and the search for kicks, and its utter lack of political conviction, "À Rebours" peddled an élitist, aristocratic hyper-aestheticism that has nothing in common with punk's anyone-can-do-this ethos. Even so, Hell seemed to be channeling Huysmans when his self-designed "Please Kill Me" T-shirt spawned the D.I.Y. movement. What Hell took from "À Rebours," above all, was the idea of a person trying to build a new reality—"making your own world," as he put it. "For me, going into rock and roll was an opportunity to deliberately design my whole world and way of life in a way that's not too distant from what des Esseintes did."

What is startling about these otherwise fatuous musings is how much they resemble the argument that Justice Anthony Kennedy mounted to reaffirm the constitutional right to abortion in Planned Parenthood v Casey (1992): "At the heart of liberty is the right to define one's own concept of existence, of meaning, of the universe, and of the mystery of human life." If there is one satirical target that Huysmans hits again and again throughout his work—perhaps because it was one that was so close to home—it is the pride of the unshriven intellect, the arrogant assumption that the mind of man can make or unmake the laws of nature, and no one epitomizes that better in our own day than those who follow Justice Kennedy in imagining that there is some legal defense for killing children in the womb.

After the undiscriminating critical success of *À Rebours*, Huysmans was clearly concerned that the satirical objects that he had written the novel to accomplish had been almost entirely misunderstood. Neither Zola nor Mallarmé nor Wilde appreciated what he had set himself to achieve in the novel. Only the Catholic novelist Barbey d'Aurevilly grasped the import of Huysmans' epidemiology of decadence: "After such a novel, it only remains for the author to choose between the mouth of a pistol or the feet of the Cross." That Huysmans chose the Cross over the pistol has enormous implications for our own cultural and spiritual predicament, where, we too, must choose between the culture of death and the culture of resurrected life and love.

III

In an attempt to make his readers understand why he had turned against naturalism and why he saw decadence as the ineluctable issue of naturalism, Huysmans set about writing a series of books with a hero named Durtal that would capture at once the true character of evil and the radical need for conversion to understand and combat evil. Thus, Huysmans chose to make the first book of the series, *Là-Bas*("The Damned") focus on Durtal writing a book about Gilles de Rais (otherwise known as "Bluebeard"), the serial child murderer, who sodomized his victims before dismembering them. Gilles de Montmorency-Laval, Baron de Rais (1405–40), was a knight and lord from Anjou, Brittany and Poitou, a leading figure in the French army, and a gallant companion-in-arms of Joan of Arc. Yet, as one of his retainers testified at Gilles's murder trial, this highly respected Marshal of France had also killed 800 children. In Gilles, Huysmans was presenting his readers with another character who was "against nature," who was intent on creating his own reality, but one whom no one could possibly mistake for an oddly lovable decadent.

And yet to show how disturbingly human this otherwise monstrous "real life" character was, Huysmans assures his readers that Gilles was not without a conscience. At his trial, after trying to shout down his prosecutors, he broke down and admitted his guilt. Indeed, he supplied the court with a voluminous written confession, detailing his egregious sins, many appalling passages of which Huysmans shares with his readers. And this highlights another aspect of the reality of evil that Huysmans is careful to impart: its humanity. Even in the case of a serial child rapist and murderer like Gilles, evil is not some aberration only committed by sociopaths incapable of remorse. On the contrary, evil is an inalienably human proclivity, whether it takes the form of murdering the born or murdering the unborn, or engaging in the dreary fornication that Huysmans has Durtal engage in with the drearily satanic Madame Chantelouve. That Huysmans goes out of his way to stress this aspect of his otherwise unspeakable subject demonstrates the earnestness of his moral vision, which is the last thing that we should expect to find in the work of the usual "decadent" writer. Speaking of the contrite Gilles, Huysmans writes:

> As he can descend no further, he tries returning on the way by which he has come, but now remorse overtakes him, overwhelms him, and wrenches him without respite. His nights are nights of expiation. Besieged by phantoms, he howls like a wounded beast. He is found rushing along the solitary corridors of the château. He weeps, throws himself on his knees, swears to God that he will do penance. He promises to found pious institutions. He does establish, at Mâchecoul, a boys' academy in honour of the Holy Innocents. He speaks of shutting himself up in a cloister, of going to Jerusalem, begging his bread on the way.

Here is the remorseful face of evil, than which there is nothing more human, and it is not one that we can afford to imagine of no moral relevance to ourselves.

IV

At the opening of *Là-Bas*, Durtal's faithful friend Des Hermies introduces the autobiographical hero. "In all your books you have fallen on our *fin de siècle*—our *queue du siècle*—tooth and nail. But, Lord! a man soon gets tired of whacking something that doesn't fight back but merely goes its own way repeating its offences. You needed to escape into another epoch and get your bearings while waiting for a congenial subject to present itself. That explains your spiritual disarray of the last few months and your immediate recovery as soon as you stumbled onto Gilles de Rais." No one should mistake this at face-value and assume that the choice of subject had been motivated by a kind of time traveler's escapism. Huysmans underscores his satirical intent when he has Durtal respond to his friend's analysis: "Des Hermies had diagnosed him accurately. The day on which Durtal had plunged into the frightful and delightful latter mediæval age had been the dawn of a new existence. The flouting of his actual surroundings brought peace to Durtal's soul, and he had completely reorganized his life, mentally cloistering himself, far from the furore of contemporary letters, n the château de Tiffauges with the monster Bluebeard, with whom he lived in perfect accord, even in mischievous amity." In Durtal, in other words, we have a character who may share something of the ignorance of Huysmans' readers when it comes to the true nature of evil, but the point of the book is to have him disabused of that ignorance. And, certainly, the horrors committed by Gilles accomplish that end amply enough, as do the blandishments of Durtal's mistress, Madame Chatalouve, who shows that the evil of the mediaeval murderer is not something confined to the "latter mediaeval age."

The lurid passages retailing Gilles's murders of children in Huysmans' novel—culled as they are from actual court documents—make for deeply disturbing reading. Yet, however disturbing, reading them will always make for a useful corrective to the moral inanity of those like Justice Anthony Kennedy who imagine that we can redefine evil out of existence, or maintain that flouting the natural law has something to do with liberty.

The Durtal novels capture the horror of evil with an unforgettable vividness; they also show how bedeviled men, whether Gilles or Gosnell or you or I, can combat evil. In his superb biography of Huysmans, Robert Baldick quotes the author himself regarding the second of the Durtal novels, *En Route*: "The plot of the novel is as simple as it could be. I've taken the principal character of *Là-Bas*, Durtal, had him converted and sent him to a Trappist monastery. In studying his conversion, I've tried to trace the progress of a soul surprised by the gift of grace, and developing in an ecclesiastical atmosphere, to the accompaniment of mystical literature, liturgy, and plainchant, against a background of all that admirable art which the Church has created."

En Route is also notable for being one of the books Oscar Wilde requested when imprisoned in Reading Gaol. Despite all of the false nonsense that has been written about that tragic figure, the profoundly remorseful Wilde would have understood what Durtal meant when he confides how "After having dragged the sickness of my soul around all the clinics of the intellect, I ended up, with God's grace, going to the only hospital where they put you to bed and really look after you—the Church." Moreover, in *En Route*, Wilde would have seen *À Rebours* in a new, more accurate light. Confessing sin is essential to understanding and abjuring sin.

Huysmans' understanding of the Church was indissolubly bound up with his understanding of Our Lady. In *L'Oblat*, he has Durtal, the reluctant convert, the sensual man who never finds temptations of the flesh easy to resist, the man profoundly conscious of his own legion flaws, finally submit wholeheartedly to the will of God. "There is much to atone for," he says. "If the divine rod is ready to chastise us, let us bare our backs for it; let us at least show a little willingness." And in this, as Baldick shows, Our Lady offers sinners vital help.

Huysmans maintained that Mary was the one human being over whom Suffering had no rights, but that in imitation of her Son she renounced this immunity, "wishing to suffer as much as it was in her power to suffer." Thus he united woman and suffering in a common rehabilitation ... for in the person of the *Regina martyrum* he represented woman no longer as Satan's catspaw, but—by virtue of her suffering—as an instrument of salvation, the glorious mediatrix and redeemer of mankind.

That all of the Durtal novels culminate in Durtal's conversion to Catholicism has not won his creator many accolades. Although Huysmans befriended many priests in his lifetime, and no one could deny the devoutness of his faith, the Church has never known what to make of him: he was always so outspoken, so critical of factitious piety. Then, again, if the Church looked on the Durtal novels with disapproving eyes, the literary world has been scarcely less critical. Huysmans' conversion is often dismissed as the opportunistic ploy of an author who wished to cash in on the reaction that followed the Dreyfus Affair. In many quarters, Huysmans will never be forgiven for the unexpected success he had with *La Cathédrale*, which sold 20,000 copies in its first month alone. In the *New Oxford Companion to French Literature* (1995), Jennifer Birkett of the University of Birmingham brings a now commonplace charge with comical crudity: "Huysmans' transition from Naturalism to Symbolism and Catholicism ... represents the political refusal of the desk-bound civil servant that Huysmans remained all his life to engage with the challenges of industrialization and democratization. It is an evasion into idealism that is linked with right-wing and regressive political factions."

This, of course, is the same charge leveled against the pro-life lobby. One can read scores of accounts of the history of abortion written in the last forty years and never see one historian show the least interest in the slaughter of the innocents. Opposition to abortion, like Huysmans' opposition to the nihilism of decadence, is only explicable in terms of right-wing reaction. Yet no one will credit Birkett's unjustifiable swipe who reads Huysmans' account of the prayer book he found at Chartres composed in the fourteenth century by Gaston Fébus, Comte de Foix, one of whose prayers exhibits the uncompromising contrition that is at the heart of Huysman's best work:

Thou who hast shaped me in my mother's womb, let me not perish ... Lord, I confess my poverty ... My conscience gnaws me and shows me the secrets of my heart. Avarice constrains me, concupiscence befouls me, gluttony disgraces me, anger torments me, inconstancy crushes me, indolence oppresses me, hypocrisy beguiles me ... and these, Lord, are the companions with whom I have spent my youth, these are the friends I have known, these are the masters I have served." And further on he exclaims, "Sin have I heaped upon sin, and the sins which I could not commit in very deed yet have I committed by evil desire.

V

The reason why the public response to the Gosnell and Planned Parenthood outrages has been so muted is that in order for us to denounce Gosnell and Planned Parenthood properly, we should have to denounce ourselves, our own connivance in evil, our own radical selfishness, our own apathy. Huysmans is careful to stress how Gilles confesses and asks God pardon for his sins: we must do the same. And we can begin by understanding the true character of abortion. What was it that Mother Theresa said at the National Prayer Breakfast in Washington in 1997? "What is taking place in America is a war against the child. And if we accept that the mother can kill her own child, how can we tell other people not to kill one another?" Then, again, at the same breakfast, this soon-to-be-saint put the matter with something of the Comte's laconic eloquence: "It is a poverty to decide that a child must die so that you may live as you wish."

Since all of Huysmans's work is a prayer, and we need prayers more than anything else to understand and respond to the evil of abortion, I shall end this essay with another apposite prayer by the Comte de Foix:

> My God and my Mercy, I am ashamed to pray to Thee for very shame of my evil conscience; give a fountain of tears to my eyes, and to my hands largess of alms and charity; give me a seemly faith, and hope, and abiding charity. Lord, Thou holdest no man in horror save the fool that denies Thee. Oh, my God, the Giver of My Redemption and Receiver of my soul, I have sinned and Thou hast suffered me!

Friendship's Garland:
Joyce and Svevo in Trieste

James Joyce and Italo Svevo: The Story of a Friendship, Stanley Price (Somerville Press). 276 pages.

That the sense of place animates good writing is a truism of which our reading continually reminds us. No Warwickshire, no Shakespeare. No London, no Dickens. No Staffordshire, no Arnold Bennett. In an essay entitled "Place in Fiction" (1956), Eudora Welty nicely captured how family engenders this ineradicable dynamic.

> There may come to be new places in our lives that are second spiritual homes—closer to us in some ways, perhaps, than our original homes. But the home tie is the blood tie. And had it meant nothing to us, any other place thereafter would have meant less, and we would carry no compass inside ourselves to find home ever, anywhere at all.

No writer better exemplifies this than James Joyce (1882–1941), whose experience as a young man in the beleaguered Joyce family in Edwardian Dublin colored nearly everything he wrote. The son of an improvident, hard-drinking father, Joyce would never forget the faith his father put in his untested abilities, and yet, as the eldest of ten in a family wracked with disarray and discord, he was also desperate to prove those abilities. In *Dubliners* (1914), his collection of short stories about the city and people that would be so vital to his art, he gave voice to this desperation with a specificity that only family-infused place could confer.

> There was no doubt about it: if you wanted to succeed you had to go away. You could do nothing in Dublin. As he crossed Grattan Bridge he looked down the river towards the lower quays and pitied the poor stunted houses. They seemed to him a band of tramps, huddled together along the river-banks, their old coats covered with dust and soot, stupefied by the panorama of sunset and waiting for the first chill of night to bid them arise, shake themselves and begone.

In *Portrait of the Artist as a Young Man* (1916), Joyce's alto-ego Stephen Dedalus declares, "I go to encounter for the millionth time the reality of experience and to forge in the smithy of my soul the uncreated conscience of my race." He also commits to his diary an entry that is often taken to be something of his young creator's artistic manifesto: "I will try to express myself in some mode of life or art as freely as I can and as wholly as I can, using for my defense the only arms I allow myself to use—silence, exile, and cunning." Of course, Joyce did become one of literature's most celebrated exiles, though it is questionable whether it was an exile entirely motivated by artistic integrity. He fled to the Continent as much to escape his father's bibulous notoriety as to find his artistic voice. Or, perhaps, one should say, he could only find his artistic voice by, first, fleeing and, then, reimagining his father's failures.

What makes Stanley Price's brilliant study of the friendship between Joyce and the Triestine novelist Italo Svevo so fascinating is that it shows how Joyce could only finish the story of his family that he had left unfinished in Dublin by settling in Trieste and befriending Svevo. In *Ulysses* (1922), Leopold Bloom, the Jewish husband and father whom Svevo was so instrumental in helping Joyce create, charts the true trajectory of Joyce's art: "Think you're escaping and run into yourself. Longest way round is the shortest way home."

One of Joyce's Parisian friends, the surrealist poet Philippe Soupault might have had Mr. Price's book in mind when he noted how Trieste "provided Joyce with a necessary detachment; he felt himself far removed from Ireland, still distinguishing images and echoes of Dublin, but seeing, feeling, and hearing better from afar that city where he had loved and suffered." Another Frenchman, the literary critic, Louis Gillet also captured the appeal of the city for Joyce when he described it as: "This pretty, good-natured Austrian city ... with [its] gaiety of the Midi ... medley of languages ... and exotic, oriental flavor." And yet what most helped the young Irishman turn his Triestine exile to such innovative artistic account was his friendship with a man who in many ways was as extraordinary as Joyce himself. As the Parisian journalist Nino Frank put it, "Perfectly Adriatic, Svevo had the Venetian Jew's mischievous good nature and sharp subtlety, which are among civilization's finest virtues." Unlike Joyce, whose bitterness could often get the better of him, Svevo never ceased to revel in the irrepressible zest of life.

Ettore Schmitz (1861–1928), took the name Italo Svevo (Italus the Swabian) to signify his mixed heritage: Triestine by language, Austrian by citizenship, and German-Jewish by ancestry. Like Joyce, he came from a big family of 16 children, 8 of whom survived, and had a father who suffered considerable financial reverses, though Svevo's father lost his money through bad investments, not through habitual overindulgence in

John Jameson Irish whisky. For 18 years, Svevo toiled as a bank clerk until he married into a family that owned a successful marine paint business. Like Joyce, who brought the first cinema to Dublin with Triestine backers, Svevo had a flair for the entrepreneurial. When the First World War broke out, he persuaded all of the war's combatants to buy his anti-corrosive paint for their warships. In 1907, two years after Joyce had settled in the city, Svevo became Joyce's pupil at the Berlitz School in Trieste to improve his English. He also became something of a father figure to the young Irish exile, playing Bloom to Joyce's Stephen Dedalus. In return, Joyce memorialized Svevo's wife, Livia by drawing on her for Anna Livia Plurabelle, the all-embracing, maternal muse of *Finnegans Wake* (1939), a statue of whom is now affectionately known in Dublin as "the floozy in the Jacuzzi." If academics around the world still hold the author of that meandering book in some awe, the plain people of Dublin have never followed suit.

When Joyce set his pupil the task of critiquing the first three chapters of *A Portrait of the Artist*, Svevo summoned the courage to admit that he was a novelist himself, though neither of his novels had been noticed by the critics. ("There is no unanimity," Svevo quipped, "like the unanimity of silence.") The friendship of the two frustrated writers was sealed when Joyce, never lavish of praise, read *A Life* (1892) and *As a Man Grows Older* (1898) and declared his pupil the successor to Anatole France. Later, Joyce would encourage Svevo to persevere with what would become his masterpiece, *The Confessions of Zeno* (1923), a fictional send-up of psychoanalysis, whose hero continuously tries and fails to give up cigarettes. For the chain-smoking Svevo himself, the worst crisis of the Great War occurred in March of 1916 when Trieste ran out of tobacco. "There was rioting," Price points out, "and when supplies were finally resumed, tobacconists' shops were broken into as smokers made sure of their fair share. Svevo did not join in the violence but he managed to buy a year's supply." In addition to artistic encouragement, Joyce also generously acted as Svevo's unpaid publicist, recommending the book to influential literary friends, whose glowing reviews turned it into an international *success d'estime*.

In return, Svevo helped refine Joyce's detailed understanding of all things Jewish. Price shows how Joyce turned this to account in the "Cyclops" section of *Ulysses*, where Bloom reminds the anti-Semitic citizen in Barney Kiernan's pub that "Mendelssohn was a jew and Karl Marx and Mercadante and Spinoza"—a litany about which Price amusingly surmises:

> His creator perhaps meant to illustrate the wide range of secular Jews. Mendelssohn was baptised a Protestant, Karl Marx rejected all religion, and was frequently anti-Semitic, associating Jews with capitalism. Spinoza was one of the few Jews ever to be excommunicated by the community, in Amsterdam, for his heretical views. Mercadante was the strangest, most esoteric choice, an early nine-

351

teenth-century Italian operatic composer, known to Joyce, but hardly anybody else, and he was not a Jew. Joyce was not above private jokes.

Joyce and Svevo, although twenty-one years apart, had much in common. They were both genuine artists, willing to suffer any setback rather than displease their importunate muses. They were both masterly at making the slings and arrows of outrageous fortune serve the alchemy of fiction. They were both fond of the ridiculous, even in the most tragic of circumstances. When Joyce was fleeing Paris in 1940 ahead of the invading Nazis, the Swiss border authorities mistook him for a Jew, doubtless confusing him with his hero, Bloom, which caused Joyce to respond: "je ne suis pas juif de Judée mais aryen d'Erin." As Price remarks, "Even in this surreal predicament, Joyce was still able to pun bilingually."

Both men were connoisseurs of cities. Joyce was deeply fond of Dublin, Trieste, and Paris, even if dismissive of Rome, which he likened to "a man who lives by exhibiting his grandmother's corpse," while Svevo was fond not only of Trieste, which before the Great War was the fourth largest city of the Austro-Hungarian Empire and one of Europe's busiest ports, but the cities where he conducted the family paint business, including Florence, Venice and London. Indeed, after residing in London, Svevo and his wife became Anglophiles, convinced, as Svevo wrote, that "English kindness and good manners ... constitute almost an unwritten law that complements [England's] civil and criminal law." For Svevo, it might be true that "Perfidious Albion has always consisted of *Gentlemen*," but "we are all perfidious when dealing with foreign countries. Remember we Italians are all descended from Machiavelli."

Although critical of colonialism, both were at home in the polyglot urbanity of the old imperial order. After the Austro-Hungarian Empire fell in 1918, Joyce was never comfortable in Trieste, which, under Italian rule, was forced to play second fiddle to Venice. Certainly, neither Joyce nor Svevo would have agreed with the caricature of the empire put about by the framers of the Versailles Treaty: for them, pre-war Trieste might have had its tensions but it was never a part of any "prison of the peoples." In this regard, they might have sympathized with Empress Zita, who when told by her husband Karl that the empire was *kaput* was incredulous: "A sovereign can never abdicate," she declared. "He can be deposed and his sovereign rights be declared forfeit. All right. That is force. But abdicate— never, never, never."

Joyce, in particular, was partial to the Austro-Hungarian Empire for the same reason that he was partial to the British Empire: it offered more civilized freedom than the nation-states concocted by the nationalists. He was particularly contemptuous of the nationalists of Ireland for betraying his beloved Parnell. "They did not throw him to the English wolves," Joyce noted in his best satirical vein: "they tore him apart themselves." Moreover, since the British Prime Minister H. H. Asquith had awarded him in 1916 an annual pension of £100 from the Civil List (or £3,500 in today's money), he was never keen on surrendering his British passport.

Both Joyce and Svevo were contented family men, largely because they had the good fortune to marry strong, forbearing, intelligent women. The art critic, Carola Giedion-Welcker, one of Joyce's closest female friends on the Continent, recalled that the learned novelist "always admired the natural behavior of his wife and listened in fascination when she intuitively and spontaneously decided matters that he had scrutinized carefully from every angle, *sine ira et studio.*" After Joyce's death, when Nora Joyce (*née* Barnacle) was asked about the many writers surrounding her husband, including Pound, Eliot, Hemingway, and Beckett, her reply was typically mocking: "Sure, if you've been married to the greatest writer of them all, you don't remember the little fellows." Svevo was fond of Nora because she reminded him that his livelihood depended on keeping the hulls of ships free of barnacles—a standing joke between the two families.

Svevo and Joyce were also bound together by the sorrows of family. The most moving chapter in *The Confessions of Zeno* involves the death of Zeno's father, which Svevo based on his painful relationship with his own father. At one point, Zeno sees in the life of the deathbed a mysteriousness that transcends alike sorrow and resentment, which leads him to conclude with his accustomed seriocomic acuity: "When you are actually dying you have other things to do than to think about death."

Joyce's last years were saddened by his daughter Lucia's accelerating schizophrenia. Lucia and her father, Carl Jung observed, "were like two people going to the bottom of a river, one falling and the other diving." Unlike Svevo, Joyce was unpersuaded by the promises of psychoanalysis, telling his friend, "Psychoanalysis? Well, if we need it, let's keep to confession." The literary critic James Wood makes an incisive point when he says that this dismissive attitude towards the new science may not have entirely disconcerted Svevo; after all, *The Confessions of Zeno*, in its whimsical way, constitutes a slyly critical pastiche, not an uncritical endorsement of psychoanalysis.

Finally, both men were lapsed members of their respective religions: Joyce, Catholicism, and Svevo, Judaism, though Svevo was later baptized and married in the Catholic Church to please his Catholic wife. One aspect of Svevo that must have appealed to Joyce was his friend's respect for religion, even if he found himself incapable of belief. In *The Confessions*, Zeno is shown studying the Christianity of his wife Augusta with some diligence before rejecting it. And yet the grounds on which he rejects it are striking.

Augusta's religion did not take time to acquire or put into practice. You bowed your knee and returned to daily life again immediately! That was all. Religion for me was a very different thing. If I had only believed, nothing else in the world would have mattered to me.

When Price says that Svevo was "hostile to all organized religion," he exaggerates what was, in fact, an attentive, even wistful skepticism. After all, when Joyce gave him the sermon passages in *A Portrait* to read, Svevo responded: "I have read them with a very strong feeling and I know in my little town a lot of people who would certainly be struck by the same feeling." Then, again, in the *Confessions*, Svevo has Zeno admit after the death of his father:

> I returned to the religion of my childhood and held to it for a long time. I imagined that my father could hear what I said ... For some time I continued these conversations with my father, which were as sweet and secret as an illicit love; to everyone else I went on laughing at religious practices, though in reality—I will confess it here—I daily with my whole heart commended my father's soul to the care of some unknown being. It is the essence of true religion that one does not need to make a loud profession of it in order to get the consolation which at certain moments one cannot do without.

As for Joyce, plundering the doctrines and rituals of the Catholic Church for his own aesthetic purposes may not have brought him any closer to practicing the faith that he had abandoned as a youth in Dublin but it did make him leery of the pitfalls of apostasy. When Stephen Dedalus' friend Cranly asks him why, with his impatience with Rome, he does not become a Protestant, Stephen replies: "I said that I had lost the faith ... but not that I had lost self-respect. What kind of liberation would that be to forsake an absurdity which is logical and coherent and to embrace one which is illogical and incoherent?"

Although Price draws freely on previous books—particularly the revised edition of Richard Ellmann's unsurpassed biography of Joyce (1982), P. N. Furbank's biography of Svevo (1966), and John McCourt's groundbreaking, *The Years of Bloom: James Joyce in Trieste 1904–1920* (2000)—he presents his subjects with such wit, insight, balance and élan that one sees them as though for the first time. He also grounds his sympathy—especially for Joyce—in an admirable refusal to be bamboozled. Apropos *Finnegans Wake*, for example, which Joyce's brother Stanislaus called a "a driveling rigma-role," Price quotes one of the novelist's more devoted acolytes, the translator Paul Léon, who admitted to a friend: "Lately I have been spending a lot of time with literature. I have been working with James Joyce ... I've found it wonderfully amusing to translate simple ideas into incomprehensible formulas and to feel it is a masterpiece."

What is remarkable about Joyce is how he persevered in his own "incomprehensible formulas" despite the reservations that even his admirers had about his "darknesses and unintelligibilities" — to use a phrase from Harriet Shaw Weaver, the novelist's patron, who supported the novelist munificently through most of the writing of *Ulysses* and *Finnegans Wake*. Not only did Weaver share her doubts — telling him at one point, "It seems to me that you are wasting your genius" — but so too did H. G. Wells, who had had nothing but praise for *A Portrait of the Artist as a Young Man*, observing that Sterne himself could not have rendered the book's Christmas dinner better and supplying the sort of praise that young novelists usually only dream about.

> Like some of the best novels in the world it is the story of an education; it is by far the most living and convincing picture that exists of an Irish Catholic upbringing. It is a mosaic of jagged fragments that does altogether render with extreme completeness the growth of a rather secretive, imaginative boy in Dublin.

By 1929, however, after fragments of *Finnegans Wake* had been published, Wells had changed his tune. In his blunt, unsparing way, he wrote the experimental author: "You have turned your back on common men, on their elementary needs and their restricted time and intelligence ... What is the result? Vast riddles." Nevertheless, Price, like Ellmann, shows that Joyce's belief in his own inerrable genius was adamantine, even if Weaver's censures impelled him to take to his bed for two days. It also helped that he had a considerable network of individuals, especially within the European *avant garde*, who seriously believed that the author of *Finnegans Wake* was beyond criticism.

Price is amusing about those figures — including the biographer Herbert Gorman and the bookseller Sylvia Beach — both of whom fled the cult. Apropos Gorman, he relates how Joyce told the American journalist that he wished *James Joyce: the First Forty Years* (1924) to be an account of the saintly novelist's martyrdom at the hands of persecuting publishers. When the galleys arrived full of unflattering references to Joyce and his family, and Joyce demanded that they be excised, Gorman cut all ties with the bowdlerizing author. One person who never left the cult was Svevo's wife Livia, who, in a memoir written after her husband's death, recalled the impact Joyce's successful promotion of *The Confessions of Zeno* had had on Svevo. "I do not remember ever having seen Ettore so radiant. It was to James Joyce, who had reappeared like a kindly star in his sky, that he owed this great satisfaction."

There are only a small number of truly first-rate books on Joyce but this is one of them. If exile helped Joyce sort out his early family life in Dublin, an inventorying integral to the springs and elaboration of his reminescential art, it was also what made him susceptible to the sycophancy that so tragically blinded him to the flaws of his later work. Yet, on this score, Price, in his generous, moving, commendable book, is right to give Elizabeth Bowen the final word:

> Let us strip from Joyce the exaggeration of foolish intellectual worship he got abroad, and the notoriety he got at home, and take him back to ourselves as a writer out of the Irish people, who received much from our tradition and was to hand on more.

A Revisionist's
Scott Fitzgerald

Paradise Lost: A New Life of Scott Fitzgerald, David S. Brown (Harvard University Press). 397 pages.

The essence of revisionist history is boldness: if one is not prepared to overturn conventional readings radically, then there is little point to the exercise—and the bolder the revisionism, the greater the stakes. David S. Brown's biography of F. Scott Fitzgerald deserves credit for taking such a bold approach. Most previous Fitzgerald biographies have been content to portray their subject as an honorable and hardworking writer of considerable talent whose inability to drink sensibly ruined his chances of writing the good books that he had it in him to write—more well-made books like *The Great Gatsby*, say, rather than potboilers like *The Beautiful and the Damned* or his often one-dimensional formulaic short stories or the ambitious but flawed *Tender is the Night*, which H. L. Mencken rightly regarded as "poor stuff indeed." Instead of the gin-soaked scribbler trying, against all odds, to wrest literary greatness from personal ruin, Brown presents Fitzgerald as a social critic, who deplored the excesses and evils of market capitalism in nearly everything he wrote. Brown thus places Fitzgerald and his work not in the context of literary art but of intellectual history.

As theses go, this is not as implausible as it may sound. After all, *The Great Gatsby* could be read through this anti-capitalist lens. Gatsby, like Fitzgerald himself, invents a persona for himself in accordance with capitalist criteria for happiness—and winds up with what T. S. Eliot called "a receipt for deceit." In this reading, for the true *dénouement* of the book, readers can look beyond Nick Carraway's conclusion about Gatsby's inability to attain his dream to the disillusioned avowals of *The Crack-up*, where the romantic in Fitzgerald comes face to face, not with "man's capacity for wonder," but with a kind of purchaser's remorse. In *My Lost City* (1932), Fitzgerald struck a distinctly Chestertonian note when, standing atop the Empire State Building, "the roof of the last and most magnificent of towers," he recalled what he describes as the city's "crowning error ... its Pandora Box," to which he gave characteristically trenchant expression: "Full of vaunting pride the New Yorker had climbed here and seen with dismay what he had never expected, that the city was not the endless succession of canyons that he had supposed but that *it had limits.*" In *Orthodoxy* (1908), Chesterton had articulated this reality with a pungency that must have stuck in Fitzgerald's youthful mind. "The moment you step into the world of facts," the Fleet Street philosopher observed, "you step into a world of limits. You can free things from alien or accidental laws, but not from the laws of their own nature."

One can entertain Brown's revisionist thesis on other grounds. Stories like "May Day" (1920), "The Diamond as Big as The Ritz" (1922), "The Rich Boy" (1926), and "Babylon Revisited" (1931) can be read as Fitzgerald's sifting through the sand on which so much of capitalist society was built, the boom and bust that reflected the remorseless cupidity of the Scotch-Irish who devised its rules—men like Mellon and Morgan, Carnegie and Frick and, indeed, Fitzgerald's own maternal grandfather, Philip McQuillan, who made a pile out of the wholesale grocery business, though it was always with his own father, whom Fitzgerald's first biographer Arthur Mizener characterized as "a quiet gentlemanly man with beautiful Southern manners," that the novelist most identified.

Nevertheless, Brown's thesis has several problems. First, market capitalism does have limits, however much overzealous traders might sometimes wish to defy them: this is precisely why capitalism sees booms and busts. Brown can hardly be credited with proving Fitzgerald a serious critic of market capitalists by reminding them of such an economic truism. Second, Fitzgerald was nothing if not a lifelong fan of the fruits of capitalism. The Plaza Hotel, Ivy League colleges, Ivy League clubs, expensive cars, expensive tipple, the French Riviera, Brooks Brothers, and Jazz Age New York were just a few of his favorite things—and none would have been possible without a market economy. Third, if Fitzgerald was aware that the privileges and pleasures on which his often fortunate characters battened came occasionally at the expense of the less fortunate, he never indulged in the class resentment typical of critics of capitalism. On the contrary, he often made no bones about his preference for writing of the more fortunate. An amusing example can be found in "May Day," where Fitzgerald describes Yale undergraduates meeting against the backdrop of hopeless socialist protest. Here, readers of a certain age will recall what a mainstay of Manhattan's class system could be found in one of its most characteristic eateries:

> Childs', Fifty-ninth Street, at eight o'clock of any morning differs from its sisters by less than the width of their marble tables, or the degrees of polish on the frying-pans. You will see a crowd of poor people with sleep in their eyes, trying to look straight before them at their food so as not to see the other poor people. But Childs'

Fifty-ninth, four hours earlier is quite unlike any Childs' restaurant from Portland Oregon to Portland, Maine. Within its pale but sanitary walls one finds a noisy medley of chorus girls, college boys, debutantes, rakes, *filles de joie*—a not unrepresentative mixture of the gayest of Broadway, even of Fifth Avenue.

If a social critic lay beneath the aesthete in Fitzgerald, he was oddly inept at showing himself. For Brown, however, the *Great Gatsby* "offered readers a peek into the imposing Plaza Hotel, informed them that pharmacies were excellent places to buy illegal hooch, and effectively contrasted the nation's new wealth-gathering with its older and presumably less material-minded ideals." Here, the shakiness of Brown's revisionist thesis becomes patent. Fitzgerald, on the one hand, is a purveyor of a kind of morose delectation and, on the other, a critic of the "new wealth-gathering," which, despite the prurience to which he caters, he contrasts "presumably" with undefined "older" and "less material-minded ideals." Fitzgerald might have famously said that "The test of a first-rate intelligence is the ability to hold two opposed ideas in mind at the same time and still retain the ability to function," but this is hardly a good definition of a coherent social critic.

Thus, it is dubious whether Fitzgerald's idea of the earthly paradise, lost or regained, had anything to do with market capitalism. Slowly drinking himself to death with his friend Ring Lardner would have been more to his taste than yearning after an American agrarianism unrealistic even in Thomas Jefferson's day. Through page after page of this misguided book, I could not help recalling something Fitzgerald once said of his spendthrift wife Zelda and himself: "We're too poor to economize. Economy is a luxury … our only salvation is in extravagance." The idea that this improvident hedonist was a secret acolyte of Thornstein Veblen and *The Theory of the Leisure Class* (1899) is comical—even if, to turn a needed buck, Fitzgerald once wrote something called "The Irresponsible Rich" (1924).

Even with Fitzgerald's contradictions, Brown might have written a good book if he were a better intellectual historian. As it is, he never brings alive the figures whom he claims taught Fitzgerald to doubt the values on which he and his acquisitive society were reared. Speaking of Henry Adams, the author of *Mont Saint Michel and Chartres* (1904), for example, Brown is not so much unenlightening as meaningless.

> Like Adams, Scott wanted to understand the source of society's disenchantment, to follow the accelerating pace of its power as it rippled through regions, peoples and cultures. Both men were interested in observing the dynamo's impact. Adams developed a particular interest in fifteenth-century European origins; Fitzgerald, by contrast, headed straight to Gotham.

No revisionist biographer capable of writing this sort of gibberish will convince us that Scott Fitzgerald took any serious interest in ideas, let alone economics. Brown may make the novelist congenial to the anti-capitalist academy—the same academy that exhorts its charges to take to the ramparts in pursuit of utopian socialism's elusive benefits—but he will not persuade anyone appreciative of the true source of Fitzgerald's elegiac art. To understand that peculiarly romantic wellspring, we have to go to another romantic—William Butler Yeats, who summed up in two verses what Brown cannot capture in nearly 400 pages:

> Man is in love and loves what vanishes
> What more is there to say?

The Catholic Apologist
in Evelyn Waugh

In *Our Age: English Intellectuals between the World Wars* (1990), Lord Noel Annan (1916–2000), the spokesman of the English liberal Establishment heaped praise on his generation for liberating John Bull from what he regarded as the prison house of Victorian values, but he also singled out one contemporary of his for sustained abuse: "Evelyn Waugh was the real deviant of my generation," Annan wrote. "He went against the grain of decent opinion; he deviated from the values we esteemed." Not only a "snob," a "reactionary," a "disillusioned romantic," a "malignant tease," and a "*deraciné* from the twenties," Waugh was what Annan called an "Augustinian Catholic." For the donnish humanitarian, Waugh was a deviant because, like St. Augustine, he believed in original sin; he believed in the reality of evil; he believed that sinful man was reliant on God's grace to help him contend not only with the evil in the world but the evil in himself. In response, Annan countered that his contemporaries had "no difficulty in finding explanations why the world [was] so full of evil." Politics and social science supplied all of the requisite explanations. His contemporaries might be "less ready" to find reasons why they themselves were "so prone to rage," to "conceit," to envy, to causing "others unhappiness in order to give [themselves] pleasure," but still they managed to find reasons, and "when things [got] bad the analyst [was] at hand." Waugh abominated psychiatry. As he told the poet John Betjeman in 1946: "People are going mad & talking balls to psychiatrists, not because of accidents to the chamber-pot in the nursery, but because there is no logical structure to their beliefs." Betjeman's reply did not dispute Waugh's point: "All I can do now is to read, pray and study the life of Our Lord. That I am doing." But the epistolary apologist in Waugh would not relent.

> One deep root of error is that you regard religion as the source of pleasurable emotions & sensations and ask the question, "Am I not getting just as much out of the Church of England as I should from Catholicism?" The question should be "What am I doing for God?" Nothing less than complete abandonment is any good. His will is plain as a pikestaff that there shall be one fold & one shepherd and

361

you spend all of your time perpetuating a sixteenth-century rift & influencing others to perpetuate it.

Needless to say, this was not the sort of apologetics in which most of Waugh's Catholic contemporaries—or ours—might engage, even those favorably disposed to that great seventeenth-century French spiritual classic *L'Abandon à la divine providence*, but it exemplifies the uncompromising force of Waugh's faith. It is also not altogether dissimilar from the tack that John Henry Newman took with Anglo-Catholics in his *Lectures on Certain Difficulties felt by Anglicans in submitting to the Catholic Church* (1850). For Newman, as for Waugh, conversion was not merely an option: it was imperative for the salvation of one's soul. When Newman's sister Jemima baulked at his conversion, speculating that it would lessen his influence in Protestant England, Newman replied in words that Waugh would have keenly understood:

> What a doom would have been mine, if I had kept the Truth a secret in my own bosom, and when I knew which the One Church was, and which was not part of the One Church, I had suffered friends and strangers to die in an ignorance from which I might have relieved them! Impossible.

Evelyn Arthur St. John Waugh (1903–66), novelist, travel writer, biographer and critic was born in Hampstead, the son of Arthur Waugh, an eminent man of letters, who for many years was the managing director of Chapman & Hall, which would become his son's publisher. Waugh's brother, Alec was a writer of popular novels. After attending the Anglican minor public school, Lancing, Waugh attended Hertford College, where he read modern history. After leaving Oxford without a degree, he became a schoolmaster, a gruesome experience, though it furnished him with the fodder he needed for his gloriously funny first novel, *Decline and Fall* (1928).

Waugh's literary star rose with dazzling celerity. *Decline and Fall* and *Vile Bodies* (1930) sold more copies in a week than all of Arthur's and Alec's books put together. His diaries document the gusto with which he enjoyed his success. Many writers can look back on robust drinking days but few persisted in them with Waugh's bacchanal abandon. His Olympian intake only decreased when he retired to country hotels to write his books or to faraway jungles to research his travelogues. But then his first wife, Evelyn Gardiner (a.k.a. She-Evelyn) left him for a man whom Waugh nicely called a "ramshackle oaf," and his bright young world toppled around him. As he told one friend, "I did not know it was possible to be so miserable and live."

After converting to Rome in 1930, Waugh spent the rest of his days trying to see himself and the world *sub specie aeternitatis*. His grandson, Alexander Waugh suggests that the novelist's conversion was simply another outrage undertaken to disconcert his father, with whom he had an unrelentingly fractious relationship; but this is false. Waugh might have relished play-acting but there was nothing make-believe about his Catholic faith. That Alexander does not grasp this elemental fact may also have something to do with his boorish swipes at the great apologist Msgr. Ronald Knox, of whom his grandfather was immensely fond. Indeed, Waugh showed the quality of his often-overlooked *caritas* when he stayed with the dying Knox in Torquay for several weeks after his friend's cancer proved ineradicable.

It is ironic that Alexander should have regarded his grandfather's respect and indeed affection for Knox as unaccountable because none of Waugh's contemporaries provides a better key to understanding the novelist's Catholic art than the learned convert and apologist, whose wit, like Waugh's wit, sprang from the uncompromising faith at his core. In a sermon delivered at St. Edmunds, Ware, Knox spoke of the Catholic religion in terms that nicely capture its appeal for Waugh. Addressing the seminarians at St. Edmund's college, Knox wrote:

> You have been born into an age of decision for the world and for the Catholic church. Before our very eyes the half faiths and the false Christianities which the Reformation brought with it are crumbling away. The number of their adherents is steadily diminishing, and even those who do not profess to adhere to them are more and more abandoning belief in the Bible, belief in revelation, belief in the Sacraments, belief in a world of rewards and punishments hereafter. And it is not only their beliefs but their moral standards that are disappearing. Especially the sanctity of marriage is being profaned; divorce is treated as a natural occurrence; no age before ours has so openly and so flagrantly set at naught the ordinance of God. And while Protestantism crumbles away, the Catholic Church is winning back ground. We Catholics, in our effort to convert England, are not like furniture removers, paid by the hour, slowly and gingerly piling things on to a van. We are like men fighting a fire, desperately keeping at bay, here and there, the flames of unbelief and of social disorder.

Granted, Knox here was addressing young men studying to become priests. Yet, for all of its delight in the anarchic, there was a steely, hieratic aspect to Waugh's art—as Ian Ker showed so brilliantly in his essay "Evelyn Waugh: The Priest as Craftsman" in *The Catholic Revival in English Literature 1845–1961* (2003), the best essay ever written about the novelist. Thus, when Knox extolls faithful Catholics as outlaws, he extolls his friend's unbiddable fidelity to a faith most of his contemporaries spurned.

> David was an outlaw in his own country; you, too, if you are faithful Catholics, still more if you are preaching the Catholic religion, will be outlaws to some extent in the world of to-day, a world which tends more and more to banish religion from its speech and its

thought. Other school have other traditions — this one has bred great soldiers, this has been a nursery of poets, there the civic virtues are practised and extolled. Our tradition is a different one, and in these days, I think, a more important one. We are a college of outlaws; those who have gone out from us were men who could set their face against the false standards of the world they lived in, who could stem the current of their times instead of being carried away with it.

Once Waugh's first marriage was annulled, as the result of She-Evelyn's adultery, Evelyn married Laura Herbert, an imperturbable nineteen-year old who spent most of her married life doting on her beloved cows. Alexander implies that Laura and Evelyn disliked their children. Evelyn, it is true, told Diana Cooper that "I can only regard children as defective adults." But the letters he wrote to his children when they were unhappy at school (especially those to Auberon) are models of parental affection, good sense and fun. He was philoprogenitive despite himself.

Most of the people who disliked Waugh in his own day disliked him not so much because of his books but because, like Annan, they found his conservatism and his Catholicism repellent, though one of his most sympathetic critics, Frances Donaldson (who wrote good books on P. G. Wodehouse and on growing up with her father, the playwright Freddy Lonsdale) was neither conservative nor Catholic. Apropos Waugh's looking after his beloved Ronnie in his last days Donaldson wrote: "When one considers how difficult he found it to endure anyone outside his own family for more than a few hours, how difficult most of us would find it to leave our own beds and live for weeks in an English hotel caring for an old, sick man, how few of us would if it came to it do it, I think this one action earned him the word *fidelis.*"

Whence came Waugh's deep, faith? In an essay recounting his conversion, "Come Inside" (1949), Waugh wrote: "Those who have read my books will perhaps understand the character of the world into which I exuberantly launched myself. Ten years of that world sufficed to show me that life there, or anywhere, was unintelligible and unendurable without God." Once Waugh came to this realization, his conversion to the Church of Rome was fairly swift and uncomplicated. The priest who received him into the Church, Monsignor Martin D'Arcy, S.J., recalled that most of their catechetical conversations revolved around reason. "I have never met a convert who so strongly based his assent on truth," the Jesuit recalled. "It was a special pleasure to make contact with so able a brain." Braininess was not the only quality that animated Waugh's Catholicism: his humility also played a part. Speaking in the same essay of his life after his conversion, Waugh wrote that it had "been an endless delighted tour of discovery in the huge territory of which I was made free. I have heard it said that some converts in later life look back rather wistfully to the fervour of their first months of faith. With me it is quite the opposite. I look back aghast at the presumption with which I thought myself suitable for reception and with wonder at the trust of the priest who saw the possibility of growth in such a dry soul."

In 1930, the year of his conversion, Waugh set out the understanding of his own place in history that would animate all of his books, whether set in Mayfair, Oxford, Europe or the jungle, an understanding inseparable from his Catholic faith.

> Today we can see ... on all sides ... the active negation of all that western civilization has stood for. Civilization—and by this I do not mean talking cinemas and tinned food, nor even surgery and hygienic houses, but the whole moral and artistic organisation of Europe—has not in itself the power of survival. It came into being through Christianity, and without it has no significance or power to command allegiance. The loss of faith in Christianity and the consequential lack of confidence in moral and social standards have become embodied in the ideal of a materialistic, mechanized state, already existent in Russia and rapidly spreading south and west. It is no longer possible, as it was in the time of Gibbon, to accept the benefits of civilization and at the same time deny the supernatural basis upon which it rests.

For both the aesthete and the convert in Waugh, Western Civilization was synonymous with the Church. At the same time, while he recognized the Church as "the analogue of a nation or country," the traveler in him recognized that its universality transcended "the clan, the tribe, the nation." Consequently, he rejected Belloc's unduly limiting dictum, "Europe is the faith, and the faith is Europe."

Although Waugh treats the Catholic faith directly in such non-fiction works as *Edmund Campion: Jesuit and Martyr* (1935), *Robbery Under Law* (1939), *The Life of the Right Reverend Ronald Knox* (1959), *A Little Learning* (1964), and his copious journalism, he also took up the faith in some of his best novels, including *Brideshead Revisited* (1945), *Helena* (1950) and *The Sword of Honour* (1966). In all of these studies of grace, Waugh shows how the life of faith actually takes root in a world hostile to but transformed by grace, the supernatural being always present in the natural world. Sebastian Flyte, Helena and Guy Crouchback all find themselves in a world radically fallen, and yet it is their persevering, grace-endowed faith that sustains them.

Even though not all of Waugh's novels make explicit reference to Catholicism, it is important to stress that there is remarkable unity in his work, before and after his conversion. As Douglas Lane Patey shows in his brilliant critical biography: Waugh "was on the road to Rome from the mid-twenties, long before the failure of his first marriage, even before the publication of his first novel." Indeed, all of the early satirical novels lay the groundwork for his conversion by showing its inescapable necessity. Moreover, all of his novels are preoccupied, to varying degrees, with something that exercises Helena in Waugh's own favorite of his novels: "Think of the misery of a whole world possessed of Power without Grace." In this, Patey shows how Waugh was influenced by Robert Hugh Benson's *Lord of the World* (1907).

Waugh's marvelously funny autobiographical novel, *The Ordeal of Gilbert Pinfold* (1957), which draws on the chloral-driven delusions he suffered on shipboard while *en route* to Cairo, is a good example of the unsparing criticism he could turn not only on the unbelieving world but himself. Mr. Pinfold, he says, "had been received into the church—'conversion' suggests an event more sudden and emotional than his calm acceptance of the propositions of his faith—in early manhood, at the time when many Englishmen of humane education were falling into communism. Unlike them, Mr. Pinfold remained steadfast. But he was reported bigoted rather than pious." If the persecution mania to which Pinfold is subjected shows the world at its most sadistic, it also shows Pinfold at his most humble. As Waugh's narrator points out: "when the leaders of his Church were exhorting their people to emerge from the catacombs into the forum, to make their influence felt in democratic politics and to regard worship as corporate rather than a private act, Mr. Pinfold burrowed ever deeper into the rock." The parallels to Waugh himself here are obvious, though it is only now that his readers can see how prescient he was about the misfortunes that lay in wait for Catholics in democratic politics.

Waugh might often have been content to pose, like Pinfold, as "a combination of eccentric don and testy colonel," offering "the world a front of pomposity mitigated by indiscretion that was as hard, bright and antiquated as a cuirass." Yet there was a deadly seriousness behind the pose: he would never flinch from being *contra mundum* when his principles were at stake. Nor did he shy away from telling the world truths that it would rather not hear. "Given propitious circumstances," he wrote in *Robbery under Law*, "men and women who seem quite orderly, will commit every conceivable atrocity ... we are all potential recruits for anarchy. Unremitting effort is needed to keep men living together at peace." For Waugh, that effort could not hope to succeed without the Christian faith. "It seems to me that in the present situation in European history," he wrote, "the essential issue is no longer between Catholicism on one side, or Protestantism, on the other, but between Christianity and Chaos."

A Definitive Dig
in the Graham Greene Quarry

Russian Roulette: The Life and Times of Graham Greene, Richard Greene (Little Brown). 591 pages.

In this witty, elegant, revelatory biography, Richard Greene states that his "book takes a very high view of Graham Greene's accomplishments, and so endorses the common opinion of three generations of writers and critics that he is one of the most important figures in modern literature." "Important" writers are not necessarily good writers; in fact, they can be rather poor ones, especially if their importance hinges on their aping or, worse, pandering to the prejudices of their age; but Greene was a good writer despite the "importance" often attributed to him. Not a stylist in the sense in which Evelyn Waugh or Ford Madox Ford were stylists, he accomplished his art—and won his popularity—by concealing his art. Moreover, he may have shared his contemporaries' fascination with the Cold War but his own personal obsessions with faith and betrayal, together with his solicitude for what one early critic nicely called the "ingloriously vicious," always set his interest in such matters apart.

Born in Berkhamsted, Herefordshire, the son of a headmaster, Graham Greene (1904–91) read history at Balliol and converted to Catholicism after marrying Vivienne Dayrell-Browning, whom he never divorced, despite his numerous extramarital affairs. While pursuing his highly successful literary career, he worked briefly for MI6 in West Africa. That both his last mistress and his estranged wife attended his funeral says something for his improbable lovableness. Asked in old age of his work, he said he had written a few good books, some of which might remind some of Flaubert. Thirty years after his death his sales remain strong.

His Catholic novels are his best, particularly *Brighton Rock* (1938), *The Power and the Glory* (1940), and *The End of the Affair* (1951), though he also wrote what he called "entertainments," including *The Stamboul Train* (1932), *The Ministry of Fear* (1943) and *Travels with My Aunt* (1969). Carol Reed directed the amusing film version of *Our Man in Havana* (1958) with Noel Coward and Alec Guinness, about the filming of which Guinness recalled: "We were put in a very gilded hotel and given vast over-decorated suites ... Merula [the actor's wife] had difficulty getting a hair-do in the hotel salon as it was always crowded with Castro's officers having their shoulder-length hair permed and their beards curled while they sat with sub-machine guns across their knees."

Greene also wrote excellent literary criticism. If he had never produced a page of fiction, he would still be remembered for his incisive readings of Henry James, François Mauriac, Henry Fielding, Walter de la Mare, and Rider Haggard, all of whose work influenced his own. Moreover, as a publisher's reader, he was instrumental in the publication of Flann O'Brien's wonderfully funny début novel, *At Swim-Two-Birds* (1939), which was fitting: Greene and O'Brien shared an outrageous sense of humor. As Richard Greene says of the novelist, his practical jokes included "ringing up a retired solicitor in Golders Green who happened also to be named Graham Greene and berating him, in various accents, for writing 'these filthy novels.'" Then, again, "he would carry with him other people's business cards, and when he spotted a friend in a restaurant, he would write lewd or inscrutable proposals on the back of a card, send it across, and watch the friend's reaction."

When Evelyn Waugh warned his friend that abandoning God in his fiction would be like P. G. Wodehouse abandoning Jeeves, he was making a shrewd point. Greene's best books would be inconceivable without their God-haunted fixation on sin. As the critic V. S. Pritchett rightly observed, Greene's greatest achievement was to revive the sense of evil in the English novel, from which it had been absent since the death of James. Greene's depiction of the exultantly evil Pinkie in *Brighton Rock* bears this out. It was also his Catholic faith that enabled him to recognize the reality of eternity, which his character Craven memorably reaffirms in the short story, "A Little Place off the Edgeware Road" (1947) when he says that "the squalid darkening street outside was only one of the innumerable tunnels connecting grave to grave where the imperishable bodies lay."

Yet when Greene left off writing directly about God in his later fiction — particularly in *The Honorary Consul* (1973) and *The Human Factor* (1978) — he still took up secular themes in terms central to his Catholic faith. Certainly, the novelist's Catholic sense of order made him appreciative of the comedy of disorder. In *The Human Factor*, Greene describes an old spy assigned to Africa being roused after nodding off at lunch.

> He opened blue, serene unshockable eyes and said, "A cat nap." It was said that as a young man somewhere in Ashanti he had inadvertently eaten human flesh, but his digestion had not been impaired. According to the story he had told the Governor, "I couldn't really complain, sir. They were doing me a great honour by inviting me to take pot luck."

Greene has not been fortunate in his biographers. Norman Sherry, whom Greene tapped to write the authorized biography, treated the novelist in three stupefying volumes as though his only claim to fame had been to churn out *romans à clef* of no discernible literary or moral significance, while Michael Shelden presented his subject as a pathological huckster, only masquerading as a Catholic to sell books. For Shelden, the real Greene was homicidal, sadomasochistic, homosexual, anti-Semitic, misogynistic, treasonous and, perhaps most ludicrously, anti-Mexican. (Both *The Power and the Glory* and *The Lawless Roads* (1939) are set in Mexico.) Richard Greene, by contrast, has succeeded in writing the best biography of the novelist by showing his subject not only fair criticism but sympathy. He also writes a lean, brisk, cinematic prose reminiscent of Greene's own, which gives his narrative its readability.

As for the effect that Greene's Catholicism had on his work, his biographer shows that it was more decisive than the novelist was prepared to admit: he "believed in there being an essential self. Greene saw *Mrs. Dalloway*, for example, not as a novel with realized characters but as a mere prose poem. In his view, this was not only an intellectual difference between Woolf's beliefs and his, but a failure of craft—her characters are defective because ontologically adrift." One could never say this of Greene's characters, most of whose reality derives from their maker's Catholic belief in material and supernatural reality.

At the same time, Richard Greene shows how the novelist was never unsusceptible to the charisma of strongmen like Omar Torrijos and Fidel Castro. His biographer is also careful not to sentimentalize Greene's relationship with the traitor Kim Philby, which even the broadminded John Le Carré found deplorable. Apropos Greene's endorsing Philby's claim that loyalty to individuals necessarily trumped loyalty to countries, his biographer is categorical: "It is an attractive thought, as nations have a lot to answer for … But as a moral principle it falls apart: it hints at tribalism and tends to justify indifference to strangers." Now, when the tribalism of our own elites ensures their hegemony over a deliberately idiotised populace, Richard Greene makes a timely point.

He also reminds one of how blatant the novelist's political misjudgments were. When one sees Greene equating Communism with Catholicism, one can never be sure whether he knew what he was saying or whether he was simply turning phrases. "Catholics and Communists have committed great crimes," the novelist has one of his characters say in *The Comedians* (1966), "but at least they have not stood aside, like an established society, and been indifferent. I would rather have blood on my hands than water like Pilate." One has to wonder whether Greene would say the same of the blood on the hands of those fellow travelers in the Vatican who have sold out the Catholic Church in China to the hardly indifferent red Chinese.

The storyteller, however, cannot be confused with the provocateur in Greene. When the double agent Castle in *The Human Factor* (1978) lands in Moscow, after his treachery is surfaced, he spends his days in the dreary flat his masters have provided him reading *Robinson Crusoe* and musing as he looks out the window: "This was not the snow he remembered from childhood, and associated with snowballs and fairy stories and games with toboggans. This was a merciless, interminable, annihilating snow, a snow in which one could expect the world to end."

Similarly, the storyteller in Greene could be prescient when it came to exposing what his biographer calls "brittle orthodoxies." His characterization of America's involvement in Vietnam is a good example. Reasonable people can debate America's conduct of the war but it is hard to argue with the narrator Thomas Fowler's assessment of the character of Alden Pyle in Greene's novel *The Quiet American* (1955): "I never knew a man who had better motives for all the trouble he caused ... impregnably armored by his good intentions and his ignorance." Anyone inclined to doubt this should dip into Sir Max Hastings's recent history of the Vietnam War, or Plato on the tragic hero, who must be neither rogue nor paragon but a "character between these two extremes ... a man ... whose misfortune is brought about not by vice or depravity, but by some error or frailty."

In describing the various manifestations of Greene's bipolar illness, Richard Greene supplies his readers with a useful key to his subject's manic restlessness, which the novelist may not have entirely understood himself but turned to good account when developing his characters. Castle, the reluctant double agent, wrestling with his family and M16 loyalties, is described, just before sleep, as "allowing himself to strike ... off on that long slow underground stream which bore him on towards the interior of the dark continent where he hoped that he might find a permanent home, in a city where he could be accepted as a citizen, as a citizen without any pledge of faith, not the City of God or Marx, but the city called Peace of Mind."

In his autobiography, *A Sort of Life*, Greene recalled his father reading Robert Browning to him as a boy and his later realizing that the poet's lines had influenced him "more than any of the Beatitudes," especially these: "Our interest's in the dangerous edge of things / The honest thief, the tender murderer / the superstitious atheist ... We watch while these in equilibrium keep / The giddy line midway." Here was proof that the novelist knew what he was about when he wrote the brilliant opening line of his autobiography: "If I had only known it, the whole future must have lain all the time along those Berkhamsted streets."

In a review of Charles Carrington's life of Kipling, Greene observed that "It is the fate of a good biographer that the reviewer neglects him for random reflections on his subject" but he also said that "Mr. Carrington has dug with effect: the quarry is exhausted, and, as Kipling would have wished, future writers need concern themselves only with the work." The same can be said of Richard Greene and his clairvoyant excavations in the hitherto misused quarry of Graham Greene's life and work.

BIOGRAPHERS

John Batchelor's Lord Tennyson

Tennyson: To Strive, To Seek, To Find, John Batchelor (Pegasus). 422 pages.

Early and late, Tennyson's theme is mortal beauty. In *The Princess* (1847), he set it to an enchanting music.

> The splendor falls on castle walls
> And snowy summits old in story;
> The long light shakes across the lakes,
> And the wild cataract leaps in glory.
> Blow, bugle, blow, set the wild echoes flying,
> Blow, bugle; answer, echoes, dying, dying, dying.

Later, as an older man, on the Isle of Wight, where he would live with his wife and two sons in his sequestered Farringford, he summoned the theme to honor his old friend and neighbor, Sir John Simeon, a good friend of Cardinal Newman.

> Nightingales sang in his woods:
> The Master was far away:
> Nightingales warbled and sang
> Of a passion that lasts but a day;
> Still in the house in his coffin the Prince of courtesy lay.

The historian James Anthony Froude spoke for many of his generation when he confessed how "Spiritually [Tennyson] lives in all our minds (in mine he has lived for nearly forty years) in forms imperishable as diamonds which time and change have no power over." The literary critic George Saintsbury corroborated this when he observed how "no age of poetry can be called the age of one man with such critical accuracy as the later Nineteenth Century is, with us, the Age of Tennyson." Even T. S. Eliot, who had rather severe reservations about the poet, allowed that he "had three qualities ... seldom found together except in the greatest poets: abundance, variety, and complete competence." What makes John Batchelor's life of the poet so admirable is that while it recreates the Victorian Tennyson with meticulous care. It also attends to those aspects of the poet's work that transcend his historical context. There are not many good biographies of Tennyson — Robert Bernard Martin's *Tennyson: The Unquiet Heart* (1980) is an exception—but Batchelor's life can now be accounted the best. Written with considerable learning, grace and panache, it should spur new interest in a poet who has much to say to our own contemporaries.

Alfred Tennyson (1809–92) was born at Somersby rectory, Lincolnshire into a rancorous, divided, unhappy family. His father, the Rev. Dr. George Clayton Tennyson, the eldest son, had been forced into the Church against his will after his father decided to make his youngest brother, Charles his heir. The resentment this bred in Tennyson's father never went away. It exacerbated his epilepsy and turned him into a violent drunkard. Indeed, Tennyson would often have to flee the rectory to flee his father's inebriated rages. Still, he never ceased to take his father's part against his paternal grandfather and uncle, both of whom disdained the Somersby Tennysons. Moreover, the distress that the patriarchal dispossession caused Tennyson's mother, Elizabeth and his other siblings drove him to join "the men of many acres" whom he otherwise despised. Such are the complicated impulses that inform the industry of talent.

In addition to division, the Tennysons suffered from madness. Mary, Tennyson's eldest sister, struggled with religious mania; his brothers Arthur and Horatio labored under recurrent mental instability; his brother Edward was actually confined to an asylum; and his youngest sister Matilda was never the same after being dropped on her head in a coal scuttle. Then, again, another brother would always introduce himself to guests by declaring, "Hello, I am Septimus: I am the morbid Tennyson."

As for Tennyson himself, he not only feared madness but longed for death. As his wife told his son Hallam when engaged in writing his father's biography, Tennyson, terrified of his father's rages, often "went out through the black night, and threw himself on a grave in the churchyard, praying to be beneath the sod himself." Then, again, the poet confessed that "In my youth I knew much greater unhappiness than I have known in later life. When I was about twenty, I used to feel moods of misery unutterable! I remember once in London the realization coming over me, of the *whole* of its inhabitants lying horizontal a hundred years hence. The smallness and emptiness of life sometimes overwhelmed me." For anyone intent on making poetry his life's work, this was useful misery. What was it that John Berryman once said? "The artist is extremely lucky who is presented with the worst possible ordeal which will not actually kill him. At that point, he's in business."

After attending Louth Grammar School, Tennyson went up to Trinity College, Cambridge, where he joined the Apostles and met the dazzling Etonian, Arthur Hallam, whose friendship and support would be crucial to his development as a poet. The son of the Whig historian Henry Hallam, Arthur was handsome, brilliant, and a budding poet in his own right. That he saw his young friend's genius from the start gave Tennyson precisely the confidence he needed to turn his considerable talents to account. Indeed, as Batchelor shows, it was Hallam who arranged publication for Tennyson's first two books, which included such classic poems as "Mariana," "The Kraken," "The Lady of Shalott," "The Lotos-Eaters," and "A Dream of Fair Women." Considering Tennyson's auspicious debut, it is easy to see why the young poet was so attached to his friend: Hallam helped Tennyson become Tennyson.

But then Hallam died suddenly in 1833 of apoplexy while visiting Vienna, and Tennyson was shattered. When Hallam's father asked for a reminiscence, the poet replied that he had "attempted to draw up a memoir of his life and character, but I failed to do him justice. I hope to be able at a future period to concentrate whatever powers I may possess on the construction of some tribute." Seventeen years later, the poet released *In Memoriam A. H. H.* (1850), a collection of 133 lyrics, which, taken together, constitute his far-ranging meditation on the meaning not only of his friend's life and death, but of his entire age's preoccupation with what Newman called the "great *apostasia*." For James Knowles, the founder of the Metaphysical Society and a good friend of Tennyson, the poem, confronting as it did the desolation of unbelief, "was the cry of the whole human race."

That two of the most eminent of Victorians—the Queen herself and Benjamin Disraeli—had a special attachment to the poem underscores the deep chord it struck with Tennyson's contemporaries. If the Queen loved the poem because it echoed her own bereavement over Prince Albert's untimely death, the romantic egotist in Disraeli saw in one of its cantos an oblique delineation of his own improbable rise to power.

> Who breaks his birth's invidious bar,
> And grasps the skirts of happy chance,
> And breasts the blows of circumstance,
> And grapples with his evil star;
>
> Who makes by force his merit known
> And lives to clutch the golden keys,
> To mould a mighty state's decrees,
> And shape the whisper of the throne

In the writing of *In Memoriam*, Tennyson would take up three of his most abiding themes: loss, change, and transcendence. Yet, while these cantos were still evolving, he would also publish a third book of verse in 1842, which included some of his greatest poems: "Break, break, break," "Ulysses," "Morte d'Arthur," "Locksley Hall," and "Tithonous." Hallam's loss might have been a bane to his personal life but it was a boon to his poetry.

Apropos the poet's rackety life in London in the 1830s and 1840s with such footloose friends as Thackeray, Edward Fitzgerald, James Spedding, Edward Lear and Carlyle, Batchelor observes: "The nomadic, chaotic Alfred

Tennyson of legend, a legend built up and lovingly transmitted for posterity by his many friends in these vagrant years, was in fact displaying an inner resolution. He was a *poet*, nothing else, and he claimed no other identity, role or mode of existence." From early youth, Tennyson also looked the poet, especially after he adopted his signature cape and sombrero. For Henry James, everything about this consummate poet was "a thousand miles away from American manufacture." However, the dark side to his steely dedication to his art was a tendency towards solipsism. As Batchelor remarks, "even with Arthur Hallam, it can often seem that what Tennyson loved was not Arthur himself, but Arthur's love of Tennyson: his own image and his own genius as reflected in Arthur's loyal admiration."

Batchelor also quotes the strictures of Edward Lear, who remarked in his friend "the anomaly of high souled & philosophic writings combined with slovenliness, selfishness, & morbid folly." In this light, Batchelor's Tennyson can sometimes remind one of that unforgettable "monster" that Ted Hughes shared with his readers in "Famous Poet," behind whose eyes one can see nothing "But the haggard stony exhaustion of a near-/Finished variety artist." Certainly, a good deal of Tennyson's later work was given over to writing narrative verse of questionable merit — *Enoch Arden* (1864) comes to mind — composed to satisfy the enormous demand for his work on the part of a public flattered that their Laureate should wish to please them. At the same time, when speaking of the later Tennyson, Batchelor never falls prey to modish condescension, agreeing with Chesterton that it was "intensely typical of Tennyson's philosophical temper that he was almost the only Poet Laureate who was not ludicrous." And he could often strike back at critics (indirectly) with epigrammatical nicety, as in *Idylls of the King*: "Never yet / Was noble man but made ignoble talk / He makes no friend who never made a foe."

Batchelor is also good at uncovering the many contradictions that animated his subject, showing how at once shrewd and gullible he could be in money matters. While one of the most successful poets who ever lived — *Enoch Arden*, for example, sold 17,000 copies on its first day of publication and over 60,000 copies after its first year, earning the poet over £8,000, an immense amount for a volume of narrative verse — he also fell for a huckster's scheme to streamline wood carving, which robbed him of his entire inheritance in a matter of months. Then, again, with loyal friends, Tennyson could be oddly cold and aloof — Edward Fitzgerald was made to endure this *froideur*, especially after fame made Tennyson more than usually grand — but in his favor it must be said that after Thackeray handed in his dinner pail, Tennyson took in his orphaned daughters. Indeed, on walks along Hampstead Heath, he would often confide in Annie Thackeray about his early poverty, self-doubts, and loneliness, proof that the adulated Laureate never entirely outgrew the unhappy boy from Somersby fleeing the spectacle of his besotted papa.

After the loss of Hallam, Tennyson became infatuated with Rosa Baring of Harrington Hall, a rich, haughty, trifling woman, whose rejection led him to write his great dramatic monologue *Maud* (1855), than which there is no poem in the language more rich and strange. (That the monologue should have ended with his deranged hero speaking of "The blood-red blossom of war with a heart of fire" must have given the poets of the Great War an eerie shudder.)

When Tennyson married Emily Sellwood, another Somersby woman, who would become his agent, muse, and secretary, he made an inspired choice, though one observer was convinced that she immured him in "the sultry, perfumed atmosphere of luxury and homage." Drawing on Ann Thwaite's excellent biography of Emily, Batchelor paints a lively portrait of this devout, talented, enterprising woman. In the partnership into which Emily entered with her necessitous husband, she might have given more than she received, but she gave without stint. In "June Bracken and Heather", written a year before his death, when Emily was seventy-seven, Tennyson wrote her a moving tribute, commending her for having "a faith as clear as the heights of the June-blue heaven / And a fancy as summer-new / As the green of the bracken amid the gloom of the heather."

Although never fond of church going and heedless of doctrinal orthodoxy, Tennyson was profoundly religious. As he told the diarist William Allingham: "Two things I have always been firmly convinced of — God — and that death will not end my existence." The loss of Hallam would deepen these certainties by infusing them with the reality of love. His later years are packed with brilliant poetry — Batchelor shows again and again how his lyrical gift never left the poet, even in his eighties, as "Crossing the Bar" so splendidly attests — but there are no verses that better sum up this love than these from *In Memoriam*:

> Love is and was my King and Lord,
>   And will be, tho' as yet I keep
>   Within his court on earth, and sleep
> Encompass'd by his faithful guard,
>
> And hear at times a sentinel
>   Who moves about from place to place,
>   And whispers to the worlds of space,
> In the deep night, that all is well.

For the great poet whose greatest poems grew out of loss and heartbreak, mortal beauty was an intimation of immortal love, and in "Vastness," a poem Tennyson wrote at the end of his life, he expressed his discovery of this liberating truth with impassioned conviction: "Peace, let it be! for I loved him, and love him for ever: the dead are not dead but alive."

George Romney:
Portrait of the Artist as a Portraitist

George Romney: A Catalogue of his Complete Paintings, Alex Kidson (Yale University Press). 960 pages.

In his magisterial study of English culture in the eighteenth century, *The Pleasures of the Imagination* (1997), the historian John Brewer made a vital point when he argued that although we might look back on the culture of the Georgians and see an enviable "order, stability and decorum," the Georgians themselves considered it "modern, not traditional," proof "that their society and way of life were changing." And he concluded that what most characterized this admirable culture was not "respectability or elegance" but "dynamism, variety and exuberance."

To immerse oneself in Alex Kidson's magnificent three-volume catalog is to see the force of Brewer's point, for no painter captures the "dynamism, variety and exuberance" of his Georgian subjects better than George Romney (1734–1802), who, together with Sir Joshua Reynolds and Thomas Gainsborough, was one of England's greatest eighteenth-century painters. Kidson's catalog has many virtues: it corrects erroneous and reveals hitherto unknown attributions; it chronicles how commissions were carried out; and it meticulously trawls account books, ledgers, sketchbooks, newspaper reports, reviews, and the writings of Romney's contemporaries to supply the contemporary background for an *oeuvre* that spans nearly 2,000 portraits. But it also shows again and again how Romney proved Brewer's point by bringing an altogether new inventiveness and élan to portraiture. As Kidson points out in the *Oxford Dictionary of National Biography*, "Romney was ... an artist who, under the cover of his professional image, experimented, developed, and reinvented himself continuously, and who in retrospect appears by temperament one of the first great modernists in British art."

After the art dealer Joseph Duveen resuscitated Romney's reputation in the early twentieth century sufficiently to make him profitably appealing to such deep-pocketed art collectors as Frick, Huntington and Gulbenkian, Romney's reputation languished, and it has only been the sedulous, exacting work of Kidson that has restored the painter to his proper place as the "bridging figure between the classicism of Reynolds and the brilliant informality of Lawrence."

The autodidact son of a Lancashire joiner, Romney chose to become an artist after reading Shakespeare and Milton, the grandeur of whose work would make an abiding impression on him. Indeed, one early augury of the exceptional portraits to come was Romney's striking portrayal of Lear stripping off his clothes on the heath—an apt theme for a portraitist keen on making portraiture truly revelatory. Although taught painting by a painter from Kendal named Christopher Steele, who bequeathed to his apprentice a delight in bold, dramatic color, Romney remained aloof from other artists. After working briefly with Steele in York, where Laurence Sterne regaled the two painters with advance readings of *Tristram Shandy* (1760), he returned to Kendal to launch his own career.

Wedding his landlady's daughter after she nursed him back to health from a fever and bore him a son, Romney would nonetheless leave his wife and children behind when he set off for London. Apparently, he had been told by Sir Joshua that "marriage spoilt an artist." His own absentee marriage notwithstanding, he always portrayed the marriages of his sitters with insightful sympathy.

Still, to beguile the guilt he felt for living apart from his family, Romney painted incessantly, conducting seven ninety-minute sittings per day and plunging into portraits without any preliminary sketches. Maintaining this manic schedule throughout the 1770s, 1780s and 1790s made him the most fashionable painter in London; it also wrecked his health. Leaving his smart residence in Cavendish Square, he returned to Kendal a broken man, though his wife took back the prodigal and nursed him for the last three years of his life. That his son (who wrote his biography) had nothing but praise for his father shows that Romney, however absentee, was not unloved.

Like all proper artists, Romney was continually dissatisfied with his art. His friend and fellow artist John Flaxman recognized that the painter's "heart and soul were engaged in the pursuit of historical and ideal painting." When Romney traveled to revolutionary France and saw the variety of historical themes that David had been commissioned to paint, his heart sank. This was the sort of grand, visionary painting that he had always wished to produce himself. Nevertheless, if the portraits gathered together in this heroic catalog show Romney's yearning to transcend the limits of portraiture, they also show that it was only within those limits that the artist in him shone.

Indeed, it is his very impatience with conventional portraiture that gives his best portraits their distinction. In his great portrait of Warren Hastings, for example, we see the former Governor-General of Bengal in 1795, seven years after Edmund Burke and his Whig associates brought a charge of impeachment against him in the House of Commons. As it happened, Hastings was acquitted on all counts, though he left his trial a shattered man. The £80,000 he had brought back with him from India—a tidy sum in Georgian England—had vanished in court costs. All he had left by the time Romney painted him was his disillusionment, which made this once redoubtable grandee not so much bitter with the world, as baffled that he should ever have imagined its prizes worth pursuing in the first place.

Then, again, there is Romney's pastel portrait of William Cowper, which shows the poet gazing away from the artist and his viewer at something beyond the canvas, proof that, he, too, like the painter, was preoccupied with yearnings that the surface of life, however fine or enticing, could never satisfy. What gives this study in desolation added poignancy is that poor Cowper was periodically convinced that he was irredeemably damned. In what amounts to an anti-portrait, Cowper's coat blends indistinguishably with the pastel's background, and his shirt and nightcap do little but isolate the poet's almost disembodied head, with its great wondering eyes and disconsolate, quizzical lips. If Romney's Hastings shows a public man come to grief, his Cowper shows a fellow artist who has seemingly never known anything but grief—for Romney, a sympathetic soul.

Another example of his ability to defy the conventions of portraiture can be seen in what Kidson rightly regards as "one of the greatest self-portraits of the eighteenth century," which hangs in the National Portrait Gallery. In this riveting *aperçu*, Romney leaves everything unfinished but the sullen, brooding gaze he turns to the viewer, which is as much an aesthetic gauntlet as a *cri du coeur*. Here is the artist weary of what he regarded as the "shackles" of portraiture, but also the proud, unhappy man contemptuous of the fashionable world on which so much of his livelihood depended.

Nevertheless, to look at the portraits in this splendid catalogue is to see how the artist in Romney continually sought to make portraiture serve his art. His wonderful portrait of Lady Louisa Lennox (1738–1830), for example, captures not only a fascinating individual—a strong, intelligent, subtle woman who cries out for a Fanny Burney or Jane Austen to do her complex beauty justice—but an entire social order, one founded on hierarchical rank and subordination, yes, but also a deep attachment to the land and people of the countryside. The wife of Lord George Henry Lennox (1737–1805), who served in the Seven Years War and later became MP for the family borough of Chichester, Lady Louisa is shown dressed in riding attire sitting with a spaniel on her lap, completely at one with her rural setting. Here are aristocratic beauty and grace removed from their usual opulent settings, but also a certain simplicity, even a sweetness. Countless books have been written about England's landed aristocracy but how few of them capture its *gentilesse* as revealingly as this casual portrait by the man whom Henry James called "the strong, deep, mellow Romney."

William Cobbett might have regarded the nobility as "these mean, these cruel, these cowardly, these carrion, these dastardly reptiles." Romney, by putting them before his viewers in a favorable, though never sycophantic light, humanizes them.

Those who wish to maintain, as the feminist historian Amanda Vickery maintains, that women in Georgian England were marginalized victims, cowering under the "smothering power" of fathers and husbands, as Vickery puts it in *Behind Closed Doors: At Home in Georgian England* (2009) must come away from Romney's pictures impressed by how well he bundles away this patriarchal tyranny, for none of his wives and daughters have the least look of victims about them. The marital portraits here—whether of Mr. and Mrs. William Lindow or Sir Christopher and Lady Elizabeth Sykes—exhibit bonds of affection and esteem. They do not corroborate the gender hysteria of our ahistorical feminists, in which aggrieved females are eternally at the mercy of despotic males. In the charming "promenade" portrait of the Sykes, for instance, it is Lady Elizabeth who leads the way, not her "stiff and business-like husband," as Kidson nicely puts it, who follows his Lady's lead with grateful docility. If there were any patriarchal oppression afoot in this household, husband and wife were ingenious at concealing it.

Another feminist myth exploded here is that eighteenth-century women were somehow overwhelmed not only by unwanted pregnancies but unwanted children. Page after page of these volumes confute that claim by showing how philoprogenitive the mothers were who sat to Romney with their children. If one of the ways that Georgian portrait painters endeared themselves to their upper-class clients was to enter into what truly mattered to them, whether their families or their estates, Romney obliged his sitters by fully entering into their delight in their children. Gainsborough and Reynolds were marvelous painters but neither painted children with anything like Romney's inimitable panache. In gratifying his clients' demand for portraits of children Romney transformed not only the mother and child portrait but the family portrait as well.

A superb example of the former is his portrait of Mrs. Anne Wilson and her Daughter, which Romney painted for Mrs. Wilson as a memento of the daughter she lost after the portrait had been commissioned. It is one of the most moving portraits he ever painted—"all abraded by sorrows we are not equipped to understand," to borrow a phrase from Scott Fitzgerald.

The best example of the latter is his delightful portrait of the Leveson-Gower children, which, in addition to being an inspired pastiche of Poussin's *Dance to the Music of Time* (1636), shows how Romney could present his juvenile subjects in the most stylized of settings without losing a scintilla of their charming spontaneity. The man who denied himself the society of his own children never passed up an opportunity to revel in that of others.

Finally, the catalog includes all of the portraits that Romney painted of his favorite sitter, Emma Hart, later Lady Hamilton, the seductively beautiful daughter of an illiterate blacksmith who would go on to enrapture Lord Nelson. (Before setting off for the Battle of Trafalgar, the great naval hero wrote his paramour: "Brave Emma! Good Emma! If there were more Emmas there would be more Nelsons.") Emma was introduced to Romney's studio in 1782 when she was 16 and he was 47. Over the next 4 years, she had nearly 200 sittings with Romney and appears in 28 portraits. For Romney, as Kidson remarks, Emma "rekindled the possibilities of portraiture itself." Here we have Emma as Circe, Mirth, Nature, Calypso, Absence, Sybil, Vestal, St Cecilia, "Spinstress" and Bacchante. Unfortunately, after Nelson died and the government refused to give her a pension, Emma ran up unrepayable debts and died at 49 in a Calais boarding house of cirrhosis of the liver—a melancholy end to a most improbable life, though it would have confirmed Romney's sense of the transience of human beauty, which he captured so splendidly in these incomparable portraits.

Life of Frank:
Samuel Johnson's Legatee

The Fortunes of Francis Barber: The True Story of the Jamaican Slave who Became Samuel Johnson's Heir, Michael Bundock (Yale University Press). 282 pages.

In his memorable poem, "At the Graveside of Henry James," W. H. Auden apostrophized the great American novelist to make a useful point:

> Master of nuance and scruple,
> Pray for me and for all writers living or dead;
> Because there are many whose works
> Are in better taste than their lives, because there is no end
> To the vanity of our calling: make intercession
> For the treason of all clerks.

Since there are indeed many writers "whose works are in better taste than their lives," when we happen upon those about whom this is not the case, we naturally welcome biographies that confirm why they elude Auden's otherwise just reproof. And since no one fits that bill better than Samuel Johnson, all readers interested in the exemplary virtues of the great lexicographer, poet, editor and critic will delight in Michael Bundock's *The Fortunes of Francis Barber.*

The Director of the Dr. Johnson's House Trust, Bundock has produced a finely researched, admirably written and altogether fascinating life, which shows how the boy who had grown up in slavery on a sugar plantation in Jamaica deeply enriched Johnson's moral and spiritual life. In addition to being a brilliant account of a relationship that might have begun as one of master and servant but ended as one of father and son, Bundock describes the full horror of the sugar plantations in Jamaica, where slaves worked from dawn to dusk six days a week under the broiling Caribbean sun and where planters presided over a system of manifold iniquity.

Francis was given as a gift to Johnson in 1752 by his friend Richard Bathurst, the son of a ruined planter who styled himself Colonel Richard Bathurst. The titles planters gave themselves caused great mirth in England, one wit noting how "They are all *Colonels, Majors, Captains, Lieutenants,* and *Ensigns.*" When Frank arrived at Johnson's house in Gough Square, he was 10 and Johnson 42. For the beleaguered lexicographer, the very presence of the young boy must have been a welcome distraction from the slow progress he was making on his Dictionary. He was also mourning the death of his wife. Then, again, he was happy that Francis had been freed. Fettered in a melancholy he could never entirely escape, he empathized with Frank. No one can read Johnson's works without seeing how abhorrent slavery was to him. Indeed, his opposition to the American colonists was rooted in his detestation of their slave-owning, impelling him to ask, "How is it that we hear the loudest yelps for liberty among the drivers of Negroes?" And as for his friend Bathurst, he was happy that giving Francis away freed him of the sin that had ruined his father. As he told Boswell, with that care for the well-being of others that was so typical of the man, "My dear friend Dr. Bathurst declared that he was glad that his father had left his affairs in total ruin, because having no estate, he was not under the temptation of having slaves."

Drawing on the voluminous papers of the planter Thomas Thistlewood, Bundock shows the extent to which plantations doubled as brothels. "Thistlewood's diary," he writes, "reveals that in 37 years in Jamaica, he had sex 3,852 times with 138 women … There was simply no question of resistance, as the women knew the consequences only too well." Those who refused were whipped. Whether Francis was sired by Bathurst is a lively question. No proof has surfaced.

John Hawkins, Johnson's first biographer notes the merriment that Frank's arrival inspired in Johnson's friends, especially since "The uses for which Barber was intended to serve … were not very apparent." After all, "Diogenes himself never wanted a servant less than Johnson seemed to do." Hawkins cited Johnson's "great bushy wig," which was "as impenetrable by a comb as a thick-set hedge" and the dust on his outer garments, which "was never known to have been disturbed by a brush." Fortunately, Frank's duties did not include seeing to it that his master was smartly turned out. Instead, he was responsible for running errands, carrying messages, greeting Johnson's guests at the door, waiting at table, and joining Johnson on his occasional rambles outside London.

Since Johnson's household included lodgers that Johnson had taken in out of charity—particularly, the bibulous doctor Robert Levet and the blind poet Anna Williams—Frank found himself in combustible company. Levet, Johnson admitted, was "a brutal fellow," even though he enjoyed his company, "for his brutality" was "in his manners, not his mind." And Williams, although a learned woman, was equally unrefined, always losing her temper and eating her meals with her fingers. The fights between Frank and Williams were fierce, Frank complaining of Williams's bossiness and Williams complaining of Frank's laziness. Indeed, Williams's rages became so unbearable that Johnson often had to flee the household. No wonder he told Hawkins that "a tavern-chair was the throne of human felicity." If Johnson enjoyed "the conflict of opinions and sentiments" in taverns, the conflicts at home were seldom jolly. In fact, Frank left Johnson's household in 1756 to join an apothecary in Cheapside. Two years later, he ran away to join the Royal Navy. Since Frank always treated Johnson as a *paterfamilias*, his decision might have been an act of rebellion, particularly as he knew how contemptuous Johnson was of the seafaring life. As Johnson told Boswell, "No man will be a sailor who has contrivance enough to get himself into a jail; for being in a ship is being in a jail, with the chance of being drowned." The letter to the radical MP John Wilkes that the great comic novelist Tobias Smollet wrote at Johnson's behest gave Johnson one of his most famous epithets.

DEAR SIR, I am again your petitioner, in behalf of that great CHAM of literature, Samuel Johnson. His black servant, whose name is Francis Barber, has been pressed on board the Stag Frigate ... and our Lexicographer is in great distress. He says the boy is a sickly lad, of a delicate frame, and particularly subject to a malady in his throat, which renders him very unfit for his Majesty's service. You know what manner of animosity the said Johnson has against you; and I dare say you desire no other opportunity of resenting it than that of laying him under an obligation. He was humble enough to desire my assistance on this occasion, though he and I were never cater-cousins; and I gave him to understand that I would make application to my friend Mr. Wilkes, who, perhaps, by his interest ... might be able to procure the discharge of his lacquey.

As it happened, although Wilkes made appeals to the Admiralty (despite his contempt for Johnson's Tory politics), Frank was only discharged after Johnson wrote an appeal himself, saying "It would be a great pleasure, and some convenience to me, if the Lords of the Admiralty would be pleased to discharge [Barber], which, as he is no seaman, may be done with little injury to the King's service."

From 1760 until Johnson's death in 1784, Frank returned to the employ of his paternal master, who prized his company and sought to help him however he could. Starting in 1767, Johnson paid Frank's fees to attend grammar school in Hertfordshire, where he studied Latin and Greek, as well as music and dancing. Johnson also shared with Frank his deep Christian faith. "I prayed with Francis," he wrote in one diary entry, "which I now do commonly, and explained to him the Lord's Prayer." That Johnson took a keen interest in Frank's education is clear from his letters, in one of which he counselled the young man: "You can never be wise unless you love reading," a truth we would be wise to instill in our own unlettered children.

Bundock draws a richly sympathetic portrait of Frank. In addition to having a certain wanderlust, he was personable and handsome. "Frank has carried the empire of Cupid farther than most men," Johnson wrote after they visited Lincolnshire, where the boy so enamored the local girls that one of them followed him back to London. In 1773, Frank married Elizabeth Ball (a pretty young white woman) and had five children, all of whom came to live with Johnson in Bolt Court. Mrs. Thrale recalled inviting Frank and his wife to a servant's ball at Streatham, at which "Frank took offense at some attentions paid his Desdemona, and walked away next morning to London in wrath." Presumably a white servant had flirted with his wife. At any rate, Frank was never altogether comfortable in the white world for which he had exchanged the black world of his captivity.

In his will, Johnson made Frank his legatee, settling an annuity on him of £70 (a tidy sum in eighteenth-century England). At his master's suggestion, Frank left London for Lichfield, Johnson's birthplace, and set up a school in the nearby village of Brantwood—a mile away from Edial, where, sixty years before, Johnson had established his own school. Nevertheless, Frank, like so many of Johnson's friends, was bad with money, and to keep the wolves from the door he was forced to sell the personal mementoes that Johnson had given him. "O how will Boswell envy me," the Canon of Lichfield Cathedral wrote Hawkins. "No less than Dr. Johnson's watch is now in my possession! ... I purchased it from Francis Barber, his black servant." This galled Hawkins because he had wanted the watch for himself. In all events, in 1801 Frank died in Stafford Infirmary, which was run, curiously enough, by the grandfather of Charles Darwin, who founded the hospital to take in dying paupers.

"The highest panegyrick that private virtue can receive," Johnson wrote in one of his *Rambler* essays, "is the praise of servants ... it very seldom happens that they commend or blame without justice." That Frank named not one but two of his sons Samuel shows the affectionate esteem in which he held his kind and loving master. Readers interested in learning why Johnson was the living refutation of Rochefoucauld's maxim that no master is a hero to his servant will find Michael Bundock's book a moving, masterly read.

James Grant
and Walter Bagehot

In 1835, the Reverend Sydney Smith, the wittiest divine ever produced by the English National Church, wrote a letter to one of his young female friends peculiarly emblematic of the English nation when it was on the brink of becoming the most powerful nation on earth. "Lucy, dear child," Smith wrote, "You are going to Boulogne, the city of debts, peopled by men who never understood arithmetic; by the time you return, I shall probably have received my first paralytic stroke, and shall have lost all recollection of you; therefore, I now give you my parting advice. Don't marry anybody who has not a tolerable understanding and a thousand a year, and God bless you, dear child."

Money, in other words, meant a great deal to the nineteenth-century English. And yet what is perhaps most remarkable about historians of the period is how few of them really grasp that truth. Indeed, in many respects, the period's most celebrated historians suffer from a kind of financial illiteracy. Who, for example, would go to E. P. Thompson, the Marxist author of *The Making of the English Working Class* (1963) for a reliable handle on how money animated that admirably dynamic society? Or Asa Briggs, who wrote highly regarded histories of the Victorians before serving as president of the William Morris society? Or even G. M. Young, whose *Victorian England: Portrait of an Age* (1953) may offer dazzling intellectual history but has little to say of the financial world of the Victorians. It is true that the prolific David Kynaston somewhat supplied this omission by writing his multi-volume history of the City of London (1995–2002), but since he writes primarily of the City as a world onto itself he does not put the financial preoccupations of the Victorians in any wider context.

Enter James Grant, the crack financial commentator and gentleman scholar, whose books on John Adams and Bernard Baruch abound with both historical and financial acumen. In his latest biography, *Walter Bagehot: The Life and Times of the Greatest Victorian*, Grant takes up the life of a man steeped in finance to show how it was precisely his appreciation of the deeply financial character of his society that enabled him to anatomize it with such discrimination and verve.

Nevertheless, Grant is highly critical not only of Bagehot's irresponsible financial prognostications (especially with regard to Overend Gurney & Co., the largest discount house in the City of London at the time, that suspended payments on 10 May, "Black Friday," 1866) but of his rather snobbish opposition to electoral reform. In the lead up to the Reform Bill of 1867, which gave the vote to the English and Welsh working classes, Bagehot tried to scuttle the bill by reminding his readers that the "lower orders" compared to "the educated 'ten thousand'" were "narrow-minded," "unintelligent," and "incurious." For Grant, "the schoolboy who had called his classmates 'the mob' had grown up to become a supercilious man. ... his contempt for his fellow man—especially the 'little people,' as Bagehot was want to call the underlings—was jarring."

This in marked contrast to the conclusion about the man's character to which Alastair Buchan, a previous biographer, was drawn. While he acknowledges that Bagehot was "haunted," as many other "liberal and moderate men of the fifties and sixties" were, as to how to grant the franchise to the working class, before Disraeli's "leap in the dark," without acquiescing in "the rule of mere numbers," he sees his hero, on balance, as having sought a solution to the dilemma that would be at once just and responsible. For Buchan, Bagehot's remedy "was a straightforward and arbitrary one: to maintain the influence of the educated classes by retaining existing £10 qualifications in general, but to make the working-class influence felt by enfranchising all ratepayers in the larger towns that had a high industrial population." For Buchan, this judicious approach was redolent of the man's moral development. "To those who knew in his forties," the biographer says,

> he seemed a figure uniquely gifted and resolved, worthy of Sir Walter Raleigh's later phrase on Shakespeare, a "man cast in the antique mould of humanity, equable, alert and gay." But this balance had been won by victories in a private campaign against himself, against arrogance, against intellectual pride and folly, against circumstance, against dejection, and ill health. In the course of the campaign, he had achieved not only simplicity and modesty but gentleness.

Grant is content to see this personal moral campaign as less than altogether successful. Who is right? I would say that both Grant and Buchan are right, in their own ways, though Grant makes perhaps the more persuasive case by showing how Bagehot's objection to "rule by mere numbers" can be seen as an objection to rule by men siring too many children.

At the same time, Grant never overlooks Bagehot's undeniable genius, which he celebrates in a narrative as fast-paced as it is toughminded. Readers interested in Victorian history, banking, English literature, constitutional government or all of the above, will revel in the critical symɔathy that Grant brings to understanding his paradoxical, exasperating, ncandescent subject.

Like Grant himself, Walter Bagehot (1826–77) was both a financier and a littérateur. After a scintillating university career at University College, London, he edited the *Economist*, invented the Treasury Bill, advocated for cabinet government and wrote two books that have never lost their appeal: *The English Constitution* (1867), which remains the "go to" book whenever royal crises arise and *Lombard Street* (1873), which Grant nicely calls "the canonical guide to stopping a run on the banks."

Bagehot was also a redoubtable prose stylist, an inspired historian and a genuinely gifted literary critic. Grant is particularly good on Bagehot's brilliant coverage of the 1848 revolution in France—written when he was all of twenty-five—as well as his dealings with Gladstone, Disraeli, and Robert Lowe, later Viscount Sherbrooke, a Coriolanus-like elitist who served as Chancellor of the Exchequer, a post which he famously likened to a "taxing machine." Why? "He is entrusted with a certain amount of misery which it is his duty to distribute as fairly as he can."

Despite Bagehot's own epigrammatic prose, some of his judgements were specious. For example, he often made glib plugs for reckless central banking:

> A panic, in a word, is a form of neuralgia, and according to the rules of science you must not starve it. The holders of the cash reserve must be ready not only to keep it for their own liabilities, but to advance it most freely for the liabilities of others. They must lend to merchants, to minor banks, to "this man and that man," whenever the security is good. In wild periods of alarm, one failure makes many, and the best way to prevent the derivative failures is to arrest the primary failure which causes them.

In our own increasingly volatile world, this has become the justification for "too-big-to-fail" economics and its misguided thinking still animates twenty-first-century central bankers. "No sooner do the banks bring down a crisis on themselves, or stock prices take a tumble," Grant writes, "than the call goes out for the Federal Reserve to infuse the market with emergency credit." And to prove his point, Grant points out that: "In his memoir of the Great Recession, *The Courage to Act*, Ben S. Bernanke, chairman of the Federal Reserve from 2006 to 2014, cited Bagehot more frequently than any living economist."

Nonetheless, when Bagehot's judgements were on the beam, they could be far-sighted. This was certainly the case when he turned his attention to the question of what sort of statesman should most effectively govern a modern parliamentary democracy. For Bagehot, no one could look dispassionately at Gladstone's career without seeing that it was not the intellectual who made the best statesman but the capable man of business. The man who most fit this pragmatic bill for Bagehot was Sir Robert Peel, who passed Catholic Emancipation, repealed the protectionist Corn Laws, and gave the English their first metropolitan police force. "In common life," Bagehot argued, in that prose, which Grant rightly compares to good civilized talk, "we continually see some men as it were scarcely separable from their pursuits ... It is so with Sir Robert Peel. So long as constitutional statesmanship is what it is now, so long as its function is the recording of views of a confused nation, so long as success in it is confined to minds plastic, changeful, administrative, — we must hope for no better man. You have excluded the profound thinker; you must be content with what you can obtain—the business gentleman."

Notwithstanding his admiration for Peel, Bagehot had his doubts about the Prime Minister's highly controversial Bank Charter Act (1844) — otherwise known as Peel's Act—which sought to avert panics by securing the gold value of the pound. As far as Bagehot was concerned, as Grant remarks, "Peel's Act served no useful purpose in tranquil times," and "in a panic, only incited the fear that the chancellor would refuse a letter to suspend it." Thus, Bagehot was not opposed to extraordinary government intervention in finance, even though others foresaw that it could prove ruinous. Grant's reading of the matter is incisive: "If we consider the ideas central to the debate—discretion versus regulation in monetary management, the problem of moral hazard—the battle has raged to this day." As this shows, the advocate of the gold standard in Peel might have made him an even better bet as a model for the modern statesman than Bagehot imagined.

Two previous biographies of Bagehot, one by his sister-in-law Mrs. Russell Barrington, and the other by Buchan, may be still worth reading but Grant's biography must now be accounted the best. It makes particularly good use of Ruth Dudley Edward's history of the *Economist*, Kynaston's recent history of the Bank of England and Bagehot's own voluminous works, which Norman St. John-Stevas collected some years ago in 15 volumes. Witty, shrewdly judged and enviably but enviably well written, Grant's life will give all of its readers, aficionados and neophytes alike, an enhanced understanding of Bagehot and the real financial world in which he and his contemporaries moved, not the vague or ideologically distorted one offered by too many historians of the English nineteenth century.

Sydney Smith would approve.

Andrew Roberts:
An Artist's Churchill

In his massive biography of Winston Churchill, Andrew Roberts recounts how Major-General Sir James Edmonds, the editor of the Government's Official War History, helped Churchill to compose *The World Crisis*, his history of the Great War by supplying him with pertinent maps and documents, after which Churchill, striding up and down his study at Chartwell, his country house overlooking the Weald of Kent, would dictate his account of events to his secretary. For Edmonds, the experience was unforgettable.

> I heard what seemed to be a spirit voice whispering to him, but the whispers were his own; he murmured each sentence over to see how it sounded before he dictated it. He took infinite pains to polish up his prose; after two or three typewritten versions, he would have four or five galley-proofs—an expensive business for his publishers ... He has the soul of an artist.

As to Churchill's artistry, Evelyn Waugh had his doubts. Although appreciative of Churchill's desire to have his histories embody a certain "magnificence," he also thought that his "historical writings ... though highly creditable for a man with so much else to occupy him, do not really survive close attention." Why? "He can seldom offer the keen, unmistakable aesthetic pleasure of the genuine artist." T. S. Eliot was somewhat less unfavorable, convinced that Churchill's "historical style possesses beauties that the charm of no other personality than his could give." Moreover, he was "honester than Macaulay." However, Eliot also saw how oratory colored Churchill's writings, especially his biography of his ancestor, John Churchill, the Duke of Marlborough.

> In a style formed by oratory, we must never expect intimacy; we must never expect the author to address us as individual readers, but always as members of a mob. The mob of course may be assumed to possess every intellectual and moral virtue, as mobs addressed by orators usually do; it may even be a select mob. That addressed in the pages of *Marlborough* is a kind of Whig-Tory amalgam, men of the world of course, used to good manners and to downright

plain speaking, virtuous but tolerant of the morals of Restoration times; recognizing the importance of good blood, but a little cynical about ancient pedigrees ... What is more important, however, than the particular constitution of the audience addressed by Mr. Churchill, is that characteristic of his kind of writing, which consists in constantly pitching the tone a little too high. At the end of a period we seem to observe the author pause for the invariable burst of hand-clapping.

Graham Greene was amusing about Churchill's fondness for the magniloquent when he said, apropos Operations Torch, the Allies' landing in Vichy-controlled Algiers and Morocco in 1942: "I imagine Churchill's reference to the services of West Africa in the war was ironic." (Churchill had said that the landing was "a majestic enterprise.") For Greene, "As far as I can see their contribution has been confined to cowardice, complacency, inefficiency, illiteracy and thirst ... People say the African is not yet ready for self-government. God knows whether he is or not: the Englishman here certainly isn't." Like many others, Malcolm Muggeridge thought that Churchill's books might have more historical than artistic value—Churchill, after all, was so often the protagonist of the history he interpreted—but he was sure that *The Second World War*, "Even more than *The World Crisis* ... will remain an imperishable monument to one who, in an age of littleness, has shown himself to be a great Englishman, a great European, and a great man."

What sets Roberts apart from other Churchill biographers is not only his revisiting of Churchill's greatness at a time when so many hitherto unreleased sources have been made available—especially the diaries of King George VI and the Soviet ambassador to London Ivan Maisky—but the genuine artistry with which he captures the character of that greatness. For so efficient an historian as Roberts, whose seamless narrative is only matched by his command of his sources, the notion that his achievement can be attributed to anything as grandiose as the "soul of the artist" might seem fanciful. Yet the artist in this scholarly, popular historian is paramount. One can see this in the enviable verve with which he weaves together the thematic strands of Churchill's life, without ever compromising the drama inherent in its chronology. Here, we see Churchill's abiding preoccupation with empire, his adoption of his father's Tory Democracy, his love of what he called "the noble English sentence," his dedication to the art of oratory, his bravery, his ebullience, his wit, his magnanimity, his fascination with history, and, most rivetingly, his prophetic understanding of the evil of Nazi tyranny, when so many around him wished to imagine it negotiable.

Then, too, Roberts is brilliant on Churchill and Stalin. *Realpolitik* is not for the faint of heart but that Churchill (of all men) should have had to keep mum about the Soviets' cold-blooded murder of 14,000 Polish officers in 1940 in the Katyn forest outside Smolensk in order to keep Stalin and the Russian army trained on defeating Hitler makes for grimly fascinating reading. Speaking of his relationship with Stalin, Churchill once said, "If my shirt were taken off now, it would be seen that my belly is sore from crawling to that man. I do it for the good of the country, and for no other reason." As Roberts remarks: "He felt the humiliation, and was widely criticized for it, especially when he shortly had to bully Britain's brave Polish allies over their post-war frontiers with Russia, but Britain needed the Soviet Union to continue to win huge victories before Operation Over-lord was launched in June." Eliot, incidentally, acted from something of the same motivation when, as a director of Faber & Faber he turned down George Orwell's savage satire on the Stalinist state, *Animal Farm* (1945).

If the historian Robert Rhodes James looked at Churchill's career before the Second World War and saw only failure, Roberts looks at the career in full and shows it to have been one in which failure and greatness went hand-in-hand. Roberts, in other words, has succeeded in showing his subject in all of his complexity and contradiction, and it is his critical sympathy that finds in these human qualities the stuff of greatness. In this regard, he has followed the painters Walter Sickert, Sir John Lavery, and, most strikingly, William Orpen, all of whose portraits of Churchill bring out his essential complexity. Churchill himself, after all, thought Orpen's portrait the most faithful ever done of him — an arresting preference considering the meditative doubt and vulnerability it depicts. But, then, Churchill was never averse to good critics. His delight in the acerbic Field Marshal Brooke, with whom he had so many titanic battles in laying out Britain's military strategy during the Second World War, is a case in point. "When I thump the table and put my face towards him what does he do? Thumps the table harder and glares back at me. I know these Brookes — stiff-backed Ulstermen and there's no one worse to deal with than that!" On nearly every page of Roberts's biography, instead of celebratory special pleading or mean-spirited detraction, one finds interpretative depth and richness. And that Roberts manages this with brisk effortlessness only shows that he has emulated Horace in exhibiting his art by concealing it.

Another proof of his artistry is the relentlessness with which he identifies the substantive and disposes of the merely malicious objections to his subject. No Churchill detractor has ever written so rigorously critical a book. Indeed, so unsparing are Roberts's strictures against his hero that it is difficult to imagine any future detractor mounting any attacks on Churchill that would match his exhaustive dossier. Of course, the misologists in the liberal academy will always fulminate against Churchill's political incorrectness, but their ability to enumerate his actual as opposed to his perceived flaws has now been blessedly obviated. In this regard, Roberts has taken Churchill's own distaste for whitewashing entirely to heart. "To do justice to a great man," Churchill once wrote, "discriminating criticism is necessary. Gush, however quenching, is always insipid."

Accordingly, the artist in Roberts shows that the misjudgments and miscalculations and simple weaknesses of the man were inseparable from his greatness. Failure, after all, is the crucible of greatness, without which it can never take shape, never free itself from the trammels of error. Churchill, Roberts shows, continually learned from his mistakes and was never averse to admitting them once they became patent. We all know the wonderful Churchillian gibe: "In the course of my life I have often had to eat my words, and I must confess that I have always found it a wholesome diet"; but few biographers have ever shown as compellingly as Roberts the good use to which Churchill put his lessons learned. As Roberts argues, "The Dardanelles catastrophe taught him not to overrule the Chiefs of Staff; the General Strike and Tonypandy taught him to leave industrial relations during the Second World War to Labour's Ernest Bevin; the Gold Standard disaster taught him to reflate and keep as much liquidity in the financial system as the exigencies of wartime would allow."

He also learned from others' failures. Whereas Asquith as Prime Minister during World War I delegated defense to, first, Fisher, and, then, Kitchener; and Lloyd George delegated the Somme and Passchendaele to Haig, with disastrous results, Churchill was shrewd enough to take control of both the premiership and defense. The daily task of winning the war, in other words, would not be delegated—a hard-and-fast principle with which Clement Atlee, Churchill's coalition partner, entirely agreed. "My own experience of the First World War, and my readings in history," Atlee wrote after the war, as Roberts points out, "had convinced me that the Prime Minister should be a man who knew what war meant, in terms of the personal suffering of the man in the line, in terms of high strategy, and in terms of that crucial issue—how the generals got on with their civilian bosses."

That Churchill had spent time in the trenches in France with the Royal Scots Fusiliers to expiate his role in the failure of the Gallipoli campaign certainly made him aware of the sufferings of the man in the line. Moreover, he had worked closely enough with generals and admirals in the First World War to ensure their respect, if not their inveterate agreement. As for his strategic smarts, he clearly recognized how crucial enlisting Roosevelt and the Americans in the war would be to winning it; what he dubbed the "special relationship," before and after Russia entered the war, would always be the lynchpin of victory. Indeed, no one would have relished this passage from Vera Brittain's classic account of her stint as a nurse during the Great War, *Testament of Youth* (1933) more than Churchill:

> I was leaving quarters to go back to my ward, when I had to wait to
> let a large contingent of troops march past me along the main road
> that ran through our camp. They were swinging rapidly towards

Camiers, and though the sight of soldiers marching was now too familiar to arouse curiosity, an unusual quality of bold vigour in their swift stride caused me to stare at them with puzzled interest. They looked larger than ordinary men; their tall, straight figures were in vivid contrast to the under-sized armies of pale recruits to which we had grown accustomed. At first I thought their spruce, clean uniforms were those of officers, yet obviously they could not be officers, for there were too many of them; they seemed, as it were, Tommies in heaven. Had yet another regiment been conjured out of our depleted Dominions? I wondered, watching them move with such rhythm, such dignity, such serene consciousness of self-respect. But I knew the colonial troops so well, and these were different; they were assured where the Australians were aggressive, self-possessed where the New Zealanders were turbulent. Then I heard an excited exclamation from a group of Sisters behind me. "Look! Look! Here are the Americans!" I pressed forward with the others to watch the United States physically entering the War, so god-like, so magnificent, so splendidly unimpaired in comparison with the tired, nerve-racked men of the British Army. So these were our deliverers at last, marching up the road to Camiers in the spring sunshine!

Churchill, as Robert shows, also learned from his successes: "The Great War cryptographic breakthroughs of the Admiralty's Room 40 taught him to back Alan Turing and the Ultra cryptanalysts; the anti-U-boat campaign of 1917 taught him the advantages of the convoy system; his advocacy of the tank encouraged him to promote the invention of new weaponry, pioneered by General Hobart and the MI(R) Directorate." As Roberts dryly observes: "He had long understood the superiority of the Mauser over the spear."

Good jokes of this sort abound in the book. When Paul Reynaud, the French prime minister before the Fall of France asked what would happen when the Germans attempted to invade Britain, Churchill replied, "I haven't thought that out very carefully, but, broadly speaking, I should propose to drown as many as possible of them on the way over, and then *"frapper sur la tête"* [knock on the head] anyone who managed to crawl ashore." When the postwar outcry for more social welfare was at its height, the Tory Democrat in Churchill was categorical: "You must rank me and my colleagues as strong partisans of national compulsory insurance for all classes for all purposes from the cradle to the grave," he insisted, though he added that everyone should work, "whether they come from the ancient aristocracy or the modern plutocracy, or the ordinary type of pub-crawler."

As for Churchill the man, Roberts shows that he was more a Regency than a Victorian figure. Certainly, his drinking recalls that bibulous age. When he told a friend that "The secret of drinking was always to drink a little too much all the time," he might have been speaking from the pages of Thomas Creevey, the Regency diarist, who chronicled the bacchanal intake of such heroic topers as the Prince of Wales and Richard Brinsley Sheridan. Churchill and his boon companion F. E. Smith would have fit perfectly in that rackety world, though Churchill, unlike Smith, was never the worse for wear for the champagne, wine, whisky and soda, port and brandy that were often his quotidian tipples. Indeed, when Smith tried to lay off the hard stuff, Churchill was notably supportive, telling his wife Clementine: "He drinks cider & ginger pop & looks ten years younger. Don't make a mock of this. He looks sad." As John Campbell's magnificent biography of Smith shows, he was one of the few men whose brilliance could match Churchill's own, though cirrhosis of the liver sent him to an early grave at fifty-eight. Another of Churchill's atavistic traits was his penchant for weeping, something he shared with such Regency figures as Pitt the Younger and Cardinal Newman. If he had a tough skin when it came to criticism, he was a pushover whenever his feelings were engaged.

Roberts shows again and again the quality of Churchill's feeling, which was rarely self-indulgent or merely sentimental. A good example is when he went to Bristol to bestow honorary degrees after air raids had killed or wounded several hundred people in the city. Jock Colville, Churchill's private secretary, recalled how the prime minister and his party "walked and motored through devastation such as I had never thought possible." Yet the bombed-out houses had Union Jacks flying in them, and when the people of Bristol gathered round Churchill they waved and cheered. Throughout the ordeal, Colville recalled, Churchill "kept murmuring to himself "Wonderful people … wonderful people.'" Afterwards, he addressed the Bristoleans through what one eyewitness recalled as "angry tears":

> I go about the country whenever I can escape for a few hours or for a day from my duty at headquarters, and I see the damage done by the enemy attacks; but I also see side by side with the devastation and amid the ruins, quiet, confident, bright, and smiling eyes, beaming with a consciousness of being associated with a cause far higher and wider than any human or personal issue. I see the spirit of an unconquerable people. I see a spirit bred in freedom, nursed in a tradition which has come down to us through the centuries, and which will surely at this moment, this turning-point in the history of the world, enable us to bear our part in such a way that none of our race who come after us will have any reason to cast reproach upon their sires.

When the Oxford Union recently debated the proposition whether "Britain should be ashamed of Winston Churchill," some in the audience might have recalled these words with shame of another sort. Since critics of the imperial Churchill are often fond of comparing him unfavorably to Mahatma Gandhi, it is useful to have Roberts quote what the least coherent critic of the Raj had to say to the British during the London Blitz: "Invite Hitler and Mussolini to take what they want of the countries you call your possessions," Gandhi wrote. "Let them take possession of your beautiful island with its many beautiful buildings. You will give all this, but neither your minds nor your souls."

Although the Tory Establishment, not to mention their Liberal and Labour colleagues, often chose to regard Churchill as a throwback to an irrecoverable past, he was much more forward-looking, indeed, prescient than he was ever given credit for being. We need only revisit the 1930s, when England, still reeling from the Great War, could not bring herself to face the growing Nazi threat. A good specimen of the country's settled aversion to war—indeed, to preparing to prevent war—can be gleaned from the conclusion of Veronica Wedgwood's highly acclaimed history at the time, *The Thirty Years War* (1938), in which she could almost have been acting as Neville Chamberlain's ventriloquist. "The war solved no problem," she wrote in her memorable conclusion.

> Its effects, both immediate and indirect, were either negative or disastrous. Morally subversive, economically destructive, socially degrading, confused in its causes, devious in its course, futile in its result, it is the outstanding example in European conflict of meaningless conflict. The overwhelming majority in Europe, the overwhelming majority in Germany, wanted no war ... They wanted peace and they fought for thirty years to be sure of it. They did not learn then, and have not since, that war breeds only war.

Here was the Munich mentality in all of its delusive moral vanity. Opposing it made Churchill enormously unpopular, especially with the country's political class. Yet unlike so many in public life, Churchill never flinched from unpopularity when principle was at stake. In light of his subject's striking integrity when it came to the defense of liberty, Roberts has taken pains to fill this biography, as he did his earlier one on the Victorian premier, Lord Salisbury, with choice precepts, and here he quotes from one of the speeches Churchill gave around the time of Munich that should be required reading not only for England's parliamentarians but ours as well.

> What is the use of Parliament if it is not the place where true statements can be brought before the people? What is the use of sending Members to the House of Commons who say just the popular things of the moment, and merely endeavour to give satisfaction to the Government Whips by cheering loudly every Ministerial platitude, and by walking through the Lobbies oblivious of the criticisms they hear? People talk about our Parliamentary institutions and Parliamentary democracy; but if these are to survive, it will not be because the Constituencies return tame, docile, subservient Members, and try to stamp out every form of independent judgment.

By sharing quotes like this with his readers, Roberts shows that he writes as a man of action, who knows the stakes of action. Indeed, one of his epigraphs makes this plain. As Churchill told guests of a luncheon in Westminster Hall in 1955: "Study history, study history. In history lie all the secrets of statecraft." No one's books exemplify the wisdom of this exhortation better than those of Andrew Roberts. To borrow a phrase that Gladstone used of Burke, they are magazines of such wisdom.

Churchill's wonderful appeal to the sense of integrity in his political colleagues notwithstanding, when Hitler reneged on the Munich agreement, and war finally became unavoidable, the pro-appeasement Tory Establishment only acknowledged Churchill's prescience with the utmost reluctance. After war was declared, the bastions of that Establishment—the House of Lords and the Carleton Club—still resounded with criticism of Churchill, and this for a reason that Roberts nicely pinpoints: "That the majority of Conservatives had been so spectacularly wrong about Hitler was not going to lessen their antagonism to him; indeed, it might have made it worse." Roberts quotes the appeaser Rab Butler to give his readers a good sampling of just how virulent the contempt for Churchill was amongst his Tory colleagues. At a drinks party after Churchill's accession, Butler remarked:

> The good clean tradition of English politics, that of [William] Pitt [the Younger] as opposed to [Charles James] Fox, had been sold to the greatest adventurer of modern political history. He had tried earnestly and long to persuade Halifax to accept the Premiership, but he had failed. He believed this sudden coup of Winston and his rabble was a serious disaster and an unnecessary one: "the pass had been sold" —by Chamberlain, Halifax and Oliver Stanley. They had weakly surrendered to a half-breed American.

While such opposition from his own party might have disheartened lesser men, it buoyed Churchill. After all, he had been making converts of naysayers all his life (with the notable exception of his father, the mercurial, unstable, brilliant Lord Randolph, who went to his grave never really seeing the point of his gifted son). Once Churchill became prime minister on 10 May 1940, he set about winning the war that his Tory colleagues had refused to allow him to prevent with a certain bellicose gaiety. "You do your worst," he taunted the Nazis, "and we will do our best." Certainly, as Roberts relates, he came to his post with unusual advantages.

> Hitler's attack turned Churchill's perceived weaknesses into priceless assets almost overnight. His obvious interest in warfare was no longer warmongering, it was invaluable. His oratorical style, which many had derided as ham-acting, was sublime now that the situation matched his rhetoric. His obsession with the Empire would help to bind its peoples together as it came under unimaginable stress, and his chauvinism left him certain that, if they could

get through the present crisis, the British would prevail over the Germans. Even his inability to fit comfortably into any political party was invaluable in the leader of a government of national unity.

When the historian in Churchill recalled his assumption of the premiership on that Friday in May, the artist in him commemorated the event in words that even the fastidious literary critic in Eliot could not have but admired. They remain some of the most moving words in all the English language. "I felt as if I were walking with destiny," Churchill wrote, "and that all my past life had been but a preparation for this hour and for this trial … I could not be reproached either for making the war or with want of preparation for it. I thought I knew a good deal about it all, and I was sure I should not fail."

In a piece entitled, "The Literature of Politics" (1955), T. S. Eliot reminded his readers that the "question of questions" with which the writer charged with making sense of politics must ultimately concern himself was this: "What is Man? what are his limitations? what is his misery and what his greatness? And what, finally, his destiny?" The artist in Roberts has written the best of all one-volume biographies of Churchill by showing that it was precisely Churchill's readiness to walk with destiny—to cooperate with it, to embody it—that made him understand very profoundly indeed, when the liberty of all Europe hung in the balance, what made for the limitations and the misery and the greatness of man.

Andrew Roberts's *Churchill: Walking with Destiny* exhibits not only an historian but an artist working at the very top of his form. It is impossible to praise too highly.

The Bantam Cock: Newman's Pugnacious Protégé

Thomas William Allies: "A Soul Temper'd with Fire", Michael Trott (Gracewing). 468 pages.

I

In 1876, apropos married Anglican priests keen on converting to Catholicism but held back by England's treatment of defectors from the Established Church as pariahs and the Church of Rome not knowing what to do with such converts, John Henry Newman spoke of how vital it was to find "some means of drawing to us so many good people, who are now shivering at our gates." Before Pope Benedict XVI established the Ordinariate in 2009, no such means had been found. Anglican priests who converted were left to shift for themselves. Some lived in want. Most kept body and soul together only by heroic struggle. Of these the most extraordinary was Thomas William Allies, who converted in 1850 after the Gorham Judgment and went on to play a pivotal role in securing Catholic education for England's Catholic schoolchildren, as well as writing wonderfully acerbic polemics and church history.

He also became an erudite defender of the Holy See when Ultramontanism was first taking shape. The sham authority of King Henry VIII's Royal Supremacy (1534) gave him a passionate taste for the genuine article. For Allies, the Holy Apostolical See was "a power, the operation of which extends over all times and climes from the day of Pentecost to the day of final judgment." Here was no summer convert. One of the more admirable aspects of the man was the pertinacity with which he remained true to the respect for authority that impelled him to convert to the Church in the first place, an authority which we also crave at a time when our synodal friends in Germany are taking sledgehammers to the magisterial Faith, not to mention the moral law.

Whenever Allies gives expression to his Ultramontane convictions, it is to urge his contemporaries to look beyond the National Church's episcopal pretensions. What was in place, we often hear him asking his readers in his controversial pieces, before the peculiar spectacle of "Queen Victoria bestowing spiritual jurisdiction on her Bishops in Europe, Asia, Africa, America, and Australia?" The answer Allies gives is of a categorical clarity.

> In the fifteen centuries which preceded Henry VIII's seizure of spiritual jurisdiction, the Church of God had appeared before the whole world as a body corporate, stretching by her episcopate, one and undivided, through all lands, both within and without the Roman empire, which was her first nursery-ground. Therein she grew amid persecution, sometimes intermitted in practice, never surrendered in principle, for two hundred and eighty-three years from the day of Pentecost to the peace of Constantino in A.D. 312. Assuredly, during that time, the State of imperial Rome—which thwarted her when it did not actively attack her—bestowed on her no mission, no jurisdiction. That mission came forth full and unfettered from the mouth of our Lord, not to Kings and civil rulers of nations, but to Apostles, as in the words, " Go and make disciples all nations," and, "Behold, I am with you all days, even to the consummation of the world"; and to the Prince of the Apostles in the presence of his brethren, "Feed My sheep," for this is the fulfilment of the promise, "To thee will I give the keys of the kingdom of heaven." That glorious martyrdom of three hundred years won, by a miraculous perseverance, a foundation of independence for the Church which should never fail.

Now when the Holy See finds itself in Erastian captivity, these elemental truths might seem dubious, but I would argue that one reason why Allies is worth reading is that he encourages us to recognize that no Erastianism, however cunning or impudent, unconscionable or destructive, can ever prevail against the Church Militant.

In *Thomas William Allies: "A Soul Temper'd with Fire"* Michael Trott has written a fascinating life of the unbiddable convert, which is as much a study of conversion as it is of failure. No one can read the book without remembering those useful words that Newman wrote about his own attitude to failure when his friend Lord Braye, an old Etonian and Christ Church man, who had converted in 1868 and went on to become Lieutenant Colonel of the Leicestershire Regiment during the South African War, complained of not accomplishing enough. "Your case is mine," Newman wrote.

> It is for years beyond numbering—in one view of the matter for these 50 years—that I have been crying out "I have laboured in vain, I have spent my strength without cause and in vain: wherefore my judgment is with the Lord, and my work with my God." Now at the end of my days, when the next world is close upon me, I am recognized at last at Rome. Don't suppose I am dreaming of com-

plaint—just the contrary. The Prophet's words, which expressed my keen pain, brought, because they were his words, my consolation. It is the rule of God's Providence that we should succeed by failure; and my moral is, as addressed to you, Doubt not that He will use you—be brave—have faith in His love for you—His everlasting love—and love Him from the certainty that He loves you.

The highest compliment that one could pay Trott's book is that it honors Newman's pastoral understanding of failure by meticulously attending to Allies's failure—not complete failure but failure enough for the spiritual success that Newman had in mind. Here is a book that anyone interested in Newman, the English Church, conversion, Ultramontanism, Catholic education or the misadventures of Erastianism will find riveting. Full of bitter wit, out-of-the-way archival learning and instructive tough-mindedness, it extenuates neither the sacrifices nor the frustrations Allies endured to defend a vision of the Church that is as worth considering today as it was over a hundred years ago. Yes, it is a vision that left many Catholics and Anglicans of his own day unpersuaded or indifferent. It is a vision that requires readers to contemplate what Newman called "God's Particular Providence" in ways that will necessarily baffle their notions of historical contingency. But it also won the ardent approval not only of Leo XIII, that most dynamic and discriminating of popes, but Cardinal Vaughan, who, after reading Allies's multi-volume *The Formation of Christendom*, deemed it "one of the noblest historical works" he had ever read. By presenting Allies without special pleading—indeed, at times, Trott is as impatient with his subject as many of his contemporaries were—he gives us as true a portrait of the man as we are likely to get. As we all know, there are few good books on Newman and his many friends but this, decidedly, is one of them.

II

Thomas William Allies (1813–1903), was born at Midsomer Norton, Somerset, the son of Thomas Allies, curate of Henbury, Bristol, and later rector of Wormington, and his wife, Frances Elizabeth Fripp, daughter of a Bristol merchant—the same independent-minded merchants who gave Edmund Burke so much trouble. Allies's mother died a week after his birth, and he was brought up by his father's second wife, Caroline Hillhouse. After attending the grammar school in Bristol, he entered Eton College in 1827, where he would win the first Newcastle scholarship. He entered Wadham College in 1828, where he was exhibitioner in 1830–3. Graduating BA with a first class in classics in 1832, he proceeded to obtain his MA in 1837, and was fellow from 1833 until 1841.

Entering the Anglican ministry the following year, Allies became a Tractarian under the influence of Newman's friend William Dodsworth, who would later follow him into the Catholic Church after the Gorham ruling. From 1840 to 1842 he was examining chaplain to Bishop Blomfield, who recoiled from his subordinate's Romish tendencies. If Allies's pugnacity, small stature and dapper dress won him the nickname of "Bantam Cock" among his amused friends, they annoyed his superiors. In 1842, Blomfield gave way to his own annoyance by giving Allies the meagre living of Launton, near Bicester.

In 1840 Allies married Eliza Hall Newman, the sister of a fellow Oxford student. Allies and his wife had five sons and two daughters. In June 1842, Allies first met Newman, of whom he would always remain deeply fond. It is true that Allies occasionally exasperated the otherwise forbearing Oratorian, but this was mostly attributable to the historian taking historical positions with which Newman could not agree. Allies, for instance, argued that there was something worth emulating in what he imagined the palmy relations between Church and State in the Middle Ages. No, Newman objected, the Church had had no golden age. Her apostolate was always with a radically fallen world. "The world is one of our three deadly enemies," Newman reminded his friend; "Did it cease to be so in the Middle Ages?"

Allies's doubts regarding the validity of the Established Church were intensified while traveling in France between 1845 and 1847 in the company of John Hungerford Pollen, the architect whose beautiful University Church on St. Stephen's Green remains a standing rebuke to the apostate Irish. When Allies published these doubts in his *Journal in France* (1848), Samuel "Soapy" Wilberforce, the epitome of the Broad Church, took predictable offense.

In 1850, having made a detailed study of the Fathers, especially Suárez's *De erroribus sectae Anglicanae*, Allies's attachment to the Established Church began to crack. For Allies, as for Newman, to be deep in history was to cease to be a Protestant. Then, again, his revulsion from the Privy Counsel's ruling on the Gorham matter regarding baptismal regeneration only reinforced his conviction that the Erastian National Church was not only schismatic but heretical, a conviction which echoed Newman's reading of the same ruling in his brilliant *Anglican Difficulties* (1850). After all, both men began their lives invested in defending the Anglican church that they would subsequently disavow.

Trott, for some reason, makes no mention of *Anglican Difficulties*, an odd omission considering how indicative it is of the shared objections that Newman and Allies had to the National Church and the Anglo-Catholics who chose to remain within its pale. Indeed, Trott holds that the *Grammar of Assent* (1870) is Newman's masterpiece, while I would give that distinction to *Anglican Difficulties*. Certainly, in the lectures Newman gave in King William Street one can see not only the apologist and historian but the satirist in Newman at the very top of their form. No more witty trouncing of the theological, historical, and intellectual claims of English Protestantism has ever been written. This is doubtless why Pusey and Keble ignored it. Indeed, this is why they ignored Allies's *Royal Supremacy* (1850). "Dr. Pusey never could be brought to face the question," Allies wrote. Instead, he "preserved silence on [the] subject, a silence which I venture to think more significant than any defiance could have been. Clearly, the subject would not bear touching but perhaps it might be *ignored*." A whole history of Anglicanism could be written based on that one *bon mot*.

Allies, to his credit, never ignored the bogus foundation on which Anglicanism was reared, though seeing the National Church for what it was caused him "intense consternation," revealing as it did "a state of things which took away from him all power from that moment any longer to defend the religious community in which he had been born and bred, and with which all his hopes of prosperity in life were inextricably blended."

In *Royal Supremacy*, Allies first exhibited his considerable polemical skills. It should be required reading for Cardinal Kasper and Cardinal Ouellet and anyone else in the Catholic swim who imagines Anglicanism compatible with Catholic Truth. As Allies himself said of the book, which he included in his omnibus, *Per Crucem ad Lucem* (1903):

> The second treatise in this volume was composed by the writer some months later in the same year, 1850, when he was still a beneficed clergyman in the Church of England, but expressly to exhibit the grounds on which he felt that he was obliged to surrender that position. This occasion of it is very distinctly stated in the Preface to it, which ends with the words, "My last act as an Anglican, and my last duty to Anglicanism, is to set forth, as I do in the following pamphlet, what has induced me to leave it." In fact, the writer could not but feel that, having thus given up five years of his life to the consideration of one question so paramount in his eyes that all thoughts, studies, and prayers were directed to the solution of it, and having published in two editions a defence of the Church of England from the charge of schism, he was bound, when he had discovered that his defence was entirely beside the mark, to avow the change of conviction, and to publish also those proofs which had had so great an effect on his own mind as to tear him up by the roots from the community in which he had lived to middle age, and transplant him into another soil.

Here, one can see, how deeply Newmanian Allies was, which is perhaps one reason why Newman was so often critical of him. Yes, as he told Archbishop Cullen in Dublin: Allies was a good scholar and published author and "would be invaluable as Greek Professor, or Latin, or Professor of Ancient History or Modern, or of Metaphysics." Yet there was another qualification that especially impressed Newman: "He is a person I value very much, and take great interest in, from the painful difficulties in which he is at present." Allies suffered profoundly as the result of his conversion—after all, like Newman himself, he was a man of talent, who could not be expected to take kindly to the mortifications of failure—and it was precisely this that most endeared him to the convert in Newman. When Newman told Allies not to complain of his suffering and simply get on with the job at hand, he might almost have been remonstrating with himself.

While Allies complained to Newman that he was too indulgent to such liberal Catholics as Lord Acton and Richard Simpson, Newman reassured him that he did so only to keep them in the fold; and, in any case, as he said, "I have … spoken out my mind to you with a freedom which I have never used towards them." Sensibly, Newman kept up good relations with both the Ultramontane and the Liberal Catholic camps, not wishing to engage in the sort of unseemly acrimony to which Kipling adverted when he recalled Walter Besant, the slum novelist telling him not to pick sides in the literary brawls of the Savile Club, where things "could get like a girls' school where they stick out their tongues at each other when they pass."

In October 1850 Allies resigned his Launton living and joined the Church of Rome, following his wife, who had taken the final step five months previously—proof that the Bristol merchant's daughter had no shortage of courage. Once in the No-Man's-Land of nineteenth-century Catholic England, Allies found himself stripped of all his former station. When he had no choice but to move to London's inelegant Golden Square, he was even forced to take in pupils. Soon thereafter, he had to move still again to The Priory, 21 North Bank, St John's Wood—later the residence of the bohemian George Eliot. Trott chronicles the mental suffering that accompanied Allies's impecunious removals by quoting from his diaries:

> During the past month I have suffered at times extreme depression of spirits; the root of this is always the same—the utter destitution of my temporal fortunes, and the hopelessness of the prospect, as if the rest of my life was to be heaping up sand hillocks by the sea-shore. The grievance is that I long to study, to produce some work for the glory of God, and I am condemned to the most anxious thoughts as to what I shall eat and what I shall drink, wherewithal I shall be clothed I and mine, and to the drudgery of teaching dunces. It is a terrible trial certainly, and has been upon me with the weight of a mountain for three years now, and in anticipation long before.

Despite these tribulations, Allies was resourceful enough—and faithful enough—to carve out a separate career for himself as an advocate for Catholic education. If he was averse to teaching other people's children, ʒe was keen on having his own children taught properly, especially since ʒe recognized, as he said, that "there is not ... a convert of Oxford or ʒambridge who is not forced into feeling ... despair and disgust at the ʒondition of scientific teaching among us, compared with that existing at ʒhe best Protestant schools."

From August 1853 until his retirement on a pension in 1890 he was secretary of the Catholic Poor School Committee. In addition, he had a decisive hand in the founding of the Notre Dame Training College, Liverpool, in 1855; the Sacred Heart Training College for Women, Wandsworth, in 1874; and St Mary's Training College for Men at Hammersmith—which would go on to become present day, St. Mary's in Twickenham at Strawberry Hill.

As honorary secretary of the Education Crisis Fund (1870–3), he proved a good fundraiser, wringing £50,000 (£100,000 in today's money) out of Catholic London to enable English Catholics to meet the demands of the 1870 Education Act. There is naturally much in Trott's book about Allies's genteel poverty when he was attempting, with strenuous futility, to launch himself as a gentleman scholar, but thanks to his advocacy for Catholic education—effective advocacy—he still managed to leave £39,359 in the bank when he handed in his dinner pail.

In 1855, Newman prevailed upon a reluctant Archbishop Cullen to allow him to appoint the English scholar the first Professor of Modern History at the Catholic University of Ireland, though it might have been providential that lack of interest on the part of students led to his giving only one lecture. When John Butler Yeats learned that his son the poet had been passed over for what might have been a well-paying professorship at Trinity College Dublin, he was unconcerned, knowing he had given "a voice to the sea cliffs." Allies was similarly better off outside the academy, even Newman's academy.

In all events, such indifference would prefigure the reading public's indifference to Allies's written work throughout his life, despite the encomia of such Catholic papers as The Dublin Review and The Month, though I would argue that there are still things in Allies's work that merit revisiting.

For instance, Allies's proposed course of lectures lay the groundwork for his *The Formation of Christendom* (8 vols., 1865–95), which the old DNB justly describes as a "work [which] trenchantly expounds the predominance in history of the see of Peter." Newman dismissed it, telling one correspondent: "it is a thousand pities that a clever man like Allies should sermonize in the way he does. We are reading him in the Refectory—and he always seems in the same place, prancing like a cavalry soldier's horse, without advancing, in the face of a mob." However, Cardinal Vaughan was nearer the mark: "If any man wishes to ennoble his own estimate of the Catholic Church let him read this book. If any man's soul is capable of rising to a lofty idea of life, let him understand the part that Christ has taken (and is still taking) in the formation of Christendom, as is shown from trustworthy sources by the pen of Mr. Allies." In the book, to take just one example bearing out Vaughan's praise, Allies speaks of the providential part God took in the world with respect to marriage, a subject about which Melanie McDonagh is brilliant in the *Spectator* (10 August 2022). Looking out at the fallen world that was so often content to ignore him, Allies writes:

> Over these unrecorded years of human life, which want their prophet and their bard, sounds yet the echo of perpetual strife. If mighty forms loom among their obscurity, and come out at length with fixed character and a strong and high civilisation, such as the Assyrian and Egyptian, the Indian and Chinese monarchies, and so many others of more or less extent and renown, we know that states have suffered change after change in a series of wars. The patriarchal ruler has given way to the conquering chief; conquest has humiliated some and exalted others. What remains intact in each country, and after all changes, is government itself. This carried on the human race.

Most readers would agree with this rudimentary division between barbarism and civilization. "But if we examine more closely this race which is thus scattered through all countries," Allies writes, "which speaks innumerable tongues, has lost the sense of its own brotherhood, worships a multitude of local gods, is divided, cut up, formed again, and torn again with innumerable wars, and has degraded a large part of itself into servitude, so as to lose as it would seem all semblance of its original unity, we yet find running through it, existing from the beginning as constituent principles which the hand of the Creator has set in it, four great goods," one of which is marriage. And here he descants on the very institution that we in our own accelerating barbarism have so tragically forsaken.

> For what hand but that of the Creator could have impressed ineffaceably upon a race, misusing as we have seen to such a degree the faculty of free-will, such an institution as marriage, in which the family, and all which descends from the family, is contained? The dedication of one man and one woman to each other for the term of their lives, for the nurture and education of the family which is to spring from them, is indeed the basis of human society, but a basis which none but its Maker could lay. It exists in perpetual contradiction to human passion and selfishness, for purposes which wisdom or the pure reason of man entirely approves, but which human frailty is at any time ready to break through and elude. If we could so entirely abstract ourselves from habit as to imagine a company of men and women thrown together, without connection with each other, without any knowledge, any conception beforehand of such an institution, and left to form their society for themselves, we

should not, I think, imagine them one and all choosing to engage themselves in such a union, resigning, respectively, their liberty, and binding themselves to continue, whatever might happen to either party, however strength and vigour might decline on one side, or grace and attractiveness on the other, in this bondage for life. Yet this institution of marriage is found established, not in a single company of human beings, but in a thousand societies of men separated by place, by language, by religion, and by government. The most highly policied among them are the strictest in maintaining its purity; and the higher you are enabled by existing records to ascend in their history, the stronger and clearer appears the conception of the duties of the married state. It is surrounded with all the veneration which laws can give it, and the blessing of religion consecrates it. Take marriage among the Romans as an instance. Their commonwealth seems to be built upon the sanctity of marriage and the power of the father. The like is the case with China, the most ancient of existing politics. There is not one nation which has gained renown or advanced in civilisation but shows, as far back as you can trace its history, this institution honoured and supported. I leave to mathematicians the task of calculating what are the chances of such an institution springing up in so great a multitude of nations according to an identical rule, guarded in all of them with whatever protection religion and law could afford, except by the fiat of a Creator in the manner described by Moses. The signet of God impressed on Adam at his origin could alone create such a mark on his race; the Maker alone lay such a foundation for it.

Allies had wanted, when a young man, to be a poet. He wrote a poet's prose. Yes, he was good at hurling polemical mud pies. He had the polemicist's hatred of cant and certainly he had much to rail against in the cant of the National Church. But he was also good at speaking of what was nearest his heart, especially when he spoke for all hearts zealous of what Dean Church called "the gifts of civilization" — which are always the gifts of God's Providence. Speaking of the gift of marriage, which helped to sustain him through so many of his trials, he concludes by saying:

> We find this institution in the course of time and in various countries debased by polygamy, and corrupted by concubinage. These aberrations testify to the force of human passion, and the wantonness of power and wealth ever warring against it, but they only enhance thereby the force of the institution's universal existence from the point of view from which I have regarded it.

We, too, can testify to "the force of the institution," though the challenges to its "universal existence" confronting us are a good deal more desperate and, indeed, diabolical than the polygamy and concubinage of Allies's nineteenth century. Still, the passage corroborates the high praise the book received from Vaughan, who rightly held that "No English work that I know exhibits the mission of the Church to the world, to the pagan world, to the civilized world, and I might add to the modern world … in a more eloquent, a more fascinating, or a more convincing manner."

Apropos Allies the poet, I should quote from a long polemical poem that the author wrote for *The Month* in 1894, with the memorable title, "The Birth, Growth and Suicide of a Heresy," which Trott nicely sums up as showing how "The fruit of Protestantism was inner emptiness, the reality underlying the surface assurance of the Victorian Establishment."

> A church dissolved by its own children's blows
> Bears witness to the source from which it rose,
> And endless error's ever-growing fruit
> Betrays the deadly nature of the root.
> What is the gospel offered to the world
> By power whose teachings from strong fleets are hurl'd?
> Or what the picture of the inward mind
> Whose outward fortune dazzles all mankind?
> Bishops on gravest doctrine disagreed,
> Sects with no bishops, preachers with no creed;
> Synods which call themselves Pan-Anglican,
> And sit and speak, and vote belief in Pan:
> A general residuum undefin'd,
> Which, each specific lost, remains behind.
> This is the cost of blood and strife, and tears;
> The grand Eureka of three hundred years.

My only regret in reading this splendid savaging—a savaging worthy of Swift—is that I did not find space for it in *The Saint Mary's Book of Christian Verse*. It must go into the revised edition.

III

In 1885 Pope Leo XIII created Allies Knight Commander of St Gregory; in 1893 he awarded him the Gold Medal for Merit. In 1903, after a long period of declining health, Allies died at his home in St John's Wood and was buried beside his wife at St Mary Magdalene's, Mortlake. One of the most acute of the Oxford converts, he could never forget the cost of conversion; after all, it was its cost that gave his conversion its vitality. In October of 1885, he showed as much by confiding to his diary:

> Strongly impressed in the night with the false estimate of one's own standing in God's sight, which yearning after intellectual distinction produces. How can I get myself entirely to realise that mental power is of itself no guarantee whatever of Divine acceptance, as little as bodily beauty or material wealth. It seems to me that even now I

have not overthrown completely the idolatry in my heart, which quite engrossed me up to the age of twenty-four, and was the root, I think, of every sin and error.

Men of learning, let alone controversialists are not inveterately given to such sensible introspection. That Allies was is a mark in his favor. It is still more proof of the deep affinity he had with Newman, who once told another notable Ultramontane, W. G. Ward: "devotion and self rule are worth all the intellectual cultivation in the world."

Saint John Henry Cardinal Newman

Thinking Aloud

Essays Critical and Historical, Volume I, John Henry Newman, Newman Millennium Edition, volume XIII, edited by Andrew Nash (Gracewing). 570 pages.

When John Henry Newman published his two-volume *Essays Critical and Historical* in 1871, a collection he had written as an Anglican on topics ranging from rationalism and the American Episcopal Church to the liberal Anglican historian Henry Hart Milman and the catholicity of the Anglican Church, the *Dublin Review* ran a notice of the collection observing how

> Fr. Newman speaks very touchingly in his Preface of his past position ... that "from various circumstances he has been obliged through so many years to think aloud." We believe he is one of the extremely few men recorded in history, to whose reputation this circumstance will prove beneficial rather than injurious.

Andrew Nash, in his exemplary edition of the first volume of the essays for Gracewing's Millennium Edition of Newman's works, points out that while Newman explained that his motive for publishing the essays was, as he said, "to reduce what is uncatholic in them," he was nonetheless "far from defensive" about them, since they served, in part, to explain his eventual disillusionment with the Anglican Church. More specifically, since his choice to republish was made after his *Apologia pro Vita Sua* (1864) had regained him so many new Anglican readers, "his strategy behind the republication," as Nash notes, "was to influence this Anglican audience — to show them, as the *Apologia* had argued throughout, that his Tractarian principles led him to Rome and therefore should lead other Anglo-Catholics to Rome too." In this regard, Nash is right to suggest that the essays can be read as an appendix to the *Apologia*.

Yet, for Nash, what is most remarkable about the essays is "how consonant" they are "with [Newman's] later Catholic faith"; indeed, "his critique of ... Protestant Christianity ... now looks strikingly perceptive, even prophetic"; and the insight they offer into "the consistency of Newman's principles and the trajectory of their development" makes them of particular interest now, when Newman is so soon to be canonized.

In republishing the essays, Newman was also sharing with his readers something of the Anglican difficulties with which he had to struggle in order to embrace what he referred to as "the one true fold of the Redeemer." Once he had sorted these difficulties out, repudiated the Anglican ministry and entered the Catholic Church, he could reaffirm the objectivity of truth because he had personified it in his own self-sacrificing conversion. One can see the force of this objectivity in a letter that he wrote to Mrs. Froude, the wife of the man to whom he dedicated the collection (Hurrell Froude's brother, William), after the last of these Anglican essays had been written in 1844. "Surely," he wrote, "the *continuance* of a person who wishes to go right in a wrong system, and not his giving it up, would be that which militated against the objectiveness of Truth — leading to the suspicion that one thing and another were equally pleasing to our Maker, where men are sincere." In thus allowing himself to be shown thinking aloud, Newman could show that he had acted faithfully on his own long-held conviction, expressed so memorably in the speech he had given on being made a cardinal, that "Liberalism in religion is the doctrine that there is no positive truth in religion, but that one creed is as good as another," a doctrine "inconsistent with any recognition of any religion, as *true*."

Nash's point about the collection confirming the consistency of Newman's thought is borne out nicely by a passage in the essay entitled "Apostolical Tradition" (1836), in which Newman reviews a book of letters between an Anglican clergyman and his Unitarian brother. There, he has occasion to observe:

> We have said that the common ground, on which these disputants erect their arguments, admits of being used in behalf of error; but we must go further. Their first principle really is inconsistent with there being any certainties in Revelation whatever; for, if nothing is to be held as revealed but what every one perceives to be in Scripture, there is nothing that can be so held, considering that in matter of fact there is no universal agreement as to what Scripture teaches and what it does not teach: and why are one man's opinions to be ruled by the readings of another? The right which each man has of judging for himself *ipso facto* deprives him of the right of judging for other inquirers. He is bound to tolerate all other creeds by virtue of the very principle on which he claims to choose his own. Thus ultra-Protestantism infallibly leads to Latitudinarianism.

Of course, this confirms one of the grounds on which Newman took issue with liberalism — its affinity with infidelity — but it is also interesting to note that this passage is not found in the original text, which is content to describe the common ground on which the brothers argued thus:

> Both parties acquiesce in the fundamental position that truth of doctrine is to be gained from Scripture by each person for himself;

and here lies the πρῶτον ψεῦδος ["primary misapprehension"] of the controversy, which in consequence becomes a trial of strength between the two individuals.

Here, the gist of the two passages may be the same, but the more detailed rewrite from 1871 is considerably more compelling. Nonetheless, both passages entirely refute those tiresome detractors of Newman, who insist that his opposition to liberalism was neither coherent nor consistent.

II

Like most good writers with something to say close to their hearts, Newman is often autobiographical in these essays, albeit in an oblique way. For example, in his essay entitled "Poetry with Reference to Aristotle's Aesthetics" (1828), he praises the poet George Crabbe (a favorite of James Joyce) by calling attention to his *Tales of the Hall* (1819), which clearly puts the reader in mind of Newman's fraught relationship with his younger brother Charles, who, although brought up in the same Anglicanism as his brother, went on to embrace the utopian socialism of Robert Owen (1771–1858).

> In the writings of [Crabbe] there is much to offend a refined taste; but, at least in the work in question, there is much of a highly poetical cast. It is a representation of the action and reaction of two minds upon each other and upon the world around them. Two brothers of different characters and fortunes, and strangers to each other, meet. Their habits of mind, the formation of those habits by external circumstances, their respective media of judgment, their points of mutual attraction and repulsion, the mental position of each in relation to a variety of trifling phenomena of every-day nature and life, are beautifully developed in a series of tales moulded into a connected narrative. We are tempted to single out the fourth book, which gives an account of the childhood and education of the younger brother, and which for variety of thought as well as fidelity of description is in our judgment beyond praise. The Waverley Novels would afford us specimens of a similar excellence. One striking peculiarity of these tales is the author's practice of describing a group of characters bearing the same general features of mind, and placed in the same general circumstances; yet so contrasted with each other in minute differences of mental constitution, that each diverges from the common starting-point into a path peculiar to himself. The brotherhood of villains in Kenilworth, of knights in Ivanhoe, and of enthusiasts in Old Mortality, are instances of this.

Apropos this lively foray into literary criticism, Nash observes that it was included in a collection otherwise given over to theological issues because,

"For Newman, the poetical and the spiritual are the same thing." Indeed, in one passage in the essay, Newman says categorically, "With Christians, a poetical view of things is a duty—we are bid to colour all things with hues of faith, to see a Divine meaning in every event, and a superhuman tendency." Certainly, the historian in Newman saw how Gibbon's inability to enter into this fundamental reality disabled him from writing any reliable history of the rise of Christianity. Resolving to treat only of the external aspects of that rise and dismissing the deep spiritual longings to which Christianity appealed as superstitious or deluded fanaticism, Gibbon would have nothing to do with this "poetical view of things." Moreover, most Christian poets of his own time and indeed, of ours, would agree that it is of the essence of good poetry, as of good faith, "to see a Divine meaning" in events.

Another essay that confirms Newman's abiding opposition to liberalism is "On the Introduction of Rationalistic Principles into Revealed Religion" (1836), which began life as Tract 73 of the *Tracts of the Times*. Nash's textual appendix shows that Newman only revised the very opening of the piece; the rest he left untouched. What he added to the original text is a witty swipe not only at Thomas Erskine (1788–1870), the Scottish Episcopalian theologian, whose writings exude Socinianism, but James Fitzjames Stephen, the skeptical circuit court judge and *litterateur*, who had descended upon Newman at the Oratory in 1865 after abusing him in *Fraser's Magazine* for falling short of what the judge superciliously referred to as the "canon of proof." Newman's addition to the opening—a fair paraphrase of Stephen's reductionist faith—is worth quoting at length.

> That is, I cannot believe anything which I do not understand; therefore, true Christianity consists, not in "submitting in all things to God's authority," His written Word, whether it be obscure or not, but in understanding His acts. I must understand a scheme, if the Gospel is to do me any good; and such a scheme is the scheme of salvation. Such is the object of faith, the history of a series of divine actions, and nothing more; nothing more, for everything else is obscure; but this is clear, simple, compact. To preach this, is to preach the Gospel; not to apprehend it, is to be destitute of living faith. Of course I do not deny that Revelation contains a history of God's mercy to us; who can doubt it? I only say, that while it is this, it is something more also. Again, if by speaking of the Gospel as clear and intelligible, a man means to imply that this is the whole of it, then I answer, No; for it is also deep, and therefore necessarily mysterious. This is too often forgotten.

A passage from this same essay, which Newman left untouched, bears out Nash's claim that these Anglican essays often tally with Newman's later Catholic faith. The proponent of the necessary complementarity between faith and reason in Newman may have enriched our understanding of this essential element of Catholic orthodoxy in many of his Catholic writings, but, first, as a conscientious Anglican, he had to disentangle reason from rationalism, a disentangling for which those who wish to dispute the accuracy of Newman's opposition to liberalism have yet to account. If understanding any complex issue requires making precise distinctions where confusions might arise, no one was ever as adept at this as Newman. Here, one can see the true genius of the man.

> As regards Revealed Truth, it is not Rationalism to set about to ascertain, by the exercise of reason, what things are attainable by reason, and what are not; nor, in the absence of an express Revelation, to inquire into the truths of Religion, as they come to us by nature; nor to determine what proofs are necessary for the acceptance of a Revelation, if it be given; nor to reject a Revelation on the plea of insufficient proof; nor, after recognizing it as divine, to investigate the meaning of its declarations, and to interpret its language; nor to use its doctrines, as far as they can be fairly used, in inquiring into its divinity; nor to compare and connect them with our previous knowledge, with a view of making them parts of a whole; nor to bring them into dependence on each other, to trace their mutual relations, and to pursue them to their legitimate issues. This is not Rationalism; but it is Rationalism to accept the Revelation, and then to explain it away; to speak of it as the Word of God, and to treat it as the word of man; to refuse to let it speak for itself; to claim to be told the *why* and the *how* of God's dealings with us, as therein described, and to assign to Him a motive and a scope of our own; to stumble at the partial knowledge which He may give us of them; to put aside what is obscure, as if it had not been said at all; to accept one half of what has been told us, and not the other half; to assume that the contents of Revelation are also its proof; to frame some gratuitous hypothesis about them, and then to garble, gloss, and colour them, to trim, clip, pare away, and twist them, in order to bring them into conformity with the idea to which we have subjected them.

Nash's gloss on this important essay is perceptive: "Through Abbot [an American Congregationalist with whose rationalism Newman took issue] and Erskine, Newman is in fact fighting a theological battle with opponents nearer home such as R. D. Hampden and others of the Liberal school of theology within the Church of England." While there were many differences between these two groups—Erskine and Abbott being comparative lone wolfs, while Hampden had the support of liberal, anti-Tractarian Oxford behind him—both Abbott and Hampden sensibly fled the field after encountering Newman's polemical artillery, Abbott devoting himself to composing children's books and Hampden to tending to his garden.

One of the most perceptive—and eloquent—of the pieces here is Newman's essay on the American Episcopal Church, in which he sought to detect some signs of life at a time when he was beginning to despair of his own highly rarefied Anglicanism at home. His findings were hardly reassuring. "To tell the truth," he confessed, "we think one special enemy to which the American Church … lies open is the influence of a refined and covert Socinianism." As Newman so discerningly recognized, what the Americans wanted, especially those smug, moneyed Americans who made up the bulk of the Episcopal Church, was a religion "which neither irritates their reason nor interferes with their comfort." Why?

> Severity whether of creed or precept, high mysteries, corrective practices, subjection of whatever kind, whether to a doctrine or to a priest, will be offensive to them. They need nothing to fill the heart, to feed upon, or to live in; they despise enthusiasm, they abhor fanaticism, they persecute bigotry. They want only so much religion as will satisfy their natural perception of the propriety of being religious. Reason teaches them that utter disregard of their Maker is unbecoming, and they determine to be religious, not from love and fear, but from good sense.

Since the character and development of Newman's principles have been deliberately misrepresented by those who wish to appropriate him and his work to advance the neo-Modernism now undermining the doctrinal, sacramental, moral and liturgical integrity of the Church, Nash's elegant and discriminating edition will serve as a welcome reminder of the Servant of Truth in Newman.

Modernism, for those unfamiliar with the term, is a program of heterodoxy that seeks to conform the Church to the intellectual, moral and social aberrations of the modern world. After Pius X released his encyclical condemning Modernism, *Pascendi Dominici Gregis*, which he delivered on the Nativity of Our Lady in 1907, the Modernists responded by conceding that: "Our religious attitude is ruled by the single wish to be one with Christians and Catholics who live in harmony with the spirit of the age." The assiduous efforts of those within the present hierarchy to conform the Church to our own age's views on homosexuality, concubinage, and abortion will give readers a fair understanding of just how Modernist some of the hierarchy has become. When we refer to Newman's prescience, it is to this that we must ultimately refer, since Modernism, of its essence, is the apotheosis of rationalism.

For another instance of Newman's introducing autobiographical sidelights into his texts, readers can consult his essay here on St. Ignatius of Antioch (*c.* 50–98/117), written for the *British Critic* in January of 1839, which prefigures how the patristic scholar in Newman found the basis for his *Essay on the Development of Christian Doctrine* (1845) in the writings of the early Fathers. Newman always laid great stress on the need to bring a certain critical sympathy to one's study of Christ and His Church in order to understand them. He faults Gibbon severely for lacking this sympathy, even though he relished the historian's prose style. As Nash shows, he also faults himself for misreading the Fathers when he first encountered them. In this regard, his criticism recalls something from one of G. K. Chesterton's detective stories, "The White Pillars Murder," in which the shrewd detective Dr. Adrian Hyde observes: "Clumsy eavesdropping must be worse than the blind spying on the blind. You've not only got to know what is said, but what is meant. There's a lot of difference between listening and hearing."

III

Since the essay on St Ignatius abounds in fairly arcane references, Nash's notes are indispensable. Indeed, his annotations throughout the volume are enviably apt, combining as they do learning, precision, succinctness and wit. For example, after quoting a bishop in St. Ignatius's time saying of heretics, "I warn you against wild beasts in human form, whom you ought not only not to receive, but, if possible, not even to fall in with; only to pray for," Newman remarks:

> So speaks a bishop of the first century, — "wild beasts in human form"; have not such terms been done into English in the nineteenth by the words of "venerable men," men of "inoffensive," "uncontroversial" dispositions?

To which Nash appends the amusing note: "Newman is being ironic; these are the epithets given, by their supporters, to Anglican writers of liberal, unorthodox opinions."

With respect to a passage from Newman's finely satirical essay on Selina, Countess of Huntingdon (1707–91), whose evangelical Methodism still flourishes in England today, Nash shows what a self-deprecatory critic of his former Tractarian allegiances—especially his *via media*—Newman could be. In his essay, Newman writes of the disciples of the Countess trying to hector their countrymen into subscribing to what became known as "The Countess of Huntingdon's Connexion," a hectoring about which Newman dryly remarks:

> Here, if we mistake not, we see the meaning of the style of certain publications [i.e., the writings of the Tractarians], to which the last seven years have given birth, and which have been accused, though more so at first than now, of intemperance and harshness, of repelling people, instead of attracting them. We suspect their writers thought that the very first point to be secured in the controversy, was the inflicting upon all readers that theirs was a whole

positive consistent objective system, which had to be mastered, not one which men already partly held and partly not, and from which they might pick and choose as they pleased, but one which they had to approach, study, enter upon, and receive or reject, according to their best judgment. They wished it to be recognized as a creed.

Nash's gloss on this is marvelous: "Newman knows perfectly well what the writers thought, being one of them himself. His pose of the detached observer is thus ironic." If Newman's detractors obsess over what they imagine his *penchant* for self-vindication, Nash points, instead, to his delicate self-mockery, which is of a piece with the appeal of his intellectual honesty.

The most well-known of Newman's detractors, Frank Turner, the former Yale professor of history, asserted that Newman only claimed to oppose liberalism to ingratiate himself with Rome's theological conservatives: his real *bête noir* was Evangelicalism. Putting aside the derisory inaccuracy of such an assertion, we can see in Newman's essay on the Countess of Huntingdon that while he might have had certain core issues with Evangelicalism, he had a soft spot for Evangelicals. Of the Countess herself, he says:

> Lady Huntingdon ... sets Christians of all times an example. She devoted herself, her name, her means, her time, her thoughts, to the cause of Christ. She did not spend her money on herself; she did not allow the homage paid to her rank to remain with herself: she passed these on, and offered them up to Him from whom her gifts came. She acted as one ought to act who considered this life a pilgrimage, not a home, — like some holy nun, or professed ascetic, who had neither hopes nor fears of anything but what was divine and unseen.

Lastly, in his essay, "Prospects of the Anglican Church" (1839), Newman shows with what fair and dispassionate generosity he could view the Oxford Movement, another sign of how these essays heralded the retrospective *élan* of the *Apologia*:

> There will ever be a number of persons professing the opinions of a movement party, who talk loudly and strangely, do odd or fierce things, display themselves unnecessarily, and disgust other people; there will be ever those who are too young to be wise, too generous to be cautious, too warm to be sober, or too intellectual to be humble; — of whom human sagacity cannot determine, only the event, and perhaps not even that, whether they feel what they say, or how far: whether they are to be encouraged or discountenanced. Such persons will be very apt to attach themselves to particular persons, to use particular names, to say things merely because others say them, and to act in a party-spirited way ... There is no warrant, however, for supposing that the agents themselves in the

present revolution of religious sentiment partake in the fault we have been specifying; though, as is natural, it is the fashion to lay it at their door. It has been the fashion; though, in spite of a certain learned dignitary in the North, we hope it is a fashion going out, to accuse them of being simple Dominics, or men who contract their notion of religious truth to a narrow range of words, and would fain burn every one who scruples to accept it.

Nash's notes here are not only informative but funny. Apropos the "certain dignitary in the North," he points out, "As the 1839 text reveals, this was George Townsend (1788–1857), low church Anglican divine extremely hostile to the Oxford Movement … Strongly anti-Catholic, in 1850 he had an audience with Pope Pius IX and attempted to convert him to Protestantism." As for Newman's reference to "Dominics," Nash writes: "i.e. like St. Dominic (1170–1221), founder of the Order of Preachers, seen by Protestants as a fanatical heresy hunter." It is commentary like this that gives Nash's edition its sparkle.

In May of 1884, when he was 83 and feeling less than spry, Newman told a correspondent: "The weakness and stiffness of my fingers react upon my brain. I have thoughts and forget them, and lose my thread of argument and any vivid impression, before I can write it down. I never could think, never profitably meditate, without my pen and now that I cannot use it freely, I cannot use my mind." This melancholy state of affairs certainly did not obtain when Newman was writing the brilliant essays that adorn this first volume of *Essays Critical and Historical*, a thinking aloud made all the more fascinating by Andrew Nash's smart, incisive, revelatory editing.

St John Henry Newman's
Apologia Revisited

In 1864, in response to the novelist Charles Kingsley's allegation in *Macmillan's Magazine* that "Truth for its own sake was never a virtue with the Roman clergy" and that "Father Newman informs us that it need not be, and on the whole ought not to be," the great convert John Henry Newman (1801–90) wrote his *Apologia Pro Vita Sua* to defend his own and his coreligionists' veracity.

Twenty years earlier, Newman had been the Anglican Church's most influential churchman, a redoubtable preacher, polemicist and educator. W. E. Gladstone said that his influence at Oxford had been one "for which perhaps, there is no parallel in the academical history of Europe, unless you go back to the twelfth century or to the University of Paris."

However, in leading the Oxford Movement's efforts to rescue the National Church from its Erastian incoherence, Newman came to see Catholicism as the true faith. His study of the early Fathers opened his eyes to what he called "the One Truth Fold of the Redeemer." If Anglicans wished to imagine the Roman Church a corruption of the Primitive Church, Newman came to see the one as an ineluctable development of the other. History converted him.

In thus converting, Newman joined a faith that most Englishmen regarded as backward, superstitious, treacherous and irrational. The bookman Augustine Birrell (1850–1933) put this view memorably when he observed how: "It was common talk at one time to express astonishment at the extending influence of the Church of Rome, and to wonder how people who went about unaccompanied by keepers could submit their reason to the Papacy, with her open rupture with science and her evil historical reputation. From astonishment to contempt is but a step. We first open wide our eyes and then our mouths."

This was Kingsley's view as well, and once he impugned Newman and his fellow Catholics, he gave the convert the opening he needed not only to refute his assailant but to explain to his contemporaries why he had left everything in the world dear to him to join what he called "the One Fold of

Christ," entering into which was like "coming into port after a rough sea." His *Apologia* would be, at once, his defense and his self-portrait.

For so agile a controversialist as Newman, refuting Kingsley was child's play. One cannot read the book without coming away pitying the man whose ill-considered accusations inspired it. Newman demolishes Kingsley. The novelist George Eliot nicely attested to this when she observed: "I have been made so indignant by Kingsley's mixture of arrogance, coarse impertinence and unscrupulousness with real intellectual incompetence, that my first interest in Newman's answer arose from a wish to see what I consider thoroughly vicious writing thoroughly castigated. But the Apology now mainly affects me as the revelation of a life."

Eliot's last point was precisely what Newman intended his readers should see in his riposte to his unscrupulous accuser. After dreading the prospect of revisiting so much harrowing ground in his controversial life, Newman resolved on what would be the book's governing principle. "I recognized what I had to do," he wrote, "though I shrank from both the task and the exposure which it would entail. I must ... give the true key to my whole life; I must show what I am, that it may be seen what I am not, and that the phantom may be extinguished which gibbers instead of me. I wish to be known as a living man, and not as a scarecrow which is dressed up in my clothes."

What makes the *Apology* such an extraordinary book is that it furnishes the "key" to the author's "whole life" not by mining the usual autobiographical quarries of family, childhood and education but by focusing on his evolving religious convictions, which, far from being deceitful or rote, were of the most guileless probity. With no confessional exhibitionism or unseemly volubility, Newman wrote the history of how his avid and exacting faith took shape in a book that merits comparison with perhaps the greatest of all Christian autobiographies, St. Augustine's *Confessions*.

Indeed, he wrote his account, partly, as he said, for "religious and sincere minds, who are simply perplexed ... by the utter confusion into which late discoveries or speculations have thrown their most elementary ideas of religion." And it was on their behalf that he invoked those "beautiful words," as he called them, of the Bishop of Hippo, who knew from bitter personal experience "the difficulty with which error is discriminated from truth, and the way of life is found amid the illusions of the world."

Some literary genius only comes of religious genius, and, Newman, like St. Paul, possessed it *in excelsis*. His *Apologia* captures this genius in all of its depth and incandescence. Indeed, in some of the greatest prose in all of English literature, prose which influenced G. K. Chesterton, Ronald Knox, Graham Greene, and Muriel Spark, Newman succeeded in showing his readers that it was not imposture that animated his conversion, but love.

Since Newman, before and after converting, served the Truth, regardless of the pressures put on him to sidestep or repudiate it, we can also see the principle of veracity in his conversion. Indeed, at the very end of the *Apologia*, he confirms this in the most unambiguous terms possible.

> To one other authority I appeal on this subject, which commands from me attention of a special kind, for it is the teaching of a Father. It will serve to bring my work to a conclusion.
>
> "St. Philip," in the words of the Roman Oratorian who wrote his Life, "had a particular dislike of affectation both in himself and others, in speaking, in dressing, or in any thing else.
>
> "He avoided all ceremony which savoured of worldly compliment, and always showed himself a great stickler for Christian simplicity in every thing; so that, when he had to deal with men of worldly prudence, he did not very readily accommodate himself to them.
>
> "And he avoided, as much as possible, having any thing to do with *two-faced persons,* who did not go simply and straight-forwardly to work in their transactions.
>
> "*As for liars, he could not endure them,* and he was *continually reminding* his spiritual children, *to avoid them as they would a pestilence.*"
>
> These are the principles on which I have acted before I was a Catholic; these are the principles which, I trust, will be my stay and guidance to the end.

Many excellent autobiographies were written in England in the tumultuous nineteenth-century—most notably by John Ruskin, Mark Pattison and Anthony Trollope—but the subtlest, deepest and most revelatory, for all its incidental reticence, was the one written by the man who has been recently declared a saint by the Church that needs his unbiddable integrity more than ever.

Newman and Liberalism

A Talk Delivered to the Elm Institute, Yale, New Haven, 8 February 2019

When John Henry Newman was given his red hat by Leo XIII in 1879, the new cardinal made a point in his "Biglietto speech" to say two things about his long career, both as a Catholic and as an Anglican. First, he meant his audience to know that he had never ceased opposing liberalism. "For thirty, forty, fifty years I have resisted to the best of my powers the spirit of liberalism," he declared. Since some in the liberal academy have an interest in misrepresenting what Newman meant by liberalism, we should let him say for himself what he meant. "

> Liberalism in religion is the doctrine that there is no positive truth in religion, but that one creed is as good as another, and this is the teaching which is gaining substance and force daily. It is inconsistent with any recognition of any religion, as *true*. It teaches that all are to be tolerated, for all are matters of opinion. Revealed religion is not a truth, but a sentiment and a taste; not an objective fact, not miraculous; and it is the right of each individual to make it say just what strikes his fancy. Devotion is not necessarily founded on faith. ... Since, then, religion is so personal a peculiarity and so private a possession, we must of necessity ignore it in the intercourse of man with man. If a man puts on a new religion every morning, what is that to you? It is as impertinent to think about a man's religion as about his sources of income or his management of his family. Religion is in no sense the bond of society.

Secondly, Newman wished his auditors to appreciate that he had waged this campaign against liberalism against a definite historical backdrop.

> Hitherto the civil Power has been Christian. Even in countries separated from the Church, as in my own, the *dictum* was in force, when I was young, that: "Christianity was the law of the land." Now, everywhere that goodly framework of society, which is the creation of Christianity, is throwing off Christianity. The *dictum* to which I have referred, with a hundred others which followed upon it, is gone, or is going everywhere; and, by the end of the century, unless the Almighty interferes, it will be *forgotten*. ... As to Religion,

433

it is a private luxury, which a man may have if he will; but which of course he must pay for, and which he must not obtrude upon others, or indulge in to their annoyance. The general character of this great *apostasia* is one and the same everywhere.

For Newman, the English Reformation had been a tragedy for the unity of Christendom because it ultimately opened the door not only to apostasy but the private judgment so essential to liberalism. And liberalism gave rise to unbelief, a species of apostasy that was at the very heart of Newman's apostolate because it was at the heart of his recognition that there could be no re-evangelization of the English people without proper Catholic education. Unbelief was also more insidious than the repudiation of Catholicism exacted by more formal apostasy because it was so much more prevalent in a society suffused with No Popery. Moreover, the unbelief that followed apostasy posed formidable problems for the newly reconstituted English Catholic Church. If three hundred years of Protestant Christianity had left the English radically hostile to Catholic Christianity, any attempt at reviving the Church in England would have its work cut out for it. Another ancillary problem, as Newman saw it, was that the English had apostatized twice. If their first apostasy had been from their traditional Catholic faith to the Protestant faith of the Tudors, their second caused them to abandon the Bible Christianity of the Established Church for the rationalism of the Enlightenment, which Newman saw as interchangeable with the liberalism that he spent his life combatting. (One can see this in his excoriating criticism of the Enlightenment historian, Edward Gibbon.) Again, in his "Biglietto" speech, there was nothing of happenstance in his speaking of his fight against liberalism in the context of what he called "the great *apostasia*." They went hand-in-hand.

The apostasy bred of liberalism—what he called "the all-corroding, all-dissolving scepticism of the intellect"—faced Newman at every turn of his long life. Indeed, it drove his two brothers away from the Christian faith, as well as many of his dearest friends. Towards the end of his life, when he peered into the future, he saw with prophetic clarity, the unprecedented scale of the general irreligion to come. "I am speaking of evils, which in their intensity and breadth are peculiar to these times," he wrote. "But I have not yet spoken of the root of all these falsehoods ... The elementary proposition of this new philosophy which is now so threatening is this— that in all things we must go by reason, in nothing by faith, that things are known and are to be received so far as they can be proved. Its advocates say, all other knowledge has proof—why should religion be an exception?"

One of the reasons why Newman held such abiding sway over his contemporaries was precisely because he spoke of the character of this new faithless rationalism with such terrible accuracy. Matthew Arnold's younger brother, Thomas, who would later teach English literature in

Newman's Catholic University in Dublin, after converting to the Church not once but twice, to the chagrin of his wife, certainly acknowledged his debt to Newman on this score. In his very first letter to the great convert in 1855, he wrote from New Zealand:

> My excuse for writing to you and seeking counsel from you, is that your writings have exercised the greatest influence over my mind. I will try to make this intelligible in as few words as possible. My Protestantism which was always of the liberal sort and disavowed the principle of authority, developed itself during my residence at Oxford into a state of absolute doubt and uncertainty about the very facts of Christianity. After leaving Oxford I went up to London, and there, to my deep shame be it spoken, finding a state of doubt intolerable, I plunged into the abyss of unbelief. You know the nature of the illusions which lead a man to this fearful state far better than I can tell you;—there is a page in your lectures on the University system where you describe the fancied illumination and enlargement of mind which a man experiences after abandoning himself to unbelief, which when I read, it seemed as if you had looked into my very heart, and given in clear outline feelings and thoughts which I had had in my mind, but never thoroughly mastered.

The passage to which Arnold refers, from Newman's *Discourses on the Scope and Nature of University Education* (1852), which would later be expanded into his classic *The Idea of a University* (1873), describes the seeming "illumination" the mind undergoes when it first "comes across the arguments and speculations of unbelievers, and feels what a novel light they cast upon what he has hitherto accounted sacred; and still more, if it gives in to them and embraces them, and throws off as so much prejudice what it has hitherto held, and, as if waking from a dream, begins to realize to its imagination that there is now no such thing as law and the transgression of law, that sin is a phantom, and punishment a bugbear, that it is free to sin, free to enjoy the world and the flesh." For Newman's part, in the midst of such factitious "illumination," such antinomian licentiousness, he never lost sight of the fact that

> Religion has its own enlargement, and an enlargement, not of tumult, but of peace. It is often remarked of uneducated persons, who have hitherto thought little of the unseen world, that, on their turning to God, looking into themselves, regulating their hearts, reforming their conduct, and meditating on death and judgment, heaven and hell, they seem to become, in point of intellect, different beings from what they were. Before, they took things as they came, and thought no more of one thing than another. But now every event has a meaning; they have their own estimate of whatever happens to them; they are mindful of times and seasons, and compare the

present with the past; and the world, no longer dull, monotonous, unprofitable, and hopeless, is a various and complicated drama, with parts and an object, and an awful moral.

What made Newman's descriptions of the life of faith so captivating to so many of his contemporaries was that they were honest about the absence of faith amongst the Victorian English. If one looks at his sermons and his letters one can see that he had grounds for suspecting that unbelief was much more widespread in his day than many imagined. Indeed, in the National Church, ravaged as it was by the latitudinarianism of liberal divines, unbelief was rampant. For the most part, when it came to the Christian faith, the Victorians tended to be not so much ill-formed as unformed: they were not so much apostate as pagan. Henry Mayhew, for example, in the course of the interviews he conducted for *London Labour and the London Poor* (1851), found that "not three in one hundred costermongers had ever been in the interior of a church, or any place of worship, or knew what was meant by Christianity." The upper classes, to whom the National Church primarily catered, may have known very much more, but whether theirs was a genuine, as opposed to merely a tribal faith was highly questionable. Certainly, Newman saw a kind of travesty of Christian faith in what he called, in one of his best Anglican sermons, "The Religion of the Day" (1839), in which there "is an existing teaching ... built upon worldly principle, yet pretending to be the Gospel, dropping one whole side of the Gospel, its austere character, and considering it enough to be benevolent, courteous, candid, correct in conduct, delicate, — though it includes no true fear of God, no fervent zeal for His honour, no deep hatred of sin, no horror at the sight of sinners, no indignation ... at the blasphemies of heretics, no jealous adherence to doctrinal truth, no especial sensitiveness about the particular means of gaining ends, provided the ends be good, no loyalty to the Holy Apostolic Church, of which the Creed speaks, no sense of the authority of religion as external to the mind: in a word, no seriousness." Newman, in other words, recognized that the Church could promote a rationalism of her own, which, in some respects, could be even more destructive than the world's rationalism.

Certainly, rationalism of both the ecclesiastical and the worldly variety is still with us, though our rationalism is infinitely more ruinous than the sort adopted by the Victorians. Victorian rationalists, after all, did not set about trying to redefine something as fundamental to the "goodly framework of human society" as marriage. What makes Newman such a lively contemporary of ours is the perspicuity with which he saw the import of this God-defying reliance on the human intellect. No one saw the battle-lines forming between Roman Catholicism and its liberal enemies as clearly as Newman. The late Yale professor Frank Turner, whose attacks on Newman's integrity serve as such a rallying cry for Newman's detractors, argued that Newman's very understanding of liberalism was flawed because it was somehow lacking in specificity. My auditors can judge for themselves whether Newman is vulnerable on this score. Certainly, throughout his long life, he took up the evils posed by liberalism with commanding acuity. "I look out, then, into the enemy's camp, and I try to trace the outlines of the hostile movements and the preparations for assault which are there in agitation against us," Newman wrote in 1858. "The arming and the manoeuvring, the earth-works and the mines, go on incessantly; and one cannot of course tell, without the gift of prophecy, which of his projects will be carried into effect and attain its purpose, and which will eventually fail or be abandoned." (The fact that Newman chose an analogy to trench warfare here is striking in light of the fate that awaited the Victorians' belief in progress in the fields of Flanders.)

Newman delineated clearly enough the main lines of the liberal philosophy that would seek to discredit and dislodge the teachings of the one holy catholic and apostolic Faith from the minds and hearts of men. "You may have opinions in religion, you may have theories, you may have arguments, you may have probabilities," Newman portrayed his rationalist liberal arguing, "you may have anything but demonstration, and therefore you cannot have science. In mechanics you advance from sure premises to sure conclusions; in optics you form your undeniable facts into system, arrive at general principles, and then again infallibly apply them: here you have Science." But for the liberal rationalists, "it is absurd for men in our present state to teach anything positively about the next world, that there is a heaven, or a hell, or a last judgment, or that the soul is immortal, or that there is a God."

In capturing the ethos of this anti-Christian rationalism so precisely, Newman captured not only the skepticism of his own age but that of ours as well.

> Well, then, if Religion is just one of those subjects about which we can know nothing, what can be so absurd as to spend time upon it? what so absurd as to quarrel with others about it? Let us all keep to our own religious opinions respectively, and be content … upon no subject whatever has the intellect of man been fastened so intensely as upon Religion. And the misery is, that, if once we allow it to engage our attention, we are in a circle from which we never shall be able to extricate ourselves. Our mistake reproduces and corroborates itself. A small insect, a wasp or a fly, is unable to make his way through the pane of glass; and his very failure is the occasion of greater violence in his struggle than before. He is as heroically obstinate in his resolution to succeed as the assailant or defender of some critical battlefield; he is unflagging and fierce in

an effort which cannot lead to anything beyond itself. When, then, in like manner, you have once resolved that certain religious doctrines shall be indisputably true, and that all men ought to perceive their truth, you have engaged in an undertaking which, though continued on to eternity, will never reach its aim; and, since you are convinced it ought to do so, the more you have failed hitherto, the more violent and pertinacious will be your attempt in time to come. And further still, since you are not the only man in the world who is in this error, but one of ten thousand, all holding the general principle that Religion is scientific, and yet all differing as to the truths and facts and conclusions of this science, it follows that the misery of social disputation and disunion is added to the misery of a hopeless investigation, and life is not only wasted in fruitless speculation, but embittered by bigotted sectarianism.

Here, one can see the satirical genius with which Newman entered into the liberal prejudices of his opponents, and it is this critical clairvoyance that makes him such an incomparable guide to the rationalism at the heart of liberalism. At the same time, if in meeting his opponents, he could play the witty barrister, putting their arguments better than they could put them themselves, he was also a redoubtable advocate for the Truth against which liberalism has always warred. Robert Pattison, in his brilliant book, *The Great Dissent: John Henry Newman and the Liberal Heresy* (1991) nicely encapsulates the upshot of this advocacy. "The great virtue of Newman's critique of liberalism is that it should exist at all," Pattison writes.

That there should be one consistent view of the world opposed to liberalism, root and branch, sharing none of its premises and despising all of its works is an inestimable benefit, for no one more than the liberal himself. Without some honest and unforgiving voice such as Newman's, the liberal would be lost in the labyrinth of his own ideology. He would smugly assume that the paradoxical tenets of his creed are what Jefferson assured them they were: self-evident truths ... The poverty of feeling without belief, the politics that is expediency, and the humanism that denies truth all fall within the scope of Newman's invective and receive from him no quarter. He treats the ugliest manifestations of liberalism with the contempt they deserve but rarely provoke. Newman is the master of those who dissent.

One can readily corroborate Pattison's point by looking at Newman's *Essay on the Development of Christian Doctrine*, which Cardinal Kasper and his liberal friends have gone to such strenuous lengths to misrepresent. There, Newman cannot have been more categorical about what he refers to as "the dogmatic principle," his abiding riposte to the clever falsehoods of liberalism.

That there is a truth then; that there is one truth; that religious error is in itself of an immoral nature; that its maintainers, unless involuntarily such, are guilty in maintaining it; that it is to be dreaded; that the search for truth is not the gratification of curiosity; that its attainment has nothing of the excitement of a discovery; that the mind is below truth, not above it, and is bound, not to descant upon it, but to venerate it; that truth and falsehood are set before us for the trial of our hearts; that our choice is an awful giving forth of lots on which salvation or rejection is inscribed; that "before all things it is necessary to hold the Catholic faith"; that "he that would be saved must thus think," and not otherwise; that, "if thou criest after knowledge, and liftest up thy voice for understanding, if thou seekest her as silver, and searchest for her as for hid treasure, then shalt thou understand the fear of the Lord, and find the knowledge of God," —this is the dogmatical principle, which is strength.

In contrast to the dogmatical principle, Newman described the objections to dogma that animates liberals, and here we have no problem understanding what Newman is describing because we encounter such convictions daily in our own lives.

That truth and falsehood in religion are but matter of opinion; that one doctrine is as good as another; that the Governor of the world does not intend that we should gain the truth; that there is no truth; that we are not more acceptable to God by believing this than by believing that; that no one is answerable for his opinions; that they are a matter of necessity or accident; that it is enough if we sincerely hold what we profess; that our merit lies in seeking, not in possessing; that it is a duty to follow what seems to us true, without a fear lest it should not be true; that it may be a gain to succeed, and can be no harm to fail; that we may take up and lay down opinions at pleasure; that belief belongs to the mere intellect, not to the heart also; that we may safely trust to ourselves in matters of Faith, and need no other guide, —this is the principle of philosophies and heresies, which is very weakness.

In thus giving such arresting expression to the stark divide between the Truth espoused by the Church and the shibboleths of liberalism, Newman was not simply framing an abstract war of ideas. An inveterately practical man, he was deeply concerned about what the issue of doctrinaire anti-Catholicism would be. "Where men really are persuaded of all this, however unreasonable," he asks, "what will follow?" For Newman, liberal relativism would not be inconsequential, and the accuracy of his predictions can be verified by our own increasingly tragic experience: it would issue in "A feeling, not merely of contempt, but of absolute hatred, towards the Catholic theologian and the dogmatic teacher. The patriot abhors and loathes the partisans who have degraded and injured his country; and the citizen of the world, the advocate of the human race, feels bitter indignation at those whom he holds to have been its misleaders and tyrants for two thousand years."

The upshot of Newman's assessment of the gains that rationalism had made since the French Revolution was sobering. "Christianity has never yet had experience of a world simply irreligious," he wrote in 1873.

> Perhaps China may be an exception. We do not know enough about it to speak, but consider what the Roman and Greek world was when Christianity appeared. It was full of superstition, not of infidelity. There was much unbelief in all as regards their mythology, and in every educated man, as to eternal punishment. But there was no casting off the idea of religion, and of unseen powers who governed the world. When they spoke of Fate, even here they considered that there was a great moral governance of the world carried on by fated laws. Their first principles were the same as ours. Even among the sceptics of Athens, St. Paul could appeal to the Unknown God. Even to the ignorant populace of Lystra he could speak of the living God who did them good from heaven. And so when the northern barbarians came down at a later age, they, amid all their superstitions, were believers in an unseen Providence and in the moral law. But we are now coming to a time when the world does not acknowledge our first principles.

In conclusion, if Newman devoted his life to anatomizing and combating the evils of liberalism, he was sensible enough to recognize that such evils would not be either easily or speedily removed. The work he initiated would have to be carried forward by others as committed to true liberty and true liberal education as he was, and it is precisely because of the necessity for this continuing charge that I am honored to have been able to address the Elm Institute today. Institutes like yours have a vital role to play in this vital fight.

Ladies and gentlemen, thank you for being such an attentive, patient, gracious audience.

Newman and the
Grace of Simplicity

Now that the canonization of Blessed John Henry Cardinal Newman nears, we have seen a good number of articles from different quarters telling us what Newman thought and did not think. Of these, the piece I found most tell-tale was the essay by Ryan Marr that appeared on 22 July 2019 on the Witherspoon Institute site in which Marr claimed, apropos the "Biglietto" Speech, that Newman had not opposed liberalism, as he explicitly stated he had "for thirty, forty, fifty years." No, he had opposed what the author ingeniously called "religious indifferentism," a claim reminiscent of the old Groucho Marx joke, in which the man caught in bed with his neighbor's wife, turns to the cuckold and says, "Who are you going to believe: me or your own eyes?"

Here is the passage to which I refer from the Witherspoon post:

> Of course, we should be careful not to conflate the "liberalism" that Newman opposed with the word as it is commonly used today. Certainly, there are errors intrinsic to contemporary political liberalism that need critiquing, but that conversation is distinct from the struggle against the spirit of liberalism *in religion*, which demands unqualified resistance. In the *Biglietto Speech*, Newman specifically described this strand of liberalism as "the doctrine that there is no positive truth in religion, but that one creed is as good as another." This outlook teaches that "[r]evealed religion is not a truth, but a sentiment and a taste; not an objective fact, not miraculous; and [that] it is the right of each individual to make it say just what strikes his fancy." As his words indicate, the preeminent object of Newman's concern was religious indifferentism.

As his words indicate? Newman's words indicate nothing of the kind. He never mentions "religious indifferentism" in the speech. Marr has not written a gloss of the speech: he has bowdlerized it.

If we believe our own eyes, *pace* what the misguided author of this post claims, we will see that Newman did oppose liberalism. We will see that the liberalism he opposed has everything to do with our own liberalism, grounded as they both are in the calamitous arrogance of rationalism. And we will see that his opposition to liberalism was not restricted to religious liberalism. As Matthew Schmitz astutely pointed out the other day in *First Things*: Newman may have "insisted that he opposed political liberalism only insofar as it sought 'to supersede, to block out, religion,' but he had an expansive definition of what this meant. ... Teetotalism was one example. He mistrusted the temperance movement because it sought to promote virtue 'without Religion ... on mere principles of utility.' Better to be a drunk [in other words] than a Benthamist."

For those who might have missed Schmitz's piece, he rightly deplored the fact that leading up to the canonization there will be two camps disputing the meaning of Newman's legacy:

> On one side will be those who venerate Newman as the patron saint of liberal Catholicism. They believe that his writings authorize dissent from, and revolutions in, Christian doctrine. In their eyes, his canonization will be a sign that what is denounced as error in one age may later be embraced as truth. On the other side will be those who have read Newman's stinging denunciations of theological and political liberalism, and therefore imagine that he favored the illiberal and ultramontane form of Catholicism that flourished during the nineteenth century. Both these images of Newman are false.

This is true as far as it goes, though one has to keep in mind that those who wish to claim that Newman was liberal and Modernist far outweigh those who claim that he was illiberal and unduly ultramontane. (Of course, he *was* ultramontane, though not excessively so.) The most prevalent false Newman is still the false Modernist Newman—the Newman, that is to say, posited by those like Marr and his friends at the Pittsburgh Newman Institute who wish to argue that Newman's thinking (especially with regard to the development of doctrine) can be cited to reconcile the Church to the modern world's most egregious moral errors.

What I should like to speak of in this essay is another Newman, one who often goes missing in such unreal debates, and that is the Newman who steered clear of the Charybdis and Scylla of liberalism and illiberalism to enter into the genuine simplicity of what he called "the one true Fold of the Redeemer."

In the sermon he placed last in his 8-volume *Parochial and Plain Sermons* (1834–43), entitled "Ignorance of Evil" (1836), Newman took pains to remind his readers that there was a profound point to God's forbidding those in paradise from eating from the Tree of Knowledge. "Our happiness as well as duty lies in not going beyond our measure—in being contented with what we are—with what God makes us," he wrote. "They who seek after forbidden knowledge, of whatever kind, will find they have lost their place in the scale of beings in so doing, and are cast out of the great circle of God's family."

In the increasingly barbarous order that has taken shape in the wake of the collapse of Christendom, knowledge, of course, is everywhere adulated, even though it is shown repeatedly to be not only evil but factitious. For Newman, this adulation was an expression of our exile from God's divine purpose, since it shows "how different is our state from that for which God made us." However, if in reading that, anyone is inclined to suppose that Newman was speaking in easy generalities, he will be quickly disabused by Newman himself, who illustrates what he means with a terrible specificity.

> [God] meant us to be simple, and we are unreal; He meant us to think no evil, and a thousand associations, bad, trifling, or unworthy, attend our every thought. He meant us to be drawn on to the glories without us, and we are drawn back and (as it were) fascinated by the miseries within us. And hence it is that the whole structure of society is so artificial; no one trusts another, if he can help it; safeguards, checks, and securities are ever sought after. No one means exactly what he says, for our words have lost their natural meaning, and even an Angel could not use them naturally, for every mind being different from every other, they have no distinct meaning. What, indeed, is the very function of society, as it is at present, but a rude attempt to cover the degradation of the fall, and to make men feel respect for themselves, and enjoy it in the eyes of others, without returning to God. This is what we should especially guard against, because there is so much of it in the world. I mean, not an abandonment of evil, not a sweeping away and cleansing out of the corruption which sin has bred within us, but a smoothing it over, an outside delicacy and polish, an ornamenting the surface of things while "within are dead men's bones and all uncleanness"; making the garments, which at first were given for decency, a means of pride and vanity. Men give good names to what is evil, they sanctify bad principles and feelings; and, knowing that there is vice and error, selfishness, pride, and ambition, in the world, they attempt, not to root out these evils, not to withstand these errors;—that they think a dream, the dream of theorists who do not know the world;—but to cherish and form alliance with them, to use them, to make a science of selfishness, to flatter and indulge error, and to bribe vice with the promise of bearing with it, so that it does but keep in the shade.

That the world and the Church should somehow not be at odds is, of course, one of the basal convictions of the Modernists. For them, the only way the Church can hope to flourish in the modern world—or the "post-modern" world, if one insists—is for the Church to accommodate the errors of the world, especially as they relate to homosexuality, concubinage, contraception, and abortion. Newman, as anyone knows who has read him with any attentiveness, would never have shown the least sympathy with such an impious project. As he said in another sermon, "Nature and Grace" (1849), with his accustomed perspicuity:

> Behold here the true origin and fountain-head of the warfare between the Church and the world; here they join issue, and diverge from each other. The Church is built upon the doctrine that impurity is hateful to God, and that concupiscence is its root; with the Prince of the Apostles, her visible Head, she denounces "the corruption of concupiscence which is in the world," or, that corruption in the world which comes of concupiscence; whereas the corrupt world defends, nay, I may even say, sanctifies that very concupiscence which is the world's corruption. Just as its bolder teachers, as you know, my brethren, hold that the laws of this physical creation are so supreme, as to allow of their utterly disbelieving in the existence of miracles, so, in like manner, it deifies and worships human nature and its impulses, and denies the power and the grant of grace. This is the source of the hatred which the world bears to the Church; it finds a whole catalogue of sins brought into light and denounced, which it would fain believe to be no sins at all; it finds itself to its indignation and impatience, surrounded with sin, morning, noon, and night; it finds that a stern law lies against it in matters where it believed it was its own master and need not think of God; it finds guilt accumulating upon it hourly, which nothing can prevent, nothing remove, but a higher power, the grace of God. It finds itself in danger of being humbled to the earth as a rebel, instead of being allowed to indulge its self-dependence and self-complacency. Hence it takes its stand on nature, and denies or rejects divine grace.

What is striking about this uncompromising assessment of matters is how much it animated Newman's own reading of England's worldly rejection of the ancient faith. Surveying the history of England before and after the English Reformation, Newman saw a people, who, after a thousand years, "grew tired of the heavenly stranger who sojourned among them"; a people who "had had enough of blessings and absolutions, enough of the intercession of saints, enough of the grace of the sacraments, enough of the prospect of the next life. They thought it best to secure this life in the first place, because they were in possession of it, and then to go on to the next, if time and means allowed. And they saw that to labour for the next world was possibly to lose this; whereas, to labour for this world might be, for what they knew, the way to labour for the next also. Anyhow, they would pursue a temporal end, and they would account any one their enemy who stood in the way of their pursuing it. It was a madness; but madmen are strong, and madmen are clever ..." For Newman, this worldly madness was of a piece with England's new "temporal end."

And so with the sword and the halter, and by mutilation and fine and imprisonment, they cut off, or frightened away from the land, as Israel did in the time of old, the ministers of the Most High, and their ministrations: they "altogether broke the yoke, and burst the bonds." "They beat one, and killed another, and another they stoned," and at length they altogether cast out the Heir from His vineyard, and killed Him, "that the inheritance might be theirs." And as for the remnant of His servants whom they left, they drove them into corners and holes of the earth, and there they bade them die out; and then they rejoiced and sent gifts either to other, and made merry, because they had rid themselves of those "who had tormented them that dwelt upon the earth." And so they turned to enjoy this world, and to gain for themselves a name among men, and it was given unto them according to their wish. They preferred the heathen virtues of their original nature, to the robe of grace which God had given them: they fell back, with closed affections, and haughty reserve, and dreariness within, upon their worldly integrity, honour, energy, prudence, and perseverance; they made the most of the natural man, and they "received their reward." Forthwith they began to rise to a station higher than the heathen Roman, and have, in three centuries, attained a wider range of sovereignty; and now they look down in contempt on what they were, and upon the Religion which reclaimed them from paganism.

As we all know, "making the most of the natural man" has served England very poorly indeed, though this would not be entirely evident until after Newman's death. He certainly would have goggled at the spectacle of England's continuing to surrender her sovereignty for what Shakespeare nicely referred to as "inky blots and rotten parchment bonds."

Nevertheless, despite his being something of a Dutch uncle with his English contemporaries, an uncle never averse to telling them the truth, even when it was least palatable, the English always respected him. He might, as Dean Church pointed out, have broken "with England and all things English in wrath and sorrow," but he was still "recognised by Protestant England as one of its greatest men." When Newman was given his red hat by Leo XIII in 1879, Church made an incisive point about the newly made cardinal and his relationship with his fellow Englishmen when he wrote in the *Guardian*, the Anglican paper of the time:

In a crowd of new Cardinals—men of eminence in their own communion—he is the only one about whom Englishmen know or care anything. His words, when he speaks, pass verbatim along the telegraph wires, like the words of the men who sway the world. We read of the quiet Oxford scholar's arms emblazoned on vestment and furniture as those of a Prince of the Church, and of his

445

motto—*Cor ad cor loquitur*. In that motto is the secret of all that he is to his countrymen. For that skill of which he is such a master, in the use of his and their "sweet mother tongue," is something much more than literary accomplishment and power. It means that he has the key to what is deepest in their nature and most characteristic in them of feeling and conviction—to what is deeper than opinions and theories and party divisions; to what in their most solemn moments they most value and most believe in.

What the English "most value and most believe in" today is anyone's guess, but surely it is not only the English who should be sufficiently moved by Newman's mastery of his "sweet English tongue" to heed what he has to tell us of the primacy of holy simplicity in the exercise of our faith. "Let us, finding ourselves in the state in which we are, take those means which alone are really left us, which alone become us," he writes in "Ignorance of Evil."

> Christ has purchased for us what we lost in Adam, our garment of innocence. He has bid us and enabled us to become as little children; He has purchased for us the grace of *simplicity*, which, though one of the highest, is very little thought about, is very little sought after. We have, indeed, a general idea what love is, and hope, and faith, and truth, and purity, though a poor idea; but we are almost blind to what is one of the first elements of Christian perfection, that simple-mindedness which springs from the heart's being *whole* with God, entire, undivided. And those who think they have an idea of it, commonly rise no higher than to mistake for it a mere weakness and softness of mind, which is but its counterfeit. To be simple is to be like the Apostles and first Christians. Our Saviour says, "Be ye harmless," or simple, "as doves." And St. Paul, "I would have you wise unto that which is good, and *simple concerning evil*." [Rom. xvi. 19.] Again, "That ye may be *blameless and harmless*, the sons of God, without rebuke, in the midst of a crooked and perverse nation." [Phil. ii. 15.] And he speaks of the "testimony of" his own "conscience, that in *simplicity* and godly sincerity, not with fleshly wisdom, but by the grace of God," he had his conversation in the world and towards his disciples.

Here is Newman's signature eloquence in all of its biblical authority. Yet, curiously enough, Marr has difficulties with such moving eloquence, claiming in his oddly philistine way that "Newman's Victorian rhetoric can sometimes sound foreign to our ears, and the density of his prose means that it can prove difficult to wade through." That anyone capable of such a sentence should be put in charge of what calls itself a Newman Institute is a puzzler, but then there is a good deal that is puzzling about the Newman Institute in Pittsburgh.

Nevertheless, those who delight in Newman's work will know that he does not write, like so many other prose stylists, to parade his mastery of style: he writes to speak "heart to heart" — to cure souls. And consequently, it is fitting that he should end this sermon — a most apposite sermon for our sophistical contemporaries — with a prayer.

> Let us pray God to give us this great and precious gift; that we may blot out from our memory all that offends Him; unlearn all that knowledge which sin has taught us; rid ourselves of selfish motives, self-conceit, and vanity, littlenesses, envying, grudgings, meannesses; turn from all cowardly, low, miserable ways; and escape from servile fears, the fear of man, vague anxieties of conscience, and superstitions. So that we may have the boldness and frankness of those who are as if they had no sin, from having been cleansed from it; the uncontaminated hearts, open countenances, and untroubled eyes of those who neither suspect, nor conceal, nor shun, nor are jealous; in a word, so that we may have confidence in Him, that we may stay on Him, and rest in the thoughts of Him, instead of plunging amid the thickets of this world; that we may bear His eye and His voice, and know no knowledge but the knowledge of Him and Jesus Christ crucified, and desire no objects but what He has blessed and bid us pursue.

Newman, Gibbon and
the Reckoning of History

The quote that one hears most often trotted out about Newman and history is: "to be deep in history is to cease to be a Protestant."

Now, even taken out of context, the quote reaffirms a good deal of what we know about Newman's relation to history. As a student of the early Church Fathers, Newman was converted from Anglican Protestantism to Roman Catholicism largely by consulting the work of the Fathers—especially, the work they did in identifying, verifying and reaffirming the *fidei depositum*– and by recognizing that the Early Church and the Catholic Church were one and the same. Of course, one of the fundamental claims made by Protestants in Newman's day was that the Catholic Church was not the same as the Early Church because it was a corruption of that primitive Church. If we look at the work of the Whig historians, from Henry Hallam and Connop Thirlwell to Henry Hart Milman and James Anthony Froude, we can see how persistently they sought to substantiate this claim. However, both the early Fathers and the later Fathers told a different tale. The Catholic Church was an authentic development, not a corruption of the Early Church. Indeed, for the convert in Newman, it was the National Church, cobbled together by Henry VIII and the first Elizabeth in the sixteenth century that was a corruption of the "one holy catholic and apostolic" faith, and not the other way round.

Yet if we put Newman's quote in its larger context, we can see that he was making an additional point, which nicely exhibits the acuity of his historical sense.

> Whatever be historical Christianity, it is not Protestantism. If ever there were a safe truth, it is this. And Protestantism has ever felt it so. I do not mean that every Protestant writer has felt it; for it was the fashion at first, at least as a rhetorical argument against Rome, to appeal to past ages, or to some of them; but Protestantism, as a whole, feels it, and has felt it. This is shown in the determination of dispensing with historical Christianity altogether, and of forming a Christianity from the Bible alone; men never would have put it aside, unless they had despaired of it. It is shown by the long

449

neglect of ecclesiastical history in England, which prevails even in the English Church. Our popular religion scarcely recognizes the fact of the twelve long ages which lie between the Councils of Nicaea and Trent, except as affording one or two passages to illustrate its wild interpretations of certain prophesies of St. Paul and St. John. It is melancholy to say it, but the chief, perhaps the only English writer who has any claim to be considered an ecclesiastical historian, is the unbeliever Gibbon. To be deep in history is to cease to be a Protestant.

In other words, for Newman, it was no accident that the Protestant English should have been content to have so zealously anti-Catholic a historian as Edward Gibbon writing their ecclesiastical history. After all, if they had paid attention to any more balanced church historian, they would have run the risk of encountering real church history; and they could not have borne that because it might very well have forced them "to cease to be Protestant."

Gibbon's animus against Christianity *per se* may not have been altogether congenial to all English Protestants; the thesis of the *Decline and Fall of the Roman Empire*, after all—which, incidentally, Gibbon pinched from Voltaire—was that Rome fell because of what Gibbon styled "the triumph of barbarism and religion," specifically, the Christian religion. Nevertheless, for English Protestants, his history did have the benefit of not contradicting the Anglican view of church history, which Newman memorably encapsulated in one of his best satirical sallies in his *Lectures on the Present Position of Catholics*. In that brilliant book, published in 1851, which I commend to all of my readers for its witty demolition of the entire No Popery house of cards, Newman got at the root of the Protestant Englishman's fanciful notions about his national identity by locating them squarely in his even more fanciful notions about the progress of the Christian faith. In his marvelous lectures, Newman explains that for English Protestants, "Christianity was very pure in the beginning, was very corrupt in the middle age, and is very pure again in England now, though still corrupt everywhere else." Moreover, as Newman observes, "in the middle age, a tyrannical institution called the Church arose and swallowed up Christianity." Fortunately, however, "the Church is alive still, and has not yet disgorged its prey, except, as aforesaid, in our own favoured country." The reason this should be the case is simple. As Newman describes it, "in the middle age, there was no Christianity anywhere at all, but all was dark and horrible, as bad as paganism, or rather much worse. No one knew anything about God, or whether there was a God or no, nor about Christ or His atonement; for the Blessed Virgin, and Saints, and the Pope, and images, were worshipped instead; and thus, so far from religion benefitting the generations of mankind who lived in that dreary time, it did them infinitely more harm than good."

Here Newman's satirical wit exposed how English Protestants resolutely refused to consider the real course of ecclesiastical history, a refusal extensively exhibited in Gibbon's *Decline and Fall,* where scoffing and mockery take the place of any equitable criticism of Christianity's true progress. It was not only the rise of Catholicism that Gibbon misunderstood but Catholicism itself. And here, again, the historian in Newman is indispensable because he shows the extent to which Gibbon was not only unsympathetic to Catholicism but intent on ignoring any evidence that might show why the Faith commanded the unprecedented allegiance it commanded.

In his *History of Latin Christianity* (1855), the liberal Anglican historian, Henry Hart Milman followed Gibbon by paying attention only to the externals of the Faith. In "Mr. Milman's View of Christianity" (1841), Newman wrote about an abiding feature of rationalist, secular accounts of the rise of Christianity.

> For the fact is undeniable, little as Mr. Milman may be aware of it, that this external contemplation of Christianity necessarily leads a man to write as a Socinian or Unitarian *would* write, whether he will or not. Mr. Milman has not been able to avoid this dreadful disadvantage, and thus, however heartily he may hate the opinions of such men himself, he has unintentionally both given scandal to his brethren and cause of triumph to the enemy. A very few words will account for this. The great doctrines which the Socinian denies are our Lord's divinity and atonement; now these are not external facts;—what he confesses are His humanity and crucifixion; these *are* external facts. Mr. Milman then is bound by his theory to dwell on the latter, to slur over the former.

Newman was adamant that if historians neglected the inner substance of the Faith, especially as it was attested by the martyrs, they would only produce a rationalist caricature of the Faith. And, indeed, if we look at most histories of Christianity that followed the baleful example of Gibbon—with the honorable exceptions of those by John Lingard and, more recently, Peter Brown and Louis Wilken—we can see that this reductionist, secular, rational bias continues to be prevalent.

In this regard, it was ironic that Gibbon should have used the Arian heresy to argue the absurdity of seeing the rise of the Church in terms of the rise of her theology because, in a fundamental way, Gibbon and all of the rationalist Liberal historians who followed him were Arians themselves. That is to say, they refused to concede that in order to write a proper history of Christianity it was necessary to include not only the human aspects of the Faith but the divine aspects as well. And by insisting that the evidence of martyrdom revealed both these aspects of the Faith, Newman was insisting that it was only by taking into consideration the Creator's particular Providence—His direct, personal, unwavering love for

His creatures– that we could understand and represent the true character of history.

Of course, Newman recognizes that such direct, personal, unwavering solicitude on the part of a loving Creator is difficult to credit, much less fathom, even by those who rejoice in His Providence. In his moving sermon, "A Particular Providence as Revealed in the Gospel" (1835), Newman responded to the vision of history that Gibbon set out in his voluminous history—a vision from which God is largely absent or present only as the result of the claims of deluded fanaticism—with a profound reminder of the one factor that gives all of human and divine history its governing purpose.

> God beholds thee individually, whoever thou art. He "calls thee by thy name." He sees thee, and understands thee, as He made thee. He knows what is in thee, all thy own peculiar feelings and thoughts, thy dispositions and likings, thy strength and thy weakness. He views thee in thy day of rejoicing, and thy day of sorrow. He sympathises in thy hopes and thy temptations. He interests Himself in all thy anxieties and remembrances, all the risings and fallings of thy spirit. He has numbered the very hairs of thy head and the cubits of thy stature. He compasses thee round and bears thee in his arms; He takes thee up and sets thee down. He notes thy very countenance, whether smiling or in tears, whether healthful or sickly. He looks tenderly upon thy hands and thy feet; He hears thy voice, the beating of thy heart, and thy very breathing. Thou dost not love thyself better than He loves thee. Thou canst not shrink from pain more than He dislikes thy bearing it; and if He puts it on thee, it is as thou would put it on thyself, if thou art wise, for a greater good afterwards. Thou art not only His creature (though for the very sparrows He has a care, and pitied the "much cattle" of Nineveh), thou art man redeemed and sanctified, His adopted son, favoured with a portion of that glory and blessedness which flows from Him everlastingly unto the Only-begotten. Thou art chosen to be His … Thou wast one of those for whom Christ offered up His last prayer, and sealed it with His precious blood. What a thought is this, a thought almost too great for our faith!

The rise of Christianity, for Newman, primarily involved those who accepted and cooperated with God's particular Providence and those who rejected and spurned it. Faith is the means by which the individual, with God's providential grace, enters into the reality of history, which, for Newman, is not simply something that concerns historians or savants: it is the bond that ties together the educated and the uneducated, the rich and the poor, the powerful and the weak, the living and the dead. Gibbon, on the other hand, is altogether too rationalist to bother about such ties. Moreover, he regarded ordinary people and their yearning for God from an aloof, contemptuous remove. "The decline of ancient prejudice exposed a very numerous portion of human kind to the danger of a painful and comfortless situation," he writes of the desuetude into which devotion to the imperial gods fell before the Incarnation:

A state of scepticism and suspense may amuse a few inquisitive minds. But the practice of superstition is so congenial to the multitude that, if they are forcibly awakened, they still regret the loss of their pleasing vision. Their love of the marvellous and supernatural, their curiosity with regard to future events, and their strong propensity to extend their hopes and fears beyond the limits of the visible world, were the principal causes which favoured the establishment of Polytheism. So urgent on the vulgar is the necessity of believing that the fall of any system of mythology will most probably be succeeded by the introduction of some other mode of superstition.

Compared to this dismissive view of "the vulgar" and their susceptibility to what Gibbon regarded as mere superstition, nothing could be more refreshing than Newman's view of the ordinary faithful. "Religion has its own enlargement, and an enlargement, not of tumult, but of peace," he writes in *The Idea of a University* (1873).

It is often remarked of uneducated persons, who have hitherto thought little of the unseen world, that, on their turning to God, looking into themselves, regulating their hearts, reforming their conduct, and meditating on death and judgment, heaven and hell, they seem to become, in point of intellect, different beings from what they were. Before, they took things as they came, and thought no more of one thing than another. But now every event has a meaning; they have their own estimate of whatever happens to them; they are mindful of times and seasons, and compare the present with the past; and the world, no longer dull, monotonous, unprofitable, and hopeless, [the world, in other words, that Gibbon presents us throughout the *Decline and Fall*) is a various and complicated drama, with parts and an object, and an awful moral.

What Newman found most objectionable about Gibbon's polemical treatment of Christianity was not that it tallied with heterodox theology—that was a given—but that it prefigured the widespread infidelity to which liberalism would give rise in the nineteenth century. Of course, in reading his various works as well as his voluminous letters, we can see how at once consistent and incisive Newman's lifelong critique of liberalism was, a critique which many scholars now working in the liberal academy are intent on discrediting. That they are attempting to do this by contending that Newman was mistaken in his opposition to liberalism because he somehow did not understand what liberalism was about will give my readers a good sense of just how mischievous and brazen this enterprise is. Indeed, in most cases, their only refutation of Newman's criticism of the very liberalism that they promote themselves is to argue that the criticism itself is inadmissible because it is unfounded. Yet in his most succinct definition, which he gave in his famous "Biglietto" speech in Rome after Leo XIII made him a cardinal on 12 May 1879, he spoke of an evil that no faithful Catholic today would ever dare deny.

> Liberalism in religion is the doctrine that there is no positive truth in religion, but that one creed is as good as another, and this is the teaching which is gaining substance and force daily. It is inconsistent with any recognition of any religion, as *true*. It teaches that all are to be tolerated, for all are matters of opinion. Revealed religion is not a truth, but a sentiment and a taste; not an objective fact, not miraculous; and it is the right of each individual to make it say just what strikes his fancy. Devotion is not necessarily founded on faith. Men may go to Protestant Churches and to Catholic, may get good from both and belong to neither. They may fraternise together in spiritual thoughts and feelings, without having any views at all of doctrine in common, or seeing the need of them. Since, then, religion is so personal a peculiarity and so private a possession, we must of necessity ignore it in the intercourse of man with man. If a man puts on a new religion every morning, what is that to you? It is as impertinent to think about a man's religion as about his sources of income or his management of his family. Religion is in no sense the bond of society.

Whenever I see liberal academic historians disputing the accuracy of Newman's definition of liberalism—most of whom follow uncritically in the footsteps of the scurrilous Frank Turner, the late Yale Professor of History, who wrote an almost pathological assault on the great convert's faith and integrity, accusing him of having been "the first great, and perhaps most enduring, Victorian skeptic"—I am reminded of something to which Yeats gave pungent expression in his poem, "The Seven Sages" (1933), where he asks

> what is Whiggery?
> A levelling, rancorous, rational sort of mind
> That never looked out of the eye of a saint
> Or out of a drunkard's eye.

No one understood how this "levelling, rancorous, rational sort of mind" animated the French Revolution better than Edmund Burke, the prophetic insights of whose works demonstrate why Newman was right to oppose the rationalism at the heart of nineteenth-century liberalism, the mischief of which is with us still in the twenty-first century.

Apropos the Revolution, it is important to note that there was no keener admirer of Burke's *Reflections on the French Revolution* (which came out in 1790, only two years after the last volume of the *Decline and Fall* appeared) than Edward Gibbon, who saw it as a necessary defense of the public order and the rights of property that the revolutionaries had so thoroughly undermined. Nonetheless, Gibbon was entirely mum on Burke's critique of the havoc wrought by the anti-Catholic ideas of the *philosophes*, ideas which were of the essence of Jacobinism. Of course, conceding the accuracy of that critique would have required Gibbon to admit the wrongheadedness of his own promotion of the same ideas in his *Decline and Fall*. In his intellectually dishonest silence, in other words, he sought to conceal his own culpability for touting such anti-Catholic ideas, all of which would become staples of nineteenth-century liberalism.

Newman, however, more than any of his contemporaries, saw the great prescience of Burke's recognition of the bloodshed and mayhem to which Enlightenment Europe's apostasy would lead, and in his lifelong opposition to liberalism we can see his debt to Burke's great anatomy of the evils of apostasy. One can demonstrate this easily enough by quoting the two men in succession. Here is Burke in a letter written to his beloved son, Richard, in 1792, in which he warned that:

> If ever the Church and the Constitution of England should fall in these Islands, (and they will fall together), it is not Presbyterian discipline, nor Popish hierarchy, that will rise upon their ruins. It will not be the Church of Rome nor the Church of Scotland—not the Church of Luther, nor the Church of Calvin. On the contrary, all these Churches are menaced, and menaced alike. It is the new fanatical Religion, now in the heat of its first ferment, of the Rights of Man, which rejects all Establishments, all discipline, all Ecclesiastical, and in truth all Civil order, which will triumph, and which will lay prostrate your Church ... If the present establishment should fall, it is this religion which will triumph in Ireland and in England, as it has triumphed in France. This religion, which laughs at creeds and dogmas, and confessions of faith, may be fomented equally amongst all descriptions and all sects; amongst nominal Catholics, and amongst nominal churchmen; and amongst those dissenters, who know little and care less about a presbytery, or any of its discipline, or any of its doctrine.

And for Newman's part, in his lecture, "On the Patristic Idea of Anti-Christ" (1835), he sets out how the French Jacobins had provided the boilerplate for the liberalism that would enter England in its wake:

> [I]n the Capital of that powerful and celebrated nation, there took place, as we all well know, within the last fifty years, an open apostasy from Christianity; nor from Christianity only, but from every kind of worship which might retain any semblance or pretence of

the great truths of religion; atheism was absolutely professed;—
and yet in spite of this, it seems a contradiction in terms to say it,
a certain sort of worship, and that, as the prophet expresses it, "a
strange worship," was introduced.

Observe what this was. I say, they avowed on the one hand
Atheism. They prevailed upon a wretched man, whom they had
forced upon the Church as an Archbishop, to come before them in
public and declare that there was no God, and that what he had
hitherto taught was a fable. They wrote up over the burial-places
that death was an eternal sleep. They closed the churches, they
seized and desecrated the gold and silver plate belonging to them,
turning, like Belshazzar, those sacred vessels to the use of their
impious revellings; they formed mock processions, clad in priestly
garments, and singing profane hymns. They annulled the divine
ordinance of marriage, resolving it into a mere civil contract to
be made and dissolved at pleasure. These things are but a part of
their enormities.

On the other hand, after having broken away from all restraint as
regards God and man, they gave a name to that reprobate state itself
into which they had thrown themselves, and exalted it, that very
negation of religion, or rather that real and living blasphemy, into
a kind of god. They called it Liberty, and they literally worshipped
it as a divinity. It would almost be incredible, that men who had
flung off all religion should be at the pains to assume a new and
senseless worship of their own devising, whether in superstition
or in mockery, were not events so recent and so notorious. After
abjuring our Lord and Saviour, and blasphemously declaring Him
to be an impostor, they proceeded to decree, in the public assembly
of the nation, the adoration of Liberty and Equality as divinities:
and they appointed festivals besides in honour of Reason.

Here was the historical context that Newman supplied for his concerns
over liberalism—a revolutionary context in which liberalism became not
only anti-religion but a religion in itself. And we can readily see how Gib-
bon's anti-Christian, rationalist history contributed to the anti-Christian,
rationalist tyranny that came to define the French Revolution, which has
provided the blueprint for all anti-Christian revolution ever since.

The redoubtable diplomatic historian, George Peabody Gooch, who
lived a splendidly long life (from 1873 to 1968) was convinced, as he said
in his magisterial *History and Historians in the Nineteenth Century* (1913) that
"Gibbon constructed a bridge from the old world to the new which is still
the highway of nations, and stands erect long after every other structure of
the time has fallen into ruins." This was truer than old Gooch could have
realized. But to appreciate just how truly he spoke, we need to consult the
prophetic historian in Newman.

Why should any of us bother ourselves about this new religion of Liberty and Equality? We should bother ourselves about it because it is the same religion to which our own rationalists subscribe, those who promote contraception and abortion, sodomy and transgenderism, gender theory and what the most impudent of them style "same-sex marriage." It is replete with notions of false liberty. It is anti-life and it is most decidedly anti-Catholic.

In conclusion, Newman is an historian worth heeding because he recognized that history is not, *pace* Gibbon, "little more than the register of the crimes, follies, and misfortunes of mankind"; it is the register of man's need for salvation—indeed, his hope for salvation—which is why Newman's own history is founded on the Cross, as we can see most brilliantly in his sermon, "The Cross of Christ the Measure of the World" (1841):

> It is the death of the Eternal Word of God made flesh, which is our great lesson how to think and how to speak of this world. His Cross has put its due value upon everything which we see, upon all fortunes, all advantages, all ranks, all dignities, all pleasures; upon the lust of the flesh, and the lust of the eyes, and the pride of life. It has set a price upon the excitements, the rivalries, the hopes, the fears, the desires, the efforts, the triumphs of mortal man. It has given a meaning to the various, shifting course, the trials, the temptations, the sufferings, of his earthly state. It has brought together and made consistent all that seemed discordant and aimless. It has taught us how to live, how to use this world, what to expect, what to desire, what to hope ...
>
> Go to the political world: see nation jealous of nation, trade rivalling trade, armies and fleets matched against each other. Survey the various ranks of the community, its parties and their contests, the strivings of the ambitious, the intrigues of the crafty. What is the end of all this turmoil? the grave. What is the measure? the Cross.
>
> Go, again, to the world of intellect and science: consider the wonderful discoveries which the human mind is making, the variety of arts to which its discoveries give rise, the all but miracles by which it shows its power; and next, the pride and confidence of reason, and the absorbing devotion of thought to transitory objects, which is the consequence. Would you form a right judgment of all this? look at the Cross.
>
> Again: look at misery, look at poverty and destitution, look at oppression and captivity; go where food is scanty, and lodging unhealthy. Consider pain and suffering, diseases long or violent, all that is frightful and revolting. Would you know how to rate all these? gaze upon the Cross.
>
> Thus in the Cross, and Him who hung upon it, all things meet; all things subserve it, all things need it. It is their centre and their

interpretation. For He was lifted up upon it, that He might draw all men and all things unto Him.

The eminent Acton scholar, Josef Althoz, who taught for many years at the University of Minnesota and edited Acton's letters to the liberal Catholic Richard Simpson, argued that Newman's "commitment to religion was too profound to allow him to submit to the rival discipline of history" and that therefore "he was ahistorical in his outlook." Keeping this great sermon on the Cross in mind, I should argue that it is precisely because of Newman's "commitment to religion"—the very essence of religion—that he understood history in ways that entirely eluded Gibbon and continues to elude all of his rationalist progeny within and outside of the Church.

Newman's *Anglican Difficulties*:
An Interview with the Editor

CATHOLIC WORLD REPORT (CWR): *Your critical edition of John Henry Newman's* Anglican Difficulties *(1850, rev. ed. 1876) is your fourth book on Newman, the previous three treating, in turn, Newman and his contemporaries, his family, and his views of history. Tell us about this latest book.*

EDWARD SHORT: Newman's *Anglican Difficulties* consists of twelve talks that he gave at the London Oratory in King William Street in 1850, five years after his conversion. His audience comprised Catholics, Anglo-Catholics, Protestants and intrigued skeptics. In addition to Catholic priests and Anglican ministers, there were convert peeresses and "hard-faced" Irishmen in attendance as well—an ecumenical mix. While the stated purpose of the lectures might have been "to clear away from the path of an inquirer objections to Catholic truth," especially Anglo-Catholic inquirers, the book is also a brilliant meditation on the Church and the World, an unsparingly satirical study of the Oxford Movement, an auto-biographical dress rehearsal for the *Apologia pro Vita Sua* (1864) and a piece of masterly prose.

Neglected for over a century by many who regarded its hard-hitting criticism of the Erastian National Church of England as merely polemical, the book can now be seen as profoundly cautionary. (*Erastian* is an eponymous word from the sixteenth-century Swiss theologian Erastus, who held that churches should be subordinate to the state.) If one of the book's animating themes is to show how worldly establishments travesty "the Ark of Salvation," Newman's *Anglican Difficulties* has perennial appeal.

"For this is the truth," he says in a famous passage: "the Establishment, whatever it be in the eyes of men, whatever its temporal greatness and its secular prospects, in the eyes of faith is a mere wreck." One can only imagine how the Anglican Establishment in Newman's day bristled at such a charge. They bristle still. Yet he was addressing them as a Dutch uncle, intent on telling them truths they needed to hear, not out of supercilious-ness or spite but charity and love. And since he, too, had once been avid to defend the Anglican Establishment there is an authority to his tough love:

We must not indulge our imagination, we must not dream: we must look at things as they are; we must not confound the past with the present, or what is substantive with what is the accident of a period. Ridding our minds of these illusions, we shall see that the Established Church has no claims whatever on us, whether in memory or in hope; that they only have claims upon our commiseration and our charity whom she holds in bondage, separated from that faith and that Church in which alone is salvation. If I can do aught towards breaking their chains, and bringing them into the Truth, it will be an act of love towards their souls, and of piety towards God.

Now that we see the Vatican subordinating the Church in China to the Chinese Communist Party, we can see that Newman's concern about Erastianism has applications well beyond the nineteenth-century Anglicanism with which he had so many issues. As he points out in the lectures, the Roman Catholic Church has always been threatened by states seeking to undermine her unique mission in the world.

One irony of Newman's reading of these matters is that the entity that he credits with having kept the Church free of any lasting imperial or state interference over the centuries was the papacy, the very entity that has become so Erastian under the pontificate of Pope Francis, though it is always reassuring to keep in mind something Newman wrote in one of his letters during the First Vatican Council when the issue of papal infallibility was being debated: "The temporal prosperity, success, talent, renown of the Papacy did not make me a Catholic, and its errors and misfortunes have no power to unsettle me."

The "see no evil" approach of so many Catholics when it comes to this problem of papal Erastianism—especially Opus Dei Catholics—only makes it worse: we have no obligation as Catholics to acquiesce in the corruption and heterodoxy that result when the papacy subordinates itself to Red China or the European Union or the American Democratic Party—all demonstrably malign establishments that would have incurred the unsparing disapproval of Newman.

✠

CWR: *You say that one of the book's major preoccupations is one of Newman's greatest themes, the relationship between the Church and the World. Can you expand on that?*

EDWARD SHORT: The theme of the Church and the World goes to the heart of the overriding theme of the lectures but also Newman's work as a whole. It exhibits the unity of his work, since he takes this theme up in so many of his other works, including his *Arians of the Fourth Century* (1833), *The Essay on the Development of Christian Doctrine* (1845), *The Idea of a University* (1870) and *A Letter to the Duke of Norfolk* (1875)

The theme also gives Newman the opportunity to reaffirm the unique mission of the Church, which the World always seeks to thwart, has indeed sought to thwart from the Church's very inception. "There was once no independent jurisdiction in religion," he writes, "but, when our Lord came, it was with the express object of introducing a new kingdom, distinct and different from the kingdoms of the world, and He was sought after by Herod, and condemned by Pilate, on the very apprehension that His claims to royalty were inconsistent with their prerogatives. Such was the Church when first introduced into the world, and her subsequent history has been after the pattern of her commencement; the State has ever been jealous of her, and has persecuted her from without and bribed her from within."

✣

CWR: *One of Newman's most winning qualities is his readiness to see matters as they are, before trying to make them what they should be. Can you give us an example of how he exhibits this quality in his lectures?*

EDWARD SHORT: A perfect example of this is Newman's readiness to concede the difficulties of conversion, not just for Anglo-Catholics, but for everyone, especially conversion to a Church so many of whose truths naturally revolt the natural man, let alone what Newman nicely refers to as the "coalition of wit and wisdom."

Here one can also see the rhetorical *élan* of the lectures, which is never more in evidence than when Newman is recommending the consequential but overlooked truth of his subject. Speaking of the hostility that the Church has always incurred, he writes: "It would be wonderful, indeed, if a teaching which embraces all spiritual and moral truth, from the highest to the least important, should present no mysteries or apparent inconsistencies," he says in his first lecture;

> wonderful if, in the lapse of eighteen hundred years, and in the range of three-fourths of the globe, and in the profession of thousands of millions of souls, it had not afforded innumerable points of plausible attack; wonderful, if it could assail the pride and sensuality which are common to our whole race, without rousing the hatred, malice, jealousy, and obstinate opposition, of the natural man; wonderful, if it could be the object of the jealous and unwearied scrutiny of ten thousand adversaries, of the coalition of wit and wisdom, of minds acute, far-seeing, comprehensive, original, and possessed of the deepest and most varied knowledge, yet without some sort of case being made out against it; and wonderful, moreover, if the vast multitude of objections, great and small, resulting from its exposure to circumstances such as these, acting on the timidity, scrupulousness, inexperience, intellectual fastidiousness, love of the world, or self-dependence of individuals, had not been sufficient

to keep many a one from the Church, who had, in spite of them, good and satisfactory reasons for joining her communion. Here is the plain reason why so many are brought near to the Church, and then go back, or are so slow in submitting to her.

In this passage, one can see that Newman does his auditors the honor of never talking down to them. Charles Lamb once described one of his fellow clerks at the South Sea House as having "the air and stoop of a nobleman," and by "stoop" he meant "that gentle bending of the body forward, which, in great men, must be supposed to be the effect of an habitual condescending attention to the applications of their inferiors." Well, Newman was certainly a great man but he had none of the great man's air or stoop. He always treats his readers as though they are on his own level. Consequently, he treats his old Anglican friends' difficulties with Catholicism with the respect they deserve, though this does not always rule out his treating them with delicious satirical irony. As he said so memorably in his final lecture, "It is no work of a day to convince the intellect of an Englishman that Catholicism is true."

Together with the respect he showed his fellows, there was also a great *caritas* about Newman, a humility suffused with solicitude for their well-being. "If I have been excessive here," he said towards the end of his lectures, "if I have confused what is defective with what is hollow, or have mistaken aspiration for pretence, or have been severe upon infirmities of which self-knowledge would have made me tender, I wish it otherwise. Still, whatever my faults in this matter, I have ever been trustful in that true Catholic spirit which has lived in the movement of which you are partakers. I have been steady in my confidence in that supernatural influence among you, which made me what I am, which, in its good time, shall make you what you shall be. You are born to be Catholics; refuse not the unmerited grace of your bountiful God; throw off for good and all the illusions of your intellect, the bondage of your affections, and stand upright in that freedom which is your true inheritance." This, by any estimate, is wonderful writing.

✤

CWR: *Most readers who have studied the Oxford Movement are familiar with Dean Church's classic history. How would you characterize Newman's own contribution to the history of the Movement? Throughout the edition, you call the reader's attention to what you believe is Newman's overlooked acuity as an historian. How does his handling of the Oxford Movement substantiate your claim that he was a redoubtable historian?*

EDWARD SHORT: Dean Church writes his history of the Oxford Movement in his classic study in 1890 and Newman writes his history in *Anglican Difficulties* in 1850. That is a gap of 40 years and yet Church, although resolutely opposed to even considering following Newman into the Church of

Rome, largely bases his account of the Movement on Newman's insights. For example, he sees the Oxford Movement as having been launched to repel what Newman saw as the depredations of liberalism, especially in its attack on what he called the "dogmatic principle." And he follows Newman in depicting the fizzling out of the Movement in Oxford as having been caused not only by Newman's secession to Rome but by the rise of liberalism in Oxford.

Yet what makes Newman's account of the Movement so much more cogent is his treatment of the claims to apostolicity of the Anglican High Church. While Church glosses over these claims, Newman demolishes them, and one of the reasons why *Anglican Difficulties* has been largely ignored by Anglo-Catholics and those who sympathize with the Anglo-Catholic position is that Newman's demolition is fairly unanswerable.

Nevertheless, commentators still seek to deny the substance of Newman's criticism of the Anglican Church. Peter Nockles, for example, argued in his book *The Oxford Movement in Context* (1991) that Newman and the Tractarians had done little that the High Church had not done in the eighteenth and early nineteenth centuries—a claim that he pinched from Frederick Meyrick, the Bursar of Trinity College—but one can see from both Newman's and Church's accounts that the Movement opposed High Churchmen as well as liberals. To try to substantiate his risible claim, Nockles went so far as to argue that Newman's reading of the Erastian character of the Anglican Church in *Anglican Difficulties* "did much to perpetuate a misconception of Orthodox teaching on church and state"—as though the disavowals of the High Church themselves when it came to their Erastianism were proof that they were not Erastian. And he did this by citing of all people, Geoffrey Faussett, the High Churchman who delated poor Edward Pusey for preaching on the Eucharist. Over the centuries, Newman has attracted many inept commentators—I am writing a rather long, excoriating book about them for my patient friends in Bedford Square—but Nockles is one of the absolute worst.

If one were to concede Nockles's point that there was no such thing as Erastianism in the Anglican Church, there should have been no basis for Anglo-Catholicism in the first place, for as Newman clearly reminds his readers: Anglo-Catholicism "has been formed on one idea, which has developed into a body of teaching of the National Church logical in the arrangement of its portions, and consistent with the principles on which it originally started. That idea, or first principle, was ecclesiastical liberty; the doctrine which it especially opposed was in ecclesiastical language, the heresy of Erastus, and in political, the Royal Supremacy. The object of its attack was the Establishment, considered simply as such."

Ecclesiastical liberty … In Newman's time, as in our own, this was a vital principle, the abrogation of which gave rise to much mischief and, indeed, much unbelief and much corruption of belief. Newman's main argument in *Anglican Difficulties* is that by remaining in the Established Church the Anglo-Catholics were betraying their core principle.

But there is a lesson here for Catholics as well. It is precisely because we witness a Catholic Church in our own time accommodating the *Zeit-geist* of progressivism that we should attend to what Newman had to say about the Anglican Church accommodating the *Zeitgeist* of liberalism in the nineteenth century. For those who clamor that the Church must somehow remake herself as the agent of what the progressives call "social justice," Newman has a withering reply: "If the Church be a kingdom, or government, not of this world, I do trust you have provided for her a message, a function, not of this world, something distinct, something special, something which the world cannot do, which 'eye hath not seen, nor ear heard, nor heart of man conceived.' It is not enough to give her morality to preach about; why a heaven-appointed Society for that? With the Bible in his hands, if that be all, I do not see why one man, if properly educated, should not preach morality as well as another, without any disturbance of the rights of the magistrate or the order of civil society."

Another interesting feature of Newman the historian is how his lectures confirm the "Catholicity" of the Catholic Church by contrasting it with the special pleading of the Anglo-Catholics. No one makes the case for Anglo-Catholicism less persuasively than the Anglo-Catholics themselves. Newman makes particularly good satirical use of the writings of William Warburton, Bishop of Gloucester (1698–1779), the pre-eminent defender of Erastianism, and William Palmer of Worcester (1803–85), the exponent of what became known as "the branch theory," according to which the Anglican Church is entitled to regard itself as "Catholic" because it is a "branch" of something the Anglo-Catholics call the "Universal Church."

✢

CWR: *You say in your introduction that the lectures constitute something of a dress rehearsal for Newman's great autobiography, the* Apologia pro Vita Sua. *Can you elaborate?*

EDWARD SHORT: Since Newman led the very Anglo-Catholic party within the Anglican Church that he criticizes so roundly in the lectures, the lectures are necessarily replete with autobiography. Newman's detractors are fond of charging him with playing fast and loose with the truth of his own role in the Oxford Movement. Indeed, they treat his *Apologia* as though it were little more than an exercise in self-vindication. Yet the fact remains that in *Anglican Difficulties*, as in the *Apologia*, Newman is unsparing when it comes to criticizing his own role in attempting to salvage the "wreck" of Anglo-Catholicism, or what he refers to as "mimic Catholicism."

One of the reasons why the Anglo-Catholic party, by and large, never responded to the lectures—other than to ignore them—is that they could never forgive Newman for repudiating the *Via Media*, about which he says in the final lecture that it may be "an interposition or arbitration between the extreme doctrines of Protestantism on the one hand, and the faith of Rome which Protestantism contradicts on the other" but "it is, from the nature of the case, but a particular form of Protestantism." Why? Its "essential idea" is "that [Catholicism] has gone into error, whereas the essential idea of Catholicism is the Church's infallibility." For Newman to state so bluntly that the "halfway house" of the *Via Media* was the manufacture of Protestantism—the very thing that the "Movement of 1833," as Newman called it, most abominated—was simply intolerable to his erstwhile Anglo-Catholic friends, though no account of the Oxford Movement can have any genuine historical or theological value that does not concede this fundamental point. The Oxford Movement, after all, was a rather rarefied game of "hunt the slipper" and the upshot was that most of its acolytes never found the slipper. Newman did, but few of his Tractarian friends followed suit.

✢

CWR: *Truth is obviously a great theme in the lectures. What is the significance of that?*

Edward Short: Newman was a Servant of Truth. He found the writing of *Anglican Difficulties* such an ordeal precisely because he knew that in swearing his allegiance to the Truth when it came to the untenability of Anglicanism he would offend and estrange many dear Anglican friends. And yet he upheld the Truth—without ever showing his erstwhile friends any mean-spiritedness. On the contrary, he shows them how Truth is the very bond of fellowship.

✢

CWR: *What can you tell us about the textual variations?*

Edward Short: They are tell-tale. Owen Chadwick's claim that the book was an overzealous convert's overzealous plug for Catholicism, a plug which the older Newman would never have made, is utterly false. "Ten years later," the church historian wrote, "Newman would not have written in this language. He was suffering … from the disease of being a new convert, of burning what once he adored." The changes that Newman made to the revised text of 1876 prove otherwise. They are syntactical, not substantive. I should only add that Dr. Andrew Nash did a superb job with the textual variants, which he identified and set out with great exacting care.

✢

CWR: *You say that the lectures are a treasure trove of Newman's brilliance as a prose stylist. Can you provide a few examples?*

Edward Short: In each of the 12 hour-long lectures, Newman includes set pieces of declamatory prose of great power, which, when one remembers that he had a lovely speaking voice, must have been enthralling to hear. That these are preserved on the printed page is a great blessing. For anyone discouraged by the rise of heterodoxy within the Church, Newman supplies an encouraging antidote:

> *Noli æmulari* Is it not written in the book of truth, that the ungodly shall spread abroad like a green bay tree, and then shall wither? that the adversary reaches out his hand towards his prey, in order that he may be more emphatically smitten? "Yet a little while, and the wicked shall not be: I passed by, and lo! he was not; I sought him, and his place was not found. Better is a little to the just than the great riches of the wicked; for the arms of the wicked shall be broken, but the Lord strengtheneth the just." So was it with the great Arian heresy, which the civil power would fain have forced upon the Church; but it fell to pieces, and the Church remained One. So was it with Nestorius, with Eutyches, with the Image-breakers, with Manichees, with Lollards, with Protestants, into whom the State would put life, but who, one and all, refuse to live. So is it with the communion of Cranmer and Parker, which is kept together only by the heavy hand of the State, and cannot aspire to be free without ceasing to be one. One power alone on earth has the gift and destiny of ever being one. It has been so of old time; surely so will it be now. Man's necessity is God's opportunity. *Noli æmulari,* "Be not jealous of the evil-doers."

Here, we can see the contrast between the Church and the World at the very heart of the lectures, on which Newman expatiates at length in terms that we can readily recognize in our own increasingly baleful experience.

> The world believes in the world's ends as the greatest of goods; it wishes society to be governed simply and entirely for the sake of this world. Provided it could gain one little islet in the ocean, one foot upon the coast, if it could cheapen tea by sixpence a pound, or make its flag respected among the Esquimaux or Otaheitans, at the cost of a hundred lives and a hundred souls, it would think it a very good bargain. What does it know of hell? it disbelieves it; it spits upon, it abominates, it curses its very name and notion. Next, as to the devil, it does not believe in him either. We next come to the flesh, and it is "free to confess" that it does not think there is any great harm in following the instincts of that nature which, perhaps it goes on to say, God has given. How could it be otherwise? who ever heard of the world fighting against the flesh and the devil? Well, then, what is its notion of evil? Evil, says the world, is whatever is an offence to me, whatever obscures my majesty, whatever disturbs my peace. Order, tranquility, popular contentment, plenty, prosperity,

advance in arts and sciences, literature, refinement, splendour, this is my millennium, or rather my elysium, my swerga; I acknowledge no whole, no individuality, but my own.

If this is the view of the world that Newman takes in the lectures, a view very much like our own, though the nineteenth century managed such things as "literature," "refinement," and "splendour" better than its twenty-first century successors, this is the view he takes of the Church:

> My dear brethren, do not think I am declaiming in the air or translating the pages of some old worm-eaten homily; as I have already said, I bear my own testimony to what has been brought home to me most closely and vividly as a matter of fact since I have been a Catholic; viz., that that mighty world-wide Church, like her Divine Author, regards, consults for, labours for the individual soul; she looks at the souls for whom Christ died, and who are made over to her; and her one object, for which everything is sacrificed—appearances, reputation, worldly triumph—is to acquit herself well of this most awful responsibility. Her one duty is to bring forward the elect to salvation, and to make them as many as she can to take offences out of their path, to warn them of sin, to rescue them from evil, to convert them, to teach them, to feed them, to protect them, and to perfect them. Oh, most tender loving Mother, ill-judged by the world, which thinks she is, like itself, always minding the main chance; on the contrary, it is her keen view of things spiritual, and her love for the soul, which hampers her in her negotiations and her measures, on this hard cold earth, which is her place of sojourning.

✤

CWR: *Any reflections in conclusion?*

EDWARD SHORT: The lectures warn readers of the great evil establishments can do when they seek to warp, appropriate or suppress the Church. Certainly, we see that all around us now. When Archbishop Vigano speaks of the criterion for the choice of so many cardinals under the present pontificate as "corruptibility," he is not speaking idly. His analysis of the captivity in which the Erastian Church now finds herself will be proven accurate.

In Newman's anatomy of the ways in which the Anglican Establishment tried to masquerade as the "Ark of Salvation" over its 300-year history, he points out the corrosive influence of secular states that should be as much a warning to Catholics as Protestants. Erastianism, after all, is not simply a Protestant problem.

Nevertheless, at the same time, Newman's lectures show his evangelizing love for his old companions in the Oxford Movement and, by extension, for everyone of good faith who seek to know and embrace the Truth of God's promises.

In his essence, Newman is not an intellectual or even a controversialist, though his books abound in intellectual fireworks and the most agile, devastating polemics. No, he is, at heart, a parish priest—a priest dedicated to the cure of souls. And the best bits of *Anglican Difficulties* show this. "Provided she can do for the soul what is necessary," he wrote of the Church that meant so much to him, "if she can but pull the brands out of the burning, if she can but extract the poisonous root which is the death of the soul, and expel the disease, she is content." Readers dismayed by how ineffectual the Church has become in defending her own God-given integrity will come away from reading the book with their faith renewed. Like so much else that Newman wrote, *Anglican Difficulties* is a testament not only to God's Truth but His Grace.

A Saint's Life

John Henry Newman was born in London at 80 Old Brook Street on 21 February 1801. His father, John Newman was a private banker in the City of London, the son of a Mayfair grocer, originally of Cambridgeshire; his mother, Jemima (née) Fourdrinier, was the daughter of a printer of Norman Huguenot stock, whose family became well known for its innovative paper making. Newman's parents married in 1799 and had six children, John Henry being the eldest, followed by two younger sons and three daughters. Of Ham House, the family's beloved summer home near Richmond, Newman recalled gazing at "candles in the windows in illumination for the victory at Trafalgar"—a fitting memory for a man who would grow up to become himself one of England's national heroes.

Given to warm personal relations—indeed, Newman had a genius for friendship—he was chary of personal avowals. In the *Apologia*, he writes of his distaste for what he called "disclosures." Yet, here and there, he revealed striking things about his youth. "I was brought up from a child to take great delight in reading the Bible," he remarked; and while he had "no formed religious convictions till [he] was fifteen … [he] had perfect knowledge of [his[Catechism." When the family moved into an elegant Georgian townhouse at 17 Southampton Place in Bloomsbury, Newman recalled "admiring the borders of the paper in the drawing rooms." His other memory of childhood was equally characteristic: he "rested," as he put it, "in the thought of two and two only supreme and luminously self-evident beings, myself and my Creator." Beauty and truth—vital prerequisites for anyone's entering into what Newman called "the Presence of the Word Incarnate"—would always attract him.

In 1808 Newman enrolled in Ealing School, where the classics master, Walter Mayers renewed his Christian faith. "From the age of fifteen, dogma has been the fundamental principle of my religion," Newman would later write in the *Apologia*, and for this he first credited Mayers. Another crucial influence was that of the Biblical scholar Thomas Scott, whom Newman admired for "his resolute opposition to Antinomianism" and his two mottoes, "Holiness rather than peace" and "Growth the only evidence of life."

In 1817, Newman went up to Trinity College, Oxford. In 1822, notwithstanding his poor degree, he was elected fellow of Oriel College, where he befriended Hurrell Froude and John Keble. He also delighted in playing Beethoven's quartets with Blanco White. (Newman was an accomplished violinist.)

At Oriel, Newman began an extensive study of the early Fathers of the Church. He also began to see more clearly the dangers of liberalism, which he described in a letter of 1832 as a "cold and scoffing theory, which says there is no great evil in the world ... and all religions are about the same." Later, in 1879, when Pope Leo XIII gave him his red hat, he would declare that he had spent "thirty, forty, fifty years" combatting liberalism, "the doctrine that there is no positive truth in religion, but that one creed is as good as another." The claim, often made by Newman's detractors, that his opposition to liberalism was inconsistent is demonstrably false.

In 1833, Newman toured the Mediterranean with Froude. After attending his first Mass in Rome, he wrote to his mother: "as I looked on, and saw ... the Holy Sacrament offered up, and the blessing given, and recollected I was in church, I could only say in very perplexity my own words, 'How shall I name thee, Light of the wide west, or heinous error-seat?'" When Froude left Rome for France, Newman decided to return to Sicily by himself, which, as he wrote, "filled me with inexpressible rapture, and to which ... [I was drawn] as by a lodestone"—for the unsuspecting pilgrim a most providential lodestone. Succumbing to typhoid fever, he cried aloud, "I have not sinned against [the] light." In the lucid intervals of fever, he told himself: "God has work for me."

After recovering from fever, with the help of a loyal Neapolitan servant named Gennaro, who had been a sailor aboard the *Victory* at the Battle of Trafalgar, Newman sailed from Palermo to Marseille on an orange boat. Becalmed in the Straits of Bonifacio, he wrote what would become known as "Lead, Kindly Light," the hymn that expresses so movingly his trust in the Light that would guide him ever after.

Returning to England in 1833, Newman joined with Froude and Keble to form the Oxford Movement, the purpose of which was to try to introduce some dogmatic coherence into the Anglican Church—which proved a quixotic, doomed enterprise. In 1834, he published the first of eight volumes of his *Parochial and Plain Sermons*. When his *via media* came to smash, partly as the result of his arguing in Tract 90 that the 39 Articles could sustain a Catholic reading, he retired to Littlemore, where he moved closer and closer to recognizing Roman Catholicism as what he called the "Ark of salvation."

In 1842, he published his *Oxford University Sermons*, which set out the truths of faith and reason denied by the rationalists of the age. In September 1843, he resigned the living of St. Mary the Virgin, where he had preached his sermons. In October of 1845, he resigned his Oriel fellowship. On 9 October, he was received into the Church of Rome. Nothing reveals the saint in Newman better than the faithful aplomb with which he left all he loved in the world to embrace and defend what he called the "one true fold of the Redeemer."

In his *Essay on the Development of Christian Doctrine* (1845), Newman showed how the history of the Catholic Church inheres in her adopting true and rejecting false developments. For Saint John Paul II, it was Newman's "passionate contemplation of truth" that enabled him to see Christ as "the light at the heart of every kind of darkness." In 1846, he showed how central the Blessed Sacrament was to his Catholic faith when he wrote of St Fidelio in Milan: "I could go into this beautiful church … all day long without tiring. … Nothing moves there but the distant glittering Lamp which betokens the Presence of our Undying Life, hidden but ever working for us."

Ordained a priest in Rome in 1847, Newman took as his patron saint the joyous Florentine St. Philip Neri and established the Birmingham Oratory. In 1848, he published *Loss and Gain*, his Oxford novel, one of whose characters speaks of the Mass as "not a mere form of words" but "the evocation of the Eternal," where Our Lord and Saviour "becomes present on the altar in flesh and blood before whom angels bow and devils tremble."

Upon settling into his new Oratorian life, Newman published his *Lectures on the Present Position of Catholics in England* (1851), an exuberant skewering of No Popery. In 1852, after helping to found the Catholic University in Dublin, for which he served as rector from 1851 to 1858, crossing the Irish Sea 56 times, he published his *Discourses on the Scope and Nature of University Education*, the blueprint for his classic, *The Idea of a University* (1873). In 1859, he wrote "On Consulting the Faithful in Matters of Doctrine," which urged that the laity be treated "with attention and consideration." Why? Because "the body of the faithful is one of the witnesses to … the tradition of revealed doctrine, and because their *consensus* through Christendom is the voice of the Infallible Church"—a heartening reminder for an age, like ours, mired as it is in episcopal failure to uphold that infallibility. In the same year, Newman helped to form the laity himself by founding the Oratory School.

Two controversies preoccupied Newman's Catholic life. In 1864, in response to Charles Kingsley's alleging that "Truth for its own sake was never a virtue with the Roman clergy" and that "Father Newman informs us that it need not be, and on the whole ought not to be," Newman wrote his *Apologia Pro Vita Sua* to defend his own and his coreligionists' veracity. "It is not pleasant to be giving to every shallow or flippant disputant the advantage over me of knowing my most private thoughts, I might even say the intercourse between myself and my Maker," Newman wrote. "But I do not like to be called to my face a liar and a knave: nor should I be doing my duty to my faith or to my name, if I were to suffer it." Newman's inspired riposte met with almost universal acclaim. Dr. Liddon, Pusey's biographer, spoke for many when he wrote: "Dr. Newman's 'Apologia' is the greatest treat I have had for a very long time indeed ... the whole is beautiful beyond words." If Newman was the greatest prose stylist of the nineteenth century, nothing exhibits this better than the *Apologia*.

Newman's other controversy concerned the First Vatican Council's adoption of the doctrine of papal infallibility. Although he thought defining the doctrine inopportune, fearing it might unsettle converts, he accepted it himself as early as 1851. In responding to W. E. Gladstone's charge that papal infallibility would impede the exercise of conscience, indeed disable English Catholics from being loyal subjects, he wrote his *Letter to the Duke of Norfolk* (1875), which "upholds," as Newman's biographer Ian Ker remarks, "the sovereignty, but not the autonomy, of the individual conscience." The conscience, in other words, needs forming, and, for Catholics, it is formed by the Church's infallible teachings, not the counsels of self will.

In 1870, Newman published his *Grammar of Assent*, which anatomizes how we arrive at certainty in religious belief. When the Ultramontane W. G. Ward read it, he was disarmed: "In the midst of our ecclesiastical differences ... it is an unspeakable comfort to me ... that on one point at least and that a most important one, I can fight under your banner." To a Jesuit who claimed that the book's reasoning failed its epistemological object, Newman replied: "Syllogizing won't meet it."

After Newman was made a cardinal, the Duke of Norfolk wrote of how "it was sometimes urged that in Newman intellectual qualities were allowed somewhat to overcloud the simplicity of Catholic faith. But it would be difficult indeed to gather from any other writer than Newman such sublime conceptions of devotion to the Mother of God or of our kindred with the saints; and in all this the high intellectual insight is blended with the most childlike tenderness. I feel very strongly that the action of the Holy See in making Newman a Cardinal brought out this great side of his character, this great lasting teaching of his life."

Another biographer, Richard Holt Hutton echoed these sentiments, writing after Newman's death on 11 August 1890: "No more impressive testimony could have been afforded to the power, sincerity, and simplicity of the great English Cardinal's life than the almost unanimous outburst of admiration and reverence from all the English churches and all the English sects." On his tombstone, the great convert had written: *Ex umbris et imaginibus in veritatem*. Since Newman's life was not only a search for and finding but a testifying to the Truth, no man could ever have had an apter epitaph.

Epilogue

Evelyn Waugh's Displaced Persons

Throughout the early Middle Ages the monks were regarded by their lay contemporaries as the intercessors for the rest of society, divided against those who gave it livelihood by toil and those who defended it by arms. The monasteries therefore were not endowed solely as shrines of adoration or homes of charity, but as houses of public prayer, and when, in the perfected, self-conscious feudal state labour-service and military service were imposed and assessed as necessary functions of different classes, the monks were regarded as executing an equally indispensable social service of intercession.

Dom David Knowles, *The Monastic Order in England: From the Times of St. Dunstan to the Fourth Lateran Council 940—1216* (1940; second edition, 1963)

My God, when I have dedicated something I have written to any human person, I am taking away something which does not belong to me, and giving it away to one who is not competent to receive it. What I have written does not belong to me. If I have written the truth, then it is "God's truth": it would be true if every human mind denied it, or if there were no human minds in existence to recognize it. ... If I have written well, that is not because Hobbs, Nobbs, Noakes and Stokes unite in praising it, but because it contains that interior excellence which is some strange refraction of your own perfect beauty, and of that excellence of which you alone are the judge. If it proves useful to others, that is because you have seen fit to make use of it as a weak tool, to achieve something in them of that supernatural end which is their destiny, and your secret.

Ronald Knox, preface to an unfinished book of apologetics, quoted in Evelyn Waugh, *The Life of Right Reverend Ronald Knox* (1959)

I

In his crowning masterpiece, *Sword of Honour*, Evelyn Waugh describes an encounter between his Catholic hero Guy Crouchback and his father Gervase, which reinforces a major theme of the trilogy written between 1952 and 1961 and revised by the author into a single-volume text or "recension,"

473

as he called it, in 1965. In this scene, Guy, on leave from his regiment, the Halberdiers, during the Second World War, and reunited with his father, says in the wake of Italy's surrender:

> "What a mistake the Lateran Treaty was. It seemed masterly at the time—how long? Fifteen years ago? What are fifteen years in the history of Rome? How much better it would have been if the Popes had sat it out and then emerged saying: 'What was all that? *Risorgimento?* Garibaldi? Cavour? The House of Savoy? Mussolini? Just some hooligans from out of town causing a disturbance. Come to think of it, wasn't there once a poor little boy whom they called King of Rome?' That's what the Pope ought to be saying today."
>
> Mr. Crouchback regarded his son sadly. "My dear boy," he said, "you're really talking the most terrible nonsense, you know. That isn't at all what the Church is like. It isn't what she's *for.*"

This realization on the part of the elder Crouchback that the Church cannot conduct herself as though she were merely a political entity is pivotal to the book. Indeed, the real theme of *Sword of Honour* is the Church and the World. How do these two seemingly irreconcilable things coexist? Before I delve into this lively matter, I should say something briefly of the treaty that inspired Guy's contempt.

The Lateran Treaty (1929), struck between the Kingdom of Italy under King Victor Emmanuel III of Italy and the Holy See under Pope Pius XI, settled the hitherto unresolved Roman Question by recognizing the Vatican City as an independent state under the sovereignty of the Holy See. The Italian government also agreed to compensate the Roman Catholic Church for the loss of the Papal States during the pontificate of Pope Pius IX. For the historian Paul Corner of the University of Siena, the treaty "was an example of the fact that Mussolini's formula, 'Everything in the State, nothing outside the State, nothing against the State,' was capable of exceptions when necessary and when political advantage was to be gained," though the advantage to Mussolini was not unalloyed. "Certainly, the agreement consolidated his position and confirmed his independence from the [Fascist] party, but it did also mean a concession; like the monarchy, the Church remained an autonomous centre of power in respect to the Fascist structure and as such put a limit to any genuinely totalitarian pretensions."

For Cardinal Bourne, the Archbishop of Westminster between the years 1903 and 1935, the treaty was welcome. As he told his English countrymen in his Easter Sunday homily:

> One thing only is necessary for sovereignty—namely, to be absolutely *sui juris*—not to be the subject of another. This sovereignty may be rooted in a purely spiritual function ... But Peter and his successors, as mortal men, must have a foothold for their feet, a place

in which to dwell, a territory in which to exercise the necessary and essential function of their purely spiritual charge and sovereignty.

In *Sword of Honour*, Gervase Crouchback writes his son a pivotal letter in which he defends the treaty. "When you spoke of the Lateran Treaty," he writes, "did you consider how many souls may have been reconciled and have died at peace as the result of it? How many children may have been brought up in the faith who might have lived in ignorance? Quantitative judgments don't apply. If only one soul was saved, that is full compensation for any amount of loss of 'face.'"

Of course, the ignominious pact into which Pope Francis and his friends in the Vatican have entered with the red Chinese offers the Church no such assurances, nor does it secure her any autonomy; but Gervase's insistence that one soul saved is full compensation for any loss of diplomatic face resonates deeply with his son and becomes the thematic means by which Waugh unifies his work.

II

Gervase's letter is also a clear echo of what John Henry Newman had written in one of his first Catholic compositions, *Anglican Difficulties* (1850), in which he had occasion to remind his readers of the Church's true charge in the fallen World:

> My dear brethren, do not think I am declaiming in the air or translating the pages of some old worm-eaten homily; as I have already said, I bear my own testimony to what has been brought home to me most closely and vividly as a matter of fact since I have been a Catholic; viz., that that mighty world-wide Church, like her Divine Author, regards, consults for, labours for the individual soul; she looks at the souls for whom Christ died, and who are made over to her; and her one object, for which everything is sacrificed — appearances, reputation, worldly triumph — is to acquit herself well of this most awful responsibility. Her one duty is to bring forward the elect to salvation, and to make them as many as she can to take offences out of their path, to warn them of sin, to rescue them from evil, to convert them, to teach them, to feed them, to protect them, and to perfect them. Oh, most tender loving Mother, ill-judged by the world, which thinks she is, like itself, always minding the main chance; on the contrary, it is her keen view of things spiritual, and her love for the soul, which hampers her in her negotiations and her measures, on this hard cold earth, which is her place of sojourning.

When Gervase dies, Guy, in pensive attendance at the requiem Mass, takes stock of the counsel he had received from his father over the years and realizes that he is at a crossroads. The besetting sin of spiritual sloth about which his father had warned him requires his attention as never before, and Waugh describes him thus discerning his way forward:

> In the recesses of Guy's conscience there lay the belief that somewhere, somehow, something would be required of him; that he must be attentive to the summons when it came. They also served who only stood and waited. He saw himself as one of the labourers in the parable who sat in the marketplace waiting to be hired and were not called into the vineyard until late in the day. They had their reward on an equality with the men who had toiled since dawn. One day he would get the chance to do some small service which only he could perform, for which he had been created. Even he must have his function in the divine plan. He did not expect a heroic destiny. Quantitative judgments did not apply. All that mattered was to recognise the chance when it offered. Perhaps his father was at that moment clearing the way for him. "Show me what to do and help me to do it," he prayed.

This, too, echoes Newman, who wrote in one of his most cherished prayers:

> God has created me to do Him some definite service. He has committed some work to me which He has not committed to another. I have my mission. ... I am a link in a chain, a bond of connection between persons. He has not created me for naught. I shall do good; I shall do His work. I shall be an angel of peace, a preacher of truth in my own place, while not intending it if I do but keep His commandments. Therefore, I will trust Him, whatever I am, I can never be thrown away. If I am in sickness, my sickness may serve Him, in perplexity, my perplexity may serve Him. If I am in sorrow, my sorrow may serve Him. He does nothing in vain. He knows what He is about. He may take away my friends. He may throw me among strangers. He may make me feel desolate, make my spirits sink, hide my future from me. Still, He knows what He is about.

III

Since *Sword of Honour*, like *Brideshead Revisited* (1945) and *Helena* (1950), is a novel about the workings of Providence in the fallen world, Guy comes to realize his "definite service" in rather an anfractuous way. And to capture this anfractuosity, Waugh deploys one of his best characters, Virginia, a prodigal, promiscuous, ingenuous creature. At the book's opening she is civilly divorced from Guy, but has also remarried and divorced someone else, and after an affair with a man named Trimmer she then finds herself not only broke and alone but saddled with an unwanted pregnancy from him. The passages in the book describing Virginia desperately searching wartime London for an abortionist—with which Waugh was helped by his friend Anne Fleming, the wife of the creator of James Bond—exhibit not only his shrewd understanding of character but his even shrewder appreciation of the dignity of human fallenness—even at its most absurd.

The last prospective abortionist she visits, for instance, has actually closed shop, the War Office having requisitioned his talents for voodoo for the war effort. Instead of performing abortions, he now casts spells on Herr Von Ribbentrop, Hitler's ambassador to Britain. When Virginia meets the man whom she wishes to kill her child, he receives her with a memorable salutation.

"Good morning. Come in. How are you? You have the scorpions?"
"No," said Virginia, "no scorpions this morning."

Readers who know their Bible will see echoes in this of Luke 10:19. "Behold, I give unto you power to tread on serpents and scorpions, and over all the power of the enemy: and nothing shall by any means hurt you." But parents of children who know their Bible will also be reminded of Luke 11:12–14: "Now suppose one of you fathers is asked by his son for a fish; he will not give him a snake instead of a fish, will he? Or if he is asked for an egg, he will not give him a scorpion, will he? If you then, being evil, know how to give good gifts to your children, how much more will your heavenly Father give the Holy Spirit to those who ask Him?" In having Dr. Akonanga of 14 Blight Street, W.2., off the Edgware Road ask after scorpions, Waugh reminds his readers in one word of what the true relationship between God and his children should be. In giving the doctor's office this definite address, Waugh makes a vital allusion to Graham Greene's short story, "A Little Place Off the Edgware Road" (1939), in which his friend speaks of "the squalid darkening street," which was "only one of the innumerable tunnels connecting grave to grave where the imperishable bodies lay." Abortion, in other words, cannot abort God's immortal work.

Of course, Waugh presents the scene to portray the sinner in Virginia, but he does so with striking compassion. The sinner in Virginia actually has a tragic dignity. Once the misunderstanding about the parcel of scorpions is sorted out, Virginia introduces herself. "'I've come as a private patient,' she said. 'You've treated lots of women. Women like myself,' she explained with her high incorrigible candour, 'who want to get rid of babies.'" Virginia may be a sinner; she may be unaware of the love that God bears for her and her baby; but she is not a canting sinner. She does not follow the ineffable Marie Stopes and prate of birth control. She does not prate of reproductive rights, like our own sinners. She calls a spade a spade. She has come to the doctor to get rid of her unwanted child.

When Virginia despairs of finding an abortionist, she looks up her former husband, having heard that he is likely to come into a considerable fortune now that his father is dead. Guy is staying with his Uncle Peregrine after a parachute injury and welcomes the society of his lively former wife. Peregrine, a droll bachelor, whose exacting Catholicism puts one in mind of Bridey's faith in *Brideshead Revisited*, is the perfect foil for Virginia, though, as Waugh shows, for all their differences, they share an unworldly honesty. Indeed, when Peregrine takes Virginia out for dinner their conversation reveals their characters' improbable similarity.

> "Peregrine, have you never been to bed with a woman?"
> "Yes, said Uncle Peregrine smugly, "twice. It is not a thing I normally talk about."
> "Do tell."
> "Once when I was twenty and once when I was forty-five. I didn't particularly enjoy it."
> "Tell me about them."
> "It was the same woman."
> Virginia's spontaneous laughter had seldom been heard in recent years; it had once been one of her chief charms. She sat back in her chair and gave full, free tongue; clear, unrestrained, entirely joyous, without a shadow of ridicule, her mirth rang through the quiet little restaurant. Sympathetic and envious faces were turned towards her. She stretched across the tablecloth and caught his hand, held it convulsively, unable to speak, laughed until she was breathless and mute, still gripping his bony fingers. And Uncle Peregrine smirked. He had never before struck success. He had in his time been at parties where others had laughed in this way. He had never had any share in it. He did not know quite what it was that had won this prize, but he was highly gratified.
> "Oh, Peregrine," said Virginia at last with radiant sincerity, "I love you."

As their conversation continues, it transpires that the promiscuous Virginia and the celibate Peregrine have something else in common. They are both, in their different ways, keenly aware of the sorrows of sex, of how desire and disorder can go hand-in-hand. When Peregrine describes the attitude towards sex that he has encountered among the denizens of Bellamy's, he could be describing the sordid liaisons to which Virginia has succumbed before and after leaving Guy.

> "I know most men go in for love affairs," he said. "Some of them can't help it. They can't get on at all without women, but there are plenty of others—I daresay you haven't come across them much— who don't really care about that sort of thing, but they don't know any reason why they shouldn't, so they spend half their lives going after women they don't really want. I can tell you something you probably don't know. There are men who have been great woman-

izers in their time and when they get to my age and don't want it any more and in fact can't do it, instead of being glad of a rest, what do they do but take all kinds of medicines to make them *want* to go on? I've heard fellows in my club talking about it."

Peregrine also reveals his recognition of Virginia's peculiar plight in taking up with the ramshackle Trimmer when he says to his dinner guest: "You only have to look at the ghastly fellows who are a success with women to realise that there isn't much point in it." Virginia is described by Waugh as listening distractedly to her interlocutor, only making "a little pagoda of the empty oyster-shells on her plate." Yet when she breaks her silence, it is to share with Peregrine how she and he are bound together by other preoccupations. "Without raising her eyes she said: '*I'm* rather thinking of becoming a Catholic.'" Peregrine receives this startling revelation with a revelation of his own.

"Oh," he said. "Why?"
"Don't you think it would be a good thing?"
"It depends on your reasons."
"Isn't it always a good thing?"
The waiter reproachfully rearranged the oyster-shells on Virginia's plate before removing it.
"Well, isn't it?" she pressed. "Come on. Tell. Why are you so shocked suddenly? I've heard an awful lot one way and another about the Catholic Church being the Church of sinners."
"Not from me," said Uncle Peregrine.
The waiter brought them their turbot.
"Of course, if you'd sooner not discuss it ..."
"I'm not really competent to," said the Privy Chamberlain, the Knight of Devotion and Grace of the Sovereign Order of St. John of Jerusalem. "Personally I find it very difficult to regard converts as Catholics."

One might be inclined to see this as simply another comic twist of Peregrine's recusant Catholicism, but Waugh actually means it as an expression of the man's humility, his appreciation of the demands of conversion. "Uncle Peregrine hesitated between his acceptance in theory of the operation of divine grace and his distant but quite detailed observation of the men and women he had known, and relapsed to his former 'I'm really not competent to say.'" The devout Catholic in Peregrine is cast in an even more interesting light when he admits to Virginia that he had thought that she was coming to his flat not to see her estranged husband but him, an admission which appeals richly to her sense of the ridiculous, though Waugh could not present his portrait of these two unlikely sinners with more winning tenderness.

479

"Well," said Uncle Peregrine, "that alters everything." He looked at her with eyes of woe. "It was Guy you've been coming to see all these last days?"

"Of course. What did you think? ... Oh, Peregrine, did you think I had Designs on *you*?"

"The thought had crossed my mind."

"You thought perhaps I might provide your third—" She used a word, then unprintable, which despite its timeless obscenity did not make Uncle Peregrine wince. He even found it attractive on her lips. She was full of good humour and mischief now, on the verge of another access of laughter.

"That was rather the idea."

Here one can see Waugh's Jamesian flare for scene making—"Dramatise it, dramatise it!" being the American novelist's constant mantra. Yet James rarely managed dialogue of this beguiling alchemy.

"But surely that would have been Wrong?"

"Very Wrong indeed. I did not seriously entertain it. But it recurred often ... You could have moved into the room Guy is in now ..."

Virginia's laughter came again, most endearing of her charms.

"Darling Peregrine. And you wouldn't have needed any of those expensive treatments your chums in Bellamy's recommend?"

"In your case," said Uncle Peregrine with his cavalier grace, "I am practically sure not."

When Virginia shares her "Designs" with Guy, the two are forced to speak of the love that their fraught relations have betrayed. "I don't love any more," says the desolate Guy, to which Virginia retorts, pleadingly: "Not me?"

"Oh, no, Virginia, not you. You must have realised that."

"It is not easy to realise when lots of people have been so keen, not so long ago. What about you, Guy, that evening in Claridge's?"

"That wasn't love," said Guy. "Believe it or not, it was the Halberdiers."

"Yes. I think I know what you mean."

The justness of their agreeing on this last point is borne out by Waugh's describing wartime London earlier in the book as a place where "every doorway held an embraced couple." For no less a critic and no less a Londoner than V. S. Pritchett, "large portions of the last war were exactly as [Waugh] describes them." Pritchett is also astute in realizing that if "Crouchback's bad wife would once have been seen [by the novelist] as a vile body; she is now discerned as a displaced person." One of the great achievements of Waugh's masterpiece is to show how all of its characters are displaced persons, though their home is not this or that English or

European place but the country St Raphael describes in the prayer that meant so much to Flannery O'Connor.

> Raphael, lead us toward those we are waiting for,
> those who are waiting for us:
> Raphael, Angel of happy meeting,
> lead us by the hand toward those we are looking for.
> May all our movements be guided by your Light and transfigured
>   with your joy.
>
> Angel, guide of Tobias, lay the request we now address to you
> at the feet of Him on whose unveiled Face you are privileged to gaze.
> Lonely and tired, crushed by the separations and sorrows of life,
> we feel the need of calling you and of pleading for the protection
>   of your wings,
> so that we may not be as strangers in the province of joy,
> all ignorant of the concerns of our country.
> Remember the weak, you who are strong,
> you whose home lies beyond the region of thunder,
> in a land that is always peaceful, always serene and bright
> with the resplendent glory of God.

Of course, the "region of thunder" has a special significance for the ineffable Apthorpe but that is another story.

In showing Guy accepting Virginia's offer of re-marriage, even with Trimmer's child in her womb, indeed, precisely because of the illegitimate child, Waugh exhibits the fruits of the conversion that Peregrine finds so improbable, though, brilliantly, the novelist presents this turning to God from the standpoint of Guy's highly conventional friend, Kerstie—from the standpoint, that is to say, of Vanity Fair.

> "You poor bloody fool," said Kerstie, anger and pity and something near love in her voice, "you're being *chivalrous*—about *Virginia*. Can't you understand men aren't chivalrous anymore and I don't believe they ever were. Do you really see Virginia as a damsel in distress?"
> "She's in distress."
> "She's tough."
> "Perhaps when they *are* hurt, the tough suffer more than the tender."
> "Oh, come off it, Guy. You're forty years old. Can't you see how ridiculous you will look playing the knight-errant? Ian thinks you are insane, literally. Can you tell me any sane reason for doing this thing?"

Here, the Catholic Guy is at a disadvantage. He knows that the unbelieving Kerstie will not enter into why he is doing what he has decided to do, knight-errantry, in the sense in which she understands the term, being something rather different from love—self-surrendering love. Yet, he perseveres.

> "Of course Virginia is tough. She would have survived somehow. I shan't be changing her by what I'm doing. I know all that. But you see there's another"—he was going to say "soul"; then realized that this word would mean little to Kerstie for all her granite proprie-ty—"there's another life to consider. What sort of life do you think her child would have, born unwanted in 1944?"
> "It's no business of yours."
> "It was made my business by being offered."
> "My dear Guy, the world is full of unwanted children. Half the population of Europe are homeless—refugees and prisoners. What is one child more or less in all the misery?"
> "I can't do anything about all those others. This is just one case where I can help. And only I, really. I was Virginia's last resort. So I couldn't do anything else. Don't you *see*?"
> "Of course I don't. Ian [Kerstie's husband] was quite right. You're insane."

That Kerstie is married to Ian Kilbannock, the fatuous journalist attached to the Halberdiers, lends her worldly view of matters an extra absurdity. For Kerstie and Ian, to love selflessly *is* insane. They might have been the people St Paul had in mind when he told the Corinthians that the preaching of the cross is only foolishness to them that perish. Still, Kerstie's spiritual philistinism nicely offsets Guy's newfound *caritas*. "It was no good trying to explain, Guy thought. Had someone said: 'All differences are theolog-ical differences'? He turned once more to his father's letter: *Quantitative judgments don't apply. If only one soul was saved, that is full compensation for any amount of loss of 'face'.*"

Anne Pasternak Slater's comments apropos Guy's decision to take Vir-ginia back are spot on. She certainly recognizes that in the eyes of the Church Guy and Virginia have never been unmarried—despite their civil divorce. One of the very best of our literary critics, she understands the deep Catholic core of the book—a core which baffled Waugh's contempo-rary critics, including Kingsley Amis, Philip Toynbee, Frank Kermode and Gore Vidal, all of whom simply found the book "reactionary," "snobbish" and "hollow." In her study of Waugh, Pasternak Slater notes how the novelist introduces a character named Mr. Goodall, a connoisseur of the recusant aristocracy, to show how a distant relative of Guy unwittingly made an illegitimate child his heir. For Goodall, in God's eyes, the child is the true heir. Guy, however, is skeptical, asking whether God's Provi-dence could ever be construed to bother itself with "the perpetuation of the English Catholic aristocracy." Goodall insists that it is concerned with such things—"And with sparrows too, we are taught." And here Pasternak

Slater makes a lively point.

Now, in Waugh's final volume, this resolution is set the right way up. Guy knowingly fathers Trimmer's bastard son, and takes him into the household of his faith, a family of inestimably greater value than the aristocracy. Moral order is established and conventional validations of legitimacy and inherited class rejected. This, incidentally, is another answer to those who accuse Waugh of snobbery.

Trimmer, after all, we have to remember, begins his protean career as a hairdresser on Cunard ships. Moreover, the accuracy of Pasternak Slater's point is borne out by the description of Gervase Crouchback that Waugh provides his readers at the book's opening.

There was nothing of the old dandy about him, nothing crusted, nothing crotchety. He was not at all what is called a "character." He was an innocent, affable old man who had somehow preserved his good humour—much more than that, a mysterious and tranquil joy—throughout a life which to all outward observation had been overloaded with misfortune. He had like many another been born in full sunlight and lived to see night fall. He had an ancient name which was now little regarded and threatened with extinction. Only God and Guy knew the massive and singular quality of Mr. Crouchback's family pride.

The elder Crouchback is one of the book's best characters, a good man whose goodness Waugh manages to capture in a few choice, deft, luminous strokes. Ian Ker, in what is the very best essay ever written about the novelist, "Evelyn Waugh: The Priest as Craftsman" (2003), notes how:

When Mr. Crouchback dies, it seems entirely appropriate that his solicitor should observe that, although none of Mr. Crouchback's furniture is "of any value," nevertheless "it was all well made." A man who has done the job of being a Catholic, of doing Catholic things, so perfectly would naturally also have well-crafted furniture.

The American author, Gore Vidal, on the other hand, speaking for many of those outside the Catholic pale, found Waugh's Catholic art unconvincing. "Satirists seldom end well," he wrote in his review of the trilogy in the *New York Times*.

The rage that fills them and makes possible their irritable art is apt to turn on themselves. Dean Swift's madness is instructive. Waugh's own experiences, recorded in his extraordinary novel "The Ordeal of Gilbert Pinfold" (1956), are in that dark tradition. For Waugh's art, the difficulties inevitably increase as he turns from present horrors to his private vision of the good life. His religious and social preferences are his own business, but when he tries to make a serious case for them in his work, he is on shaky ground. Even the prose—so precise in its malice when he is on the attack—grows solemn and hollow when he tries to celebrate goodness and love and right action. One might say of him, to paraphrase James on Meredith, that he does the best things worst.

"Shaky ground"? The ground on which Waugh founded his Catholic art is man's inalienable failure, his radical need for God's grace and redemption. There is no more solid ground than that. Of course, if critics blind to the "mysterious and tranquil joy" that animates the faithful Gervase find Vidal's strictures plausible, they will miss out on the power and appeal of the book. As for satirists not ending well, Waugh died on Easter Sunday after Easter Sunday Mass surrounded by his family, a spry, devout, accomplished man. Only a fool would regard such an end as bad.

IV

Virginia's conversion is another instructive riposte to Peregrine's comical scrupulosity. "In Westminster Cathedral," Waugh writes, "Virginia made her first confession. She told everything; fully, accurately, calmly, without extenuation or elaboration. The recital of half a lifetime's mischief took less than five minutes. 'Thank God for your good humble confession,' the priest said. She was shriven. The same words were said to her as were said to Guy. The same grace was offered. Little Trimmer stirred as she knelt at the side-altar and pronounced the required penance; then she returned to her needlework." It is precisely the forthcoming naturalness of Virginia's unburdening of her sins that puts Peregrine's scruples in their necessary light. We can ponder the mystery of absolution all we like—or we can simply go to confession. Virginia chooses the latter. "That evening she said to Uncle Peregrine, as she had said before: 'Why do people make such a *fuss*? It's all so easy. But it is rather satisfactory to feel I shall never again have anything to confess as long as I live.'" Of course, in a new penitent, imagining that one confession will suffice for the conversion of the natural man might be a piece of understandable deludedness, but for Waugh, and for his readers, Virginia's peace of mind is edifying. It even impresses Peregrine. "Uncle Peregrine made no comment," Waugh notes. "He did not credit himself with any peculiar gift of discernment of spirits. Most things which most people did or said puzzled him, if he gave them any thought. He preferred to leave such problems in higher hands."

In describing Virginia's experience as a catechumen, Waugh offers his readers a portrait of conversion that should encourage even the most zealous of sinners to repent of their sins. Here, we have no Rex Mottram attempting to rig what ought to be the surrender, the unconditional surrender of conversion, but only the ingenuousness of assent.

Presently she said: "I've finished my lessons, you know.'"

"Lessons?"

"Instructions. Canon Weld says he's ready to receive me any time now."

"I suppose he knows best," said Uncle Peregrine dubiously.

"It's all so easy," said Virginia. "I can't think what those novelists make such a fuss over — about people 'losing their faith.' The whole thing is clear as daylight to me. I wonder why no one ever told me before. I mean it's all quite obvious really, isn't it, when you come to think of it?"

"It is to me," said Uncle Peregrine.

"I want you to be my godfather, please. And that doesn't mean a present — at least not anything expensive." She plied her needle assiduously, showing her pretty hands. "It's really you who have brought me into the Church, you know."

"I? Good heavens, how?"

"Just by being such a dear," said Virginia.

Here, the operation of Providence in the world, which Peregrine found so inscrutable in his earlier encounter with Virginia, becomes manifest. And that Waugh manages to pull this off with two characters who would not be out of place in his earlier Mayfair comedies is a mark of his consummate late artistry.

V

Most readers revel in *Sword of Honour* because of its high comedy. Apthorpe, Ritchie-Hook, and Ludovic are comic characters of a Falstaffian richness. Yet the comedy inherent in these farcical figures is unredeemed until we meet with Virginia's divine comedy. This is a comedy, as I have tried to show, with its own peculiar hilarity, but it is also a comedy suffused with grave purpose. It certainly gives Waugh the opportunity to end his trilogy on a note of profound hope — the hope of conversion in a world riddled with despair. And Virginia's decision to have, not abort her child, is at the heart of that conversion

After deciding to accept Trimmer's child as his heir, Guy seeks to help a few displaced Jews whom he has befriended. He has come to love his neighbor as he loves himself. The same desire to follow God's commandments that had converted him from a tribal to a true Catholic now enables him to look beyond the desolations of the smart set.

Accordingly, when Guy meets with one of his Jewish friends for the last time before she is taken away for her almost certain murder, the two descant on the nature of war, which turns out to be rather similar to the nature of original sin. While Guy tries to assure Mme Kanyi that someone who has been pursuing her will make no trouble for her, she demurs, and in her demurral, in a few offhand, simple utterances, she conjures up centuries of Jewish persecution. She also drives home what St Jerome deplored as the treacherousness of the human heart. Guy may be able to leave the debâcle of Crete behind him, but Mme Kanyi very likely will not. "You are leaving," she says. "There was a time when I thought that all I needed for happiness was to leave. Our people feel that. They must move away from evil. Some hope to find homes in Palestine. Most look no farther than Italy—just to cross the water, like crossing the Red Sea." For Mme Kanyi and her Jewish friends, fleeing evil is never easy, and this gives her an insight into the nature of evil hitherto unsuspected by Guy. "Is there any place that is free from evil," she asks.

> "It is too simple to say that only the Nazis wanted war. These Communists wanted it too. It was the only way in which they could come to power. Many of my people wanted it, to be revenged on the Germans, to hasten the creation of the national state. It seems to me there was a will to war, a death wish, everywhere. Even good men thought their private honour would be satisfied by war. They could assert their manhood by killing and being killed. They would accept hardships in recompense for having been selfish and lazy. Danger justified privilege. I knew Italians—not very many perhaps—who felt this. Were there none in England?"
> "God forgive me," said Guy. "I was one of them."

Faced with the aboriginal calamity of Guy's fallenness, one is grateful for Waugh's last joke, replete as it is with his Catholic sense of grace, indeed, his Catholic sense of hope. At the novel's end, Arthur Box-Bender, Guy's brother-in-law, who has always thought the Catholic faith nonsense, has been having trouble with his son. What is wrong with the son?

> Divorce? Debt? No, something odder than that. He'd gone into a monastery.

In summing up the novel, Frank Kermode argued that it only showed how "the whole matter of Catholic England and its hereditary defenders" was a "myth," to which Waugh clung to give some order to what he regarded as an otherwise disastrous world. Despite the novelist's best efforts, *Sword of Honour* only proved that the "force" of the myth was "diminishing." After all, at the book's end, "Priests are corrupt, England dishonoured; and the heir of Broome is sinking into despair until moved to virtuous action by the plight of displaced persons ... whom he could not save." Failure, in other words, in Kermode's jejune reading, discredits Christian hope. Waugh, of course, knew otherwise. Yes, he admitted in the preface that he had written, unwittingly, "an obituary for the Roman Catholic Church in England," loathing as he did the depredations of Vatican II. Yet at the same time the very fact that he has the son of Box-Bender enter the monastery at the end of the book affirms his recognition of the truth of something Newman had occasion to say in his "Sermon on the Liturgy" (1830): "Hope is the patient subdued tranquil cheerful thoughtful waiting for Christ."

INDEX

Index

Alfred 155; and Committee of Public Safety 154; and confiscation of Church property, after vilifying clergy 155; and Crabbe, George 152; and death of son, Richard 152–3; and Declaration of Right 151; and dissidence of dissent of American Protestantism 287–8; and Doyle, William 256; and evil 149; and family as "touchstone of good governance" 149, 150, 151–2, 157; and Flaubert, Gustav 157; and French Revolution as baleful precedent 163; and Gordon Riots 177, 239; and Hazlitt, William 150, 235–6, 240; and Ireland 153; and Irishry 237–8; and Langford, Paul 162, 240; and Locke, F. P. (biographer) 152; and *Magna Carta* 151; and Namier, Lewis 239; and Napoleon 153; and natural law 149–50, 151, 158–9; 160; and O'Brien, Conor Cruise 238; and "pattern of private life" 161; 236; and Paine, Thomas 156, 159; and *philosophes* 149–50, 238; and prescience 153; and Price, Richard 154; and rationalist arrogance 157; and rationalist constitutionalism 156–7; and Reynolds, Joshua 152; and rights of man 159, 160; and Robespierre 154; and Roman Catholicism 152, 162; and Rousseau 159; and "stamp of our forefathers" 159; and Swift, Jonathan 239; and Third Estate 154; and wife Jane Mary née Nugent 352 on *ancient regime* 157; on bad laws 237; on *Cecilia* (1782) by Fanny Burney 152; on Christianity and the Divine Wisdom 161; on corruption 162; on demands of maintenance of liberty 239; on inheritance 149, 161–2; on Jacobinism 153; on *philosophes* 157–8; on marriage 160–1; on popular will 239; on revolutionaries' "genius for self-promotion" 158–9; on outlawing of Roman Catholic Mass 237–8 on people as true legislator 240; on

revolution and abuse of language 239; revolutionary parvenus 154–5; on social order as compact between living and dead 238; on Terror, Jacobin 154; on tyranny of bad laws 237; on virtue 162, 239; on virtuous polity 239

WORKS: *Reflections on the Revolution in France* (1791), 149, 151, 154, 155; *An Appeal from the New to the Old Whigs* (1791) 149, 156; *A Letter to a Noble Lord* (1796) 154; *Letter on a Regicide Peace* (1796) 160

Burney, Fanny on Burke, Edmund 152
Butler, Joseph 36
Byron, George Gordon, Lord 5, 85, 128

Calhoun, John C. and the outlawing of slavery 192
Campbell, John 400
Causley, Charles 30
Cervantes 82
Chapman, Raymond 13, 28–9
Chapman, R. W. on Johnson, Samuel 134
Chateaubriand on anarchy in French Revolution 155
Chesterfield, Philip Dormer Stanhope, fourth Earl of 70, and Adams, Abigail 120–1
Chesterton, Gilbert Keith 5, 8, 44–5, 165, 224; and influence of "Lepanto" on Jennings, Elizabeth 88, on Hardy, Thomas 16, 32; on Lambeth Conference 219; on Stopes, Marie 219; on Schoolmen 320; on Tennyson, Lord Alfred 378
WORKS: *The Well and the Shallows* (1935) 219; *The Victorian Age in Literature* (1913) 16; *Autobiography* (1936) 16; "The White Pillars Murder" 425
Church, Richard William 413, 445, 462
Churchill, John, Duke of Marlborough 281
Churchill, Sir Winston, and ability to learn from successes 399; and ability to make converts of naysayers 402; and assessments by Butler, Rab

491

218; and mixed communions 220; and Müller, Cardinal Gerhard 231–2; and Newman, St. John Henry 69, 218, 226–7; and Norton, Charles Eliot 224–5; and Orwell, George and *Animal Farm* (1945) 397; and Ouellet, Cardinal Marc 229; and questions of tradition, belief and unbelief 75; and religious philistinism 225; and religious poetry 76–7; and Russell, Bertrand 224; and Russia 225–6; and sense of sin 40; and Shakespeare 70–1; and Socinianism, American 221; and Scott, Sir Walter 218; and Stevenson, Robert Louis 217; and Stopes, Marie 219; and style 72; Tennyson, Lord 67; Temple, William, Archbishop of York 219–20; and tradition 75; and unbelief 39, 226–7; and Vauvenargues 70; and Walpole, Horace 70; and wit, dry 221
on Andrewes, Lancelot 78; on Arnold, Matthew 38; on Baudelaire, Charles 68–9; Beerbohm, Sir Max 223–4; on Christian culture, fragility of 230–1; on Churchill, Winston 395–6; on contraception 219; on conversion 226–7; on culture and religion 230; on difference between reviewer and critic, 1–2; on Donne, John 75; on Greene, T. H. 69; on Hardy, Thomas 38–9; on Herbert, George 71–2; on Hopkins, Gerard Manley 72; on humanism 69–70; on Marivaux 70; on Moliere 70; on political solutions to unbelief 226; on prosody 74; on religious sense 73; on reputation for learning 222; on requirements for literary critic 72; on rhetoric, 4; on Pascal, Blaise 76; on Pius XII 78–9; on Rossetti, Christina 76–9; on Swinburne, Algernon 67–8, 220–1; on Southwell, SJ, St. Robert 76
POEMS: "East Coker," 25, 92; "Little Gidding" 39, *Ash-Wednesday* 39, *Four Quartets* 39: "Journey of the Magi" 39, 223; *The Waste Land* 38, 39
CRITICISM: *The Use of Poetry and the*

Use of Criticism 38; *After Strange Gods* 38–9; *The Sacred Wood* (1920) 69; *For Lancelot Andrewes* (1928), 69; *Selected Essays* (1932, 1934, 1951) 69; *On Poetry and Poets* (1957) 69, 179; "Tradition and the Individual Talent" 72, 114; *The Metaphysical Poets* (1926) 72, 112; "The Aims of Education" 73; "Shakespeare and the Stoicism of Seneca" 75; "The Pensées of Pascal" 76; "What Dante Means to Me" (1950) 82; "Christianity and Communism" (1932) 170, 225–6; ; "Revival of Christian Imagination" 217; *The Complete Prose of T. S. Eliot* 217–32; The Criterion 218; "Virgil and the Christian World" 223; "Towards a Christian Britain" 227–8; *Notes Towards the Definition of Culture* (1948) 230; "Second Thoughts on Humanism" 320; "The Literature of Politics" 403
PLAYS: *The Confidential Clerk* 2–3
Eliot, Valerie 68
Eliot, Vivienne 39, 114
Ellmann, Richard 62
Elton, Geoffrey, on history's inability to prove truth of universals 312; on humanists 319–20
Emerson, Ralph Waldo 44, 63
Empson, William and "malign neo-Christianity" 76

Family 7, 63, 73, 88, 122, 123, 127, 129, 144, 149, 150, 151, 156, 157, 160, 163, 165–6, 167, 169, 170–1, 172, 173, 174, 211, 227, 228, 231, 236, 238, 278, 279, 280, 296, 333, 334, 336, 349, 350–1, 353, 355–6, 364, 376, 412, 433, 454, 483, 484
Fathers of the Church 83, 311, 313, 321, 408, 425, 429, 449, 470
Fielding, Sir John 178
Fitzgerald, Francis Scott 357–60
Fitzgerald, Penelope 5
Flaubert, Gustav 295; 317; 341; and *Bouvard and Pecuchet* (1881) 157; on ignorance of history 295

Fontenelle 70
Ford, Mark 21
Franklin, Benjamin 178
Freud, Lucian 61
Froude, James Anthony 8, 316, 375

Gardner, Helen 139
Garigue-Lagrange, Reginald 224
General Election of 1892 243
George V, King of England 6
Gibbon, Edward 2, 145, 170, 365, 422, 425, 439, 449, 450, 451, 452, 453, 455, 456, 458
Gibson, James 13
Gielgud, John 92
Gillray 152
Gioia, Dana 30, 81; 97–115; and Auden, Wystan Hugh 101; and Bishop, Elizabeth 100; and Brubeck, Dave 101; and comedy, flare for 106; and the Cross 110; and Dante 113; and the dead 98; and desire 100, 101, 102, 103, 104, 105, 10, 110, 111, 113, 114; and Donne, John 112; and Eliot, T. S. 100, 101, 112, 114; and Ewart, Gavan 106; and Falstaff 108; and Fitzgerald, Penelope 108; and Fitzgerald, Robert 98, 100; and Fraser, Lady Antonia 101; and Frost, Robert 101; and Graves, Robert 98, 105; and Gray, Thomas 112; and Hardy, Thomas 101–2; and Hughes, Ted 110; and Jeffers, Robinson 101; and Johnson, Samuel 106, 108; and Jonson, Ben 112; and Kees, Weldon 101; and Larkin, Philip 98–9, 101; and Lauridsen, Morten 101; and loss 101, 103, 109, 111, 114; and love 112, 114–15; and MacMillan, James 101; and Marvell, Andrew 103; and music 99, 113; and preoccupation with form 98, 107; and Rilke 248; and Roget, Peter 106; and Shakespeare 101, 103, 113–14; and Sonoma Valley 101; and Stevens, Wallace 100, 101; and St. Thomas Aquinas 97, 108; and storytelling 109–10; and Swift, Jonathan 107;

and symbols 99; and Tennyson 112; and Tomlinson, Charles 112; and Trevor, William 110; and words, 107–8, 109
POEMS "The Lost Garden" 30, 103–4; "The Road" 97; "Interrogations at Noon" 97–8; "All Souls" 98; "Autumn Inaugural" 99, 100; "Psalm to Our Lady Queen of the Angels" 99; *Daily Horoscope* (1986); *The Gods of Winter* (1991); "New Year" 101; "The Apple Orchard" 102, 104; "The Lunatic, The Lover and the Poet" 104; "Nothing Is Lost" 104; "Counting the Children" 104–5; "Money" 105; "Progress Report" 106; "Words, Words, Words" 107; "The Litany" 107; "Words" 107; "Speaking of Love" 108–9; Special Treatments Ward" 110–11; "Prayer" 111; "An Old Story" 111; "The Present" 112; "Prophecy" 114; "Marriage of Many Years" 114–15; CRITICISM; "Can Poetry Matter?" (1991) 110

Goethe 5, 82
Gogol, Nikolai 82
Goldsmith, Oliver 8
Gooch, George Peabody 456
Gordon, Lord George 177
Gordon Riots 177–9
Gothic 28–9; and Clark, Kenneth 289; and Gothic Revival 287–90; and Newman, St. John Henry on form 290; and Pugin, Augustus 289, 290; and Ruskin, John 289–90; and "The Nature of Gothic" and Ruskin's definition of Gothic 289–90; and *The Stones of Venice* (1851–3) 289; and Upjohn, Richard 289; and Trinity Episcopal Church in New York City 289–90
Gower, George Granville William Sutherland-Leveson, 3rd Duke of Sutherland 335–6
Grant, James 8, and Bagehot, Walter 391–4; and prose style, enviable but enviable 394

495

Moore, George 2
Moore, Marianne 85–6
Morris, William, 1st Viscount
Nuffield 168
Motley, John Lothrop 63
Mozart 82
Müller, Cardinal Gerhard, on the
question of contraception 231–2
Murray, William, 1st earl of
Mansfield 178

Napoleon 155
Nash, Andrew 419, 421, 422, 423, 425,
426, 427, 465
Nathanson, Bernard 211
Natural Law 149, 150, 151, 159, 160, 186,
212, 177, 277, 298, 345
New Critics 58
Newman, St. John Henry 8, 152,
165; and Allies, Thomas William
405–15; and Arnold, Thomas
434–5; and American Episcopal
Church 424; and Anglo-Catholics
463–4; and apostasy 15; and Birrell,
Augustine 429; and Chesterton,
G. K. 425; and conscience 472;
and devotion to the Mother of
God 472; and "delicious satirical
irony" of *Anglican Difficulties* 462;
and editing of *Anglican Difficulties*
459–68; and dogmatic principle
438–9; and Eliot, George 430; and
epitaph 472; and Erastianism 406,
407, 460, 463, 464; and Fathers of
the Church 83, 311, 313, 321, 408,
425, 429, 449, 470; and Gibbon,
Edward 422, 425, 434, 449, 450, 451,
452, 453, 455, 456, 457, 458; and
Gladstone, W. E. 472; and Hardy,
Thomas 35–7; and humility 69; and
Huntingdon, Selina Countess of
425–6; and Hutton, R. H. 472; and
Modernism, Pius X and *Pascendi
Dominici Gregis* (1907) 424; and Ker,
Ian 16, 363, 472, 483; and Kingsley,
Charles 429; and liberalism 433–40;
and Mayhew, Henry and ignorance
of Christianity among London

poor 436; and Oxford Movement
426; and Norfolk, 15th Duke of 472;
and Pattison, Robert and *The Great
Dissent: John Henry Newman and the
Liberal Heresy* (1991) 438; and Pollen,
John Hungerford 408; and prophetic
historian 456–7; and primitive man
186; and Revealed Truth, as opposed
to rationalism 423; and reviews and
reviewing, disdain for 3; and St.
Augustine 430; and St. Ignatius of
Antioch and the need to read Fathers
with critical sympathy 424–5; and St.
Philip 431, 471; and satirical genius
with which he mocks the follies of
his rationalist opponents 437–8;
and satirical send-up of English
Protestantism 450–1; and satirical
self-mockery 425–6; and satirical
skewering of Oxford Movement 459;
and Scott, Thomas 469; and Servant
of Truth 465; and Socinianism 421,
424; and Southern, R. W. 309–10, 313;
and "sovereignty of Truth" 69; and
Turner, Frank 426; and unbelief 27;
and unbelief and liberalism 434; and
unbelief among Victorians 436; and
unbelief among Greeks and Romans,
440; and unbelief and "ecclesiastical
liberty" 463–4; and ultra-
Protestantism and Latitudinarianism
420; and variance between Fathers
and Councils of the Scholastic
tradition and Anglican theology 313;
and *Via Media*, repudiation of 465;
and Ward, W. G. 472; and "fountain-
head of warfare between the Church
and the World" 444; and *Zeitgeist*,
Anglican Church's capitulation to
464
on church and state 295–6; on Church
and the World 466–7; on conversion
227; on knowledge 310
WORKS: "Lead, Kindly Light" 35–6;
Anglican Difficulties (1850) 37, 313,
362, 408, 409, 420, 259, 462, 463,
464, 454, 468, 475; *Apologia Pro Vita
Sua* (1864) 40–1, 167, 309, 419, 426,